T0295782

POVERTY AND PROFICIENCY

The Cost of and Demand for Local Public Education

A Textbook in Education Finance

POVERTY AND PROFICIENCY

The Cost of and Demand for Local Public Education

A Textbook in Education Finance

Editor

John Yinger
Syracuse University, USA

 World Scientific

NEW JERSEY · LONDON · SINGAPORE · BEIJING · SHANGHAI · HONG KONG · TAIPEI · CHENNAI · TOKYO

Published by

World Scientific Publishing Co. Pte. Ltd.

5 Toh Tuck Link, Singapore 596224

USA office: 27 Warren Street, Suite 401-402, Hackensack, NJ 07601

UK office: 57 Shelton Street, Covent Garden, London WC2H 9HE

Library of Congress Cataloging-in-Publication Data
Names: Yinger, John, 1947– editor.
Title: Poverty and proficiency : the cost of and demand for local public education :
    a textbook in education finance / edited by John Yinger.
Description: New Jersey : World Scientific, 2019. | Includes bibliographical references.
Identifiers: LCCN 2019020068 | ISBN 9789811201608 (hardcover) |
    ISBN 9789811202698 (paperback)
Subjects: LCSH: Education--United States--Finance. | Public schools--United States--Finance. |
    Education--Demographic aspects--United States. | Property tax--United States. |
    Poor children--Education--United States. | Poverty--United States.
Classification: LCC LB2825 .P598 2019 | DDC 370.973--dc23
LC record available at https://lccn.loc.gov/2019020068

British Library Cataloguing-in-Publication Data
A catalogue record for this book is available from the British Library.

For any available supplementary material, please visit
https://www.worldscientific.com/worldscibooks/10.1142/11316#t=suppl

Desk Editors: Herbert Moses/Sylvia Koh

Typeset by Stallion Press
Email: enquiries@stallionpress.com

In memory of Bill Duncombe

About the Editor

John Yinger is Trustee Professor of Public Administration and Economics at the Maxwell School, Syracuse University and is also director of Maxwell's Education Finance and Accountability Program. Professor Yinger received his PhD in economics from Princeton University. His research has covered a variety of topics in state and local public finance (especially education finance) and urban economics (especially discrimination in housing). He can be contacted at jyinger@maxwell.syr.edu.

Contents

Part 8: School Infrastructure   625

Appendices

Introduction

John Yinger

*Departments of Public Administration and International
Affairs and of Economics,
Syracuse University, Syracuse, NY*
jyinger@maxwell.syr.edu

This book brings together my teaching notes and research on education finance. This collection could serve as a textbook for a graduate course in education finance or as supplemental readings for a graduate course on state and local public finance or on education policy.[1]

The questions addressed in this book are important. Is the property tax an equitable way to finance elementary and secondary education? How much more does it cost to reach a state's education targets in a high-poverty school district than in a rich district? What design for state education aid best meets a state's student performance objectives? How much more does it cost to buy housing in a high-quality school district than in a low-quality one? Should small school districts be consolidated? What is the best way to fund school infrastructure? My hope is that this book will encourage many students, and perhaps some scholars, to address these and related questions.

Much of the research reprinted in this book is co-authored. Indeed, I owe a profound debt to William Duncombe, who is a co-author on more than

---

[1]The lecture slides for my masters and Ph.D. classes on state and local public finance are available in Yinger (2020).

half of the chapters in this book.[2] My other co-authors also made major contributions to this book, for which I am grateful.[3]

This book has eight parts: Local Public Finance, The Property Tax, Cost Functions for Public Education, The Demand for Public Education, State Aid to Education, School Quality and Property Values, School District Consolidation, and School Infrastructure. In some cases, the articles fit into more than one of these topics. Chapter 8, for example, shows now a provision of the property tax in New York State affects education demand, but it includes estimation of education cost functions. Moreover, the other chapters in Part 4 focus on education demand, but they also discuss and estimate education cost functions along the way.

The two chapters in Part 1 provide background on the U.S. federal system with a focus on public elementary and secondary schools. Chapter 1, "Overview of the Property Tax in the United States," explains the organization and funding of local governments, describes and analyzes the local property tax, and discusses many variations in property tax design across states. This chapter is a compilation and expansion of my teaching notes on many aspects of the property tax. It also presents a new approach to the incidence of the property tax on owner-occupied housing. Chapter 2, "Bidding and Sorting," presents the standard analysis of household location and housing price determination in a system of local governments.[4] One feature of this system, namely the sorting of high-income households into high-quality school districts, has important implications for education costs and demands — and for economic inequality.

Part 2 turns to more detailed analysis of various features of the property tax. Chapter 3, "Property Tax Capitalization," explains a key feature of a system of local governments and competitive housing markets, namely, the capitalization of property taxes into house values. This capitalization is defined as a situation in which the price of housing declines as the local property tax rises, while all else remains equal.[5] (As discussed in Part 6, school quality is also capitalized into housing values.) Chapter 4, "Is the

---

[2]William Duncombe passed away in May 2013. Appendix D, which appears at the end of this book, provides information about his career.

[3]I would also like to thank Kitty Nasto, without whom this book would not have been possible. She assisted me on book-related tasks too numerous to name.

[4]Chapter 2 draws heavily on Ross and Yinger (1999). More recent literature is reviewed in Yinger (2015).

[5]This chapter draws on the analysis of property tax capitalization in Yinger *et al.* (1988).

Property Tax a Benefit Tax? The Case of Rental Housing," which is co-authored with Robert J. Carroll, explores the incidence of the property tax on rental housing. This chapter shows that because they are mobile, renters bear only a small portion of the property tax burden in the Boston area. This finding contradicts the view (discussed in Chapters 1 and 2) that the property tax is a "benefit tax," which is a tax that serves simply as a price for local public services.

Part 3 turns to education cost functions. A cost-function indicates the spending required for a school district to reach a given student-performance target using best practices. As a result, these chapters examine variation in spending across school districts, controlling for student performance and accounting for school district efficiency.[6] Chapter 5, "Are Education Cost Functions Ready for Prime Time? An Examination of their Validity and Reliability," is co-authored with William Duncombe. It explores the strengths and weaknesses of cost functions for studying education, exposes some misconceptions about district-level education production functions, and estimates cost functions for Missouri. Chapter 6, "The No Child Left Behind Act: Have Federal Funds Been Left Behind?" is co-authored with William Duncombe and Anna Lukemeyer.[7] This chapter estimates education cost functions for Kansas and Missouri and shows that, in light of these cost functions, federal funding through the No Child Left Behind Act (NCLB) "cannot come close to funding high standards without implausibly large increases in school-district efficiency." Moreover, this chapter shows that NCLB gave states an incentive to keep their standards low.[8]

Chapter 7, co-authored with William Duncombe, is titled "How Much More Does a Disadvantaged Student Cost?" This chapter explains why student disadvantage is an important cost factor in providing public education.

---

[6]School district efficiency cannot be directly observed, and several different approaches are available to bring it into the analysis. Starting with Duncombe *et al.* (1996), my co-authored articles accounted for efficiency by including in the cost function an efficiency index calculated using Data Envelopment Analysis. In 2003, however, my co-authors and I decided that a better approach is to estimate cost functions that control for variables with a conceptual link to efficiency. Duncombe and Yinger (2011), reproduced as Chapter 5, and Duncombe *et al.* (2015) review the literature on alternative approaches to accounting for efficiency and other issues that arise in estimating cost functions.

[7]Anna Lukemeyer passed away in 2018. Among other things, she brought extensive knowledge of state education court cases to our joint research (Lukemeyer 2003). She will be missed. For information on Profession Lukemeyen's publications, see https://www.maxwell.syr.edu/cpr/efap/Anna_Lukemeyer/.

[8]Lukemeyer *et al.* (2008) provide further analysis of NCLB using cost functions.

It also shows how to estimate education cost indexes that account for student disadvantage and shows that these costs indexes are comparable to the extra weights for pupils from poor families or with other disadvantages that appear in many state education aid formulas. This chapter also estimates education cost functions and pupil weights for New York State.

This book brings in the demand for education in Part 4. The chapters in this part include cost-function estimation, including estimation of school district efficiency. As these chapters show, information from a cost function is necessary for a correctly specified demand analysis. These chapters also show that the general issues raised by the demand for education are common across many states, while many of the details are state-specific.[9]

Chapter 8, "The Unintended Consequences of Property Tax Relief: New York State's STAR Program," which is co-authored with Tae Ho Eom, William Duncombe, and Phuong Nguyen-Hoang, shows that local voters in New York State changed their behavior when a state-funded property tax exemption altered their incentives. These behavioral responses led to significant unintended consequences.[10]

Chapter 9 is titled "Education Finance Reform, Local Behavior, and Student Performance in Massachusetts." It is co-authored with Phuong Nguyen-Hoang. This chapter estimates cost and demand functions for Massachusetts. The twist is that this analysis is used to show that a major education finance reform in the state led to a significant increase in student performance. Chapter 10, "Making Do: State Constraints and Local Responses in California's Education Finance System," which is co-authored with William Duncombe looks at the case of California, where school districts are heavily constrained by state policy. This chapter shows that, despite

---

[9]A follow-up to the article reproduced in Chapter 8, Nguyen-Hoang and Yinger (2018b), shows that the behavioral economics concepts of salience and framing can help to explain the price elasticities in a model of the demand for school quality.

[10]Chapter 8 includes estimates of the so-called flypaper effect, which is the impact of $1 of state aid on the demand for education relative to the equivalent increase in voter income. Further analysis of the data behind Chapter 8 by Nguyen-Hoang and Yinger (2018a) finds that these estimates of the flypaper effect are too high because of a scaling problem in the voter income variable. The flypaper effects should be about 15, not 50. This problem does not affect the other estimates in the chapter. A flypaper effect of 15 implies that about $0.30 of every dollar of aid is spent on education and the rest is used for tax relief. Nguyen-Hoang and Yinger also show that the behavioral economics concepts of salience and framing can help to explain variation in the flypaper effect over time and across school districts.

these constraints, local voters respond to the same types of incentives as local voters in other states.

Part 5 focuses on state aid to education. The first chapter in this part, Chapter 11, "State Aid and the Pursuit of Educational Equity: An Overview," introduces this topic. It describes the various types of state aid formulas, examines the role of cost adjustments in state aid design, explains the roles of local taxes and school district efficiency, and describes the aid formulas and court cases in many different states. Chapter 12, "School Finance Reform: Aid Formulas and Equity Objectives," which is co-authored with William Duncombe, provides a detailed explanation of various school finance formulas. This chapter shows, using data from New York State, that a so-called power-equalizing aid formula provides less assistance to high-need districts than does an equal-cost foundation aid formula. It also shows that even with improvements in district efficiency, large increases in aid to needy districts are needed to meet even a minimal performance standard. Chapter 13, co-authored with Helen F. Ladd, explores the philosophical basis for a policy of aiding needy school districts. The final chapter in this part, Chapter 14, "Capitalization and Equalization: The Feedback Effects of Foundation Aid for Schools," asks whether the property value changes induced by state aid reform alter the aid a district will receive in later years. The focus is on lump-sum aid delivered through a foundation aid formula. This chapter shows that in the case of foundation aid, these feedback effects are likely to be small or non-existent.

One key issue in evaluating state education aid reforms is whether those reforms boost student performance, particularly in high-need school districts. Cost function studies address this issue to some degree because they estimate the relationship between spending and performance. Chapter 9, for example, uses estimated cost and demand functions to simulate the impact on student performance of a major state aid reform in Massachusetts. In addition, Chapter 11 discusses some of the literature on state aid reform and student test scores. Since these chapters first appeared, several scholars have published articles on this issue using data sets that follow student performance for many years (see Jackson *et al.*, 2016; Hyman, 2017; and Lafortune *et al.*, 2018). These articles provide strong evidence that a well-designed state aid reform has positive long-term academic and employment consequences for the affected students, especially those in high-need districts.

Homebuyers are willing to pay more to live in a school district with better schools. This "school quality capitalization" is the subject of Part 6.

Chapter 15, "The Capitalization of School Quality into House Values: A Review," is co-authored with Phuong Nguyen-Hoang. This chapter provides a review of the literature on this topic. Studies in many different places find evidence for this type of capitalization. The other chapter in this part, Chapter 16, is titled "The Impact of State Aid Reform on Property Values: A Case Study of Maryland's Bridge to Excellence in Public Schools Act." This chapter is co-authored with Il Hwan Chung and William Duncombe. It shows that a major education finance reform in Maryland had significant impacts on house values, especially in the neediest districts.

School District Consolidation is one of the most dramatic changes in school organization over the past century. Indeed, over this period, the number of school districts has declined by over 90 percent. The chapters in Part 7 examine the potential cost savings from consolidation and look into the impact of consolidation on property values. Chapter 17, "The Benefits and Costs of School District Consolidation: What Recent Research Reveals about Potential Cost Savings," co-authored with William Duncombe, provides an accessible overview of the research on these topics. Chapter 18, "Does School District Consolidation Cut Costs?," which is also co-authored with William Duncombe, makes use of a unique panel data set for rural school districts in New York State to obtain precise estimates of the cost impacts of consolidation, including both adjustment costs and costs related to enrollment change. This study finds large cost savings for small districts, but little cost savings for the consolidation of two districts each with enrollments of 2,000 pupils or more.

Chapters 19, "How Does School District Consolidation Affect Property Values: A Case Study of New York" co-authored with William Duncombe and Pengju Zhang, estimates the extent to which consolidation affects house values. The focus on house values accounts for household attitudes toward consolidation, which may reflect not only cost savings, but also other factors, such as changes in travel time or access to teachers, that do not appear in the school budget.

The final part of this book addresses the topic of School Infrastructure. Chapter 20 is titled "School District Responses to Matching Aid Programs for Capital Facilities: A Case Study of New York's Building Aid Program." It is co-authored with Wen Wang and William Duncombe.[11] This chapter

---

[11] Wen Wang passed away in 2017. He made valuable contributions to the topic of this book, namely, education finance in the United States (see Wang and Duncombe, 2009, Wang and Zhao, 2011, and Zhao and Wang, 2015). Professor Wang also published extensively on education finance in China and on local government finance generally in both the

estimates a model of school infrastructure spending in New York State, which supports this spending though a state matching grant. It shows that most school districts respond to the price incentive created by this matching grant. Despite the fact that the matching rate is higher for needy districts, however, these districts do not respond to this incentive, presumably because their other needs are so great. The last chapter, Chapter 21, "Still Unknown: The Impact of School Capital on Student Performance," explains what is needed to estimate the impact of school infrastructure on student performance, and shows that some claims in recent research on this topic are not correct.

This book also has four appendices. Appendix A, "Present Value and Discounting with Applications to Local Public Finance," provides a review of the algebra of present value and discounting with some applications that are relevant to the material in this book. These applications include the income method for assessing property, the setting of pension benefits, and the pricing of municipal bonds.

Appendix B, "The State and Local Lunch Group," was originally written for a conference honoring the career of Professor Helen "Sunny" Ladd, but this appendix sheds light on the start of my career, too. Not only did Sunny and I collaborate on several projects early in our careers, we also were both part of a network of young scholars in Cambridge, Massachusetts, from the mid-1970s to the mid-1980s who met to discuss topics in local public finance and who formed many different partnerships to pursue publications on these topics. This appendix identifies these partnerships. One of the publications that arose from my connections to the State and Local Lunch Group (SLLG) appears in this book as Chapter 13, co-authored with Helen Ladd and another (Yinger *et al.*, 1988) is the source of most of the material in Chapter 3. However, every chapter in this book builds on what I learned from working with the talented scholars who participated in the SLLG.[12]

Appendix C is a tribute to my public finance professor at Princeton, Wallace Oates. Many of the chapters in this book build on ideas that I first learned about in his course — and cannot seem to stop thinking about. Finally, Appendix D is a tribute to my frequent co-author, William

United States and China. He will be missed. For more information on Professor Wang's publications, go to http://cpr.maxwell.syr.edu/efap/index.html.

[12]Another SLLG-linked publication (Bradbury *et al.*, 1984) explores local public cost functions and fiscal disparities across towns in Massachusetts. Because towns provide K-12 education in Massachusetts, my research on education cost functions (Part 3 of this book) and on state aid to education (Part 5) builds on this article.

Duncombe, who passed away in 2013. This appendix also contains a list of Bill's publications in education finance and provides links to additional information about his career.

Housekeeping Notes

1. The authors' affiliations at the beginning of each chapter refer to their affiliations in 2019, not to their affiliations at the time the re-printed article was first published.
2. References at the end of each chapter that are now published but were forthcoming or in working paper form at the time the re-printed article was first published have been updated. Associated publication dates have also been updated in the text.
3. Citations referring to articles that are reprinted in this book are indicated in the reference lists in square brackets. A reference for Duncombe and Yinger (2005), for example, is entered as:

    Duncombe, William D., and John Yinger. 2005. "How much more does a disadvantaged student cost?" *Economics of Education Review* 24(5) (October): 513–532. [Chapter 7]

4. The original version of Chapter 11, which appeared in a book (Yinger, 2003), did not have its own reference list. The reference list for Chapter 11 in this book is excerpted from the overall reference list in Yinger (2003).
5. Chapter 11 was originally published as an overview chapter in an edited volume, namely, Yinger (2003). As such, it often refers to the chapters in that volume. To avoid confusion, all these chapter references have been converted to standard references. Instead of (Duncombe and Johnston, Chapter 5), for example, the text in Chapter 11 now reads (Duncombe and Johnston, 2003). In addition, the Duncombe and Johnston study and all the other studies in Yinger (2003) have been added to the reference list for Chapter 11.

References

Bradbury, Katharine L., Helen F. Ladd, Mark Perrault, Andrew Reschovsky, and John Yinger. 1984. State aid to offset fiscal disparities across communities. *National Tax Journal* **37**(2): 151–170.

Duncombe, William D., John Ruggiero, and John Yinger. 1996. Alternative approaches to measuring the cost of education, In H. F. Ladd (ed.), *Holding Schools Accountable: Performance-Based Reform in Education*, Washington DC: The Brookings Institution.

Duncombe, William D., Phuong Nguyen-Hoang, and John Yinger. 2015. Measurement of cost differentials. In M. E. Goertz and H. F. Ladd (eds.), *Handbook of Research in Education Finance and Policy*, pp. 260–278, 2nd edition, New York: Routledge.

Duncombe, William D., and John Yinger. 2011. Are education cost functions ready for prime time? An examination of their validity and reliability. *Peabody Journal of Education* **86**(1): 28–57. [Chapter 5]

Hyman, Joshua. 2017. Does money matter in the long run? Effects of school spending on educational attainment. *American Economic Journal: Economic Policy* **9**(4): 256–280.

Jackson, C. Kirabo, Rucker C. Johnson, and Claudia Persico. 2016. The effects of school spending on educational and economic outcomes: Evidence from school finance reforms. *The Quarterly Journal of Economics* **131**(1): 157–218.

Lafortune, Julien, Jesse Rothstein, and Diane Whitmore Schanzenbach. 2018. School finance reform and the distribution of student achievement. *American Economic Journal: Applied Economics* **10**(2) (April): 1–26.

Lukcmeyer, Anna. 2003. *Counts as Policymakers: School Finance Reform Litigation.* El Paso: LFB Scholarly Publications.

Lukemeyer, Anna, William D. Duncombe, and John Yinger. 2008. Dollars without sense: The mismatch between the no child left behind act accountability system and title I funding. In R. D. Kahlenberg (ed.), *Improving on No Child Left Behind: Getting Education Reform Back on Track*, pp. 19–102, New York: The Century Foundation.

Nguyen-Hoang, Phuong and John Yinger. 2018a. The flypaper effect: Methods, magnitudes, and mechanisms. Working Paper, Center for Policy Research, Syracuse University, July.

Nguyen-Hoang, Phuong and John Yinger. 2018b. How salience and framing alter the behavioral impacts of property tax relief. Working Paper, Center for Policy Research, Syracuse University, May.

Ross, Stephen and John Yinger. 1999. Sorting and voting: A review of the literature on urban public finance. In P. Cheshire and E. S. Mills (eds.), *Handbook of Urban and Regional Economics*, pp. 2001–2060, vol. 3, Applied Urban Economics, North Holland: Elsevier.

Wang, Wen and William Duncombe. 2009. School facilities funding and capital outlay distribution in the states. *Journal of Education Finance* **34**(3): 324–350.

Wang, Wen and Zhirong Zhao. 2011. Fiscal effects of local option sales taxes on school facilities funding: The case of North Carolina. *Journal of Public Budgeting, Accounting, and Financial Management* **23**(4): 507–533.

Yinger, John. 2015. Hedonic markets and sorting equilibria: Bid-function envelopes for public services and neighborhood amenities. *Journal of Urban Economics* **86**(March): 9–25.

Yinger, John. 2020. *Lecture Notes in State and Local Public Finance.* World Scientific: Singapore.

Yinger, John, Howard S. Bloom, Axel Boersch-Supan, and Helen F. Ladd. 1988. *Property Taxes and House Values: The Theory and Estimation of Intrajurisdictional Property Tax Capitalization.* Boston: Academic Press.

Zhao, Zhirong and Wen Wang. 2015. Local option sales tax, state capital grants, and disparity of school capital outlays: The case of Georgia. *Journal of Public Budgeting, Accounting, and Financial Management* **27**(2): 129–152.

Part 1
Local Public Finance

Chapter 1

The Property Tax in the United States

John Yinger

*Departments of Public Administration and International
Affairs and of Economics, Syracuse University,
Syracuse, NY, United States*
jyinger@maxwell.syr.edu

1. Introduction

The property tax is the main source of tax revenue for local governments
in the United States. This tax is, among other things, a crucial source of
funding for counties, cities, and school districts. This chapter provides a
non-technical overview of this important tax. Section 2 describes the U.S.
federal system and the extent to which its many types of local government
rely on the property tax. Section 3 explains the basic design of the property
tax, property tax incidence and efficiency, and the administration of the
property tax, including issues that arise in determining whether this tax
is administered fairly. The basic principles of the property tax are shared
throughout the U.S., but many variations in the design of the tax are used
in some jurisdictions but not others. These variations, which include tax
classification, homestead exemptions, circuit breakers, and tax limitations,
are discussed in Section 4. The final section reviews some key lessons about
the property tax for policy makers to consider. This chapter is largely
descriptive, although it introduces some of the behavioral issues considered
in subsequent chapters.

2. Background on the U.S. Federal System

The United States has a unique federal system characterized by a large role
for state and local governments, at least relative to the role for state and local
governments in other countries. The property tax is a key revenue source for
the local governments in this system.[1] This section provides an overview of
this system as background for the role of the property tax.

2.1. *Constitutional Foundations*

The broad themes of the U.S. federal system are established by the U.S. Constitution and the 50 state constitutions. A key feature of this system is that
the U.S. Constitution gives states and the federal government equal standing
as constitutional units. The Constitution assigns some responsibilities to the
federal government and others to states. Section 1 of the Constitution, for
example, gives the U.S. Congress the power, among other things, "to coin
Money" and "to provide and maintain a Navy." On the other hand, the Tenth
Amendment says that "The powers not delegated to the United States by
the Constitution, nor prohibited by it to the States, are reserved to the
States respectively, or to the people." The federal government cannot tell
states how to behave on matters within their purview. Of course, the federal
government can, and sometimes does, give states a financial incentive to
behave in a certain way, but it cannot dictate state behavior.

The constitutional basis for the U.S. federal system provides broad
themes, but it does not provide specifics. The specifics are worked out
through legislation and the courts. Thus, the boundaries between federal and
state authority are subjects of active debate and often change in one direction
or the other. In the case of education, for example, the federal Elementary
and Secondary Education Act of 1965 greatly increased the amount of federal
education aid to states. This aid was provided with relatively few strings.
The No Child Left Behind Act (NCLB), which was signed into law in 2002,
not only increased federal education aid to states, but also gave states a
strong financial incentive to implement new accountability standards based
on standardized tests. Most observers regard this foray of federal programs
into state education policy as a mixed success, at best, and NCLB was
replaced with the much less intrusive Every Student Succeeds Act in 2015.[2]

---

[1]Youngman (2016) describes the history of the property tax in the United States.
[2]Duncombe, Lukemeyer, and Yinger (2008) provide an evaluation of the accountability
system in NCLB.

2.2. *Types of Local Government*

Local governments are created under the rules established by each state. These rules vary across states, but the broad outlines are similar across the country. Local governments include counties, townships, municipalities, school districts, and special districts. In general, every location in a state is in a county, a township, and a school district, whereas many locations are outside of municipalities and special districts, and special districts may overlap. In most states, cities, boroughs, towns, and villages are all called municipalities. Figure 1 provides a map of the units of a local government in a hypothetical U.S. state.

Variations on this general theme are common. According to the 2012 Census of Governments, there are no townships in the South and West and

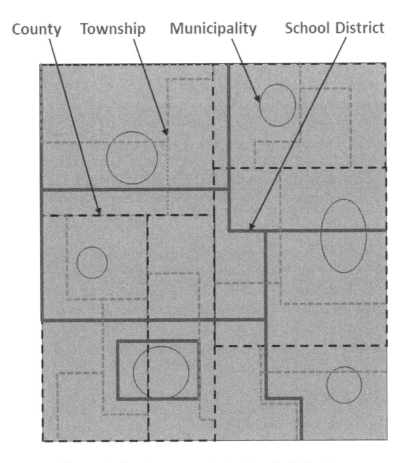

Figure 1   Local governments in a hypothetical state.

no counties in Connecticut, Rhode Island, and the District of Columbia.[3] Townships are called towns in New York State, and they do not exist within that state's cities.[4]

The Census defines an independent local government as one with its own taxing power, usually in the form of a property tax. A dependent unit of government does not have its own taxing power and can be thought of as an agency in another government. States differ widely in their use of independent special purpose governments. New York City has over 100 dependent agencies, for example, whereas the equivalent units of government (including libraries, schools, and transit) are independent districts in Chicago.

The U.S. has a large number of independent special districts: 37,203 in 2012. This number has grown considerably over the years; only 12,319 independent special districts existed in 1952. The number of special districts varies widely across states. Eleven states (California, Colorado, Illinois, Kansas, Missouri, Nebraska, New York, Oregon, Pennsylvania, Texas, and Washington) each have over 1,000 special districts. The most common types of special districts are fire protection districts (5,865), water supply districts (3,522), housing and community development districts (3,438), and drainage and flood control districts (3,248).

In some cases, such as water supply districts or drainage and flood control districts, special districts are established to account for spillovers across municipalities. In other cases, special districts may be set up to avoid property tax limits (Zhang, 2018).[5]

School districts are organized in many different ways. DC, Maryland, North Carolina, Alaska, and Hawaii have no independent school districts, and Hawaii has only one school district, which is part of the state government. Another 16 states have a combination of dependent and independent school districts. In New York, for example, schools are a department of city government in Buffalo, New York City, Rochester, Syracuse, and Yonkers, but are independent units of government everywhere else in the state. Virginia has one independent and 135 dependent school systems. Louisiana has 69 independent school districts and one dependent school system.

---

[3]The Census of Governments is the source for all the governmental descriptions in this chapter. See U.S. Census Bureau (2013).
[4]"Towns" are also not municipal governments in the New England States, Minnesota, and Wisconsin; "boroughs" are not municipal governments in Alaska.
[5]Section 4.6 discusses property tax limits, which usually do not apply to special districts.

Thanks to school district consolidation (see Part 7 of this book), the number of school districts in the country has declined steadily for many years, from 67,355 in 1952 to 12,880 in 2012. Consolidation is still an issue in some states in which many small districts remain.

Figure 2 summarizes the level and change in local governments over the last 60 years. Table 1 illustrates the wide variation in the types of local governments in different states, and Figure 3 describes across-state variation in school district arrangements.

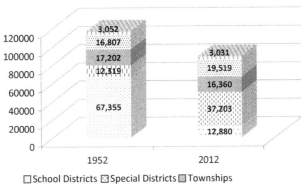

Figure 2   Number of governments, by type of government, 1952 and 2012.
Source: U.S. Bureau of the Census, 2013.

Table 1   Local governments in selected states, 2012.

State	Total	County	Town	Muni.	School	Special
Alaska	177	14	0	148	*0	15
California	4,350	57	0	482	*1,025	2,786
Hawaii	21	3	0	1	1(Dp)	17
Illinois	6,968	102	1,431	2,729	905	3,232
Mass.	852	5	298	53	*84	412
Nebraska	2,581	93	419	530	272	1,267
New York	3,454	57	929	617	*679	1,172
Penn.	4,905	66	1,546	1,015	514	1,764
Texas	4,856	254	0	1,214	*1,079	2,309
Virginia	497	95	0	229	*1	172

Notes: Muni. = municipal; * = also has dependent school districts; Dp = the only school district is a state-level dependent district.
Source: U.S. Census of Governments.

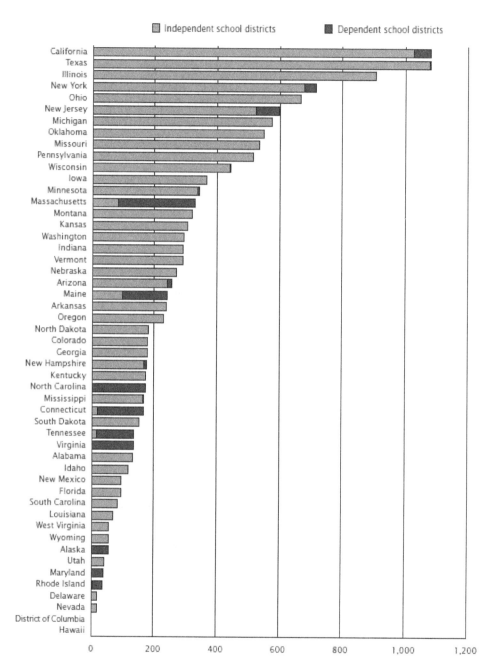

Figure 3 Total number of public school systems by state, 2012.

Source: Hogue, 2013.

2.3. *Local Government Budgets*

The main services provided by local governments are elementary and secondary (K-12) education, police, and fire protection. These governments also make significant contributions to the provision of health care, income maintenance, highways, community colleges, recreation, environmental protection, community development, and housing.[6] For the nation as a whole, local revenue comes mainly from local taxes (41.4 percent), state aid (31.8 percent) and charges and miscellaneous revenue (22.6 percent) (see Figure 4). The property tax provides the lion's share (72.1 percent) of local taxes (see Figure 5).

The property tax plays a particularly important role in the financing of K-12 education. As explained by McGuire, Papke, and Reschovsky (2015), the exact contribution of the property tax is difficult to determine because the Census data refer only to independent school districts and because some property taxes have rates set by the state and are classified as state taxes by the Census (see Section 4.6).[7] After estimating the property taxes for schools from parent governments, McGuire *et al.* find that in 2010–2011 local sources provided 43.1 percent of school K-12 school revenue, states provided 44.1 percent, and the federal government provided 12.5 percent. Moreover,

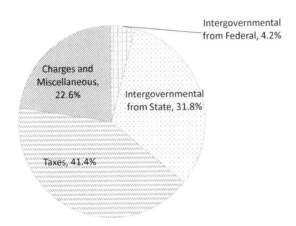

Figure 4   Sources of local general revenue, 2014.

---

[6]For more information on local government spending, see https://www.census.gov//govs/local/.

[7]For more detail on budgets of independent school district see "2015 Public Elementary — Secondary Education Finance Data," which is available at: https://www.census.gov/data/tables/2015/econ/school-finances/secondary-education-finance.html.

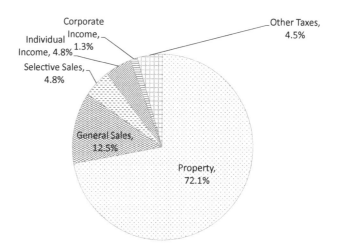

Figure 5   Local taxes, 2014.

local property taxes supplied 82.1 percent of this local revenue. Because of its central funding role, the property tax has a large impact on the demand for local public education. This topic is explored in Part 4 of this book.

Opinion polls find that the property tax is the least popular of all major taxes.[8] However, the shares of school funding and of all local funding provided by the property tax vary widely across states, and states have many tools to alter the magnitude and distribution of property tax revenue. For example, state policy makers can increase state education aid, particularly to needy school districts. This step shifts some of the burden for funding local schools onto state taxes and enables school districts to cut property taxes or at least to cut back on their growth. Part 5 of this book takes a close look at state aid for education. States also can give local governments access to other revenue sources, such as user fees, a sales tax, or an income tax.[9] In addition, state policy makers can pass a variety of property tax

---

[8]In 2005, Gallup asked a sample of households "Which do you think is the worst tax — that is, the least fair?" Forty-two percent of these households said it was the property tax. Only 20 percent of households selected next tax on the list, the federal income tax. Milton Friedman quipped that this lack of popularity arises "for one simple reason: It's the only tax left on the books for which people have to write a big check." (These poll results and this quotation come from Fox (2017)) Support for Friedman's view comes from Cabral and Hoxby (2012) who argue that the property tax is less salient for households who pay through escrow accounts, which avoid a large one-time payment. Cabral and Hoxby "find that areas in which property taxes are less likely to be salient are areas with higher property tax rates" (p. 26).

[9]McGuire, Papke, and Reschovsky (2015) provide an overview of alternative funding sources for schools. Ohio allows school districts to levy an income tax, for example, with parameters largely set by the state. Ross and Nguyen-Hoang (2013) find that districts

relief measures to lessen the property tax burden on vulnerable groups, such as the elderly. Two such programs, homestead exemptions and circuit breakers, are discussed in Sections 4.3 and 4.4, respectively. Finally, many states have property tax limitation measures that lower the level or growth of property taxes. These measures, and their impact on property tax revenue, are discussed in Section 4.6.

3. Introduction to the Local Property Tax

3.1. *The Basic Design of a Property Tax*

The property tax is levied on all private residential, commercial, and industrial properties in a jurisdiction, with the exception of properties owned by non-profit organizations, such as churches and universities.[10] The tax base is the market value of property, as estimated by a public official called an assessor. The tax payment, T, on the ith parcel equals the jurisdiction's nominal tax rate, m, multiplied by the parcel's assessed value, A; that is,

$$T_i = mA_i \qquad (1)$$

The nominal tax rate is sometimes called a mill rate (hence the symbol m) because it is often expressed in terms of mills. In the dictionary, a "mill" is defined as one tenth of a cent or one thousandth of a dollar. A "mill rate" is the dollars of tax per $1,000 of assessed value. A tax rate of 20 mills, for example, indicates that a house assessed for $100,000 must pay a tax of $(20)(\$100) = \$2,000$. This example makes it clear that a 20 mill tax rate corresponds to a 2 percent tax rate, so one can also say that a mill equals one tenth of a percent.

The mill rate is usually set by elected officials, such as the members of the school board or the mayor and the city council. In some cases, particularly in school districts, it must be ratified directly by the voters. As discussed in Section 4.6, many states place some limits on property tax rates and may entirely eliminate local control.

In philosophical terms, the property tax is a tax on private property wealth, or at least on property wealth in the form of real estate, including

---

adopting the income tax substitute away from property taxes but also increase their total revenue. Duncombe and Yinger (2001) provide a formal look at many ways to provide property tax relief.

[10]In a few jurisdictions, a property tax is levied on mobile homes, inventory, machinery, or automobiles. For information on this (small) component of the property tax, see LILP (2018).

land.[11] The market value of property, which is the amount of money the property could command in a competitive market, is an objective measure of this wealth, and therefore constitutes a clear, fair, easy-to-understand tax base. A property tax is ideal for local governments, because it funds services that directly benefit local voters. Voters are therefore in a good position to decide if the benefits from further services are worth the associated property tax cost. Moreover, voters have an incentive to monitor local officials to ensure that local public services are provided in a cost-effective manner. In addition, the property tax is a relatively stable revenue source because property values generally do not fluctuate very much from year to year. The so-called Great Recession of 2008 to 2010 was an exception to this rule, because it involved large declines in house values and hence in the property tax base.[12] However, the unique circumstances of this episode are unlikely to be replicated.[13]

3.2. *Property Tax Incidence*

The two most basic questions about any tax are who bears the tax burden (incidence) and the extent to which the tax alters taxpayer behavior (distortion). This section considers incidence and Section 3.3 considers distortion.

Any tax incidence question has two parts. The first part is to determine who bears the burden of a tax, that is, whose real opportunities are diminished because the tax is in place. A progressive tax is one in which the tax burden as a share of income increases as income rises. With a proportional tax, this burden is the same at all income levels, and with a regressive tax this burden falls with income. The second part is to select an equity standard and determine whether the tax meets that standard, or at least moves closer toward that standard than alternative taxes. The first part is a "positive" question, which means that it can, at least in principle, be tested against the evidence. The second part is a "normative" question, which means that reasonable people with different values may disagree on the most appropriate equity standard.

---

[11]Youngman (2016) reviews the philosophical issues raised by the property tax, including the arguments for using the market value of property as the tax base.
[12]Chernick and Reschovsky (2017) examine revenue sources in 112 large cities and their overlapping jurisdictions. They find an increase in property tax revenues from 2006 to 2009 followed by a decline of 8.5 percent from 2009 to 2012. The decline in property values was much larger than this, but they show "that local governments are able to (partially) offset the decline in property values by raising nominal millage rates and that in some cities only a fraction of changes in market value are ever incorporated into the property tax base." In addition, they find that many cities increased fees to offset lower property tax revenue.
[13]For more on these circumstances, see Mian and Sufi (2015).

The two most widely used equity standards are the "ability to pay principle" and the "benefit principle." The ability to pay principle says that the tax burden should increase, or at least not decline, as income rises. People with a greater ability to pay should bear a larger tax burden. Taxes with a proportional or progressive incidence meet this principle, albeit to different degrees, but a regressive tax does not. The benefit principle says that a tax should be paid by the same people who benefit from the services funded by the tax. These two principles are not inconsistent with each other, although most tax debates focus on one or the other.

In the case of the property tax, the positive component of the incidence question has proven to be difficult to answer, in part because incidence is an inherently difficult topic and in part because there are several different ways to think about property tax incidence.

The standard approach is to consider the incidence of a national property tax with a broad base, often characterized as "wealth," and a single rate. A formal analysis of this case can be found in Zodrow (2001, 2014).[14] The legal incidence of a tax falls on the people required to write the tax checks to the government, whereas the economic incidence falls on the people whose real opportunities are diminished because the tax is in place. In some cases, the people bearing the legal incidence of a tax can change their behavior in a way that alters prices or wages and thereby shifts the economic incidence onto other people. In the case of the property tax, property owners write the tax checks, and the amount of property is fixed, at least in the short run. With a fixed supply, the price of property cannot change, and property owners are unable to shift the tax to tenants, consumers, or workers. In other words, property owners bear the economic burden of the tax. When all types of property are considered, property ownership increases with income, so this analysis concludes that the property tax is progressive.

In the long run, of course, the amount of property may change due to the net impact of construction and demolition. As a result, the price of property may change, thereby allowing suppliers of property to shift some of the tax burden to renters, workers, or consumers. The annual net change in the amount of property is small, however, relative to the property stock, so this type of shifting is generally regarded as too small to reverse the progressivity conclusion.

Another approach is to focus on owner-occupied housing. In this case, most house sales involve existing housing, and the tax burden inevitably falls

---

[14] A property tax is not literally a tax on wealth, but it applies to most property wealth so the "wealth"-based analysis by Zodrow and other scholars is instructive. Fisher (2015) provides an overview of the literature.

largely on homeowners. The first question with this approach is whether the property tax payment grows with a homeowner's income. With a constant tax rate, as in a single jurisdiction, this question becomes whether the tax base, house value, increases or decreases relative to income as income goes up. If it increases, then high-income people pay a larger share of their income in property taxes than do low-income people and the property tax on owner-occupied housing is progressive. If it decreases, then the opposite is true and this portion of the tax is regressive.

As it turns out, economists have conducted extensive research on the relationship between house value and income. The key concept is the income elasticity of demand for housing, which is the ratio in the previous paragraph expressed in percentage terms. An income elasticity above 1.0, for example, indicates that housing consumption increases faster than income as income goes up — which implies that the property tax is progressive. The vast majority of studies find, however, that this income elasticity is less than one (see Goodman, 1988 or Zabel, 2004). This result implies that the property tax on owner-occupied housing is regressive.[15] This regressivity is a key motivation for the property tax relief programs discussed in Sections 4.3 and 4.4.

The property tax on owner-occupied housing is even more regressive when the variation in property tax bases across jurisdictions is considered. The basic principle of incidence analysis is that the economic burden of a tax falls on people whose real opportunities are diminished when the tax is imposed. In the case of property tax variation, the actual property tax rate is not a good measure of tax burden, because this rate is set by local voters. It makes no sense to say that the property tax imposes a higher burden on homeowners in Jurisdiction A who select a 3 percent property tax rate than on homeowners in Jurisdiction B who select a 2 percent rate. Instead, the appropriate measure of the tax burden in a jurisdiction is the property tax rate that would be required to raise a given amount of revenue per capita, such as the state-wide average.[16] This measure depends on the property tax base, but it does not depend on the jurisdiction's actual property tax rate and is outside the control of local voters.

---

[15]Section 3.5 shows that this regressivity is often magnified when assessments are not kept up to date.

[16]This burden is the inverse of "revenue-raising capacity," which indicates the amount of revenue a district would raise at a given tax burden, based on factors outside its control. See Ladd and Yinger (1991) for a discussion of this concept. An additional factor not considered here but treated at length in Parts 3 and 5 of this book is that the spending required to achieve a given government performance target may vary from one jurisdiction to the next.

In New York State, for example, the poorest decile of school districts has \$182,948 in property value per pupil, whereas the richest decile has \$1,491,480 (New York State Education Department (NYSED, 2017).[17] Suppose school districts are expected to raise half of the revenue for K-12 schools. To raise \$9,443 per pupil, which is half of state-wide average spending, the least wealthy districts would have to levy a property tax of 5.2 percent, whereas the wealthiest districts would only need a rate of 0.6 percent. Incidence analysis usually expresses the tax burden as a share of income. In the case of property taxes, an income-based analysis must account for the fact that some portion of the property tax on property other than owner-occupied housing is exported to non-residents. NYSED indicates that income per pupil is \$71,530 in the poorest decile of districts and \$523,508 in the richest. After a rough accounting for exporting, I find that the poorest districts would have to pay 13.2 percent of their income to reach average spending, but the richest districts would only have to pay 1.2 percent.[18] Regardless of whether property value or income is the base, these calculations obviously describe a very regressive property tax system.

This analysis of inter-jurisdictional equity is incomplete, however, because it fails to account for state aid to localities, which may offset this regressivity to some degree. In the case of K-12 education, the property tax is part of an education finance system, which should be evaluated as a whole. As it turns out (see Part 5), the main education aid program in most states makes use of a foundation formula, which sets a district's aid equal to a spending target, called the foundation spending level, minus an expected local contribution, all in per pupil terms. The expected local contribution equals an expected property tax rate, which is the same for all districts, multiplied by the districts' property value per pupil.[19] If this formula is implemented without extra provisions, it completely offsets the regressivity

---

[17]These are figures for 2014–2015. The pupil count gives extra weight to high school students and students with disabilities and a lower weight to kindergarteners.

[18]These calculations, which are based on the data in NYSED (2017), assume that the income elasticity of demand for housing is 0.5 and that half of the property tax burden on property other than single-family housing is paid by non-residents. The resulting export ratios (non-resident taxes divided by resident taxes) range from 0.0 in the poorest districts to 0.52 in the richest districts. The burdens equal the spending target divided by the product of income and the sum of one and the export ratio. For a detailed analysis of export ratios, see Ladd and Yinger (1991), who find an export ratio of 0.62 for the property tax in the average large city.

[19]Some states require schools to levy the specified property tax rate, whereas others do not. The ability of districts in some states to levy a tax rate below the level in the foundation aid formula affects school quality, but it is irrelevant for determining a district's capacity.

from the property tax up to the foundation spending level. Up to this level, in other words, the burden of the education finance system is proportional to house value, not regressive. Beyond this level, however, the regressivity remains. In this example, the tax burden is expressed as a share of house value. Even with a foundation aid formula, the tax burden is likely to be regressive with respect to income.

Although most states use a foundation formula for education aid, the foundation spending levels, the details of the foundation aid program, and the use of other aid programs vary widely across states. As a result, the spending level at which the education finance system switches to severe regressivity and the degree of regressivity below that level also vary widely. Moreover, states provide far less aid to other types of local government, and this aid rarely makes use of a foundation formula. Aid to non-school local governments therefore does little to offset the fundamental regressivity of the property tax as a funding source for these governments.

A third approach to property tax incidence highlights the impact of tax changes on the current owners of property. This approach builds on the notion of "property tax capitalization," which is the subject of Chapter 3 and of Yinger *et al.* (1988). The value of an asset, say a house, is the present value of the net benefits from owning it. Property taxes certainly affect these net benefits, so an increase in the property tax results in a decline in the value of the house. The larger the property tax increase and the longer it is expected to last, the larger the decline in the house's value. This link between property taxes and house values has been documented by many scholarly studies.

The existence of property tax capitalization shifts the focus of incidence analysis to property owners at the time property taxes change. Owners at that time cannot escape the tax change that applies to their house. If they stay in their house, they pay the tax change directly, and if they sell their house, they pay the tax change in the form of a capital gain or loss in the sales price. Moreover, if they do decide to move, the people who buy their house do not bear any of the burden of the property tax increase because the higher taxes are offset by a lower sales price. According to the capitalization approach to property tax incidence, therefore, the burden of any property tax change falls on the owners of property at the time of the change in the jurisdiction where the change took place.[20] If a shopping mall shuts down, for example, and the affected jurisdiction raises its property tax rate to make

---

[20]Public services are also capitalized into house values, but this type of capitalization is more complicated because different households place different values on public services. In

up for the lost revenue, then the burden of this rate increase falls on all property owners in the jurisdiction when the rate goes up.

Despite the plausibility of the capitalization approach and the extensive empirical evidence supporting it, however, most scholars and policy makers simply ignore it, perhaps because its implications are often counter-intuitive (see Chapter 3). A better tactic, it seems to me, is to focus on the progressivity or regressivity of taxes that have been in place for a long time, and to apply the capitalization approach to short-term tax changes. The equity of a property tax revaluation that is followed by a return to an assessment system with no updates, for example, should be evaluated on the basis of the capital gains and losses it creates. Tax changes that are expected to be in place for a long time should be evaluated primarily on the basis of their progressivity or regressivity, but the short-term benefits and costs they generate are certainly worth noting.

One important application of this approach is economic development. With full capitalization, lower property tax rates lead to higher property values and hence to no net advantage in attracting business for a low-tax jurisdiction. This argument helps to explain why scholars have not found consistent evidence to support the view that property tax rates affect economic development and why some careful studies do not find any such impact at all (e.g., Wassmer and Anderson, 2001; Srithongrung and Kriz, 2014). Even in the case of property tax abatements negotiated on a case-by-case basis, which are discussed in Section 4.1, landowners may be able to charge more for land because everyone knows that abatements are likely. Poor information about abatements might leave an opening for them to be effective in some cases, but with good information the only way out of the dilemma caused by capitalization may be for the jurisdiction to buy land itself and then to sell or lease it to new businesses at below-market prices.

A fourth approach is to ask whether property tax payments are closely aligned with the benefits from the public services that are funded by the property tax. If this is true, then the incidence of the tax falls on the people who benefit from the services it funds. Some scholars who believe that there is a close connection between property tax payments and service benefits call the property tax a "benefit tax" and argue that the standard approach to tax incidence is no longer appropriate. As Fisher (2009, p. 14) puts it: "If property taxes serve as benefit taxes ..., it does not

---

contrast, every household is willing to pay $1 to save $1 of property taxes. See Chapter 2 and Part 6.

make sense to consider the incidence of the tax separate from the provision of
public services, because the tax simply reflects the demand for the services,
with each taxpayer paying the cost of the desired consumption of local public
services" (see also Oates and Fischel, 2016).

For two reasons, I do not find the benefit tax argument to be convincing.[21]
First, the argument inappropriately blends the positive and normative
components of incidence analysis. Even if the property tax is a benefit
tax (a positive conclusion), policy makers may still be concerned about the
progressivity or regressivity of the tax (a normative conclusion). Moreover,
the benefit principle (a normative standard) may be relevant to policy makers
even if the property tax is not a benefit tax (a positive outcome). Concluding
that a tax is a benefit tax instead of a tax with burdens and benefits that
do not line up does not make the benefit principle any more relevant or
compelling. Contrary to the statement by Fisher, therefore, it makes perfect
sense to "consider the incidence of the tax separate from the provision of
public services" even if this conclusion holds.[22]

Scholars do not generally bring in the value of services received when
they estimate the incidence of other taxes, and taking this step does not
obviate the interest in the distribution of the tax burden by income class.
Suppose the property tax is a benefit tax. Then, for the reasons discussed
above, people who live in a jurisdiction with a relatively large property tax
base per capita still face a much lower property tax burden than people who
live in a property-poor jurisdiction. The regressivity of this outcome may be
of interest to scholars and policy makers and cannot be washed away with
the "benefit tax" label.

Second, it is possible to identify the assumptions under which a benefit
tax would arise, and these assumptions turn out to be extreme. Some people
trace the benefit tax idea back to Tiebout (1956), whose famous article
argued that people shop for a community just like they shop for commodities.
The Tiebout model assumes away both the housing market and the property
tax, but these dimensions were added by Hamilton (1975). In other words,
Hamilton devised a model with housing and a property tax in which the
property tax operates like the price for entering a community, which implies

---

[21] A third reason is offered by Zodrow (2014). He points out that even if the property tax
is a benefit tax for people who move into a community, it is not a benefit tax with respect
to property tax changes for the residents of a community.

[22] Although I disagree with Fisher (and several other scholars) concerning benefit taxes, I
recommend the rest of his article on property taxes (2009) and his textbook on state and
local finance (2015).

that the property tax is a benefit tax. Hamilton's key assumptions are:
(1) the per-unit cost of public services is constant, (2) the supply of housing
is perfectly elastic, and (3) the people in a community set a zoning rule at
exactly their own preferred level of housing consumption.

Ross and Yinger (1999) show formally that the property tax is a benefit
tax under these assumptions.[23] However, they also show that these assumptions are not consistent with the available evidence. As demonstrated by the
studies in Part 3 of this book, for example, the cost of local public education
is often much higher in poor communities than in rich communities. Variation
in public service costs breaks the exact match between property taxes and
public service demand, which is required for a benefit tax. Without this
exact match, households bid more for housing in low-cost communities, all
else equal, so the price of entry is no longer confined to the property tax
payment.[24] Violations of the Hamilton assumptions do not eliminate the correlation between property tax payments and public service benefits, but they
do eliminate the exact match that is required for the benefit tax designation.

Ross and Yinger also show that if Hamilton's assumptions do hold, then
every household will live in its most preferred community, and nobody will
bid up the price of housing in any other community, including a community
with higher-quality public services. The large literature showing that higher-
quality local public services such as education leads to higher house values,
including the studies in Part 6 of this book, therefore provides evidence
contradicting the benefit tax view of the property tax.[25]

Some scholars have argued that the benefit tax approach applies to both
renters and owners. As shown by Carroll and Yinger (1994; reproduced

---

[23] A non-technical version of the Ross–Yinger argument is provided by Chapter 2 of this
book.

[24] State aid to local governments complicates this analysis. In principle, state aid could
offset variation in local public service costs and it could help to account for externalities
that spill over from one jurisdiction's public services to other locations. In practice,
however, state aid does not appear to be closely matched with these costs or these
externalities.

[25] The capitalization of property tax rate differences across jurisdictions due to differences
in commercial and industrial property is consistent with the benefit tax view of the
property tax. A household also can lower the price it faces for local public services by
moving to a jurisdiction where the average house value is greater than the value of the
house it buys. A price cut of this type will affect house values, but it is ruled out by the
zoning assumption required for the property tax to be a benefit tax. In other words, this
price cut does not materialize when zoning requires entering households to buy a house
with the same value as the ones owned by the higher-income households who already live
there.

as Chapter 4 of this book), the empirical evidence does not support this argument. Renters are fairly mobile, so landlords cannot raise rents to cover their property taxes unless the property taxes provide services that renters value. Carroll and Yinger derive and estimate a model that incorporates this logic. They find that in the average jurisdiction in the Boston area, renters pay only 15 percent of the property tax while landlords pay the rest. In other words, there is a correlation between property taxes in rents and public service benefits to renters, but landlords pay a large share of the property tax without receiving the associated public service benefits. The exact tax benefit match required by the benefit tax view does not exist.

3.3. *Property Tax Distortion*

Taxes alter the behavior of affected parties. Starting from the standard proposition that a market economy yields efficient outcomes, at least without monopolies or externalities, behavioral responses to taxes lead to distortions, that is, to deviations from these efficient outcomes. In the case of owner-occupied housing, property taxes are paid by people who buy houses or by homeowners who pay for renovations that increase the assessed value of their house. Because of these tax payments, homebuyers and homeowners are willing to pay less to builders or renovators for any given house or renovation, which is a source of distortion. A similar distortion applies to non-residential property.

The quantity of housing in a given house can be measured by the "housing services" it delivers, which is equivalent to its rental value. One way to characterize the distortion is that the property tax prevents the purchase of some units of housing services even though the homebuyer or homeowner is willing to pay more for those services than the supplier requires to supply them. The sum of the difference between willingness to pay and required return across all units of housing services that are not purchased because of the property tax is called the excess burden of the tax. The excess burden from the property tax is difficult to measure. One general equilibrium simulation model (Sullivan, 1985), which considers a broad range of property tax effects, estimates that the excess burden equals 6.5 percent of property tax revenue.[26]

A reasonable objective for policy makers is to minimize this type of distortion. All taxes cause distortion, and economists generally argue that distortion from a given tax more than doubles when the tax rate doubles.

---

[26] For a formal analysis of efficiency with a property tax, see Yinger (1999).

Assuming equal tax bases, for example, a system in which tax A and tax B each have 2 percent tax rates leads to less distortion than a system in which tax A has a 4 percent rate and is the only tax. As a result, this objective calls for a balanced revenue system, without any taxes that cause major distortions. This approach does not require balance at every level of government, but instead requires balance in the federal system as a whole. Heavy, but not exclusive reliance on the property tax at the local level may be consistent with a distortion-minimizing objective, so long as other levels of government rely on different tax sources.

The possibility that the property tax is a benefit tax is relevant to this discussion. Recall that one of the conditions for the property tax to be a benefit tax is that the residents in a community set the zoning barrier at exactly their optimal level of housing. In other words, this condition assumes that there is no tax distortion in the housing market. As pointed out earlier, this condition, along with the other conditions required for the property tax to be a benefit tax, is extreme. In the case of zoning, for example, the residents of a community have an incentive to set the zoning barrier above their optimal housing level to shift the burden of the property tax onto new residents (see Ross and Yinger, 1999). In short, the property tax might not cause distortion in the housing market under some assumptions, but those assumptions are very unlikely to be met.

3.4. *Assessment Methods*

In order to implement a property tax, a local government must solve the administrative problem that the market value of a property is not observed unless the property is sold in a competitive market, which is not true for most properties in most years. This problem is solved through the office of a tax assessor, who is given the job of estimating the market value of every property in every year. The assessor's estimate of a property's market value is its assessed value, A.

An assessor has three principal tools for estimating the market value of a property.[27] One tool, often called the market data method, has three steps: (1) collect information on properties that did sell along with information on property and neighborhood characteristics for all houses; (2) run a regression analysis of sales price on property and neighborhood characteristics for

---

[27] For a more detailed discussion of assessment methods, see New York State Department of Taxation and Finance (2012).

houses that sold; (3) predict the sales prices of properties that did not sell on the basis of their property and neighborhood characteristics and the regression-based estimates of the extent to which those characteristics affect sales prices.[28] This approach works best when many sales can be observed, as for owner-occupied housing in a city or large suburb.

The second tool, called the income method, is to estimate the market value of a property based on the income it generates.[29] In general, the market value of any asset, which is what a willing buyer would pay for it, is the present value of the sum of net benefits from owning it. Information on the flow of net benefits and on the discount rate can therefore be used to calculate a market value. This tool is particularly useful for rental property, such as an apartment building, because this type of property rarely sells but generates a clear stream of rental benefits.[30]

The third tool, called the cost method, is to estimate the market value of property based on the average cost per square foot of building a comparable structure. With this tool, the cost of land must be added separately, and adjustments must be made for depreciation and perhaps other factors. The conceptual foundation for this approach comes from a basic result in microeconomics, namely, that in a competitive market, the long-run equilibrium price of a product is the minimum point on its long-run average cost curve. This approach is best suited for properties, such as factories, that do not sell very often and that do not have easily predicted flows of net benefits, although it is sometimes applied to residential property.

3.5. Assessment Equity

Assessment practices may vary from one jurisdiction to the next, and they sometimes even vary within a jurisdiction. Consequently, the mill rate in one jurisdiction is not necessarily comparable to the mill rate in another

---

[28]A large academic literature, called housing hedonics, focuses on housing and neighborhood traits as determinants of house values, which is, of course what assessors do, too. See Part 6 of this book. Recent lessons from this literature might prove helpful to assessors.

[29]Appendix B provides a more detailed explanation of the income method.

[30]A New York State law regarding the assessment of condominiums constitutes a particularly blatant and unfair misuse of the income method. To be specific, this law requires assessors to use the income method for condominiums, even though no rental stream can be observed. Rental streams for comparably sized apartments are used instead, even though this procedure vastly underestimates condominium sales prices. No adjustment for the sales price of comparable condominiums is permitted. See NYSDTF (2017).

jurisdiction. Moreover, the fact that two houses in the same jurisdiction pay the same mill rate does not imply that they face the same tax burden. To facilitate comparisons across properties, both across jurisdictions and within a single jurisdiction, we need another concept, namely the effective property tax rate.

The effective property tax rate, t, is defined to be the tax payment, T, as a share of the market value of a property, V. For the ith parcel,

$$t_i \equiv \frac{T_i}{V_i} \tag{2}$$

Remember that assessed value, A, is only an estimate of V, so A_i and V_i need not be equal. Now combining equations (1) and (2), we find that

$$t_i \equiv \frac{T_i}{V_i} = \frac{mA_i}{V_i} = m\left(\frac{A_i}{V_i}\right) \tag{3}$$

In words, the effective tax rate equals the mill rate multiplied by the assessment/sales ratio. An assessment/sales ratio of 1.0 or 100 percent corresponds to full value assessment, that is, to setting assessments equal to market values.

Now consider two jurisdictions with the same mill rate but differing assessment practices. To be specific, suppose one set's assessments at 50 percent of market value and the other sets assessments at 100 percent of market value. Clearly the real burden of the property tax, t, is only half as large in the first jurisdiction, because, in effect, only half of the market value of each property is being taxed. Similarly, even within a jurisdiction where all the properties face the same nominal tax rate or mill rate, unequal assessment practices can lead to higher effective tax rates on some properties than on others. Equation (3) provides a general way to correct for assessment practices and hence to compare effective tax rates both across any two jurisdictions and between any two properties in the same jurisdiction.

The main objective of an assessment system within a jurisdiction is to minimize differences in assessment/sales ratios across taxpayers. Recall that taxpayers all face the same mill rate, so if they have different assessment/ sales ratios, they will also have different effective property tax rates. This is not fair. As a starting point, every taxpayer in a jurisdiction should face the same effective property tax rate. Some of the policies discussed in Section 4 result in unequal effective property tax rates across taxpayers, but this is a feature of these policies. In the case of assessing, however, it is a bug, not a feature. It is not fair for one homeowner to have a significantly higher effective tax rate than her neighbor simply because the assessor was not equally accurate in estimating the market values of the two houses.

The ability to pay principle discussed in Section 3.2 leads to a concern about "horizontal equity" and "vertical equity." Horizontal equity exists when taxpayers with the same tax base, in this case property value, pay the same tax. Different assessments for houses with the same market value obviously violates this standard. Vertical equity exists when taxpayers with a larger tax base pay a higher tax rate — or at least not a lower one. With accurate assessments, the tax payment is a constant proportion of property value for all taxpayers. This outcome is called a proportional tax and it satisfies a weak version of the vertical equity standard.[31] If assessments are not updated for many years (and are not even updated when a property sells), then the effective tax rate is determined by the growth in property value. Property with relatively rapid value growth will experience a falling effective tax rate relative to other property. Because the price of expensive houses tends to grow at a faster rate than the price of inexpensive houses, this lack of updating often leads to lower effective tax rates on expensive houses — a clear violation of the vertical equity standard.[32]

The most widely used measure of assessment fairness is called the "coefficient of dispersion" or COD. The COD for a given taxing jurisdiction is calculated using the following formula:

$$\text{COD} = \frac{100}{M} \left(\frac{\sum_i \left| \frac{A_i}{V_i} - M \right|}{N} \right) \tag{4}$$

where A_i/V_i is the assessment/sales ratio for the ith parcel, M is the median A/V ratio, and N is the number of parcels. This measure indicates the extent to which assessment accuracy varies from one property to the next. A COD value below 10 is often used as an indication of assessment equity in an established residential area, although higher values are regarded as acceptable in more complicated market environments (New York State Department of Taxation and Finance (NYSDTF, 2018a).

---

[31]This statement depends on the value judgment that the property tax base, namely, market value, is the appropriate standard for determining progressivity, proportionality, or regressivity. An alternative value judgment is that income is the appropriate standard. As discussed in Section 3.2, a residential property tax is regressive relative to income — even with accurate assessments.

[32]If a homeowner or landlord fails to pay property taxes, the assessing jurisdiction can foreclose on the property. Property acquired by the government in this way is often vacant and unmaintained for a long time. Over-assessment of low-valued properties may lead to concentrated foreclosure and neighborhood decline in low-income neighborhoods. See, for example, Atuahene and Hodge (2018).

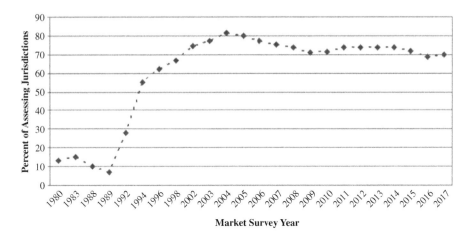

Figure 6 Percent of county city and town assessing jurisdictions with assessment uniformity, 1980–2017.

Notes: In measuring assessment equity for 1994 and subsequent survey years, acceptable levels of the coefficient of dispersion (COD) statistic were increased for the more rural assessing units. Recent reassessment programs that were reviewed and verified for the 1996 and subsequent surveys were deemed uniform.

Source: New York Department of Taxation and Finance, 2018a.

Assessors are elected officials in some places, but most assessors are now appointed and the level of professionalism in assessing has increased steadily over time. As a result, the quality of assessing, in terms of its accuracy in predicting market values, has also increased. This trend is the result of both pressure from voters for more fair and accurate assessments and, in many cases, of state policies that encourage or require assessment improvements. Figure 6 provides some evidence on this point from New York State. This figure indicates that assessment quality increased dramatically in the 1990s, but about 30 percent of assessing districts still fail to meet the COD standards set by New York State.

Assessment quality is influenced not only by the quality of the assessors, but also by several features of the property tax system.[33] The first feature to consider is the right of property owners to appeal their assessment to an assessment review panel. A property owner may be able to lower her assessment by presenting evidence that this assessment is significantly higher than the recent sales prices of comparable property. If this appeal is rejected, a property owner also can bring her appeal to court. Because

---

[33]Eom (2008) finds that assessment uniformity increases with the salary of the assessor, an indicator of assessor quality, after accounting for the potential endogeneity of the salary variable.

appeals are costly for the assessing jurisdiction, this right of appeal serves as an incentive for accurate assessments. Appeals are also expensive for a property owner, however, so they may not be widely used even when assessments are inaccurate. In Cook County, Illinois, for example, the COD for single-family houses reached a maximum of 35 in 2011, which is far above professional norms (Grotto, 2017a). Despite this inaccuracy, only 6.3 percent of homeowners appealed their tax assessment during a year in the 2009 to 2013 period. In addition, only 3.0 percent of homeowners received an assessment adjustment and only 1.3 percent received an adjustment through a subsequent legal proceeding (Johnson, 2015).[34]

A second feature is the average A/V ratio. In principle, this feature should not matter. After all, assessments can be fair on the basis of the COD if all houses are assessed at 10 percent or at 100 percent of their market value. The variation in the A/V ratio is what matters, not the level. Scholars have found, however, that in practice, a system with a median A/V close to 1.0 tends to have a lower COD than a system with a much lower median (Eom, 2008). Perhaps because fractional assessments are more difficult to compare to market information, deviations from the median A/V ratio are more likely to arise when that ratio is below 1.0.

This finding is relevant for policy because some states require A/V ratios other than 1.0. According to a survey conducted by Eom (2008), 44 percent of the states call for 100 percent assessment, that is, an A/V ratio of 1.0, whereas other states call for A/V ratios ranging from 4.5 percent (North Dakota) to 70 percent (Connecticut). Several states also do not impose a specific A/V target. States with a low target or no target at all could improve the quality of their assessments by raising the target to 100 percent assessment or by enforcing their "target" more vigorously.

Many states also impose requirements concerning the frequency of revaluations, that is, of a comprehensive re-assessment of all the property in a jurisdiction. According the Eom survey (2008), 13 states require annual re-assessment, 26 states require re-assessment at a longer interval, and nine states leave re-assessment up to the local taxing jurisdiction.[35] New York State was in the latter category in 1999, when only 50 percent of assessing jurisdictions had revalued within the previous five years and 18 percent of these jurisdictions had not revalued in the previous 20 years (Eom, 2008).

---

[34]Because higher-income homeowners are more likely than low-income households both to appeal their assessment and to receive an assessment adjustment, appeals may increase vertical inequity in a jurisdiction with inaccurate assessments. See Grotto (2017b).
[35]The other two states did not respond to this survey.

A revaluation every four years is now a requirement for state financial assistance, however, and a majority of assessing districts have completed or scheduled a revaluation (NYSDTF, 2018a).

Eom (2008) finds, not surprisingly, that assessment quality increases with the frequency of revaluation.[36] It follows that a state can increase the quality of its local governments' assessments by requiring a revaluation every one to three years. Because revaluations are costly, revaluation every year may not be warranted, but the equity gains from more accurate assessments justify the imposition of a revaluation requirement. Chapter 3 provides a more detailed discussion of the gains from maintaining accurate assessments.

A fourth feature of any assessment system is the way assessment districts are defined. Assessment is conducted at the county level in some states, but at a lower level in others. New York State provides a striking example of the latter approach because it has 983 assessing units (NYSDTF, 2018a). Several hundred of these units are so small that they share an assessor with another unit or have a part-time assessing board. Moreover, assessing units for towns and villages in New York overlap, so that village residents pay taxes based on one assessed value to their village and taxes based on another assessed value to their county, town, and school district. Larger, non-overlapping districts would obviously be more professional and more cost effective.

The main reason a proliferation of assessing units is costly, however, is that assessing is characterized by substantial economies of scale (Sjoquist and Walker, 1999; Eom, 2008). Because they have more information at their disposal, assessors in larger districts are able to estimate market values with more accuracy, and hence provide more uniform assessments. According to Sjoquist and Walker, a 10 percent increase in the number of parcels results in a 6.2 percent decrease in the cost of assessing per parcel. This estimate implies that cutting the number of assessing districts in New York in half, which corresponds to doubling the number of parcels per district, would result in a 33.9 percent decrease in the state-wide cost of assessing. Shifting to county assessment units might cut the state's total assessing costs at least in half.

A fifth feature of some state's property tax systems is an assessment cap, which sets a maximum annual increase in a property owner's assessed value. In California, for example, Proposition 13 limits assessment increases to 2 percent but resets assessed values to market values upon resale.[37] This

---

[36] To be precise, assessment uniformity decreases with the number of years since the last revaluation and with whether an assessing unit was revalued within Eom's sample period.

[37] To be precise, the limit is the lesser of 2 percent and the increase in California's consumer price index.

limit was passed in 1978 with house values in 1975 as the base. As a result, people who have remained in the same house for 40 years have seen their assessments rise by $[(1.02)^{40} - 1] = 120.8$ percent, whereas people who move into a house after 40 years of 10 percent annual housing appreciation (this is California!) face an assessment (equal to market price) that has increased $[(1.10)^{40} - 1] = 4,425.9$ percent. If these two houses had the same A and V to begin with, then the owner of the second house faces a property tax payment (and an effective property tax rate) that is $4,425.9/120.8 = 36.6$ times as high as that of the first house! The U.S. Supreme Court has ruled that this type of tax variation based on length of residency is legal. I think it undermines faith in local governments because it results in neighbors paying such different property taxes for similar houses. For more, see Sexton, Sheffrin, and O'Sullivan (1999).

Assessment caps also cause distortion by discouraging households from moving. Florida addresses this problem by making the assessment-cap benefit portable, that is, by allowing households to retain an assessment below market value if they move within a state.[38] The problem with this approach is that it magnifies the tax advantage for long-term state residents relative to new residents. A fairer approach, in my view, would be to retain portability while setting a minimum assessed value for long-term state residents equal to a fraction, say 50 percent, of market value.

Note that assessment growth caps are similar to assessments that are not updated frequently. In both cases, some homeowners receive a property tax break every year compared to other homeowners. An assessment cap gives this bonus to existing homeowners compared to new homeowners, whereas fixed assessments give this bonus to existing homeowners in neighborhoods with rising house values compared to both new homeowners and existing homeowners in neighborhoods with declining house values. A key difference between these two assessment scenarios is that when a jurisdiction-wide revaluation takes place, existing homeowners in a jurisdiction with an assessment cap are not affected, whereas homeowners in neighborhoods with property value growth, who benefited from fixed assessments, receive a capital loss and homeowners in neighborhoods with property value declines receive a capital gain. These gains and losses are fair for long-time residents, because they simply take back the capital gains or reimburse the capital

---

[38]Details of the Florida portability policy can be found at http://www.pcpao.org/SOH. html. The assessment break that can be transferred to a new house cannot exceed $500,000 and is prorated if a household's new house has a lower market value than its old house.

losses in previous years. These gains and losses are not fair for households who purchased homes shortly before the revaluation however, because these households did not receive these gains and losses in the past. This analysis is presented in more detail in Chapter 3.

4. Variations on the Basic Design

Every state alters the basic design of a property tax in one way or another. One state, Minnesota, uses a progressive rate structure. Other states add various forms of exemptions or alter their rate structure in various ways. This section describes some of the major property tax variations.[39] Later chapters provide additional related analyses. Chapter 8, for example, considers the impact of property tax exemptions on the demand for local public education in New York, and Chapter 10 explores the impacts of property tax limitations on education finance in California.

4.1. *Classification*

Some states allow local governments to impose different effective tax rates on different types of property. This policy is known as property tax classification. In most cases, classification leads to a higher tax rate on business than on residential property.

Classification laws have pros and cons. On the plus side, classification with a higher tax rate on business property can shift some of the property tax burden in a low-income city onto non-residents, many of whom benefit from city services. For example, some city businesses are owned by people who live in the suburbs but work in the city. In addition, some city businesses are owned by shareholders who live around the country. A higher tax rate on business property will shift some of the tax burden away from city residents and onto these relatively high-income non-residents. As discussed in Section 3.2, the incidence of the property tax is difficult to determine, and some of the taxes on business property might be shifted to consumers or workers. Thus, property tax classification with a higher tax rate on business property would undoubtedly lead to an increase in tax exporting, but the extent of this increase is not known.

---

[39]This list of property tax variants in this section is not comprehensive. For other variants, primarily having to do with business property, see LILP (2018). In addition, Youngman (2016) discusses the tax treatment of open space and farmland.

A possible disadvantage of classification is that it is generally set up with a higher tax on business property — and may therefore discourage economic development. As noted in Section 3.2, however, scholars have found that a city's business property tax rate has little or no impact on economic development. Nevertheless, many local governments give property tax abatements to individual businesses to attract or retain them. Further discussion of this *ad hoc* classification, with a lower rate on business property, appears later in this section.

Classification can be implemented either by allowing different nominal tax rates for different types of property or by allowing different assessment–sales ratios for different types of property. Both methods are used, although the first is far more popular. Equation (3) demonstrates that these two methods are equivalent. A 20 percent higher effective tax rate (t) for business, for example, can be implemented either by multiplying m in equation (3) by 1.2 or by multiplying (A/V) in equation (3) by 1.2.

An unusual form of classification, called the Homestead Tax Option or HTO is authorized in New York State.[40] About 75 jurisdictions have taken advantage of this option. The HTO allows assessing units that complete a state-approved revaluation to preserve the levy shares that existed before revaluation. If business property provided 50 percent of the levy before revaluation, then passing the HTO would keep business property's share at 50 percent, even if business property only made up 40 percent of the post-revaluation assessments. Accomplishing this outcome requires a higher post-revaluation nominal tax rate — and hence a higher effective property tax rate — on business property than on residential property.

The problem is that this arrangement focuses on levy shares instead of effective property tax rates. In many parts of New York, the value of business property has not been growing as fast as the value of residential property. As a result, the only way to keep the business share fixed, at 50 percent in my example, is to gradually raise the effective property tax rate on business. As a result, some jurisdictions with the Homestead Option have experienced steadily rising effective property tax rates on business property. Because classification has pros and cons, it might make sense under some circumstances to balance them by selecting an effective property tax rate for business property that is somewhat higher than the residential property tax rate. It makes no sense, however, to say that the net benefits from classification are rising over time so the gap between the business

---

[40]For more detail on the HTO, see Yinger (2012), upon which this section draws.

and residential rates should rise as well. Moreover, it certainly makes no sense to implement a policy in which this rate gap is likely to go up continually and without limit. In addition, businesses like predictability, so it might be hard to attract business to locations where the effective property tax rate on business property is following an uncertain but probably upward path.

Another type of classification imposes a higher tax rate on land than on buildings. This approach builds on the work of an 18th-century economist, Henry George, who argued that taxes on land are non-distortionary, because the amount of land is fixed, and fair, because land ownership is concentrated among high-income households. Modern versions of this argument appear in Brueckner (1986) and Oates and Schwab (1997), and many economists find this scheme appealing.

The only evidence about this approach comes from Pennsylvania. According to Banzhaf and Lavery (2010), as of 2000, 18 cities in Pennsylvania used a split-rate tax with a higher tax rate on land. Because the value of land is not directly observed, this approach is difficult to administer, and five of these cities, including Pittsburgh, had dropped it by 2010. Existing studies of the Pennsylvania experience suggest that these slit-rate taxes have decreased urban sprawl (Banzhaf and Lavery, 2010) and increased the price of land (as measured by its assessed value), particularly land in residential use (Yang, 2018). Because of the limited evidence about their effects and their administrative challenges, land taxes of this type do not appear to be gaining in popularity — despite their support among economists.

Finally, *ad hoc* classification can arise in two ways. The first way is through poor assessment practices. In the case of Boston, for example, inaccurate assessments resulted in higher effective property tax rates on business than on residential property.[41] This situation was difficult to remedy, because a shift to equal assessments would have required voters to accept an increase in residential property tax rates. The situation was resolved when Massachusetts allowed Boston and other local governments to implement an official classification scheme, which prevented residential tax rates from rising (see Yinger *et al.*, 1988).

---

[41]This type of *ad hoc* classification can be expensive for a city because businesses can appeal their taxes — and often win — on the grounds that their rate is higher than the residential rate. This double benefit for firms was common in Boston before revaluation (Yinger *et al.*, 1988). Because of capitalization, the relatively high business property tax rates allowed firms to buy property at low prices and then to win lawsuits based on these high rates. Courts did not find this unfair, because they did not consider capitalization.

The second way *ad hoc* classification can occur is through the use of property tax abatements, that is, property tax breaks for selected businesses. These abatements are popular, but the available evidence indicates that they are not effective in attracting business to a jurisdiction (Kenyon, Langley, and Paquin, 2012; Bartik, 2017). This lack of effectiveness may be due in part to the capitalization effects discussed in Section 3.2. Moreover, a property tax break to Firm A shrinks the overall property tax base and raises the property tax rate that other property owners must pay unless Firm A would not have moved to the jurisdiction without the tax break. Unfortunately, neither public officials nor citizens can determine whether this condition holds. As a result, public officials claim that the tax breaks they hand out create jobs and voters do not realize that this claim is probably not true. This logic may explain why so many jurisdictions use property tax abatements despite the evidence that they are ineffective.

4.2. *Payments in Lieu of Property Taxes*

All states exempt property owned by non-profit organizations from the property tax, so long as this property is used for non-profit purposes. These non-profits make use of city services, however, so the lack of property tax revenue from non-profits can put a strain on a city's budget. This issue is particularly important in a few cities that have a great deal of tax-exempt property, in the form of university buildings, places of worship, or the offices of social service agencies. Although the value of non-profit property is difficult to estimate, some studies conclude that non-profit property makes up 7 to 10 percent of total property value in Philadelphia, Boston, Baltimore, and New York City (Kenyon and Langley, 2010).

To offset the loss of property tax revenue, many cities make other arrangements, including special property tax assessments for certain services, such as sewer hook-ups; fees for services; negotiated payments in lieu of taxes (PILOTs); or negotiated services in lieu of taxes. These approaches are not possible in all cities, because PILOTs are voluntary agreements and because fees and special assessments are not always authorized. For additional information on these arrangements, see Kenyon and Langley (2010).

4.3. *Homestead Exemptions*

Many state policy makers are concerned about the burden of the property tax on people with relatively inexpensive houses. This concern is consistent with the view, discussed in Section 3.2, that the property tax on owner-occupied housing is regressive. To ease this burden, many states have implemented homestead exemptions, the subject of this section, and/or circuit breakers, the subject of Section 4.4.

A homestead exemption exempts the first $X of a house's value from the property tax, where X is a value set by the government. This value varies from state to state and sometimes from one local jurisdiction to another. A homestead exemption may be expressed as the first $X of assessed value, but states recognize that they must adjust for variation in assessment practices. In other words, states that set an exemption in terms of assessed value allow the value of this exemption to vary across districts so that it equals the same market value in every assessing district. For analytical purposes, therefore, it is appropriate to specify a homestead exemption in terms of market value. Thus, homeowner i's tax payment with a homestead exemption is

$$T_i = t^*(V_i - X_i) \tag{5}$$

where t^* is the property tax rate in the homeowner's jurisdiction. This rate applies to each dollar of house value above X. If X_i is larger than V_i, as it often is in a few states, then homeowner i pays no property tax.

Almost all states have some kind of special exemptions for the elderly, for people with disabilities, and/or for veterans. About 20 states have exemptions for all homeowners. Moreover, a few states also make an assumption about the share of rent that covers property taxes and on that basis provide a homestead exemption to renters. The latest information on homestead exemptions by state is provided by the Lincoln Institute of Land Policy (LILP, 2018).

As shown in Figure 7, Panel A, homestead exemptions change the property tax from a proportional tax to a progressive tax relative to the house-value tax base. The horizontal axis is the tax base and the vertical axis is the effective tax rate, defined as T_i/V_i. In this figure, the rate with no exemption, t^*, is 2 percent for all households. With the exemption, $X, which is $40,000 in this figure, the effective tax rate is zero for homeowners with house values at or below $X and gradually increases until it approaches t^* at high house values. This tax schedule is obviously very progressive.

Panel B of Figure 7 describes the tax schedule with a homestead exemption using household income as the base. Following the discussion of household housing demand in Section 3.2, this figure is based on the assumption that the income elasticity of demand for housing is 0.5. This panel shows that the homestead exemption reduces the regressivity of the property tax substantially at low incomes and slightly at high incomes. The example in this panel even includes a progressive segment where the

J. Yinger

Panel A: House Value as the Base

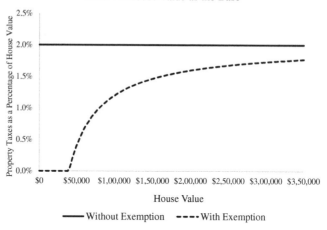

Panel B: Household Income as the Base

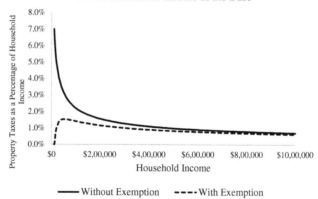

Panel C: Income as the Base; Varying House Values

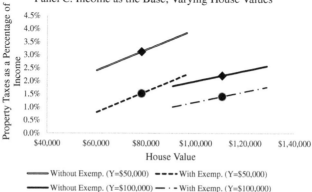

Figure 7   Property tax schedules with an exemption.

tax burden increases with income, but this segment does not appear with significantly lower values of the exemption.

As shown in Panel C of Figure 7, the impact of an exemption also depends on the ratio of income to house value. The square markers in this panel indicate points that also appear on the solid line in Panel B; the round markers indicate points that appear in the dashed line in Panel B. Variation around these markers shows that holding income constant, the tax burden as a share of income increases with house value. In other words, an exemption program does not reward homeowners who decide to buy expensive housing relative to their income.

An unusual variant on this design appears in New York State's School Tax Relief Program, STAR, which gives all homeowners an exemption for school property taxes. Under this program the amount of the exemption, X, is adjusted to be higher in counties with above-average sales prices for single-family houses. As a result of this provision, called the Sales Price Differential Factor (SPDF), the exemption is over three times as high in the richest counties in the state than in the average county (see Chapter 8). By subsidizing people who live in high-cost locations, the SPDF has the dubious distinction of under-mining both the efficiency and the fairness of the property tax.

One key feature of some homestead exemptions, including STAR, is that the local governments using them are reimbursed by the state for the lost revenue. An unreimbursed exemption requires a jurisdiction to raise its tax rate in order to collect the same amount of revenue it would have collected if the exemption were not in place. With a reimbursed exemption, however, the state compensates the taxing jurisdiction for the property tax revenue lost because of the exemption.

The problem with this reimbursement is that it lowers the price of local government services and thereby gives the affected local government an incentive to raise property taxes and increase spending. Suppose a local government increases its tax rate by 1 percent. Then a household with a house worth $\$V$ will pay $(0.01)(V - X)$ more in property taxes, but thanks to state reimbursement, the local government will receive $(0.01)(V)$. In other words, the taxpayer's share of the tax increase is only $(V - X)/V$. In the case of STAR, the value of X in most school districts is \$30,000, so a taxpayer with a \$90,000 house pays only two-thirds of a tax increase, which is equivalent to a 33 percent reduction in the price of education. Not surprisingly, school districts responded to this incentive (Rockoff, 2010; Eom *et al.*, 2014). The analysis in Eom *et al.* (reproduced as Chapter 8) finds that these incentives increased school property taxes in New York State by almost 14 percent.

This incentive to increase spending could easily be eliminated through a minor change in the design of a homestead exemption. The tax savings from the exemption is t^*X, where t^* is the local government's property tax rate. Replacing t^* with $\bar{t}$, the average property tax rate in the state or region, would eliminate this incentive because a local government could not increase the compensation it receives from the state by increasing its own tax rate.[42] To the best of my knowledge, no state uses this revised design.

4.4. *Circuit Breakers*

A circuit breaker is a policy ensuring a property tax payment does not exceed a certain fraction of the taxpayer's income. The flow of taxes, like a flow of electricity, is cut off once it reaches an undesirable level. To be specific, a circuit breaker provides a tax break (usually through an income tax credit) if a household's property tax payment, t^*V, exceeds a given share, β, of its income, Y. The credit, CB, is a selected percentage, α, of the difference between these two amounts. For taxpayer i,

$$
\begin{aligned}
CB_i &= \alpha(t^*V_i - \beta Y_i) \quad \text{if } (t^*V_i - \beta Y_i) > 0 \\
CB_i &= 0 \qquad\qquad\qquad \text{if } (t^*V_i - \beta Y_i) \leq 0
\end{aligned}
\tag{6}
$$

Equation (6) describes a "single-threshold" circuit breaker, where the threshold, β, is the same for all households. With $\alpha = 1$ and $\beta = 0.035$, for example, the credit equals the entire property tax payment above 3.5 percent of the taxpayer's income. Many states use a "multiple-threshold" design instead, with a higher value of β for lower-income households. In addition, some states use a "sliding-scale" design, which caps property tax payments as a percentage of income, with a higher percentage for lower-income households. This design is equivalent to equation (6) with $\beta = 0$ and a value of α that decreases with household income. Circuit breakers are typically "refundable" income tax credits, which means that a taxpayer can receive the full credit even if he or she does not owe any income tax. Bowman *et al.* (2009) describe and analyze the full range of circuit breaker designs.

About half of the states have circuit breakers for elderly homeowners and/or elderly renters. All homeowners and renters are eligible for a circuit breaker in a few states. For more information on the use of this policy, see LILP (2018).[43] Because renters do not write property tax checks, a circuit

---

[42]Another way to weaken this incentive (but cause other problems) is to limit property tax rate increases. A limit of this type was implemented in New York State in 2011. See Section 4.6.

[43]Yinger (2015) presents an evaluation of a circuit breaker proposal in New York State.

breaker cannot apply to renters unless it includes an assumption about the share of rent that covers the property tax on the apartment. As discussed in Section 3.2, this share is difficult to estimate, and the rental shares in circuit breaker laws vary considerably across states.

The tax schedules for a single-threshold circuit breaker are illustrated in Figure 8. Panel A shows the tax schedule with respect to property value, assuming α equals 1 and β equals 0.035. The horizontal axis is the value of a taxpayer's home (or corresponding rental measure) and the vertical axis is the effective property tax rate after the credit. The horizontal line at 2 percent (t^*) is the tax rate that would apply to all property without any circuit breaker or other relief. This is, of course, a proportional tax relative to the base, V. This figure, which describes a circuit breaker (CB) at two different income levels (Y), reveals that a CB has one progressive element and one regressive element relative to the property tax base. The progressive element is that the tax relief kicks in sooner at lower income levels. The regressive element is that the tax relief increases with house value.

Panel B of Figure 8 contains the comparable schedule with income as the base at two different house values (V). This panel shows that a CB changes the schedule from highly regressive to proportional up to the cut-off income defined by equation (6) but has no impact on regressivity after that income level. As in the case of a homestead exemption, the main effect of a CB is to provide substantial tax savings to low-income households. At a given income level, however, a CB, unlike an exemption, provides greater savings to households with higher house values. Panel C of Figure 8 makes this point in another way. This panel shows how variation in house value affects property taxes as a percentage of income, holding income constant. At any given income level, tax relief is not provided below a certain house value. Above that value, however, tax relief increases significantly as income rises.

Circuit breakers are designed to help people who have a hard time paying property taxes out of their current income. This design makes the property tax more progressive and is particularly helpful for low-income people who experience a temporary loss of income. Nevertheless, circuit breakers have two serious weaknesses.

First, circuit breakers reward households who decide to buy or rent expensive housing relative to their income. This point is illustrated by Figure 8. In all three panels, the tax relief provided to households at a given income level increases with house value. People who buy an expensive house relative to their income may have trouble paying their property taxes out of their income, but no equity principle justifies a tax break to them relative to

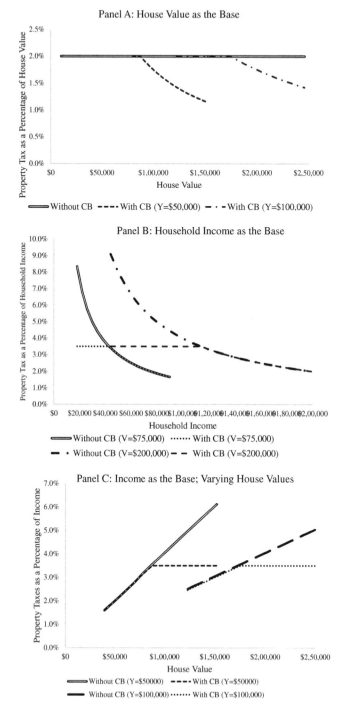

Figure 8   Property tax schedules with a circuit breaker.

their more frugal neighbors. It is simply not fair to give a larger tax break to a household with a more expensive house, holding income constant.[44]

The second weakness is that a circuit breaker gives a tax break to many households who do not really need assistance. Some people like circuit breakers, for example, because they help some "empty-nesters," who are parents whose children have left home. A circuit breaker helps these people stay in the house where they raised their children even after they retire and experience a loss of income. However, these people could borrow against the value of their house to support their income needs. A tax break from the government simply subsidizes their children's inheritance, which is not a pressing fairness concern. Another example is that people who live in an area where house values have risen rapidly, such as a newly popular vacation area, may experience an increase in their property taxes relative to their income and therefore have difficulty paying their property tax bill. These people also experience a significant capital gain on their house, against which they could borrow. These newly wealthy households do not need the tax relief provided by a circuit breaker. In short, a circuit breaker is a less cost-effective way to ease the burden of property taxes on low-income households than are property tax exemptions, because circuit breakers give tax relief to many people who may have a cash-flow problem but who do not need tax relief.[45]

A better approach to these cash-flow problems is to implement a "tax deferral program," which allows empty-nesters or people in areas where property value have increased dramatically or elderly homeowners to put off paying any increase in their property taxes until the house is sold or passed on to the homeowner's heirs. At that time, the postponed property taxes and accumulated interest are paid to the government. About two dozen states have a program of this type (LILP, 2018), usually with limited eligibility. More extensive use of this approach appears to be warranted.

Finally, a circuit breaker, like a state-compensated homestead exemption, may give some taxpayers an incentive to vote for higher spending on local public services. A taxpayer who qualifies for a circuit breaker only pays a share, $(1 - \alpha)$ according to equation (6), of any increase in local property taxes. This lowering of the tax share is equivalent to a price subsidy, and it may lead voters to want more spending on the subsidized good, that is, on local public services. Evidence of this type of effect is provided by Fisher and

---

[44] Circuit breakers also cause distortion because they lower the price a household must pay to upgrade its housing.

[45] For a more positive review of circuit breakers, see Bowman *et al.* (2009).

Rasche (1984). Because a circuit breaker does not apply to all households even in a given jurisdiction, it does not appear to elicit behavioral responses as large as those elicited by a state-funded homestead exemption.

4.5. *Tax Increment Financing*

Tax increment financing (TIF) is a property tax tool designed to promote community economic development.[46] With this tool, a zone is designated around an economic development project, such as a convention center or industrial park. Then any increase in the property taxes in that zone is reserved for further development in the zone, such as streets or parks or additional business activity. The basic idea of TIF is that the property tax increases in the zone would not have occurred without the economic development project. However, the impact of the project is not known, and the change in property tax revenue could be far above or far below the component of the change the project causes. As a result, TIFs are usually implemented in areas where property values are rising for reasons other than the economic development project. This strategy ensures that some money for economic development will be available even if the core project does not have a significant impact on property values.

The problem with this approach, of course, is that it removes an unpredictable amount of revenue from the property tax stream that is used to fund basic city services, such as police and fire services. A good example of this problem is provided by Nguyen-Hoang (2014), who studies the impact of TIFs in Iowa, which has 2,200 TIF districts. In the Iowa case, a TIF district can claim the entire property tax increase in the district, regardless of the service to which the property tax revenue is devoted. Any increase in school property taxes in the district, therefore, goes to the TIF district, not to the schools. Proponents of this design say that the spillover development outside the zone that is caused by the TIP project will boost school revenues despite this design. Opponents say that this spillover is likely to be small or non-existent so the TIF design simply takes some property tax growth away from schools. Nguyen-Hoang finds that "greater use of TIF is associated with reduced education expenditures" (p. 536). This effect is larger in poorer

---

[46]Youngman (2016) provides a more detailed examination of TIF districts. Her analysis supports the conclusion that TIFs have serious limitations as an economic development tool — a conclusion highlighted by the case of California, which pioneered TIF districts in the 1950s but ended new TIF projects in 2011.

school districts. Nguyen-Hoang recommends several TIF reforms, such as allowing school districts to opt out of TIF programs.

4.6. *Tax Limits*

Local officials are typically not free to set, or ask voters to ratify, any property tax rate they want. Because of state rules, these officials are likely to face a limit on the rate for their jurisdiction or a limit on the rate for all the local jurisdictions that serve a given location. They also may face a limit on revenue growth or expenditure growth. In some cases, these limits are so strict that the property tax is effectively transformed into a state tax, that is, into a tax that cannot be altered at all by local officials. For a complete catalogue of the various types of limits, see Kioko (2011). All of these limits are examples of state rules that restrict the revenue of local governments. In principle, states could make up for these restrictions by giving local governments more aid, but this is rarely the case. Instead, local governments must cut services, set up special districts that collect property taxes but are beyond the reach of tax limits (Zhang, 2018), or turn to other revenue sources they control, such as fees and fines.[47] These alternative revenue sources appear to me to be more regressive than property tax revenues.

Perhaps the best-known limit is Proposition 13 in California, which was passed by voters in 1978 and which is often said to have set off a revolt against the property tax in other states. This proposition restricts the total local property tax rate across all jurisdictions in a given location to 1 percent. Proposition 13 and similar propositions in other states were often passed on the assumption that restricting property tax revenue would force local governments to be more efficient. The evidence, which is reviewed in Downes and Figlio (2015), says otherwise. All else equal, tax limits lead to lower-quality public services.

Although local governments cannot override the Proposition 13 tax limit, they can levy a parcel tax, that is, a fixed tax on each parcel, if two-third of the voters approve.[48] Because of this high approval threshold, only 59 cities

---

[47]According to the Tax Policy Center, "[c]harges and miscellaneous fees, such as water, sewerage, and parking meter fees collected by municipal or county governments, provided ... 23 percent of general revenue" for local governments in 2014. This share has been slowly increasing over time. See https://www.taxpolicycenter.org/briefing-book/what-are-sources-revenue-local-governments.

[48]With a supermajority vote, voters can override the 1 percent limit to pay for capital costs. See Chapter 10.

and 114 school districts passed a parcel tax between 2003 and 2012, and the parcel tax provided a very small share of local revenue (Sonstelie, 2014). The behavioral consequence of this parcel tax are explored in Chapter 10. So far as I know, California is the only state to allow a parcel tax, which imposes the same tax on a mansion, a shack, a huge factory, and a mom-and-pop store. This design ensures that a parcel tax violates the vertical equity standard, which makes it a poor substitute for the property tax.

A tax limitation in New York reveals that tax limits may result in other types of inequity, as well. In 2011, New York State passed a limit on the percentage increase in the property tax levy. Although the actual cap is quite complicated, because it adjusts for many features of a school district's budget, the basic idea of the cap is to limit increases in a district's property tax revenue to 2 percent per year.[49] Because wealthy school districts receive less state aid, they rely more heavily on property taxes than do poor districts, and their property tax levies — and hence their allowable levy increase — are much larger in absolute terms. A few wealthy downstate suburbs collected over $30,000 per pupil in property tax revenue in 2011–2012, whereas the Upstate Big Three (Buffalo, Rochester, and Syracuse) collected about $3,700. The tax cap therefore allows these rich districts to collect $30,000 × 0.02 = $600 more per pupil the next year; the Big Three can only raise their revenue by $3,700 × 0.02 = $74. Over the next 25 years the average downstate suburb will be allowed to raise its revenue by almost $14,000 per pupil, but the Upstate Big Three will only be able to raise their revenue by a little over $2,000 per pupil. Without a dramatic (and unlikely) shift in state aid toward poorer districts, therefore, the fiscal disparities across school districts in New York State are going to keep growing and growing.[50] A similar equity problem arises with a property tax rate limit, such as the 1 percent limit imposed by Proposition 13 in California. Some jurisdictions are wealthy and can raise a great deal of revenue at this rate, but poor districts, which are likely to have higher costs, may find their revenue falls far short of what they need.

Another well-known limit is Proposition 2½ in Massachusetts, which was passed in 1980 and which limits both the effective municipal property tax

---

[49] To be precise, the limit is the lesser of 2 percent and the rate of inflation. Voters can override the limit with a 60 percent supermajority vote. See NYSDTF (2018b).

[50] Actually, New York State went in the opposite direction for two years by awarding a "property tax freeze credit" to jurisdictions that implemented an efficiency plan and did not exceed the levy limit. This credit paid for the levy increases in eligible districts, and therefore gives local jurisdictions an incentive to increase their levy up to the limit. Moreover, it added a regressive component to state support for local governments.

rate and the annual increase in property tax revenue to $2^1/_2$ percent, with an adjustment for new development. This limit has a significant impact because municipalities in Massachusetts, called cities and towns, provide a comprehensive set of local public services, including K-12 education plus police and fire protection. This limit has an override provision, and quite a few municipalities, particularly wealthy ones, have voted to set higher rates. An insightful analysis of the decision to override is provided by Bradbury, Mayer, and Case (2001).

Finally, several education finance reforms have, among other things, transformed some or all of the local school property tax into a state tax, with a single rate set by the state and with state control over the tax revenue. Examples include reforms in Kansas (Duncombe and Johnston, 2004) and Michigan (Cullen and Loeb, 2004).

5. Policy Conclusions

The property tax is the mainstay of local government revenue in the United States. Although the basic design of a property tax is simple, both the administrative details and the variations on the basic design are complex and lead to complex behavioral responses from the people affected, including taxpayers, businesses, assessors, and other public officials. Anyone studying local public finance needs to be aware of these complexities in the design and administration of the property tax. Moreover, as discussed in many of the following chapters, an extensive literature examines behavioral responses to these complexities, with plenty of room for additional contributions.

The property tax is a valuable component of the tax system that funds the U.S. federal system. This system would undoubtedly be less fair and less efficient without it. Nevertheless, the property tax could certainly be improved in many different ways.[51]

The most important property tax challenge is to make sure assessments are as accurate as possible. States can help meet this challenge by requiring (and subsidizing) high assessment standards and frequent revaluations and by making sure that assessing districts are large enough, say counties, to take advantage of economies of scale. Local governments can help meet this challenge by hiring professional assessors, being transparent about assessing methods, and making it easy for taxpayers to contest their property tax bills. As discussed in Chapter 3, allowing assessments to become out of date creates

---

[51]Reschovsky (2017) provides an alternative, but overlapping, list of property tax reforms.

fairness problems that are difficult to resolve. Fairness problems also arise with legislated limits on assessment growth, which favor long-term residents over new residents. These problems could be mitigated by setting minimum allowable assessment/sales ratios.

A second key challenge is to find ways to manage the property tax burden. States should provide sufficient education aid so that school districts can meet state educational standards at a reasonable property tax rate. Because the property tax is so regressive across school districts, this lesson applies with particular force for districts with low wealth. A well-designed foundation aid formula, which is discussed in Part 5 of this book, can minimize or even eliminate this regressivity.

When property tax rates in a state are high relative to similar states, elected officials should consider either increasing state aid to local governments or else allowing school districts and other local governments to levy other broad-based taxes. Property tax limits are a popular way to keep property taxes down. Unless they are accompanied by state aid increases or access to other revenue sources, they often lead to cuts in essential services and magnify the unfair revenue disparities between rich and poor jurisdictions.

A third challenge is to improve the fairness of the property tax across taxpayers with different incomes. The most pressing equity problem is that a standard property tax places a high burden on low-income homeowners. Most states ease this burden using homestead exemptions or circuit breakers for certain groups, such as the elderly and veterans, or for all taxpayers. Both of these policies make the property tax more progressive. A circuit breaker is the less appealing policy of the two because, at any given income level, it gives larger benefits to people who buy larger houses and because it gives benefits to some people who do not really need the help, including people who have experienced a rapid rise in house value. A better approach is to combine a homestead exemption, with a property tax deferral plan. To increase progressivity relative to income, the exemption amount could be higher for households with lower incomes.[52]

A fourth challenge is to align the property tax with a jurisdiction's economic development objectives. Scholars and policy makers appear to have

---

[52] A plan varying the exemption amount with income presumably would be administered like a sliding-scale circuit breaker, namely, as an income tax credit. This shift in administration would facilitate the use of a state-wide or regional average tax property rate, instead of the taxpayer's local property tax rate, in calculating the credit amount, thereby eliminating the price incentive associated with a state-compensated property tax exemption.

different views about this challenge. Most scholars argue that property tax breaks for businesses are not an effective economic development policy, and yet the local public officials who decide such things all seem to hand them out anyway. The key issue, it seems to me, is that firms are unlikely to move into a jurisdiction in response to property tax cuts or abatements because the savings from lower property taxes are likely to be offset by increases in land prices. Industrial parks on land owned by the jurisdiction provide one possible way out of this dilemma.

Tax increment financing is another popular economic development tool. This tool is based on two faulty premises. The first faulty premise is that all the growth in the property tax base in the zone around a development arises because of that development. In fact, many TIF projects are placed in locations that already have rapidly growing property values. The second faulty premise is that the best use of the tax increment in the TIF zone is always for the TIF project. In fact, cities might have much better uses for that revenue. A more sensible approach, in my view, is to identify projects worthy of governmental support and then to design a budget that supplies the appropriate amount of money for each project.

Overall, the existing evidence indicates that the best way to harness the property tax for economic development is to preserve the tax base, i.e., to minimize property tax abatements, and to use the available revenue to provide the public services, such as good schools, that make a jurisdiction attractive to people or firms that might want to move there.

Although the basic formula for a property tax is simple, the property tax is in fact a complex revenue source, with many variants that raise complex issues for policy makers to address. The chapters in the rest of this book provide further insight into many of these issues. They also show that in evaluating the property tax, as well as other topics in state and local government finance, broad themes are often shared across states, whereas each state, and often each local government, comes up with its own details. Scholars studying local public finance in the United States would be well advised to look for both themes and variations.

Acknowledgments

I am grateful to Yilin Hou, Daphne Kenyon, Yusun Kim, Jerry Miner, Andy Reschovsky, Joan Youngman, and Bo Zhao for helpful comments on drafts of this chapter.

References

Atuahene, Bernadette A., and Timothy R. Hodge. 2018. Stategraft. *Southern California Law Review* **91**(2) (January): 263–302.

Banzhaf, H. Spencer and Nathan Lavery. 2010. Can the land tax help curb urban sprawl? Evidence from growth patterns in Pennsylvania. *Journal of Urban Economics* **67**(2): 169–179.

Bartik, Timothy J. 2017. *A New Panel Database on Business Incentives for Economic Development Offered by State and Local Governments in the United States*. W.E. Upjohn Institute for Employment Research, February.

Bowman, John H., Daphne A. Kenyon, Adam Langley, and Bethany P. Paquin. 2009. Property tax circuit breakers: Fair and cost-effective relief for taxpayers. Policy Focus Report, Lincoln Institute for Land Policy. Available at: https://www.lincolninst.edu/sites/default/files/pubfiles/property-tax-circuit-breakers-full_0.pdf.

Bradbury, Katharine, Christopher J. Mayer, and Karl E. Case. 2001. Property tax limits, local fiscal behavior, and property values: Evidence from Massachusetts under Proposition 2½. *Journal of Public Economics* **80**(2): 287–311.

Brueckner, Jan K. 1986. A modern analysis of the effects of site value taxation. *National Tax Journal* **39**(1): 49–58.

Cabral, Marika and Caroline Hoxby. 2012. The hated property tax: Salience, tax rates, and tax revolts. NBER Working Paper 18514, November.

Carroll, Robert J. and John Yinger. 1994. Is the property tax a benefit tax? The case of rental housing. *National Tax Journal* **47**(2): 295–316. [Chapter 4]

Chernick, Howard and Andrew Reschovsky. 2017. The fiscal condition of U.S. cities: Revenues, expenditures, and the 'Great Recession'. *Journal of Urban Affairs* **39**(4): 488–505.

Cullen, Julie Berry and Susanna Loeb. 2004. School finance reform in Michigan: evaluating proposal A. In J. Yinger (ed.), *Helping Children Left Behind: State Aid and the Pursuit of Educational Equity*, pp. 215–250, Cambridge, MA: MIT Press.

Downes, Thomas and David Figlio. 2015. Tax and expenditure limits, school finance, and school quality. In Helen F. Ladd and Margaret E. Goertz (eds.), *Handbook of Research in Education Finance and Policy*, pp. 392–407, 2nd edition, New York: Routledge.

Duncombe, William D. and Jocelyn Johnston. 2004. The impacts of school finance reform in Kansas: Equity is in the eye of the beholder. In J. Yinger (ed.), *Helping Children Left Behind: State Aid and the Pursuit of Educational Equity*, pp. 147–194, Cambridge, MA: MIT Press,.

Duncombe, William D. and John Yinger. 2001. Alternative paths to property tax relief. In W.E. Oates (ed.), *Property Taxation and Local Government Finance*, pp. 243–294, Lincoln Institute of Land Policy.

Duncombe, William D., Anna Lukemeyer, and John Yinger. 2008. Dollars without sense: The mismatch between the no child left behind act accountability system and title I funding. In R. D. Kahlenberg (ed.), *Improving on No Child Left Behind: Getting Education Reform Back on Track*, pp. 19–102, New York: The Century Foundation.

Eom, Tae Ho. 2008. A comprehensive model of determinants of property tax assessment quality: Evidence in New York state. *Public Budgeting and Finance* **28**(1): 58–81.

Eom, Tae Ho, William D. Duncombe, Phuong Nguyen-Hoang, and John Yinger. 2014. The unintended consequences of property tax relief: New York state's STAR program. *Education Finance and Policy* **9**(4): 446–480. [Chapter 8]

Fisher, Ronald C. 2009. What policy makers should know about property taxes. *Land Lines* (January): 8–14.

Fisher, Ronald C. 2015. *State and Local Public Finance*, 4th edition, Routledge.

Fisher, Ronald C. and Robert H. Rasche. 1984. The incidence and incentive effects of property tax credits: Evidence from Michigan. *Public Finance Review* **12**(3): 291–319.

Fox, Justin. 2017. Why economists love property taxes and you don't. *Bloomberg*, November 28. Available at: https://www.bloomberg.com/view/articles/2017-11-28/why-economists-love-property-taxes-and-you-don-t.

Goodman, Allen C. 1988. An econometric model of housing price, permanent income, tenure choice, and housing demand. *Journal of Urban Economics* **23**(3): 327–353.

Grotto, Jason. 2017a. An unfair burden. *Chicago Tribune*, June 10. Available at: http://apps.chicagotribune.com/news/watchdog/cook-county-property-tax-divide/assessments.html.

Grotto, Jason. 2017b. The problem with appeals. *Chicago Tribune*, June 10. Available at: http://apps.chicagotribune.com/news/watchdog/cook-county-property-tax-divide/appeals.html.

Hamilton, Bruce W. 1975. Zoning and property taxation in a system of local governments. *Urban Studies* **12**: 205–211.

Hogue, Carma. 2013. Government organization summary report: 2012. U.S. Bureau of the Census Report G12-CG-ORG, September. Available at: https://www.census.gov/library/publications/2013/econ/g12-cg-org.html.

Johnson, Randall K. 2015. Who wins residential property tax appeals? *Columbia Journal of Tax Law* **6**(2): 209–240.

Kenyon, Daphne A. and Adam H. Langley. 2010. Payments in lieu of taxes: Balancing municipal and nonprofit interests. Policy Focus Report, Lincoln Institute of Land Policy, November. Available at: https://www.lincolninst.edu/publications/policy-focus-reports/payments-lieu-taxes.

Kenyon, Daphne A, Adam H. Langley, and Bethany P. Paquin. 2012. Property tax incentive pitfalls. *National Tax Journal* **65**(4): 1011–1021.

Kioko, Sharon M. 2011. Structure of state-level tax and expenditure limits. *Public Budgeting and Finance* **31**(2): 43–78.

Ladd, Helen F. and John Yinger. 1991. *America's Ailing Cities: Fiscal Health and the Design of Urban Policy*, Updated Edition, Baltimore: Johns Hopkins University Press.

Lincoln Institute of Land Policy. 2018 (updated annually). Significant features of the property tax. Available at: http://datatoolkits.lincolninst.edu/subcenters/significant-features-property-tax/about.aspx.

McGuire, Therese J., Leslie E. Papke, and Andrew Reschovsky. 2015. Local funding of schools: The property tax and its alternatives. In Helen F. Ladd and Margaret E. Goertz (eds.), *Handbook of Research in Education Finance and Policy*, pp. 376–391, 2nd edition, New York: Routledge.

Mian, Atif and Amir Sufi. 2015. *House of Debt: How They (and You) Caused the Great Recession, and How We Can Prevent It from Happening Again* Chicago: University of Chicago Press.

New York State Department of Taxation and Finance. 2012. Assessment equity. Available at: https://www.tax.ny.gov/research/property/reports/ratio/uniformassmntstd/index.htm.

New York State Department of Taxation and Finance. 2017. "Volume 7 — opinions of counsel SBEA No. 81. Available at: https://www.tax.ny.gov/pubs_and_bulls/orpts/legal_opinions/v7/81.htm.

New York State Department of Taxation and Finance. 2018a. Assessment equity in New York: Results from the 2017 market value survey. Available at: https://www.tax.ny.gov/research/property/reports/cod/2017mvs/index.htm.

New York State Department of Taxation and Finance. 2018b. New York state's property tax cap. Available at: https://www.tax.ny.gov/research/property/cap.htm.

New York State Education Department. 2017. Analysis of school finances in New York state school districts, 2014–2015. Available at: http://www.oms.nysed.gov/faru/PDFDocuments/2016_Analysis_a.pdf.

Nguyen-Hoang, Phuong. 2014. Tax increment financing and education expenditures: The case of Iowa. *Education Finance and Policy* **9**(4): 515–540.

Oates, Wallace E. and Robert M. Schwab. 1997. The impact of urban land taxation: The pittsburgh experience. *National Tax Journal* **50**: 1–21.

Oates, Wallace E. and William A. Fischel. 2016. Are local property taxes regressive, progressive, or what? *National Tax Journal* **69**(2): 415–434.

Reschovsky, Andrew. 2017. The future of U.S. public school revenue from the property tax. Lincoln Institute Policy Brief, September. Available at: https://www.lincolninst.edu/publications/policy-briefs/future-us-public-school-revenue-property-tax.

Rockoff, Jonah. 2010. Local response to fiscal incentives in heterogeneous communities. *Journal of Urban Economics* **68**(2): 138–147.

Ross, Justin M. and Phuong Nguyen-Hoang. 2013. School district income taxes: New revenue or a property tax substitute? *Public Budgeting and Finance* **33**(2): 19–40.

Ross, Stephen and John Yinger. 1999. Sorting and voting: A review of the literature on urban public finance. In P. Cheshire and E. S. Mills (eds.), *Handbook of Urban and Regional Economics*, pp. 2001–2060, vol. 3, Applied Urban Economics, North Holland.

Sexton, Terri A., Steven M. Sheffrin, and Arthur O'Sullivan. 1999. Proposition 13: Unintended effects and feasible reforms. *National Tax Journal* **52**(1): 99–112.

Sjoquist, David L. and Mary Beth Walker. 1999. Economies of scale in property tax assessment, *National Tax Journal* **52**(2): 207–220.

Sonstelie, Jon. 2014. California's parcel tax. Working Paper, Lincoln Institute of Land Policy, September. Available at: https://www.lincolninst.edu/publications/working-papers/californias-parcel-tax.

Srithongrung, Arwiphawee and Kenneth A. Kriz. 2014. The impact of subnational fiscal policies on economic growth: A dynamic analysis approach. *Journal of Policy Analysis and Management* **33**(4): 912–928.

Sullivan, Arthur M. 1985. The general-equilibrium effects of the residential property tax: Incidence and excess burden. *Journal of Urban Economics* **18**(2): 235–250.

Tiebout, Charles M. 1956. A pure theory of local expenditures. *Journal of Political Economy* **64**: 416–424.

Wassmer, Robert W. and John E. Anderson. 2001. Bidding for business: New evidence on the effect of locally offered economic development incentives in a metropolitan area. *Economic Development Quarterly* **15**(2): 132–148.

Yang, Zhou. 2018. Differential effects of land value taxation. *Journal of Housing Economics* **39**: 33–39.

Yinger, John. 1999. Capitalization and efficiency. In A. Panagariya, P. Portney, and R. Schwab (eds.), *Environmental and Public Economics: Essays in Honor of W. E. Oates*, pp. 310–326, Elgar, Edward Publishing, Inc.

Yinger, John. 2012. Four flaws in New York State's property taxes and how to fix them: The homestead option. It's Elementary Column, July. Available at: http://maxwell.syr.edu/cpr/efap/it_s_elementary.

Yinger, John. 2015. A circuit breaker for New York state? It's Elementary Column, March. Available at: http://maxwell.syr.edu/cpr/efap/it_s_elementary.

Yinger, John, Howard S. Bloom, Axel Börsch-Supan, and Helen F. Ladd. 1988. *Property Taxes and House Values: The Theory and Estimation of Intrajurisdictional Property Tax Capitalization*, Academic Press.

Youngman, Joan. 2016. *A Good Tax: Legal and Policy Issues for the Property Tax in the United States*. Lincoln Institute of Land Policy.

Zabel, Jeffrey A. 2004. The demand for housing services. *Journal of Housing Economics* **13**(1): 16–35.

Zhang, Pengju. 2018. The unintended impact of tax and expenditure limitations on the use of special districts: Politics of circumvention. *Economics of Governance* **19**(1): 21–50.

Zodrow, George R. 2001. The property tax as a capital tax: A room with three views. *National Tax Journal* **54**(1): 139–156.

Zodrow, George R. 2014. Intrajurisdictional capitalization and the incidence of the property tax. *Regional Science and Urban Economics* **45**: 57–66.

Chapter 2

Bidding and Sorting*

John Yinger

*Departments of Public Administration and International
Affairs and of Economics, Syracuse University, Syracuse, NY, United States*
jyinger@maxwell.syr.edu

1. Introduction

One of the central questions in local public finance is: **How do households select a community in which to live?** This chapter provides an intuitive overview of the academic literature on this question. It draws heavily on the more technical presentation in Ross and Yinger (1999).[1] Scholars have also considered two related questions: How do communities select the level of local public services and tax rates? Under what conditions is the community-choice process compatible with the local voting process? These two questions are not addressed here, but they are covered in Ross and Yinger.

The literature on community selection is often traced back to a famous paper by Tiebout (1956), who argued that people shop for a community, just as they shop for other things. This process came to be known as "shopping with one's feet." The Tiebout model became very influential both because it identified an important type of behavior to be studied and because it concluded that the process of allocating people to communities has certain desirable properties. To be specific, Tiebout claimed that this process, like any unfettered market process (without externalities) is efficient. As it turns

---

*This chapter is reproduced from "Bidding and Sorting," In J. Yinger (ed.), *Housing and Commuting: The Theory of Urban Residential Structure*, pp. 361–384. World Scientific Publishing, 2018.
[1]See Ross and Yinger (1999) for extensive references to the literature.

out, Tiebout's analysis was highly simplified, and indeed left out both the housing market and the property tax, which is the main source of local revenue in the United States. Thus, many people regard this analysis as unrealistic and reject its efficiency conclusion, but others think that this conclusion is still correct, at least to a first approximation.

This chapter provides an intuitive review of the literature since Tiebout. It begins by addressing the way a household decides how much to pay for housing in a given community, called bidding, and what happens when different types of households compete for housing, called sorting. The chapter also introduces an important empirical phenomenon, called capitalization, which is a test of bidding and sorting models, and explores the normative issues first raised by Tiebout. A key example of capitalization, namely property tax capitalization, is explored in Chapter 3.

2. Bidding

The central positive question addressed in this chapter is: **How does the housing market allocate households to communities when local public services and property taxes vary from one community to the next?** A broad consensus has emerged concerning the appropriate way to analyze this question. This consensus has general applicability to any country with active housing markets, reasonably mobile households, and multiple local governments that exhibit some variation in public service levels or tax rates. It evolved from the insight made famous by Tiebout, namely that households care about local public services and local taxes and compete for entry into the most desirable communities. This consensus has two components: bidding and sorting.

Bidding analysis builds on a variety of assumptions that roughly characterize urban areas in the United States. First, this analysis assumes that households fall into distinct income-taste classes and that all households care about their consumption of housing, public services, and other goods. Households within a class are considered to be identical in their demands for these things, but many classes may exist. Households are also assumed to be mobile, that is, to be able to move costlessly from one jurisdiction to another. In other words, short-run barriers to mobility are ignored. This assumption implies that an equilibrium cannot exist unless all people in a given income-taste class achieve the same level of satisfaction or, to use the economist's term, of utility. In other words, any household that does not reach as high a utility level as do similar households will have an incentive to move, and this type of moving behavior will lead to a situation in which all similar households have the same utility (and no household has an incentive to move).

All households who live in a jurisdiction are also assumed to receive the same level of public services, and residence in a jurisdiction is assumed to be a precondition for the receipt of public services there.[2] Each urban area is assumed to have many local jurisdictions, which have fixed boundaries and vary in their local public service quality and property tax rates. Finally, in most models, households are homeowners, not renters, and local public services are financed through a local property tax.

These assumptions are used to understand where people live and how much they pay for housing. Thus, they are introduced in a basic analysis of the housing market in which households compete with each other for access to the most desirable locations. In this context, the most desirable locations are those with the best combination of high-quality public services and a low property tax rate. Households compete for entry into desirable locations by **bidding** against each other for housing. To proceed with our analysis, therefore, we must consider bidding behavior in a housing market.

An analysis of bidding behavior depends on four key concepts. Housing is measured in units of **housing services**, which provide an index of the size and quality of a housing unit. For our purposes, we can think of housing services as simply the size a house in square feet, adjusted for the quality of the design, fixtures, and appliances. The **price per unit of housing services** is the associated price concept per unit time, say per year. The **rent** for a housing unit equals the price per unit of housing services multiplied by the number of units of housing services the unit contains. If the unit is an apartment, this rent is equivalent to the annual contract rent. If the unit is owner-occupied, this rent is not observed in the market place but is implicit. The **value** of a housing unit is the amount someone would pay to own that unit; it equals the present value of the flow of net rental services associated with ownership.[3]

---

[2]These two assumptions do not always apply. The quality of schools or of police protection may vary within a jurisdiction, and some people have access to charter schools or other public services in jurisdictions where they do not live (see for example, Reback, 2005).

[3]For an asset with a long life, such as a house, the present value formula reduces to a simple form. Specifically, the value of a house, V, equals the annual rental flow, R, divided by an annual discount rate, say r; that is, $V = R/r$. In this context, r is sometimes called the capitalization rate, because it translates an annual flow, R, into an asset or capital value, V. For more on these concepts and on bid functions, see Chapters 3 and 19.

The price per unit of housing services is assumed to be constant in a given jurisdiction. However, this price (and hence both rent and value) varies across jurisdictions as the quality of public services and the local property tax rate varies. Consider first the case of a single income/taste class, that is, of an urban area in which all households are alike. Because households are mobile, as well as alike, each household must achieve the same utility level. As a result, households who live in jurisdictions with relatively desirable service-tax packages must pay for the privilege in the form of higher housing prices; otherwise, these households would be better off than households in other jurisdictions and those other households would have an incentive to move. Another way to put this is that households who end up in jurisdictions with relatively undesirable service-tax packages must be compensated in the form of relatively low housing prices. This analysis can be summarized in the form of a **bid function**, which indicates the maximum amount a household would pay to live in a jurisdiction as a function of the desirability of the service-tax package there.

This logic is summarized in Figures 1 and 2. In Figure 1, a household's bid, expressed as a price per unit of housing services, is on the vertical axis and the quality of local public services is on the horizontal axis. In this figure, the property tax rate is held constant. As the quality of public services goes up (holding taxes constant), households' bids for housing go up. In other words, people are willing to pay more for housing in a jurisdiction with better public services. Figure 2 plots household bids as a function of the

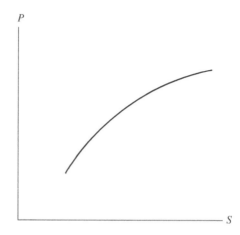

Figure 1 Housing bids as a function of public service quality (holding the property tax rate constant).

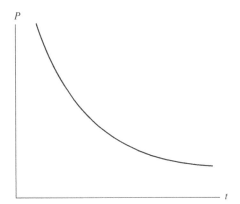

Figure 2 Housing bids as a function of the property tax rate (holding public service quality constant).

property tax rate (holding public service quality constant). The higher the property tax rate, the lower the bid, all else equal.

3. Sorting

Figures 1 and 2 describe the housing bids for one type of household but do not reveal how different types of households are sorted into jurisdictions. Because all households are obviously not alike, an extension to multiple household types — and to sorting — is critical for understanding a federal system with multiple local governments.

The key to understanding sorting is to recognize that bid functions like the one in Figure 1 are **steeper** for some types of households than for others. The steepness of a bid function indicates the extent to which a household type's bids for housing increase when the quality of public services increases. The steepness of a bid function matters because landlords (or housing sellers) prefer to sell to the household type that is willing to pay the most per unit of housing services. Thus, as shown in Figure 3, households with relatively steep bid functions win the competition for housing in locations where the quality of public services, S, is relatively high, and households with relatively flat bid functions win the competition for housing in locations where the quality of public services is relatively low. For example, the group with the steepest bid function in this figure wins the competition for all levels of public service quality above $S3$.

J. Yinger

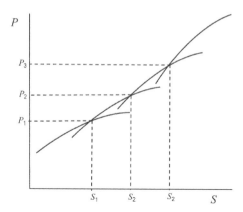

Figure 3   Consensus bidding and sorting.

Under normal circumstances, high-income households have steeper bid functions than low-income households. In other words, high-income households are willing to pay more for an **increment** in public service quality. This does not mean that high-income households intrinsically value service quality more than do low-income households; instead, it simply means that high-income households, who after all have greater resources, increase their bids for housing by a greater amount when service quality goes up.

This relationship between income and bid-function steepness implies that high-income households live in locations with relatively high quality public services, a situation often called "normal" sorting, because it is the usual outcome.[4] This situation is illustrated by Figure 3 when the steeper bid functions (the ones to the right) belong to a higher-income classes and the flatter bid functions (the ones to the left) belong to a lower-income class. In this case, it is clear that the highest-income households win the competition for housing in the highest-service jurisdictions.

Figure 3 also reveals that low-income households win the competition for housing in jurisdictions with relatively low public service quality, such as the jurisdictions providing quality below $S1$. How, one might ask, can low-income people ever outbid high-income people for housing? The key to answering this question is to remember that bids are expressed per unit of housing

---

[4] "Normal" sorting based on access to worksites is discussed in Yinger (2018, Chapter 7).

services. Hence low-income people win the competition because they bid a high amount **per unit of housing services** but consume a relatively low **quantity** of housing services. If housing services are measured in square feet, then low-income people select small apartments or double up so that they consume very few square feet per capita. In Figure 3, low-income households bid more per square foot than high-income households in jurisdictions with low levels of S, and a landlord (or seller) in those jurisdictions can make more money by renting (selling) to low-income people who double up than to high-income people who do not.

The logic of sorting implies that jurisdictions tend to be **homogeneous** in terms of income and preferences. The link to income is not exact. Some households with high incomes but weak preferences for public services might bid the same amount for an increment in public services as do low-income households with a strong preference for public services — and hence end up in the same community. Nevertheless, because income is a key determinant of public service demand, and hence of housing bids, this analysis predicts that the households in a given community will tend to have similar incomes.

However, this analysis does not rule out the possibility of heterogeneous jurisdictions, as defined by bid-function slopes. In fact, if a jurisdiction provides a level of public service quality at which the bid functions of two groups cross, both groups are content to live there. This situation is illustrated by $S1$, $S2$, and $S3$ in Figure 3. At each of these public service levels, two groups bid the same amount for housing, so a jurisdiction delivering any of these service levels will contain two household types. Moreover, it is possible to have a sorting outcome in which many different household types bid the same amount per unit of housing services in a relatively large jurisdiction, such as a central city, and hence all live there.

The sorting analysis in Figure 3 does not consider property taxes. As it turns out, this is entirely appropriate because property taxes do not affect sorting even though they affect bids. The outcome reflects the fact that all household types, regardless of income or preferences, are willing to pay $1 to avoid $1 of property taxes. The same cannot be said for public service quality. Some groups are willing to pay more than others for an improvement in service quality, which is precisely why the bid functions in Figure 3 do not all have the same slope.

Although property taxes do not affect sorting, it is instructive to draw another version of Figure 3 that has property taxes built in. To take this step, we must first consider Figure 4, which presents a household's demand curve

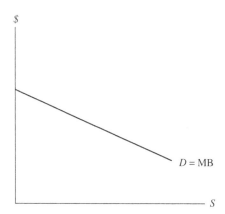

Figure 4   The demand for local public services.

for local public services. Recall that a demand curve indicates the **marginal** benefit from some good or service, that is, the amount a household (or set of households) is willing to pay for an additional unit of that good or service. In Figure 4, a household receiving a relatively low service quality is willing to pay a relatively high amount for an increment in service quality, whereas a household receiving a relatively high service quality is only willing to pay a relatively small amount for a comparable increment. In other words, the marginal willingness to pay for local public service quality declines as service quality increases.

Although the marginal willingness to pay declines with service quality, the marginal cost of service quality is constant or increasing. With constant returns, it takes the same property tax increase to fund a one-unit increase in service quality whether one starts from a low or high public service quality in Figure 4. As service quality increases, therefore, the net willingness to pay for an increment in public service quality declines and may eventually become negative. At very high levels of service quality, in other words, the small benefit from an increment in quality may be outweighed by the required property tax increase. With an upward sloping marginal cost curve for public services, this offset occurs at a lower level of service quality.

This situation is illustrated in Figure 5, which now has community income on the horizontal axis and housing bids on the vertical axis.[5] In this figure, one must distinguish between the income of a class of households

---

[5] A more general version of this analysis employs an index of the demand for local public services, not just income, on the horizontal axis (see Ross and Yinger, *op. cit.*).

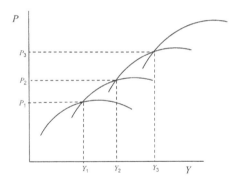

Figure 5   Consensus bidding and sorting net of taxes.

searching for housing, which determines the slope of their bid function, and the income of an existing community, Y, which determines the service quality and property tax rate there. As community income increases, the demand for public service quality increases, but any increase in service quality must be funded with higher property taxes. As a result, bid functions now increase at relatively small levels of service quality, but then become flatter and eventually decline as service quality increases. Figure 5, like Figure 3, illustrates that household types with relatively steep bid function (presumably high-income households) win the competition for housing in jurisdictions with relatively high service quality.

With this approach, one can derive a condition for "normal" sorting. This condition depends on three elasticities: θ, the income elasticity of demand for S; μ, the price elasticity of demand for S; and α, the income elasticity of demand for H. The condition is that normal sorting will occur whenever[6]

$$-\frac{\theta}{\mu} > \alpha.$$

A typical estimate of θ is 0.5 and a typical estimate of μ is -0.1. The literature on housing demand suggests that $\alpha \approx 0.4$. Since $0.5/0.1 = 5.0$ is clearly greater than 0.4, the condition for normal sorting is very likely to be met.

One might ask what the demand for housing has got to do with it. In this model, the ratio of θ to μ is the income elasticity of willingness to

---

[6]This condition first appeared in Henderson (1977).

pay for S, that is, the extent to which willingness to pay for S increases with income. The income elasticity of demand for H, α, indicates how housing consumption increases with income. Since a household must win the competition by demanding more **per unit of H**, an increase in willingness to pay for **S** does not lead to a winning bid if it is spread out over a much larger number of units of **H**. This condition just indicates whether the increase in willingness to pay for S that comes with a higher income leads to a higher P, or whether H increases so fast with income that this higher willingness to pay is spread out over so much more H that it does not result in a higher P.

Some scholars have extended this analysis to consider a continuous distribution of demands, instead of placing households into discrete income-taste classes.[7] This approach adds another source of heterogeneity: a jurisdiction contains a certain chunk of the distribution of demands, not just one or more taste classes.

In addition, this approach helps with the interpretation of across-jurisdiction differences in bids. In the standard model, the difference in bids between two jurisdictions does not correspond to the difference in bids for any particular income-taste class, unless that class occupies both jurisdictions. In other cases, this difference understates the willingness to pay of the higher-demanding class for the difference in services and it overstates the willingness to pay of the lower-demanding class.

But if there is a distribution of demands, the difference in bids between jurisdictions can be interpreted as the willingness to pay of the marginal household — that is, of the household that is just indifferent between the two jurisdictions.

Thanks to sorting, the observed market price function is the highest bid at each public service level, which is called the bid-function envelope. An envelope is, of course, a mathematical concept, and under some assumptions, the form of this envelope can be derived from the form of the underlying bid functions. One such derivation is provided by Yinger (2015) based on constant-elasticity demand functions for public services and housing. An example of this form, which can be estimated, is illustrated in Figure 6. Virtually all the parametric forms used in the literature are special cases of the form Yinger derives.

---

[7]This approach is developed in Epple *et al.* (1984). Associated estimating techniques are presented in Epple *et al.* (2010).

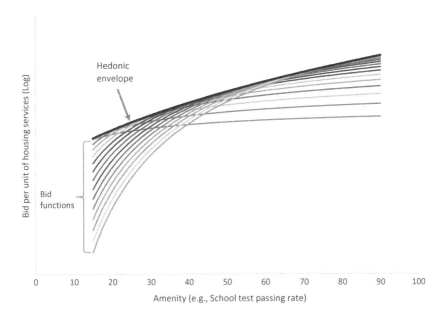

Figure 6   Illustrative bid functions and hedonic envelope.

4. Capitalization

This consensus analysis of the allocation of households to jurisdictions leads to the clear predictions that rents will increase with public service quality and that property values will be higher in communities with higher public service quality and or lower property tax rates, all else equal. These predictions are illustrated in Figure 2 (for property taxes) and Figures 3 and 6 (for public services). The term "capitalization" is used to describe this phenomenon. The annual flows of public services and property taxes are said to be capitalized into the value of houses in the associated jurisdiction.

  A large literature tests this prediction. Virtually all studies of the topic find that the value of key public services, such as elementary and secondary education, are capitalized into the price of housing. Nguyen-Hoang and Yinger (2011) provide a review of the literature on school quality capitalization. These studies are estimating the envelope of the underlying bid functions, so they do not reveal the bids (or willingness to pay) of any particular household type.[8] Nevertheless, the almost universal finding of

---

[8]See Chapters 18 and 20 for more discussion of this issue.

significant public service capitalization indicates that people are willing to pay more to live in locations where public services are better.

According to almost all of the relevant studies, property taxes also appear to be capitalized into house values (see the reviews in Yinger *et al.*, 1988; Ross and Yinger, 1999; and Chapter 3 of Yinger, 2018). It is helpful to distinguish between two definitions of property tax capitalization: The capitalization of current property taxes and the capitalization of the present value of expected future property taxes. Bids on housing reflect expectations about future events, and house buyers' expectations about the future flow of property taxes are likely to be fully capitalized into house values. Scholars observe current taxes, however, not tax expectations. If property taxes are expected to change in the future, current tax differences will not be fully capitalized into house values. Consider, for example, a community with a large shopping center that has been contributing property taxes but is now about to close. Homebuyers are likely to recognize that the relatively low property tax rates in that community cannot be sustained, so their bids for housing will reflect a tax rate that is higher than the one observed at the time of their home purchase. In other words, the present value of expected future taxes is fully capitalized into house values but the present value of the flow associated with the current tax rate is not. This issue is discussed in more detail in Chapter 3.

5. The Hamilton Approach

An alternative approach to sorting was proposed by Hamilton (1975). This approach adds several additional assumptions.

First, it assumes that housing suppliers respond to any variation in the price of housing across communities by expanding the supply of housing in communities with higher prices. This assumption implies, unlike the conventional view, that the price of housing will not be higher in a community with higher public service quality or lower property tax rates.

Second, it assumes that a unit of public services costs the same in every jurisdiction. This assumption rules out the possibility that the cost of public services depends on the characteristics of the people in a jurisdiction. The cost of public services cannot, for example, decline with household income. Without this assumption, low-income households might bid up the price of housing in high-income communities in order to gain access to the low-cost services provided there.

Third, this approach assumes that a jurisdiction can use zoning restrictions to set the consumption of housing at exactly the optimal level.[9] This assumption is important because it rules out the possibility that low-income households want to move into high-income communities in order to take advantage of the large tax bases there. After all, the property tax a household pays depends not only on its own property value but also on the average value of the property in its jurisdiction.

A more formal statement of this issue requires a new concept, namely, a household's **tax share** for local public services. In the case of a private commodity, a household can purchase as much as it wants at the posted market price. In the case of a local public service, however, the amount a household pays for an increment in service quality depends on the property tax system. The tax share is simply the household's share of any increase in property taxes needed to fund an increase in public service quality. Even for a given type of household, this tax share can vary widely across jurisdictions, in part because some jurisdictions have more expensive houses and in part because some jurisdictions have far more commercial and industrial property than others. The tax share is lower in a district with a great deal of commercial and industrial property because much of the burden of any school tax increase falls on commercial and industrial taxpayers, not on homeowners.

The amount a homeowner must pay for a one-unit increase in a public service equals her tax share multiplied by the public service's marginal cost. This product is called the **tax price**. For the purposes of this discussion, the marginal cost will be set to one, so the tax price equals the tax share. In fact, however, the marginal cost of public services varies widely across jurisdictions (see for example, Duncombe and Yinger, 2005).

The easiest way to derive an expression for a tax share is to combine a single voter's property tax payment with the local government budget constraint. A household's property tax payment, T, equals an effective property tax rate, t, multiplied by the value of the household's property, V, or $T = tV$. A local government must set spending per household, E, equal to the property tax rate multiplied by average property value per

---

[9]Zoning tools do not, of course, literally determine housing consumption. However, Hamilton and others argue that the wide range of zoning tools (setback requirements, lot-size restrictions, and so on) enable local governments to control housing consumption with a high degree of precision (see Ross and Yinger, 1999).

household, $\bar{V}$, or $E = t\bar{V}$.[10] This government budget constraint implies that the tax rate must equal spending divided by the tax base or $t = E/\bar{V}$. Substituting this tax rate into the household's tax payment leads to the expression $T = E(V/\bar{V})$. This result implies that the tax share equals $(V/\bar{V})$. The amount someone spends on a private good is the quantity of the good multiplied by the price. In this case, the quantity of the local public services is E, and its "price" is $(V/\bar{V})$.

Now we can return to the issue of sorting. Consider a household with a house value (V) equal to \$100,000. If it lives in a community where the average property value (V^*) equals \$50,000, then its tax share is 2, whereas if it lives in a community where the average property value equals \$200,000, its tax share is only 0.5. In other words, moving from the first community to the second is equivalent to cutting the price it pays for local public services by 75 percent! Obviously, the household will make this move unless the price of housing is higher in the second community. The Hamilton assumption rules out this type of move, and hence the need for price variation across communities, by forcing all households in a given community to purchase the same value of housing. The household in this example cannot move into the second community under the Hamilton assumption because everyone in that community must purchase a house worth \$200,000. Thus, an equilibrium can be attained with the same housing price in both communities.

With the Hamilton assumptions, the sorting diagram takes yet another form, as shown in Figure 7. Two features of this figure should be emphasized. First, every household lives in the jurisdiction that provides the service-tax package it is willing to pay the most for, which is, by definition, its optimal service-tax package. This outcome is efficient because no household can gain by moving to another jurisdiction. Thus, the Hamilton assumptions reproduce Tiebout's main normative result, namely that a system of local governments is efficient. Second, in Figure 6 the price of housing is the same in every community. Because every household lives in its optimal community, no household bids up the price of housing anywhere else. In other words, **the Hamilton assumptions ensure that there is no capitalization.** The price of housing does not reflect the quality of local public services or the local property tax rate.[11]

---

[10]This analysis can easily be extended to consider state aid and other local revenue sources (see Ross and Yinger, 1999).

[11]The Hamilton assumptions do not rule out the capitalization into house values of variation in effective property tax rates due to variation in the amount of commercial and industrial property.

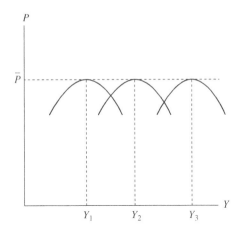

Figure 7 Hamilton bidding and sorting.

A simple test of the validity of the Hamilton model, therefore, is to determine whether service capitalization exists. As discussed in the previous section, the vast majority of studies on this topic find evidence of public service capitalization, and thereby reject the Hamilton model. In my judgment, the Hamilton model is clever and helpful because it identifies the assumptions that would have to hold for capitalization to disappear. Nevertheless, this model should clearly be rejected as an accurate portrayal of the American federal system.

6. Normative Analysis

The lasting fame of Tiebout derives primarily from his claim that "voting with one's feet" is analogous to shopping for a commodity and leads to efficient provision of local public services. The literature has struggled with questions of efficiency and equity ever since.

7. Efficiency

Although the Tiebout model did not incorporate either a housing market or a property tax, Hamilton (1975) shows that the same result can be obtained from a model with these features, so long as his assumptions about housing suppliers and zoning are satisfied. In particular, the Hamilton assumptions imply that every community is homogeneous, in the sense that it contains a single income-taste class, and that voters select the level of local public services as if it had a constant price, just like a private good. Thus, the Tiebout analogy to shopping in a private market place is preserved and the efficiency properties of that type of shopping are attained.

The Hamilton approach has been widely cited as proof that our system of local governments is at least approximately efficient. However, as shown earlier, the key prediction of the Hamilton model, namely, no capitalization, is resoundingly rejected by dozens of studies on the topic. As a result, it makes no sense to accept the Tiebout/Hamilton conclusion that a system with many independent local governments is fully efficient.

Instead, two key conclusions emerge from the literature. The first, which is in the spirit of Tiebout and Hamilton, is that setting up a federal system with many independent local governments has profound efficiency advantages over a centralized system in which the quality of local public services is the same everywhere. This efficiency advantage arises because the demand curve for local public services, which is illustrated in Figure 4, varies widely across households.

Consider the two households in Figure 8. Household 1 has a low income and a low demand curve, $D1$, and household 2 has a high income and a high demand curve, $D2$. Each household's demand curve indicates its marginal benefit from public services, so its total benefit from any particular public service level is the area under its demand curve up to that service level. Now suppose MC is the cost per unit of public services for both households.

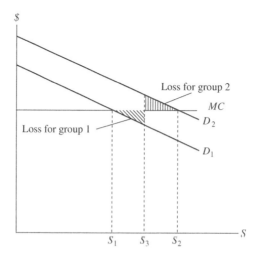

Figure 8   Inefficiency due to heterogeneity.

Then each household would prefer to have the level of service at which its marginal benefit (its demand curve) equals its marginal cost ($=MC$). Thus, household 1 would prefer to live in a jurisdiction with service level $S1$, and household 2 would prefer to live in a jurisdiction with service level $S2$. If each household succeeds in finding such a jurisdiction, the outcome is efficient, in the sense that no other arrangement (short of redistribution) would make either household better off.

With a single local government, however, both households would be forced to consume the same level of local public services, say $S3$. In this situation, the level of local public services would be too high for household 1 and too low for household 2. To be specific, the units of public services between $S1$ and $S3$ would be delivered to household 1 even though the marginal benefit from each of those unit falls below the marginal cost household 1 must pay. The loss to household 1 is the indicated shaded area. The units of public services between $S3$ and $S2$ would not be delivered to household 2 even though the marginal benefit from each of those unit falls above the marginal cost household 2 must pay. The loss to household 2 is the indicated shaded area. In short, moving from separate, homogeneous jurisdictions to a single jurisdiction leads to significant losses for both household types. Or, to put it another way, allowing one jurisdiction to break up into smaller, more homogeneous jurisdictions result in net benefits to both types of households and is therefore an efficient thing to do.[12]

The second key conclusion is that despite the efficiency of many local governments compared to a single local government, our actual system of local governments is not nearly as efficient as it could be. In fact, dozens of capitalization studies reject the Tiebout/Hamilton assumptions and hence reject their conclusion of full efficiency. Instead, our system has several sources of inefficiency that could, at least in principle, be corrected or offset by the actions of higher levels of government.

---

[12]The low-demand household type (1) is likely to have a relatively low house value and the high-demand household type is likely to have a high house value. As a result, household type 1 is likely to have a low tax share (and hence a low tax price) compared to household type 2. Both household types prefer the level of services at which marginal benefit equals tax price. Within a single community, this difference raises the preferred service level of household type 1 and lowers the preferred service level of household type 2. In fact, with this adjustment, both household types might prefer service level S3 or something close to it. This analysis does not change the fact that type 2 households would gain from moving to a homogeneous jurisdiction, where their tax share would be 1.0.

Two potential sources of inefficiency are particularly important.[13] First, local governments are not nearly as homogeneous as the idealized Tiebout/Hamilton view implies. Indeed, as shown earlier, heterogeneous communities are possible, even likely, in the consensus bidding/sorting analysis. Moreover, it can be shown a large central city is likely to provide a level of public services below the efficient level. If so, state or federal subsidies to city governments could actually enhance efficiency.[14]

Second, unless all the Hamilton assumptions are satisfied, the property tax, like other taxes, distorts household behavior and leads to a deviation from the efficient level of local public services. Scholars do not agree on the best way to eliminate this distortion.[15]

8. Equity

When local governments have considerable autonomy, as in the United States, and sorting occurs, some jurisdictions have much higher incomes and tax bases than others and end up with much higher quality public services. This effect is magnified by the fact that high-income jurisdictions tend to have favorable environments for providing public services and hence relatively low public service costs.[16] Moreover, the high value of houses in high-income communities implies that, compared to low-income communities, those communities can raise a given amount of property tax revenue at a relatively low property tax rate.

Because the system of local governments is established by higher levels of government, by the states in the United States, for example, higher levels of government bear ultimate responsibility for the nature of this system. As a result, higher levels of government may be concerned with variation in local public services, and may want to compensate local governments for unfavorable fiscal factors that are outside their control, such as a low tax

---

[13]Several other sources are discussed in the literature. First, the sorting process might not allocate households to communities in an optimal way (see Wildasin, 1986). Second, local governments might themselves behave in an inefficient way (again, see Wildasin). Third, property tax and public service capitalization may prevent local voters from acting in an efficient manner (see Ross and Yinger, 1999; Yinger, 1999).

[14]For more on this argument, see Ross and Yinger, *op. cit.*

[15]Great Britain experimented with a community-specific head tax as a way to avoid this distortion, but found that it was not only unpopular, but also ran into some of the efficiency problems discussed in footnote 13 (see Ross and Yinger, 1999).

[16]Environmental factors are discussed at length in Ross and Yinger (1999) and Duncombe and Yinger (2005).

base, high input prices, or a harsh environment. This compensation by a state can take the form of an intergovernmental aid program that accounts for tax-base and cost differences across communities or of institutional changes, such as regional tax-base sharing or allowing cities to tax suburban commuters.

Fairness issues assorted with bidding and sorting have long been rec-ognized in the case of education, both by academics and policy makers. Moreover, many American states, often in response to a court ruling, now provide higher grants per pupil to school districts with lower property values per pupil. Some grant systems are designed to bring all school districts up to a minimum spending level, and others are designed to ensure that all districts that levy the same property tax rate will receive the same spending per pupil. No existing grant system eliminates the correlation between property wealth and school spending, but some of them undoubtedly lower this correlation significantly.[17]

The consensus bidding model also raises a different sort of equity issue that is related to the **timing** of ownership, not to the income distribution. To be specific, an unanticipated change in service quality or property taxes in one jurisdiction relative to others leads to capital gains or losses for the owners of property there at the time of the change. In fact, if capitalization is complete, the capital gain or loss equals the present value of the stream of annual changes in service benefits or taxes, and these owners bear the entire burden of the change. Moreover, households who buy a house from one of these owners in the future bear no burden at all because these future buyers will be compensated for higher taxes or lower service quality in the form of lower housing prices. As a result, capitalization creates classes of households based on the timing of their home purchase, instead of their income or wealth. Some policies are unfair because they arbitrarily benefit or harm people in some of these time-dependent classes relative to others.

Consider, for example, a community in which poor assessing practices lead to effective property tax rates that vary widely from one house to another.[18] In this situation, an unanticipated revaluation that brings all houses to the same effective tax rate will result in capital losses for houses that were previously under assessed and to capital gains for houses that were previously over assessed. These gains and losses are largely arbitrary and hence unfair; a longtime owner whose house was previously under assessed could be said to be paying back tax breaks in the form of a capital loss,

---

[17]See Yinger (2004) for further discussion of equity issues in education.
[18]This example is discussed in detail in Yinger *et al.* (1988).

but the same loss falls on a recent buyer who gained nothing at all from the past under assessment. One cannot avoid this problem, however, by retaining the poor assessing system, because such a system hands out regular, small, unannounced effective tax rate cuts or increases as it allows assessments to diverge from market values. The resulting incremental gains and losses also are arbitrary, and hence unfair. The only way out of this dilemma is to pay the one-time fairness cost of revaluation and then keep assessments up to date in the future.

9. Conclusions

In sum, state and federal governments making decisions about a federal system face many challenges in designing the appropriate policies. Many people have the general presumption that decentralization promotes efficiency at the expense of fairness. However, this presumption should not be pushed too far. Some policies to promote decentralization may enhance efficiency while violating some standards for fairness, but other decentralization policies may enhance efficiency and fairness simultaneously. Moreover, the conclusion that decentralization tends to promote efficiency does not imply that any particular federal system is as efficient as it could be. Indeed, state and federal governments may find many ways to promote efficiency even in a fairly decentralized federal system.

References

Duncombe, W. D. and J. Yinger. 2005. How much more does a disadvantaged student cost? *Economics of Education Review* **24**(5): 513–532. [Chapter 7]

Epple, D., R. Filimon, and T. Romer. 1984. Equilibrium among local jurisdictions: Toward an integrated treatment of voting and residential choice. *Journal of Public Economics* **24**(3): 281–308.

Epple, D., M. Peress, and H. Sieg. 2010. Identification and semiparametric estimation of equilibrium models of local jurisdictions. *American Economic Journal: Microeconomics* **2**(4): 195–220.

Hamilton, B. W. 1975. Zoning and property taxation in a system of local governments. *Urban Studies* **12**: 205–211.

Henderson, J. V. 1977. *Economic Theory and the Cities.* New York: Academic Press.

Nguyen-Hoang, P. and J. Yinger. 2011. The capitalization of school quality into house values: A review. *Journal of Housing Economics* **20**(1): 30–48. [Chapter 15]

Reback, R. 2005. House prices and the provision of local public services: Capitalization under school choice programs. *Journal of Urban Economics* **57**(2): 275–301.

Ross, S. L. and J. Yinger. 1999. Sorting and voting: A review of the literature on urban public finance. In Cheshire, P. and E.S. Mills (eds.), *Handbook of Urban and Regional Economics, Applied Urban Economics,* vol. 3, pp. 2001–2060. North-Holland: Elsevier.

Tiebout, C. M. 1956. A pure theory of local expenditures. *Journal of Political Economy* **64**(5): 416–424.

Wildasin, D. E. 1986. *Urban Public Finance*. London: Harwood Academic Publishers.

Yinger, J. 1999. Capitalization and efficiency. In Panagariya, A., P. Portney, and R. Schwab (eds.), *Environmental and Public Economics: Essays in Honor of Wallace E. Oates*, pp. 310–326. Northampton: Edward Elgar Publishing Inc.

Yinger, J. 2004. State aid and the pursuit of educational equity: An overview. In Yinger, J. (ed.), *Helping Children Left Behind: State Aid and the Pursuit of Educational Equity*, pp. 3–57. Cambridge, MA: MIT Press. [Chapter 11]

Yinger, J. 2015. Hedonic markets and sorting equilibria: Bid-function envelopes for public services and neighborhood amenities. *Journal of Urban Economics* **86**: 9–25.

Yinger, J. 2018. *Housing and Commuting: The Theory of Urban Residential Structure*. World Scientific Publishing.

Yinger, J., H. S. Bloom, A. Boersch-Supan, and H.F. Ladd. 1988. *Property Taxes and House Values: The Theory and Estimation of Intrajurisdictional Property Tax Capitalization*. Boston: Academic Press.

Part 2
The Property Tax

Chapter 3

Property Tax Capitalization*

John Yinger

*Departments of Public Administration and International
Affairs and of Economics, Syracuse University, Syracuse, NY, United States*
jyinger@maxwell.syr.edu

1. Introduction

A famous article by Oates (1969) first tested the hypothesis that house values
depend on local public service quality and on local property tax rates, a
phenomenon known as capitalization.[1] His strong evidence for capitalization
in a sample of communities in New Jersey stimulated dozens of additional
studies on the topic.

This chapter covers the subsequent literature on property tax capitalization. It focuses on the approach and evidence in Yinger *et al.* (1988),
henceforth referred to as *PTHV*. The chapter considers conceptual and
empirical issues that arise in estimating property tax capitalization and
discusses the important, but often counterintuitive implications of property
tax capitalization for public policy.

---

*This chapter is reproduced from "Property Tax Capitalization," In J. Yinger (ed.),
Housing and Commuting: The Theory of Urban Residential Structure, pp. 385–397. World
Scientific Publishing, 2018.
[1]Oates was not the first to look at property tax capitalization, but he was the first to
estimate tax and service capitalization in one unified framework. Earlier citations on
property tax capitalization are provided by Yinger *et al.* (1988). More recent studies are
reviewed in Ross and Yinger (1999).

2. The Theory of Property Tax Capitalization

Property tax capitalization arises from the basic equality between the value of an asset, in this case a house, and the present value of the stream of net benefits from owning it. Without property taxes, the amount someone is willing to pay for a house is the present value of the rental benefits from ownership, or

$$V = \sum_{y=1}^{L} \frac{\hat{P}H}{(1+r)^y} = \frac{\hat{P}H}{(1+r)} + \frac{\hat{P}H}{(1+r)^2} + \cdots + \frac{\hat{P}H}{(1+r)^L}, \qquad (1)$$

where $\hat{P}$ is the price of housing services not considering taxes, H is housing services (quality adjusted square feet), r is the real discount rate, and L is the expected lifetime of a house.

This equation can be simplified considerably with some simple algebra:

$$V(1+r) = \hat{P}H + \frac{\hat{P}H}{(1+r)} + \frac{\hat{P}H}{(1+r)^2} + \cdots + \frac{\hat{P}H}{(1+r)^{L-1}}$$

and

$$V - V(1+r) = -\hat{P}H + \frac{\hat{P}H}{(1+r)^L}$$

or

$$V[1 - (1+r)] = \hat{P}H[(1+r)^{-L} - 1]$$

or

$$V = \hat{P}H \left(\frac{1 - (1+r)^{-L}}{r} \right) = \frac{\hat{P}H}{r'}, \qquad (2)$$

where

$$r' = \frac{r}{1 - (1+r)^{-L}}. \qquad (3)$$

This derivation leads to a very important simplification. If the value of rental services is constant (in real terms) over time and the lifetime of housing, L, is large, then $r = r'$ and

$$V = \frac{\hat{P}H}{r}.$$

(4)

Now we can add property taxes, which are an annual expense that lowers property values.

$$V = \sum_{y=1}^{L} \frac{\hat{P}H}{(1+r)^y} - \sum_{y=1}^{N} \frac{\beta'tV}{(1+r)^y} = \frac{\hat{P}H}{r} - \frac{\beta'tV}{r'}.$$

(5)

In this equation, β' is the "*degree* of property tax capitalization," defined as the impact of a $1 increase in the present value of the property tax stream on the value of a house. If β' equals 0.5, for example, then a $1 increase in the present value of property taxes leads to a $0.50 decrease in the value of a house. The reason for the "prime" will be clear in a moment.

Now you can see the source of the term "capitalization." The annual flow of property tax payments shows up in a "capital" or asset value, namely V, using the logic of discounting. Indeed, the denominator in an asset pricing expression, r or r' here, is often called the capitalization rate.

Note also that we do not require the expected lifetime of property taxes to be the same as the expected lifetime of the house. The reason for this will become clear shortly.

As you can see, equation (5) is not in final form because V is on both sides. So let's solve for V.

$$V \left(1 + \frac{\beta't}{r'}\right) = \frac{\hat{P}H}{r}$$

or

$$V = \frac{\hat{P}H}{r\left(1 + \frac{\beta't}{r'}\right)} = \frac{\hat{P}H}{r + \left(\frac{r}{r'}\beta'\right)t} = \frac{\hat{P}H}{r + \beta'[1 - (1+r)^{-N}]t}$$

or

$$V = \frac{\hat{P}H}{r + \beta t} = \frac{\hat{P}H}{r\left(1 + \frac{\beta}{r}t\right)}.$$

(6)

The coefficient to be estimated, β, is the expression in front of t, so it includes both β' and the impact of different expectations about the lifetime of a house and of property taxes. This explains why we need both β and β'; the first is what we estimate but the second is the underlying degree of capitalization. It is still not obvious why we need to consider expectations — hold on.

3. Estimating Property Tax Capitalization

Although equation (6) is fairly simple, it has proven to be difficult to estimate for several reasons.

First, it involves a nonlinear relationship between t and V, even after taking logarithms, so it cannot be estimated with linear regression methods. As a result, existing studies use various approximations or nonlinear estimating techniques. To be specific, after taking logs, the estimating equation is

$$\ln\{V\} = \ln\{\hat{P}\} + \ln\{H\} - \ln\{r\} - \ln\left\{1 + \frac{\beta}{r}t\right\}. \tag{7}$$

In this equation, the first term is a function of locational characteristics of housing and the second term is a function of the structural characteristics of housing. Because r does not vary across houses, it is just the constant term.

More importantly, it is impossible to separate β and r. We will return to this point below. Moreover, the ratio β/r, which is the coefficient of interest, enters in a nonlinear way. One possible approach is to estimate equation (7) — and β/r — using nonlinear methods.

Another possibility is to use the standard approximation that $\ln(1 + a) \approx a$ when a is small, say 0.1. With this approximation, the appropriate tax variable is simply t by itself (and its estimated coefficient is β/r). The accuracy of this approximation depends on the value of $a = \beta t/r$. Suppose $t = 0.01$, $\beta = 0.3$, and $r = 0.03$. In this case, $a = 0.1$, and this approximation is reasonably accurate. But if t or β is any larger, then the quality of this approximation may not be very good. Moreover, a researcher cannot know the value of β ahead of time, and therefore cannot know if this is a reasonable approach to take.

Nevertheless, many studies simply enter t or $\ln\{t\}$ as the tax variable. The use of $\ln\{t\}$, the approach in Oates, is particularly troubling because it has no connection to equation (7). The errors introduced by these inaccurate approximations are not known. In my view, this approach is unsatisfactory: The theory here is clear and empirical work should make use of it.

Another approach, which is possible with panel data containing at least two time periods, is to use a difference form of the equation. With two time periods,

$$V_1 = \frac{\hat{P}H}{r + \beta t_1} \quad \text{and} \quad V_2 = \frac{\hat{P}H}{r + \beta t_2}$$

so

$$V_1 - V_2 \equiv \Delta V = \frac{\hat{P}H}{r + \beta t_1} - \frac{\hat{P}H}{r + \beta t_2} = \hat{P}H \left(\frac{1}{r + \beta t_1} - \frac{1}{r + \beta t_2} \right)$$

$$= \hat{P}H \left(\frac{\beta(t_2 - t_1)}{(r + \beta t_1)(r + \beta t_2)} \right)$$

$$= \left(\frac{\hat{P}H}{r + \beta t_1} \right) \left(\frac{\beta \Delta t}{r + \beta t_2} \right) = V_1 \left(\frac{\beta \Delta t}{r + \beta t_2} \right)$$

so

$$\frac{\Delta V}{V_1} = \left(\frac{\beta \Delta t}{r + \beta t_2} \right). \tag{8}$$

This equation can be estimated with nonlinear methods, where, as before, the coefficient of interest is β/r.

In *PTHV*, this equation is used to study intra-jurisdictional capitalization, that is, the capitalization of effective property tax rate differences within a community. To remove the impact of intra-jurisdictional tax differences/changes, and of other factors that vary over time, the dependent variable is deflated using a housing price index. This removes from V the impact of any change in the average effective tax rate (among other things) and leaves just the impact of the change in the deviation from the average tax rate.

To be more specific, let us express the effective tax rate as $t = \bar{t} + (t - \bar{t})$ and put an asterisk on V to remind us that it has been deflated using a price index. Then equation (8) becomes

$$\frac{\Delta V^*}{V_1^*} = \left(\frac{-\beta \Delta t}{r + \beta t_2} \right)$$

$$= \frac{-\beta((\bar{t}_2 - \bar{t}_1) + [(t_2 - \bar{t}_2) - (t_1 - \bar{t}_1)])}{r + \beta[\bar{t}_1 + (\bar{t}_2 - \bar{t}_1) + (t_2 - \bar{t}_2)]}. \tag{9}$$

The price-index adjustment implies that $(\bar{t}_2 - \bar{t}_1) = 0$; in other words the impact of district-level changes in effective tax rates has been removed from the dependent variable. In addition, revaluation, if it is done carefully, leads to an outcome in which every house has approximately the same effective tax rate after revaluation, which implies that $(t_2 - \bar{t}_2) = 0$. Introducing these two equations into equation (9) results in the following simple form[2]:

$$\frac{\Delta V^*}{V_1^*} = \frac{-\beta((t_2 - \bar{t}_2) - (t_1 - \bar{t}_1))}{r + \beta \bar{t}_1} = \frac{-\beta \Delta t^*}{r + \beta \bar{t}_1} = b \Delta t^*, \qquad (10)$$

where

$$\Delta t^* = (t_2 - \bar{t}_2) - (t_1 - \bar{t}_1)$$

$$b = \frac{-\beta}{r + \beta \bar{t}_1}. \qquad (11)$$

Equation (11) provides an interpretation for the estimated coefficient, b. Solving equation (11) for β, we find that

$$\beta = \frac{br}{1 - b\bar{t}_1}. \qquad (12)$$

Thus, with an estimate of b, data on $\bar{t}_1$, and an assumption about the r, one can obtain an estimate of β.

Equation (12) corrects an error in *PTHV*. The algebra in that book mistakenly ignores the $b\bar{t}_1$ term in the denominator of (12). As we will see below, this mistake implies that the book *understates* the value of β from the linear model by about 30 percent.

Second, the value of the discount rate, r, is not observed, and the form of equations (7)–(9) precludes separate estimation of r and β. Most studies follow Oates by estimating a value of β/r, assuming a value for r, and then calculating the implied value of β. The trouble with this approach is that the value of β depends on an untested assumption and different studies use different values of r. In fact, the most extreme estimates in the literature, in either direction, are driven largely by extreme assumptions about r.

Moreover, scholars are amazingly careless about r, often using a nominal interest rate, when the theory clearly shows that a real rate, say 2–4 percent, is needed.

A real rate equals the nominal or market rate minus anticipated inflation. *PTHV* starts with a long-run, low-risk nominal rate (as for an investment in housing) and then subtracts anticipated inflation based on a study of the factors that determine inflation expectations. This leads to a 3 percent real discount rate for the 1970s.

---

[2]Note that it is possible to estimate (9) as a nonlinear equation with t^* instead of t and with the assumption that $(\bar{t}_2 - \bar{t}_1)$ (see *PTHV*). These nonlinear results are virtually identical to the results obtained with equation (10).

Third, the asset-pricing logic behind equations (7), (8), and (10) requires assumptions about house buyers' expectations. To be specific, this logic predicts that a \$1 increase in the present value of future property taxes will lead to a \$1 decline in house value (i.e., $\beta' = 1$), but it does not say that current tax differences will be fully capitalized (i.e., $\beta = 1$) *if they are not expected to persist.*

Virtually all the literature estimates the capitalization of *current* property tax differences. Under the assumption that current tax differences will persist indefinitely, the assumption that $\beta = 1$ makes perfect sense. In fact, however, current differences may not be expected to persist. In this case, we can use the result derived earlier, namely,

$$\beta = \beta'[1 - (1+r)^{-N}], \tag{13}$$

where N is the length of time current tax differences are expected to persist. The theory indicates that $\beta' = 1$, but the estimated β clearly need not equal 1, and indeed need not equal the same value under all circumstances.

For example, if current property tax differences across (or within) communities are expected to disappear in 10 years and $r = 0.03$, then (13) implies that the estimated β will be only 26 percent even if $\beta' = 1$.

Fourth, because $t = T/V$, one must treat t as endogenous. This endogeneity is both definitional (t is a function of the dependent variable) and behavioral (factors that are unobserved by the researcher but observed by the assessor may influence V may also influence T). *PTHV* develops a model of assessor behavior to identify some instruments and then uses either nonlinear two-stage least squares (for equation (9)) or 2SLS (for equation (10)).

Fifth, one must be careful about omitted variable bias, particularly with equation (7). Good data are needed. This is not quite such a big problem with double-sales data, which are used for equations (9) and (10). Even in that case it could arise, however, so data on additions and renovations are desirable.

Note that omitted variable bias is a bigger problem with equation (7) than with (10), because the latter removes all jurisdiction-level variation. In other words, deflating V eliminates the possibility that the estimated impact of a change in t is biased by the omission of other changes at the jurisdiction level, such as changes in public service quality or transportation costs.

Sixth, there is the problem of itemization. If a taxpayer itemizes her deductions, then she gets to deduct property taxes. So a \$1 increase in the present value of property taxes does not really cost this taxpayer \$1.

Perhaps this is reflected in capitalization. In fact, however, mortgage interest payments are also deductible, so an income tax correction applies to both the numerator and denominator of the estimated coefficient, β/r. If s is the marginal income tax rate, this ratio with full deductibility of interest is $[\beta(1-s)]/[r(1-s)] = \beta/r$. So it is not clear that income taxes need to be considered.

Nevertheless, one might also argue that the denominator is really the opportunity cost of investing in housing, not the mortgage interest rate. This opportunity cost can be thought of as the return on other low-risk, long-term investments, and it is unaffected by deductibility. An alternative view, therefore, is that estimated capitalization should be lower for itemizers than for non-itemizers. For a more detailed treatment of this issue, see de Bartolomé and Rosenthal (1999).

4. Estimates of Property Tax Capitalization

Virtually every study of property tax capitalization finds a statistically significant negative impact of property taxes (or property tax changes) on house values. The vast majority these studies use data from the United States, but a few use data from Canada. Estimates of β vary widely, but if r is set at 3 percent, the estimates of β for the best studies fall between 15 and 60 percent (see *PTHV*).

No study yet provides a definitive estimate of β', but several recent studies provide some evidence that it is close to 100 percent.

5. Property Taxes and House Values

PTHV is based on double-sales data in Massachusetts for observations before and after revaluation. These revaluations took place in the 1970s. Recall that the $t = m(A/V)$, so when assessment practices are poor, as they were in Massachusetts, effective tax rates vary widely. Revaluation brings effective tax rates into line so there are big changes in effective tax rates, that is, in Δt both upward and downward. This study takes advantage of the large variation Δt to identify the impact of t on house values.

In Waltham, the community with the best data (i.e., the most complete set of controls for housing characteristics and renovations), the *PTHV* estimate of β equals 21.1 percent with nonlinear 2SLS (equation (9)) and 22.2 percent with the 2SLS approximation (equation (10)). These results are

Table 1 Corrected estimates of capitalization in Waltham for property taxes and house values.

	Nonlinear version	Linear version (equation (9))
Estimate of b	7.4233	7.0433
Value of $\bar{t}_1$	0.0420	0.0420
Value of $1 - b\bar{t}_1$	0.6882	0.7042
Original β	0.2227	0.2113
t-statistic	5.0	5.6
Corrected β	**0.2227**	**0.3000**
Understatement (%)	31.2	29.6
Implied N (years)	13.2	12.1

based on 353 double-sales observations and are highly significant. Similar results were obtained for 6 other communities.

As noted earlier, one would expect β to be 26 percent if β' equals 1.0 and current tax differences are expected to last only 10 years. Because of the legal pressure to revalue in Massachusetts, the 10-year horizon is very reasonable. These estimates correspond to a horizon of 8.5 and 8.0 years, respectively.

As noted earlier, however, these linear estimates are not quite correct, and need to be divided by the denominator of equation (12). Corrected estimates for Waltham are given in Table 1. Because the correction depends on the effective tax rate, the magnitude of the correction would not be exactly the same in the other communities.

Thus, the linear estimates β for Waltham reported in *PTHV* understate the corrected estimates by about 30 percent. The corrected estimates are consistent with $\beta' = 1$ if people expected pre-revaluation differences in effective tax rates to last for 13.2 and 12.1 years, respectively.

6. Eisenberg

Eisenberg (1996) looks at the capitalization of property taxes in Syracuse before revaluation, when the rates varied considerably. He uses a version of equation (7). He picks up on a point in *PTHV* that someone borrowing up to her limit to buy a house gets capitalization built into her bid: every increase in property taxes must be offset by a decrease in bid, i.e., in housing price. He also follows up on the point that the capitalization story is cleanest for non-itemizers.

Eisenberg conducted a survey of several hundred residents. He found out if they itemized and if they had borrowed up to their limit. He estimated the degree of capitalization for non-itemizers who were borrowed up to their limit and found that $\beta = 1.0$, exactly 1.0! He also asked households about their expectations concerning revaluation. However, nobody expected Syracuse to revalue (unlike in Massachusetts), so expectations proved not to matter. de Bartolomé and Rosenthal (1999), also account for itemization. They argue that previous studies have not properly specified the role of federal income taxes, but that the resulting errors work in different directions and roughly cancel out on net. Thus, their estimate of capitalization for non-itemizers, about 0.40, is not as high as Eisenberg's.

7. Tax Capitalization and Public Policy

Tax capitalization has some bizarre implications for public policy.

If property taxes are fully capitalized, then any tax changes show up in house values immediately and *there is no way to escape* them. A homeowner with a tax increase must either stay and pay the higher tax or leave and suffer a capital loss. Moreover, the loss is the *full present value* of the future increases in taxes. Homeowners who experience a cut in taxes get a capital gain.

In theory, the gains and losses are effective when a policy change is announced, but in practice there may be some time before information is complete or people really believe that the change will be implemented. The implication for studying capitalization is that the estimated rate of capitalization may be small right after tax changes are announced and then grow to its maximum after implementation.

There is some evidence to support this notion in *PTHV*. Anticipated property tax changes have a small, but significant impact on house values. However, the degree of capitalization is quite small until tax changes have been fully implemented.

This evidence supports the view that lags in implementation may allow owners to escape some, or even most, of the impact of property tax changes if (a) there is a lag between announcement and implementation and (b) they act right after announcement.

Now consider *assessment reform*. Assessment reform leads to capital gains for some (those whose houses were over-assessed relative to other houses) and to capital losses for others (those whose houses were under-assessed). For long-term residents, these changes are fair. A resident who has been under-assessed for a long time has been given, in effect, a loan from the city and revaluation just claims back this loan.

But for new residents, these changes are not fair. If someone bought a high-effective-tax-rate house one day and the change is announced the next, this person has a huge capital loss even though she did not benefit at all from the poor assessment system. In fact, capitalization implies that this person paid a premium for her house.

One way to minimize this fairness problem may be to have a long lag between announcement and implementation. As explained earlier, this lag may allow owners at the time of announcement to escape some of the burden of the tax changes. Moreover, this fairness problem does not arise if houses are revalued upon re-sale, which they were not in Massachusetts or Syracuse.

So a revaluation imposes some unfair gains and losses in order to restore faith in the property tax and local government and to ensure fairness in the future. This trade only makes sense if assessments are updated regularly. Otherwise, small gains and losses are handed out each year as assessment errors mount, which is unfair and undermines the case for reform.

In addition, poor assessments lead to court cases, which the city usually loses. Someone can buy a property cheap because its property taxes are relatively high and then sue the city to get a rebate because of unfairly high taxes. This happened with business property in Boston, to the tune of tens of millions of dollars. The only way to avoid this crazy situation is to keep assessments up to date!

In the case of Proposition 13, assessment growth is fixed at 2 percent, so the assessment/sales ratio, and hence t, declines over time for long-term owners. This cannot be turned into a capital gain because houses are revalued upon sale. But it still represents a gift to owners who stay (and discourages mobility). The U.S. Supreme Court said this was legal, and California voters like the reward to long-term residents. I do not think it is fair.

Another application is to state aid. If a jurisdiction gets aid and cuts its property taxes (we will ignore service impacts for now), this leads to a capital gain to residents. Because aid is sometimes based on property values, there is a strange *feedback* here: low property values lead to more aid which leads to higher property values which leads to less aid.

As Inman (1978) has pointed out, this leads to problems with a power-equalizing aid program. This type of program gives a higher matching rate to lower-wealth jurisdictions. This higher matching rate raises property values in lower-wealth jurisdictions and therefore leads to lower aid for them as time goes on. In other words, the property-value impacts undermine the objectives of the aid program. This feedback effect does not arise with another important type of aid called foundation aid, however (see Chapter 14). Foundation aid provides higher block grants (not higher matching rates) to lower-wealth jurisdictions, but with a fixed budget for the program, the amount of aid they receive is not altered by property value effects, should they arise.

References

de Bartolomé, C. A. M. and S. S. Rosenthal. 1999. Property tax capitalization in a model with tax-deferred assets, standard deductions, and the taxation of nominal interest. *The Review of Economics and Statistics* **81**(1): 85–95.

Eisenberg, E. 1996. Intrajurisdictional property tax capitalization rates. Ph.D. Dissertation (Unpublished), Department of Public Administration, Syracuse University.

Inman, R. P. 1978. Optimal fiscal reform of metropolitan schools: Some simulation results. *American Economic Review* **68**(1): 107–122.

Oates, W. E. 1969. The effects of property taxes and local public services on property values: An empirical study of tax capitalization and the Tiebout hypothesis. *Journal of Political Economy* **77**(6): 957–971.

Ross, S. L. and J. Yinger. 1999. Sorting and voting: A review of the literature on urban public finance. In Cheshire, P. and E. S. Mills (eds.), *Handbook of Urban and Regional Economics, Applied Urban Economics*, vol. 3, pp. 2001–2060. North-Holland: Elsevier.

Yinger, J., H. S. Bloom, A. Boersch-Supan, and H. F. Ladd. 1988. *Property Taxes and House Values: The Theory and Estimation of Intrajurisdictional Property Tax Capitalization*. Boston: Academic Press.

Chapter 4

Is the Property Tax a Benefit Tax?
The Case of Rental Housing*

Robert J. Carroll[†] and John Yinger[‡,§]

[†]*US National Tax Quantitative Economics and Statistics Group,*
Ernst and Young
[‡]*Departments of Public Administration and*
International Affairs and of Economics,
Syracuse University, Syracuse, NY, United States
[§]*jyinger@maxwell.syr.edu*

Is the property tax a benefit tax? This paper tests the benefit-tax hypothesis for rental housing. In the case most favorable to this hypothesis, namely with mobile tenants, relatively high property taxes cannot be directly reflected in rents but can be indirectly reflected to the extent that they lead to relatively high-quality public services. This indirect shifting equals tenants' willingness to pay for the public service increment. Even in this case, however, the property tax is not a benefit tax unless the tax rate is set so indirect shifting equals a landlord's tax increase. This second condition is not met in the Boston area in 1980; on average, indirect shifting covers only about $0.11 of a $1.00 increase in property taxes.

1. Introduction

Scholars disagree about whether a local property tax is a benefit tax, in the sense that the tax burden coincides with benefits from the services it finances.

*This chapter is reproduced from "Is the Property Tax a Benefit Tax? The Case of Rental Housing," *National Tax Journal*, **47**(2), June 1994, pp. 295–316.

All views expressed are those of the authors alone and do not represent the views of the Department of the Treasury. We thank James Alm, Gib Metcalf, Douglas Holtz-Eakin, Harvey Rosen, several anonymous referees, and the participants in the public finance seminar at Duke University for valuable comments on earlier drafts of this paper. We are also grateful to Katharine Bradbury and Andrew Reschovsky for providing data.

This debate is important because a benefit tax causes no efficiency loss and satisfies the widely held principle that the people who benefit from a service should pay for it. Mieszkowski and Zodrow (1989, p. 1140) argue, for example, that "the benefit view obtains only if zoning ... is sufficiently binding" and then "reject the assumption of perfect or binding zoning and conclude that a national system of property taxes is distortionary." In contrast, Fischel (1992, p. 171), building on the work of Hamilton (1975), claims that "the property tax becomes merely a fee for local public services and thus has no dead weight loss." This paper provides evidence on this debate for the case of rental housing.[1]

A necessary condition for the property tax to be a benefit tax is that those who bear a higher property tax burden than others in the same urban area must receive correspondingly higher benefits from public services. Indeed, the core of the benefit-tax concept is that a household must pay a higher property tax "fee" in order to obtain higher-quality public services. The claim that the property tax is a benefit tax, therefore, can be tested by determining whether the burden of property tax differences across communities in an urban area falls on the people who benefit from the accompanying differences in public service quality. To put it another way, this claim can be tested with a model of the balanced-budget incidence of rental property tax differentials within an urban area.[2] This paper develops and tests such a model.

As first pointed out by Orr (1968, 1970), the incidence of the property tax on rental housing can be estimated, at least in part, by examining the relationship between property taxes and apartment rents.[3] The only way for landlords to shift the tax onto tenants is to charge relatively high rents in communities where property taxes are relatively high. This focus on property tax differentials cannot determine the incidence of the average property tax rate, but is sufficient for a test of the benefit-tax notion.

Existing studies of the relationship between rents and property taxes implicitly assume that tenants are not fully mobile. Renters do not pay property taxes directly, and mobile renters would not be willing to pay a higher rent simply because property taxes are higher. Renters do consider

---

[1] For a recent review of this debate, and an alternative empirical test of the benefit view, see Wassmer (1993).

[2] Balanced-budget incidence has been used to refer to a variety of incidence concepts in the literature. For clarity, we use the definition provided by Musgrave and Musgrave (1989), in which the combined effects of tax changes and benefit changes are taken into account.

[3] See also Coen and Powell (1972) and Orr (1972).

public service quality when deciding where to live, however, so that differentials in public service quality, which are made possible in part by differences in property tax rates, can be a source of tax shifting even with fully mobile renters. This general equilibrium effect, which is the focus of this paper, has not been considered in any previous research.

Section 2 reviews prior research on the incidence of property taxes on rental housing. Section 3 develops a model of balanced-budget incidence that combines an analysis of renters' decisions, an equation to determine the value of an apartment building, a community's budget constraint, and a simple analysis of the determinants of median rent. This model can be tested with a hedonic equation for rent determination and a measure of public service quality. The fourth section presents our strategy for obtaining the required measure of service quality and estimating a hedonic equation and describes our data. All these components are assembled in the fifth section, which presents the estimation results and discusses their implications for the incidence of property tax differentials and for the benefit view of the property tax. The final section summarizes our main conclusions.

2. The Literature

Table 1 depicts the principal features and conclusions of studies examining the incidence of the property tax on rental housing. These studies do not reach a consensus about the portion of the tax that is shifted onto renters.

In addition to neglecting the general equilibrium effect modeled below, these studies encounter several methodological problems, all of which we address in our own regressions. First, several studies employ an inadequate set of housing attributes and are therefore subject to omitted variable bias. Second, most studies use expenditure as a measure of public service quality. As explained below, this approach is, at best, a rough approximation. Third, most researchers include only education and omit sanitation, police and fire protection, transportation, and other public services, all of which may influence renters' bids for housing.

Another problem common to the studies is that some of the explanatory variables, such as the tax rate, may be simultaneously determined with rent, thereby introducing simultaneity bias. As shown below, correcting for this simultaneity can alter the results substantially. Finally, despite the availability of general functional forms for hedonic regressions, these studies use fairly restrictive forms.

Table 1 Empirical studies of the incidence of property tax differentials on rental housing.

	Orr (1968)	Heinberg and Oates (1970)	Orr (1970)	Hyman and Pasour (1973)	Dusansky, Ingber, and Karatjas (1981)
Incidence of Tax	Fails to find evidence of shifting.	Fails to find evidence of shifting.	Shifting of 46 percent of tax.	Shifting of 60 percent of tax.	Shifting of between 62 and 110 percent depending on assumption of time horizon and discount rate.
Study Characteristics					
Unit of observation	Municipality	Municipality	Municipality	Municipality	Municipality
Geographic area	Boston MSA	Boston MSA	Boston MSA	North Carolina	Suffolk County, NY
Time period	1960	1960	1960	1970	1970
Sample size	31	23	31	115	62
Model Specification					
Dependent variable	Median gross rent per median rooms of all housing units.	Median gross rent per median rooms of all rental units.	Median gross rent and median gross rent per median rooms of all rental units.	Median gross rent.	Median gross rent.
Property tax variable(s)	Equalized property tax rate for all property.	Equalized property tax rate for all property.	Equalized property tax rate for all property.	Equalized property tax rate for all property.	Equalized property tax rate for all property.
Public service variable(s)	Education expenditures per pupil.	Education expenditures per pupil.	Education expenditures per pupil.	Municipal and education expenditure per capita.	Education expenditures per pupil.
Structural characteristics	1	1	2	1	1
Locational characteristics	2	2	3	6	2
Estimation Procedure[a]	OLS	OLS, 2SLS	OLS, 2SLS	OLS	2SLS, 3SLS

Notes: [a]OLS = ordinary least squares, 2SLS = two-stage least squares, and 3SLS = three-stage least squares.

3. Property Taxes, Service Quality, Rents, and Apartment Values

This section analyzes the extent to which property tax differentials across communities are shifted onto renters. The model has two principal components: the renter's choice of a community and the landlord's valuation of an apartment building. These two components are tied together with two others: the community budget constraint and the determinants of median rent.

3.1. *The Renter's Choice of a Community*

The starting point of our analysis is a renter's maximization problem. Following Yinger (1982, 1985), we assume that each renter selects a community based on rent and public service level. Property taxes do not enter the renter's problem directly because renters do not pay a property tax bill. The renter's problem is to select a composite good, housing, and a level of public services to

$$\text{Maximize} \quad U(Z, H, S)$$
$$\text{Subject to} \quad Y = Z + P(S)H, \tag{1}$$

where Z = a composite good with a price of unity, H = units of housing services, S = quality of local public services *per capita*, Y = renter's income, and $P(S)$ = price per unit of housing services, which is a function of S. Note that $R(S) = P(S)H$ equals apartment rent.[4]

In his role as a mover, a renter chooses S indirectly through his choice of a community; that is, renters select their preferred quality of public services by "voting with their feet." Although the property tax does not appear in the renter's problem, the public service level, S, clearly depends on the property tax rate (among other things), so that property taxes can have an indirect influence on P and hence on renters' choices.

The key first order conditions of this problem concern the choices of Z and S. In particular, the renter sets

$$\frac{\partial U / \partial S}{\partial U / \partial Z} = (\partial P / \partial S) H. \tag{2}$$

---

[4]Throughout this paper, the concept of housing services, H, is used for ease of presentation; equivalent results could be derived, however, with a more general notation in which rents were a function of S; of other locational variables, such as distance to employment centers; and of structural housing characteristics, such as the number of rooms. In fact, our hedonic regression (described below) uses this type of general form.

The left side of equation (2) is the marginal rate of substitution between S and Z, or, because Z is the numeraire, the marginal benefit from S in dollar terms. The right side is the marginal cost of S, that is, the increase in the cost of housing from moving to a community with better public services.

Equation (2) is a maximization condition for a single renter when $P(S)$ is given. Following the logic of an urban model, this equation also can be interpreted as an equilibrium condition, for the price of rental housing, assuming perfectly mobile renters. Unless the price of rental housing varies across communities, that is, across different levels of S, according to equation (2), some communities will be relatively attractive to renters and rental prices will be bid up there.[5] The housing market reaches equilibrium only when renters pay for the privilege of living in a high-service community and are compensated for living in a low-service community.[6]

3.2. A Landlord's Valuation of an Apartment Building

The second component of the model is the determination of market value. Because landlords do pay property tax bills, the amount they are willing to pay for an apartment building equals the present value of the net rental income it yields minus the present value of the property tax payments on the building. Formally, the market value of an apartment building with an expected life of N years is

$$V = \sum_{n=1}^{N} \frac{P(S)H - T}{(1+r)^n} \tag{3}$$

where V = market value, T = annual property tax payment, and r = real interest rate. Assuming that N is large and noting that the annual property tax payment equals the effective property tax rate, t, multiplied by house

---

[5]The application of urban model concepts to public services and rents is discussed in more detail in Yinger (1985).
[6]To the extent that renters in different communities have different incomes or tastes, this relationship may not be exact; housing services will still command a higher rent in a community with better services, all else equal, but observed differences in rents may not equal any particular group's valuation of public service quality. In this paper, we assume that the bids of existing residents apply to marginal changes in S.

value, equation (3) becomes[7]

$$V = \frac{P(S)H - tV}{r} \quad \text{or} \quad V = \frac{P(S)H}{(r+t)}. \tag{4}$$

3.3. *The Community Budget Constraint*

The service level and the effective property tax rate are tied together through a community's budget constraint. By definition, spending *per capita, E*, equals service quality *per capita, S*, multiplied by the average cost per unit of service quality, *C*. Moreover, spending must equal revenue, which consists of property taxes and miscellaneous other revenue. Thus, a community's budget constraint is

$$E = (S)(C) = t\bar{V} + M \quad \text{or} \quad S = \frac{(t\bar{V} + M)}{C} \tag{5}$$

where $\bar{V}$ = the *per capita* property value in a community and M = local revenue *per capita* from sources other than the property tax.

3.4. *Median Rent*

The final component of our model is a simple supply-and-demand analysis of a community's median rent, the dependent variable in our empirical work. The median rent in a community is a function of the service quality and property tax rate there, and it equals the price per unit of H in the community multiplied by the community's median apartment "size," say $\hat{H}$. Before it can be applied to median rent, however, our theory must be modified, because tenants may not be perfectly mobile and because the median apartment size (unlike the size of a given apartment) may change as the price per unit of H changes.[8] To account for these possibilities, let us distinguish between housing bids, P, and actual housing prices, say P^*. Actual rents, R^*, are the product of P^* and $\hat{H}$.

---

[7]Instead of assuming that N is large, r can be replaced with r^*, which is the infinite-horizon discount rate that is equivalent to rate r with lifetime N. See Yinger *et al.* (1988). Note also that this formulation assumes that the effective property tax rate is held constant over time, which implies that assessments are kept up to date.

[8]We do not consider the possibility that an individual landlord will alter the level of H in her apartments in response to a change in P. This type of response is possible but is likely to be small in magnitude.

Consider the following demand and supply curves:

$$\hat{H}_D = \hat{H}_D[P^* - P(S)]$$
$$\hat{H}_S = \hat{H}_S[P^*(1-t)]. \tag{6}$$

The direct impact of t on P^* and R^* can be found by totally differentiating equation (6) with respect to t and P^* and setting the change in $\hat{H}_D$ equal to the change in $\hat{H}_S$. Let $\mu(\sigma)$ stand for the price elasticity of demand (supply).[9] Then these steps lead to

$$P_t^* = \frac{dP^*}{dt}\frac{1}{P^*} = \frac{1}{1-t-\frac{\mu}{\sigma}} \tag{7}$$

and

$$R_t^* = \frac{dR^*}{dt}\frac{1}{R^*} = \frac{1+\mu}{1-t-\frac{\mu}{\sigma}}. \tag{8}$$

Equation (7) is a standard incidence result.[10] The higher σ and the lower the absolute value of μ, the higher the impact of a tax increase on the price of housing and hence the greater the shifting of the tax onto tenants. If tenants are perfectly mobile, that is, if μ is infinite, landlords bear the entire burden of the tax increase.

Equation (8) contains a surprise, however. If μ, is less than minus one, the impact of t on R^* is *negative*. Hence, the estimated value of R_t^* provides a test of the hypothesis that tenants' demand for housing is elastic. This is an important test for a theory such as ours that depends on the existence of tenant mobility.

The impact of S on P^* and R^* can be found by totally differentiating equation (6) with respect to S and P^* and equating the two quantity changes. The results are

$$P_S^* = \frac{dP^*}{dS}\frac{1}{P^*} = \frac{P_S}{1-\frac{\sigma}{\mu}}, \tag{9}$$

where $P_S = (dP/dS)/P$, and

$$R_S^* = \frac{dR^*}{dS}\frac{1}{R^*} = \frac{P_S(1+\sigma)}{1-\frac{\sigma}{\mu}}. \tag{10}$$

---

[9]These are not ordinary price elasticities; instead, they are elasticities of median H, not total H, with respect to price.
[10]This result can be compared to an equation in McDonald (1993, p. 110), which refers to a unit tax, instead of the *ad valorem* tax considered here.

These equations provide the key to the indirect shifting of property taxes onto rents, which occurs when property tax increases are used to improve service quality. Equation (9) reveals not only that this indirect shifting depends on the extent to which tenants are willing to pay for a service quality increment, as measured by P_S, but also that the extent of this indirect shifting actually *decreases* as σ goes up. In other words, the supply elasticity has the opposite impact on indirect shifting of the property tax as it has on direct shifting. This result is obtained because indirect shifting occurs as the demand curve, not the supply curve, is pushed up. For a given increase in the demand curve, the more elastic the supply curve, the smaller the increase in price.

It follows that an increase in σ can either increase or decrease landlords' share of a property tax increase, depending on whether direct shifting or indirect shifting dominates.

Equation (10) reveals that, unless housing supply is fixed, one cannot extract the impact of service quality on housing bids from a regression of rents on service quality without accounting for variation in median apartment "size" or $\hat{H}$. A standard hedonic regression for apartment rents controls for $\hat{H}$ by including as control variables all observable housing characteristics, such as the median number of rooms. However, our model calls for the reduced-form impacts of S and t on R^* when $\hat{H}$ is allowed to vary across jurisdictions, that is, without controlling for housing characteristics. Results from a standard hedonic regression will be presented for comparison purposes.[11]

3.5. *The Complete Model*

To bring direct and indirect shifting into our analysis, we must rewrite equation (4) based on actual prices, not housing bids, and recognize that changes in t affect S through the community budget constraint, equation (5). The result is

$$V = \frac{P^*[S(t), t]H}{r + t}. \tag{11}$$

Equation (11) reveals that a change in the property tax affects the market value of an apartment building in three ways: through its impact on the denominator,

---

[11] Technically speaking, both μ and σ can be shown to be equal the sum of an elasticity that applies to the observed components of H and one that applies to the unobserved components of H. A regression that includes housing characteristics as control variables implicitly sets equal to zero the elasticities associated with observed components. A regression that excludes housing characteristics can be used to find the total elasticities.

through its direct impact on P^*, and through its impact on S and hence its indirect impact on P^*. Because the t in the denominator of equation (11) comes directly from the landlord's tax payment, the first effect can be called the direct tax effect. It always is negative; for a given rental flow, higher property taxes lead to a lower market value. The other two effects, which can be called the direct and indirect rental effects, usually are positive, and can vary from one community to another.[12] Higher taxes lead to better services, for example, but the extent of the increase in services, and hence the extent of the indirect impact on rents, depends on a community's public service costs.

The net impact of a property tax increase on the value of an apartment building depends on all three effects. At the margin, this net impact is the change in market value relative to a $1 change in the present value of the property tax stream. Totally differentiating equation (11) and the present value of the property tax stream, T/r, we find that[13]

$$\frac{dV}{d(T/r)} = \frac{r[\epsilon(r+t) - t]}{t[\epsilon(r+t) + r]} \tag{12}$$

where $\epsilon = [(\partial P^*/\partial S)(\partial S/\partial t) + (\partial P^*/\partial t)] \times (t/P^*)$, which is the elasticity of P^* with respect to t, that is, the sum of the direct and indirect rental effects.

One of the terms in ϵ is $(\partial S/\partial t)$, which can be derived from the budget constraint, equation (5). In differentiating equation (5), we divide property into residential and business; we assume that residential property values are defined by equation (11) with $\hat{H}$ instead of H; and we allow adjustments in $\hat{H}$ in response to changes in P^*. Based on the evidence in Wheaton (1984), we also assume that business rents remain constant.[14] With these assumptions, we find that

$$\frac{\partial S}{\partial t} = \frac{r\bar{V} + t(r+t)\bar{V}_R R_t^*}{(r+t)(C - t\bar{V}_R R_S^*)} \tag{13}$$

where $\bar{V}_R$ is residential property value *per capita*.[15]

---

[12] As explained below, the indirect effect can be negative under some circumstances.

[13] Equations (7) and (8) are derived by noting that V is a function of t, totally differentiating $V = V(t)$ and $tV = tV(t)$, and rearranging terms. H is held constant, because we are looking at the taxes on a given apartment building.

[14] Wheaton (1984) finds that the rent per square foot for class-A office space in the Boston area in 1980 is not a function of the community's property tax rate. Thus, his study applies to the same time and place as ours. McDonald (1993) finds that rents do reflect property taxes to some degree, but his study covers intrajurisdictional tax differences in Chicago.

[15] This analysis assumes that an increase in the property tax goes entirely to higher service quality and not to a reduction in other taxes. This assumption is reasonable in the case of Massachusetts, where municipalities are not allowed to levy any broad-based taxes except the property tax. In another state one might want to amend the model to consider

Equation (12) describes the incidence of a change in the property tax in one community holding constant the property tax everywhere else. The first requirement for the property tax to be a benefit tax is that any increase in property taxes be fully shifted to tenants. If the expression in equation (12) is zero, that is, if asset values are not affected by a property tax increase, then this full shifting occurs. In this case, the direct and indirect rental effects and the resulting increase in asset value exactly offset the direct tax effect. If this expression is negative, which implies that the rental effects are smaller than the direct tax effect, landlords bear some of the burden of a property tax increase.

Equations (12) and (13) demonstrate that the extent to which property tax increases are shifted to tenants is not the same in every community. A community's property tax rate, cost index, average property value, and average residential property value, all influence the degree of shifting. At a given tax rate, for example, a tax increase results in a smaller increase in service quality, and hence in a smaller indirect rental effect, in a high-cost community than in a low-cost community. This variation is a significant departure from standard incidence analysis.

The possible outcomes for a community can be summarized by the relationship between ϵ and $[t/(r + t)]$. A property tax increase is partially shifted onto tenants if ϵ falls between 0 and $[t/(r + t)]$, exactly shifted to tenants if ϵ equals $[t/(r + t)]$, and overshifted onto tenants if ϵ exceeds $[t/(r + t)]$. These results indicate that tenants bear the entire burden of the tax increase when the sum of the direct and indirect rental effects, which is measured by ϵ exactly offsets the direct tax effect, which is measured by $[t/(r + t)]$. A property tax increase is exactly paid by landlords only if ϵ equals zero, which requires that tenants receive no benefit from an increment in public service quality (so the indirect rental effect is zero) and that either $\mu = -\infty$ or $\sigma = 0$ (so the direct rental effect is zero), and it is overshifted onto landlords if ϵ is below zero. A negative ϵ implies that a property tax increase has such a negative impact on a community's average property value that it results in a decline in service quality that is sufficiently large not only to make the indirect rental effect negative but also to make it larger in absolute value than the direct rental effect, which always is positive.[16]

---

substitution between tax sources. Even in Massachusetts, there might be some tendency to substitute property taxes for licenses and fees, but we do not consider this possibility.

[16]If the decline in service quality is so large that ϵ is less than $[-r/(r+t)]$, then an increase in the property tax rate actually causes a decline in the property tax payment for a given apartment building. In this extreme case, the sign of the expression in equation (14) must

Although R_t^* and R_S^* can be estimated, ϵ cannot be calculated without making an assumption about either μ or σ. It will prove useful to consider two extreme cases. The first case is defined by $\mu = -\infty$, that is, by a horizontal demand curve. In this case, which is used in our earlier analysis of renter community choice, equation (7) reveals that $P_t^* = 0$. It follows from equation (8) that $\sigma = -R_t^*$ and from equations (9) and (10) that $P_S = P_S^* = R_S^*/(1+\sigma)$. The second case is defined by $\sigma = \infty$, that is, by a horizontal supply curve. In this case, equation (7) reveals that $P_t^* = 1/(1-t)$; equation (8) reveals that $\mu = [R_t^*(1-t) - 1]$; equation (9) reveals that $P_S^* = 0$; and equation (10) reveals that $P_S = -R_S^*/\mu$. Substituting these results into equation (13), the definition of ϵ and equation (12), yields the burden on landlords.

With neither μ nor σ infinite and with estimates of R_t^* and R_S^*, we have two equations (8) and (10), in three unknowns, $P_S, \mu,$ and σ. Solving equation (8) for μ as a function of σ, we find that

$$\mu = \frac{R_t^*(1-t) - 1}{1 + \frac{R_t^*}{\sigma}}. \tag{14}$$

If R_t^* is less than zero (a test of tenant mobility), the demand elasticity will not be negative as required unless σ is greater than the absolute value of R_t^*. With any value of σ above $-R_t^*$ we can use equation (14) to find μ and equation (10) to find P_S as a function of μ and σ:

$$P_S = R_S^* \left(\frac{1 - \frac{\sigma}{\mu}}{1 + \sigma} \right). \tag{15}$$

We do not simulate with equations (14) and (15), however, because cases 1 and 2, defined above, bracket the shifting possibilities.[17]

Finally, note that equation (12) indicates whether landlords or renters bear the burden of a marginal change in a community's property tax, but it does not measure the incidence of an existing tax differential. The incidence

---

be reversed, since the only way to raise money is to lower the effective property tax rate. When ϵ is this small, therefore, there always is overshifting onto tenants.

[17] If the indirect rental effect dominates the direct rental effect, increasing σ results in less shifting onto tenants, and setting $\sigma = -R_t^*$ results in the maximum degree of shifting. This value of σ implies that $\mu = -\infty$ (case 1). If the direct rental effect dominates, setting $\sigma = \infty$ (case 2) results in the maximum degree of shifting onto tenants.

measure for an existing differential is

$$\text{landlord share} = \frac{V(t) - V(\bar{t})}{\frac{T(t)}{r} - \frac{T(\bar{t})}{r}}, \tag{16}$$

where the arguments indicate that V and T/r are evaluated at a community's actual tax rate, t, and at the metropolitan average tax rate, $\bar{t}$.[18] Equation (16) requires an estimate of the apartment value that would prevail under the average tax rate, $V(\bar{t})$. Our estimating procedure is presented below.

3.6. *Net Benefits to Tenants*

The public services considered in this paper are received by the tenant, not the landlord. For any given increase in t, the net benefits to a tenant equal the present value of the associated increase in service benefits, or $(\partial P/\partial S)(\partial S/\partial t)(H)(dt)/r$, minus the increase in the present value of rents, which is the expression in equation (12) plus one. Using equation (15), the definition of ϵ and the change in t required to alter (tV/r) by \$1, we find that this net benefit, NB, is

$$NB = \frac{(r+t)^2[tP_t^*(\frac{\sigma}{\mu} - 1) - \epsilon(\frac{\sigma}{\mu})]}{t[\epsilon(r+t) + r]} \tag{17}$$

The second requirement for a property tax to be a benefit tax is that the net benefits to tenants be zero, that is, that the payments made by tenants in the form of higher rents exactly cover the benefits they receive in the form of better services. According to equation (17), this requirement is met if $\mu = -\infty$ (case 1 above), $\sigma = 0$, or $\epsilon = t(\sigma - \mu)/[(1 - t)\sigma - \mu]$. Under the first two circumstances, the indirect rental effect exactly equals tenant willingness to pay for the service quality increment and the direct effect is zero. In the last circumstance, the value of the service quality increment is not fully reflected in rents, but the direct effect exactly makes up the difference.

---

[18]We use the average property tax rate weighted by the share of property value in each community. This formulation is preferred to a simple average because the weighted average will reflect the share of capital in each community.

Finally, note that if $\sigma = \infty$ (case 2 above), the net benefits defined by equation (17) must be negative; that is, rents must increase by more than tenants' valuation of public services.[19]

3.7. *When is the Property Tax a Benefit Tax?*

Equations (12) and (13) reveal that a community's decisions affect the incidence of the property tax. To maximize their market value, landlords would select the tax rate at which $\epsilon = [t/(r + t)]$.[20] At this rate, any additional increase in property taxes would lead to an increase in rents that exactly offset the landlord's increase in taxes; that is, any additional increase would be borne entirely by tenants, as required for a benefit tax.

However, renters will not in general prefer the same tax rate as landlords. As pointed out by Stiglitz (1983) and Yinger (1985) and confirmed by equation (17), perfectly mobile tenants are indifferent to property tax increases, regardless of the tax rate.[21] This indifference at the margin, which also arises with perfectly immobile landlords, is the second requirement for a benefit tax. Without perfect mobility, tenants prefer to increase the tax rate until their net benefit from a further increase equals zero, that is, until the second benefit-tax condition is met. As shown earlier, their preferred tax rate is defined by $\epsilon = t(\sigma - \mu)/[(1 - t)\sigma - \mu]$.

These results imply that the property tax is unlikely to be a benefit tax.[22] If $\mu = -\infty$, or if $\sigma = 0$, tenants' net benefits equal zero regardless of the local property tax rate. Thus, the two benefit-tax conditions derived here will be satisfied so long as the property tax rate is set at landlords' preferred level. Landlords do not select the property tax rate, however, and they may have little political power. Indeed, if they are non-residents, they do not

---

[19]In this case, $\epsilon = t/(1 - t) = tP_t^*$. Plugging this expression into equation (17) proves the result in the text.

[20]This is easier said than done; ϵ itself is a complicated nonlinear function of t and an explicit expression for t cannot be derived from our equations.

[21]This statement does not imply that tenants are indifferent across communities. A tenant selects a community where rents are determined by people in his income-taste class, that is, where the impact of services and taxes on rents equals his own willingness to pay. See Yinger (1985). This is, of course, the heart of the benefit-tax idea, namely that taxes serve as a price when people shop for a community.

[22]The two conditions presented here are necessary but not sufficient for the property tax to be a benefit tax. These conditions apply to property tax differentials, not to the average property tax rate in a metropolitan area. Even if the two conditions in the text were met, the property taxes associated with the average rate might be paid by landlords, which is another violation of the benefit-tax notion.

even get to vote. Thus, the tax rate is more likely to be set at the level that renters or homeowners prefer.[23] Moreover, without either perfectly mobile tenants or immobile landlords, the property tax rate *cannot* be set to satisfy the benefit-tax conditions for both landlords and tenants; that is, the two conditions are incompatible.[24]

4. Estimation Strategy

In this section we explain our strategy for estimating both public service quality, S, and a hedonic equation in which R^* is a function of S and t. These steps allow us to calculate the net burden of a property tax on both landlords, equation (12), and tenants, equation (17). In addition, we describe our simulation procedure for finding $V(\bar{t})$ and hence for calculating the incidence of existing tax differences, as given by equation (16).

4.1. *Public Service Quality*

Our procedure for estimating C was developed by Bradbury *et al.* (1984) and refined by Ladd and Yinger (1991). It recognizes, following Bradford, Malt, and Oates (1969), that the cost of public services depends on environmental factors as well as on the cost of inputs. A city with relatively old housing, for example, must spend more to deliver the same degree of fire protection to its citizens than must other cities. Thus, the procedure begins by estimating, for a cross section of cities, the impact of environmental cost factors on city spending, controlling for other factors that influence public service quality, such as income and tax price. A cost index for each city can then be calculated using the actual environmental characteristics of the city and the estimated impacts of these factors on service costs.

---

[23] Net benefits to tenants from a tax increase equal their willingness to pay for the associated service quality increment minus the increase in rents. The burden on landlords equals their increased tax payment, $1, minus the increase in rents. Hence, the difference between net benefits to tenants and net benefits to landlords provides a benefit-cost test for a tax increase; if this difference is negative, the costs exceed the benefits. It is ironic that with mobile tenants, the benefit-cost test will be met only if the tax rate is set at the level landlords prefer — even though landlords do not receive any of the benefits. This benefit-cost test applies to benefits to tenants, not benefits for all residents of a community; costs might exceed benefits provided to tenants but be less than benefits provided to all residents.

[24] The two expressions for ϵ cannot both be satisfied with a positive σ and a negative μ unless $(1-r)/r \le t < (1-r)$, which places t far above any observed values. The equality applies if and only if $\sigma = \infty$.

To be specific, the analysis begins with a standard demand function for local public services, in which service quality is a function of median income, Y; tax price, which equals the median tax share, $V/\bar{V}$, multiplied by the (constant) cost per unit of service quality, C; and intergovernmental aid plus other non-property-tax revenue, M. Assuming a multiplicative form for this demand function, we obtain the following expenditure equation (excluding M, for simplicity)[25]:

$$E = (S)(C) = kY^\theta \left(\frac{V}{\bar{V}}\right)^\gamma C^{\gamma+1}. \tag{18}$$

Following Ladd and Yinger (1991), the cost function is assumed to take the form

$$C = l \left(\prod_{i=1}^{k} C_i^{\alpha_i}\right) \tag{19}$$

where l is an index of input costs and C_i represents an environmental cost factor, such as the poverty rate or the share of housing that is old. Substituting equation (19) into equation (18) and taking logarithms yields a functional form that can be estimated with ordinary least squares. The cost index is competed using equation (19); the estimated price elasticity, γ; and the coefficients of the cost variables.[26] The final step is to obtain a measure of service quality, S, using equation (5), that is, by dividing each community's *per capita* expenditure by its cost index.[27]

4.2. The Hedonic Equation

The next step is to use the measure of service quality, S, in a hedonic equation of the rental housing market. We obtain R_i^* and R_S^* from the results of the

---

[25] For detailed discussions of expenditure equations, see Inman (1979), Rubinfeld (1987), or Ladd and Yinger (1991).

[26] First, the price elasticity is used to obtain the α_i's (i.e., $\alpha_i = \beta_i/(\gamma+1)$). Then the cost index, C, is computed directly from equation (19).

[27] This formulation assumed that the error term in the expenditure regression does not reflect management quality. If it did, then the service quality measure would be biased upward in poorly managed cities and downward in efficient cities. To deal with this problem, we also used an alternative measure of service quality, namely predicted expenditure (based on our expenditure regression) divided by cost. This alternative measure yields essentially identical results. We conclude that our service quality measures are not subject to this bias. Note also that, due to data limitations, this paper follows Bradbury *et al.* (1984) by computing a general index for all services. Ladd and Yinger (1991) are able to compute a cost index for general expenditures and separate cost indices for police and fire services.

hedonic. We use the Box–Cox approach, which has been widely employed in the housing literature and which allows us to estimate the appropriate functional form instead of imposing it.[28]

4.3. *The Incidence of Existing Property Tax Differentials*

With the cost indexes and the hedonic prices, the incidence of a marginal change in the property tax rate can be calculated directly from equations (12) and (13). In carrying out these calculations, we set the real interest rate at ten percent.[29]

Calculating the incidence of existing property tax differentials from equation (16) is more difficult. This incidence depends on $V(\bar{t})$, which is the value of V in equation (11) when t is set equal to $\bar{t}$. Finding $V(\bar{t})$ is complicated, however, because it requires an estimate of the value of S that would exist if t were set to $\bar{t}$, $S(\bar{t})$, which equals the actual S multiplied by the ratio of revenue received with a tax rate of $\bar{t}$ to actual revenue. Revenue at $\bar{t}$ depends on the impact of t and S on rents, which is specified by the hedonic equation.[30] This equation is solved with a simulation procedure that assumes, as does equation (13), that the average size of apartments adjusts

---

[28]Recent studies relying on the Box–Cox (1964) method include Goodman (1978, 1988) and Halversen and Pollakowski (1981). We apply the Box–Cox transformation to both the dependent and some of the explanatory variables, with different values of λ for each side of the equation. This approach has the advantage that widely used log-linear and semi-log models are special cases of our procedure. Box–Cox parameters can be obtained through maximum likelihood estimation (MLE) or nonlinear two-stage least squares (NLTSLS). See Spitzer (1982). Although MLE is most frequently used, Amemiya and Powell (1981) recommend NLTSLS because MLE estimates generally are inconsistent because of the endogeneity introduced into the model from the use of the Box–Cox transformation of the dependent variable. Finally, Spitzer (1984) shows that the t-statistics for the Box–Cox MLE are not scale invariant. To solve this problem, we follow Spitzer by dividing each explanatory variable to which the Box–Cox transformation is applied by its geometric mean.

[29]As explained in Yinger *et al.* (1988), this approach states rents in real terms so one must use a real interest rate. They estimate that the real rate was three percent around 1970; real interest rates appear to have increased since then and, in the case of rental housing, should include maintenance, depreciation, and perhaps other factors, although in a model of changes income taxes cancel. A reasonable real rate for 1980 therefore probably would be between five and seven percent. We use a somewhat higher rate to increase the chance that the property tax will be a benefit tax; raising the rate raises the share of the tax borne by tenants. The effect of the interest rate is small, however, and our average burdens on landlords and tenants change by only a couple percentage points when the rate is lowered to five percent.

[30]The hedonic without structural characteristics is used so that the simulated changes in S and t affect both prices and quantities of H.

to changes in housing price and the rental value of business property remains constant.[31] The final step in the simulation is to calculate the landlords share in equation (16) by substituting $S(\bar{t})$ into the estimated hedonic equation.[32]

4.3.1. *The data*

Data for 147 towns and cities in the Boston SMSA in 1980 are used to estimate the hedonic equation. Descriptions of the variables, their means, and their standard deviations are given in Table 2.[33] The dependent variable is median gross rent, which includes actual or imputed utility payments by renters. The explanatory variables are grouped into three categories: public service quality and the tax rate, structural characteristics of housing, and community amenities.

4.3.2. *Service quality and tax rate*

The two variables most important to this analysis are the public service level, SQUALITY, and the effective property tax rate, TAXRATE. The calculation of SQUALITY is described above. As noted earlier, the coefficient of TAXRATE provides a test of the hypothesis that tenants are mobile.[34]

---

[31] In addition, we assume that changes in P and H occur in both the rental and sales markets. An appendix with full explanation of our simulations, as well as the simulation program, is available upon request from the authors.

[32] For this step we use the hedonic equation with structural characteristics to hold H constant to the extent possible with our data and we ignore the estimated effect of t on rents. Because the coefficients of S still reflects changes in the unobserved components of H, this approach should be regarded as an approximation that holds exactly only if $\mu = -\infty$ and $\sigma = 0$. In this case, the estimated impact of S on rents only reflects changes in prices and the direct effect of t on rents is zero. (Hence, one must assume that the estimated effect reflects some omitted non-tax variable).

[33] Many of the variables used here were originally collected for Bradbury *et al.* (1984). This data set has been supplemented with variables from the 1980 census and other sources.

[34] In Massachusetts, 1980 tax payments were based on a 1980 nominal tax rate and a 1978 assessed value. TAXRATE is the 1980 effective property tax rate in a community. Because of widespread poor assessing practices (see Yinger *et al.*, 1988), the available estimates of market values, called "equalized values," are inaccurate for 1978 but had improved considerably by 1980, so we defined TAXRATE as the 1980 nominal tax rate multiplied by the 1980 ratio of assessed value to equalized value for residential property. This measure is divided by the ratio of 1980 to 1978 total assessed value to correct for changes in nominal rates associated with changes in aggregate assessed values. This correction has a significant effect on TAXRATE only in communities that revalued between 1978 and 1980. This correction is not quite right because it is based on total, not residential, assessed values, so we explored other definitions of the tax variable. In particular, we repeated our analysis with effective rates based on 1978 equalized values, with 1978 total, instead of residential,

Table 2 Description of variables used for estimation of hedonic equation, their means and standard deviations (147 municipalities).

Variable	Description	Mean (Standard deviation)
Dependent		
RENT	Median gross rent in 1980, annual.	$3,627 (647)
SQUALITY	Index of public service quality, all municipal services.	756 (163)
TAXRATE	Effective property tax rate for residential housing in 1980.	2.48 (1.09)
Structural Characteristics		
MEDROOMS	Median number of rooms in rental housing structures in 1980.	4.19 (0.46)
RENTAGE	Fraction of 1980 rental units built before 1950.	0.45 (0.15)
UNITS	Fraction of structures with two or fewer rental units in 1980.	0.65 (0.18)
UTILITY	Fraction of rental units that include utility costs as part of rent.	0.77 (0.11)
Neighborhood Amenities		
DENSITY	1980 population divided by square miles of land area.	2.265 (3.255)
RENTER	Fraction of year-round housing units that are rental units.	0.27 (0.15)
POPRAT	Rate of population change defined as 1980 population divided by 1970 population.	1.11 (0.25)
DISTANCE	Linear distance to the Boston central business district (in miles).	21.29 (10.34)
RTE128	Linear distance to Route 128 (in miles).	7.94 (6.01)

Note: SQUALITY was estimated from the expenditure determination model.

Sources: Sources include the *1980 Census of Population and Housing*. Massachusetts Taxpayers' Foundation, and the Massachusetts Department of Revenue.

4.3.3. *Structural characteristics*

Rents are a function of the structural characteristics of housing, as well as of public service quality. As explained earlier, these variables are left out of our

---

effective rates, and with an effective rate that was updated using information from 1980 to 1988, by which time assessment practices in Massachusetts were reasonably accurate. Details of this updating procedure are available from the authors. These alternate tax variables do not alter our own principle results.

principal reduced-form equations, but are presented here for completeness. RENTAGE measures the age of the rental housing stock. As Galster (1987) points out, differences in the age of housing structures typically indicate differences in construction technology, type and efficiency of mechanical systems (plumbing, heating, and wiring), and the time over which the structure has been subject to normal wear and tear and weathering. MEDROOMS indicates the size of rental units. Older and smaller rental units are expected to command lower rents.

The fraction of buildings with two or fewer rental units, UNITS, controls for the size of apartment buildings. UTILITY is the fraction of units that include utilities as part of rent. This variable is not included to correct for the impact of utilities on rents because the dependent variable is median gross rent which, by definition, includes utility payments. Instead, it controls for the presence of housing characteristics associated with the inclusion of utilities in rents. For example, landlords who live in their buildings may be more likely than the owners of large apartment buildings to include utilities in rent because the two- or three-family houses they occupy are not equipped with separate utility meters. Moreover, several studies have identified a positive relationship between housing upkeep and owner-occupancy. See Galster (1987). Thus, UTILITY may be a good proxy for the presence of well-maintained apartments because of owner-occupancy.

4.3.4. *Community amenities*

The community amenity variables describe the character and relative location of communities. These variables are included in our reduced-form equations under the assumption that community characteristics do not change in response to changes in housing price. Densely populated communities, as measured by DENSITY, are likely to have higher congestion, which leads to lower rents, other things equal. Communities with a high percentage of rental housing, as measured by RENTER, tend to be more centralized, lower-income communities with more transient populations, less stable neighborhoods, and less upkeep of properties.[35] Consequently,

---

[35]Factors that alter the median apartment size, including housing price, may alter the percentage renter in a community. We tested for this possibility with the test developed by Hausman (1978, 1983), using percent elderly as an instrument, and found that percent renter is indeed endogenous. As a result, we treat percent renter as endogenous in the full hedonic equation and interpret it as a determinant of median apartment size to be excluded from the hedonic equation without structural characteristics. We also discovered, however, that including percent renter in the hedonic regression without structural characteristics has virtually no impact on our incidence results.

communities with a high proportion of renters are expected to have lower rents. Communities characterized by large influxes of population, as measured by POPRAT, may face temporary upward pressure on rents.[36]

DISTANCE and RTE128 depict the proximity of a community to the central business district (CBD) of Boston and the major beltway for the Boston metropolitan area, respectively. We expect rents to reflect the high premium placed on short commuting distances. Consequently, rents are expected to be higher closer to the CBD and to Route 128, both of which are employment centers.

5. Results

This section presents the estimation results for the service quality measure and the hedonic equation fpr rental housing and discusses the implications of these results for the incidence of property tax differentials.

5.1. *Expenditure Determination Model*

The expenditure determination model differs from that used by Bradbury *et al.* (1984) only in functional form. The results of the two models are similar, and therefore are only summarized briefly here.[37] The town of Lincoln has the lowest cost index at 0.67, while Hull has the highest at 1.63. These figures imply that Hull would have to spend 63 percent more than the average municipality to maintain an average service quality, whereas Lincoln could obtain average- quality services even if it spent 33 percent less than average. Weston has the highest level of public service quality, while Lawrence has the lowest. Boston has the eighth highest cost index in the metropolitan area.

---

[36]The vacancy rate also was included in an early version of the model. Since the hedonic equation is a reduced form of the supply and demand sides of the rental housing market, the vacancy rate might provide an indication of the availability of rental housing. However, the coefficient for this variable was close to zero and statistically insignificant. Dropping this variable did not affect the results of the model. Three communities in the Boston area had some form of rent control. In order to control for the effects of rent control policies on rents, we included a dummy variable for these communities and also deleted them from the estimation, but neither approach affected the results of the model. Our final results include these communities and exclude the dummy variable.

[37]Unlike Bradbury *et al.* (1984), we use a multiplicative functional form, include 1980 population as an explanatory variable, and adjust the cost index to account for the price elasticity. The last step raises the variance of the cost index. Detailed results of our expenditure model are available upon request.

Note that high residential property tax rates do not necessarily lead to high public service quality. Even though Boston has the second-highest property tax rate in the Boston SMSA, for example, its service quality index ranks it only in the top one-third. As explained earlier, a city's revenue depends on its property tax base and its intergovernmental aid, as well as on its property tax rate, and its ability to translate revenue into services depends on its public service cost index.

5.2. *Hedonic Equation*

The hedonic regression results are presented in Tables 3 and 4. Table 3 contains the regression without structural housing characteristics, which is used for our incidence calculations. Both tables display estimates from several estimation techniques for comparison purposes. The estimates of the Box–Cox (1964) parameters indicate that linear and log-linear functional forms are not appropriate.[38]

The structural variables tend to have the expected signs and are statistically significant.[39] The results for the community amenities are somewhat more mixed. The most interesting results are for DISTANCE and RTE128. The coefficient for DISTANCE is negative, as expected, and statistically significant, but the coefficient of RTE128 is positive and statistically insignificant, perhaps indicating the negative amenities of noise and pollution close to this heavily traveled beltway.

---

[38] Following standard practice, variables expressed as proportions (MEDROOMS, RENT-AGE, UNITS, UTILITY, and RENTER) are not transformed for the Box–Cox procedure. Note also that the MLE estimate of λ_1, the Box–Cox (1964) parameter for the dependent variable, differs somewhat from the NLTSLS estimates. The estimate for λ_2, the Box–Cox estimate for the explanatory variables, is not very sensitive to the estimation approach, but does change somewhat when, as explained below, we control for the endogeneity of RENTER and TAXRATE.

[39] UTILITY has a positive impact on rents and is statistically significant, but this result is biased if UTILITY and RENT are simultaneously determined. This type of simultaneity could arise if, for example, high-rent apartments tend to have utilities included in rent, while low-rent apartments do not. We investigated this simultaneity using Hausman tests (1978, 1983) and found no evidence that it exists. Variables indicating the general use of particular types of equipment used for heating housing units or water, or the use of various types of air conditioning units were used as additional instruments for these tests.

Table 3 Hedonic equation without structural characteristics.

Variable	OLS	2SLS	Box–Cox		
			MLE	A-P NL2SLS[a]	A-P NL2SLS[b]
λ_1			0.63	0.21	0.45
			(0.40)	(0.88)	(0.99)
λ_2			0.99^c	1.10^c	1.08
			(0.44)	(0.79)	(0.66)
INTERCEPT	3101.4	3796.8	0.046	0.038	0.054
	(421.9)	(525.9)	(0.021)	(0.026)	(0.028)
SQUALITY	1.34^c	1.07^c	0.265^c	0.255^c	0.257^c
	(0.33)	(0.36)	(0.069)	(0.071)	(0.075)
TAXRATE	−7927.9	-26142^c	−0.046	−0.045	-0.148^c
	(4911.8)	(9194)	(0.030)	(0.031)	(0.047)
DENSITY	-36.0^c	−10.9	−0.011	−0.008	−0.003
	(21.4)	(24.8)	(0.014)	(0.018)	(0.013)
POPRAT	308.9	193.8	0.097	0.097	0.097
	(223.9)	(239.3)	(0.069)	(0.068)	(0.071)
DISTANCE	-28.1^c	-26.7^c	-0.136^c	-0.127^c	-0.145^c
	(7.9)	(8.3)	(0.047)	(0.060)	(0.059)
RTE128	6.35	5.68	0.009	0.010	0.011
	(10.23)	(10.75)	(0.016)	(0.016)	(0.017)
R^2	0.22	0.22	0.22	0.21	0.15

Notes: [a]Nonlinear two-stage least squares is used to control for endogeneity implicit in the use of the Box–Cox transformation on the dependent variable. Second degree polynomials and cross products of the exogenous variables are used as instruments.
[b]Nonlinear two-stage least squares is used to control for the endogeneity implicit in the use of the Box–Cox transformation on the dependent variable, and for the correlation between and TAXRATE and the error term. Second degree polynomials and cross products of the exogenous variables, as well as the variables used to estimate the cost index are used as instruments.
[c]Statistically significant at the 95 percent level (two-tailed); standard errors are in parentheses.

The coefficient of SQUALITY in Table 3 indicates, as expected, that rents are higher in communities with higher-quality public services. Also, as expected, the coefficient of TAXRATE is negative, but it is not always significant. Both coefficients increase in absolute value when housing characteristics are excluded.

These results could be biased because of the endogeneity of the tax rate or service quality variables. We examined this possibility using the specification tests developed by Hausman (1978, 1983), with separate tests

R. J. Carroll & J. Yinger

Table 4 Hedonic equation with structural characteristics.

Variable	OLS	2SLS	Box–Cox MLE	Box–Cox A-P NL2SLS[a]	Box–Cox A-P NL2SLS[b]
λ_1			0.78[c]	0.99[c]	1.06[c]
			(0.30)	(0.49)	(0.52)
λ_2			1.06[c]	1.09[c]	1.18[c]
			(0.40)	(0.44)	(0.49)
INTERCEPT	−464.5	287.4	−0.260	−0.252	−0.231
	(468.2)	(558.7)	(0.097)	(0.098)	(0.101)
SQUALITY	0.81[c]	0.66[c]	0.163[c]	0.167[c]	0.177[c]
	(0.24)	(0.25)	(0.050)	(0.051)	(0.051)
TAXRATE	−3656	−13,813[c]	−0.023	−0.021	−0.072[c]
	(3610)	(6701)	(0.022)	(0.022)	(0.030)
MEDIAN ROOMS	782.4[c]	751.1[c]	0.890[c]	0.904[c]	0.854[c]
	(101.3)	(104.7)	(0.124)	(0.129)	(0.131)
RENTAGE	−513.2	−458.2	−0.145	−0.146	−0.119
	(315.3)	(319.6)	(0.090)	(0.090)	(0.094)
UNITS	−1097.1[c]	−1176.7[c]	−0.301[c]	−0.303[c]	−0.342[c]
	(356.5)	(324.4)	(0.102)	(0.102)	(0.107)
UTILITY	2765.6[c]	2677.6[c]	0.778[c]	0.775[c]	0.790[c]
	(322.4)	(334.7)	(0.091)	(0.091)	(0.093)
DENSITY	−48.5[c]	−25.9	−0.013	−0.012	−0.006
	(22.6)	(22.1)	(0.015)	(0.015)	(0.012)
RENTER	−408.8	−817.2[c]	−0.109	−0.116	−0.173
	(448.5)	(492.9)	(0.127)	(0.127)	(0.130)
POPRAT	−193.5	−286.3	−0.054	−0.056	−0.054
	(164.2)	(174.0)	(0.052)	(0.052)	(0.050)
DISTANCE	−22.1[c]	−21.1[c]	−0.105[c]	−0.104[c]	−0.103[c]
	(5.9)	(5.9)	(0.035)	(0.036)	(0.037)
RTE128	2.45	0.34	0.0039	0.0038	0.0047
	(7.19)	(7.44)	(0.011)	(0.011)	(0.011)
R^2	0.63	0.62	0.63	0.62	0.61

Notes: [a]Nonlinear two-stage least squares is used to control for endogeneity implicit in the use of the Box–Cox transformation on the dependent variable. Second-degree polynomials and cross products of the exogenous variables are used as instruments.
[b]Nonlinear two-stage least squares is used to control for the endogeneity implicit in the use of the Box–Cox transformation on the dependent variable, and for the correlation between TAXRATE and RENTER and the error term. Second-degree polynomials and cross products of the exogenous variables, as well as the variables used to estimate the cost index and percent elderly are used as instruments.
[c]Statistically significant at the 95 percent level (two-tailed); standard errors are in parentheses.

for SQUALITY and TAXRATE.[40] The null hypothesis of no specification error is rejected for TAXRATE but not for SQUALITY. Consequently, we re-estimate our Box–Cox (1964) equation with nonlinear two-stage least squares (NLTSLS) to control for the endogeneity of TAXRATE. The results of NLTSLS estimation also are reported in Tables 3 and 4. The coefficient for SQUALITY is still positive and significant and is similar in magnitude to that obtained from other specifications. The coefficient for TAXRATE is still negative and is now statistically significant.[41] This result supports the hypothesis that demand is elastic. The NLTSLS results are used in our calculations.

5.3. *Incidence of Property Tax Differentials*

Table 5 presents frequency distributions and summary statistics for the net impact of a $1 property tax increase on landlords, as given by equation (12), and on tenants, as given by equation (17). Results are presented for the two cases defined earlier: case 1 sets $\mu = -\infty$ and case 2 sets $\sigma = \infty$. The landlord burden columns also include case 1A, which assumes not only that $\mu = -\infty$ but also that $\sigma = 0$.[42]

The table indicates that landlords bear a large share of the burden of a property tax increase in all communities in all cases. To be specific, landlords bear, on average, $0.909 for every $1.00 property tax increase in case 1,

---

[40]Equation (5) provides guidance for choosing the additional instruments required for these tests. First, the same set of variables determines S and f. Second, only variables relevant for S and t that do not influence rents should be instruments. Accordingly, our instruments were *per capita* income, equalized value *per capita*, the cost index, state aid *per capita*, federal general revenue sharing *per capita*, other federal aid *per capita*, aid to regional school districts *per capita*, and *per capita* local revenue from non-property tax sources. The results from these tests are available upon request.

[41]The coefficient of TAXRATE also might be negative because higher taxes are correlated with unobserved management inefficiency. However, our correction for this problem, explained in footnote 27, has little impact on this coefficient. This negative sign also could reflect either the fact that renters care about property taxes for some reason other than their connection to service levels or a correlation between property taxes and some variable omitted from our equation. We have no way to determine whether either of these possibilities applies. We also asked whether factors that might affect mobility affect the coefficients of SQUALITY and TAXRATE. Interaction terms with income, poverty, percent black, and percent elderly all were insignificant.

[42]This subcase is contradicted by the negative sign of the tax variable unless one assumes that this sign reflects omitted variables, not a demand response to higher housing prices.

Table 5 Burden of a $1 property tax increase.

	Burden on landlords			Burden on tenants	
	Case 1	Case 1A	Case 2	Case 1	Case 2
Mean	$0.909	$0.892	$0.844	$0.00	$0.156
Median	0.918	0.905	0.843	0.00	0.157
Maximum	0.982	0.974	0.896	0.00	0.253
Minimum	0.703	0.672	0.747	0.00	0.104
Number of communities with a burden between					
$0.00 to 0.20	0	0	0	147	138
0.20 to 0.40	0	0	0	0	9
0.40 to 0.60	0	0	0	0	0
0.60 to 0.70	0	0	2	0	0
0.70 to 0.80	5	6	9	0	0
0.80 to 0.90	41	61	138	0	0
0.90 to 0.95	78	68	0	0	0
0.95 to 1.00	23	10	0	0	0

Notes: Burden on landlords is defined by equation (12). Burden on tenants is defined by equation (16). Case 1 is defined by $\mu = -\infty$; case 1A adds $\sigma = 0$; case 2 is defined by $\sigma = \infty$.

$0.892 in case 1A, and $0.844 in case 2. The minimum burden in an individual community, which appears in case 2, is $0.747. It follows that property tax rates are set far from the levels preferred by landlords, and therefore far from the level required for the property tax on rental housing to be a benefit tax.

The remaining columns of Table 5 present the net impact of a property tax increase on tenants, including the value of the resulting service quality improvements. As shown earlier, the assumed infinite elasticity of demand in case 1 implies that the net burden on tenants is zero. In case 2, the net burden on tenants from a $1.00 increase in property taxes is $0.156, on average, with a minimum of $0.104 and a maximum of $0.253. So long as tenants are highly mobile relative to landlords, therefore, the net burden of a property tax increase on tenants is likely to be very small. To put it another way, tenant mobility ensures that, at the margin, the property tax operates like a benefit tax from the point of view of tenants. Tenant mobility does not ensure, however, that the tax rate is set so that tenants receive $1 of benefits for every $1 increase in property taxes.

We cannot determine the true values of μ and σ. If μ actually equals $-\infty$, the property tax is not a benefit tax, because t is not set at the level landlords prefer, that is, because the first condition is not met. In fact, this condition is not even close to being satisfied as landlords pay $0.909, on average, for a $1 increase in property taxes. Moreover, if σ actually equals ∞, the property tax is not a benefit tax because the two necessary conditions are incompatible. The average burden on landlords is lower in this case, namely $0.844 for every $1 increase in property taxes, but the average net burden on tenants also is significant, namely $0.156.

Regardless of one's assumptions about the housing price elasticities, therefore, our analysis of two necessary conditions reveals that the property tax is far from being a benefit tax both on average and in every community. The principal explanation for this outcome is that a $1.00 property tax increase results in a service quality improvement that is worth far less than $1.00 to tenants. Either property taxes are not set at an optimal level or the marginal benefits to other city residents, presumably homeowners, far exceed their tax costs.

The net impact on landlords of existing property tax differentials, as represented by equation (16), also is high. (Because the benefits to tenants associated with these tax differentials are difficult to calculate, no attempt was made to calculate the associated net impacts on tenants.) On average, landlords bear 45 percent of existing property tax differentials. Because of differences across communities in the cost index, in the property tax base, and in the effective property tax rate, however, the burden on landlords varies greatly across communities.[43] These results provide further evidence that the property tax on rental housing is not a benefit tax.[44]

6. Conclusion

According to the "new view" of the property tax, property tax differentials will be borne by renters only to the extent that renters are immobile relative to the other actors in the rental housing market. This paper shows that when associated changes in service quality are recognized, some of the burden

---

[43]Nine communities have a landlord share above 100 percent and 16 have negative landlord shares; that is, their service and tax differences from the average community have a very large positive impact on rents.

[44]These results may have implications for the overall balanced-budget (incidence of the property tax. Courant (1977) shows that the incidence of tax deviations may not cancel out because of nonlinearities in the production function for real estate. This paper shows that the balanced-budget incidence of property tax differentials may influence the average incidence because of the dependence of differential incidence on community characteristics. If landlords bear a relatively large share of the tax in communities with above-average rates, which we find to be the case, then the burden of the average property tax rate understates the average burden of the property tax on landlords.

of these differentials falls on renters even if they are mobile. This shifting occurs because tenants are willing to pay higher rents to receive the better services purchased by higher property taxes. However, fully mobile tenants (or tenants facing a fixed housing supply) are indifferent to an increase in the property tax because the benefits from the associated service quality increase are exactly offset by an increase in rent. Thus, the property tax causes no distortion in the behavior of such tenants.

Even with fully mobile tenants, however, the property tax is not a benefit tax unless the rent increases caused by a property tax increase (through a service quality increase) exactly equal the increase in the landlord's tax payment. Otherwise, landlords pay some of the tax increase without receiving the service quality increment; this tax burden on landlords is a source of distortion. In our sample, a $1.00 property tax increase results in a rent increase of only about $0.15, on average, even with infinitely elastic housing supply. The magnitude of the resulting tax burden on landlords varies from one community to another. As noted earlier, for example, there is more shifting onto tenants in a community with low public service costs than one with high public service costs, all else equal. Nevertheless, rent increases never fully compensate landlords for tax increases, and the maximum rental increase in a single community is only $0.25. This conclusion is confirmed by a simulation of the burdens placed on landlords from existing tax differentials across communities; on average, higher rents offset only 55 percent of the tax differences paid by landlords. In our sample, therefore, the property tax on rental housing falls far short of being a benefit tax, even under assumptions that make the benefit-tax outcome most likely.

References

Amemiya, Takeshi and James L. Powell. 1981. A comparison of the box–cox maximum likelihood estimator and the non-linear two-stage least squares estimator. *Journal of Econometrics* **17**: 351–381.

Box, G. and D. Cox. 1964. An analysis of transformations. *Journal of the Royal Statistical Society, Series B* **26**: 211–243.

Bradbury, Katharine, Helen Ladd, Michael Perrault, Andrew Reschovsky, and John Yinger. 1984. State and to offset fiscal disparities across communities. *National Tax Journal* **37**: 151–170.

Bradford, David F., R. A. Malt, and Wallace E. Oates. 1969. The rising cost of local public services: some evidence and reflections. *National Tax Journal* **22**: 185–202.

Coen, Robert M. and Brian J. Powell. 1972. Theory and measurement of the incidence of differentials property taxes on rental housing. *National Tax Journal* **25**: 211–216.

Courant, Paul N. 1977. A general equilibrium model of heterogeneous local property taxes. *Journal of Public Economics* **8**: 313–327.

Dushansky, Richard, Melvin Ingber, and Nicholas Karatjas. 1981. The impact of property taxation on housing values and rents. *Journal of Urban Economics* **10**: 240–255.

Fischel, William A. 1992. Property taxation and the tiebout model: evidence for the benefit view from zoning and voting. *Journal of Economic Literature* **30**: 171–177.

Galster, George C. 1987. *Homeowners and Neighborhood Reinvestment.* Durham, NC: Duke University Press.

Goodman, Allen C. 1978. Hedonic prices, price indices, and housing markets. *Journal of Urban Economics* **5**: 471–484.

Goodman, Allen C. 1988. An econometric model of housing price, permanent income, tenure choice, and housing demand. *Journal of Urban Economics* **23**: 327–53.

Halversen, Robert and Henry O. Pollakowski. 1981. Choice of functional form for hedonic price equations. *Journal of Urban Economics* **10**: 37–49.

Hamilton, Bruce. 1975. Zoning and property taxes in a system of local governments. *Urban Studies* **12**: 205–211.

Hausman, Jerry. 1978. Specification tests in econometrics. *Econometrica* **46**: 1251–1272.

Hausman, Jerry. 1983. Specification and Estimation in NonLinear Simultaneous Equations." In Griliches and Intriligator (eds.), *Handbook of Econometrics*, Volume 2, pp. 391–445. New York: North-Holland.

Heinburg, John D. and Wallace E. Oates. 1970. The incidence of differential property taxes on urban housing: a comment and some further evidence. *National Tax Journal* **23**: 92–98.

Hyman, D. N. and E. C. Pasour, Jr. 1973. Property tax differentials and residential rents in North Carolina. *National Tax Journal* **26**: 303–307.

Inman, Robert. 1979. The fiscal performance of local governments: an interpretative review. In P. Mieszkowski and M. Straszheim (eds.), *Current Issues in Urban Economics*, pp. 270–321. Baltimore: John Hopkins University Press, 1979.

Ladd, Helen F. and John Yinger. 1991. *America's Ailing Cities: Fiscal Health and the Design of Urban Policy*, Updated ed. Baltimore: John Hopkins Press.

McDonald, John F. 1993. Incidence of the property tax on commercial real estate: the case of downtown Chicago. *National Tax Journal* **66**: 109–120.

Mieszkowski, Peter and George R. Zodrow. 1989. Taxation and the tiebout model. *Journal of Economic Literature* **27**: 1098–1146.

Musgrave, Richard A. and Peggy B. Musgrave. 1989. *Public Finance: In Theory and Practice*, 5th Edition. New York: McGraw Hill.

Orr, Larry L. 1968. The incidence of differential property taxes on urban housing. *National Tax Journal* **21**: 253–262.

Orr, Larry L. 1970. The incidence of differential property taxes on urban housing: a response. *National Tax Journal* **23**: 99–101.

Orr, Larry L. 1972. The incidence of differential property taxes on urban housing: reply. *National Tax Journal* **25**: 217–220.

Rubinfeld, Daniel L. 1987. The economics of the local public sector. In Alan Auerbach and Martin Feldstein (eds.), *Handbook of Public Economics*, vol. 2, pp. 1–76. New York: North-Holland.

Spitzer, John J. 1982. A primer on box–cox estimation. *Review of Economics and Statistics* 307–313.

Spitzer, John J. 1984. Variance estimates in models with the box–cox transformation: implications for estimation and hypothesis testing. *Review of Economics and Statistics* **66**: 645–652.

Stiglitz, Joseph E. 1983. The theory of local public goods twenty-five years after tiebout: a perspective. In George S. Zodrow (ed.), *Local Provision of Public Services: The Tiebout Model After Twenty-Five Years*, pp. 17–54. New York: Academic Press.

Wassmer, Robert W. 1993. Property taxation, property base, and property value: an empirical test of the new view. *National Tax Journal* **66**: 135–160.

Wheaton, William C. 1984. The incidence of inter-Jurisdictional differences in commercial property taxes. *National Tax Journal* **37**: 515–527.

Yinger, John. 1982. Capitalization and the theory of local public finance. *Journal of Political Economy* **90**: 917–943.

Yinger, John. 1985. Inefficiency and the median voter: property taxes, capitalization, heterogeneity, and the theory of the second best. In John M. Quigley (ed.), *Perspectives on Local Public Finance and Public Policy*, vol. 2, pp. 3–30. Greenwich, CT: JAI Press.

Yinger, John, Howard S. Bloom, Axel Borsch-Supan, and Helen F. Ladd. 1988. *Property Taxes and House Values: The Theory and Estimation of Intrajurisdictional Property Tax Capitalization*. New York: Academic Press.

Part 3
Cost Functions for Public Education

Chapter 5

Are Education Cost Functions Ready for Prime Time? An Examination of Their Validity and Reliability[*]

William Duncombe[‡] and John Yinger[†,§]
*†Departments of Public Administration and
International Affairs and of Economics,
Syracuse University, Syracuse, NY, United States*
§*jyinger@maxwell.syr.edu*

This article makes the case that cost functions are the best available methodology for ensuring consistency between a state's educational accountability system and its education finance system. Because they are based on historical data and well-known statistical methods, cost functions are a particularly flexible and low-cost way to forecast what each school district must spend to meet the standards in a state's accountability system. However, the application of cost functions to education must confront several challenges in both data collection and estimation methodology. This article describes the strengths and weaknesses of various ways to address these challenges and illustrates how the reliability and forecasting accuracy of cost functions can be tested using data for Missouri school districts.

1. Introduction

Every state faces the challenge of creating an education finance system that is consistent with its educational accountability program. The accountability program sets student performance targets that school districts are expected

---

[*]This chapter is reproduced from "Are Education Cost Functions Ready for Prime Time? An Examination of their Validity and Reliability," *Peabody Journal of Education: Issues of Leadership, Policy and Organizations*, **86**(1), 2011, pp. 28–57.
[‡]Deceased.

to meet, and, for consistency, the education finance system should provide every district with the resources it needs to meet these targets. This article explains how educational cost functions can be used to address this problem, explores the challenges facing researchers estimating educational cost functions, responds to recent criticism of the cost-function approach, provides estimates of education cost functions for the state of Missouri, and tests the accuracy of these estimates. Overall, we make the case that cost functions are the best available methodology for ensuring consistency between a state's educational accountability system and its education finance system.

2. Education Cost Functions

Production and cost functions are key microeconomic tools for understanding how various inputs are translated into a given output. A production function explains output as a function of input levels, and the related cost function explains a firm's costs as a function of its output and the input prices it faces. These tools have been extensively used to study education and other public services. At the school district level, for which a full list of inputs is difficult to observe, cost functions are the principal tool for studying educational production.[1] In this case, the key outputs are measures of student performance on state tests and graduation rates. The key input price is the salary a district must pay to attract teachers.

Any application of cost functions to education must address several challenging issues. First, it must select the outputs on which to focus. Second, any estimation of a cost equation must recognize the difference between costs and spending, which, as discussed next, is school-district efficiency. Third, educational cost depends not only on input prices but also on student characteristics, such as the poverty rate and the share of students with limited English proficiency. These characteristics are sometimes known as "fixed inputs," because they are outside a school district's control. Fourth, estimation of an education cost equation must recognize that both measures of student performance and teachers' salaries are influenced by school district decisions

---

[1]Education cost functions have been estimated for Arizona (Downes and Pogue, 1994), California (Duncombe et al. 2008; Imazeki, 2008), Illinois (Imazeki, 2001), New York (Duncombe et al., 2008; Duncombe and Yinger, 2000, 2005b), Texas (Gronberg et al., 2004; Imazeki and Reschovsky, 2004a, 2004c), and Wisconsin (Reschovsky and Imazeki, 2001).

and are therefore, to use the statistical term, endogenous. To obtain unbiased results, studies that estimate cost functions must account for this endogeneity. Finally, a cost function study must select an appropriate functional form.

2.1. *Selection of Outputs*

For the problem on which this article focuses, namely, the consistency of accountability and finance systems, it is appropriate to select an output measure or measures that are central to a state's school accountability system. In most cases, these measures will indicate student performance on key state-administered tests (such as English, reading, or mathematics) and perhaps graduation rates. One approach would be to focus on the end point — high school test scores — and another would be to look at average scores over several grades.

Yet another approach, which has appeared both in the scholarly literature and in a few state accountability systems, is to focus on levels of student performance, not measured, say, by the share of students passing a state test but measured instead by the *change* in student performance over time, often referred to as a value-added measure. This approach is difficult to implement in a cost study, however, because a value-added approach requires test score information on the same cohort in different grades — information that is not generally available. Moreover, value-added measures provide noisy signals about student performance, particularly in small school districts (Kane and Staiger, 2002).

To understand why a value-added approach is difficult to implement, consider a standard Cobb-Douglas value-added production function in which student performance depends on the starting point (i.e., the previous year's performance) plus current year inputs:

$$S_T = S_0 \left(\prod_{t=1}^{T} A(L_t)^\alpha (K_t)^\beta e_t \right) \varepsilon = S_{T-1}(L_T)^\alpha (K_T)^\beta e_T, \tag{1}$$

where S represents student performance, L is labor, K is capital, α and β are output elasticities for labor and capital, e_t is a random error associated with period t, and ε is a time-invariant error term for the district. (The subscript for the district is implicit.) The cost function associated with this production function, which can be estimated in log form, is [2]:

$$C = a(S_T)^{1/(\alpha+\beta)}, \tag{2}$$

---

[2]For a derivation, see Henderson and Quandt (1980, p. 85).

where

$$\alpha = (\alpha + \beta) \left(\frac{W^{\alpha} r^{\beta}}{A S_{T-1} e_T \alpha^{\alpha} \beta^{\beta}} \right)^{1/(\alpha+\beta)}, \tag{3}$$

where W is the price of labor, r is the price of capital, and $(\alpha + \beta)$ measures returns to quality scale (Duncombe and Yinger, 1993). With a value-added approach, therefore, the log of S_{T-1} should be included in the estimating equation, with a predicted negative sign.

In this derivation, S_{T-1} is the previous year's score for the cohort observed in year T. If S_T is an eighth-grade score in 2000, for example, then S_{T-1} cannot be measured by either eighth-grade scores in 1999 or seventh-grade scores in 2000. Instead, it must be measured by the seventh-grade scores in 1999. The accumulated inputs for the previous cohort (eighth grade in 1999) and for the next cohort (seventh grade in 2000) have no impact on the current cohort (eighth grade in 2000) and are not an approximation for the term in the model. With a few exceptions, data for a correctly specified value-added cost model are not available, so this approach can be used in only a few states.[3] Implementation of "growth models" in a number of states to comply with No Child Left Behind (NCLB) may increase the feasibility of value-added cost functions over the next decade.

2.2. *School-District Efficiency*

The second issue at the heart of the problems addressed in this article is the difficulty of measuring school district efficiency. A cost equation indicates how much a school district would have to spend to achieve a given student performance level if it used the best available technology, that is, the best available teaching methods and management practices. "Cost" by this definition cannot be observed, however; instead, a researcher observes actual spending, which may not reflect the best available technology. To put it another way, spending may exceed cost because some districts deviate from the best available technology. Districts that deviate from the best available technology are defined to be "inefficient." No study can identify the determinants of a school district's "costs," therefore, without controlling for school-district efficiency.

More formally, education costs (C) depend on student performance (S); resource prices (W), such as teacher salaries; student enrollment (N); and

---

[3]In their studies of Texas *et al.* (2004a, 2004c) and Gronberg *et al.* (2004) used measures of value-added across 1 or 2 years.

student need measures (P); that is, $C = f(S, W, N, P)$. Now let e stand for school district efficiency in delivering S. Without loss of generality, we can set the value of e at 1.0 in an efficient district, so that e has a value between zero and one in a district that does not use current best practices. With this scaling, the cost/efficiency equation is:

$$E = \frac{C}{e} = \frac{f(S, W, N, P)}{e}. \tag{4}$$

Moreover, a district that does not use best practices $(e < 1)$ must spend more than an efficient district $(e = 1)$ to achieve the same level of performance (S), all else equal.

Unfortunately, however, the concept of "efficiency" in the education context is widely misunderstood. To understand why, consider first the case of firms producing a single output (or multiple outputs produced with totally separate inputs). In this case, an inefficient firm is one that does not use the best available technology to produce the output. Inefficient practices include using an outmoded machine or sending executives on expensive vacations, and "inefficient" is a synonym for "wasteful."

When a firm produces multiple outputs with some sharing of inputs, however, the concept of "inefficiency" applies to the firm's production of each output, not to the firm as a whole, and "inefficiency" and "waste" may no longer be equivalent. Consider farms that grow corn and beans in the same fields, a practice used by Native Americans to give the beans a place to climb. One farm might use extra person power, and hence be inefficient, in growing corn because it takes great care not to trample the beans. This type of efficiency has nothing to do with waste; instead, it has to do with the farm's trade-off across the two outputs. A farm that is inefficient in this sense may, of course, also be wasteful by using an outmoded tractor, for example, but there is no logical connection between these two components of inefficiency.

Multiple outputs and input sharing are inherent features of production in public education; the same teachers and classrooms, supported by the same administrative services, provide many different outputs. These outputs include student performance on standardized tests, graduation rates, and student performance in art, music, athletics, and citizenship. In this setting, an analyst can ask if a school district is inefficient in producing English and math performance, but one must recognize that this type of inefficiency reflects both spending to promote other outputs and the use of outmoded techniques or other forms of waste. For example, a school district that is efficient in delivering student performance in mathematics might not be efficient in delivering student performance in English or art. Indeed, spending on art may have little impact on mathematics performance, so that it is a source of inefficiency in the production of mathematics. A good art or music program may, of course, contribute to students' general conceptual skills with some spillover to mathematics, but in most cases spending on these programs will not have as large an impact on mathematics scores as more spending on instruction in mathematics. No existing study has been able to separate these two types of inefficiency.

Misunderstanding about the concept of inefficiency in education leads to many incorrect statements in both the public debate and the scholarly literature. School districts with high spending levels and low performance are often called "inefficient," even if their high spending reflects the relatively high wages they must pay to attract teachers or the added costs of educating disadvantaged students (an issue discussed further in the next section). After accounting for labor market conditions and student characteristics, school districts that spend more than other districts with the same student performance on English and mathematics tests are sometimes called "wasteful." In fact, however, districts that spend more than other districts with the same English and math performance may simply be providing relatively high levels of student performance along other dimensions, such as graduation rates or music skills. Of course, these districts may also be using outmoded techniques or being wasteful in some other way, but spending numbers alone cannot determine whether this is true.

Scholars have used a variety of methods to control for school-district efficiency in the estimation of a cost function. Because efficiency cannot, by definition, be directly observed, all of these methods control for efficiency indirectly. One method is to estimate the cost function with district fixed effects, which control for all district characteristics, including efficiency, that do not vary over time (Downes and Pogue, 1994). The limitations of this approach are that it requires panel data; that it cannot control for district efficiency that varies over time; and that, by removing all cross-section variation, it undermines a researcher's ability to estimate the impact on costs of S, W, N, and P.

The second approach begins with the estimation of a cost frontier based on the lowest observed spending for obtaining any given student performance, using a technique called data envelopment analysis (DEA). The next step is to calculate each district's deviation from this spending as an index of inefficiency and then to control for this measure in an estimated cost function (Duncombe *et al.* 1996; Duncombe and Yinger, 2000; Reschovsky and Imazeki, 2001).[4] This approach has two key limitations. First, because the frontier is estimated with data on S and C, it relies on the functional form assumptions in DEA to identify the role of efficiency, assumptions that cannot be tested. Second, a standard DEA index of "inefficiency" reflects both cost and efficiency differences across districts. As a result, this approach may lead to underestimated coefficients of cost variables, such as student poverty, because a portion of the impact of these variables on costs may be captured by the estimated coefficient of the "inefficiency" index.

The third approach is to identify factors that have a conceptual link to efficiency and then to control for them in a cost function regression. A limitation of this approach is that these conceptual links cannot be directly tested. Nevertheless, a strong case can be made for the inclusion of two types of efficiency controls. First, some district characteristics might influence the incentives for voters to monitor school officials or for school officials to adopt best practices. For example, Imazeki and Reschovsky (2004a) controlled for efficiency using a measure of competition from other public schools, which might influence the behavior of school officials. Second, some district characteristics, such as median household income or tax price, might influence voters' demand for measures of school-district performance other than S. Because efficiency can only be defined relative to specific measures of school district performance, in this case S, any spending to obtain other measures of performance is, by definition, inefficient.[5] Income and tax price are examples of variables that help control for this type of inefficiency (Duncombe and Yinger, 2000, 2005a, 2005b).

---

[4]Ruggiero (1998) showed how to separate cost and efficiency factors in DEA, but his approach requires far more observations than are available for any state because each district must be compared with other districts that have the same performance and the same cost factors. A multistage DEA-based approach has been used by McCarty and Yaisawarng (1993), Ray (1991), and Ruggiero (2001). Another approach is a stochastic frontier regression (Alexander *et al.*, 2000; Gronberg *et al.*, 2004). Ondrich and Ruggiero (2001) showed, however, that stochastic frontier regression produces the same results as an OLS regression except that the intercept has been shifted up to the frontier. As a result, this approach does not remove biases caused by omitting controls for efficiency.

[5]In a cost-function context, it is not possible to separate inefficiency associated with "wasteful" spending from inefficiency associated with spending on performance measures other than those included in S. It follows that a given school district could be deemed inefficient in providing one measure of student performance, say, math and English scores, and efficient in providing another, say, art and music.

3. Controlling for Student Characteristics and Other External Cost Factors

Scholars have long recognized that the cost of education depends on many factors outside a school district's control. These factors include the wage environment, student enrollment, and the concentration of disadvantages among the student population. Duncombe and Yinger (2007b) have provided a detailed review of the scholarly literature on these factors.

A typical cost-function study controls for teacher wages (either measured by a private wage or treated as endogenous), student enrollment and student enrollment squared, a measure of poverty among the students (such as the percentage eligible for a free or reduced price lunch), and a measure of the share of students who speak English as a second language. In most studies, these variables are highly significant and have a large impact on education costs. A study of New York by Duncombe and Yinger (2005b) found, for example, that the cost of bringing a poor child up to a given education performance standard is more than twice as high as the cost for a non-poor child.

3.1. *Addressing Endogeneity*

An estimated education cost function includes school outputs on the right side. Because these outputs are jointly determined with spending, however, they need to be treated as endogenous. This endogeneity is a great challenge for cost functions studies. The standard solution to an endogeneity problem is to estimate the model using instrumental variables. To be a valid instrument, a variable must help explain observed school outputs while not affecting school spending in any other way. Not surprisingly, variables with these two characteristics are difficult to find. Studies that use teacher wages as a cost factor also should treat this variable as endogenous.

Some early studies, including some of our own, used income and tax-price as instruments for school outputs. These variables satisfy one characteristic of a good instrument: they are demand variables that influence a community's choice of output levels. As it turns out, however, these variables do not satisfy the other main characteristic of a good instrument; because they affect the demand for many outputs, they show up as a determinant of efficiency in the cost function for any subset of outputs. In other words, they are invalid instruments because they are direct determinants of spending.

A more promising approach is to identify districts that are similar to a district and use their exogenous characteristics of instruments. The decisions of voters and school officials set their targets for good performance in part by observing comparison districts, but the exogenous characteristics of these districts do not influence the district's spending in any other way.[6] Because any cost analysis focuses on specific performance measures and other performance measures show up in inefficiency, this approach is most compelling when the performance measure in the cost function either covers the most publicized measures in the state, such as those included in the state's accountability program. This approach is used (and, to the extent possible, tested) in the regressions presented next.

3.2. *Functional Form*

A final challenge is to select a functional form for the cost model. This form reflects underlying assumptions about the technology of production, such as the degree of substitution between inputs, economies of scale, and the interaction between school and non-school factors. Most education cost studies have used a simple multiplicative cost function, which works well in practice but which imposes limits on both factor substitution and economies of scale.[7] By contrast, Gronberg *et al.* (2004) used a flexible cost function that does not impose significant restrictions on production technology. This approach adds many variables to the cost model, however, which makes it more difficult to identify cost effects with precision.[8]

---

[6]Scholars face a trade-off with this approach. If the "similar" districts are literally neighbors, then their exogenous characteristics might be correlated with unobservable sorting factors shared with the district that defines the observation, thereby creating an endogeneity problem. If the "similar" districts are too far away geographically, however, they may not be part of the district's comparison group so that their traits have no explanatory power in the first stage regression. In this article we compromise between these two extremes by selecting the traits of districts in the same labor market area.

[7]Most studies use a variant of the Cobb-Douglas function, which is multiplicative in form. The Cobb-Douglas function assumes that the elasticity of substitution between all inputs is equal to one and that the elasticity for economies of scale is constant at all levels of output.

[8]One of the most popular flexible cost functions used in empirical research is the translog cost function. A translog cost model includes squared terms for each input price and outcome, and adds interaction terms between all factor prices, and outcomes. Gronberg *et al.* (2004) also included a number of interaction terms between outcomes, teacher salaries, and non-school factors. In all, they have more than 100 variables in their cost function for Texas compared to 18 variables in the Texas cost model estimated by Imazeki and Reschovsky (2004a).

4. Criticism by Costrell, Hanushek, and Loeb

The article by Costrell *et al.* (2008; henceforth CHL) criticizes cost functions on several grounds. Many of these criticisms can also be found in Hanushek (2005) and Loeb (2007). This section presents our responses to the CHL analysis.

4.1. *Lack of an Alternative*

Our main disagreement with CHL is that they do not propose an alternative approach to solving the problem posed at the beginning of this article, namely, the compatibility between a state's education finance and school accountability systems. We do not claim that cost functions are perfect or that the challenges they pose are easily met, but we do claim that they are a logically compelling and empirically reasonable way to address this problem. We do not know of any other method that provides an alternative approach that is nearly as complete or compelling. No such alternative is identified by CHL. In fact, one of the authors in previous work (Hanushek, 2005) argued that decisions "on the right balance among different government programs and between public and private spending along with structuring the schools and their incentives is rightfully the province of the democratic appropriations process and not consultants hired by interested parties" (p. 2). In other words, Hanushek believes that better designs of school finance systems to support adequacy will emerge from the political process, not from research on the cost of adequacy.

Complex empirical challenges appear in many types of policy problems. To prepare a budget, for example, every state needs a macroeconomic forecasting model and method for forecasting revenue. Economists certainly do not all agree on the best way to estimate a model of this type. Nevertheless, states all have procedures for creating and debating such a model — and for using its forecasts in their budgets. According to Voorhees (2004), states vary widely in methods and institutional arrangements for revenue forecasts. Some states set up a council of economic advisers, others rely on university experts, and a large number of states produce their forecasts using econometric methods. While state revenue forecasts by state agencies are influenced by politics (Bretschneider *et al.*, 1989), they are informed by technical forecasts developed using a variety of methods (Kuo and Liang, 2004; Mocan and Azad, 1995; Shkurti, 1990).

The estimation of education costs, which is required to make education finance and accountability systems compatible, is also a fundamental problem for state policymakers, and cost functions provide the best available estimating method. States need to find ways to develop cost function studies, supplemented with appropriate other methods, which can inform the design of their state aid systems, just as they have found ways to incorporate macroeconomic forecasting models into their budgeting process. Rejecting cost functions because they are imperfect without providing an alternative is like rejecting the use of macroeconomic models for revenue forecasting and thereby turning the forecasting process back over to politicians.

We should make it clear that we have no trouble with the development of other methods for estimating what it would take to meet a state's accountability standards. Formal evaluations of various programs that look at costs and impact on performance, for example, would be helpful contributions. In fact, we have argued that states should take a more active role in initiating evaluations and helping school districts determine which programs are the most cost effective (Duncombe *et al.*, 2008). But existing evidence about program impacts and costs is limited, and this type of evidence cannot replace a comprehensive cost measure obtained through a cost regression.[9]

We also do not believe, as CHL (2008) seem to suggest we do in their last paragraph (p. 221), that cost function studies indicate the amount of money that will "guarantee student success or at least the opportunity for student success" according to the state's standards. Cost functions can be used to estimate the spending required to meet a performance standard if a district uses best practices, but the district may not use best practices, and even if it does, a cost function only provides an estimate, not a guarantee. Nevertheless, we do believe that cost function studies are the best currently available method for estimating the cost of reaching any given performance target.

4.2. *Interpretation of an Expenditure Equation*

CHL also argue that a regression with expenditure as the dependent variable cannot be given a cost interpretation. On this point our disagreement with them is profound. Equation (1) in this article shows that spending equals costs divided by efficiency. If efficiency is not correlated with the variables

---

[9]On this point we are at least in agreement with Loeb (2007), who said that "the primary drawback of this method," which she called the "evidence-based" approach, "is that the research base is not strong enough to support it" (p. 13).

that determine cost, then a regression of spending on cost variables yields unbiased estimates of the cost parameters. If efficiency is correlated with these variables, then the methods discussed earlier are needed to insulate the coefficients of the cost variables from omitted variable bias. In either case, the cost variables have clear, legitimate cost interpretations. The coefficient of the poverty variable, for example, indicates the impact of an increase in poverty on the spending that is required to achieve any given level of student performance.

CHL give this coefficient, which they label β_3, a different interpretation. As they put it (where FRL stands for free and reduced price lunch, a common poverty variable),

> The estimated coefficient β_3, represents the additional spending, on average, among districts with higher percentages of FRL students, holding other variables constant. In essence it indicates what districts with different levels of poverty are spending. It does *not* represent the extra *cost* required to achieve any given performance level for FRL students. All a positive β_3, coefficient in equation (1) [not presented here] would reflect is a tendency of either the state or the district to spend more heavily when there is a greater proportion of students in poverty, while any similar tendency to spend less on poor students would yield a negative coefficient. This interpretation of β_3, holds regardless of whether extra spending is required to increase performance or is effective at doing so. (pp. 205–206)

This is simply not correct. CHL have forgotten the end of their own first sentence in this quotation. Performance is held constant. Moreover, in the estimating framework presented earlier, efficiency is held constant as well. So this coefficient does have a cost interpretation.

The cost equation presented by CHL is linear. This specification assumes that the impact of an increment in student poverty on the cost of education is constant, controlling for performance and efficiency. If this assumption is not correct, then the coefficient of a poverty variable estimated with their equation might give a biased estimate of the impact of poverty on costs. The problem, however, is with their linear specification, not with the cost function method. In fact, most studies estimate a multiplicative equation, which is much more reasonable on conceptual grounds; in this case, the coefficient of the poverty variable indicates the percentage increase in cost that accompanies an increase in the share of students from poor families. No published cost function study of which we are aware estimates a cost function that is linear.

CIIL (2008) go on to argue that "deviations from average spending of comparable districts — are simply redefined as deviations from 'cost.' That is why the 'cost' estimates carry the logically incoherent implication that half the districts spend less than is necessary to achieve what they have achieved" (p. 212). We disagree. Cost based on best practices is defined as the minimum spending to achieve a given student performance, not as average spending. No cost study either claims or implies that "half the districts spend less than is necessary to achieve what they have achieved." Instead, cost studies control for performance and for differences in the cost environment in different school districts, and then assume that remaining variation in spending reflects variation in efficiency. With this approach, it is possible to construct an estimated efficiency index, which is 1.0 in the most efficient district (which is the one with the lowest spending after accounting for cost variables) and lower than 1.0 in other districts.

Of course, errors may arise in the efficiency index if the regression is misspecified, if the efficiency controls are inadequate, or if some cost factors have been omitted from the regression. But these are the types of problems that confront any estimating problem, not just this one. In other words, this approach only yields an estimate of efficiency, but, contrary to the claims of CHL, it is a logically coherent one.

4.3. *Production Functions as an Alternative to Cost Functions*

Finally, CHL argue that cost functions are not credible because a "production function" estimated with the same data yields extremely different results.[10] Normally, a production function relates output, in this case student performance, to inputs. The great challenge facing this application of production functions is that it requires a comprehensive set of inputs, which is difficult to observe at the district level. In fact, we know of no study that has attempted to estimate a district-level production function with measures of teachers and teacher quality, administrators and administrator quality, maintenance staff, and supplies. To avoid measuring these inputs, CHL use student performance as the dependent variable and spending per pupil as the key explanatory variable. In effect, this approach assumes that spending is a proxy for the bundle of inputs that a school district selects.

---

[10]Imazeki (2008) made this argument, too. She claimed that "if the data and model were perfect (i.e., correctly specified with no unobservable variables or measurement error), the final cost estimates from the cost function and production function should be similar" (p. 102). This is simply not correct. As discussed next, spending and inputs are not the same thing and there is no reason at all to expect the final cost estimates from a misspecified production function to yield cost estimates that are similar to those from a cost function.

This approach, namely, using spending as a measure of inputs, runs into two serious problems: extreme assumptions about production technology and measurement error.

4.3.1. *Extreme assumptions about production technology*

To see what assumptions are required for this approach to make sense, consider a simple production function for student performance, S, with two inputs, K and L. The prices of these inputs are P_K and P_L, so spending, E, equals $(P_K K + P_L L)$. Hence the production function is:

$$S = f\{E\} = f\{P_K K + P_L L\}. \tag{5}$$

With this formulation, spending on K is assumed to have the same impact on S as spending on L. In other words, the marginal products of the two inputs are

$$\frac{\partial S}{\partial K} = f'P_K \quad \text{and} \quad \frac{\partial S}{\partial L} = f'P_L. \tag{6}$$

Now the slope of an isoquant is found from the total differential of the production function with dS set equal to zero. In symbols,

$$dS = 0 = \frac{\partial S}{\partial K}dK + \frac{\partial S}{\partial L}dL = f'P_K d_K + f'P_L dL. \tag{7}$$

This equation leads directly to the slope of an isoquant:

$$\frac{dK}{dL} = -\frac{P_L}{P_K}. \tag{8}$$

This is the first sign of trouble. Isoquants are supposed to depend only on technology, not on prices.

The slope of the government's iso-cost lines are found by totally differentiating the cost equation given earlier, namely, that $E = (P_K K + P_L L)$, and setting $dE = 0$.

$$dE = 0 = P_K dK + P_L dL \quad \text{or} \quad \frac{dK}{dL} = -\frac{P_L}{P_K}. \tag{9}$$

This equation signals more trouble. The isoquants and the iso-cost lines have exactly the same slope; in other words, they are tangent everywhere! This means that, with this approach, all combinations of K and L are assumed to be equally efficient.

These problems extend to the case of more than two inputs. This approach requires the assumptions that spending of every input is equally productive and that any combination of inputs, including a value of zero for every input except one, is equally productive.

A cost function, in contrast, can be directly derived from standard production functions without imposing any such unrealistic assumptions on production technology. A cost function does require the measurement of input prices. If resource prices for some types of resources, such as materials and supplies, exhibit little variation across districts, however, they can be dropped from a cost-function estimation without imposing any constraints on the underlying production technology.

4.3.2. *Measurement error in the key explanatory variable*

As discussed earlier, efficiency, e, in equation (1) cannot be directly observed, so it is not possible to separate cost and spending. This fact causes trouble for a production function, which is intended to describe the best available technology. The fact that the measured spending variable reflects waste as well as best-practices spending implies that there may be a large measurement error in this variable. It would not be surprising, therefore, to find an estimated impact of spending on performance that was close to zero.[11]

One cannot avoid this problem by saying that the regression picks up the average link between spending and performance. With errors in the key variable, the estimated coefficients are biased and inconsistent. One way to solve the problem would be to use an instrumental variables technique. To the best of our knowledge, this has never been attempted. Moreover, an instrument might be impossible to find. To isolate the cost component of spending, which is the effect one is trying to estimate, one needs an instrument that helps explain the link between inputs and spending. However, any instrument that meets this first test for a good instrument inevitably fails the second test, which requires no direct link between the instrument and the dependent variable, in this case district performance. An empirical implementation of equation (5) also could include controls for variables associated with inefficiency, but this approach does not provide a general solution to the errors-in-variables problem. There may be a way out of this conundrum, but we do not know what it is, and it certainly has not been provided by people using this approach.

---

[11]In addition, we find it ironic that CHL, who are so critical of the treatment of efficiency in cost function studies, do not find fault with the production function approach, which faces much more severe challenges in dealing with efficiency.

Cost function studies may also face an errors-in-variables problem in measuring their key explanatory variable, namely, performance. This problem has an entirely different source, of course, namely, the random component in test-based measures of student performance. The difference is that this problem can be accounted for by the instrumental-variables procedures that are common in these studies. In the case of cost functions, instrumental variables that meet the above two tests can be identified. Moreover, policymakers are often interested in the performance index itself, which is not measured with error, instead of in the underlying student skills. Cost functions face no errors-in-variables problem for performance measures interpreted in this way.

Finally, cost function studies also face the possibility of omitted-variable bias if they do not control for efficiency. Because efficiency cannot be directly measured, no cost function study can definitively rule out this possibility. As discussed earlier, however, cost function studies have used a variety of different approaches to minimize this type of bias.

4.3.3. *Conclusion*

In short, it is not possible to estimate a production function at the school district level using spending as a measure of "inputs" without making the assumption that spending on every input is equally productive and that all input combinations are equally efficient. These are extreme, indeed, ridiculous assumptions, which the cost function approach does not have to make. Moreover, the production function approach magnifies the problem of accounting for efficiency because it automatically incorporates inefficiency into the definition of the key explanatory variable, namely spending per pupil. This creates a difficult errors-in-variables problem that has no obvious solution. To the best of our knowledge, the people who have used this approach have made no attempt to address this problem. In contrast, cost function studies do not employ an explanatory variable that reflects inefficiency by definition, and, as discussed earlier, they have used a range of methods to incorporate efficiency into the estimating equation.

5. Cost Function Estimates for Missouri

In the remainder of the article we illustrate how the validity and reliability of cost functions can be tested using cost function estimates for school districts in Missouri. The cost function estimates in this article are based on data from 2000 to 2005, which include three years prior to NCLB and three years after its passage. The implementation of NCLB during the middle of our time series poses a significant challenge to forecasting accuracy because pre-NCLB years will generally be used to fit the model and post-NCLB years will be used to test the forecasts. In this section we describe the data and measures, methodology, and cost function results.

5.1. *Data and Measures*

The cost function estimates provided in this article are based on a number of databases. Most of the data are produced by the Missouri Department of Elementary and Secondary Education (DESE). This section is organized by the type of variables used in the cost model, and summary statistics for key variables in 2005 are reported in Table 1 for most school districts in Missouri (sample size in 2005 was 516).[12]

5.1.1. *Per-pupil spending*

The dependent variable used in the cost function is per-pupil operating spending. To broadly reflect resources used in the production of education in Missouri school districts, the spending measure is based on "current operating cost" (COC) developed by DESE. COC includes total instructional and support spending minus total capital outlay and several revenue categories (food service sales, state food service aid, federal food service aid, and receipts from other districts). In addition, transportation spending was removed since it is affected by factors, such as sparsity of the population, weather conditions, and road conditions, which are not likely to affect instructional spending. Our measure of per pupil spending in the average district in the state was approximately $6,100 in 2005.[13]

---

[12]Data for approximately five school districts are not available. See Duncombe (2007) for a more in-depth discussion of the variables used in this cost model.

[13]Special education services in St. Louis County and Pemiscot County are provided by special school districts serving these counties. Total spending, counts for special education students, and counts of students receiving subsidized lunch in these two special school districts are assigned to the regular school districts in each county using the share of county enrollment in each regular school district. For example, if a regular school district had 10% of St. Louis County enrollment, then it would be assigned 10% of the spending, 10% of special education students, and 10% of the subsidized lunch students in the special district serving St. Louis County.

Table 1 Descriptive statistics for variables used in cost model, Missouri school districts (2005).

Variables	Average	Standard deviation	Minimum	Maximum
Per pupil spending	$6,112	$1,513	$3,907	$16,434
Student performance measure	25.6	7.2	4.8	53.5
Cost variables				
Teacher salaries	$27,460	$3,290	$21,201	$40,055
Student poverty (Percent subsidized lunch students)	46.1	16.0	4.7	95.1
Race-poverty interaction (Poverty variable multiplied by percent African American)	2.9	10.1	0.0	96.2
Percent special education students	16.7	4.0	3.4	43.4
Enrollment	1607.7	3568.4	49.8	38682.5
K12 districts (1 = yes; 0 = no)	0.86	0.34	0.00	1.00
Efficiency-related variables				
Fiscal capacity	$61,631	$41,074	$20,399	$410,166
Per pupil property values				
Per pupil income	$63,962	$35,112	$2,652	$394,463
State aid/income ratio	0.0594737	0.062326	0.00	1.144402
Other monitoring variables				
Percent of adults that are college educated (2000)	0.13	0.08	0.03	0.67
Percent of population 65 years or older (2000)	0.15	0.04	0.04	0.32
Percent of housing units that are owner occupied (2000)	0.77	0.08	0.42	0.95
Local tax share (median housing price/average property values)	1.23	0.49	0.25	2.91
Sample size		516		

Sources: Missouri Department of Elementary and Secondary Education; U.S. Census Bureau.

5.1.2. *Student performance measure*

The student performance measures used in the cost function are based on Missouri Assessment Program exams in math and communication arts administered by DESE. These are criterion-referenced exams in three grades for each subject area (Grades 4, 8, 10 for math, and Grades 3, 7, and 11 for communication arts). The information reported on these exams is the percent of students reaching certain thresholds in performance: (Step 1, progressing, near proficient, proficient, and advanced). The measure used in the cost model is the average of the share of students reaching proficiency for each exam. Although the majority of districts in Missouri serve the full range of grades, there are 73 districts serving kindergarten to eighth grades. We impute high school exam results for students attending K-8 districts.[14]

5.1.3. *Teacher salaries*

Costs of providing education services vary across districts, in part, because of differences in prices that districts have to pay for resources, such as teachers. Some districts may have to pay more than other districts to attract similar teachers, because of a higher cost of living, fewer amenities in the area, and more difficult working conditions. Because teachers are the principal resource used to produce education, we include a measure of teacher salaries in the cost model.[15] To ensure that the teacher salary measure is comparable across districts, we use data on individual teachers to develop a salary measure that controls for differences in average education and experience across districts.[16] We treat this salary variable as endogenous using private sector salaries and student enrollment in the labor market area as instruments.

5.1.4. *Student measures*

A key variable in a cost model is the number of students served by the district. Student counts are used both directly as a variable in the cost model and to transform other variables into per-pupil measures. The student count measure used in this article is an average of the enrollment estimates in September and January. We use the average of these two enrollment counts to provide a measure of average enrollment for the year. Average

---

[14]K8 students attending only one K12 district are assigned the high school proficiency rates for math and communication arts in this K12 district. In a few cases students in a K8 district attended two K12 districts for high school. To assign a high school performance measure to a K8 district, we constructed a weighted average of proficiency for high school math and communication arts exams, where the weight is based on relative enrollment. For example, assume students in the K8 district A attended K12 Districts B and C, where the enrollment in District B is 6,000, and enrollment in District C is 4,000. Then the high school performance assigned to District A is based on a weighted average of high school performance in Districts B and C, where the weights are 60% and 40%, respectively.

[15]Although other professional staff are key resources as well, variation in other professional salaries across districts are typically highly related to variation in teacher salaries (correlation over 0.75). We include only teacher salaries in the cost model.

[16]To control for variation in education and experience across districts, the natural logarithm of teacher salaries is regressed on the log of total experience, and an indicator variable for whether the teacher has a graduate degree. We use the regression to estimate average salaries for teachers in each district with the statewide average experience (between 0 and 5 years) and the statewide average percentage of teachers with a graduate degree.

enrollment provides a better estimate of the underlying enrollment of the district during the year and is less sensitive to unusual results associated with a single enrollment count. To account for the nonlinear relationship between enrollment and per-pupil spending we include enrollment and enrollment squared.[17]

One of the key factors affecting the cost of reaching performance targets is the number of students requiring additional assistance to be successful in school. Poverty has consistently been found to be negatively correlated with student performance (Ferguson and Ladd, 1996; Haveman and Wolfe, 1994). Poverty measures should accurately capture the percentage of a district's students living in low-income households. The most commonly used measure of poverty in education research is the share of students receiving free or reduced price lunch in a school, because this measure is produced annually.[18] To reduce the potential instability in this measure, especially in small districts, we use a two-year average of the subsidized lunch percentage.

The one change in specification for cost variables across the cost models we estimate (Models 1 and 2) is the inclusion of an interaction term between the share of subsidized lunch students and the share of African American students. To improve forecasting accuracy we tried several interactions of other variables with the subsidized lunch rate and as well as a quadratic specification.[19] The interaction with the share of African American students produced the most accurate forecasts of those we tried. This variable accounts for the possibility that the social disadvantages students bring to school are more severe among low-income African American students than among low-income White students.

---

[17]In other cost function estimates we have used a series of dummy variables to capture different enrollment size categories. Although this is a flexible way of measuring the relationship between spending and enrollment, the forecasting accuracy of models using these variables was slightly worse than using a quadratic relationship for enrollment. We also checked forecasting accuracy when a cubic term is included in the model and did not find it improved accuracy (and it was statistically insignificant).

[18]Another measure of child poverty is the child poverty rate produced by the Census Bureau every 10 years as part of the *Census of Population*. Although this measure is updated on a biennial basis, the updates are based on the decennial Census estimates, which implies that they may be quite inaccurate by the end of every decade. We found that the subsidized lunch rate in 2000 had a correlation of over 0.7 with the Census child poverty rate.

[19]We also tried interactions of the subsidized lunch rate with pupil density, enrollment, and percent college educated adults. Only the interaction with percentage African American and with pupil density were statistically significant. When a quadratic specification for subsidized lunch was tried, the coefficient on the squared term was not significant.

Students with special needs often require additional services and support, which can substantially increase school spending. Counts of special education students with individualized education programs are collected by DESE. To measure special education, we calculated total special education students as a share of enrollment. Another student characteristic that can affect the cost of bringing students up to a given performance level is a lack of English fluency, often called limited English proficiency (LEP). Unfortunately, the LEP data for Missouri do not appear to be accurate enough to use in this study.[20]

5.1.5. *Efficiency-related measures*

Costs are defined as the minimum spending of school resources required to provide students an opportunity to reach a given level of student performance. However, the dependent variable in the cost model is per-pupil spending. As discussed earlier, inefficiency in the cost function context can include both waste and a district's choice to focus on non-tested subject areas (e.g., art, music, or athletics). Although it is not possible to measure efficiency directly, it is possible to control for it indirectly, and thereby to minimize the possibility of omitted variable bias in the cost coefficients.

Our approach is to include in the cost function variables that have been linked to efficiency in previous research. The literature on managerial efficiency in public bureaucracies suggests three broad factors that might be related to productive inefficiency: fiscal capacity, competition, and other factors affecting voter involvement in monitoring government (Leibenstein, 1966; Niskanen, 1971; Wyckoff, 1990). Research on New York school districts indicates that taxpayers in districts with high fiscal capacity, as measured by property wealth, income, and state aid, may have less incentive to put pressure on district officials to be efficient, or may be more apt to spend money on non-tested subjects (Duncombe *et al.*, 1997; Duncombe

---

[20]Unlike subsidized lunch, there are no federal standards on how LEP students are measured, and typically no auditing process to assure that the data are accurate. In Missouri, student language data are collected in the Limited English Proficient Student Census (or English Language Learners Census) in October of each year. To evaluate the accuracy of the LEP data collected by Missouri, we compared this data to an alternative measure available in the *2000 Census of Population* — the percentage of students, who live in a household where English is not spoken well at home. The LEP measure supplied by school districts in Missouri is not highly correlated ($r = 0.30$) with the Census measure, suggesting that there are inconsistencies in how districts are classifying and reporting LEP students.

and Yinger, 2000). Property values are measured by assessed value for real property (residential, agricultural, and commercial and industrial) and personal property. The measure of income used in the analysis is adjusted gross income, which is provided by the Missouri Department of Revenue to DESE based on information from Missouri income tax returns.[21] We use a measure of state aid per pupil supporting basic operations divided by per-pupil income.[22] Previous studies have also found that voter's incentive and capacity to monitor operations in school districts and their demand for a broad set of school performance measures may differ depending on the education level of residents, the share of senior citizens in the population, the share of owner occupied housing, and the share of school taxes paid by the typical voter (local tax share). Per-pupil property values are published by DESE, and the other variables are from the *2000 Census of Population*.

5.2. *Cost Function Estimates*

We estimate a constant-elasticity cost model using log linear 2SLS regression to account for the potential endogeneity of student performance and teacher salaries. To select instruments we use the average of exogenous variables related to student performance (percentage of Hispanic and percentage of African American students) and salaries (private sector salaries and enrollment size) in other districts in the same labor market area. The strength of instruments is tested using a weak instrument test based on partial F-statistics (Bound *et al.*, 1995). A threshold of 10 is often recommended for acceptable instruments, although lower thresholds are acceptable in some cases (Stock and Yogo, 2005). For the models presented in Table 2, all of the partial F-statistics are above 10. For the models in Table 3, the partial F-statistics on teacher salaries are between 6 and 9.[23] To check for the possible effect of weak instruments on the accuracy of 2SLS

---

[21] The income data lags several years, so that the income data from the 2002 calendar year are used for the 2004–2005 school year.

[22] The state aid measure includes minimum guarantee aid (basic formula) and aid for free and reduced price lunch students.

[23] The model was estimated with xtivreg2 in STATA (Schaffer, 2005). Another weak instrument test involves comparing Kleibergen-Paap rk statistic to critical values established by Stock and Yogo (2005). Although this comparison is not technically correct given non-i.i.d errors, Baum *et al.* (2007) argued that this is a reasonable approximation. The Kleibergen-Paap rk statistic is generally below the critical values established by Stock and Yogo (2005) for 10% relative bias. In other words, this test would suggest the potential for weak instruments in both Models 1 and 2.

estimates, we reran the cost function models using two of Fuller's k-class estimators ($a = 1$, $a = 4$), which are considered to be better estimators when instruments are weak (Murray, 2006). Because the results using the Fuller estimators are very similar to those with 2SLS, we report the 2SLS results. Second, we tested for overidentifying restrictions using a Hansen J-test (Baum *et al.* 2007), and found that we could not reject the null

Table 2 Cost function estimates for different years for Missouri school districts (model 1).

Variables	2000–2005	2000–2002	2001–2003	2002–2004
Intercept	−6.07793	−5.51048	−4.70453	−6.57974*
Student performance measure[a]	0.30329*	0.28074*	0.24449*	0.30029*
Cost variables				
Teacher salaries[a]	1.41207**	1.27558**	1.19364**	1.41729**
Student poverty (percent subsidized lunch students)	0.00519**	0.00453**	0.00464**	0.00525**
Percent special education students	0.00188	0.00215	0.00202	0.00129
Enrollment[a]	−0.69238**	−0.60763**	−0.61445**	−0.68291**
Enrollment squared[a]	0.03830**	0.03331**	0.03380**	0.03782**
K12 districts (1 = yes; 0 = no)	0.12652**	0.11427**	0.12468**	0.13081**
Efficiency-related variables				
Fiscal capacity				
Per pupil property values[a]	0.00203	0.01290	0.02656	0.00992
Per pupil income[a]	0.18073**	0.21961**	0.21876**	0.20799**
State aid/income ratio	1.27080**	1.94095**	1.88658**	1.57542**
Other monitoring variables				
Percent of adults that are college educated (2000)	0.26049	0.20842	0.26867	0.19820
Percent of population 65 years or older (2000)	−0.27082	−0.26372	−0.32357	−0.29627
Percent of housing units that are owner occupied (2000)	−0.19776**	−0.18511*	−0.17242*	−0.17325*
Local tax share (median housing price/average property values)[a]	−0.07631**	−0.07936**	−0.07424**	−0.07969**
2001	−0.00156	−0.00141		
2002	−0.01508	−0.01403	−0.01129	
2003	−0.03204		−0.02738*	−0.01824**
2004	−0.05741**			−0.04437**
2005	−0.03711			

(*Continued*)

Table 2   (*Continued*)

Variables	2000–2005	2000–2002	2001–2003	2002–2004
Instrument tests:				
Partial *F*-statistics:				
Student Performance measure	25.93	26.04	24.28	21.90
Teacher salaries	15.53	16.74	13.23	12.13
Overidentification test (*p*-value)	0.09	0.07	0.03	0.11
Sample size	3068	1520	1538	1546

Notes: Estimated with linear 2SLS regression with the log of per pupil current operating cost (minus transportation spending) as the dependent variable. The performance measure and teacher salaries are treated as endogenous variables with instruments based on exogenous variables for other districts in the same labor market area and census district type (see text). Robust standard errors are used for hypothesis testing (controlling for clustering at the district level).
*indicates a coefficient significantly different from zero at the 5% level.
**indicates a coefficient significantly different from zero at the 10% level.
[a]Expressed as a natural logarithm.

hypothesis that the instruments are uncorrelated with the error term at the 5% level.

Table 2 presents results of the basic cost function (Model 1) estimated for four periods — the full sample (2000–05) and several 3-year periods used to check forecasting accuracy (2000–02, 2001–03, 2002–2004). Table 3 presents the results for an alternative model (Model 2), which was specified based on analysis of forecasting errors associated with the basic model.

In general, per-pupil spending has the expected relationship with the independent variables in the cost function (Table 2) and the estimated coefficients are statistically significant from zero. The coefficient on the student performance measure ranges from 0.24 to 0.30 and indicates that a 1% increase in performance (as measured by a composite of proficiency rates for communication arts and math tests) is associated with a 0.24% to 0.3% increase in per pupil spending, controlling for the other variables in the cost function. Teachers' salaries are positively related to per-pupil spending; a 1% increase in teachers' salaries is associated with a 1.19% to 1.41% increase in per pupil expenditures holding other factors constant. The share of students in poverty and in special education is positively related to spending, and the poverty measure is significantly different from zero at the 5% level. The coefficients on the enrollment measures suggest significant

Table 3 Cost function estimates for different years for Missouri school districts (Model 2).

Variables	2000–2005	2000–2002	2001–2003	2002–2004
Intercept	−4.14437	−3.53610	−2.00864	−5.06573
Student performance measure[a]	0.37845**	0.41108**	0.29732**	0.34819**
Cost variables				
Teacher salaries[a]	1.28134**	1.19568**	1.06783**	1.38386**
Student poverty (percent subsidized lunch students)	0.00407**	0.00389**	0.00345**	0.00424**
Poverty variable multiplied by percent African American	0.00004**	0.00006**	0.00005**	0.00004**
Percent special education students	0.00199*	0.00255*	0.00249**	0.00152
Enrollment[a]	−0.67788**	−0.64316**	−0.62510**	−0.68362**
Enrollment squared[a]	0.03743**	0.03540**	0.03458**	0.03768**
K12 districts (1 = yes; 0 = no)	0.13825**	0.12209**	0.13833**	0.14873**
Efficiency-related variables				
Fiscal capacity				
Per pupil property values[a]	−0.00575	−0.02046	0.00327	−0.00880
Per pupil income[a]	0.12808**	0.14464**	0.12579**	0.13064**
State aid/income ratio — low[b]	−0.06880**	−0.06517**	−0.07083**	−0.06756**
State aid/income ratio — high[b]	0.19155**	0.20328**	0.16506**	0.19913**
Other monitoring variables				
Percent of adults that are college educated (2000)	−0.12248	−0.37317	−0.15399	−0.00828
Percent of adults college educated squared	0.61936	0.96208**	0.88190**	0.42890
Percent of population 65 years or older (2000)	−1.57258*	−1.36373	−1.66517*	−1.89970**
Percent of population 65 years or older squared	4.33299*	3.58088	4.51787*	5.28648**
Percent of housing units that are owner occupied (2000)	−0.20794*	−0.18841	−0.19921*	−0.18570
Local tax share (median housing price/average property values)[a]	−0.09174**	−0.10032**	−0.09421**	−0.09629**
Local tax share squared[a]	0.03805	0.04170	0.05111**	0.03997
2001	−0.00196	0.00194		
2002	−0.00249	−0.00054	0.00100	
2003	−0.01484		−0.00906	−0.01323*

(*Continued*)

Table 3 (*Continued*)

Variables	2000–2005	2000–2002	2001–2003	2002–2004
2004	−0.04103			−0.03731**
2005	−0.02453			
Instrument tests:				
Partial *F*-statistics:				
Student Performance measure	19.35	20.08	17.33	14.97
Teacher salaries	8.01	7.99	6.95	6.57
Overidentification test (*p*-value)	0.09	0.07	0.03	0.11
Sample size	3068	1520	1538	1546

Notes: Estimated with linear 2SLS regression with the log of per pupil current operating cost (minus transportation spending) as the dependent variable. The performance measure and teacher salaries are treated as endogenous variables with instruments based on exogenous variables for other districts in the same labor market area and census district type (see text). Robust standard errors are used for hypothesis testing (controlling for clustering at the district level).
*indicates a coefficient significantly different from zero at the 5% level.
**indicates a coefficient significantly different from zero at the 10% level.
[a]Expressed as a natural logarithm.
[b]Low ratio is a ratio below 0.05 and high ratio is above 0.2.

economies of size with the cost minimizing enrollment level between 8,000 and 9,000 students.

Turning to the efficiency-related variables, the fiscal capacity measures have the expected positive relationship with per-pupil spending, which may indicate greater inefficiency or more demand for a broader array of educational services. The coefficients for state aid and per-pupil income are statistically significant from zero at conventional levels. A higher share of senior citizens in the population, a higher share of owner-occupied housing in the district, and a higher local tax share are associated with lower spending, with the latter two variables statistically significant. The share of college-educated adults is associated with higher spending but is not statistically significant.

6. Evaluating Reliability and Predictive Validity of Cost Functions Estimates

Cost functions, like production functions, are a general tool, which can be used for several types of empirical analyses. For example, cost functions have been used for program evaluation (Duncombe and Yinger, 2007a); policy analysis (Eom *et al.*, 2014; Wang *et al.*, 2011); and to forecast spending required to meet performance targets, such as those associated with NCLB (Duncombe *et al.*, 2008; Imazeki and Reschovsky, 2004b, 2006). It is in this later role, as a tool for forecasting the costs of reaching adequate student performance, or so-called cost of adequacy, that cost functions have been recently criticized (Costrell *et al.*, 2008; Hanushek, 2005). In this section, we describe the criteria and measures for evaluating the reliability and predictive validity of cost functions and illustrate their application using our cost function estimates for Missouri school districts (Duncombe, 2006).

6.1. *Reliability*

An important criteria for evaluating any measure is reliability, which can be defined as the "consistency and repeatability" of a measure (Trochim, 2001, p. 88). Reliability is typically estimated by comparing consistency of measures of the same phenomenon at different times (test–retest reliability), by different raters (inter-rater reliability), or using different items measuring the same phenomenon (internal consistency). Of the three types of reliability, test–retest reliability seems the most appropriate for forecasting. Test–retest reliability could be evaluated by comparing forecasts derived from cost functions estimated from different periods. Barring some major change in the education system (e.g., NCLB), we should expect that the regression coefficients on the key cost variables and the composite cost indices that were derived from these variables, should be highly related.

To examine test–retest reliability we estimate cost indices from the last three regression models presented in Tables 2 and 3. A cost index indicates how much more or less a particular district needs to spend compared to a district with average characteristics to provide its students an opportunity to reach the same performance level.[24] For example, a cost index of 120 indicates that a district will require 20% more spending than the average district to reach any student outcome level. The correlations between cost

---

[24] For each variable a district can influence (outcome measure and efficiency-related variables), the estimated coefficient of the cost model is multiplied by some constant, typically the state average for that variable. For each cost factor outside of district control, the estimated coefficient from the cost model is multiplied by the actual values for the district. The sum of the products for factors outside and within district control is used to predict costs in a district with average outcomes and efficiency. Predicted costs are also calculated for a hypothetical district, which has average values for all variables in the cost model. Predicted spending in each district is divided by spending in this average district (and multiplied by 100) to get the overall cost index.

Table 4 Comparison between cost indices for different years for
Missouri school districts (Model 1) averages by census region.

	2000–2002	2001–2003	2002–2004
Model 1:			
Large central cities	112.3	110.0	114.0
Medium cities	92.0	90.6	91.9
Urban fringe of large cities	96.6	95.3	96.3
Urban fringe of medium cities	84.2	84.3	83.7
Large town	86.9	86.6	86.8
Small town	91.5	91.5	91.0
Rural metro	94.3	93.9	93.7
Rural non-metro	106.1	106.6	106.6
Model 2:			
Large central cities	150.2	138.0	140.6
Medium cities	88.0	88.1	89.0
Urban fringe of large cities	103.9	101.2	102.1
Urban fringe of medium cities	82.1	83.2	82.3
Large town	88.0	88.2	87.3
Small town	92.2	92.0	91.5
Rural metro	93.0	93.6	93.5
Rural non-metro	105.4	105.5	105.6

indices from the different cost models are very high (more than 0.99)
suggesting high consistency in cost function estimates across different years.
When average cost indices are compared across Census district type there
is also a high degree of consistency (Table 4). As expected large central
cities have the highest costs as well as sparsely populated rural districts
(rural non-metro). The largest difference across Models 1 and 2 are for large
central cities and districts on the urban fringe of large cities. Several districts
in these categories have very high concentrations of low-income and African
American students.

6.2. *Predictive Validity*

The appropriate validity criteria to evaluate cost functions depend on the
purpose for which they are used. If cost functions are used in program
or policy evaluation, then the appropriate criterion is internal validity,
which involves ruling out alternative explanations for the causal connection
between the program and outcome (Barrow and Rouse, 2005). If cost
functions are used for prediction purposes, then they should be evaluated on
predictive validity. Predictive validity measures how well a measure predicts
"something it should theoretically be able to predict" (Trochim, 2001, p. 68).

Predictive validity is closely related to the concept of forecasting accuracy, which measures how well a forecast of a phenomenon fits the actual values. The predictive validity criteria focuses on the accuracy of the bottom-line spending estimate associated with a particular level of student performance, not on identifying "successful" education strategies.

In selecting a forecasting method, it is important to consider the time-frame and objectives of the forecast (Armstrong, 2001, 2005; Bretschneider, 1985). Forecasting the spending associated with a particular performance level are typically made for the medium term (2–5 years), and the estimates need to be able to adjust to relatively large changes in key factors affecting student performance and the education environment (e.g., poverty, enroll-ment size, etc.). In addition, most of the variation used to estimate the cost function forecasting model is cross-sectional because long time-series are not generally available. Bretschneider labeled these types of forecasts as "predic-tion" forecasts (p. 6), because "they focus on specific policy issues, tend to be one-shot in nature, or . . . re-occur irregularly, and have a variable or arbitrary lead time" (p. 6). For prediction-type forecasts where the underlying theoretical model is known and data are cross-sectional, econometric models are typically recommended (Armstrong, 2005, 2006; Bretschneider, 1985).

Forecasts are principally evaluated on forecasting accuracy and bias (Armstrong, 1985, 2001; Makridakis *et al.*, 1983). "The real test of a forecasting model is its out-of-sample forecasting ability" (Chatfield, 1996, p. 506). Out-of-sample tests of forecasting accuracy generally involve dividing the sample into two (Tashman, 2000). The first period (fit period) is used to estimate the forecasting model and the second period (test period) is used to test the accuracy of the model (Tashman, 2000, p. 438). Multiple tests of forecasting accuracy can be done depending on the timeframe of the forecast (how many years in the future) and the length of the time series. For example, if six years of data are available and three years of data are needed to estimate the forecasting model, then it is possible to estimate three one-year-out forecasts, two two-year-out forecasts, and one three-year-out forecast.[25] The accuracy measures from similar forecasts can be averaged and compared across forecasts of different time horizons.

---

[25] Another decision is whether to keep the 1st year of the model fit period fixed (rolling origin evaluations) or to keep the period used to estimate the forecasting model fixed (rolling window evaluations). Rolling origin evaluations use the maximum data available to fit the model, whereas rolling window evaluations create a more equal comparison across different forecasts (Tashman, 2000). We use a rolling window forecast based on 3 years of data for this article.

Normally, we would expect that the longer the time horizon, the less accurate the forecast.

To evaluate forecasting accuracy (and bias) the actual value for a test period is subtracted from the forecasted value and divided by the actual value to produce an estimate of the percent error (PE) of the forecast. Forecasting bias can be measured by taking the mean or median PE. If the average PE is primarily positive (negative), then the forecast is overestimating (underestimating) actual values. Forecasting accuracy can be assessed by taking the absolute value of the percent error for each observation and calculating the mean or median absolute PE.[26]

The accuracy of a forecasting model is commonly compared to a simple alternative model, usually called a naïve forecast. The most common version of a naïve forecast is to assume that the forecast this period is equal to the actual value for the previous period (no change). Thiel's U-statistic compares a forecast to this simple naïve forecast (Armstrong, 1985).[27] Since cost of adequacy forecasts have to be able to adjust with changes in student performance standards and key cost variables, a more appropriate naïve forecast would be based on a simple model of spending regressed on the student performance index, teacher salaries, and a student poverty measure.

Tables 5 and 6 report estimates of forecasting bias and accuracy for several different forecasts for Model 1 (second panel). For 1-year-out forecasts we averaged three different forecasts, and for 2-year-out forecasts we averaged two forecasts. These forecasts were compared to those from a naïve model where per-pupil spending was regressed on student performance, teacher salaries, and the subsidized lunch rate (first panel).[28] The forecasts from Model 1 reported in Table 5 overestimated spending on average by 5%

---

[26]The average absolute PE has been criticized as having a bias favoring underestimates compared to overestimates (Armstrong, 1985). An alternative is to divide the error by the average of the forecast and actual values rather that the actual values. Armstrong (1985) called this the adjusted mean absolute PE.

[27]The Theil U-statistic is commonly measured as the square root of the ratio of the square of the PE divided by the square of the PE for the naïve forecast. The PE of the naïve forecast is actual value in this period minus the actual value for the last period divided by the actual value for this period. If the Theil U-statistic is below 1, then the forecast does better than the naïve forecast. See Collopy and Armstrong (2000) for a discussion of alternative versions of the Theil U-statistic.

[28]Per-pupil spending, student performance and teacher salaries are logged. The fit of the model was weak (adjusted $R^2 = 0.064$).

Table 5 Estimates of forecasting bias and accuracy (Difference between predicted and actual as a percentage of actual) Missouri school districts.

Distribution	Bias (percent error)			Accuracy (absolute percent error)		
	1-year	2-year	3-year	1-year	2-year	3-year
Naïve Forecast:						
Mean	−2.5	0.0	−1.9	13.7	14.6	15.1
Median	−1.5	1.7	−0.2	11.2	12.4	12.4
Model 1:						
Mean	5.7	5.5	4.8	11.2	10.9	11.3
Median	5.3	5.3	4.2	9.0	8.8	9.4
1st percentile	−24.9	−22.5	−30.0	1.0	0.1	0.1
10th percentile	−9.6	−9.3	−11.9	2.7	1.8	1.8
25th percentile	−3.5	−3.3	−4.5	4.7	4.3	4.4
75th percentile	13.3	12.9	12.6	14.4	14.8	14.8
90th percentile	20.0	19.7	19.4	20.7	20.3	20.3
99th percentile	32.6	31.8	32.4	32.6	33.6	33.6
Model 2:						
Mean	0.6	0.7	−0.5	9.0	8.9	9.0
Median	0.2	0.7	−0.9	7.5	7.3	7.5
1st percentile	−25.8	−25.0	−28.9	0.9	0.7	0.2
10th percentile	−12.8	−13.1	−14.9	2.4	2.4	1.4
25th percentile	−6.3	−6.4	−8.0	4.1	4.2	3.5
75th percentile	8.0	7.8	7.3	12.4	12.2	12.8
90th percentile	14.5	14.0	14.4	17.8	17.5	18.7
99th percentile	26.4	25.8	25.4	28.7	28.1	30.8

Note: Average of forecasts by time horizon. For 1-year horizon, this is an average of 3 forecasts, for 2-year horizon an average of 2 forecasts, and for 3-year horizon this is just one forecast.

(first two lines of panel 2), which compares to a much lower level of bias using the naïve forecasts (panel 1). The forecasts from Model 1 are more accurate than the naïve forecasts with average error of 11 percent compared to 14 percent to 15 percent for the naïve forecasts. Approximately 90 percent of districts have errors of 20 percent or less using Model 1, which compares to errors of 30 percent using the naïve forecast (not reported).

Table 6 indicates that forecasts from Model 1 are particularly inaccurate and biased for two types of districts — large towns and medium cities. These districts tend to have low poverty rates and costs as indicated by cost indices well below 100 (Table 4). They also have high income and property wealth and low levels of state aid. It is not surprising that these districts have student performance levels well above average. Using PE as the

Table 6 Estimates of forecasting bias and accuracy (Difference between predicted and actual as a percentage of actual) Missouri school districts, by type of district.

Distribution	Bias (percent error)			Accuracy (absolute percent error)		
	1-year	2-year	3-year	1-year	2-year	3-year
Model 1:						
Large central cities	−5.8	−5.9	−7.5	5.8	5.9	7.5
Medium cities	19.3	19.0	18.2	19.3	19.0	18.2
Urban fringe of large cities	2.3	2.0	1.0	11.2	11.2	11.4
Urban fringe of medium cities	7.4	7.4	6.5	10.2	10.3	9.7
Large town	31.2	30.5	30.7	31.2	30.5	30.7
Small town	6.0	5.7	5.0	10.1	9.9	9.8
Rural metro	6.6	6.3	5.8	10.6	10.3	10.5
Rural non-metro	5.6	5.4	4.8	11.3	11.0	11.6
Model 2:						
Large central cities	0.1	0.4	−1.4	2.6	2.9	2.2
Medium cities	11.0	11.3	10.2	11.7	12.2	11.1
Urban fringe of large cities	−2.7	−2.9	−3.8	10.0	9.9	9.9
Urban fringe of medium cities	0.0	0.5	−1.2	7.2	7.3	6.6
Large town	20.8	20.7	21.5	20.8	20.7	21.5
Small town	0.1	0.2	−0.6	7.5	7.5	7.5
Rural metro	1.2	1.1	0.1	8.6	8.2	8.8
Rural non-metro	0.8	0.9	−0.4	9.2	9.1	9.3

Note: Average of forecasts by time horizon. For 1-year horizon, this is an average of 3 forecasts, for 2-year horizon an average of 2 forecasts, and for 3-year horizon this is just one forecast.

dependent variable it is possible to assess whether there are factors that are systematically associated with forecasting error. Table 7 presents the results when PE is regressed on the variables in the cost model. PE is positively (and significantly) associated with enrollment (over most enrollment ranges) and the fiscal capacity measures — per-pupil income, property wealth, and the state aid-income ratio. These results suggest that the cost function may be overestimating the efficiency effects from higher fiscal capacity and the higher costs associated with diseconomies of scale. PE is negatively related to the performance index, teacher salaries, subsidized lunch, and share of adults with a college education. Because several cost function variables are systematically related to forecasting error, modifications to the cost function could potentially reduce error. We tried several nonlinear specifications for the variables previously identified and interaction terms particularly between the cost variables. Although most of these changes to the model were not statistically significant, we have included in Model 2 (Table 3) changes

Table 7 Factors associated with forecasting bias for Missouri school districts by type of district.

Variables	Model 1	Model 2
Intercept	4.366**	4.979**
Student performance measure[a]	−0.029**	−0.026**
Cost variables		
Teacher salaries[a]	−0.775**	−0.539**
Student poverty (percent subsidized lunch students)	−0.002**	−0.001**
Poverty variable multiplied by percent African American		0.000**
Percent special education students	−0.001	0.001
Enrollment[a]	0.213**	0.079**
Enrollment squared[a]	−0.011**	−0.003**
K12 districts (1 = yes; 0 = no)	−0.013	−0.015
Efficiency–related variables		
Fiscal capacity		
Per pupil property values[a]	0.144**	0.003
Per pupil income[a]	0.104**	0.022
State aid/income ratio	2.733**	
State aid/income ratio–low[b]		−0.008
State aid/income ratio–high[b]		−0.042
Other monitoring variables		
Percent of adults that are college educated (2000)	−0.208**	−0.286**
Percent of adults college educated squared		0.653**
Percent of population 65 years or older (2000)	0.024	0.401
Percent of population 65 years or older squared		−0.982
Percent of housing units that are owner occupied (2000)	−0.043	−0.071
Local tax share (median housing price/average property values)[a]	0.016	−0.001
Local tax share squared[a]		0.018*
Adjusted R^2	0.372	0.096
Sample size	1548	1548

Notes: Estimated with OLS. Bias is calculated using cost model for 2000–2002. The bias is calculated for 2003–2005.
*Indicates a coefficient significantly different from zero at the 5 percent level.
**Indicates a coefficient significantly different from zero at the 10 percent level.
[a]Expressed as a natural logarithm.
[b]Low ratio is a ratio below 0.05 and high ratio is above 0.2.

that were statistically significant in some of the models and helped improve forecasting accuracy.

As indicated in Tables 5 and 6, Model 2 significantly improves prediction validity over Model 1 (and the naïve forecasts). For the typical district these forecasts have less than 1 percent bias and the accuracy of the forecasts have improved approximately 20 percent compared to Model 1 and 40 percent compared to the naïve forecast. Model 2 improves forecasting accuracy particularly for medium cities (40 percent improvement) and large towns (30 percent). When we regress PEs from Model 2 on variables in the cost model, the model fit (adjusted R^2) drops from 37 percent for Model 1 to 10 percent (Table 7). Although there is still much room for improvement in forecasting accuracy, we have illustrated how systematic analysis of forecasting errors can be used to improve forecasting accuracy and reduce bias.

So far we have focused on expenditure forecasts. We now turn to an investigation of the cost component of these forecasts. As discussed earlier, efficiency cannot be measured directly, but we can use conceptual arguments to separate cost and efficiency variables. Scholars largely agree, for example, that labor market conditions, enrollment, and concentrated poverty, all of which are beyond the control of school officials, should be treated as cost variables. Based on this separation, we can then use our model to make forecasts of the impact of changes in a district's cost environment on its spending, accounting for change in student performance. If this cost portion of our model is working well, the forecasts for districts with large changes in cost factors should be as accurate as the forecasts for districts with small changes in cost factors.

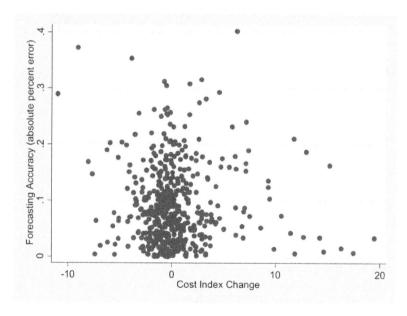

Figure 1   Comparison of changes in the cost index for a district with forecasting accuracy: 3-year-out forecast for Missouri school districts (2005).

To implement this "reasonableness" test, we estimated our cost model for 2000–02, calculated cost-index changes from 2002 to each of the following three years, and estimated forecasting accuracy for 2003 (1-year-out forecast), 2004 (2-year-out forecast), and 2005 (3-year-out forecast) for each district. If the regression is accurately capturing the role of costs, we would expect to see no systematic relationship between change in the cost index and forecasting accuracy. In other words, we would not expect districts with large changes in education costs to have lower forecasting accuracy than districts with small changes in costs. Figure 1, which presents a scatter plot of our results for the 3-year-out forecasts, shows that forecasting error does not depend on the magnitude of the cost change ($r = -0.07$). Comparable figures for the 1-year-out and 2-year-out forecasts are similar. These results suggest that our estimated cost model provides not only fairly accurate forecasts of spending but also fairly accurate estimates of the cost component of spending, regardless of the magnitude of the change in costs.

7. Conclusions

School finance systems designed to support state accountability programs should, to be effective and fair, account for differences across school districts in the underlying cost of reaching performance standards. Cost functions are one of several ways that have been developed to estimate these cost differentials. By utilizing historical data and strong statistical methods, cost functions are a particularly flexible and low-cost way to forecast required spending associated with a state's accountability system. However, the application of cost functions to education must confront several challenges in both data collection and estimation methodology. We describe approaches for addressing these challenges and highlight their strengths and weaknesses.

Recently cost functions have been criticized as a tool for estimating required spending associated with performance standards on several grounds (Costrell *et al.*, 2008; Hanushek, 2005; Loeb, 2007). Critics argue that cost functions do not adequately control for efficiency differences across districts, so that their estimates cannot be given a cost interpretation. CHL point to the large differences in results between cost functions and production functions using spending to measure inputs as evidence of the inadequacy of cost functions. We argue that this criticism misses the mark in several ways. First, the cost variables in a cost function can be given a cost interpretation because the cost function controls for student performance and the omitted variable problem associated with inefficiency. Although much work remains to be done to improve efficiency controls in cost functions, it is inaccurate to suggest that no effort to account for efficiency has been made. The fact that production functions produce different estimates is also not an indicator of the weakness of cost functions but instead indicates the serious measurement problems that arise when spending is used as a composite measure of inputs in a production function. We demonstrate that to use spending in this way requires extreme, indeed, ridiculous assumptions about production technology.

Another fundamental problem with the criticisms of CHL is that they do not propose an alternative approach to forecasting the best-practice spending required to support student performance standards. Although we do not claim that the cost function approach provides perfectly accurately forecasts of required spending, we do not know of any other method that is as comprehensive and allows for low-cost testing of forecasting accuracy.

In the second half of the article we illustrate how the reliability and forecasting accuracy of cost functions can be tested using data for Missouri school districts. We show how these forecasts can be improved by examining the determinants of forecasting error and using this analysis to modify the cost model. We also provide some evidence to suggest that these forecasts accurately capture the cost component of spending.

The development of cost functions to support state school finance systems is analogous to the development of econometric models to forecast macroeconomic variables to support state revenue forecasts and budget development. States have taken steps over the years to improve these forecasts by combining forecasts of different types and developing institutional capacity within the state government to develop and evaluate forecasts. Although state and local governments have been much slower in developing forecasting models for key expenditure areas, the growing cost burdens associated with major federal programs, such as Medicaid and NCLB, suggest the expenditure forecasting may become more common. The question is not whether these types of forecasts should be done but how best to establish institutions to support the development and continued improvement of expenditure forecasts. Deschamps (2004) described the use of an independent forecasting agency and technical workgroups in the state of Washington to support the development of entitlement forecasts. We think similar steps should be taken by states to support the development and refinement of spending forecasts to support the state education accountability system.

References

Alexander, C. D., Gronberg, T. J., Jansen, D. W., Keller, H., Taylor, L. L., and Treisman, P. U. 2000. *A Study of Uncontrollable Variations in the Costs of Texas Public Education* (Summary Report Prepared for the 77th Texas Legislature). Austin: Charles A. Dana Center, The University of Texas at Austin.

Armstrong, J. S. 1985. *Long-Range Forecasting: From Crystal Ball to Computer.* New York, NY: Wiley & Sons.

Armstrong, J. S. 2001. Standards and practices for forecasting. In J. Armstrong (ed.), *Principles of Forecasting: Handbook for Researchers and Practitioners*, pp. 679–732. Norwell, MA: Kluwer Academic.

Armstrong, J. S. 2005. Forecasting principles and methods. *Foresight* **1**: 29–35.

Armstrong, J. S. 2006. *Findings from Evidence-Based Forecasting: Methods for Reducing Forecast Error.* Unpublished Paper, Wharton School, University of Pennsylvania, Philadelphia.

Barrow, L. and Rouse, C. 2005. *Causality, Causality, Causality: The View of Education Inputs and Outputs from Economics* (Federal Reserve Bank of Chicago Working Paper, WP 2005–15). Chicago, IL: Federal Reserve Bank of Chicago.

Baum, C., Schaffer, M., and Stillman, S. 2007. Enhanced routines for instrumental variables/GMM estimation and testing. *Stata Journal* **7**: 465–506.

Bound, J., Jaeger, D. A., and Baker, R. 1995. Problems with instrumental variables estimation when the correlation between the instruments and the endogenous explanatory variable is weak. *Journal of the American Statistical Association* **90**: 443–450.

Bretschneider, S. 1985. *Forecasting: Some New Realities* (Occasional Paper No. 99). Syracuse, NY: Syracuse University, Metropolitan Studies Program.

Bretschneider, S., Gorr, W., Grizzle, G., and Klay, E. 1989. Political and organizational influences on the accuracy of forecasting state government revenue. *International Journal of Forecasting* **5**: 307–319.

Chatfield, C. 1996. Model uncertainty and forecast accuracy. *Journal of Forecasting* **15**: 495–508.

Collopy, F. and Armstrong, J. S. 2000. *Another Error Measure for Selection of the Best Forecasting Method: The Unbiased Absolute Percentage Error.* Unpublished Paper. Available from http://www.forecastingprinciples.com/paperpdf/armstrong-unbiasedAPE.pdf.

Costrell, R., Hanushek, E., and Loeb, S. 2008. What do cost functions tell us about the cost of an adequate education? *Peabody Journal of Education* **83**: 198–223.

Deschamps, E. 2004. The impact of institutional change on forecast accuracy: A case study of budget forecasting in Washington State. *International Journal of Forecasting* **20**: 647–657.

Downes, T. and Pogue, T. 1994. Adjusting school aid formulas for the higher cost of educating disadvantaged students. *National Tax Journal* **67**: 89–110.

Duncombe, W. 2006. Responding to the charge of alchemy: Strategies for evaluating the reliability and validity of costing-out research. *Journal of Education Finance* **32**: 137–169.

Duncombe, W. 2007. *Estimating the Cost of Meeting Student Performance Standards in the St. Louis Public Schools.* Report prepared for the Board of Education for the City of St. Louis. Available from http://cpr.maxwell.syr.edu/efap/Costing_Out/Duncombe_technical%20report4.pdf.

Duncombe, W. and Yinger, J. 1993. An analysis of returns to scale in public production, with an application to fire protection. *Journal of Public Economics* **52**: 49–72.

Duncombe, W. and Yinger, J. 2000. Financing higher student performance standards: The case of New York State. *Economics of Education Review*, **19**: 363–386.

Duncombe, W. and Yinger, J. 2005a. *Estimating the Costs of meeting student performance outcomes adopted by the Kansas State Board of Education* (Report prepared for The Kansas Legislative Division of Post Audit). Syracuse, NY: Syracuse University.

Duncombe, W. and Yinger, J. 2005b. How much does a disadvantaged student cost? *Economics of Education Review* **24**: 513–532. [Chapter 8]

Duncombe, W. and Yinger, J. 2007a. Does school district consolidation cut costs? *Education Finance and Policy* **2**: 341–375. [Chapter 22]

Duncombe, W. and Yinger, J. 2007b. Measurement of cost differentials. In E. Fiske & H. F. Ladd (eds.), *Handbook of Education Finance and Policy*, pp. 238–256. Mahwah, NJ: Erlbaum.

Duncombe, W., Lukemeyer, A., and Yinger, J. 2008. Dollars without sense: The mismatch between the No Child Left Behind Act accountability system and Title I funding. In R. D. Kahlenberg (ed.), *Improving on No Child Left Behind: Getting Education Reform Back on Track*, pp. 19–102. New York, NY: The Century Foundation.

Duncombe, W., Miner, J., and Ruggiero, J. 1997. Empirical evaluation of bureaucratic models of inefficiency. *Public Choice* **93**: 1–18.

Duncombe, W., Ruggiero, J., and Yinger, J. 1996. Alternative approaches to measuring the cost of education. In H. F. Ladd (ed.), *Holding Schools Accountable: Performance-Based Reform in Education*, pp. 327–356. Washington, DC: The Brookings Institution.

Eom, T. H., Duncombe, W., Nguyen–Hoang, P. and Yinger, J. 2014. The Unintended Consequences of Property Tax Relief: New York's STAR Program, *Education Finance and Policy* **9**(4) (Fall): 446–480. [Chapter 4].

Ferguson, R. F. and Ladd, H. F. 1996. How and why money matters: An analysis of Alabama Schools. In H. F. Ladd (ed.), *Holding Schools Accountable: Performance-Based Reform in Education*, pp. 265–298. Washington, DC: The Brookings Institution.

Gronberg, T., Jansen, W., Taylor, L. L., and Booker, K. 2004. *School Outcomes and School Costs: The Cost Function Approach*. College Station, TX: Texas A&M University. Available from http://www.schoolfunding.info/states/tx/march4%20cost%20study.pdf.

Hanushek, E. 2005. *The Alchemy of 'Costing Out' and Adequate Education*. Paper presented at the Adequate Lawsuits: Their Growing Impact on American Education conference, Cambridge, MA.

Haveman, R. and Wolfe, B. 1994. *Succeeding Generations: On the Effects of Investments in Children*. New York, NY: Russell Sage.

Henderson, J. and Quandt, R. 1980. *Microeconomic Theory: A Mathematical Approach*, 3rd edition. New York, NY: McGraw-Hill.

Imazeki, J. 2001. *Grade-Dependent Costs of Education: Evidence from Illinois*, Draft Paper. San Diego, CA: San Diego State University.

Imazeki, J. 2008. Assessing the costs of adequacy in California public schools: A cost function approach. *Education Finance and Policy*, **3**: 90–108.

Imazeki, J. and Rechovsky, A. 2004a. *Estimating the Costs of Meeting the Texas Educational Accountability Standards* (Report for Texas Joint Select Committee on Public School Finance). Available from http://www.investintexasschools.org/schoolfinancelibrary/studies/files/2005/january/reschovsky_coststudy.doc.

Imazeki, J. and Reschovsky, A. 2004b. Is No Child Left Behind an un (or under) funded federal mandate? Evidence from Texas. *National Tax Journal* **57**: 571–588.

Imazeki, J. and Reschovsky, A. 2004c. School finance reform in Texas: A never ending story. In J. Yinger (ed.), *Helping Children Left Behind: State Aid and the Pursuit of Educational Equity*, pp. 251–281. Cambridge, MA: MIT Press.

Imazeki, J. and Reschovsky, A. 2006. Does No Child Left Behind place a fiscal burden on states? Evidence from Texas. *Education Finance and Policy* **1**: 227–246.

Kane, T. J. and Staiger, D. O. 2002. The promise and pitfalls of using imprecise school accountability measures. *Journal of Economic Perspectives* **1**: 91–114.

Kuo, Y. and Liang, K. 2004. Human judgments in New York State sales and use forecasting. *Journal of Forecasting* **23**: 297–314.

Leibenstein, H. 1966. Allocative efficiency vs. x-efficiency. *American Economic Review* **56**: 392–415.

Loeb, S. 2007. *Difficulties of Estimating the Cost of Achieving Education Standards* (Working Paper 23). Seattle: Center on Reinventing Public Education, Evans School of Public Affairs, University of Washington.

Makridakis, S., Wheelwright, S., and McGee, V. 1983. *Forecasting: Methods and applications*. New York, NY: Wiley & Sons.

McCarty, T. A. and Yaisawarng, S. 1993. Technical efficiency in New Jersey school districts. In H. O. Fried, C. A. Knox Lovell, and S. S. Schmidt (eds.), *The Measurement of Productive efficiency: Techniques and Applications*, pp. 271–287. New York, NY: Oxford University Press.

Mocan, H. N. and Azad, S. 1995. Accuracy and rationality of state general fund revenue forecasts: Evidence from panel data. *International Journal of Forecasting* **11**: 417–427.

Murray, M. 2006. Avoiding invalid instruments and coping with weak instruments. *Journal of Economic Perspectives* **20**: 111–132.

Niskanen, W. A. 1971. *Bureaucracy and Representative Government*. Chicago, IL: Aldine-Atherton.

Ondrich, J. and Ruggiero, J. 2001. Efficiency measurement in the Stochastic Frontier model. *European Journal of Operational Research* **129**: 432–442.

Ray, S. C. 1991. Resource use in public schools: A study of Connecticut. *Management Science* **37**: 1520–1628.

Reschovsky, A. and Imazeki, J. 2001. Achieving education adequacy through school finance reform. *Journal of Education Finance* **26**: 373–396.

Ruggiero, J. 1998. Non-discretionary inputs in data envelopment analysis. *European Journal of Operational Research* **111**: 461–468.

Ruggiero, J. 2001. Determining the base cost of education: An analysis of Ohio school districts. *Contemporary Economic Policy* **19**: 268–279.

Schaffer, M. 2005. *XTIVREG2: Stata Module to Perform Extended IV/2SLS, GMM and AC/HAC, LIML and k-class Regression for Panel Data Models* (Statistical Software Components S456501). Boston, MA: Boston College Department of Economics.

Shkurti, W. 1990. A user's guide to state revenue forecasting. *Public Budgeting & Finance* **10**: 79–94.

Stock, J. H. and Yogo, M. 2005. Testing for weak instruments in linear iv regression. In D. W. K. Andrews and J. H. Stock (eds.), *Identification and Inference for Econometric Models: Essays in Honor of Thomas Rothenberg*, pp. 80–108. Cambridge, UK: Cambridge University Press.

Tashman, L. 2000. Out-of-sample tests of forecasting accuracy: An analysis and review. *International Journal of Forecasting* **16**: 437–450.

Trochim, W. 2001. *The Research Methods Knowledge Base*, 2nd edition, Cincinnati, OH: Atomic Dog.

Voorhees, W. R. 2004. More is better: Consensual forecasting and state revenue forecast error. *International Journal of Public Administration* **27**: 651–671.

Wang, W., Duncombe, W., and Yinger, J. 2011. School District Responses to Matching Aid Programs for Capital Facilities: A Case Study of New York's Building Aid Program. *National Tax Journal* **64**(3) (September): 759–794. [Chapter 20]

Wyckoff, P. 1990. The simple analytics of slack-maximizing bureaucracy. *Public Choice* **67**: 35–67.

Chapter 6

The No Child Left Behind Act: Have Federal Funds Been Left Behind?*

William Duncombe[‡], Anna Lukemeyer[‡], and John Yinger[†,§]

[†]*Departments of Public Administration and International
Affairs and of Economics, Syracuse University, Syracuse, NY, United States*
[§]*jyinger@maxwell.syr.edu*

The federal No Child Left Behind Act (NCLB) imposes new requirements on state education systems and provides additional education funding. This article estimates education cost functions, predicts the spending required to support NCLB standards, and compares this spending with the funding available through NCLB. This analysis is conducted for Kansas and Missouri, which have similar education environments but very different standards. We find that new federal funding is sufficient to support very low standards for student performance, but cannot come close to funding high standards without implausibly large increases in school-district efficiency. Because of the limited federal funding and the severe penalties in NCLB when a school does not meet its state's standards, states have a strong incentive to keep their standards low. NCLB needs to be reformed so that it will encourage high standards.

1. Introduction

The No Child Left Behind Act of 2001 (NCLB) both imposes mandates on states and gives them more federal education funding. NCLB is therefore

---

*This chapter is reproduced from "The No Child Left Behind Act: Have Federal Funds Been Left Behind?" *Public Finance Review*, **36**(4), July 2008, pp. 381–407.
[‡]Deceased.

not an *unfunded* mandate, but the money it provides may not be sufficient for states to fully achieve the standards it sets. Using data from Kansas and Missouri, this article estimates education cost functions, calculates the extra costs required to meet the NCLB standards, and compares these extra costs to the increases in federal funding.

The movement toward accountability in elementary and secondary education began well before NCLB. Indeed, accountability was a major part of education reform in most states during the 1990s (Ladd, 2001). By 2001, over forty states had school report cards, over half had school performance ratings, and many provided assistance or sanctions for low-performing schools (Meyer *et al.*, 2002). When NCLB became law in January 2002, the federal government became seriously involved for the first time in setting broad parameters, implementation timelines, and sanctions for state accountability systems (Erpenbach, Forte-Fast, and Potts, 2003).

With a few exceptions (Driscoll and Fleeter, 2003; Imazeki and Reschovsky, 2004b, 2006), however, estimates of the costs of NCLB are far from precise or complete (GAO, 2003; Mathis, 2003; Robelen, 2005). Moreover, a few states, including Utah and Connecticut, have passed legislation to ignore provisions of NCLB that require state funding or have sued the federal government for inadequate funding (Archer, 2005; Sack, 2005). In a recent survey of state education officials, over two-thirds cited adequacy of federal funding for NCLB as a moderate or serious challenge that has affected their ability to assist schools not making adequate yearly progress (Center on Education Policy, 2006). The decline in education grants in the President's 2008 Budget (OMB, 2007) has raised additional concerns about the sufficiency of federal funding for meeting the increasing standards set by NCLB.

Building on the work of Driscoll and Fleeter (2003) and especially Imazeki and Reschovsky (2004a, 2006), this article estimates the spending by school districts that is necessary to comply with NCLB standards and compares this spending with funding provisions in Title I of NCLB. Specifically, we estimate cost functions for Kansas and Missouri, and use the results to predict the spending required to provide students the opportunity to reach NCLB standards. Because of lack of consensus on the fiscal responsibility of the federal government (Robelen, 2005), we develop several alternative estimates of the Title I funding gap. Kansas and Missouri provide a particularly interesting case study, because both states share many similarities in their education environment but differ significantly in the stringency of their accountability standards. They are also states with significant diversity in school district size and demographics but have student performance and spending levels similar to the national average (NCES, 2006).

2. Education Accountability and NCLB

While the merits of education accountability systems have been debated extensively in the academic literature (Ladd, 2001; Hanushek and Raymond, 2001), the implications of the different choices for school finance systems have received much less attention. In this section we discuss the key decisions in designing an education accountability system, the accountability design in NCLB, and the fiscal implications of accountability.

2.1. *Design of Education Accountability Systems and NCLB*

Education accountability is an application of performance management to education. Key choices in the design of a performance management system include: accountability for whom; accountability for what; and the consequences of success or failure. Education accountability systems focus on holding either students or school personnel (teachers and administrators) accountable. Students are held accountable for passing a certain set of classes or for reaching a certain score on specified tests. Students who fail to meet the standards may not be allowed to graduate from high school or might receive a different type of high school degree.

School or school-district accountability systems hold school personnel accountable for student performance, as measured by student test scores, graduation rates, or gains in test scores (Ladd, 2001; Hanushek and Raymond, 2001). Programs can differ in the extent to which they consider the impact on the standards of factors outside the control of school district personnel, such as concentrated poverty. For example, some systems set standards for a district relative to other schools with approximately the same poverty rate and enrollment.

All accountability systems require performance to be measured on a regular basis. NCLB requires states to implement math and reading exams in third through eighth grades and in at least one grade in high school by 2005–2006, and science exams once in elementary, middle, and high school by 2007–2008. In addition, districts are required to report participation rates on the exams and graduation rates from high school. Moreover, NCLB requires districts to collect and report assessment information by racial, socioeconomic, and special needs sub-groups.

162 W. Duncombe, A. Lukemeyer & J. Yinger

NCLB sets as its target that *all* students reach proficiency on these measures by 2013–2014. States are provided a fair amount of discretion in defining the level of performance that is "proficient" and in setting intermediate performance targets for years before 2013–2014. Thus, states have an incentive to set low proficiency levels and to backload required proficiency improvement (Kim and Sunderman, 2004; Ryan, 2003). To highlight differences in the stringency of accountability standards, Figure 1 compares the intermediate targets and actual performance levels for Kansas and Missouri. In 2002, Kansas set the proficiency level for its students at about 50 percent compared to 13 percent in Missouri.[1] While for both states the average student was well above these targets through 2004, the average proficiency rate in Missouri was less than 40 percent of the rate in Kansas.

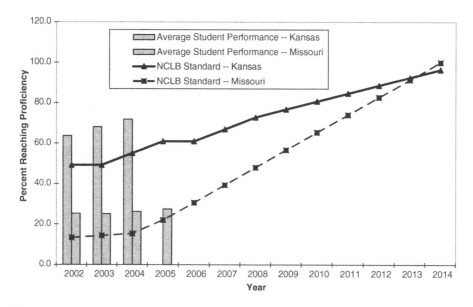

Figure 1 Average student performance compared to NCLB intermediate targets in Kansas and Missouri.

Sources: Kansas State Department of Education and Missouri Department of Elementary and Secondary Education.

---

[1]The NCLB standards in Figure 1 are average proficiency rates on three math and three readings exams. Kansas also uses a graduation rate standard of 75 percent, which is why the combined index is less than 100 percent. Both states also include participation rates in exams and attendance rates in their standards, but we ignore these rates because they are already high in most districts.

Since all states must reach 100 percent proficiency by 2014, a much faster improvement in performance is required in Missouri than in Kansas.

NCLB requires states to make adequate yearly progress (AYP) until 2014. Rules for determining AYP have evolved over the last five years, and states are now allowed several paths to establishing AYP (Center on Education Policy, 2006; Erpenbach, Forte-Fast, and Potts, 2003). Recent changes have made determining AYP much more complex (Hoxby, 2005) and can significantly reduce the performance improvement required of a school below the performance targets (Center on Education Policy, 2006).

In our analysis of the funding impacts of NCLB, we use the intermediate performance targets set for each year, rather than the requirements to make AYP. First, the requirements to make AYP, which can vary significantly across states and even across schools, are difficult to duplicate. Second, these accommodations just postpone the ultimate requirement of reaching 100 percent proficiency by 2014. If schools are going to have a reasonable probability of getting close to this standard, then they need to make significant improvements in the intervening years.

The penalty component of NCLB uses high stakes and punitive consequences for schools receiving Title I funding and not making AYP.

> After two years, students in failing schools are allowed to choose another public school (including a charter school) within the same district. After three years, the students ... can receive tutoring (at public expense) from an outside provider, public or private. Those schools that fail for four consecutive years must replace school staff, and those that fail for five years in a row must essentially surrender control to the state government, which can in turn reopen the school as a charter school, turn over management to a private company, or take over the school itself. (Ryan, 2003, 10)

In 2006–2007 schools faced for the first time closure or reorganization if they had not made AYP. The stringency of these sanctions is likely to create a significant response in many schools. Some of these responses, such as a focus on math and reading (Davis, 2006), are likely to meet program goals, whereas others, such as test score inflation (Koretz, 1996) or actual cheating (Jacob and Levitt, 2003), may be undesirable.

2.2. *Education Accountability and State Budgets*

Several commentators have examined whether NCLB is an underfunded mandate (Peyser and Costrell, 2004; Mathis, 2003). Existing studies on this topic differ widely in terms of what costs are included and how these costs are calculated (Robelen, 2005). The potential costs of implementing an education accountability system include the costs of the testing system, of enforcing the consequences, and of making the required changes in the school finance system.

Testing costs are relatively small and easy to calculate. Most states had math and reading exams in place before NCLB, and a few states, such as Texas, had exams from third through eighth grade. Estimates for testing costs have ranged from $5 million to $25 million (Hoxby, 2002; GAO, 2003; Driscoll and Fleeter, 2003). The costs of enforcing NCLB sanctions are more difficult to calculate. For schools that fail, NCLB requires districts to develop school improvement plans, provide funding for supplemental services, or provide access to another school in the district. Ultimately, states may be required to reconstitute schools. NCLB also requires districts to hire only highly qualified teachers, and Driscoll and Fleeter (2003) estimate that this requirement will cost approximately forty dollars per pupil in Ohio.

The amount that state and local governments must pay to reach NCLB standards may be large, especially if standards are high, as in Missouri. Any cost calculation is bound to be controversial because scholars do not agree on several issues: how should spending needed to reach a given student performance level using current best practices be determined; what are the extra costs for reaching a performance standard in districts with a high concentration of disadvantaged students; and what is the extent to which an accountability program can boost school-district efficiency. In a recent analysis for Ohio, Driscoll and Fleeter (2003) estimate that "intervention costs" represent over 95 percent of additional costs from NCLB and average $760 per pupil. In a study of NCLB in Texas, Imazeki and Reschovsky (2006) estimate that meeting AYP associated with a passing rate of 70 percent would require $4.4 billion of additional spending, or $1,064 per pupil. National estimates of states' costs to implement NCLB range from $8 billion (Peyser and Costrell, 2004) to $150 billion (Mathis, 2003).

3. Costing Out NCLB

Several approaches for estimating the cost of reaching a given student performance standard have been developed (Baker, 2006), and adequacy studies have been carried out in at least thirty states (Hoff, 2005).[2] We use the so-called cost function method to estimate the spending required to meet

---

[2]Cost functions are criticized by Hanushek (2005) and defended by Baker (2006) and Duncombe (2006). Hanushek's (2005) claim that cost-functions ignore efficiency is belied by

NCLB standards. In this section, we discuss data and measures, present cost function results, and estimate the cost of meeting NCLB standards in Kansas and Missouri.

3.1. *Data Sources and Measures*

Applied to education, the term "cost" stands for the minimum spending, based on current best practices, needed for the students in a district to reach a given performance level. Because we have data on spending, not costs, the cost function approach must control for school district efficiency; that is, we must recognize that not all districts use current best practices. To model the relationship between spending, student performance, and other important characteristics of school districts, a number of education researchers have employed one of the tools of production theory in microeconomics, namely, cost functions.[3] A cost function for school districts relates five factors to spending per pupil: student performance; the price of school resources, such as teacher salaries; the district's enrollment; student characteristics that affect educational performance, such as poverty; and factors that affect school district efficiency.

The cost function estimates in this article are based on three years of data for three pre-NCLB years (1999–2000 to 2001–2002) for school districts in Kansas and Missouri plus either two years (Kansas) or three years (Missouri) after the passage of NCLB. Most of the data are supplied by the state education departments in Missouri and Kansas. This section is organized by major category of variables, and summary statistics are reported in Table 1.

District Expenditures. The dependent variable used in the cost function is inflation-adjusted district operating expenditures per pupil.[4] In Kansas, our measure includes expenditures for six functional areas: instruction, student support, instructional support, school administration, general administration, operations and maintenance, and other.[5] Our measure for Missouri is

---

the efficiency corrections in Duncombe and Yinger (2000, 2005a), Duncombe, Lukemeyer, and Yinger (2003), and Imazeki and Reschovsky (2004a).

[3]Cost function studies have been conducted in other states, including New York (Duncombe and Yinger, 2000, 2005a; Duncombe, Lukemeyer, and Yinger, 2003), Arizona (Downes and Pogue, 1994), Texas (Imazeki and Reschovsky, 2004a, 2004b, 2006; Gronberg *et al.*, 2004), and Wisconsin (Reschovsky and Imazeki, 1998).

[4]The measure of inflation is the CPI for urban wage earners, with a base-year of 2000.

[5]Spending on special education, transportation, vocational education, food service, and school facilities is excluded. Details are discussed in Duncombe and Yinger (2005b).

Table 1 Descriptive statistics for variables used in cost models.

	Kansas (2004)		Missouri (2005)	
Variables	Mean	Standard deviation	Mean	Standard deviation
Per pupil spending (inflation-adjusted)	$6,400	$1,200	$5,405	$1,338
Performance measure	71.8	7.9	25.6	7.2
Cost variables				
Teacher salaries (inflation-adjusted)	$36,093	$2,701	$24,282	$2,909
Percent free lunch students	26.7	11.3		
Percent subsidized lunch students			46.1	16.0
Poverty variable multiplied by pupil density	5.1	22.5	16.6	70.9
Adjusted percent bilingual headcount	4.2	7.4		
Enrollment	1485.5	3834.2	1670.7	3568.4
Enrollment categories (share of districts in each category)				
Under 100 students	0.013	0.115	0.050	0.219
100 to 150 students	0.040	0.197	0.047	0.211
150 to 250 students	0.110	0.314	0.132	0.339
250 to 500 students	0.301	0.459	0.203	0.403
500 to 1,000 students	0.254	0.436	0.238	0.427
1,000 to 1,500 students	0.087	0.282	0.093	0.291
1,500 to 2,500 students	0.087	0.282	0.089	0.285
2,500 to 5,000 students	0.060	0.238	0.085	0.285
5,000 to 15,000 students	0.030	0.171	0.041	0.198
Over 15,000 students	0.017	0.128	0.021	0.145
Efficiency-related variables				
Per pupil income	$87,950	$31,021	$63,962	$35,112
Per pupil property values	$57,065	$43,629	$61,631	$41,074
State aid ratio	0.08	0.10	0.06	0.06
Local tax share	1.62	0.88	1.23	0.49
College education variable (2000)	17.97	6.75	13.11	8.05
Percent of population 65 or older (2000)	16.84	5.47	15.19	4.25
Percent of housing units that are owner occupied (2000)	88.59	5.66	77.28	8.02
Sample size	299		516	

Note: State aid variable is per pupil state aid divided by per pupil income. For Kansas, this variable also includes federal aid. Teacher salaries in Kansas are estimated for teacher with average experience and in Missouri based on teachers with five years or less of experience. Inflation adjustment is using the CPI for urban wage earners (2000 base).

current expenditures, which excludes capital, debt service, special education, and transportation.

Student Performance. For Kansas, our measures of student performance come from the state accountability system, Quality Performance and Accreditation (QPA). We use the share of students reaching proficiency on criterion-referenced exams in math and reading in three grades (fourth, seventh, and tenth for math, and fifth, eighth, and eleventh for reading). The QPA also includes a cohort graduation rate.[6] To construct an overall measure of student performance, we calculate a simple average of these seven measures. For Missouri, the key exam scores used to assess AYP are proficiency rates for three math and three reading exams (grades third, seventh, and eleventh for communication arts, and grades fourth, eighth, and tenth for math). Our measure of performance is an average of these scores.

Student Enrollment. For Kansas we use the enrollment measure in the General State Aid formula, namely, fulltime equivalent students (FTE). This measure equals total enrollment from first to twelfth grades plus half of total enrollment in kindergarten and pre-kindergarten programs. For Missouri we construct a rough measure of average daily membership by averaging enrollment in September and January.

Student Need. Cost functions usually include student need measures for child poverty, limited English proficiency (LEP), and special education. The poverty measures used most often in state aid formulas are the percent of students receiving a free lunch (Kansas) or a subsidized lunch (Missouri). While the reliability of these measures has been challenged, especially for secondary students, they generally track closely with the child poverty rate produced by the Census Bureau.[7] Some national evidence suggests that student performance is significantly worse in high-poverty inner city schools than in high-poverty rural schools (Olson and Jerald, 1998). To explore this possibility, we create another variable, namely, the percent free (or subsidized) lunch students multiplied by pupils per square mile, a measure of urbanization.

We do not have a consistent source of LEP data across states or even across school districts within some states. In Missouri, LEP measures are

---

[6]The graduation rate equals the number of graduates in a given year divided by total graduates plus dropouts in this year and the three previous years.

[7]The correlation between the share free lunch (Kansas) or subsidized lunch (Missouri) and the Census child poverty rate in 2000 is about 0.70 for both states.

not used in the state aid formula, and consistent data are not collected. An alternative variable from the Census is the percent of students who live in a household where English is not spoken well at home, which is consistently lower than LEP rates calculated by states. This variable was not statistically significant and was dropped. In Kansas, the LEP measure in the state aid formula is flawed, so we use data on the bilingual headcount reported to Kansas State Department of Education.

Measures of special education students are problematic because of the potential for over-classification of special education students to increase state aid (Cullen, 2003). To avoid this potential endogeneity, we remove spending on special education from our dependent variable and do not include the share of special education students as an explanatory variable.

Teacher Salaries. Teacher salary is the most important resource price affecting school district spending. In addition, teacher salaries are highly correlated with salaries of other certified staff, so that teacher salaries serve as a proxy for all staff salaries. To develop a comparable salary measure across districts, data on individual teachers are used to predict what teacher salaries would be in each district if teachers had average experience and education.[8]

Efficiency Indicators. Some school districts may have higher spending than others relative to their level of student achievement not because of higher costs, but because of inefficient use of resources. In our cost analysis, as in any other, this inefficiency can take two forms, which cannot be separated. First, some districts may be inefficient because they do not use current best practices. Examples of this type of inefficiency include poor management practices or excess compensation for school officials. Second, some districts may choose to focus on subject areas, such as art, music, and athletics, with a limited impact on test score performance in math and reading or on the graduation rate. As in any other study of production and cost, inefficiency can only be defined with respect to the production of certain, specified outputs. Once measures of student achievement have been selected, additional spending by a district relative to the spending by comparable districts with the same achievement levels by those measures is an indication of inefficiency.

---

[8]Specifically, the natural logarithm of a teacher's salary is regressed on the logarithm of their total experience and indicator variables (0–1) for whether they had a master's, doctorate, or law degree (Kansas) or had a graduate degree (Missouri). Teacher salaries are also inflation-adjusted.

Because efficiency cannot be measured directly, we include in the cost model variables that have a conceptual link to efficiency and that have been found to be significant in previous cost/efficiency studies. These variables include fiscal capacity and factors affecting voter involvement in monitoring local government. Research on New York indicates that taxpayers in districts with high property wealth, income, and state aid may have less incentive to put pressure on district officials to be efficient or may be more apt to spend money on non-tested subjects (Duncombe and Yinger, 2000). In addition, voters might have more incentive and capacity to monitor operations in school districts with relatively more college-educated adults, more elderly residents, a larger share of households that own their own homes, or where the typical voter pays a larger share of school taxes (median housing price over per pupil property values).

3.2. *Cost Function Estimates*

The cost function for school districts in Kansas and Missouri are estimated using log-linear multiple regression techniques. Because spending, performance, and salaries may be set simultaneously in the budgeting process, we treat student performance and teacher salaries as endogenous variables using an instrumental variable method (two-stage least squares).[9] Hypothesis testing is done with robust standard errors (controlling for district-level clustering).

The cost function results in Table 2 indicate that the relationships between the different variables and per pupil spending fit expectations and are generally statistically significant. To start, a 1 percent increase in student performance is associated with a 0.50 percent increase in per pupil expenditures in Kansas, and a 0.37 percent increase in Missouri.

Turning to the cost variables, we find that a 1 percent increase in teacher salaries is associated with a 0.68 percent increase in per pupil expenditures

---

[9]In both states, the instrument for salaries is an index of private wages in the district's labor market. Other instruments in Kansas are based on averages (of test proficiency rate, percent real property, log of teacher salaries) or maximums (graduation rate, per pupil personal property, and per pupil total value) in districts in neighboring counties, and in Missouri are averages for districts in the same labor market area (enrollment, percent African American students, and percent Hispanic students). Our instruments pass tests for over-identification (Wooldridge, 2003) and generally pass a weak instrument test (Bound, Jaeger, and Baker, 1995). The instruments for the outcome variable for Kansas have a fairly low partial F-statistic (3.3), but the F-statistic is statistically different from zero at conventional levels.

Table 2   Cost function estimates for Kansas and Missouri school districts.

Variables	Kansas (2000–2004)	Missouri (2000–2005)
Intercept	−2.11360	−7.00420**
Performance measure	0.50124**	0.36817*
Cost variables		
Teacher salaries	0.67969**	1.25667*
Percent free lunch students	0.00435*	
Percent subsidized lunch students		0.00549*
Poverty variable multiplied by pupil density	0.00055	0.00000*
Adjusted percent bilingual headcount	0.00158**	
K-12 districts (1 = yes)		0.11902*
Consolidated districts (1 = yes)	0.21058*	
Enrollment categories		
100 to 150 students	−0.12166*	−0.15733*
150 to 250 students	−0.22828*	−0.32205*
250 to 500 students	−0.36138*	−0.47308*
500 to 1,000 students	−0.42874*	−0.59449*
1,000 to 1,500 students	−0.50830*	−0.67928*
1,500 to 2,500 students	−0.56852*	−0.75076*
2,500 to 5,000 students	−0.56608*	−0.82422*
5,000 to 15,000 students	−0.51823*	−0.84564*
Over 15,000 students	−0.62161*	−0.81584*
Efficiency-related variables		
Per pupil income	0.13505*	0.19209*
Per pupil property values	0.05599*	−0.00735
Total aid/income ratio	0.78701*	1.23551*
Local tax share	−0.02146	−0.09089*
Percent of adults that are college educated (2000)	−0.00423*	0.24879
Percent of population 65 or older (2000)	−0.00209	−0.37339**
Percent of housing units that are owner occupied (2000)	−0.00145	−0.16346
Year indicator variables		
2001	−0.01176	−0.00095
2002	−0.00464	−0.01005
2003	−0.04626	−0.02675
2004	−0.08047	−0.05696*
2005		−0.04433
Sample size	1463	3068

Note: Estimated with linear 2SLS regression with the log of per pupil operating spending (Kansas) or current spending (Missouri) as the dependent variables. Performance and teacher salaries are treated as endogenous variables with instruments based on variables for adjacent counties for Kansas, and for labor market areas for Missouri (see text). Robust standard errors are used for hypothesis testing (controlling for clustering at district level). The performance index, teacher salaries, per pupil income, per pupil property values, and local tax share are logged. *indicates statistically significant from zero at 5 percent level. **indicates statistically significant from zero at 10 percent level.

in Kansas and a 1.25 percent increase in Missouri. The coefficients on the poverty variables and the bilingual variable for Kansas have the expected positive sign and are statistically significant, but the coefficient on the density-poverty interaction is not significant at conventional levels. In the case of Missouri, the subsidized lunch and its interaction with density are both statistically significant with the expected sign. These results correspond to an average poverty weight, defined as the percent increase in spending for a child in poverty, of fifty-five in Kansas and sixty-four in Missouri, with higher weights in central cities. Weights of this type often appear in state aid formulas (Duncombe and Yinger, 2005a). The implied weight for a bilingual student in Kansas is sixteen.

As expected, the operating costs are higher for smaller school districts. School districts in Kansas with 100 or fewer students (the omitted category) are almost 57 percent more expensive to operate than districts with 1,500 to 5,000 students, and in Missouri they are 82 percent more expensive than districts with 2,500 to 5,000 students (Table 3). For both states, economies of scale are largely exhausted by the time a district reaches about 2,500 pupils.

Several efficiency variables also prove to be important. Income and state aid have the expected positive sign and are statistically significant in both states. As expected, the tax-share variable has a negative coefficient in both states, but it is significant only in Missouri. In addition, our results suggest that efficiency in Kansas declines with property values and increases with the share of adults who have a college education and that efficiency in Missouri increases with the share of adults who are age sixty-five or older.

The year dummy variables capture changes in spending over time holding student performance and cost factors constant. One possible interpretation of these variables is that they capture changes in efficiency in the average school district. In both states, we find that spending decreases with time, a sign of increasing efficiency. This decrease is 8 percent in Kansas over a four-year period, which corresponds to an efficiency improvement of about 2 percent per year (with compounding), and 4.4 percent in Missouri over a five-year period, which corresponds to an annual efficiency improvement of 0.9 percent. These year variables are not statistically significant, however, so this is only weak evidence of efficiency gains.

These cost results can be translated into cost indexes, which indicate how much more a district needs to spend than the average district to reach the same performance level (Duncombe and Yinger, 2005a). In Kansas and Missouri, large central cities have the highest costs because of both high poverty and above-average wage costs. We estimate that to reach the same

Table 3 Per pupil spending increases required to support a particular NCLB standard by census district types.

	Actual expenditures per pupil	Percent increase in predicted spending to reach NCLB standard in		
		2007	2009	2011
Kansas				
Total state	$6,118	−1.9	5.0	10.3
Census district type				
Large central cities	$6,112	8.7	16.4	22.3
Medium cities	$6,079	−7.5	−0.9	4.0
Urban fringe of large cities	$5,535	−7.1	−0.5	4.5
Urban fringe of medium cities	$5,615	−5.9	0.8	5.9
Large town	$6,456	0.1	7.2	12.6
Small town	$6,105	−0.9	6.2	11.5
Rural metro	$7,029	−3.5	3.3	8.5
Rural non-metro	$5,901	−5.4	1.3	6.4
Missouri				
Total state	$6,248	18.5	35.5	49.5
Census district type				
Large central cities	$8,742	61.0	84.1	103.2
Medium cities	$5,873	10.8	26.8	39.9
Urban fringe of large cities	$6,813	9.4	25.1	38.0
Urban fringe of medium cities	$4,720	10.8	26.7	39.8
Large town	$5,399	11.8	27.8	41.0
Small town	$5,446	18.0	35.0	48.9
Rural metro	$5,328	11.7	27.7	40.9
Rural non-metro	$5,653	19.3	36.4	50.5

Note: Actual expenditures per pupil are for operating spending in Kansas for 2004, and for current expenditures in Missouri for 2005 in nominal dollars, calculated as student weighted averages.

performance standard as the average district, these cities would need to spend 9 percent more in Kansas and 20 percent more in Missouri. Costs in some rural districts (rural metro in Kansas and rural non-metro in Missouri) are about 7 percent more than in the average district, due primarily to their small size. The lowest costs are in suburban districts (urban fringe or medium cities), because of below-average poverty and economies of size.

3.3. *Predicting the Cost to Meet NCLB Standards*

The cost function results can be used to estimate the amount each school district must spend to reach a given performance standard, holding its efficiency constant at its current level. We estimate the spending required to meet intermediate NCLB targets in 2007, 2009, and 2011. Table 3 reports required spending increases by Census district type, based on the standards set by Kansas and Missouri and our estimated cost functions.

A comparison of the required spending increases highlights the difference in standards between the two states. To meet 2007 NCLB standards, spending in the average district (weighted by enrollment) will not have to increase at all in Kansas but will have to increase 18.5 percent in Missouri. By 2011, the spending increase in Kansas would need to be 10 percent compared to 50 percent in Missouri. In both states, the estimated required spending increases for the large central cities are particularly high.[10] These increases range from 9 percent in 2007 to 22 percent in 2011 in Kansas and from 61 percent in 2007 to 103 percent in 2011 in Missouri. In Kansas, rural districts are favored in the formula (Duncombe and Yinger, 2005b), so they do not need a spending increase, on average, to reach 2007 standards, and need only a 6 percent to 9 percent increase to meet the 2011 standards. In contrast, the Missouri aid formula does not make significant adjustments for economies of size, and the projected spending increase to meet the 2011 standards in rural districts ranges from 41 to 51 percent.

4. Determining Whether NCLB Is Under-Funded

Title I has been the principal federal compensatory aid program for four decades. In this section, we examine whether NCLB is under-funded.

4.1. *Determining Whether NCLB Is Under-Funded*

The issue of under-funding depends largely on the federal responsibility for funding the accountability provisions of NCLB. While testing and administrative costs associated with NCLB are not inconsequential, they are relatively small. Costs associated with providing students the services and support to meet the higher standards are potentially much larger, and their magnitude depend on the efficiency improvements generated by NCLB. To our knowledge only two studies have done detailed estimates of costs of meeting NCLB performance standards (Driscoll and Fleeter, 2003; Imazeki and Reschovsky, 2006).

---

[10]The Census classification for the large central cities was modified to include only the cities with above-average costs (St. Louis, Kansas City, Hickman Mills, and Center). The other districts (Park Hill and Northern Kansas City) are included in the category for medium cities.

The federal responsibility with regard to funding NCLB is a matter of debate. Section 9527(a) of NCLB can be interpreted as protecting states and districts from implementing any provisions of NCLB that are unfunded.

> Nothing in this title shall be construed to authorize an officer or employee of the Federal Government to mandate, direct, or control a State, local educational agency, or school's curriculum, program or instruction, or allocation of State or local resources, or mandate a State or any subdivision thereof to spend any funds or incur any costs not paid for under this act.

A group of school districts and the State of Connecticut have filed suits arguing that this provision prevents the U.S. Department of Education (DOE) from requiring compliance with NCLB requirements that are not fully funded by federal aid (Hendrie, 2005). In contrast, DOE argues, in part, that states bear the primary responsibility for funding education and that they can avoid NCLB requirements by declining federal aid to education. Title I was designed only to supplement state compensatory education, says DOE, and the federal government has no obligation to fully fund the costs of meeting these requirements.[11]

While courts may ultimately decide the issue, we build on the cost-function approach of Imazeki and Reschovsky (2006) to examine four scenarios with regard to the fiscal responsibility of the federal government. Assuming broad federal responsibility, Title I funds can be compared to the projected spending to meet NCLB standards. Narrowing the focus to only the post-NCLB responsibility, the increase in Title I funds since 2001 can be compared to the increase in spending associated with the higher performance standards. If Title I is viewed as just a compensatory education program, Title I funds could be compared to costs associated with bringing low-income children up to the standard. Finally, the increase in Title I funds could be compared to the increase in costs associated with raising performance of low-income children from their current levels up to NCLB standards in a particular year.

Tables 4 and 5 provide estimates of the four scenarios. We assume no increase in real dollars in Title I funding after 2005, based on the relatively small increases in Title I funding in 2007 and in the President's 2008 Budget (OMB, 2007). For the second and fourth scenarios, some districts already

---

[11]The suits are *Pontiac School District v. Spellings*, Case No. 2:05-CV-71535 (E. D. Mich 2005); *Connecticut v. Spellings*, Case No. 3:05-CV-1330 (D. Conn 2005). As of this writing, the district court ruled against the school districts in *Pontiac S.D.* They have appealed.

Table 4 Title I aid in 2005 as a share of required spending, spending increase, and spending to support poverty in Kansas school districts.

	NCLB standard in		
	2007	2009	2011
	Title I as percent of required spending		
Total state	3.0	2.8	2.6
Census district type			
Large central cities	5.9	5.5	5.2
Medium cities	2.3	2.2	2.1
Urban fringe of large cities	2.2	2.1	2.0
Urban fringe of medium cities	2.0	1.9	1.8
Large town	4.5	4.2	4.0
Small town	3.7	3.5	3.3
Rural metro	3.1	2.9	2.8
Rural non-metro	2.0	1.8	1.7
	Title I increase as percent of required spending increase		
Total state	65.2 (33.4)	27.3 (71.3)	20.9 (88.7)
Census district type			
Large central cities	50.3 (100.0)	16.4 (100.0)	11.4 (100.0)
Medium cities	15.4 (33.3)	55.5 (66.7)	11.2 (66.7)
Urban fringe of large cities	47.5 (34.8)	12.0 (60.9)	8.5 (87.0)
Urban fringe of medium cities	27.2 (20.0)	39.2 (80.0)	26.0 (100.0)
Large town	105.1 (50.0)	21.9 (83.3)	14.8 (100.0)
Small town	135.6 (42.9)	22.5 (73.8)	34.5 (90.5)
Rural metro	45.4 (30.4)	32.7 (70.8)	22.0 (86.3)
Rural non-metro	55.5 (30.0)	18.8 (72.0)	12.8 (94.0)

(*Continued*)

Table 4   (*Continued*)

	NCLB standard in		
	2007	2009	2011
	Title I as percent of spending required to support children in poverty		
Total state	8.3	7.8	7.4
Census district type			
Large central cities	8.0	7.4	7.1
Medium cities	8.9	8.3	7.9
Urban fringe of large cities	7.9	7.4	7.0
Urban fringe of medium cities	7.6	7.1	6.8
Large town	8.9	8.3	7.9
Small town	8.9	8.3	7.9
Rural metro	8.5	7.9	7.5
Rural non-metro	7.6	7.1	6.8
	Title I change as percent of required spending increase to support children in poverty		
Total state	725.4 (29.6)	119.5 (75.7)	60.5 (96.6)
Census district type			
Large central cities	34.3 (100.0)	18.0 (100.0)	13.4 (100.0)
Medium cities	27.9 (33.3)	96.1 (66.7)	691.2 (100.0)
Urban fringe of large cities	6390.6 (30.4)	62.0 (73.9)	44.4 (91.3)
Urban fringe of medium cities	70.7 (20.0)	36.2 (60.0)	18.7 (80.0)
Large town	134.9 (50.0)	38.1 (83.3)	26.7 (100.0)
Small town	570.4 (35.7)	78.5 (78.6)	62.8 (100.0)
Rural metro	96.0 (27.3)	129.5 (75.8)	55.0 (96.3)
Rural non-metro	383.9 (26.0)	177.1 (74.0)	54.5 (98.0)

Note: Calculated as simple district averages. The share of districts needing extra funds is in parentheses.

Table 5 Title I aid in 2005 as a share of required spending, spending increase, and spending to support poverty in Missouri school districts.

	NCLB standard in		
Census district type	2007	2009	2011
	Title I as percent of required spending		
Total state	4.1	3.6	3.3
Census district type			
Large central cities	2.7	2.4	2.2
Medium cities	2.6	2.3	2.1
Urban fringe of large cities	2.2	2.0	1.8
Urban fringe of medium cities	3.0	2.6	2.4
Large town	2.5	2.2	2.0
Small town	4.4	3.9	3.5
Rural metro	2.7	2.4	2.2
Rural non-metro	4.8	4.2	3.8
	Title I increase as percent of required spending increase		
Total state	13.9 (93.4)	6.4 (99.0)	8.0 (100.0)
Census district type			
Large central cities	2.9 (100.0)	2.1 (100.0)	1.7 (100.0)
Medium cities	9.1 (100.0)	3.0 (100.0)	2.0 (100.0)
Urban fringe of large cities	8.7 (83.1)	5.1 (94.9)	34.9 (100.0)
Urban fringe of medium cities	15.6 (91.7)	3.5 (100.0)	2.3 (100.0)
Large town	3.1 (66.7)	6.2 (100.0)	3.6 (100.0)
Small town	10.7 (93.0)	5.6 (100.0)	3.7 (100.0)
Rural metro	7.4 (93.8)	3.8 (100.0)	2.6 (100.0)
Rural non-metro	17.2 (95.6)	7.6 (99.3)	5.3 (100.0)

(*Continued*)

Table 5   (*Continued*)

Census district type	NCLB standard in		
	2007	2009	2011
	Title I as percent of spending required to support children in poverty		
Total state	6.6	5.7	5.2
Census district type			
Large central cities	3.2	2.8	2.5
Medium cities	4.7	4.1	3.7
Urban fringe of large cities	5.0	4.4	4.0
Urban fringe of medium cities	5.8	5.1	4.6
Large town	5.3	4.6	4.2
Small town	7.0	6.1	5.5
Rural metro	5.4	4.8	4.3
Rural non-metro	7.2	6.3	5.7
	Title I change as percent of required spending increase to support children in poverty		
Total state	32.4 (96.9)	10.2 (100.0)	6.7 (100.0)
Census district type			
Large central cities	3.5 (100.0)	2.5 (100.0)	2.0 (100.0)
Medium cities	23.8 (100.0)	6.2 (100.0)	3.9 (100.0)
Urban fringe of large cities	25.4 (86.4)	11.9 (100.0)	6.5 (100.0)
Urban fringe of medium cities	36.3 (100.0)	6.9 (100.0)	4.7 (100.0)
Large town	42.0 (100.0)	9.8 (100.0)	6.2 (100.0)
Small town	22.8 (100.0)	8.4 (100.0)	5.9 (100.0)
Rural metro	22.5 (100.0)	6.6 (100.0)	4.6 (100.0)
Rural non-metro	38.6 (97.3)	11.3 (100.0)	7.6 (100.0)

Note: Calculated as simple district averages. The share of districts needing extra funds is in parentheses.

spend enough to meet the new standards, so we also indicate (in parentheses) the share of districts needing extra Title I funds.

If the federal fiscal responsibility is to fund a significant share of the spending required to meet NCLB standards, then Title I funding is inadequate in both Kansas and Missouri. Title I funds as a percent of projected spending range from 3 percent (2007) to 2.6 percent (2011) in Kansas and 4.1 percent to 3.3 percent in Missouri (first panel of Tables 4 and 5). Title I funding covers a larger share of spending in large central cities in Kansas, but still represents a small fraction of the estimated spending to meet NCLB standards.

If the increase in Title I funds since 2001 is compared to the increase in spending to move to NCLB standards in 2007, 2009, or 2011, the Title I funding shares are considerably higher (second panel). In Kansas, this share is 65.2 percent in 2007 but drops to 20.9 percent in 2011. The comparable shares in Missouri are 14 percent and 8 percent. The highest shares are for the large and small towns in Kansas, where the increase in Title I funds provides more than enough money to meet 2007 standards, on average. Even for these districts, however, the Title I funding share is below 35 percent by 2011.

An alternative way to look at federal responsibility is to focus on the compensatory education objective of Title I. The third panel compares Title I funds to the total spending needed to bring low-income students up to a given standard. The share of compensatory education costs covered by Title I funds is only about eight percent in Kansas in all three years and between five and six percent in Missouri. Increases in Title I cover a larger share of the added spending districts must make to support low-income children. As shown in the fourth panel the increase in Title I in Kansas more than covers the added costs of disadvantaged students in 2007 and 2009, but by 2011 Title I's share drops to 60.5 percent. In Missouri, with its higher standards, Title I covers 32.4 percent of these added expenses in 2007, but this percentage declines to 6.7 by 2011.

4.2. *School-District Efficiency Increases Required to Meet NCLB Standards*

If the new federal funds provided through Title I are not sufficient to bring a district up to the NCLB standards, then school officials can reach these standards either by becoming more efficient or by receiving additional revenue from the property tax or state aid. To obtain additional perspective on NCLB, we now examine the increase in efficiency that is required for school districts to reach the NCLB standards after accounting for their increased federal aid.

Recall that spending equals costs divided by efficiency. We can observe current spending, and we can forecast the spending required to meet a NCLB standard assuming efficiency does not change. Then we can calculate the percentage change in efficiency that is required to bring spending required to meet the NCLB standard down to the sum of current spending plus the increase in Title I funding.[12]

Because the Kansas NCLB standards are low, the required efficiency improvement in Kansas also is relatively low. The average district would not have to improve its efficiency at all to reach the 2007 standard in Kansas, and the required efficiency improvement is 2.7 percent to reach the 2009 target and 7.9 percent to reach the 2011 target. As discussed earlier, we find some weak evidence that, in the average district, efficiency increased about 2 percent per year between 2000 and 2004. If efficiency improvements at this rate were to continue, it would take another four years, that is, until 2008, to reach the efficiency level required for the 2011 standards. These optimistic assumptions do not bring all districts up to the standard, however. We find that 10 percent of school districts could not reach even Kansas's low 2011 standard without an increase in efficiency of 18 percent or more.

Because of Missouri's relatively high NCLB standards, efficiency in the average district would have to increase 19.4 percent to meet the 2007 standard, 36.6 percent to meet the 2009 standard, and 50.8 percent to meet the 2011 standard. Our cost model finds possible efficiency improvements in Missouri from 2000 to 2005 but they are very small, less than 1 percent per year, and are not statistically significant. Moreover, in Missouri, as in Kansas, we estimate that 25 percent of districts could not reach the 2011 standard without an efficiency boost of at least 63.7 percent, and 10 percent could not reach this standard without a boost of 80 percent or more. There is no evidence that increases of this magnitude are possible.

---

[12]Current spending, $E(S)$, equals cost to meet current performance, $C(S)$, divided by efficiency, e, which has a maximum of 1.0. Now let $C(S^*)$ be the cost required to meet a standard, S^*. Then at the current efficiency level, spending required to meet the standard is $C(S^*)/e = E(S^*)$, which we can forecast based on our cost model. Let T be the increase in Title I funding. Then we want to solve for a new efficiency level, e^*, at which $[C(S^*) - T]/e^* = E(S)$. Now $C(S^*)/e^* = [C(S^*)/e][e/e^*] = E(S^*)[e/e^*]$. So $e^* = [E(S^*)e - T]/E(S)$. We report $(e^* - e)/e$ in the text.

5. Conclusions and Policy Recommendations

With the passage of the No Child Left Behind Act, the federal government became seriously involved for the first time in regulating state accountability systems. This article uses education cost functions to estimate the spending required to support NCLB standards in Kansas and Missouri and compares this spending with the funding available through NCLB.

We find that the increase in Title I aid falls far short of the spending increases required to meet 2011 state NCLB standards. In fact, this aid covers only 20.9 percent of the required increase in spending per pupil in Kansas and only 8 percent in Missouri. We also find that the increase in Title I does not fully cover the added costs associated with helping children in poverty. Based on the 2011 state NCLB standards, the Title I increase covers 60.5 percent of these additional costs in Kansas and only 6.7 percent of these costs in Missouri. Even unprecedented improvements in school district efficiency would not close these large gaps.

Our results differ for Kansas and Missouri largely because Kansas has a much lower standard for student performance. Thus, NCLB creates an unpleasant choice for states: avoid the NCLB sanctions by setting low standards for student performance or avoid NCLB sanctions by setting high standards and significantly raising state and/or local taxes to ensure that these standards can be reached. The severity of the NCLB sanctions therefore undermines the approach many states, including Missouri, were using before NCLB, namely, to set high standards and to phase them in, using relatively weak sanctions, over a long period of time.

The impact of these incentives can be seen in Missouri, where in January 2006 the Missouri State Board of Education approved new cut-offs for the state tests that "should result in more students scoring at the 'proficient' and 'advanced' levels" (Missouri Department of Elementary and Secondary Education, MDESE, 2006). In 2005, 30 percent of students reached proficiency in reading and 25 percent in math; under the new standards these percentages are expected to rise to 44 and 43 percent, respectively.

Thus, the problem with NCLB is not that it is an under-funded mandate. A state can meet the NCLB mandates with existing Title I funds if it sets student-performance standards low enough. Instead, the problem with NCLB is that it gives states a strong incentive to dumb their standards down. This incentive undermines the main purpose of NCLB, which is "to ensure that all children have a fair, equal, and significant opportunity to obtain a *high-quality* education and reach, at a minimum, proficiency on *challenging* State academic achievement standards and state academic assessments" (NCLB, Section 1001; emphasis added). This perverse incentive could be eliminated, of course, by more federal funds, so it is accurate to say that NCLB does not provide the funding needed to meet its own objectives. Because NCLB does not actually set standards, however, we cannot measure the degree to which it is under-funded in this sense.

Any re-authorization of NCLB should remove the perverse incentive at the heart of the current legislation. States should not be rewarded, in the sense of avoiding NCLB sanctions, for setting low standards. One possibility is to calibrate state standards based on their correlation with National Assessment of Education Progress test scores, the only national tests currently available for a random sample of students in each state. More specifically, a revised NCLB could give the Secretary of Education authority to rank state standards and establish a process that would allow states to appeal their rank. States with stricter standards could then be given either more funding or lower sanctions when they fail to meet their standards.

Another possible reform in NCLB is to weaken the sanctions considerably so that no state is pushed to lower its standards. This is, of course, what NCLB already does in the short run by basing sanctions on a flexible definition of AYP. The current system only postpones the day of reckoning, however, because states are still expected to bring all their schools up to their specified standards by 2014. Shifting to a simplified version of AYP as the ultimate target would lessen the pressure for high-standard states to lower their standards.

NCLB also does not adequately recognize the high costs of educating disadvantaged students. There is some irony here because Title I is an act dedicated to "improving the academic achievement of the disadvantaged." Nevertheless, we find that the extra funds provided by NCLB would be insufficient to meet the educational needs of low-income students even if they were exclusively devoted to these students, which they are not. Moreover, the use of sub-groups increases the chance that schools serving disadvantaged students will fail (Kim and Sunderman, 2004). Although the objective of these requirements, namely, to ensure that all children are brought up to the standards, is laudable, their consequence is that schools serving disadvantaged students face some perverse incentives (Ryan, 2003) and are more likely than other schools to be sanctioned for reasons outside their control. To avoid this unfair situation, NCLB needs to increase the extent to which its funds are directed toward disadvantaged students and/or reward states that provide the additional funds that schools with disadvantaged students require.

References

Archer, Jeff. 2005. Connecticut files court challenge to NCLB. *Education Week* **25**(1): 23–27.

Baker, Bruce D. 2006. Evaluating the reliability, validity and usefulness of education cost studies. Paper prepared for the O'Leary Symposium, Chicago, IL. February 17.

Bound, John, David A. Jaeger, and Regina M. Baker. 1995. Problems with instrumental variables estimation when the correlation between the instruments and the endogenous explanatory variables is weak. *Journal of the American Statistical Association* **90**(430): 443–450.

Center on Education Policy. 2006. *From the Capital to the Classroom.* Washington DC. September.

Cullen, Julie Berry. 2003. The impact of fiscal incentives on student disability rates. *Journal of Public Economics* **87**(7/8): 1557–1589.

Davis, Michelle. 2006. Study: NCLB leads to cuts in some subjects. *Education Week* **25**(30): 5–14.

Downes, Thomas A. and Thomas F. Pogue. 1994. Adjusting school aid formulas for the higher cost of educating disadvantaged students. *National Tax Journal* **47**(1): 89–110.

Driscoll, William and Howard Fleeter. 2003. Projected cost of implementing the federal "No Child Left Behind Act" in Ohio. Report prepared for the Ohio Department of Education, December.

Duncombe, William, D. 2006. Responding to the charge of alchemy: Strategies for evaluating the reliability and validity of costing-out research. *Journal of Education Finance* **32**(2): 137–169.

Duncombe, William, D. Anna Lukemeyer, and John Yinger. 2003. Financing an adequate education: The case of New York. In William Fowler (ed.), *Developments in School Finance: 2001–02,* Washington DC: National Center for Education Statistics. [Chapter 9]

Duncombe, William, D. and John Yinger. 2000. Financing higher student performance standards: The case of New York State. *Economics of Education Review* **19**: 363–386.

Duncombe, William, D. and John Yinger. 2005a. How much more does a disadvantaged student cost? *Economics of Education Review* **24**(5): 513–532. [Chapter 7]

Duncombe, William, D. and John Yinger. 2005b. *Estimating the Cost of Meeting Student Performance Outcomes Adopted by the Kansas State Board of Education.* A study prepared for the Kansas Division of Legislative Post Audit.

Erpenbach, William J., Ellen Forte-Fast, and Abigal Potts. 2003. *Statewide Educational Accountability Under NCLB.* Washington, DC: Council of Chief State School Officers.

Governmental Accounting Office (GAO). 2003. *Characteristics of Tests will Influence Expenses; Information Sharing may Help States Realize Efficiencies.* GAO-03-389. Washington, DC.

Gronberg, Timothy J., Dennis W. Jansen, Lori L. Taylor, and Kevin Booker. 2004. *School Outcomes and School Costs: The Cost Function Approach.* College Station, TX: Texas A&M University.

Hanushek, Eric. 2005. The alchemy of "costing out" an adequate education. Paper presented at the conference *Adequate Lawsuits: Their Growing Impact on American Education.* Cambridge, MA: Harvard University. October.

Hanushek, Eric and Margaret E. Raymond. 2001. The confusing world of educational accountability. *National Tax Journal* **54**(2): 365–384.

Hendrie, Caroline. 2005. NCLB cases face hurdles in the courts. *Education Week* **24**(34): 1.

Hoff, David J. 2005. The bottom line. *Quality Counts 2000. Education Week* **24**(17): 29–36.

Hoxby, Caroline M. 2002. The cost of accountability. *NBER Working Papers*, No. 8855, Cambridge, MA.

Hoxby, Caroline M. 2005. Inadequate yearly progress: Unlocking the secrets of NCLB. *Education Next* **5**(3): 46–51.

Imazeki, Jennifer and Andrew Reschovsky. 2004a. Estimating the costs of meeting the Texas Educational accountability standards. Unpublished Manuscript.

Imazeki, Jennifer and Andrew Reschovsky. 2004b. Is No Child Left Behind an un (or under) funded federal mandate? Evidence from Texas. *National Tax Journal* **57**(3): 571–588.

Imazeki, Jennifer and Andrew Reschovsky. 2006. Does No Child Left Behind place a fiscal burden on states? Evidence from Texas. *Education Finance and Policy* **1**: 27–246.

Jacob, Brian A. and Steven D. Levitt. 2003. Rotten apples: An investigation of the prevalence and predictors of teacher cheating. *Quarterly Journal of Economics* **118**(3): 843–877.

Kim, Jimmy and Gail L. Sunderman. 2004. *Large Mandates and Limited Resources: State Response to the No Child Left Behind Act and Implications for Accountability.* (Cambridge, MA: The Civil Rights Project).

Koretz, Daniel M. 1996. Using student assessments for educational accountability. In Eric Hanushek and Dale W. Jorgenson (eds.), *Improving America's Schools: The Role of Incentives*, Washington DC: National Academy Press.

Ladd, Helen F. 2001. School-based educational accountability systems: The promise and pitfalls. *National Tax Journal* **54**(2): 385–400.

Mathis, William. 2003. No Child Left Behind: Costs and benefits. *Phi Delta Kappan* **84**(9): 679–686.

Meyer, Lori, Greg F. Orlofsky, Ronald A. Skinner, and Scott Spicer. 2002. The state of the states. *Quality Counts 2002.* Building blocks for success: state efforts in early childhood education. *Education Week* **21**(17): 68–70.

Missouri Department of Elementary and Secondary Education (MDESE). 2006. State Board of Education revises scoring standards for MAP exams. News Release. January 13.

National Center for Education Statistics (NCES). 2006. *Digest of Education Statistics, 2005.* Washington, DC: NCES.

No Child Left Behind Act. 2001. §1001, 20 U.S.C. §6301.

Office of Management and Budget. 2007. *Budget of the United States.* Washington, DC: U.S. Government Printing Office.

Olson, Lynn and Craig D. Jerald. 1998. Barriers to success. *Education Week* **17**(17): 9.

Peyser, James and Robert Costrell. 2004. Exploring the costs of accountability. *Education Next* (2): 22–29.

Reschovsky, Andrew and Jennifer Imazeki. 1998. The development of school finance formulas to guarantee provision of adequate education to low-income students. In W. J. Fowler, Jr. (ed.), *Developments in School Finance 1997: Does Money Matter?* pp. 121–148. Washington, DC: National Center for Educational Statistics.

Robelen, Erik W. 2005. Uncertain costs. *Education Week* **24**(17): 34.

Ryan, James E. 2003. The perverse incentives of the No Child Left Behind Act. *2003 Public Law and Legal Theory Research Papers*. No. 03–17.

Sack, Joetta L. 2005. Utah passes bill to trump "No Child Left Behind." *Education Week* **24**(33): 22–25.

Wooldridge, Jeffrey M. 2003. *Introductory Econometrics: A Modern Approach*. 2nd edition. Mason, OH: South-Western, Thomson Learning.

Chapter 7

How Much More Does a Disadvantaged Student Cost?[*]

William Duncombe[‡] and John Yinger[†,§]

[†]*Departments of Public Administration and*
International Affairs and of Economics,
Syracuse University, Syracuse, NY, United States
[§]*jyinger@maxwell.syr.edu*

This paper provides a guide to statistically based methods for estimating the extra costs of educating disadvantaged students, shows how these methods are related, and compares state aid programs that account for these costs in different ways. We show how pupil weights, which are included in many state aid programs, can be estimated from an education cost equation, which many scholars use to obtain an education cost index. We also devise a method to estimate pupil weights directly. Using data from New York State, we show that the distribution of state aid is similar with either statistically based pupil weights or an educational cost index. Finally, we show that large, urban school districts with a high concentration of disadvantaged students would receive far more aid (and rich suburban districts would receive far less aid) if statistically based pupil weights were used instead of the *ad hoc* weights in existing state aid programs.

1. Introduction

Both scholars and policy makers have recognized that it costs more to achieve any given level of student performance when the students are disadvantaged

---

[*]This chapter is reproduced from "How Much More Does a Disadvantaged Student Cost?" *Economics of Education Review* **24**(5), October 2005, pp. 513–532.
[‡]Deceased.

than when they are not. Nevertheless, scholars and policy makers tend to use different methods to account for these extra costs. This paper provides a guide to statistically based methods for estimating the extra costs of educating disadvantaged students, shows how these methods are related, and compares state aid programs that account for these costs in different ways.

Many scholars have addressed educational costs through the use of an education cost index, which operates much like a cost-of-living index. Specifically, an education cost index indicates the amount a district must spend relative to the average district to obtain the same performance target. Several scholars also have proposed that these cost indexes be used in state education aid formulas, and in particular, that higher-cost districts should receive more aid, all else equal.

Educational costs are also considered by many state aid programs, but cost indexes are rarely used.[1] Instead, state aid formulas give extra weight to students in high-cost categories, such as poor students or students with limited English proficiency (LEP). Because state aid is based on the number of weighted students in a district, this approach, like a cost index, results in higher aid for districts with more disadvantaged students. If the extra weight for a poor student is 20 percent, for example, then a district in which half the students are poor will receive 10 percent more aid than a district with no poor students, all else equal.

This paper is organized as follows. Section 2 provides background on the scholarly literature and the use of pupil weights in existing state aid formulas. Section 3 provides a guide to calculating pupil weights. This section shows how cost indexes and pupil weights are related, devises a new method for estimating pupil weights, and shows how pupil weights can be incorporated into an aid formula. Section 4 uses data from New York State to illustrate the consequences of various approaches to estimating pupil weights. In particular, this section shows which types of districts gain, and which types lose, when measures of expenditure need or associated state aid payments are based on pupil weights instead of on a cost index. The final section presents conclusions and policy implications.

---

[1] A state aid formula incorporating a regression-based cost index was implemented for towns (including overlapping school districts) in Massachusetts in the 1980s (Bradbury *et al.*, 1984).

2. Background

The idea that educational costs depend on student characteristics can be traced back to the famous article by Bradford, Malt, and Oates (1969), which showed that the cost of providing public services depends on the environment in which the services are delivered. Scholars who have applied this notion to education include Bradbury, Ladd, Perrault, Reschovsky, and Yinger (1984), Ratcliffe, Riddle, and Yinger (1990), Downes and Pogue (1994), Ladd and Yinger (1994), Courant, Gramlich, and Loeb (1995), Duncombe, Ruggiero, and Yinger (1996), Duncombe and Yinger (1997, 1998, 2000), Reschovsky and Imazeki (1998, 2001, 2003), Duncombe and Johnston (2004), and Imazeki and Reschovsky (2004).

Existing scholarly work on pupil weights includes Reschovsky and Imazeki (1998), Duncombe (2002), and Duncombe, Lukemeyer, and Yinger (2003). Reschovsky and Imazeki start by estimating an education cost function. Then they use the estimated parameters to predict total spending in each district. One of the variables in their cost regression is the share of poor students (as measured by the share of students eligible for a free or reduced-price lunch). Next they set this variable at a low value (the value below which it has no impact on costs) and predict total spending again. Finally, they obtain a weight for each district by finding the difference between these two predictions, which is the impact of actual poverty in the district on total spending, and dividing this difference by the number of poor students in the district. They find that in both the mean and median district the extra weight for a poor student is 1.59.

Duncombe *et al.* (2003) use a similar approach to calculate the cost of bringing a student with a given disadvantage up to the average performance in the state. This approach also results in a different weight in each school district. They estimate that the extra weight for a poor student is 1.10 in the upstate Big Three cities (Buffalo, Syracuse, and Rochester) and 0.98 in both New York City and the average suburban district. The LEP weight is 1.12 in the Big Three, 1.15 in New York City, and about 1.10 in the average suburb.

Some scholars (e.g., Guthrie & Rothstein, 1999) have criticized the cost-function approach and have proposed alternatives. One alternative that has appeared in consultants' report for several states is to ask professional educators to identify the programs necessary to reach a given performance standard in a school with many disadvantaged students and then to calculate the cost of these programs. This so-called "professional judgment" approach was recently used in Maryland, for example (Maryland Commission on Education Finance, Equity, and Excellence, 2002). In our judgment, however, a cost function makes the best use of available information and is the preferred approach.[2] For discussions of the strengths and weaknesses of various methods, see Baker, Taylor, and Vedlitz (2004) and Duncombe, Lukemeyer, and Yinger (2004).

As shown in Tables 1 and 2, many state aid programs account for the higher costs of educating disadvantaged students.[3] Table 1 indicates that the weighted-pupil approach is used to adjust the main operating aid formula for poverty in 15 states, for students with LEP in nine states, and for students with handicaps in 14 states. The legislated extra weights for students with these disadvantages vary widely across states. Among the states that adjust for poverty, 11 use weights of 0.3 or below, whereas Maryland uses a weight of 1.0 and New Hampshire's weight reaches 1.0 under some circumstances. The LEP weights vary from 0.06 to 1.2. Virtually all of these weights fall well below the values estimated by scholars. The weights for handicaps vary widely, depending on the handicap to which they apply, and no attempt is made to summarize them. Overall, this table testifies both to the intuitive appeal of the weighted-pupil approach to aid and to the need for a systematic approach to determining the weights.

A legislated pupil weight may not be used in all state aid programs, and it may be subject to various restrictions. Thus, the effective weight may differ from the legislated weight. Table 2 provides information on effective or implicit poverty weights calculated in several different ways. This table reveals wide variation in effective poverty weights across states. Alaska, Connecticut, and New Jersey, for example, provide more than twice as much aid for high-poverty districts as for low-poverty districts, whereas New Hampshire provides less aid to high-poverty districts despite a relatively high extra weight (42.6 percent) for poor pupils. Moreover, no state has an

---

[2]This does not imply, of course, that the cost-function approach is without challenges. It may be difficult to find the necessary data, for example, and, as discussed below, difficult choices must be made about the best way to specify the cost equation and the best estimating technique.

[3]The information in this table is based on legislative language in various published sources and web sites, so it may not be complete or include all the latest aid revisions. We are grateful to Yao Huang for compiling this information.

Table 1 Legislated pupil weights in selected state aid programs.

State	Pupil weight for		
	Poverty[a]	LEP[a]	Handicap[b]
Alaska			Yes
Arizona		0.06	Yes
Colorado	0.115–0.3		
Connecticut	0.25[c]	0.1	
Delaware			Yes[d]
Florida		0.201	Yes
Georgia			Yes
Idaho		[c,d]	Yes[d]
Iowa		0.19	Yes
Kansas	0.1	0.2	
Kentucky	0.15[c]		
Louisiana	0.17		
Massachusetts	0.343–0.464[c]		Yes
Maryland	1.0	1.2	
Minnesota	0.01–0.6[c]		
Mississippi	0.05		
Missouri	0.22		
New Hampshire	0.5–1.0		
New Mexico	0.0915		Yes
Oklahoma	0.25		Yes
Oregon	0.25	0.5	Yes
South Carolina			Yes
Texas	0.2[c]	0.1	Yes
West Virginia			Yes

Notes: [a]The weights in these two columns indicate the percentage by which aid for a student in the relevant category (poor or limited English proficiency (LEP)) exceeds aid for a student not in the category.
[b]Weights for students with handicaps vary widely depending on the nature of the handicap.
[c]These states also provide categorical grants for students in this category.
[d]These states adjust aid per teacher unit for weighted pupils, which is similar to standard pupil weights.

Source: Compiled by Yao Huang based on the sources cited in Huang (2004).

effective poverty weight as high as the estimated weight in the scholarly literature.[4]

---

[4]The figures in Table 2 predate the new aid program in Maryland; this new program may be an exception to this claim.

Table 2 Implicit poverty weights in state aid programs, 2001–2002.

State	Implicit poverty weights		Per pupil spending: Ratio of high poverty district to average district[c]	Per pupil state aid: Ratio of high poverty districts to average district[c]
	Estimate 1 (%)[a]	Estimate 2 (%)[b]		
Alabama	3.1	2.7	0.90	1.00
Alaska				1.97
Arizona	2.0	0.0	0.79	1.10
Arkansas	2.0	10.6	1.23	1.03
California	5.5	6.5	0.69	1.12
Colorado	25.8			1.02
Connecticut	37.1	3.6	1.01	2.04
Delaware				1.22
Florida				1.10
Georgia	1.9			1.06
Idaho				1.10
Illinois	22.3	1.9	0.34	1.20
Indiana	20.1	1.2	0.83	1.34
Iowa	2.6	2.5	1.13	0.99
Kansas	15.8			1.16
Kentucky	25.5			1.16
Louisiana	19.7			1.03
Maine				1.04
Maryland	23.5	16.9	1.16	1.69
Massachusetts	52.5			1.60
Michigan	20.3	13.0	0.98	1.13
Minnesota	35.8	27.2	1.63	1.35
Mississippi	4.9	17.2	0.80	1.01
Missouri	36.0			1.26
Montana				1.15
Nebraska	15.0			1.19
Nevada		0.1	0.00	1.52
New Hampshire	42.6			0.98
New Jersey	31.9	46.3	1.48	2.17
New Mexico	13.8	0.6	1.25	1.01
New York	19.6			1.07
North Carolina	14.6			1.09
North Dakota				1.13
Ohio	17.2	9.1	1.38	1.39
Oklahoma	32.1			1.06
Oregon	17.1			1.23
Pennsylvania		1.2	0.44	1.33
Rhode Island	25.4			1.55

(*Continued*)

Table 2   (*Continued*)

| State | Implicit poverty weights | | Per pupil spending: Ratio of high poverty district to average district[c] | Per pupil state aid: Ratio of high poverty districts to average district[c] |
	Estimate 1 (%)[a]	Estimate 2 (%)[b]		
South Carolina	16.3	11.2	0.93	1.01
South Dakota				1.26
Tennessee	2.7			1.05
Texas	27.7			1.16
Utah	4.6	7.5	1.39	1.00
Vermont	3.7			1.56
Virginia	15.1	12.1	0.99	1.27
Washington	7.7	12.6	0.77	1.12
West Virginia				1.04
Wisconsin	10.0			1.30
Wyoming	3.0			1.55

Sources: [a]Carey (2002). Poverty, funding per low-income student divided by state and local funding per student.
[b]Baker and Duncombe (2004). Compensatory aid per child (5–17 years old) in poverty divided by total spending per pupil.
[c]Baker and Duncombe (2004).

The principle of aid adjustments for student disadvantage has been endorsed by several state supreme courts (Lukemeyer, 2004). In a 1990 decision that called for a more equitable educational finance system, for example, the New Jersey State Supreme Court first required the state "to assure that poorer urban districts' educational funding is substantially equal to that of property-rich districts" and then declared that "[t]he level of funding must also be adequate to provide for the special educational needs of these poorer urban districts and address their extreme disadvantages" (Abbott v. Burke, 1990, p. 385). A similar argument appeared in a recent decision by the highest court in New York State (Campaign for Fiscal Equity v. New York, 2003).

3. How to Calculate Pupil Weights

Pupil weights are designed to indicate the extra expense associated with students in particular categories, holding student performance constant.

In principle, these weights should be related to actual experience, that is, to the extra expenses that districts must actually pay to bring disadvantaged students up to a given standard. The existing literature brings in actual experience by deriving pupil weights from the estimated parameters of a standard education cost function. This section begins by exploring various ways to use standard education cost functions to determine the added cost per disadvantaged student in a state, expressed as a share of the cost for a student with no disadvantages. An alternative approach is to specify an education cost function so that the pupil weights can be estimated directly. The second part of this section explores this approach. The third part shows how to incorporate pupil weights into a state aid formula.

3.1. *Pupil Weights Based on a Standard Education Cost Function*

Consider the following cost function, which is similar to the formulation in most of the papers cited earlier:

$$S_j = \alpha_0 T_j^{\alpha_T} Z_j^{\alpha_Z} P_j^{\alpha_P} \exp\left\{\sum_i \beta_i C_j^i\right\}, \tag{1}$$

where S_j equals spending per pupil in district j; T equals a vector of student test scores and perhaps other performance measures; Z equals other control variables, such as those designed to control for district efficiency; P equals the price of the key input, namely teachers; C_j^i equals the share of students in cost category i in district j; and α and β indicate coefficients to be estimated. In particular, β_i indicates the percentage change in spending associated with a one percentage point increase in C_j^i. By taking logarithms and adding an error term, this equation can be estimated with standard linear regression techniques. Because they are directly influenced by district actions, T and P should be treated as endogenous (see Duncombe & Yinger, 1997, 1998, 2000; Reschovsky & Imazeki, 1998).

Once equation (1) has been estimated, a standard cost index is found in two steps. The first step is to calculate the spending required in each district to reach a given performance target, called expenditure need, assuming that districts differ only in their cost characteristics. This step is accomplished by setting the variables in T at the same performance level for all districts ($\tilde{T}$); setting the variables in Z at the state average for all districts ($\bar{Z}$); setting P at the required wage level for each district ($\hat{P}$), based on exogenous factors, such as the regional wage level; and setting student characteristics in C at their actual value in each district.[5] Then with the estimated values of the coefficients, a and b, substituted for the parameters in equation (1), α and β, one obtains this expenditure need in each district, $\hat{S}_j$. In symbols,

$$\hat{S}_j = a_0 \tilde{T}^{a_T} \bar{Z}^{a_Z} \hat{P}_j^{a_P} \exp\left\{\sum_i b_i C_j^i\right\}. \tag{2}$$

The second step is to divide $\hat{S}_j$ by its value in a district with average required wages and average student characteristics, say $\hat{S}_{j*}$, which is defined as[6]

$$\hat{S}_{j*} = a_0 \tilde{T}^{a_T} \bar{Z}^{a_Z} \hat{\bar{P}}^{a_P} \exp\left\{\sum_i b_i \bar{C}^i\right\}. \tag{3}$$

Equations (2) and (3) lead to a cost index for each district, I_j. This index equals 1.0 in a district with average characteristics, is above 1.0 in relatively high-cost districts, and is below 1.0 in relatively low-cost districts. A district with a value of 1.5, for example, has educational costs that are 50 percent above those in a district with average characteristics. The formula for a cost index is

$$I_j = \frac{\hat{S}_j}{\hat{S}_{j*}} = \frac{(\hat{P}_j)^{a_P} \exp\left\{\sum_i b_i C_j^i\right\}}{(\hat{\bar{P}})^{a_P} \exp\left\{\sum_i b_i \bar{C}^i\right\}}. \tag{4}$$

Note that the T and Z terms are the same in every district, so they cancel when the expression for I_j is written out.

One complicating factor is that educational cost indexes sometimes account for economies and diseconomies of enrollment scale, as well as for teacher costs and student disadvantages. These types of adjustments are somewhat more controversial than others. There is extensive evidence, for example, that small districts have higher costs per pupil than middle-sized districts (see Andrews, Duncombe, & Yinger, 2002). This can be interpreted as a cost difference, but it can also be interpreted as a sign that the small districts have refused to consolidate with their neighbors and thereby to

---

[5] A note on notation: A "^" indicates a spending level "required" to reach a performance target under some specified set of conditions (or a wage level required to attract teachers), a "~" indicates a policy parameter, and a "‾" indicates a mean value. In a few cases, the first and last symbols both appear, indicating the mean of a predicted value.

[6] An alternative base in this type of calculation is the value of $\hat{S}_j$ in the average district. This alternative base leads to similar results, but we find it less appealing because it shifts the focus away from the average values of the student characteristics on which the weights are based.

lower their costs.[7] Similarly, there is evidence that large districts have higher costs than middle-sized districts. This difference may reflect diseconomies of district scale, but it might also reflect mismanagement that arises in some large districts but not in others. Because these issues are not our primary concern in this paper, we calculate pupil weights without considering enrollment. We include enrollment variables in our cost regressions, but we treat them as Z variables. As a result, they are simply set at the average value for all districts and have no impact on the cost indexes or pupil weights.

As shown by Reschovsky and Imazeki (1998) and Duncombe (2002), district-specific pupil weights can be calculated using reasoning similar to that behind a cost index. The first step is to calculate required spending in each district, assuming now that a district has no disadvantaged students at all, that is, that every variable in C has a value of zero. In this calculation, as in a cost-index calculation, T and Z are held constant and P is allowed to vary across districts. If district j had no disadvantaged students, in other words, its expenditure need would be

$$\hat{S}_j^0 = a_0 \tilde{T}^{a_T} \bar{Z}^{a_Z} \hat{P}_j^{a_P}. \tag{5}$$

The second step is to find the extra spending in the district because of the presence of students with disadvantage i. This can be found by comparing required spending once disadvantage i is considered with required spending when, as above, one assumes that no students have this disadvantage, or

$$\Delta \hat{S}_j^i = a_0 \tilde{T}^{a_T} \bar{Z}^{a_Z} \hat{P}_j^{a_P} \exp\{b_i C_j^i\} - a_0 \tilde{T}^{a_T} \bar{Z}^{a_Z} \hat{P}_j^{a_P} = \hat{S}_j^0 \left(\exp\{b_i C_j^i\} - 1 \right). \tag{6}$$

The district-specific weight, W_j^i, is the extra cost per student with disadvantage i in district j expressed as a share of spending on students with no disadvantages.[8] To find this weight, equation (6) must be divided by the share of students with this disadvantage and by $\hat{S}_j^0$, or

$$W_j^i = \frac{\Delta \hat{S}_j^i}{\hat{S}_j^0 C_j^i} = \frac{(\exp\{b_i C_j^i\} - 1)}{C_j^i}. \tag{7}$$

---

[7] In spite of these problems, about one-third of the states give more aid to small or sparsely settled districts. See Huang (2004)

[8] If the data made it possible to identify students with multiple disadvantages (which ours do not), then each combination of disadvantages could be treated as a separate cost category.

District-specific weights do not appear in any state aid formula. Instead, states use state-level weights for each category of student disadvantage. The district-specific weight in equation (7) can be translated into a statewide rate by averaging it across districts. The simulations in the next section examine statewide weights that are both simple averages and enrollment-weighted averages.

A key question for us to address is: How do measures of a district's expenditure need based on a cost index differ from those based on pupil weights? As discussed earlier, expenditure need equals the amount a district must spend to meet a given performance target, as defined by a set of values for the T variables. Using equation (2), we know that expenditure need in district j equals the amount a district with average costs must spend to reach these performance targets multiplied by district j's cost index, or

$$\hat{S}_j = \hat{S}_{j*} I_j = \hat{S}_{j*} \frac{(\hat{P}_j)^{a_P} \exp\left\{\sum_i b_i C_j^i\right\}}{(\bar{\hat{P}})^{a_P} \exp\left\{\sum_i b_i \bar{C}^i\right\}}$$

$$= a_0 \tilde{T}^{a_T} \bar{Z}^{a_Z} (\hat{P}_j)^{a_P} \exp\left\{\sum_i b_i C_j^i\right\}. \tag{8}$$

Because $\exp\{a\} \approx (1+a)$ when a is small, we can also write

$$\hat{S}_j \approx a_0 \tilde{T}^{a_T} \bar{Z}^{a_Z} (\hat{P}_j)^{a_P} \left(1 + \sum_i b_i C_j^i\right). \tag{9}$$

In the case of pupil weights, the base spending concept refers to spending required to meet a given performance standard assuming no disadvantaged students but actual wages, namely, $\hat{S}_j^0$ as defined by equation (5). Total expenditure need in district j equals $\hat{S}_j^0$ multiplied by the weighted number of students, and student need per pupil (written with a W superscript to emphasize the role of weighting, or $\hat{S}_j^W$) equals $\hat{S}_j^0$ multiplied by weighted pupils relative to actual pupils, or, using equation (7),

$$\hat{S}_j^W = \hat{S}_j^0 \frac{N_j\left(1 + \sum_i W_j^i C_j^i\right)}{N_j}$$

$$= a_0 \tilde{T}^{a_T} \bar{Z}^{a_Z} \hat{P}_j^{a_P} \left(1 + \sum_i W_j^i C_j^i\right)$$

$$= a_0 \tilde{T}^{a_T} \bar{Z}^{a_Z} \hat{P}_j^{a_P} \left[1 + \sum_i \left(\exp\{b_i C_j^i\} - 1\right)\right]. \tag{10}$$

Using the same approximation as before, we can also write

$$\hat{S}_j^W \approx a_0 \tilde{T}^{a_T} \bar{Z}^{a_Z} \hat{P}_j^{a_P} \left[1 + \sum_i \left(1 + b_i C_j^i - 1 \right) \right]$$

$$= a_0 \tilde{T}^{a_T} \bar{Z}^{a_Z} \hat{P}_j^{a_P} \left(1 + \sum_i b_i C_j^i \right) \tag{11}$$

which is the same as equation (9). In other words, cost indexes and the associated district-specific weights yield approximately the same measures of expenditure need for each district. In one special case, namely, when there is only one category of disadvantage, there is no need for approximation: according to equations (8) and (10), these two approaches yield exactly the same measure of expenditure need.

The accuracy of the approximation used in this derivation diminishes as the cost impact of disadvantaged students in a district increases. This cost impact equals the product of the share of students in category i, C_j^i, and the estimated impact of students in this category on costs, b_i, summed over categories of disadvantage, or $\sum_i b_i C_j^i$. Because this approximation is used to derive both equations (9) and (11), however, it is not clear how this feature of the approximation affects the difference between these two equations. Switching to state-level weights adds another type of approximation to the mix, one that hurts districts with district-specific weights above the state average. In a later section, we use data from New York to explore the nature of these approximations by identifying the types of districts that are put at a disadvantage by the use of various state-level weights instead of a cost index.

3.2. Pupil Weights Estimated Directly from an Education Cost Function

The pupil weights in the previous section are approximations because the functional form of a standard education cost function differs from the algebraic form of a student-weight calculation. One way to avoid these approximations, therefore, is to re-specify the education cost function so that it estimates the pupil weights directly.

Consider a cost function of the following form:

$$S_j = \left(e^{\gamma^0} T_j^{\gamma_T} Z_j^{\gamma_Z} P_j^{\gamma_P} \right) \left(1 + \sum_i \omega_i C_j^i \right) \tag{12}$$

where the γ's and the ω's are parameters to be estimated and, as before, T and P are treated as endogenous. This cost function can be estimated with nonlinear two-stage least-squares. The ω's are the pupil weights we are after; with this form they can be estimated directly. Let g stand for an estimate of a γ parameter and w stand for the estimate of a ω parameter. Then, drawing on our earlier notation, with a "D" superscript to indicate direct estimation, expenditure need in district j is

$$\hat{S}_j^D = \left(e^{g^0}\tilde{T}_j^{g_T}\bar{Z}_j^{g_Z}\hat{P}_j^{g_P}\right)\left(1 + \sum_i w_i C_j^i\right). \tag{13}$$

Recall the approximation noted earlier, namely, that $\exp\{a\} \approx (1+a)$ when a is small. With $a = \sum_i w_i C_j^i$, this approximation translates equation (12) into equation (1), or vice versa. Despite this algebraic connection between the two equations, however, they are substantially different in practice. Compared to equation (1), the nonlinear equation (12) requires a more complicated estimating procedure but results in a dramatic simplification in the calculation of weights and student needs.

The obvious question to ask at this point is whether equation (1) or (12) is a better specification of the cost function, that is, which one provides a better explanation for variation in school costs.[9] This is, of course, an empirical question, which we address in a later section. However, a specification test alone cannot determine which approach is best for policy purposes. If the two approaches lead to similar results, then one must weigh the benefits of a relatively simple estimating equation (equation (1)) against the benefits of a relatively simple pupil-weight calculation (equation (12)). We return to this issue in our conclusion.

3.3. *Pupil Weights in State Aid Formulas*

The most common type of state aid formula is a foundation formula, which is used to some degree in 43 states (Huang, 2004). This type of formula is designed to bring all districts up to a minimum spending level. Another type of aid formula is a so-called "guaranteed tax base" plan, which is the main aid formula in three states and which is combined with a foundation plan in 10 others. Except in the case of Missouri, which relies exclusively on a GTB

---

[9]The specifications in (1) and (12) are not the only possible ones. In fact, some scholars, such as Gyimah-Brempong and Gyapong (1991), have used a more general specification.

formula, the weights in Table 1 refer to foundation plans.[10] Following the emphasis in existing state aid programs, we focus exclusively on the role of pupil weights in a foundation formula.[11]

A foundation formula sets aid per pupil at the difference between an expenditure target, $\tilde{S}$, and the amount of money a district can raise at a standard tax rate, a rate set by state policy makers. This amount of money is the tax rate, $\tilde{t}$, multiplied by the district's tax base, V_j. To be specific,

$$A_j = \tilde{S} - \tilde{t}V_j. \tag{14}$$

A more general approach is to select an educational performance target and then to base the formula on the expenditure needed to reach this target. Suppose $\tilde{S}$ is the expenditure needed to reach the desired level of student performance *in a district with average costs*, namely $\hat{S}_{j*}$, as defined by equation (2). Then, as shown by Ladd and Yinger (1994), a cost index, I_j, can be added to yield a performance-based foundation aid program:

$$A_j = \hat{S}_{j*}I_j - \tilde{t}V_j = \hat{S}_j - \tilde{t}V_j. \tag{15}$$

With this approach, total aid to a district obviously equals aid per pupil multiplied by number of pupils.

Pupil weights are designed to replace some, but not all, of the cost index. Specifically, pupil weights do not account for differences in teacher costs or in enrollment effects across districts. (A few states, namely, Colorado, Florida, Maryland, Massachusetts, and Texas, combine pupil weights with an adjustment for teacher costs or the cost of living.)[12] To bring in pupil weights, therefore, one needs to use a spending base that reflects teacher wages but not student characteristics, namely, $\hat{S}_j^0$ as defined by equation (5).[13] Moreover,

---

[10] Texas is one of the 10 states with a first-tier foundation formula and a second-tier GTP formula. It uses pupil weights in both tiers. See Huang (2004).
[11] The widespread use of foundation plans reflects, among other things, a widespread emphasis on an adequacy objective in recent state supreme court decisions concerning education finance. See Lukemeyer (2002, 2004).
[12] This information was provided by Yao Huang.
[13] In principle, one could also include enrollment effects in this baseline spending number. Baseline spending also sets the efficiency variables at their statewide average values. A higher efficiency standard could be selected, but this would only scale the results; as explained earlier, it is not appropriate to include variation in efficiency across districts, since this variation reflects decisions by school district officials.

the number of weighted pupils is

$$N_j^W = N_j + \sum_i W^i N_j C_j^i = N_j \left(1 + \sum_i W^i C_j^i \right). \tag{16}$$

Pupil weighting applies only to the expenditure target in a foundation aid formula, not to the expected local contribution. Introducing pupil weights therefore leads to the following formula for aid per (unweighted) pupil:

$$A_j = \hat{S}_j^0 \frac{N_j^W}{N_j} - \tilde{t} V_j. \tag{17}$$

In this formula, the ratio of weighted to unweighted pupils plays the role of the student-need component of an education cost index. The wage component of $\hat{S}_j^0$ multiplied by this ratio is equivalent to a full cost index.

4. Results for New York State

To examine the implications of different approaches to estimating the cost of disadvantaged students, we now use data from New York State for the 2000–2001 school year to compare the distribution of state aid using equation (15) with the aid using equation (17) and various forms of pupil weights. As shown in Table 3, we have data for 678 school districts and have classified these districts into eight categories ranging from New York City to small rural districts upstate.[14] These districts differ substantially in terms of enrollment, wages, and the share of students with various disadvantages. This table shows, for example, that the share of students who applied for a free or reduced-price lunch, a commonly used measure of poverty, ranges from 74.9 percent in New York City to 11.2 percent in downstate suburbs. In addition, districts vary widely in their child poverty rates and in their concentrations of students with LEP or in special education. The special education variable, which provides one way to measure the share of students with disabilities, is discussed in more detail below.

The last column of Table 3 presents a student performance index, which we will use in our cost estimation. This index combines the passing rates on elementary and secondary math and reading tests. The elementary tests cover both fourth and eighth grades, and the secondary exams, called

---

[14]The major sources of data are various publications from the New York State Education Department and New York State Office of the Comptroller. Child poverty rates and population are from the 2000 Census of Population.

Table 3 Description of New York school districts, 2001.

	Number of districts	Average enrollment	Average teacher salary ($)	Percent child poverty	Percent subsidized lunch (K6)	Percent LEP[a]	Percent special education[b]	Student performance index[c]
Large cities								
New York City	1	1,069,141	39,561	34.90	74.86	12.32	7.41	103
Yonkers	1	24,847	47,237	31.31	59.72	16.42	8.52	107
Upstate big three	3	35,575	33,113	46.46	74.53	6.76	9.46	96
Small cities								
Downstate	7	5647	47,947	16.62	33.48	7.73	6.07	148
Upstate	49	4324	34,848	25.39	41.73	2.23	6.68	145
Suburbs								
Downstate	168	3387	46,082	8.80	11.22	3.20	4.85	169
Upstate	242	2450	35,004	13.24	19.39	0.32	4.44	160
Rural								
Upstate	207	1113	33,135	21.57	29.09	0.22	4.33	156
Statewide	678	1657	35,413	14.67	21.81	0.00	4.72	161

Notes: Except in column 1, statewide figures are for the median district.

[a]LEP stands for "limited English proficiency".

[b]The share of students who require placement for 60 percent or more of the school day in a special class, or require special services or programs for 60 percent or more of the school day, or require home or hospital instruction for a period of more than 60 days.

[c]Index reflects passing rates on elementary middle school and high school tests; maximum possible value is 200.

Regents exams, are given twice as much weight because students must pass them to graduate from high school.[15] The resulting index can range from 0 (no students pass any test) to 200 (all students pass every test).[16]

4.1. *Cost Indexes*

We begin by estimating standard education cost models. These models use the functional form given in equation (1), with operating spending per pupil as the dependent variable and selected performance variables and student characteristics as key explanatory variables. These regressions also account for the possibility that school officials do not deliver the selected performance variables at the lowest possible cost — that it, that their decisions may result in inefficiency. Several approaches to the issue of efficiency, each with limitations, have been proposed.[17] Following Duncombe *et al.* (2003), our

---

[15] For more information on this index, see Duncombe *et al.* (2003). This index is treated as endogenous. We used geographic proximity to identify instruments. Specifically, our list of potential instruments consists of averages, minimum and maximum values for adjacent school districts for various measures of fiscal capacity (income, school aid, and property wealth), student need (poverty, LEP, subsidized lunch, and special education), physical conditions (pupil density, population density, and enrollment), and student performance (test scores). To select instruments from this list, we used three standard rules. The instruments must (1) make conceptual sense, (2) help to explain the endogenous explanatory variables, and (3) not have a significant direct impact on the dependent variable. We also implemented an over-identification test (Woolridge, 2003) to check the exogeneity of our final set of instruments and the Bound, Jaeger, and Baker (1995) procedure to check for weak instruments. The latter procedure is not formally specified for a model like ours, so we examined various combinations of the instruments and used the set that produced the highest F-test for most endogenous variables. In most cases, the F-statistic was 5.0 or above, indicating reasonably strong instruments for that endogenous variable. When estimating equation (12) we use the same instruments selected for estimating (1).

[16] Alternative cost functions, which yield similar results, could be estimated with each passing rate entered separately or with the addition of a drop-out rate variable. See, for example, Duncombe and Yinger (1997, 1998, 2000).

[17] One alternative approach, which yields similar results, is to include in the cost model a measure of efficiency based on Data Envelopment Analysis. See Duncombe *et al.* (1996), Duncombe and Yinger (1997, 1998, 2000), and Reschovsky and Imazeki (1997, 2001, 2003). This approach identifies efficiency based on a functional form restriction instead of on the basis of assumed linkages between efficiency and certain school district characteristics. Another approach is to collect panel data and to estimate district fixed effects, which control for al time-invariant district characteristics, including efficiency (Downes and Pogue, 1994). This approach is not suitable for our purposes, because the cost impact of across-district variation in student characteristics is captured by the fixed effects and the limited remaining variation make it difficult, if not impossible, to obtain precise estimates of the b_i coefficients.

approach is to include explanatory variables that have a conceptual link to efficiency. We argue, for example, that districts with relatively loose budget constraints, as measured by their property value, income, and state aid (all on a per-pupil basis), have less incentive to be efficient in delivering any given set of student performance outcomes.

We estimate four versions of this model. These models are distinguished by (a) the variable used to measure economic disadvantage and (b) whether special education students are included. We use two different variables to measure economic disadvantage: the child poverty rate in the school district, which is provided by the Census every two years, and the number of students in grades K-6 who sign up for a free lunch or for a reduced-price lunch.[18] The latter variable fluctuates significantly from year to year, so we use a two-year average in all of our estimations.

Although these two variables are correlated, they are by no means identical.[19] As shown in Table 3, for example, the subsidized lunch variable tends to have a substantially larger value than the child poverty variable. Moreover, the two variables have different strengths and weaknesses. The Census poverty variable has the desirable feature that it cannot be manipulated by school officials, but it is not available every year, it is often excluded from data bases maintained by state education departments, and we have no evidence about its accuracy in years not covered by a decennial Census. The subsidized lunch variable has the advantages that it is available every year, is included in many state data bases, and covers a broader population than does the poverty variable. This variable has the disadvantage, however, that it reflects parental participation decisions, and perhaps even school management policies. Given these contrasting strengths and weaknesses, we do not believe that either variable dominates the other and we present results using each of them.

One final difference between the two variables arises when another measure of student disadvantage, the share of students with LEP, is added to the cost model. As shown below, this LEP variable is highly significant

---

[18]The free lunch and reduced-price lunch programs are separate, but we combine them in all our analyses. Eligibility rules and funding for these lunch programs are provided by the federal government. Subsidized lunches are also offered after sixth grade, but many eligible students do not sign up for them, so a subsidized lunch variable for non-elementary grades does not appear to be useful.

[19]For the year 2000, for example, the correlation between the share of K-6 students who sign up for a subsidized lunch and the child poverty rate is 0.773. Correlations in other years are similar.

in cost models that include the Census poverty variable. In contrast, this variable is not close to significant in models that include the subsidized lunch variable.[20] Thus, in case of New York, the subsidized lunch variable appears to capture the cost effects both of poverty and of LEP, and the LEP variable is dropped from the models in which the subsidized lunch variable appears.

The second distinction is whether the model includes a third measure of student disadvantage, namely, the share of students in a special education program. We focus on a measure of students with relatively severe disabilities, because these students have a relatively large impact on educational costs and because the identification of these students is largely insulated from district discretion.[21] To be specific, this variable indicates the share of students who require placement for 60 percent or more of the school day in a special class, or who require special services or programs for 60 percent of more of the school day, or who require home or hospital instruction for a period of more than 60 days. As we will see, this variable is highly significant when it is included in a cost regression. However, this variable does not provide a full analysis of the extra costs imposed by student disabilities. It does not include students with relatively minor disabilities, for example, and it does not recognize the wide variations in spending required for different students in the special education category. Moreover, some states prefer to treat special education with categorical grants, instead of incorporating them into basic measures of expenditure need and operating aid. As a result, we present all of our results with and without special education students in the analysis.

These cost models include several cost variables in addition to student characteristics, namely, teacher salaries (treated as endogenous)[22] and

---

[20]To be specific, the coefficient is small in magnitude, occasionally negative, and never significant at even the 40 percent confidence level.

[21]Although our data set includes a few other measures of student disability, they are not measured consistently across districts and may be manipulated by district officials.

[22]The teacher wage variable was first limited to teachers with five years or less of experience. Teacher wages for individual teachers were then regressed on teacher experience and whether the teacher had a graduate degree. The results of this regression were used to construct a predicted teacher salary for each district for a teacher with statewide average experience (among those with no more than 5 years of experience) and average probability of a graduate degree. The potential instruments for this variable are pupil density in the district, private wages in professional occupations, unemployment rate, concentration of area teachers in the district, and the average (maximum and minimum) salaries of adjacent districts. The final list was selected using the rules presented in an earlier footnote.

student enrollment categories. The omitted enrollment category is districts
with enrollment below 1000 students. As explained earlier, we do not include
enrollment effects in our analyses of education costs, expenditure need, or
state aid.

Selected parameter estimates from the cost models are presented in
Table 4. (Full results for two of these cost models are presented in
Appendix A.[23]) The performance index is highly significant in all cases,
and the teacher wage variable has an elasticity close to unity. The student
characteristics also have large, statistically significant impacts on costs. A
school district's costs increase with the share of students in poverty (whether
measured by Census poverty or subsidized lunches), with LEP, or with a
severe handicap. As noted earlier, the LEP variable is not close to significant
in models that use the subsidized lunch variable so it has been dropped from
these models.

The second panel of Table 4 presents results for equation (12), which
provides direct estimates of the pupil weights. This equation also performs
well, and the results in this panel are similar to those in the first panel. We
conducted specification tests to determine whether equation (1) (the first
two panels) or equation (12) (the last panel) provides a better fit for any
given column.[24] We find that neither one of these models can be rejected in
favor of the other; that is, there is no statistical basis for selecting one of
them. This choice must be made on other grounds.

We then use the cost models in Table 4 to calculate cost indexes, using the
approach presented earlier. Our cost indexes reflect teacher wage costs (based
on exogenous factors only) and student characteristics. Not surprisingly, the
resulting cost indexes vary widely by district category. The first panel of
Table 5 presents cost indexes based on the Census poverty and LEP variables.
As shown in Table 5, our first cost index ranges from about 94 in upstate

---

[23]The two regressions in this Appendix A table, along with comparable regressions for
other models, which are not presented, indicate that the performance index always has
the expected positive impact on costs and is statistically significant. The three efficiency
variables also have the expected signs and are significant in most cases, and all districts
in all enrollment classes except the largest have significantly lower costs per pupil than
districts in the smallest enrollment class.

[24]We use the specification tests in Davidson and MacKinnon (2004, Chapter 15) for non-
nested nonlinear regression models. Intuitively, these tests set up a regression that combines
an initial and an alternative specification to determine whether the alternative adds any
explanatory power.

Table 4 Estimated performance and cost coefficients.

	Without special education		With special education	
	Census poverty	Subsidized lunch	Census poverty	Subsidized lunch
Standard cost models[a]				
Performance index	0.0073	0.0105	0.0079	0.0140
	(2.87)	(3.12)	(3.26)	(3.2)
Average teacher salary[b]	1.0006	1.4030	0.9392	1.3541
	(8.06)	(15.07)	(8.82)	(13.87)
Percent child poverty (2000)[c]	1.3071		1.1424	
	(4.06)		(4.17)	
Two-year average LEP[c]	0.9883		0.9908	
	(2.09)		(2.46)	
K6 subsidized lunch rate[c]		0.9819		1.1258
		(3.78)		(3.68)
Special education students[c,d]			1.9547	1.7762
			(3.34)	(2.63)
Direct estimate of pupil weights[e]				
Performance index	0.0075	0.0117	0.0079	0.0142
	(2.85)	(3.00)	(3.32)	(3.07)
Average teacher salary[b]	1.0045	1.5639	0.9520	1.5519
	(7.93)	(9.69)	(9.13)	(8.11)
Percent child poverty (2000)[c]	1.6672		1.5915	
	(3.21)		(3.11)	
Two-year average LEP[c]	1.3078		1.4236	
	(1.81)		(2.07)	
K6 subsidized lunch rate[c]		1.6896		2.1452
		(2.36)		(1.96)
Special education students[c,d]			2.6440	3.0157
			(2.69)	(1.75)

Notes: [a]Estimated with linear two-stage least-squares regression, with the student performance and teacher salaries treated as endogenous. Operating spending per pupil is the dependent variable; *t*-statistics are in parentheses. Full results for the first two columns of Panel 1 are in Appendix A.
[b]For fulltime teachers with 1–5 years of experience. Expressed as a natural logarithm.
[c]Variables expressed as percentages. Coefficients are similar to elasticities.
[d]The share of students who require placement for 60 percent or more of the school day in a special class, or require special services or programs for 60 percent or more of the school day, or require home or hospital instruction for a period of more than 60 days.
[e]Estimated with nonlinear two-stage least-squares regression. Other features are the same as in note a.

Table 5   Cost index results.[a]

	Standard cost function		Direct weight estimation	
	Without special education	With special education	Without special education	With special education
Using Census poverty and LEP				
Large cities				
New York City	170.2	172.0	165.4	169.9
Yonkers	159.2	166.3	155.9	164.3
Upstate big three	135.5	143.6	131.0	141.8
Small cities				
Downstate	140.3	141.7	141.1	140.0
Upstate	110.8	113.9	110.6	112.6
Suburbs				
Downstate	114.8	115.1	114.7	113.7
Upstate	93.8	93.9	93.7	92.7
Rural				
Upstate	93.6	93.0	93.8	91.8
Using percent of students receiving subsidized lunch				
Large cities				
New York City	195.7	233.9	207.6	222.3
Yonkers	157.5	199.1	176.1	194.9
Upstate big three	142.8	181.7	148.4	160.0
Small cities				
Downstate	146.0	165.8	165.1	173.5
Upstate	108.7	130.3	121.1	128.4
Suburbs				
Downstate	108.8	111.9	111.9	111.8
Upstate	86.7	93.2	94.0	93.7
Rural				
Upstate	84.4	96.0	94.8	96.0

Note: [a]These indexes incorporate cost adjustments for teacher salaries and student needs, but not for enrollment. A district with statewide average characteristics has an index value of 100.

suburbs and rural districts to 170.2 in New York City. This index also has relatively high values in Yonkers, the Big Three, and downstate small cities, and intermediate values in downstate suburbs and upstate small cities. The other cost indexes in the first panel exhibit similar patterns, with slightly more variation across types of district when the special education variable is included.

The second panel of Table 5 presents cost indexes based on the share of students in grades K-6 who applied for a free or reduced-price lunch. The cost indexes in this panel exhibit a larger variance than those in the first panel; the range in the first column, for example, is from 84.4 in the upstate rural districts to 195.7 in New York City. Moreover, the index for New York City exceeds 200 if special education students are included or if the pupil weights are estimated directly.

4.2. *Pupil Weights*

Our next step is to calculate statewide pupil weights and to extract the pupil weights estimated using equation (12). The results are in Table 6. All the weights in this table are above 1.0, indicating that the cost of educating a student with any one of the three disadvantages we observe is more than twice as high as the cost of educating a student with none of these disadvantages. These weights are therefore higher than the weights used by any state except Maryland (see Tables 1 and 2). Moreover, the weights for special education students are all above 1.8.

In every case, the pupil weight goes up as one moves from column 1 to column 2 or from column 2 to column 3. In other words, enrollment-weighted weights are larger than weights for the average district, and directly estimated weights are larger than the weights calculated from a standard education cost function. In addition, the poverty weights in the first and third models, which are based on the Census child poverty variable, decline by a small amount when students requiring special education are added to the analysis, whereas the LEP weight increases slightly when this change is made. Overall, this poverty weight ranges from 1.22 to 1.67, the LEP weight ranges from 1.01 to 1.42, and the special education weight varies from 2.05 to 2.64.

Table 6 also presents estimated weights using the number of students applying for a subsidized school lunch. Without either the special education variable or a direct estimating procedure, the extra weight for an economically disadvantaged student is higher with the child poverty variable than with the subsidized lunch variable. If the pupil weights are estimated directly or if the special education variable is included in the estimation, the weight based on subsidized lunch is larger, sometimes considerably larger, than the weight based on Census poverty.

Table 6 Estimated pupil weights.

	Simple average	Enrollment-weighted average	Directly estimated
Using Census poverty and LEP			
Without special education			
Child poverty	1.415	1.491	1.667
LEP	1.007	1.030	1.308
With special education			
Child poverty	1.224	1.281	1.592
LEP	1.009	1.033	1.424
Special education	2.049	2.081	2.644
Using share of students signed up for *subsidized lunch*			
Without special education			
K6 free and reduced price lunch share (2-year average)	1.108	1.294	1.690
With special education			
K6 free and reduced price lunch share (2-year average)	1.361	1.552	2.145
Special education	1.853	1.880	3.016

4.3. *Expenditure Need*

Tables 7 and 8 compare expenditure-need calculations using various approaches to the cost of disadvantaged students. Table 7 is based on the Census child poverty variable; Table 8 uses the subsidized lunch variable. The baseline in all cases is expenditure need with a full cost index, which we regard as the most direct approach with the clearest conceptual foundation. Our objective is to determine how much expenditure need diverges from this baseline when pupil weights are used. As explained earlier, pupil weights approximate a cost-index approach, so our objective is equivalent to calculating which categories of districts are placed at a disadvantage by this type of approximation. All our calculations include an adjustment for teacher wages.

The first row in each panel of Tables 7 and 8 compares aggregate expenditure need using the weights identified in each column with aggregate expenditure need using a standard cost index. A value below 1 indicates that aggregate expenditure need falls below the baseline value and a value above 1 indicates that aggregate expenditure need is higher with those weights than with the baseline cost index.

Table 7   Estimated expenditure need with pupil weights relative to baseline, using Census child poverty variable.

Regions	No student needs adjustment	Pupil weights (simple average)	Pupil weights (enrollment-weighted average)	Poverty and LEP weights = 1 special education weight = 2[a]	Directly estimated pupil weights
Without special education					
Ratio of total cost with this adjustment to spending with full cost index	0.713	0.956	0.967	0.898	1.004
Large cities					
New York City	0.592	0.923	0.939	0.847	0.991
Yonkers	0.611	0.931	0.945	0.866	1.000
Upstate big three	0.583	0.921	0.938	0.833	0.986
Small cities					
Downstate	0.764	0.980	0.990	0.937	1.027
Upstate	0.734	0.973	0.985	0.909	1.018
Suburbs					
Downstate	0.880	0.995	1.000	0.970	1.019
Upstate	0.899	1.001	1.006	0.972	1.019
Rural					
Upstate	0.814	0.992	1.002	0.941	1.024
With special education					
Ratio of total cost with this adjustment to spending with full cost index	0.650	0.930	0.940	0.900	1.019
Large cities					
New York City	0.539	0.890	0.903	0.851	1.003
Yonkers	0.539	0.889	0.901	0.856	1.003
Upstate big three	0.514	0.876	0.889	0.832	0.988
Small cities					
Downstate	0.687	0.955	0.963	0.931	1.041
Upstate	0.662	0.945	0.955	0.912	1.031
Suburbs					
Downstate	0.796	0.980	0.985	0.966	1.038
Upstate	0.830	0.991	0.996	0.975	1.039
Rural					
Upstate	0.761	0.979	0.986	0.951	1.044

Note: [a]Special education weight of 2 only applies in the model with special education students (lower panel).

Table 8 Estimated expenditure need with pupil weights relative to baseline, using subsidized lunch variable.

	No student needs adjustment	Pupil weights (simple average)	Pupil weights (enrollment-weighted average)	Poverty and LEP weights = 1 special education weight = 2[a]	Directly estimated pupil weights
Without special education					
Ratio of total need with this adjustment to total need with full cost index	0.580	0.922	0.962	0.914	1.079
Large cities					
New York City	0.453	0.875	0.926	0.874	1.070
Yonkers	0.509	0.914	0.962	0.942	1.100
Upstate big three	0.437	0.862	0.913	0.835	0.058
Small cities					
Downstate	0.635	0.966	1.006	0.977	1.119
Upstate	0.588	0.947	0.990	0.916	1.113
Suburbs					
Downstate	0.813	0.986	1.007	0.992	1.066
Upstate	0.804	1.004	1.028	0.981	1.096
Rural					
Upstate	0.687	0.985	1.020	0.947	1.124
With special education					
Ratio of total need with this adjustment to total need with full cost index	0.470	0.852	0.899	0.802	1.075
Large cities					
New York City	0.353	0.790	0.845	0.734	1.044
Yonkers	0.396	0.830	0.883	0.801	1.083
Upstate big three	0.327	0.758	0.811	0.686	1.009
Small cities					
Downstate	0.525	0.911	0.957	0.877	1.136
Upstate	0.476	0.882	0.931	0.810	1.118
Suburbs					
Downstate	0.699	0.951	0.978	0.935	1.100
Upstate	0.714	0.985	1.016	0.938	1.145
Rural					
Upstate	0.595	0.952	0.996	0.877	1.162

Note: [a]Special education weight of 2 only applies in the model with special education students (lower panel).

The first column in Table 7 shows how much expenditure need diverges from the baseline when student characteristics are not accounted for at all. In the first panel, without special education, this approach lowers aggregate expenditure need substantially, namely, by almost 30 percent, compared to the baseline and places large cities at a significant disadvantage. To be specific, the expenditure-need numbers for New York City, Yonkers, and the Big Three fall about 40 percent below the baseline. In contrast, this approach leads to expenditure needs that are only about 10 percent below the baseline in suburbs, both upstate and downstate.

The introduction of pupil weights brings the expenditure-need calculations much closer to the baseline for all types of districts. As shown in the second and third columns of the first panel in Table 7, expenditure need falls no more than 8 percent below the baseline for big cities, and no more than 1 percent below the baseline for suburbs (on average), when estimated statewide pupil weights are used. Because the enrollment-weighted average weights tend to be larger than the simple average weights, the use of an enrollment-weighted average boosts expenditure need and narrows the divergence from the baseline. Indeed, the results in the third column of Table 7 reveal almost no divergence from the baseline outside the large cities. The divergence in the large cities is about 6 percent.

One simple approximation to estimated weights that is similar to the program passed in Maryland is to use a weight of 1.0 for both poverty and LEP. The fourth column of the first panel in Table 7 indicates that this approach provides a reasonable approximation to estimated weights in the suburbs, where expenditure need is about 3 percent below the baseline, but only a rough approximation in the big cities, where expenditure need falls about 15 percent below the baseline. Finally, as shown in the last column of this panel, a calculation using weights that are directly estimated comes very close to matching the results of a cost-index calculation. Indeed, with this approach, New York City and the Big Three are only 1 percent below the baseline and no group of districts falls above or below the baseline by as much as 3 percent. This result is not surprising; as shown earlier, cost indexes and directly estimated pupil weights are approximately the same thing.

The second panel of Table 7 provides comparable results based on a cost model with special education students included. The results from this model are similar to those in the first panel, although the first two models (with no weights and with simple average weights) and the last model (with directly estimated weights) diverge from the baseline somewhat more than the comparable models in the first panel. With enrollment-weighted weights, for example, the big cities now fall about 10 percent below the baseline.

Table 8 presents results from an alternative pair of models that use the subsidized lunch variable instead of the child poverty and LEP variables in both the baseline cost-index approach and in all the calculations with pupil weights. This table reveals that leaving out weights altogether results in an even larger divergence from the baseline with the subsidized lunch variable than with the Census poverty variable. Results in the other columns are similar to the comparable ones in Table 7, particularly those based on directly estimated pupil weights. Recall that with a single cost variable, as in the first panel of Table 8, a district-specific weight is identical to a cost index. Hence, the only source of deviations from the baseline in the second and third columns of this panel is the averaging procedure. The results in these two columns therefore demonstrate that moving from district-specific weights to statewide weights is unfair to high-cost districts, particularly large cities, and that an enrollment-weighted average is preferable to a simple average.

One contrast between Tables 7 and 8 can be found in the fourth column of the panel with special education. In this case, the use of rounded weights (1.0 for subsidized lunch, 1.0 for LEP, and 2.0 for special education) leads to a much larger underestimate of expenditure need, particularly in the big cities, in Table 8 than in Table 7. This understatement is implicitly predicted by the relevant directly estimated weights in Table 6, which are 2.1 for subsidized lunch and 3.0 for special education.

4.4. *Foundation Aid*

As explained earlier, expenditure-need calculations feed into foundation aid formulas. Thus, baseline state aid is the aid a district would receive with a foundation aid formula that incorporates a full cost index. Our simulations define a baseline aid program by setting the student performance index at 160, which is the current state average. Tables 9 and 10 show how switching to pupil weights alters state aid for each category of district compared to this baseline. To make the columns comparable, we hold the total budget constant (that is, equal to the baseline amount) in all cases by raising or lowering the foundation level.[25] Results for a baseline aid program defined

---

[25]These simulations set the required local property tax rate, $\bar{t}$, at 1.5 percent, which is lower than the rate in most districts. Alternative tables that hold the foundation level constant and allow the state aid budget to change are available from the authors upon request, as are tables with a performance standard of 140 instead of 160.

Table 9   State aid relative to baseline for a given state aid budget using Census child poverty rate and LEP rate.

	No student needs adjustment	Pupil weights (simple average)	Pupil weights (enrollment- weighted average)	Poverty and LEP weights = 1 special education weight = 2[a]	Directly estimated pupil weights
Without special education					
Large cities					
New York City	0.780	0.957	0.963	0.928	0.983
Yonkers	0.800	0.965	0.969	0.952	0.994
Upstate Big Three	0.788	0.959	0.965	0.917	0.979
Small cities					
Downstate	1.136	1.050	1.046	1.079	1.046
Upstate	1.049	1.028	1.028	1.021	1.019
Suburbs					
Downstate	1.579	1.096	1.079	1.190	1.035
Upstate	1.459	1.084	1.071	1.146	1.026
Rural					
Upstate	1.230	1.062	1.058	1.078	1.031
With special education					
Large cities					
New York City	0.781	0.949	0.952	0.934	0.981
Yonkers	0.767	0.944	0.946	0.937	0.981
Upstate Big Three	0.761	0.937	0.940	0.916	0.966
Small cities					
Downstate	1.099	1.052	1.048	1.065	1.045
Upstate	1.034	1.027	1.026	1.023	1.018
Suburbs					
Downstate	1.527	1.121	1.108	1.165	1.045
Upstate	1.490	1.120	1.109	1.151	1.037
Rural					
Upstate	1.280	1.089	1.083	1.096	1.040

Notes: Performance standard is set at an index value of 160; required local tax rate is set at 1.5 percent.
[a]Special education weight of 2 only applies in the model with special education students (lower panel).

by a student performance index of 140 are very similar to those in Tables 9 and 10.

As in Tables 7 and 8, the first column of these two tables indicates the impact of ignoring student characteristics. In Table 9, which examines aid

Table 10   State aid relative to baseline for a given state aid budget using share of students signed up for subsidized lunch.

	No student needs adjustment	Pupil weights (simple average)	Pupil weights (enrollment-weighted average)	Poverty and LEP weights = 1 special education weight = 2[a]	Directly estimated pupil weights
Without special education					
Large cities					
New York City	0.740	0.937	0.950	0.942	0.980
Yonkers	0.846	0.988	0.996	1.039	1.017
Upstate Big Three	0.727	0.925	0.938	0.896	0.969
Small cities					
Downstate	1.186	1.078	1.072	1.109	1.058
Upstate	0.039	1.038	1.036	0.999	1.032
Suburbs					
Downstate	1.972	1.145	1.092	1.170	0.976
Upstate	1.699	1.153	1.113	1.121	1.014
Rural					
Upstate	1.312	1.106	1.090	1.050	1.052
With special education					
Large cities					
New York City	0.707	0.918	0.935	0.905	0.965
Yonkers	0.803	0.972	0.985	1.007	1.009
Upstate Big Three	0.662	0.880	0.896	0.842	0.930
Small cities					
Downstate	1.195	1.112	1.111	1.150	1.097
Upstate	1.032	1.053	1.056	1.022	1.053
Suburbs					
Downstate	2.067	1.225	1.174	1.326	1.055
Upstate	1.927	1.281	1.237	1.306	1.112
Rural					
Upstate	1.430	1.190	1.178	1.155	1.124

Notes: Performance standard is set at an index value of 160; required local tax rate is set at 1.5 percent.

[a]Special education weight of 2 only applies in the model with special education students (lower panel).

programs based on the Census poverty and LEP variables, this step would cut the aid of the big-city districts by 20 percent or more (compared to the baseline) and would greatly boost the aid of all other categories of districts. Indeed, both the upstate and downstate suburbs would receive at least 46 percent more aid, on average, with this approach than with the baseline approach.[26]

The next four columns show that introducing pupil weights would bring all categories of districts much closer to their baseline aid. Indeed, regardless of which pupil weights are used, the big cities would all be within 8 percent of their baseline aid. In all cases, both the upstate and the downstate suburbs receive more aid with pupil weights than with the baseline cost index. In columns 2–4, the aid in these districts is between 6 and 20 percent above the baseline. Not surprisingly, the divergence from the baseline is smallest with directly estimated weights (the last column). Indeed, in this case, aid to large cities and suburbs is always within 4.5 percent of the baseline amount.

Note that the use of either averaged or rounded weights is less disadvantageous to large cities in Table 9 than in Table 7. This result reflects the fact that Table 9 holds the state aid budget constant and thereby, in effect, eliminates the absolute decline in expenditure need in the earlier table. Finally, a comparison of the two panels of Table 9 indicates that deviations from baseline aid are somewhat larger when special education is included in the analysis. However, the difference between a result in the second panel and the comparable result in the first panel is rarely above 2 percentage points.

As shown in Table 10, the patterns across districts are similar when the subsidized lunch variable is used instead of the Census poverty and LEP variables. In most cases, the divergence from baseline is somewhat larger in Table 10 than for the comparable result in Table 9, particularly when special education is included. With rounded weights and special education, for example, the Big Three fall 8 percentage points below the baseline when child poverty is used but 16 points below the baseline with subsidized lunch. Most of the other differences are considerably smaller than this.

5. Conclusions and Policy Implications

There is widespread agreement among scholars, policy makers, and state courts that school districts with relatively high concentrations of

---

[26]One implication of these findings is that moving from an aid program without pupil weights to an equal-budget aid program based on a cost index or on statistically based pupil weights would result in a dramatic redistribution of aid from suburbs to large cities. If a state has a hold-harmless provision, that is, a provision to ensure that no district experiences a drop in aid, aid to large cities cannot be raised to the level specified by a cost-adjusted foundation aid program without a large increase in the state aid budget.

disadvantaged students should receive relatively more state aid per pupil, all else equal. In the academic literature, the state-of-the-art approach is to estimate an education cost function that includes measures of student disadvantage, to calculate an education cost index on the basis of this estimation, and then to introduce this education cost index into a foundation aid formula. Although a few state aid formulas contain elements of the cost-index approach, most state aid formulas adjust for the presence of disadvantaged students using pupil weights. Pupil weights appear to be more appealing to policy makers than the more abstract notion of an education cost index. The key problem is that, in almost every case, the weights that appear in state aid formulas are determined on an *ad hoc* basis and are far below the weights estimated by scholars.

We show that a state aid formula using pupil weights can be thought of as an approximation for a state aid formula using a cost index. The closeness of this approximation cannot be determined *a priori*, but it can readily be calculated on the basis of an estimated education cost function. We show that a state aid formula combining pupil weights and teacher wage cost adjustments derived from a standard cost function distributes aid in a way that is approximately the same as an aid formula based on a cost index. For the large, urban school districts where most disadvantaged students are concentrated, aid based on statistically based pupil weights provides a reasonable approximation for aid based on the preferred cost-index approach. These two approaches differ somewhat more in their treatment of suburban and rural school districts, which receive almost 20 percent more aid with some types of weights than with a cost index. Finally, switching to a nonlinear cost function that estimates pupil weights directly yields an aid formula that closely approximates the baseline approach in almost every case. Indeed, with directly estimated weights, aid to big cities never falls more than 4 percent below baseline aid (and aid to suburban districts falls within 5 percent of the baseline), unless special education is included in the formula and subsidized lunch is the measure of poverty.

The pupil weights we estimate are much larger than the weights that appear in any state aid formula except for Maryland's. In a typical aid formula, the extra weight for a pupil from a poor family or with LEP is about 25 percent. We estimate that these extra weights should be between 111 and 215 percent. The use of pupil weights obviously results in a much poorer approximation of our preferred aid formula when these lower weights are used. At the extreme, defined by extra weights of zero, the aid received by large urban districts falls at least 20 percent below the baseline level, and the aid received by suburban districts may exceed the baseline by over

100 percent. The low weights used in most state aid programs yield results not too different from this extreme case. The key problem, therefore, is not the use of pupil weights per se; it is the use of pupil weights that are far below the levels supported by the evidence.

We estimate similar weights for the Census poverty and subsidized lunch variables. We also conclude that in New York the LEP variable need not be included in an aid formula based on the subsidized lunch variable, at least not when the weight on the subsidized lunch variable is high enough, but find that rounded weights of 1.0 for both subsidized lunch and LEP provide a reasonable approximation to a cost-index approach. We also estimate an extra weight of at least 185 percent for a student in special education, but this weight obviously is linked to our special education variable and may not apply to the special education variables that appear in state aid formulas.

Overall, public officials who design state aid formulas face two key choices regarding disadvantaged students.[27] The first choice is whether to account for the extra cost of educating these students using a cost index or pupil weights. Judging from the choices states have made so far, the use of pupil weights appears to be a more appealing approach, and we show that, for most districts, it can result in aid amounts that closely approximate the aid amounts from a formula based on a cost index, which is the approach many scholars prefer.

The second choice is how to select pupil weights. The *ad hoc* process used in most states is not up to the task. Indeed, the weights used by most states are far below the weights estimated in this paper and by other scholars. These low weights result in aid payments that support far lower levels of student performance in school districts with more disadvantaged students than in other school districts. This outcome violates the key objective of a foundation aid formula, namely, to bring all districts up to the same minimal performance standard. Finally, we find that any pupil weights based on an estimated cost function provide a reasonable approximation to the use of a full education cost index, but that an even better approximation can be obtained using pupil weights estimated directly from a nonlinear cost function. We find no statistical basis for preferring a standard cost function to this nonlinear version, so the choice of method depends on whether policy makers prefer the complexity of the weight calculation with a standard cost function to the complexity of a nonlinear estimating procedure.

---

[27] Another key choice, which is not examined in this paper, is whether to use a teacher wage index. Even with accurate pupil weights, an aid formula would not be fair to high-wage locations unless in it included a wage index or a cost-of-living index. Only about a dozen states have this type of index now (Huang, 2004).

A state aid program is not consistent with student performance objectives
unless it accounts for the higher cost of reaching a performance target in
districts with a relatively large share of disadvantaged students. The use
of state aid formulas with extra weight for disadvantaged students is a
reasonable approach to this problem, but the fairness of this approach can
be greatly enhanced through the use of statistically based pupil weights.

Acknowledgments

The authors are grateful to the Rockefeller Foundation for financial support.

Appendix A. Results of Education Cost Models

Estimated with linear two-stage least-squares regression, with student
performance and teacher salaries treated as endogenous; operating spending
per pupil is the dependent variable

Variables	With Census poverty		With subsidized lunch	
	Coefficient	t-statistic	Coefficient	t-statistic
Constant	−2.6253	−2.53	−7.4910	−5.47
Performance index	0.0073	2.87	0.0105	3.12
Efficiency variables[a]				
Full value	0.0000	9.31	0.0000	10.30
Aid	0.8583	3.05	0.6872	2.39
Income	0.0000	1.55	0.0000	−0.70
Average teacher salary[b]	1.0006	8.06	1.4030	15.07
Percent child poverty (2000)[c]	1.3071	4.06		
Two-year average LEP[c]	0.9883	2.09		
K6 subsidized lunch rate[c]			0.9819	3.78
Enrollment classes[d]				
1000–2000 students	−0.0823	−3.31	−0.0859	−3.28
2000–3000 students	−0.0896	−3.00	−0.0957	−3.15
3000–5000 students	−0.1067	−2.87	−0.1218	−3.35
5000–7000 students	−0.0915	−2.27	−0.1110	−2.73
7000–15,000 students	−0.1019	−2.12	−0.1208	−2.53
Over 15,000 students	0.0236	0.22	0.0308	0.27
Adjusted R-square[d]	0.485		0.457	

Notes: [a]Calculated as the difference between district value and the average in peer group
[b]For fulltime teachers with 1–5 years of experience. Expressed as a natural logarithm.
[c]All variables expressed as a percentage. Coefficients are similar to elasticities.
[d]The base enrollment is 0–1000 students. The coefficients can be interpreted as the percent
change in costs from being in this enrollment class compared to the base enrollment class.

References

Abbott v. Burke 1990. 119 N.J. 287, 575 A.2d 359 (New Jersey 1990) (*Abbott II*).

Andrews, M., Duncombe, W. D., and Yinger, J. 2002. Revisiting economies of size in education: are we any closer to a consensus? *Economics of Education Review* **21**(3), 245–262.

Baker, B. and Duncombe, W. 2004. Balancing district needs and student needs: The role of economies of scale adjustments and pupil need weights in school finance formulas. *Journal of Education Finance* **29**, 195–222.

Baker, B. D., Taylor, L., and Vedlitz, A. 2004. *Measuring Educational Adequacy in Public Schools*. Report prepared for the Texas School Finance Project, March. Available at: http://www.capitol.state.tx.us/psf/1_22_04/Measuring%20Educational%20Adequacy.pdf; Last accessed 7/21/04.

Bound, J., Jaeger, D. A., and Baker, R. 1995. Problems with instrumental variables estimation when the correlation between the instruments and the endogenous explanatory variables is weak. *Journal of the American Statistical Association* **90**, 443–450.

Bradbury, K. L., Ladd, H. F., Perrault, M., Reschovsky, A., and Yinger, J. 1984. State aid to offset fiscal disparities across communities. *National Tax Journal* **37**, 151–170.

Bradford, D., Malt, R. A., and Oates, W. E. 1969. The rising cost of local public services: some evidence and reflections. *National Tax Journal* **22**(2), 185–202.

Campaign for Fiscal Equity (CFE), v. The State of New York. 2003. (Not yet filed), June 26.

Carey, K. 2002. *State Poverty Based Education Funding: A Survey of Current Programs and Options for Improvement*. Washington, DC: Center on Budget and Policy Priorities.

Courant, P. N., Gramlich, E., and Loeb, S. 1995. A report on school finance and educational reform in Michigan. In Downes, T. A. and Tests, W. A. (eds.), *Midwest Approaches to School Reform*, pp. 5–33. Chicago: Federal Reserve Bank of Chicago.

Davidson, R. and MacKinnon, J. G. 2004. *Econometric Theory and Methods*. New York: Oxford University Press.

Downes, T. A. and Pogue, T. F. 1994. Adjusting school aid formulas for the higher cost of educating disadvantaged students. *National Tax Journal* **67**, 89–110.

Duncombe, W. D. 2002. *Estimating the Cost of an Adequate Education in New York*. Center for Policy Research Working Paper No. 44, The Maxwell School, Syracuse University, Syracuse, NY, February.

Duncombe, W. D. and Johnston, J. M. 2004. The impacts of school finance reform in Kansas: equity is in the eye of the beholder. In Yinger, J. (ed.), *Helping Children Left Behind: State Aid and the Pursuit of Educational Equity*, pp. 147–193. Cambridge, MA: MIT Press.

Duncombe, W. D., Lukemeyer, A., and Yinger, J. 2003. Financing an adequate education: The case of New York. In Fowler, W. J., Jr. (ed.), *Developments in School Finance: 2001–2002*. Washington, DC: US Department of Education, National Center for Education Statistics June. [Chapter 9]

Duncombe, W. D., Lukemeyer, A., and Yinger, J. 2004. *Education Finance Reform in New York: Calculating the Cost of a 'Sound Basic Education in New York City*. Center for Policy Research Policy Brief 28/2004, Syracuse University, Syracuse, NY. Available at: http://cpr.maxwell.syr.edu/CPR_Policy_Brief_Series.aspx; Last accessed 10/14/2019.

Duncombe, W. D., Ruggiero, J., and Yinger, J. 1996. Alternative approaches to measuring the cost of education. In Ladd, H. F. (ed.), *Holding Schools Accountable: Performance-based Reform in Education*, pp. 327–356. Washington, DC: The Brookings Institution.

Duncombe, W. D. and Yinger, J. 1997. Why is it so hard to help central city schools? *Journal of Policy Analysis and Management* **16**(1), 85–113.

Duncombe, W. D. and Yinger, J. 1998. School finance reform: aid formulas and equity objectives. *National Tax Journal* **51**(2), 239–262. [Chapter 12]

Duncombe, W. D. and Yinger, J. 2000. Financing higher student performance standards: the case of New York State? *Economics of Education Review* **19**, 363–386.

Guthrie, J. W. and Rothstein, R. 1999. Enabling 'adequacy' to achieve reality: translating adequacy into state school finance distribution arrangements. In Ladd, H. F., Chalk, R. & Hansen, J. (eds.), *Equity and Adequacy in Education Finance: Issues and Perspectives*, pp. 209–259. Washington, DC: National Academy Press.

Gyimah-Brempong, K. and Gyapong, A. O. 1991. Production of education: are socioeconomic characteristics important factors? *Eastern Economic Journal* **17**, 507–521.

Huang, Y. 2004. Appendix B: a guide to state operating aid programs for elementary and secondary education. In Yinger, J. (ed.), *Helping Children Left Behind: State Aid and the Pursuit of Educational Equity*, pp. 331–351. Cambridge, MA: MIT Press.

Imazeki, J. and Reschovsky, A. 2004. School finance reform in Texas: a never ending story? In Yinger, J. (ed.), *Helping Children Left Behind: State Aid and the Pursuit of Educational Equity*, pp. 251–281. Cambridge, MA: MIT Press.

Ladd, H. F. and Yinger, J. 1994. The case for equalizing aid. *National Tax Journal* **47**(1), 211–224. [Chapter 13]

Lukemeyer, A. 2002. *Courts as Policymakers: School Finance Reform Litigation*. New York: LFB Scholarly Publications.

Lukemeyer, A. 2004. Financing a constitutional education: views from the bench. In Yinger, J. (ed.), *Helping Children Left Behind: State Aid and the Pursuit of Educational Equity*, pp. 59–85. Cambridge, MA: MIT Press.

Maryland Commission on Education Finance, Equity, and Excellence. 2002. *Final Report*. Baltimore: Maryland Commission on Education Finance, Equity, and Excellence. Available at: http://mlis.state.md.us/other/education/; Last accessed 6/14/04.

Ratcliffe, K., Riddle, B., and Yinger, J. 1990. The fiscal condition of school districts in Nebraska: is small beautiful? *Economics of Education Review* **9**, 81–99.

Reschovsky, A. and Imazeki, J. 1998. The development of school finance formulas to guarantee the provision of adequate education to low-income students. In Fowler, W. J., Jr. (ed.), *Developments in School Finance, 1997: Does Money Matter?* pp. 121–148. Washington, DC: US Department of Education, National Center for Educational Statistics.

Reschovsky, A. and Imazeki, J. 2001. Achieving educational adequacy through school finance reform. *Journal of Education Finance* **26**(4), 373–396.

Reschovsky, A. and Imazeki, J. 2003. Let no child be left behind: determining the cost of improving student performance. *Public Finance Review* **31**, 263–290.

Woolridge, J. M. 2003. *Introductory Econometrics: A Modern Approach* 2nd edition, Mason, OH: South-Western.

Chapter 8

The Unintended Consequences of Property Tax Relief: New York's STAR Program[*]

Tae Ho Eom[†], William Duncombe[¶],
Phuong Nguyen-Hoang[‡], and John Yinger[§,||]

[†]*Department of Public Administration,*
Yonsei University, Seoul, Korea
[‡]*Public Policy Center and School of Urban and Regional Planning,*
University of Iowa, Iowa City, IA 52242, United States
[§]*Departments of Public Administration and International Affairs and of*
Economics, Syracuse University, Syracuse, NY, United States
[||]*jyinger@maxwell.syr.edu*

New York's School Tax Relief Program, STAR, provides state-funded property tax relief for homeowners. Like a matching grant, STAR changes the price of education, thereby altering the incentives of voters and school officials and leading to unintended consequences. Using data for New York State school districts before and after STAR was implemented, we find that STAR increased student performance, school district inefficiency, and school spending by 2 to 4 percent in most districts, leading to an average school property tax rate increase of 14 percent. The STAR-induced tax rate increases offset about one third of the initial STAR tax savings and boosted property taxes for business property. STAR did little to offset the existing inequities in New York State's education finance system, particularly compared to an equal-cost increase in state aid. This article should be of interest to policy makers involved in property taxes or other aspects of education finance.

[*]This chapter is reproduced from "The Unintended Consequences of Property Tax Relief: New York State's STAR Program," *Education Finance and Policy*, **9**(4), Fall 2014, pp. 446–480.
[¶]Deceased.

1. Introduction

Thanks to a relatively low state share of funding for education and a wide range in property values per pupil, New York State has long faced the dual problem of high property tax rates and severe funding disparities across school districts. In 1997, New York State enacted a state-funded homestead exemption, the School Tax Relief Program (STAR), to provide property tax relief for homeowners. Although it was not recognized in the policy debates at the time STAR was passed, the use of state tax sources to lower the school property tax burden on homeowners significantly alters the way public schools are financed and magnifies the funding disparities. Moreover, the design of STAR has resulted in unintended consequences for spending, property tax rates, and student performance. This impact on school finance and these unintended consequences are the subjects of this paper.

These issues were first raised by Duncombe and Yinger (1998a, 2001). Building on the equivalence theorems of Bradford and Oates (Oates, 1972; Bradford and Oates, 1971a,b), Duncombe and Yinger argued that the STAR homestead exemption was equivalent to a form of matching aid. Like matching aid, STAR lowers voters' tax prices and therefore is likely to increase the demand for education (as measured by student performance) and lead to higher education spending and higher property tax rates. Duncombe and Yinger also argued that the STAR-induced decline in tax price lowers voters' incentives to monitor school officials and therefore may result in less efficient school districts. In this paper we estimate the impact of STAR on student performance, school district expenditures, and school property tax rates. Our estimates also provide indirect evidence about the effect on efficiency.

Many studies find that tax prices have a significant impact on the demand for local services.[1] Fisher and Rasche (1984), Addonizio (1990, 1991), and Rockoff (2010) explore the impact of property tax relief programs on school spending. The first two of these studies examine a circuit breaker implemented in Michigan in the 1970s that altered tax prices. Both studies find evidence that these tax-price changes had a significant impact on public spending. Rockoff (2010) examines STAR. He finds that replacing 10 percent of school property taxes with STAR funds would raise school spending by

---

[1]For reviews of this literature, see Rubinfeld (1987), Ladd and Yinger (1991), Duncombe (1996), and Fisher and Papke (2000).

1.6 percent.[2] These studies all estimate the elasticity of expenditure per pupil with respect to tax price. This approach has the practical advantage of not requiring a measure of the final output (in the sense of Bradford, Malt, and Oates, 1969) of education, such as student test scores. It also has a major disadvantage, however: It cannot examine directly how an expensive state property tax relief program has affected student performance or provide any evidence about its impact on efficiency.

In contrast to the previous literature, this study estimates a demand model and a cost model based on a measure of student performance. The paper is organized into five sections. In the next section we provide some basic information on the STAR program and how tax savings have been distributed across regions in the state. We then present the conceptual foundation of the paper, which involves models of demand, cost, and efficiency. In Section 4, we describe our data and empirical methods. Estimation results are presented in Section 5, as well as simulations of the impacts of STAR on student performance, spending, educational costs, and property tax rates. We conclude with some suggestions for reforms in the STAR program to minimize its unfairness and unintended consequences.

2. The Structure of STAR and the Distribution of STAR Benefits

The STAR program provides partial exemptions from school property taxes for owner-occupied primary residences.[3] The basic STAR exemption is available to all taxpayers who own their primary residence in New York State, including owners of one-, two-, and three-family houses, condominiums, cooperative apartments, mobile homes, or residential dwellings that are part of mixed-use property. Renters receive no exemption. An enhanced STAR exemption is available for homeowners above age 64. An income limit has always been part of enhanced STAR and was added to the basic STAR in 2012.

The basic exemptions were $10,000 in 1999–2000, $20,000 in 2000–2001, and $30,000 in 2001–2002 and thereafter. The enhanced exemption was set at $50,000 starting in 1998–1999 and was gradually raised to $62,200 in

---

[2]Rockoff (2010) sets district tax price equal to one minus the fraction of local property taxes paid by STAR; this formulation differs from the one derived herein.

[3]This discussion of STAR draws on New York State Department of Taxation and Finance (2013a,b,c,d), New York State Division of the Budget (2013), and Office of the New York State Comptroller (2012). See these citations for more details.

2012–2013. A homeowner's savings equal the exemption amount multiplied by the school property tax rate in the homeowner's school district. As of FY 2012, this STAR savings cannot increase by more than 2 percent per year. STAR has special provisions for the "big five" cities, New York City (NYC), Buffalo, Rochester, Syracuse, and Yonkers, in which schools are a department of city government and there is no separate school tax rate. The STAR exemption is 50 percent of the basic exemption for NYC and 67 percent of the basic exemption for the other four districts; this exemption applies to all city property taxes, not just those devoted to schools.

STAR exemptions are subject to two adjustments in many districts. First, to make them an equivalent share of market value, they are adjusted based on the assessment/sales ratio in each assessing unit. Second, they are adjusted upward by a "sales price differential factor" (SPDF) in counties in which the median residential sales price exceeds the statewide median sales price.[4] The higher exemptions resulting from the SPDF are primarily in so-called downstate counties, which include NYC and its suburbs, plus the rest of Long Island.

Because NYC, unlike other districts, raised a large share of its school revenue from an income tax, the original legislation also provided an income tax credit to all NYC residents, including renters. In addition, a STAR income tax rebate equal to 30 percent of the savings from the basic STAR exemption was implemented for all homeowners in the state in 2007. This rebate was eliminated in FY 2009. Elderly homeowners received a higher rebate during this period.

As summarized in Figure 1, these provisions generate extensive variation in STAR exemptions both over time and across districts. Time variation results from the phase-in and the income tax rebate in 2007–2009, which was equivalent to an increase in the exemption. The SPDF results in variation across district and time.[5] The basic exemption in Westchester County, for example, reached as high as 3.31 times the minimum amount in 2011.

Although New York has several other property tax exemption programs, STAR is unique in two ways (Office of the New York State Comptroller,

---

[4]The first adjustment simply ensures the benefits of the STAR exemptions do not depend on assessing practices. The SPDF cannot fall below 1.0, so it provides higher exemptions in high-housing-value districts but does not change exemptions elsewhere. All districts in downstate counties have a SPDF greater than one. Moreover, a homeowner's exemption cannot drop by more than 11 percent even when housing prices drop.

[5]Although not shown in the figure, the special treatment of the big five districts also yields variation across districts.

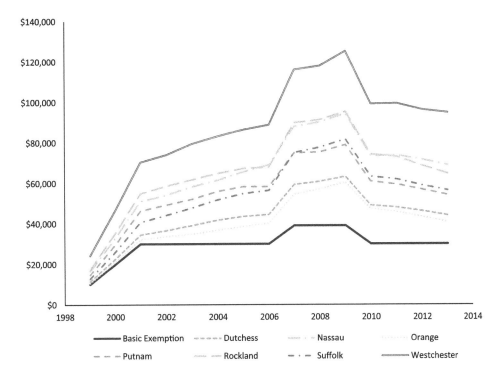

Figure 1 STAR exemptions in various counties, including rebates.

2012). First, it is the only exemption funded by the state. STAR exemptions lower a homeowner's tax bill, and the state writes a check to the school district for the lost revenue. All other exemptions erode the local tax property base and shift the burden of the tax toward property owners not eligible for the exemptions. Second, STAR is unique in terms of its scope and the size of the exemption. Although some other exemption programs have applied to a significant number of taxpayers, including 650,000 veterans and 180,000 senior citizens, none of them has come close to the breadth of the STAR program, which applies to about 3.3 million taxpayers. The cost of STAR has risen from $1.5 billion in 2002 to $3.3 billion in 2012.[6] These features also stand out at the national level. Most states have some form of property tax exemption but only a few other states, including Indiana and Massachusetts, have general property tax exemptions with state reimbursement (Duncombe and Yinger, 2001).

---

[6]The STAR income tax rebate was estimated to have added an additional $1.1 billion to the cost of STAR in 2008 (Mauro, 2008).

Table 1   School district STAR savings by NYSED regions.

	STAR savings per pupil ($)			STAR savings as % of state aid			STAR savings as % of total operating spending		
	2002	2006	2011	2002	2006	2011	2002	2006	2011
Downstate small cities	1,498	2,061	2,090	39.7	50.1	49.2	10.7	11.3	9.7
Downstate suburbs	1,316	1,669	1,856	37.6	41.8	39.5	9.9	9.9	8.9
Yonkers	1,190	1,546	1,414	13.6	18.3	15.3	8.4	9.0	8.1
Big three	318	393	369	4.1	3.8	4.7	3.0	2.9	2.2
Upstate small cities	841	1,047	1,012	13.9	15.2	11.6	8.2	8.1	6.4
Upstate rural	773	1,024	1,034	11.1	12.8	10.2	7.7	7.9	6.2
Upstate suburbs	1,010	1,244	1,295	20.8	22.6	19.7	10.5	10.3	8.6

Notes: This table presents savings from both basic and advanced STAR exemptions. The available data do not allow us to separate between the two exemptions.

Source: Authors' calculations.

As shown in Table 1, STAR revenues or savings increased from 2002 (the first year in which the basic STAR was fully implemented) to 2006 and 2011. In 2011, STAR provided property tax relief per pupil ranging from $2,090 in the downstate small cities to $369 in the upstate big three districts (Buffalo, Rochester, and Syracuse). These large cities received relatively less benefit from STAR because of their high renter populations and because they receive no benefit from the SPDF. Compared with other school districts, STAR, as a percent of state aid and total operating expenditures, was the largest for downstate small city school districts followed by their downstate suburban peers.

3.   Conceptual Foundations

The sole objective of STAR was to provide property tax relief, but STAR has many unintended consequences because it alters voters' tax prices. A voter's tax price reflects the interplay between the voter's budget constraint and the government budget constraint. In this section we derive an expanded tax price that reflects both STAR and school district efficiency and incorporates this tax price into demand and cost/efficiency models. We show that STAR has direct impacts on the demand for school quality and indirect impacts on demand that arise through STAR's effect on efficiency.

3.1. *The Demand for School Quality*

Let V stand for the market value of a voter's home and t indicate the effective property tax rate. Without STAR, the property tax payment would be tV. STAR exempts the first X dollars of market value from tax, so the property tax payment with STAR is $t(V - X)$. As noted earlier, the value of X in our sample period was \$30,000 in most districts in most years of full implementation, but was sometimes adjusted upward for high county sales prices.[7] If Y is a voter's income and Z is spending on everything except school property taxes, then a voter's budget constraint with STAR is

$$Y = Z + t(V - X). \tag{1}$$

The school district faces a cost function, $C\{S\}$, where C is total cost per pupil and S is measure of school quality. As discussed subsequently, we select measures of S that are linked to New York State's accountability system. The derivative of this function, $\partial C/\partial S$, equals marginal cost, MC. Spending per pupil, E, equals $C\{S\}$ divided by district efficiency, e. This efficiency measure, which is discussed more fully in what follows, is scaled to equal 1.0 in a fully efficient district (i.e., in a district that makes full use of the best available technology for producing S) and to fall below one in less efficient districts. Hence, this formulation indicates that inefficient districts spend more than the amount indicated by $C\{S\}$ to obtain a given level of S.

District revenue comes from property taxes and lump-sum state aid.[8] Now let $\bar{V}$ indicate total property value per pupil and A indicate state aid per pupil. Then the district budget constraint is

$$E \equiv \frac{C\{S\}}{e} = t\bar{V} + A. \tag{2}$$

Because the state compensates a district for revenue lost through the STAR exemptions, these exemptions have no impact on the district budget constraint. In other words, the district loses $t\bar{X}$ to the STAR exemptions but receives $t\bar{X}$ in compensation from the state.

---

[7] The adjustment for assessing practices is not relevant here because our model is already based on market values, not assessed values.

[8] The largest operating aid program in New York uses a foundation formula, which gives more aid to districts with lower property wealth per pupil or a higher student poverty rate. See https://stateaid.nysed.gov/. Our empirical work combines revenue from all operating aid programs.

Solving equation (2) for t and substituting the result into equation (1) yields

$$Y + A\left(\frac{V}{\bar{V}}\right)\left(1 - \frac{X}{V}\right) = Z + \frac{C\{S\}}{e}\left(\frac{V}{\bar{V}}\right)\left(1 - \frac{X}{V}\right). \tag{3}$$

Tax price, TP, is what an increment in S costs a voter, so it can be derived by differentiating a voter's spending (the right side of equation (3)), by S:

$$TP \equiv \frac{\partial\,\text{Spending}}{\partial S} = \frac{dC}{dS}e^{-1}\left(\frac{V}{\bar{V}}\right)\left(1 - \frac{X}{V}\right) = (MC)e^{-1}\left(\frac{V}{\bar{V}}\right)\left(1 - \frac{X}{V}\right). \tag{4}$$

The direct impact of STAR appears in the last term of equation (4). An exemption, X, is equivalent to a matching aid program with a matching rate $m = X/V$. This matching rate varies across districts and across time because of the phase-in, the SPDF, the temporary income tax rebate, and variation in V. Throughout this paper, we refer to X/V as the implicit STAR matching rate and $(1 - X/V)$ as the STAR tax share or STAR component of tax price.

In a standard median-voter model, the demand for school quality, S, is a function of median income (as augmented by state aid), of median tax price, and of various demographic factors. In a district of homeowners, the median tax price is equation (4) with V defined to be median house value. Within a district, STAR cuts every homeowner's tax share by $X/\bar{V}$, so it does not change the order of demands — or the identity of the median voter. As pointed out by Rockoff (2010), renters complicate this analysis; the introduction of STAR exemptions for homeowners but not renters could change the identity of the median voter. Following the theoretical literature (reviewed in Ross and Yinger, 1999), we assume renters do not care about (or vote on) S because any benefits or costs from a change in S will be offset by a change in rents.[9] Interpreting equation (1) as the median voter's budget

---

[9]This approach is supported by studies (e.g., Duncombe and Yinger, 2011) that find no impact of renter concentration on price elasticities. We cannot test this hypothesis about renters, however, so an alternative interpretation of our approach is that we use key elements of a demand model to approximate voting outcomes concerning school quality in different districts. Brunner and Ross (2010) also find voting outcomes are affected by household heterogeneity within a jurisdiction, a factor roughly captured by our district fixed effects and other controls.

constraint, using a standard multiplicative form for demand, and adding a flypaper effect, f, we find[10]

$$S = K(D)^\phi \left(Y + fA \left(\frac{V}{\bar{V}}\right)\left(1 - \frac{X}{V}\right)\right)^\theta \left((MC)e^{-1}\left(\frac{V}{\bar{V}}\right)\left(1 - \frac{X}{V}\right)\right)^\mu$$

(5)

where K is a constant, D represents demographic demand determinants, θ is the income elasticity of demand, and μ is the (negative) price elasticity of demand. Our principal hypothesis is that the STAR term, $(1 - X/V)$, is a price variable and therefore has a negative coefficient.

Tax price in equation (5) has four components: marginal cost, (the inverse of) efficiency, tax share, and STAR. These components all enter tax price in the same way but may have different elasticities in practice. Voters may be more aware of, and hence more responsive to, the STAR component than to the tax-share component, for example, because they must apply for the STAR rebate. Thus, we estimate all four elasticities and use them in our simulations. To simplify the presentation, however, we use a single elasticity in the text.

Equation (5) also reveals that STAR affects the value of aid to voters. In the standard model, the value of state aid to a voter depends on the voter's tax share, that is, on the voter's share of the money saved by cutting local taxes (Oates, 1972; Duncombe and Yinger, 2011). This effect explains why tax share appears in the augmented income term. Equation (5) shows that STAR exemptions also lower a voter's valuation of aid. We later test for this effect, which is discussed in Duncombe and Yinger (1998a, 2001) and Rockoff (2010).

3.2. *Educational Cost and School Efficiency*

Equation (2) indicates district spending, E, is the ratio of costs, C, to efficiency, e. Following standard practice (Downes and Pogue, 1994; Duncombe and Yinger, 1997, 1998b, 2000, 2005, 2008, 2011; Reschovsky and Imazeki, 1998, 2001, 2003), we assume educational cost depends, in a multiplicative way, on teacher salaries, W, student enrollment, N, and pupil characteristics, P. Following Duncombe and Yinger (2011), we also

---

[10]For a review of the literature on the flypaper effect, see Hines and Thaler (1995); for a recent contribution, see Roemer and Silvestre (2002).

identify returns to quality scale (as defined in Duncombe and Yinger, 1993). In symbols,

$$C\{S\} = \kappa S^\sigma W^\alpha N^\beta P^\lambda \qquad (6)$$

where k is a constant and σ measures returns to quality scale; $\sigma < 1.0$ indicates increasing returns and $\sigma > 1$ indicates decreasing returns. With this cost function, marginal cost is not constant:

$$MC \equiv \frac{\partial C\{S\}}{\partial S} = \sigma \kappa S^{\sigma-1} W^\alpha N^\beta P^\lambda. \qquad (7)$$

In our framework, inefficiency arises when a district is wasteful or when it spends money on an educational outcome other than the ones specified in S. These two types of inefficiency cannot be separated (in our model or any other). Our approach is to identify variables conceptually linked to either or both of these types of inefficiency and to include them in an efficiency equation. As shown subsequently, this approach allows us to estimate e and to determine STAR's indirect impact on demand, which operates through efficiency.

As pointed out by Duncombe, Miner, and Ruggiero (1997) and Duncombe and Yinger (1997, 1998b), income may affect efficiency in two ways. First, a higher income may weaken voters' incentives to monitor school officials. Second, a higher income may encourage voters to push for a broader set of objectives. Because efficiency must be defined relative to spending on a particular objective, such as student performance on certain tests, spending to promote other objectives is, by definition, inefficient. Given this role of voter demand and monitoring, we use the same definition of income in the efficiency equation as in the demand equation.

These studies also provide evidence that a tax-price decrease, like an income increase, weakens voters' incentives to monitor school officials and boosts their demand for a broad set of objectives. Thus, tax price also belongs in the efficiency equation. As in the case of income, the role of voter behavior in this analysis indicates the tax-price term in the efficiency equation, like the one in the demand equation, should reflect tax share, marginal cost, and STAR.[11]

---

[11]We exclude the efficiency component of tax price from the efficiency equation. It makes no sense to argue that voters will monitor school officials more actively when a low level of monitoring leads to inefficiency. An additional complexity is that MC refers to the marginal cost of S, whereas inefficiency includes spending on school quality measures other than S. If these other measures and S have similar cost functions, then $MC\{S\}$ is likely to be correlated with, and hence is a good proxy for, the MC of these other measures. In other

Because e reflects demand for school quality measures other than those in S, we use the same form for the efficiency equation as we use for the demand-for-S equation (5), namely, a multiplicative form based on augmented income and tax price. This approach not only has a clear conceptual foundation, but also, as we will show, facilitates identification of key parameters. For expositional purposes (but not in our estimations), we assume the flypaper effect is the same in the efficiency equation as in the demand equation. Determinants of efficiency other than augmented income and tax-price, which are discussed in the following, are represented by M. This approach leads to efficiency equation (8), where γ is the income elasticity of efficiency, δ is the price elasticity of efficiency, and k is a constant:

$$e = kM^{\rho} \left(Y + fA \left(\frac{V}{\bar{V}} \right) \left(1 - \frac{X}{V} \right) \right)^{\gamma} \left((MC) \left(\frac{V}{\bar{V}} \right) \left(1 - \frac{X}{V} \right) \right)^{\delta}. \quad (8)$$

Based on the literature, we expect that a higher augmented income leads to less efficiency ($\gamma < 0$) and that a higher tax price leads to more efficiency ($\delta > 0$).

Efficiency cannot be measured directly, but its determinants can be incorporated into the estimation of a cost function (Duncombe and Yinger, 2001). Substituting equations (6)–(8) into the definition of E in equation (2), we find:

$$E = k^{*}(S^{\sigma - \delta(\sigma - 1)})(W^{\alpha}N^{\beta}P^{\lambda})^{1-\delta} \left(M^{-\rho} \left(Y + fA \left(\frac{V}{\bar{V}} \right) \left(1 - \frac{X}{V} \right) \right)^{-\gamma} \right.$$
$$\left. \times \left(\left(\frac{V}{\bar{V}} \right) \left(1 - \frac{X}{V} \right) \right)^{-\delta} \right) \quad (9)$$

where k^{*} combines the constants in equations (6)–(8). Taking logs and, for augmented income, using the simplification that $\ln\{1 + \alpha\} \approx \alpha$ when α is less than one, yields our estimating equation:

$$\ln\{E\} = \ln\{k^{*}\} + (\sigma - \delta(\sigma - 1)) \ln\{S\} + \alpha(1 - \delta) \ln\{W\} + \beta(1 - \delta) \ln\{N\}$$
$$+ \lambda(1 - \delta) \ln\{P\} - \rho \ln\{M\} - \gamma \ln\{Y\}$$
$$- \gamma f \left[\left(\frac{A}{Y} \right) \left(\frac{V}{\bar{V}} \right) \left(1 - \frac{X}{V} \right) \right] - \delta \ln \left\{ \frac{V}{\bar{V}} \right\} - \delta \ln \left\{ 1 - \frac{X}{V} \right\}. \quad (10)$$

---

cases, $MC\{S\}$ may not influence e at all. However, dropping the impact of $MC\{S\}$ on e has little impact on our results.

This equation identifies all the parameters in equations (6) and (7) except the constant terms, which are not needed to calculate cost and efficiency indexes. The efficiency price elasticity, δ, equals the negative of the coefficient of the tax-share variable. Once δ is known, the values of the cost parameters, α, β, and λ, can be determined from the coefficients of the cost variables. Because δ is expected to be positive, omitting this correction is likely to result in an *understatement* of the impact of wages, enrollment, and student characteristics on educational costs. The efficiency income elasticity, γ, is the negative of the coefficient of $\ln\{Y\}$, and the flypaper effect, f, is the coefficient of the aid variable divided by $-\gamma$. The economies-of-scale parameter, σ, can be found using the coefficient of $\ln\{S\}$ and the estimate of δ.

The three components of tax-price in equation (8), like those in equation (5), may not have the same elasticities. We can estimate separate elasticities for the last two terms, but not for the first, which appears in all the coefficients in the first line of equation (10). We assume that the elasticity of e with respect to MC equals the estimated elasticity of e with respect to $V/\bar{V}$.[12]

An alternative approach to estimating efficiency was developed by Ray (1991) and McCarty and Yaisawarng (1993). It involves two steps.[13] The first step is to estimate the minimum spending frontier for any combination of student outcomes using Data Envelopment Analysis (DEA).[14] DEA produces an index that captures variation across districts in both efficiency and educational costs. The second step is to regress the DEA index on cost variables and on variables thought to influence efficiency. The coefficients of this regression can then be used to remove the impact of the cost variables from the DEA index, leaving a measure of efficiency. DEA is designed to identify production frontiers with multiple outputs; it is not

---

[12]In principle, the value of γ might differ for the tax-share components in augmented income, but separate γs cannot be identified, and voters are only concerned about their net impact.

[13]Ruggiero (1996) shows how to develop a DEA measure that directly removes the impact of cost factors. We have not used this clever approach because it requires a very large data set.

[14]DEA uses linear programming to determine a "best-practice frontier" for production. It was developed by Farrell (1957), Charnes, Cooper, and Rhodes (1978), and Fare and Lovell (1978). Strengths and weaknesses of DEA are discussed in Seiford and Thrall (1990) and Ruggiero (1996). DEA is popular for evaluating productive efficiency in the public sector because it handles multiple outputs, is non-parametric, and can be applied to both production and cost.

necessary or appropriate with a single output, as in the case of our education-performance index, and is difficult to incorporate into a model of cost and demand.

3.3. *Implications of the Link between Demand and Efficiency*

Once equation (10) has been estimated, two approaches are available for estimating the demand equation (5), and hence for determining the indirect impact of STAR on demand through efficiency. The first approach is to use the estimated parameters from equation (10), along with equations (6) and (8), to calculate indexes of MC and e for every district. The problem with this approach is that both MC and e (through MC) are functions of S, so that these two variables are endogenous by definition. Moreover, it may be impossible to find instruments for addressing this endogeneity because variables correlated with the impact of scale economies in MC and e, which operate through S, are, by definition, correlated with the dependent variable, namely, S.

The second approach is to exploit the multiplicative form of these equations to solve for S, that is, to eliminate S from the right side of the demand equation. This approach complicates the interpretation of the estimated parameters in the demand equation, but it eliminates the troublesome type of endogeneity just described. The first step in this approach is to calculate indexes for the exogenous components of cost and efficiency, that is, the components that do not involve S:

$$C^* = \sigma \kappa^* W^\alpha N^\beta P^\lambda \tag{11}$$

and

$$e^* = k^{**} M^\rho \left(Y + fA \left(\frac{V}{\bar{V}} \right) \left(1 - \frac{X}{V} \right) \right)^\gamma \left(C^* \left(\frac{V}{\bar{V}} \right) \left(1 - \frac{X}{V} \right) \right)^\delta \tag{12}$$

where κ^* is defined so that C^* equals 1.0 in the average district and k^{**} is defined so that e^* equals 1.0 in the most efficient district. This scaling alters the constant term in our demand regression, but does not alter any other estimated coefficient.

Now substituting equations (6) and (8) into equation (5) and making use of equations (11) and (12), we can write the demand function as:

$$S = K^*(D)^{\phi*} \left(Y + fA \left(\frac{V}{\bar{V}} \right) \left(1 - \frac{X}{V} \right) \right)^{\theta*} \left((C^*)(e^*)^{-1} \left(\frac{V}{\bar{V}} \right) \left(1 - \frac{X}{V} \right) \right)^{\mu*}$$

$$\tag{13}$$

where

$$\theta^* = \frac{\theta}{1 - \mu(\sigma - 1)(1 - \delta)}; \quad \mu^* = \frac{\mu}{1 - \mu(\sigma - 1)(1 - \delta)}; \quad \text{and}$$

$$\phi^* = \frac{\phi}{1 - \mu(\sigma - 1)(1 - \delta)}. \tag{14}$$

Equation (13) can be estimated by taking logs and using the approxima-tion for the aid term derived earlier. The values of σ and δ come from the estimation of equation (10). Equation (14) can be used to find μ, θ, and ϕ. Note that $\theta = \theta^*$ and $\mu = \mu^*$ when there are constant returns to quality scale ($\sigma = 1$).

Because e^* depends on augmented income and tax-price, substituting equation (12) into equation (13) yields another form for the demand function, namely,

$$S = K^{**} M^{-\rho\mu^*} \left(Y + f A \left(\frac{V}{\overline{V}} \right) \left(1 - \frac{X}{V} \right) \right)^{\theta^* - \gamma\mu^*}$$

$$\times \left((C^*) \left(\frac{V}{\overline{V}} \right) \left(1 - \frac{X}{V} \right) \right)^{\mu^*(1-\delta)}. \tag{15}$$

Equation (15) has two important implications. First, when efficiency is omitted from the demand equation, the estimated "income" elasticity is $(\theta^* - \gamma\mu^*)$ and the estimated "price" elasticity is $\mu^*(1 - \delta)$, which are smaller (in absolute value) than θ and μ, respectively (or than θ^* and μ^*).

The same issues arise when e is omitted from an expenditure form of the demand equation, which is equation (15) multiplied by MC/e with the assumption of constant returns to scale ($\sigma = 1$). With this approach, which is used by Rockoff (2010) and implemented here, the coefficient is $[\theta - \gamma(\mu + 1)]$ for the income term and $[\mu - \delta(\mu + 1)]$ for the tax-price term.[15] Even with constant returns, the estimated coefficients cannot be interpreted as income and price elasticities of demand unless γ and δ are assumed to be zero. Including district fixed effects and regional time trends to account for efficiency, the Rockoff (2010) strategy does not eliminate the extra terms in these coefficients because e is directly affected by STAR and varies over time in each district.

The Rockoff approach provides a demand interpretation for an expendi-ture equation that is quite different from the cost/efficiency interpretation we give to equation (9). Nevertheless, these two interpretations are not

---

[15]This step also adds 1 to the exponent of the C^* ($=MC$) term.

inconsistent. Under the demand interpretation, an expenditure equation explores the demand for a broad but unspecified set of educational outcomes, whereas we explore cost and efficiency in providing a specific school performance index. A finding that the demand for a broad set of education outcomes increases with district income or decreases with district tax price implies that an income increase or a tax-price decrease encourages a district to provide a broader set of educational outcomes, which is equivalent to becoming more inefficient in delivering the performance index in our analysis. Overall, both interpretations are legitimate, but the cost interpretation has the advantage that it does not require the assumptions that σ equals 1 and that γ and δ equal zero.[16]

The second implication of equation (15) is that, even with constant returns, the impact of STAR on the demand for S has two direct components, a price effect and a change in the value of A, and two indirect components, which operate through efficiency. By lowering tax price, STAR gives a direct boost to demand, but it also lowers efficiency, which indirectly results in lower demand. The net impact of these two responses is summarized by the $\mu(1 - \delta)$ exponent. The (negative) price elasticity, μ, indicates the direct effect; it is offset to some degree by the product of δ, which is positive, and μ. In addition, by lowering the value of aid to a voter, STAR lowers demand, but this drop in augmented income also leads to higher efficiency, which indirectly boosts demand. The net impact of these two responses is summarized by the $(\theta - \gamma\mu)$ exponent. The positive income elasticity, θ, is offset, at least in part, by the product of γ (negative) and μ.

The simulations in a later section incorporate the exact form of these indirect effects but it is instructive at this point to examine them using calculus approximations. With constant returns, differentiating equation (15) with respect to $m = X/V$ reveals that the impact of STAR on S is[17]

$$d\ln\{S\} = -\left(\frac{(\theta - \gamma\mu)f A\left(\frac{V}{V}\right)}{Y + fA\left(\frac{V}{V}\right)} + \mu(1 - \delta)\right)\left(\frac{X}{V}\right). \qquad (16)$$

---

[16] These assumptions about these three parameters might hold with the unspecified broad school performance measure in the demand interpretation even if they do not hold with the specific measure in the cost interpretation, but there is no way to determine whether or not this is true.

[17] These derivatives are evaluated at $m = 0$ (which corresponds to a starting point without STAR), with $dm = X/V$ (which corresponds to implementing STAR), and with $\sigma = 1$.

The first term in equation (16) is the net income effect and the second term is the net price effect. The second term shows the direct positive price impact of STAR on S, $-\mu$, is offset to some degree by the indirect effect, $\mu\delta$, that arises because STAR has a price impact on efficiency, which in turn affects S. Without constant returns, θ and μ in equation (16) must be replaced by θ^* and μ^* as defined by equations (14) and (15).

Using the expenditure form of the demand equation, again with constant returns, we can also derive the impact of STAR on E:

$$d\ln\{E\} = -\left(\frac{(\theta - \gamma(\mu+1))fA\left(\frac{V}{\overline{V}}\right)}{Y + fA\left(\frac{V}{\overline{V}}\right)} + \mu - \delta(1+\mu)\right)\left(\frac{X}{V}\right). \quad (17)$$

In this case, the elasticity expressions in the numerators summarize the direct impacts of STAR on efficiency and the direct and indirect impacts of STAR on S and hence on C.[18]

The district budget constraint, equation (2), implies

$$dt = \left(\frac{d\ln\{E\}}{\frac{X}{V}}\frac{E}{\overline{V}}\right)\left(\frac{X}{V}\right) = d\ln\{E\}\left(\frac{E}{\overline{V}}\right). \quad (18)$$

Not surprisingly, the impact of STAR on property taxes has the same sign as its impact on spending, regardless of scale economies. Finally, we can differentiate equation (6) to determine the impact of STAR on school district efficiency. The result with $\sigma = 1$ is[19]:

$$d\ln\{e\} = -\left(\frac{\gamma fA\left(\frac{V}{\overline{V}}\right)}{Y + fA\left(\frac{V}{\overline{V}}\right)} + \delta\right)\left(\frac{X}{V}\right). \quad (19)$$

STAR raises efficiency by cutting the value of aid to voters (the first term) but also lowers efficiency by lowering voters' tax prices (the second term). Without constant returns, the coefficient in the numerator of the first term becomes $[\gamma + \theta^*(\sigma - 1)\delta]$ and the coefficient in the numerator of the second term becomes $[\delta + \mu^*(\sigma - 1)\delta]$. The increase in S caused by STAR raises the marginal cost of S, thereby boosting efficiency and offsetting, at least in part, the drop in efficiency associated with the STAR implicit matching rate.

---

[18]Without constant returns, the coefficients in the numerators become $[(\theta^* - \gamma\mu^*)(\sigma(1-\delta)+\delta) - \gamma]$ (first term) and $[\mu^*(1-\delta)(\sigma(1-\delta)+\delta) - \delta]$ (second term).
[19]Without constant returns, the coefficient in the numerator becomes $[\gamma + \theta^*(\sigma-1)\delta]$ (first term) and $[\delta + \mu^*(\sigma - 1)\delta]$ (second term).

Table 2   Changes in key variables from 1999 to 2011 by NYSED region.

Region	Tax share	STAR tax share	Effective tax rate	Real per pupil operating spending	Student performance index
			1999		
Downstate small cities	0.583	1	1.974	19,024	56.6
Downstate suburbs	0.485	1	1.835	18,979	66.8
Yonkers	0.674	1	1.854	18,526	40.3
Big three	0.448	1	1.446	14,138	41.8
Upstate small cities	0.408	1	1.864	13,242	57.6
Upstate rural	0.365	1	1.543	13,043	59.7
Upstate suburbs	0.418	1	1.766	12,694	63.6
Average district	0.419	1	1.720	14,474	62.5
			2006		
Downstate small cities	0.506	0.810	1.563	21,467	71.7
Downstate suburbs	0.422	0.848	1.413	21,050	81.4
Yonkers	0.551	0.836	1.072	19,419	52.2
Big three	0.486	0.710	1.601	15,296	46.7
Upstate small cities	0.420	0.673	2.166	14,547	68.1
Upstate rural	0.322	0.667	1.777	15,512	70.9
Upstate suburbs	0.387	0.734	2.032	14,206	75.9
Average district	0.380	0.738	1.801	16,390	74.8
Percent change since 1999	−9.3	−26.2	4.7	13.2	19.7
			2011		
Downstate small cities	0.495	0.820	1.627	21,000	73.9
Downstate suburbs	0.460	0.856	1.592	22,192	81.9
Yonkers	0.641	0.841	1.259	16,782	55.7
Big three	0.434	0.729	1.540	16,144	51.1
Upstate small cities	0.371	0.710	1.930	14,932	68.9
Upstate rural	0.256	0.714	1.546	16,931	71.9
Upstate suburbs	0.327	0.765	1.856	15,241	77.2
Average district	0.344	0.769	1.700	17,497	75.7
Percent change since 1999	−17.9	−23.1	−1.2	20.9	21.1

Notes: Tax share is $(V/\bar{V})$; STAR tax share is $(1 - X/V)$; effective tax rate is equal to total property tax revenues divided by total equalized property values; and student performance index is simple average of non-dropout rates, Regents diploma rates, and percent of students reaching proficiency levels in grade 8 reading and grade 8 mathematics.

Source: As indicated in Table 3.

4. Data and Measures

Our conceptual framework calls for the estimation of the cost/efficiency (equation (10)) and the demand (equation (13)). In this section we describe our data and our strategy for estimating each of these equations. Our sample is most New York school districts for the academic years 1998–1999 to 2010–2011. This period is ideal for studying STAR because it includes one year before STAR was implemented — and New York's tests, accountability measures, and school aid system remained fairly stable over this period.[20] We exclude New York City from the sample because of both missing data for some variables and the fact that most of the STAR benefit to New York City comes in the form of an income tax rebate. We exclude non-k-12 districts, because we are using performance measures that include test scores in grade 8. After dropping a few observations with missing variables, the final sample includes 8,038 observations. The number of districts in the sample ranges from 607 to 627 over the sample period.[21]

Table 2 describes changes in tax-price components and other key variables before and after STAR was implemented. The first column shows that in all regions, tax share $(V/\bar{V})$ was lower in 2006 and 2011 than in 1999. The second column indicates that the average STAR tax share across districts was 77 percent in 2011, which is equivalent to a matching rate of 23 percent, and ranged from 71 percent in small city districts outside the New York City region (upstate) to 86 percent in suburban districts near NYC or on Long Island (downstate). This difference, which tends to favor needy districts, would be much greater were it not for the SPDF. Table 2 also shows that the average effective property tax rate increased by 17.7 percent from 1999 to 2006 and by 7.9 percent from 1999 to 2011. Real spending per pupil increased by 13.2 percent from 1999 to 2006 and by 21 percent from 1999 to 2011, and student performance (discussed subsequently) increased between 19.7 and 21.1 percent. Our objective is to determine the extent to which these changes can be attributed to STAR.

Table 3 provides summary statistics and sources for all of the variables we use in our estimations. The dependent variable in the expenditure model is spending per pupil. We use two spending measures: current expenditures and operating expenditures. Current expenditures are derived

---

[20]The federal No Child Left Behind Act was passed in 2001, but including federal aid has little impact on the results.

[21]Our results are virtually unchanged if we reduce the sample to create a balanced panel.

Table 3 Summary statistics (1999–2011).

	Mean	Standard deviation	Min	Max	Source
Key variables					
Current expenditures per pupil	16,726	4,297	9,718	79,252	(1)
Operating expenditures per pupil	15,788	4,054	9,164	74,269	(1)
Adjusted performance index 1 (S_1)	70.7	13.8	15.8	100	(1)
Adjusted performance index 2 (S_2)	75.8	11.6	29.2	98.2	(1)
Cost-related variables					
Teacher salary (1–5 year experience)	21,781	9,279	1	61,744	(1), (4)
Enrollment (average daily membership)	2,746	3,435	60	46,550	(1)
Percent of students with severe disabilities	1.4	0.8	0	7.5	(1)
Percent of LEP students	1.7	3.4	0	33.2	(1)
Percent of free lunch students	27.0	17.4	0	89	(1)
Demand/efficiency-related variables					
Local tax share ($V/\bar{V}$)	0.40	0.15	0.02	1.05	(1), (2)
STAR tax share ($1 - X/V$)	0.75	0.14	0.17	1	(1), (2)
State aid term $[(A/Y)(V/\bar{V})(1 - X/V)]$	0.02	0.02	0.0001	0.38	(1), (2)
Income per pupil	129,887	117,775	27,725	1,962,731	(1)
Percent of college graduates	25.7	14.1	4.9	83.4	(1), (2)
Percent of youths (aged 5–7)	17.4	2.5	4.5	30.7	(1), (2), (3)
Percent of owner-occupied housing units	81.0	11.4	20.0	100	(1), (2), (3)
Percent of seniors (aged 65 and over)	14.8	3.3	3.1	38.9	(1), (2), (3)
Instrumental variables (IVs)					
Average percent of high cost students in the rest of the county	1.3	0.4	0	3.1	(1), (4)
Average percent of LEP students in the rest of the county	2.2	2.3	0	8.5	(1), (4)
Annual county average salary of manufacturing jobs	49,560	14,837	21,882	103,054	(4)
STAR tax share with 1999 property values (X_{IV})	0.8	0.1	0.46	1	(1), (2), (4)
Adjusted state aid ratio with 1999 property values (A_{IV})	0.02	0.02	0.000031	0.38	(1), (2), (4)

Notes: Monetary variables (e.g., state highway spending per capita, federal apportionments per capita) are adjusted for inflation (using state and local government price indexes published by the Bureau of Economic Analysis) and in 2010 dollars. Performance index 1 is simple average of percent of students reaching proficiency levels in fourth-grade reading and mathematics, in eighth-grade reading and mathematics, percent of Regents diploma recipients and non-dropout rates.

Sources: (1) New York State Education Department (NYSED); (2) American Community Survey (ACS); (3) U.S. Censuses in 1999 and 2009 (The annual values for inter-census years between 1999 and 2009 were interpolated by using the linear growth rate between 1999 and 2009.); and (4) U.S. Census, County Business Patterns.

by subtracting payments on debt service from total expenditures, whereas operating expenditures equal current expenditures minus transportation spending. Because transportation spending is not directly related to student performance and involves a unique set of cost factors (such as district area and population density), the effects of STAR on operating expenditures are our primary concern.

Student performance is a key variable in both the expenditure and demand functions. Our approach is to design performance indexes that (1) cover a range of student performance measures, (2) are linked to the types of measures in previous studies and in the New York school accountability system, and (3) are based on variables measured consistently across the years in our panel. In 1998–1999, New York initiated a new testing system, which is focused on testing student proficiency, particularly in math and English. The examinations are central to New York State's accountability system and New York State Education Department (NYSED) publishes the test results as part of each school's annual report card. This system was used throughout our sample period. Our first index, S_1, is the equally weighted average percentage of students reaching the state's proficiency standard on math and English exams in fourth and eighth grades. Our second index brings in the share of students receiving a Regents Diploma by passing at least five Regents exams and the share of students not dropping out of high school (=100 − dropout rate).[22] More specifically, this index, S_2, is the equally weighted average of the components in the first index together with Regents Diploma rates and non-dropout rates.[23] Our preferred measure is S_2 because it is more comprehensive.

One complication is that starting in 2009–2010, NYSED raised the scores required for a student to be judged "proficient," called "cut scores," leading to a substantial drop in proficiency levels across the state. For 2009–2010 and 2010–2011, therefore, we calculated adjusted proficiency rates based on the cut scores that applied before these years.[24]

---

[22] Dropout refers to "any student, regardless of age, who left school prior to graduation for any reason except death and did not enter another school or high school equivalency preparation program or other diploma program" (NYSED, 2003).

[23] Although combining outcome measures requires an arbitrary decision about the weights, we do not find that our results are sensitive to the weights we use. New York's accountability system focuses on the same test outcomes included in our performance index, and an estimate of a cohort graduation rate. Because a consistent measure of a cohort graduation rate is not available during our sample period, we used the non-dropout rate instead.

[24] To correct the proficiency rates for a change in the cut score, we assume the distribution of student scores in each district follows a normal distribution. We then approximate the cumulative standard normal with: $F\{Z\} = 1/[1 + \exp\{-1.702\,Z\}]$, where $Z = (X - \mu)/\sigma$,

Teacher salary data come from the "personnel master file" produced by NYSED. Our salary variable is the average salary a district pays to teachers with one to five years of experience, controlling for the actual experience and education of the teachers in that district. This variable captures the relative generosity of a district's salary schedule instead of the average quality of a district's teachers, at least as measured by experience and education. Measures of student characteristics include the share of students eligible for a free lunch (a measure of student poverty), the share of students classified as having limited English proficiency (LEP), and the share of students having severe disabilities defined as requiring teacher consultation services or spending at least 60 percent of their time out of their regular classroom.[25] The measure of enrollment is average daily membership adjusted for the residency of the student. Following standard practice, we allow a nonlinear relationship between per pupil spending and enrollment. Based on Rockoff (2010) and Duncombe and Yinger (2011), we also include the change in district enrollment. Because it takes time for a district to adjust to a new enrollment level, an increase in enrollment lowers costs per pupil (and a decrease in enrollment raises costs per pupil) in the short run. Demographic factors included in our regressions include income per pupil and the shares of the population that graduated from four-year college, youth (5–17 years of age), homeowners, and seniors (over age 64).[26]

5. Empirical Methods and Results

5.1. *Methodology*

We estimate the structural expenditure and demand models in equations (10) and (13). We treat the STAR tax share, $(1 - X/V)$, and the adjusted aid

---

X is the test score, and μ and σ are its mean and standard deviation, respectively. The proficiency rate at any given Z is $(1 - f\{Z\})$. Because our data set includes μ for each test in each district, we can use this equation to solve for σ using the observed new cut score, X_{NEW}, and the associated proficiency rate. With this estimate of σ we can then calculate $Z_{OLD} = (X_{OLD} - \mu)/\sigma$, where X_{OLD} is the old cut score. The proficiency rate at the old cut score is $(1 - F\{Z_{OLD}\})$. More detailed notes on this procedure are available from the authors.

[25] These variables are logged in our expenditure regressions. These variables have somewhat higher standard errors if they are not logged, but other results are not affected.

[26] We do not have annual data for median household income. If differences between income per pupil and median household income are constant over time, they are captured by our district fixed effects and other controls; if not, the use of income per capita represents another reason to say that our approach only approximates the underlying public choice mechanism.

ratio, $[(A/Y)(V/\bar{V})(1 - X/V)]$, as endogenous variables in both models because STAR-induced changes in spending or student performance may be capitalized into property values. Our instruments substitute predicted V and $\bar{V}$ into the above expressions. These predictions are 1999 values inflated by the Case-Shiller home price indices for New York published by the Federal Reserve Bank of St. Louis. This approach allows us to capture growth in V and $\bar{V}$ while removing the impact of X. For ease of reference, these two instrumental variables (IVs) for STAR tax share and adjusted aid ratio are referred to as X_{IV} and A_{IV}, respectively.

Following the literature in education cost functions (reviewed in Duncombe and Yinger, 2008), we also treat both the teacher salary variable and student performance measure as endogenous in the expenditure model, because unobserved school district traits may affect spending and student performance as well as salaries.[27] The IV for the teacher salary variable is the average manufacturing wage in a district's county. Following Duncombe and Yinger (2011) and Nguyen-Hoang and Yinger (2014), the IVs for student performance are exogenous traits of school districts in the rest of a district's county. A district's own choices are likely to be influenced by the choices of nearby districts, and the choices of nearby districts are influenced by their exogenous traits. The specific IVs we use are the average percentage of high-cost students (i.e., those with severe disabilities) and of LEP students in the rest of the county. We also examine the appropriateness of these IVs using two instrument tests: overidentification and weak instrument tests. We discuss the results of these tests in detail in the next section. Also, we use the Fuller's (1977) estimator ($k = 4$), which, according to Hahn, Hausman, and Kuersteiner (2004), proves to be less subject to potential bias from weak instruments than two-stage-least squares.

The regressions also include demographic factors. The expenditure regression accounts for a district's share of college graduates and of youth. These shares could influence either the monitoring of school officials or the demand for student performance measures other than the ones captured by our indexes. The demand regression accounts for the percent of housing-units that are owner-occupied and the share of the population over age 64; a relatively high share of owners might signify a cohesive community with a higher commitment to high-quality public schools, and a relatively high share

[27]Moreover, one possible type of inefficiency, as defined here, is overly generous teacher salaries. Treating these salaries as endogenous ensures the salary variable only picks up costs, not inefficiency.

of elderly voters might lead to the opposite effect. Because efficiency and demand are related concepts, no theoretical argument can clearly assign any of these four demographic traits to one of our equations over the other. We have assigned them to maximize explanatory power, but other assignments lead to little change in our main results.

Finally, the structural models are estimated with district and year fixed effects. In the expenditure regression, the district fixed effects control for unobserved, time-invariant district traits that influence efficiency or cost. In the demand regression, they control for unobserved time-invariant district traits that influence the demand for school quality as measured by our index. These factors include those who might lead households with certain incomes to sort into districts with certain school performance outcomes.[28] These fixed effects do not, of course, rule out the possibility that our results are affected by unobserved time-varying district traits but we believe the most important time-varying district traits are already included in our regressions.

For both regressions, our hypothesis tests are conducted with robust standard errors adjusted for clustering at the school district level.[29]

5.2. *Empirical Results*

Table 4 presents the results of the expenditure model for both current and operating expenditures (as dependent variables) together with two performance indices described earlier. The results are similar across the four columns of this table. Most of the variables are statistically significant at the 5 percent or 1 percent level. Our preferred specification is in column 4, which refers to operating expenditures and the performance index that includes Regents Diploma rates and non-dropout rates. We find educational spending increases with the share of students eligible for a free lunch or who have severe disabilities. The impact of LEP students on spending is close to zero and not significant. Enrollment and spending have the expected U-shaped relationship, but the squared term is not significant. Spending per

---

[28]Households may sort across districts with different school quality based on unobservable traits, resulting in "Tiebout bias" (reviewed in Ross and Yinger, 1999). This possibility is addressed with our fixed effects. A second-order bias could arise if unobserved household traits are correlated with changes in school quality but the changes we observe do not result in significant reordering of school quality rankings, and we control for many time-varying variables.

[29]Because the demand model includes two variables (predicted cost and efficiency) derived from the expenditure model, it is possible the standard errors are biased. In fact, however, bootstrapped robust standard errors are actually lower than the ones in the table.

Table 4 Structural cost function results (1999–2011) (Dependent variable: Logged education expenditures per pupil).

	Current expenditures		Operating expenditures	
	Performance index 1	Performance index 2	Performance index 1	Performance index 2
Variable	(1)	(2)	(3)	(4)
Performance measure[a]	*0.38*	*0.62*	*0.34*	*0.55*
	$(2.49)^{**}$	$(2.56)^{**}$	$(2.27)^{**}$	$(2.31)^{**}$
Cost-related variables				
Teacher salary[a]	*0.20*	*0.21*	*0.20*	*0.21*
	$(4.32)^{***}$	$(4.35)^{***}$	$(4.40)^{***}$	$(4.42)^{***}$
Percent of free lunch students[a]	0.014	0.016	0.013	0.015
	$(2.90)^{***}$	$(2.95)^{***}$	$(2.72)^{***}$	$(2.76)^{***}$
Percent of LEP students*	−0.0020	−0.0014	−0.0020	−0.0015
	(-1.02)	(-0.70)	(-1.03)	(-0.75)
Percent of students with severe disabilities[a]	0.010	0.011	0.0098	0.010
	$(2.56)^{**}$	$(2.57)^{**}$	$(2.46)^{**}$	$(2.44)^{**}$
Enrollment[a]	−0.58	−0.53	−0.66	−0.62
	$(-2.78)^{***}$	$(-2.46)^{**}$	$(-3.20)^{***}$	$(-2.90)^{***}$
Enrollment squared[a]	0.0078	0.0044	0.013	0.010
	(0.56)	(0.31)	(0.95)	(0.70)
Percent three-year log enrollment change if positive	−0.035	−0.035	−0.034	−0.035
	$(-8.28)^{***}$	$(-8.25)^{***}$	$(-8.24)^{***}$	$(-8.20)^{***}$
Percent three-year log enrollment change if negative	−0.026	−0.027	−0.025	−0.026
	$(-5.21)^{***}$	$(-5.30)^{***}$	$(-5.06)^{***}$	$(-5.12)^{***}$
Efficiency-related variables				
STAR tax share $(1 - X/V)$[a]	*−0.11*	*−0.10*	−0.12	−0.11
	$(-2.11)^{**}$	$(-1.97)^{**}$	$(-2.28)^{**}$	$(-2.15)^{**}$
Adjusted aid ratio $[(A/Y)(V/\bar{V})(1 - X/V)]$	*2.06*	*2.00*	2.02	*1.97*
	$(5.62)^{***}$	$(5.76)^{***}$	$(5.50)^{***}$	$(5.61)^{***}$
Local tax share[a]	−0.041	−0.040	−0.042	−0.041
	$(-2.21)^{**}$	$(-2.15)^{**}$	$(-2.27)^{**}$	$(-2.21)^{**}$
Income per pupil[a]	0.036	0.031	0.037	0.033
	$(2.31)^{**}$	$(1.96)^{**}$	$(2.39)^{**}$	$(2.07)^{**}$
Percent of college graduates	0.00039	0.00054	0.00054	0.00070
	(0.35)	(0.50)	(0.49)	(0.65)
Percent of youths	0.0034	0.0042	0.0031	0.0038
	$(1.65)^{*}$	$(1.93)^{*}$	(1.49)	$(1.73)^{*}$
Selected structural parameters				
σ for performance	0.29^{*}	0.60^{**}	0.25^{*}	0.53^{**}
δ_1 for STAR tax share	0.11^{**}	0.10^{**}	0.12^{**}	0.11^{**}
δ_2 for local tax share	0.07^{***}	0.04^{**}	0.07^{***}	0.04^{**}

(Continued)

Table 4 (*Continued*)

Variable	Current expenditures		Operating expenditures	
	Performance index 1 (1)	Performance index 2 (2)	Performance index 1 (3)	Performance index 2 (4)
γ for income	−0.04***	−0.03**	−0.04**	−0.03**
f for flypaper effect	53.5**	63.8*	51.3**	59.8**

Notes: There are 8,058 observations. All financial measures are inflation-adjusted in 2010 dollars. Regressions are estimated with year and district fixed effects, the Fuller ($k = 4$) estimator, and robust standard errors adjusted for clustering at the school district level. Coefficients in **bold italics** are treated as endogenous with five IVs: the average percentage shares of high cost and LEP students in the rest of the county (for performance measures); logged annual county average salary of manufacturing jobs (for teacher salary), X_{IV} and A_{IV} constructed with growth-adjusted property values in 1999 (for the STAR tax share and adjusted aid ratio). Numbers in parentheses are *t*-statistics.
[a]Variable is log-transformed.
***Statistically significant at the 1% level; **statistically significant at the 5% level; *statistically significant at the 10% level.

pupil is also strongly affected by short-run changes in enrollment. After the adjustment in equation (10), these results also apply to educational costs.

Turning to the efficiency variables, we find the reduction in the tax share caused by an increase in STAR encourages spending on school outputs other than those in our index, which indicates lower efficiency as defined in this paper. In contrast, STAR also lowers the value of existing state education aid to voters and therefore leads to less spending on these other outputs, that is, to more efficiency. Our simulations in the next section explore the net impact of these two effects. We also find, as expected, that a lower non-STAR tax share or higher district income leads to inefficiency, again because they encourage spending on outputs other than those in our index and/or because voters have lower incentives to monitor school officials. This type of spending is also encouraged by a more educated population.

These results are derived from estimations with IVs. On the basis of the Hansen (1982) *J* test (*p* values from 0.61 to 0.97), we fail to reject the null that the IVs are jointly valid (i.e., our IVs are jointly exogenous). Our IVs are also strongly correlated with the endogenous variables. As reported in Table 5, they are highly significant with expected signs in the first stages of the two-stage estimations.[30] Moreover, the *F*-statistics in the first-stage

[30]The Kleibergen–Paap *rk* statistics for these regressions are above 4.5, but there is no direct test for weak IVs for multiple endogenous regressors and robust standard errors.

Table 5   First-stage regression results of column 4 of Table 4.

IVs	Dependent variables			
	Performance index 2	Teacher salary	STAR tax share	Adjusted aid ratio
Average percent of LEP students	0.0099	0.031	0.039	0.0010
in the rest of the county	$(3.15)^{***}$	$(2.54)^{**}$	$(16.69)^{***}$	$(5.94)^{***}$
Average percent of high cost	0.0017	0.074	−0.0081	−0.00022
students in the rest of the county	(0.45)	$(2.77)^{***}$	$(-2.54)^{**}$	(-0.79)
Logged annual county average	−0.040	0.30	0.079	0.0012
salary of manufacturing jobs	$(-2.23)^{**}$	$(2.74)^{***}$	$(5.93)^{***}$	(0.91)
X_{IV}	−0.16	0.28	1.41	0.012
	$(-5.04)^{***}$	(0.95)	$(40.21)^{***}$	$(4.61)^{***}$
A_{IV}	−0.52	−1.64	0.47	1.18
	$(-1.97)^{**}$	(-1.53)	$(2.59)^{***}$	$(25.09)^{***}$

Note: Other variables in these first-stage regression results are not reported.
***Statistically significant at the 1% level; **statistically significant at the 5% level.

regressions of our IVs range between 21.6 and 1,205, higher than the rule-of-thumb threshold value of 10 suggested in Staiger and Stock (1997). These statistics, together with use of the Fuller ($k = 4$) estimator, suggest our results are highly unlikely to be biased by weak IVs.

The results of the expenditure model can be used to derive the structural parameters in equation (10), which are reported in the second panel in Table 4. The (significant) economies of quality scale parameter (σ) is 0.53, which indicates strong economies of quality scale for New York school districts in delivering our measure of school quality. The efficiency elasticity for the STAR tax share (δ_1 is nearly three times as large as that for local tax share (δ_2) (0.11 versus 0.04). This difference, which is significant at the 1 percent level, indicates an increase in STAR induces double the impact on efficiency compared to an equivalent increase in the standard tax share. This result suggests a high-visibility policy, such as STAR, has a larger impact on voters' perceptions of tax share than do differences in $V/\bar{V}$. The efficiency elasticity for income (γ) and the flypaper effect in the efficiency equation (f) indicate an increase in community income is associated with slightly lower efficiency and the efficiency loss is much higher for an equivalent increase in state aid.

Because operating expenditures are of primary interest, Table 6 presents the results of the demand model for the two performance indices associated with operating expenditure estimations. The two STAR variables are treated as endogenous using the instruments described earlier.[31] In our preferred regression (column 2), the elasticity of performance with respect to the STAR tax share is -0.63 and is highly significant. The adjusted aid ratio is also highly significant. The other coefficients in Table 6 are generally significant and have the expected signs. For example, the tax price variables for the local tax share and cost index are negatively related to demand, and higher efficiency is associated with greater demand for student performance. The coefficient of per pupil income is positive and significant.

In the second panel of Table 6, we report the structural parameters in equation (13). For our preferred specification, the price elasticities equal -0.19 for the tax share and -0.57 for the STAR tax share.[32] As in the case of the expenditure equation, tax shares in the highly visible STAR program appear to elicit a greater response than standard tax shares. Somewhat surprisingly, the price elasticity for inefficiency, -4.22, is even larger; voters in districts that provide a relatively wide range of services and/or are wasteful select a significantly lower level of the services in our school performance index. The income elasticity of demand for our index is small, 0.15. The flypaper effect is 52.10, which indicates that \$1 of tax-share-adjusted state aid has the same impact on demand as \$52.10 of voter income. This estimate is much larger than the estimate in previous studies, but not quite as large as the estimate in Table 4. Except for the cost index coefficient, all of these parameters are statistically significant.

For purposes of comparison, Table 7 presents reduced form estimates similar to those in Rockoff (2010). The estimating equation is 15 multiplied by MC/e, assuming constant returns to quality scale ($\sigma = 1.0$). When the STAR tax share variable (which Rockoff calls the community tax price) is treated as endogenous, our estimated elasticity, -0.15, is similar to his (-0.23). Without an endogeneity correction, his estimated coefficient for the adjusted aid ratio, 0.88, is also similar to our result in column 1, at 0.78.[33]

---

[31]These instruments are significant in the first-stage regression and the associated F-statistics range from 53.4 to 219.0 — signs that the demand equation is not subject to weak instrument bias.

[32]This price elasticity is about twice as large as the elasticity estimated by Wang, Duncombe, and Yinger (2011) for open-ended matching grants for school capital spending in New York.

[33]Rockoff estimated a regression that treated this variable as endogenous but does not present the results. The form of this variable in Rockoffs equation (7) is the same as ours, but the form listed in his Table 2 is different. If he used the latter form, our results are not comparable to his.

Table 6 Demand results (1999–2011) (Dependent variable: Logged performance index).

Variable	S_1 (1)	S_2 (2)
Adjusted income		
Income per pupil[a]	0.33	0.17
	$(5.74)^{***}$	$(7.18)^{***}$
Adjusted aid ratio	**16.7**	**8.81**
	$(4.96)^{***}$	$(6.14)^{***}$
Tax price variables		
STAR tax share[a]	**−1.16**	**−0.63**
	$(-6.02)^{***}$	$(-7.59)^{***}$
Local tax share[a]	−0.39	−0.22
	$(-5.67)^{***}$	$(-6.95)^{***}$
Cost index[a]	−0.026	−0.034
	(-0.62)	(-1.29)
Efficiency index[a]	8.64	4.67
	$(5.57)^{***}$	$(7.12)^{***}$
Preference variables		
Percent of owner-occupied housing units	0.00085	0.00037
	$(3.28)^{***}$	$(2.15)^{**}$
Percent of senior citizens (aged 65 or over)	−0.0099	−0.0068
	$(-5.01)^{***}$	$(-5.57)^{***}$
Average percent of LEP students in the rest of the county	0.029	0.017
	$(5.51)^{***}$	$(5.00)^{***}$
Average percent of high cost students in the rest of the county	0.0049	0.000039
	(0.85)	(0.01)
Selected structural parameters		
μ_1 for local tax share	-0.31^{***}	-0.19^{***}
μ_2 for STAR tax share	-0.92^{***}	-0.57^{***}
μ_3 for efficiency	-6.84^{***}	-4.22^{***}
μ_4 for cost	-0.02	-0.03
θ for income	0.26^{***}	0.15^{***}
f for flypaper effect	50.2^{***}	52.1^{***}

Notes: There are 8,060 observations. S_1 and S_2 are performance indices 1 and 2. Regressions are estimated with year and district fixed effects, the Fuller ($k = 4$) estimator, and robust standard errors adjusted for clustering at the school district level. Coefficients in ***bold italics*** are treated as endogenous. The two IVs for the adjusted aid ratio and STAR tax share are those constructed with growth-adjusted property values in 1999. Cost and efficiency indices in this table are derived based on regressions in columns 3 and 4 of Table 4, using equations (11) and (12).
[a]Variable is log-transformed.
***Statistically significant at the 1% level; **statistically significant at the 5% level.

Table 7 Reduced-form expenditure results (1999–2011) (Dependent variable: Logged operating expenditures per pupil).

STAR tax share $(1 - X/V)^{\text{a}}$	−0.011	−**0.14*****	−**0.15*****
	(−0.83)	(−**7.28**)	(−**8.10**)
Adjusted aid ratio	0.78***	1.34***	**1.39*****
$[(A/Y)(V/\bar{V})(1 - X/V)]$	(4.28)	(5.61)	(**5.96**)
Cost-related variables			
Average county manufacturing salary^{a}	0.053***	0.054***	0.054***
	(3.51)	(3.56)	(3.55)
Percent of free lunch students^{a}	0.0041*	0.0030	0.0029
	(1.86)	(1.35)	(1.29)
Percent of LEP students^{a}	0.0014	0.0013	0.0013
	(1.60)	(1.47)	(1.46)
Percent of students with severe	0.0071***	0.0065***	0.0064***
disabilities^{a}	(5.07)	(4.53)	(4.48)
Enrollment^{a}	−0.85***	−0.82***	−0.82***
	(−8.89)	(−8.44)	(−8.38)
Enrollment squared^{a}	0.027***	0.029***	0.029***
	(4.18)	(4.42)	(4.44)
Percent three-year log enrollment	−0.030***	−0.031***	−0.031***
change if positive	(−12.71)	(−13.22)	(−13.21)
Percent three-year log enrollment	−0.017***	−0.018***	−0.019***
change if negative	(−10.06)	(−10.89)	(−10.93)
Efficiency-related variables			
Local tax share^{a}	−0.049***	−0.063***	−0.064***
	(−5.27)	(−6.39)	(−6.51)
Income per pupil^{a}	0.038***	0.064***	0.067***
	(5.57)	(8.19)	(8.35)
Percent of college graduates	−0.00023	0.00059	0.00067
	(−0.49)	(1.24)	(1.40)
Percent of youths	0.0019**	0.0017**	0.0017**
	(2.26)	(2.04)	(2.01)

Notes: Coefficients in **bold italics** are treated as endogenous using the IVs described in the text. Numbers in parentheses are *t*-statistics.
^{a}Variable is log-transformed.
***Statistically significant at the 1% level; **statistically significant at the 5% level.

Because our estimate of δ is small, the discussion after equation (15) implies the coefficient of the STAR tax share variable would yield an accurate price elasticity of demand if σ were equal to 1.0. Because our estimate of σ is below one, however, this STAR coefficient appears to underestimate the underlying structural parameter (μ_2 in Table 6) by more than 70 percent.

5.3. Simulating the Net Effects of STAR

Table 8 presents simulated impacts of STAR on student performance, school district efficiency, school spending, and property tax rates. These impacts are based on the results in the last column of Table 4 and the second column of Table 6 combined with data on individual districts and the equations derived earlier.[34] Although the derivatives in equations (16) to (19) provide some helpful initial intuition about these calculations, they are approximations and they make two assumptions not used for Table 8, namely, equal flypaper effects in the cost/efficiency and demand equations and equal elasticities for the various components of tax price.[35]

As shown in panel A of Table 8, we estimate that STAR resulted in a statewide average increase in spending of 4.34 percent. This spending effect ranged from 2.54 percent in Yonkers to 5.42 percent in upstate rural districts. In addition, STAR resulted in an across-district average decline of 2.61 percent in the efficiency with which our student performance index is delivered. The average operating spending was $17,666 in 2011 and there were about 1.63 million students in the state's public schools outside of New York City. The total efficiency loss, $17,666 \times 1.63$ million $\times 0.0316$, comes to about $750 million. As explained earlier, this efficiency loss may include waste in the traditional sense but we suspect that it mainly reflects the fact that the incentives in STAR lead voters to push for spending on objectives other than the ones in our index. In other words, STAR induced school districts in New York State to increase their annual spending on objectives other than boosting standard test scores and keeping students in high school by three quarters of a billion dollars. Although these other objectives are valued by voters, the state's expressed interest in these test

---

[34]We calculate the impact of STAR using equations (2), (5), and (6)–(8), with separate coefficients for each tax-price term and with separate flypaper effects for the efficiency and demand equations. These equations are used to derive the percentage changes in $S, C, e, E,$ and t when the STAR matching rate goes from zero to X/V. These equations are then combined with our estimates of the parameters and data from school districts in the state to obtain the results in Table 7. A technical appendix containing these equations is available from the authors. Simulation results with our alternative performance measure or without our cut-score correction are similar to those in Table 8.

[35]These simulations do not account for property tax capitalization, which has complex, but secondary, impacts on the results in Table 8. With capitalization, for example, higher STAR exemptions lead to higher values for owner-occupied property, which lowers the STAR implicit matching rate and raises the tax share (since its numerator includes other types of property). These changes have offsetting effects. We hope to conduct formal simulations with capitalization in future research.

Table 8 Simulated impacts (%) of STAR on sending, efficiency, performance, and property taxes.

Region	E	e	C	S	t	Offset
Panel A: STAR Exemptions in 2011						
Downstate small cities	3.22	−1.99	1.17	2.13	4.68	19.52
Downstate suburbs	2.58	−1.60	0.93	1.70	3.64	20.02
Yonkers	2.54	−1.53	0.97	1.77	6.54	34.54
Upstate big three	4.55	−2.68	1.74	3.19	29.74	77.42
Upstate rural	5.42	−3.21	2.01	3.68	22.15	44.83
Upstate small cities	5.37	−3.18	2.00	3.67	19.33	39.95
Upstate suburbs	4.29	−2.58	1.58	2.90	11.69	32.35
Statewide mean	4.34	−2.61	1.60	2.94	13.85	34.29
Median district	3.82	−2.32	1.41	2.58	7.93	28.05
Panel B: STAR Exemptions in 2011 Plus 30 Percent Income Tax Rebate						
Downstate small cities	4.39	−2.68	1.58	2.90	6.48	19.03
Downstate suburbs	3.47	−2.14	1.25	2.29	4.93	19.66
Yonkers	3.42	−2.05	1.30	2.38	8.92	34.18
Upstate big three	6.33	−3.69	2.41	4.43	46.73	82.12
Upstate rural	7.76	−4.51	2.84	5.24	32.79	43.31
Upstate small cities	7.68	−4.45	2.82	5.21	29.86	39.41
Upstate suburbs	5.97	−3.54	2.19	4.02	17.49	32.17
Statewide mean	6.10	−3.60	2.23	4.11	20.57	33.64
Median district	5.23	−3.16	1.91	3.51	11.09	27.43

Notes: E = expenditure per pupil; e = efficiency index; C = best practices spending; S = student performance index; t = effective property tax rate; Offset = share of original tax break (tX) offset by property tax rate increase.

Source: Authors calculations based on estimation results.

scores and graduation rates as central elements of its accountability program implies this is an expensive unintended consequence of STAR. This efficiency cost could be higher or lower, of course, for another set of performance objectives.

Because the increase in E is greater than the decrease in e, the definition in equation (2) implies that STAR boosts best-practice spending, C. This result is also presented in Table 8. Because of our estimated economies of quality scale (i.e., $\sigma < 1$), this increase in C leads to a more-than-proportional increase in S. In fact, the average across-district impact of STAR on S was 2.94 percent. Moreover, the increases in S were somewhat greater in some needier districts, such as the upstate big three (3.19 percent) or upstate rural districts (3.68 percent), than they were in the wealthy downstate suburbs (1.70 percent). Thus, one surprising unintended consequence of STAR is that it slightly moderated performance disparities across districts in the state.

One important exception is Yonkers, which is a needy district but received a below-average boost in its performance from STAR.

An accompanying unintended consequence that works in the other direction appears in the last two columns of Table 8. This column shows that STAR boosted property tax rates in all types of districts. The across-district average increase was 13.85 percent, and the increase ranged from only 3.64 percent in the downstate suburbs to 29.74 percent in the upstate big three. In other words, the moderation of performance disparities was accompanied by a disproportionate increase in the property tax rates in the neediest districts. This property tax increase actually offset a large share of the initial STAR tax savings in many districts.[36] This offset ranges from 77.42 percent in the upstate big three to 19.52 percent in downstate small cities. Moreover, these property tax increases apply to all property, including property that does not receive a STAR exemption. By raising the property tax rate on business property, STAR contributes to the widespread perception that New York State in general and upstate New York in particular is not friendly to business.

Panel B of Table 8 provides comparable simulations with a 30 percent boost in the STAR exemptions, as with the 2007–2009 income tax rebate program. This increase leads to a 33 to 43 percent increase in the first four columns of this table. The statewide average impact of STAR on student performance, for example, rises from 2.94 to 4.11 percent (an increase of 40 percent). The impacts on upstate tax rates are somewhat larger than this, but in most cases the offset to the initial STAR savings actually goes down, even though the tax rate changes are larger, because the initial savings are 30 percent larger in this case.

These simulated impacts can be compared to the post–pre differences in Table 2, which reflect both STAR and other factors. This comparison suggests that STAR helps to explain the increased student performance, district spending, and property tax rates over the 1999–2011 period. Between 1999 and 2006, for example, the average impact of STAR on performance, 2.94 percent, accounts for about 14 percent of the overall performance increase in the state, 21.1 percent. STAR explains even more, over one fifth, of the 20.9 percent increases in spending. The average across-district increase

---

[36]The STAR tax savings is tX. The impact on a voter's tax payment from a change in t (=dt) with STAR in place is $(dt)(V - X)$. The entry in Table 8 is $dt(V - X)/(tX)$.

in property tax rates was 7.9 percent, which is somewhat more than half of the predicted average change in Table 8. This result suggests that some other factors, such as the recession, partially offset STAR's unintended impact on property tax rates.

6. Conclusions and Policy Implications

A state education finance system consists of local property taxes, state-funded property tax exemptions, state aid to education, and sometimes other revenue sources. Each of these components alters both the incentives facing voters and school officials, and the distributions of educational outcomes and tax burdens. Proposed changes to any component of this system should be evaluated in terms of its impact on the system as a whole.

By all accounts, elected officials in New York State thought that STAR would simply provide homeowners with some relief from their school property taxes. These officials did not recognize that by significantly lowering voter's tax prices, STAR would also initiate behavioral changes by voters and school officials and thereby result in many unintended consequences, some of which offset the original intent of the program. To be specific, we find that STAR has led to substantial increases in property tax rates and has provided homeowners with far less property tax relief than advertised. In the median district, tax rate increases have offset 28 percent of the initial tax savings. We also find that STAR has had significant, unintended impacts on student performance, school district efficiency, and school spending. In the median district, STAR increased spending by 3.8 percent, decreased efficiency by 2.3 percent, and raised performance by 2.6 percent.

Although the distribution of STAR compensation from the state is profoundly inequitable, STAR has a small equalizing impact on student performance because the price subsidies in poor upstate cities are so large. We estimate, for example, that STAR resulted in a 3.7 percent increase in student performance in small upstate cities, compared with only 1.7 percent in downstate suburbs. This equalization comes at a price, of course, as it is accompanied by higher property tax rate increases in poor districts than in wealthy districts. In the upstate big three districts, for example, our estimates imply that STAR-induced property tax rate increases have offset three quarters of the initial property tax relief for homeowners and raised the effective property tax rate on business property by more than 25 percent. Moreover, STAR has led to a smaller decline in inter-district performance

disparities than would have occurred if the STAR funds had been placed
in the state aid program implemented in 2007 but effectively canceled after
New York entered the recession two years later.[37]

A revised STAR program with a more equitable formula for exemption
amounts, and hence with more equitable impacts on student performance,
could be designed. One approach would be to eliminate the SPDF; another
would be to set exemption amounts consistent with a cost-adjusted power
equalizing formula.

The design of STAR also encourages school districts to increase spending,
both in ways that boost the measures of student performance that are
included in the state's accountability program and in other ways that cannot
be identified. These spending increases are not necessarily bad but they are
unintended and are therefore not the products of thoughtful analysis or
policy design.

The STAR price incentives that led to these effects could easily be
eliminated by reimbursing a district based on a state-determined property
tax rate, perhaps the statewide average, rather than the property tax rate
selected by the district. This change would, in effect, convert STAR from an
open-ended matching grant to a lump-sum grant. As noted earlier, New York
recently took a step in this direction by limiting the growth in exemption
benefits to 2 percent annually.

Finally, our analysis shows that property tax relief programs and state
aid reforms can have complex impacts on school district behavior, even when
they are not intended to do so. We urge state policy makers to recognize these
effects and to design programs that — intentionally — lead to the types of
behavior the policy makers are attempting to promote.

Acknowledgments

Our colleague, William Duncombe, passed away in May 2013. He was a
vital member of the team that produced previous drafts of this paper,
and his contributions remain central to this draft. We are grateful to the
Rockefeller Foundation for financial support given to the Education Finance

---

[37] A description of the 2007 New York State aid formula, including its large cost adjustment
for students from poor families, can be found at https://statcaid.nysed.gov/generalInfo/.
The implicit matching rates in STAR are also less equalizing than the matching rates
in a guaranteed-tax-base program, which is used in several states, particularly if a cost
adjustment is included (see Duncombe and Yinger, 1998b).

and Accountability Program at The Maxwell School. We are also grateful for helpful comments from Bruce Baker and two anonymous referees and for data assistance from Bob Bifulco, Eric Brunner, Christian Burger, Alexander Falevich, Lincoln Groves, Nuno Mota, Judson Murchie, Sun Jung Oh, Judith Ricks, and Pengju Zhang.

References

Addonizio, Michael F. 1990. School aid and property tax relief: Some evidence of conflicting incentives. *Journal of Education Finance* **16**(1): 37–48.

Addonizio, Michael F. 1991. Intergovernmental grants and the demand for local educational expenditures. *Public Finance Review* **19**(2): 209–232. doi:10.1177/109114219101900205

Bradford, David F. and Wallace E. Oates. 1971a. The analysis of revenue sharing in a new approach to collective fiscal decisions. *Quarterly Journal of Economics* **85**(3): 416–439. doi:10.2307/1885931

Bradford, David F. and Wallace E. Oates. 1971b. Towards a predictive theory of intergovernmental grants. *American Economic Review* **61**(2): 440–448.

Bradford, David F., Richard A. Malt, and Wallace E. Oates. 1969. The rising cost of local public services: Some evidence and reflections. *National Tax Journal* **22**(2): 185–202.

Brunner, Eric J. and Stephen L. Ross. 2010. Is the median voter decisive? Evidence from referenda voting patterns. *Journal of Public Economics* **94**(11): 898–910. doi:10.1016/j.jpubeco.2010.09.009

Charnes, Abraham, William W. Cooper, and Edwardo Rhodes. 1978. Measuring the efficiency of decision making units. *European Journal of Operational Research* **2**(6): 429–444. doi:10.1016/0377-2217(78)90138-8

Downes, Thomas A. and Thomas Pogue. 1994. Adjusting school aid formulas for the higher cost of educating disadvantaged students. *National Tax Journal* **47**(1): 89–110.

Duncombe, William D. 1996. Public expenditure research: What have we learned? *Public Budgeting & Finance* **16**(2): 26–58. doi:10.1111/1540-5850.01067

Duncombe, William D., Jerry Miner, and John Ruggiero. 1997. Empirical evaluation of bureaucratic models of inefficiency. *Public Choice* **93**(1): 1–18. doi:10.1023/A:1017910714756

Duncombe, William D. and John Yinger. 1993. An analysis of returns to scale in public production, with an application to fire protection. *Journal of Public Economics* **52**(1): 49–72. doi:10.1016/0047-2727(93)90104-2

Duncombe, William D. and John Yinger. 1997. Why is it so hard to help central city schools? *Journal of Policy Analysis and Management* **16**(1): 85–113.

Duncombe, William D. and John Yinger. 1998a. An analysis of two educational policies in New York State: Performance standards and property tax relief. In James H. Wyckoff (ed.), *Educational Finance to Support Higher Learning Standards*, pp. 98–137. Albany: New York State Board of Regents.

Duncombe, William D. and John Yinger. 1998b. School finance reform: Aid formulas and equity objectives. *National Tax Journal* **51**(2): 239–262. [Chapter 12]

Duncombe, William D. and John Yinger. 2000. Financing higher student performance standards: The case of New York State. *Economics of Education Review* **19**(4): 363–386.

Duncombe, William D. and John Yinger. 2001. Alternative paths to property tax relief. In William E. Oates (ed.), *Property Taxation and Local Government Finance*, pp. 243–294. Cambridge, MA: Lincoln Institute of Land Policy.

Duncombe, William D. and John Yinger. 2005. How much more does a disadvantaged student cost? *Economics of Education Review* **24**(5): 513–532. [Chapter 7]

Duncombe, William D. and John Yinger. 2008. Measurement of cost differentials. In Edward Fiske and Helen F. Ladd (eds.), *Handbook of Education Finance and Policy*, pp. 238–256. New York: Routledge.

Duncombe, William D. and John Yinger. 2011. Making do: State constraints and local responses in California's education finance system. *International Tax and Public Finance* **18**(3): 337–368. [Chapter 10]

Färe, Rolf and C. A. Knox Lovell. 1978. Measuring the technical efficiency of production. *Journal of Economic Theory* **19**(1): 150–162. doi:10.1016/0022-0531(78)90060-1

Farrell, Michael J. 1957. The measurement of productive efficiency. *Journal of the Royal Statistical Society. Series A (General)* **120**(3): 253–290. doi:10.2307/2343100

Fisher, Ronald C. and Leslie E. Papke. 2000. Local government responses to education grants. *National Tax Journal* **53**(1): 153–168.

Fisher, Ronald C. and Robert H. Rasche. 1984. The incidence and incentive effects of property tax credits: Evidence from Michigan. *Public Finance Review* **12**(3): 291–319. doi:10.1177/109114218401200302

Fuller, Wayne A. 1977. Some properties of a modification of the limited information estimator. *Econometrica* **45**(4): 939–954. doi:10.2307/1912683

Hahn, Jinyong, Jerry Hausman, and Guido Kuersteiner. 2004. Estimation with weak instruments: Accuracy of higher-order bias and MSE approximations. *Econometrics Journal* **7**(1): 272–306. doi:10.1111/j.1368-423X.2004.00131.x

Hansen, Lars P. 1982. Large sample properties of generalized method of moments estimators. *Econometrica* **50**(4): 1029–1054. doi:10.2307/1912775

Hines, James R. and Richard H. Thaler. 1995. Anomalies: The flypaper effect. *Journal of Economic Perspectives* **9**(4): 217–226. doi:10.1257/jep.9.4.217

Ladd, Helen F. and John Yinger. 1991. *America's Ailing Cities: Fiscal Health and the Design of Urban Policy*. Baltimore, MD: Johns Hopkins University Press.

Mauro, Frank. 2008. *Testimony before the Senate Standing Committee on Local Government Assembly Standing Committee on Real Property Taxation Public Hearing on Proposed Legislation Addressing Real Property Taxation Issues*. Latham, NY: New York Fiscal Policy Institute.

McCarty, Therese A. and Suthathip Yaisawarng. 1993. Technical efficiency in New Jersey school districts. In Harold Fried, C.A. Knox Lovell, and Shelton S. Schmidt (eds.), *The Measurement of Productive Efficiency: Techniques and Applications*, pp. 172–288. New York: Oxford University Press.

New York State Department of Taxation and Finance. 2013a. *Exemptions from Real Property Taxation in NYS: County, City and Town Assessment Rolls* (years 2009–12). Available www.tax.ny.gov/research/property/reports/exempt/yyindex.htm (where yy is a 2-digit year indicator). Accessed 26 October 2013.

New York State Department of Taxation and Finance. 2013b. *STAR*. Available www.tax.ny.gov/pit/property/star/index.htm. Accessed 26 October 2013.

New York State Department of Taxation and Finance. 2013c. *STAR Differentials*. Available www.tax.ny.gov/pit/property/star/diff.htm. Accessed 26 October 2013.

New York State Department of Taxation and Finance. 2013d. *Summary of Tax Provisions* (various years). Available www.tax.ny.gov/research/stats/statistics/policy-special/summary_provisions/summary_of_provisions.htm. Accessed 4 June 2014.

New York State Division of the Budget. 2013. *School Tax Relief Program*. Available www.budget.ny.gov/pubs/archive/fy1112archive/eBudget1112/fy1112littlebook/Star .pdf. Accessed 26 October 2013.

New York State Education Department (NYSED). 2003. *Understanding Your School Report Card 2003: Guide to Secondary School Assessments*. Available www.emsc. nysed.gov/repcrd2003/information/secondary/guide.html. Accessed 4 June 2014.

Nguyen-Hoang, Phuong and John Yinger. 2014. Education finance reform, local behavior, and student performance in Massachusetts. *Journal of Education Finance* **39**(4): 245–270. [Chapter 9]

Oates, Wallace E. 1972. *Fiscal Federalism*. New York: Harcourt Brace Jovanovich.

Office of the New York State Comptroller. 2012. *School Tax Relief (STAR) Program*. Available www.osc.state.ny.us/localgov/audits/swr/2013/star/global.pdf. Accessed 26 October 2013.

Ray, Subhash C. 1991. Resource-use efficiency in public schools: A study of Connecticut data. *Management Science* **37**(12): 1620–1628. doi:10.1287/mnsc.37.12.1620

Reschovsky, Andrew and Jennifer Imazeki. 1998. The development of school finance formulas to guarantee the provision of adequate education to low-income students. In William J. Fowler (ed.), *Developments in School Finance, 1997: Does Money Matter?* pp. 121–148. Washington, DC: U.S. Department of Education, National Center for Education Statistics.

Reschovsky, Andrew and Jennifer Imazeki. 2001. Achieving educational adequacy through school finance reform. *Journal of Education Finance* **26**(4): 373–396.

Reschovsky, Andrew and Jennifer Imazeki. 2003. Let no child be left behind: Determining the cost of improving student performance. *Public Finance Review* **31**(3): 263–290. doi:10.1177/1091142103031003003

Rockoff, Jonah. 2010. Local response to fiscal incentives in heterogeneous communities. *Journal of Urban Economics* **68**(2): 138–147. doi:10.1016/j.jue.2010.03.010

Roemer, John E. and Joaquim Silvestre. 2002. The flypaper effect is not an anomaly. *Journal of Public Economic Theory* **4**(1): 1–17. doi:10.1111/1467-9779.00085

Ross, Stephen L. and John Yinger. 1999. Sorting and voting: A review of the literature on urban public finance. In Paul Cheshire and Edwin S. Mills (eds.), *Handbook of Regional and Urban Economics*, vol. 3, Applied Urban Economics, pp. 2001–2060. Amsterdam: Elsevier B.V.

Rubinfeld, Daniel L. 1987. The economics of the local public sector. In Alan J. Auerbach and Martin Feldstein (eds.), *Handbook of Public Economics*, vol. 2, pp. 571–645. Amsterdam: Elsevier Science Publishers.

Ruggiero, John. 1996. Efficiency of educational production: An analysis of New York school districts. *Review of Economics and Statistics* **78**(3): 499–509. doi:10.2307/2109797

Seiford, Lawrence M. and Robert M. Thrall. 1990. Recent developments in DEA: The mathematical programming approach to frontier analysis. *Journal of Econometrics* **46**(1): 7–38. doi:10.1016/0304-4076(90)90045-U

Staiger, Douglas and James H. Stock. 1997. Instrumental variables regression with weak instruments. *Econometrica* **65**(3): 557–586. doi:10.2307/2171753

Wang, Wen, William D. Duncombe, and John Yinger. 2011. School district responses to matching aid programs for capital facilities: A case study of New York's building aid program. *National Tax Journal* **64**(3): 759–794. [Chapter 20]

Part 4
The Demand for Public Education

Chapter 9

Education Finance Reform, Local Behavior, and Student Performance in Massachusetts[*]

Phuong Nguyen-Hoang[†] and John Yinger[‡,§]

*†Public Policy Center and School of Urban and Regional Planning,
University of Iowa, Iowa City, IA 52242, United States
‡Departments of Public Administration and
International Affairs and of Economics,
Syracuse University, Syracuse, NY, United States
§jyinger@maxwell.syr.edu*

This study examines the impact on student performance of the education finance reform enacted in 1993 in Massachusetts and of school districts' institutional structure. Estimating education expenditure and demand functions, this study presents evidence that changes in the state education aid following the education reform resulted in significantly higher student performance. Also, school officials and voters in the dependent school districts in Massachusetts respond to fiscal incentives in much the same way as those in independent school districts in other states. Finally, there are significant differences between regular school districts (coterminous with a single municipality) and regional school districts (consisting of more than one).

1. Introduction

Massachusetts provides an excellent setting to advance an understanding of education finance reform. The Massachusetts Education Reform Act (MERA), which was enacted in June 1993, introduced a new state education

---

[*]This chapter is reproduced from "Education Finance Reform, Local Behavior, and Student Performance in Massachusetts," *Journal of Education Finance*, **39**(4), 2014, pp. 297–322.

aid program, Chapter 70, and both the level and the distribution of state
aid across local school districts changed substantially over the next several
years. More specifically, Chapter 70 aid more than doubled in real terms
between 1994 and 2010, and the aid formula has gradually shifted more
aid to the neediest districts. In addition, education in the state is delivered
through school districts that are fiscally dependent on their municipalities.
Many of these districts, called regular districts, are coterminous with
one municipality; others, called regional districts, consist of two or more
municipalities (i.e., cities or towns).

Recent studies in this journal by Fahy (2011, 2012) examined equity
implications of the state's 2007 changes in Chapter 70 aid formula. Unlike
these two studies, we explore three different questions. First, we ask
whether the fiscally dependent school districts in Massachusetts respond
to fiscal incentives in the same way as fiscally independent districts in
other states.[1] Second, we examine how regional school districts are different
from regular districts in terms of education costs or student performance.
The Regional Advisory Commission (RAC), which was established by the
Massachusetts Legislature in 2009, argues that regionalization leads to
cost savings (Regional Advisory Commission, 2010), whereas others are
concerned that regionalization leads to a loss of local control (Storrow, 2010).
Our analysis sheds light on this debate.[2] Third, we estimate the impact of
education finance reform on student performance. A principal goal of MERA
and subsequent changes in Chapter 70 was to boost student performance,
particularly in high-need districts (i.e., those with high education costs), and
we ask whether this goal was achieved.

Our analysis is based on education expenditure and demand functions
that reflect the unique institutional features of the Massachusetts education
finance system. The expenditure function estimation is built on cost and

---

[1] Unlike Downes's (2000) estimation of spending levels by school districts across states, we
focus only on Massachusetts school districts and compare our results with previous studies
in other states adopting similar estimation approaches.

[2] This article also contributes to the existing literature on school district consolidation of
which regionalization is a form. District consolidation in theory has both size economies
(i.e., undiminished quality over a range of enrollment, increased dimension, teacher and
staff specialization, price benefits, and increased learning) and diseconomies (i.e., higher
transportation costs, labor relation effects, lower motivation and effort for both staff and
students, and lower parental involvement) (Duncombe and Yinger, 2007). Although a few
studies have explored the impact of school district consolidation on educational costs and
student performance (e.g., Berry and West, 2010; Duncombe and Yinger, 2007), there is a
lack of previous scholarly work on the effects of regionalization in Massachusetts on school
expenditures and student performance.

efficiency functions. We estimate these functions with a panel of data from 2001 to 2006, and we employ the estimated coefficients to simulate the effect of Chapter 70 aid on student performance. We find that local voters in Massachusetts, as in other states, responded to income and price incentives. More specifically, increases in Chapter 70 aid raised school district inefficiency and boosted voter demand for student performance. Overall, our results imply that both the recent large increases in Chapter 70 aid and the changes in its allocation led to substantial increases in student performance for all districts. However, the performance increase in the neediest, or highest education-cost, districts is small relative to the increase in low-need districts. We also find that regular and regional school districts differed in several important ways.

Our results complement the findings in a report by Downes *et al.* (2009). This report compares the change in student performance in districts with low spending prior to MERA with the change in districts with high spending before MERA. Student performance increased considerably more in the former type of district. Downes *et al.* also estimate a regression to explain the change in student performance before and after MERA as a function of district characteristics. This approach is designed to approximate a production function; in contrast, our approach is to formally derive and estimate expenditure and demand functions.[3]

The remainder of this article proceeds as follows. The section that follows provides background on MERA and school financing in Massachusetts. The section following that presents the modeling framework. Next, the data used in empirical work are described. The results are then discussed. The simulation of the impact of Chapter 70 aid on student performance is then presented.

2. MERA and Education Financing in Massachusetts

2.1. *History of Educational Legal Challenges*

Since the 1971 court ruling in *Serrano v. Priest*, in which the California Supreme Court held that the state's property-tax-based school funding system was unconstitutional, the vast majority of states have experienced legal challenges to their education finance system (Evans *et al.*, 1997; Lukemeyer, 2004). In Massachusetts, education reformers launched a series

---

[3]See Duncombe and Yinger (2011a) for a discussion of the strengths and weaknesses of production and cost approaches to the study of education performance at the district level.

of lawsuits in an attempt to improve the equity and adequacy of educational funding for financially disadvantaged school districts. The series began with the case of *Webby v. Dukakis* (1978) and continued with *Levy v. Dukakis* (1989), which was brought by public school students in Worcester, Carver, Revere, and Rockland. These two cases challenged the constitutionality of the state's school finance system. Shortly after the *Webby* case was brought up, the legislature enacted the School Funds and State Aid to Public Schools in 1978 and the Basic Skills Improvement Policy Act of 1979, which were designed to set standards for students' minimal competency in elementary language arts and mathematics. The legislature later passed the Act Improving the Public Schools of the Commonwealth, or Chapter 188, in wake of the *Levy* suit. These acts, however, did little to change the education finance system (Dee and Levine, 2004). Moreover, the economic recession that hit the state hard by the late 1980s widened the disparities between wealthy and poor districts.

In response to this situation, education reformers combined the preceding two lawsuits to bring a new lawsuit, popularly known as *McDuffy v. Robertson* (1993). The Supreme Judicial Court in Massachusetts handed down the *McDuffy* decision on June 15, 1993. This decision declared that the school funding system in Massachusetts was unconstitutional and required the legislature to provide for an "adequate" education. Shortly after the court decision, the legislature enacted MERA, under which the state committed substantial new resources to public education and altered the distribution of state education aid. These changes were codified in Chapter 70, which specifies a new state education aid program.

2.2. *District Types and School Funding System*

The public educational system in Massachusetts is dominated by regular and regional school districts. These two types constitute 87 percent (285 out of 329) of the districts in the state.[4] The former serve only (and are coterminous with) one municipality, whereas the latter are composed of two or more municipalities under a shared supervisory roof. Most of the regional school districts were established in the 1950s and 1960s on a voluntary basis (Peterson, 1964).[5] School districts, both regular and regional, can be full-grade range (K–12), 6–12, or K–6 districts.

---

[4]There are a number of regional vocational-technical and county agricultural schools.
[5]The most recently established regional district is Manchester-Essex, which came into existence on June 1, 2000.

Massachusetts is one of a few states in which a large majority of school districts are fiscally dependent on a parent government.[6] Popularly elected school committees are responsible for the operational management of the districts, including regulating student attendance, setting curricula, and teacher hires and fires. However, it is their municipal governments that assume financial responsibility for the delivery of both school and non-school public services.[7] They are required to contribute to the state-determined foundation level of school funding in inverse proportion to their capacity to pay determined based on property values.[8] Let us take, for example, Tisbury and Lawrence school districts, with property taxable values per pupil of over $8 million and $0.257 million, respectively, in fiscal year 2006. Although Tisbury was required to contribute as much as nearly 92 percent of the foundation level this year, Lawrence's local contributions were as little as 2.7 percent of the foundation level. Member cities and towns make their required contributions to their regional districts, but Chapter 70 does not specify how to allocate contributions among member communities in a regional district (Massachusetts Department of Elementary and Secondary Education, 2008).

As in other states, municipalities in Massachusetts rely heavily on property taxes. However, property taxes in this state are subject to the constraints imposed by Proposition $2^{1}/_{2}$, which was passed in 1982. This proposition places a permanent cap of 2.5 percent (the levy ceiling) on the effective property tax rate, and limits nominal annual growth in property tax revenues to 2.5 percent (the levy limit). The levy limit can be raised by growth in the property tax base or by overrides passed by local residents.[9] Proposition $2^{1}/_{2}$ has been binding on many municipal governments in

---

[6]Other such states are Alaska, Connecticut, Maine, Maryland, North Carolina, Rhode Island, Tennessee, and Virginia (U.S. Census Bureau, 2002). School districts may be county dependent (e.g., North Carolina), city or town dependent (e.g., Connecticut, Massachusetts), or mixed (e.g., Tennessee).

[7]The division of authority between the school committee and the municipality may lead to confusion about who is responsible for improving the quality of local services unrelated to education (Barron *et al.*, 2004).

[8]As this required level of funding is only a minimum, city and town governments and thus their school districts are allowed to add to this amount.

[9]Municipal governments can assess taxes in excess of levy limits and levy ceilings using debt exclusions, capital outlay expenditure exclusions, or special exclusions. The first two types of exclusions are intended to raise funds for debt service or capital project costs, respectively. Although both of these exclusions require voter approval, a special exclusion, whereby an additional levy is temporarily added to the levy limit or ceiling, does not (Massachusetts Department of Revenue, 2005).

Massachusetts. According to our calculations, the percentage of school districts constrained by Proposition 2½ increased steadily from 35.6 percent to 47.5 percent during our sample years between 2001 and 2006.[10]

Chapter 70 aid is designed to fill in the difference between expected municipal contributions and the foundation funding level. Following MERA, the state increased Chapter 70 education aid to school districts substantially from nearly $1.3 billion in 1993 to over $3.2 in 2006. As we will explore in greater detail, the distribution of Chapter 70 aid changed markedly to help high-need districts with high educational costs. Starting in 2001, Chapter 70 aid funds were cut for several school districts. Although inflation-adjusted[11] Chapter 70 aid per pupil shrank for only 19 percent of school districts between 2001 and 2002, more than 80 percent of them received lower per-pupil Chapter 70 aid, in real terms, in 2003 than in 2002. The declining trend culminated in an absolute 20 percent reduction in fiscal 2004 Chapter 70 aid for over 50 percent of school districts, and a Chapter 70 aid diminution of under 20 percent for another 20 percent of districts. However, Chapter 70 aid has started to pick up for several districts since 2005. The proportion of districts receiving larger real Chapter 70 aid per pupil increased from 15 percent in 2005 to 30 percent in 2006.

3. Modeling Framework

3.1. *Expenditure Function*

Drawing on the standard approach to educational cost functions reviewed in Golebiewski (2011), we specify C_S, total education operating cost per pupil, as a function of student performance (S), input prices (W), and other district factors outside the control of school officials (N):

$$C_S = h_1 S^\delta W^\mu N^\lambda \tag{1}$$

where h_1 is a constant. The variables in N in equation (1) fall into three categories: enrollment, student characteristics, and district types by grade range. First, following a large literature (Andrews *et al.*, 2002), we specify cost as a quadratic function of enrollment. Second, variables representing

---

[10] A school district is considered to be constrained if its tax levy is within 0.1 percent of the levy limit.

[11] We adjust Chapter 70 aid by government price indexes computed by the Bureau of Economic Analysis, U.S. Department of Commerce. The comparisons are made on a year-on-year basis.

student body characteristics include the percentage of English language learner (ELL) students, special education students, and low-income students. It may cost districts more to provide extra English classes for ELL students, to compensate for the disadvantages of students from poor families, and to accommodate special needs for students with disabilities. Third, we include dummy variables for full-grade range (K–12) and 6–12 districts, with K–6 districts being the omitted category.

A cost function describes required spending if a district uses best practices — that is, if it is efficient. Cost is unobserved; actual, or observed, total operating expenditures per pupil (E) incurred by a school district depend on both C_S and its efficiency (e).

$$E = C_S/e = h_1 S^\delta W^\mu N^\lambda / e \tag{2}$$

A district's budget constraint requires its spending to equal its revenue. Given that the district's revenue comes mostly from property taxes and Chapter 70 aid, we have

$$E = \kappa \times t\bar{V} + A \quad \text{or} \quad t = (E - A)/\kappa\bar{V} \tag{3}$$

where t is the effective tax rate in a school district, $\bar{V}$ is total taxable property value per pupil, and A is Chapter 70 aid per pupil. As indicated earlier, school districts in Massachusetts are fiscally dependent on their municipalities for funding (on top of state education aid), and κ represents the share of property tax levies spent on schools. Thus, $0 \le \kappa \le 1$, and $\kappa = 1$ or $\kappa = 0$ means that *all* property tax revenues are spent on school or non-school services, respectively.

As in many education cost studies, we assume that the median voter is decisive in a community's choice of public sector output. The median voter is usually identified as a citizen with the median income who lives in and owns the house with the median value (Bergstrom and Goodman, 1973). The median voter's budget constraint is

$$Y = Z + tV \tag{4}$$

where Y is his/her income, Z is a composite good, and V is the median house value. Substituting equation (3) into equation (4) yields

$$Y + \frac{A}{\kappa}\left(\frac{V}{\bar{V}}\right) = Z + \frac{C_S}{\kappa e}\left(\frac{V}{\bar{V}}\right) \tag{5}$$

The left side of equation (5) is the median voter's income augmented by the product of Chapter 70 aid, tax share ($V/\bar{V}$), and the inverse of the educational share of property taxes, κ. The tax share indicates how much the median voter must pay to raise one more dollar spent per pupil. The higher the property value, the more the voter contributes to spending on education in his district. Tax share is a part of tax price, P^T, which is the dollar amount the median voter pays for an incremental increase in student performance S. Tax price is determined by differentiating the right side of equation (5) with respect to S.

$$P^T = \frac{dC_S}{dS}(\kappa e)^{-1}\left(\frac{V}{\overline{V}}\right) = MC(\kappa e)^{-1}\left(\frac{V}{\overline{V}}\right) \qquad (6)$$

where MC is the marginal cost of increasing student performance by one unit. MC is derived by differentiating equation (1) with respect to S.

$$MC = \frac{dC_S}{dS} = h_1 \delta S^{\delta-1} W^\mu N^\lambda \qquad (7)$$

We now turn to efficiency, e, in equation (2), which refers to the resources a production process consumes to yield a certain output, given the current technology. Suppose that a private firm produces a single output (or multiple outputs with totally separate inputs). It is inefficient when it uses outmoded technology and/or spends extravagantly on non-productive activities, such as executive vacations. For this firm, inefficiency is synonymous with waste. Efficiency, however, is different for a production entity or process with multiple outputs and shared use of inputs. Production in public education has these inherent features. It has several educational outputs, such as student performance on math, English, and music. These outputs share many inputs, namely teachers, classrooms, and other school facilities. The concept of efficiency then applies to *each output*, not to the whole production entity. Also, inefficiency and waste are no longer equivalent as in the single-output case. Consider two districts (A and B) with the same cost factors. Suppose that district A spends more, in per-pupil terms, to obtain the same level of math performance as district B. District A's greater spending could reflect both more spending to promote other outputs than math and the use of outmoded technology or other forms of waste. The fact that district A is more inefficient in production of math performance than district B does not necessarily imply that district A is more inefficient as a whole. In fact, it may be more efficient in other outputs than district B. In sum, the inefficiency of an output in a multi-output and input-sharing production process consists of two components: trade-offs across outputs and waste. Both of these components underlie all discussions about efficiency in this article. Particularly, the efficiency that changes in response to inducing factors (e.g., income or tax price) pertain only to the outputs we specify in S.

As efficiency is unobserved, there are three popular approaches to controlling for efficiency. First, fixed effects can be used (as in Downes and Pogue, 1994) to eliminate efficiency, which is assumed to be constant over time. The use of fixed effects, however, does not deal with efficiency factors that do change over time. Also, fixed effects models make it difficult to estimate the variables of interest that have limited (or no) temporal variation. Our estimation models do include time-invariant variables of interest (e.g., a dummy variable for regional school districts); we do not, therefore, adopt this approach to addressing efficiency. The second approach is to use non-parametric data envelopment analysis (DEA) to come up with cost/efficiency indices, which are then included in the expenditure function (Duncombe and Yinger, 2000). However, the use of DEA, which accounts for non-discretionary cost factors, may result in the underestimation of their coefficients in equation (2). To identify the role of efficiency, the DEA approach relies on functional form assumptions that cannot be tested (Duncombe and Yinger, 2011a). DEA also cannot distinguish between inefficiency and statistical noise (Murillo-Zamorano, 2004).

The third approach to controlling for efficiency, which we use in this article, is to model factors with conceptual links to efficiency. These factors represent incentives that influence the behavior of voters and school officials. Because efficiency cannot be measured, these links cannot be tested directly. We can determine, however, whether the relationship between these factors and spending is consistent with these conceptual arguments. Consider first the monitoring behavior of local voters. Higher wage rates may induce voters to substitute away from monitoring school districts and work more, thereby resulting in more district inefficiency. However, higher income also has an income effect, creating incentives for voters to work less and monitor districts more, which increases efficiency. Tax price may affect monitoring as well. If voters have to pay more in taxes for a unit increase in educational output, they have greater incentives to monitor the district and thus make it more efficient.

In addition, higher income and lower tax price may induce voters to demand a broader range of school services than those specified in S, which is the first component of inefficiency. Thus, an association between income or tax price and spending controlling for S could represent the impact of these variables on the demand for school performance measures other than those in S (such as programs for art and music when S measures math

and English test scores), or it could represent a decline in the monitoring of
school officials.

This analysis leads to an equation in which efficiency is a function of tax
price[12] and income augmented by state aid, as in the left side of equation (5):

$$e = h_2 \left(Y + f_e \frac{A}{\kappa} \left(\frac{V}{\bar{V}} \right) \right)^\alpha \left(\frac{1}{\kappa} \right)^\beta \left(MC \frac{V}{\bar{V}} \right)^\psi M^\rho \tag{8}$$

where h_2 is a constant. We add the flypaper effect, f_e, for Chapter 70
aid.[13] M is a vector of demographic factors other than income and tax
price that influence district efficiency. More specifically, the two demographic
monitoring variables in M are the percentages of families with school-age
children (ages 6 to 17) and the shares of owner-occupied housing units.
Families with school-age children tend to monitor districts more closely for
the benefits of their children, thus increasing efficiency. A large body of
literature reviewed in Nguyen-Hoang and Yinger (2011) shows that school
quality is capitalized into property values; as a result, homeowners may push
their districts to be efficient and thereby to boost school quality without
increasing property taxes. M also includes a dummy variable indicating
whether a district is regional or regular.[14] As the primary objectives of
regionalization are greater efficiency and thus cost savings, we explore
whether these objectives materialize in practice.

Substituting equation (7) into equation (8), and the new equation (8) into
equation (2), and then taking logs of equation (2), using the approximation
rule that $\ln(1 + a) \approx a$ when a is close to 0) yields

$$\ln E = h_3 + (\psi + \delta(1 - \psi)) \ln S + \mu(1 - \psi) \ln W$$
$$- \psi \ln \left(\frac{V}{\bar{V}} \right) - \alpha \ln Y - \alpha f_e \frac{1}{\kappa} \frac{A}{Y} \left(\frac{V}{\bar{V}} \right)$$
$$- \beta \ln \left(\frac{1}{\kappa} \right) + \lambda(1 - \psi) \ln N - \rho \ln M + \varepsilon \tag{9}$$

---

[12]For ease of exposition, the two tax price components of MC and $(V/\bar{V})$ are represented
with a single elasticity in equation (8). Our regressions are, however, not constrained by
this exposition.

[13]The flypaper effect is a phenomenon in which lump-sum state aid positively affects
recipient governments' spending more than an equivalent rise in personal income does.
The flypaper effect has been found in several recent studies (Acosta, 2010; Brooks and
Phillips, 2010; Deller et al., 2007). See Hines and Thaler (1995) for a review of earlier
studies.

[14]This dummy variable might also be a cost factor. However, because most of the major cost
drivers are already accounted for, the cost effect of this variable is likely to be negligible.

where h_3 is a constant, and ε is the error term. We do not know what voters perceive about the use of additional property tax revenue for schools, which is given by κ. We therefore start by assuming that κ is constant across districts and estimating $\alpha f_e / \kappa$.

Given that a municipality in Massachusetts delivers school and non-school services, its non-school cost can affect its efficiency in, or cost of, educational production. A municipality with a higher cost of non-school municipal services, C_M, may reserve less of its property tax levies for school services and attempt to be more efficient in its delivery of education, thereby incurring smaller education expenditures per pupil. In other words, non-school costs, C_M, may be negatively related to κ. C_M might also work as a proxy for unobserved school cost factors. In this case, a higher C_M may be associated with greater education expenditures, holding efficiency constant. Since we do not know *a priori* the nature of C_M, we let the data tell us about this by estimating equation (10) with C_M instead of $(\frac{1}{\kappa})$.

$$\ln E = h_3 + (\psi + \delta(1 - \psi)) \ln S + \mu(1 - \psi) \ln W - \psi \ln \left(\frac{V}{\bar{\bar{V}}} \right)$$

$$- \alpha \ln Y - \alpha f_e \frac{1}{\kappa} \frac{A}{Y} \left(\frac{V}{\bar{\bar{V}}} \right)$$

$$+ \beta \ln(C_M) + \lambda(1 - \psi) \ln N - \rho \ln M + \varepsilon \tag{10}$$

The coefficient of C_M, β, can have a positive or negative sign in equation (10). If it is negative, we will interpret its coefficient as an indicator of variation in κ across school districts. We will interpret a positive β as an indication that C_M is a proxy for unobserved cost factors. As reported later, β turns out to be positive and significant.

In estimating equation (10), we treat S as endogenous because E and S are both outcomes from the same set of local decision makers. We employ the Fuller-k estimator ($k = 4$) with instrumental variables (IVs) to eliminate this possible endogeneity bias. This Fuller-k estimator is less subject to bias from weak instruments than two-stage-least-squares (2SLS) and limited information maximum likelihood (Hahn *et al.*, 2004). Following Duncombe *et al.* (2008), the IVs for the student performance index, S, are based on the yardstick competition model (Besley and Case, 1995), which argues that government decisions about service levels are influenced by the decisions of comparison jurisdictions.[15] We designate all of the other districts in the

---

[15]This theory of yardstick competition has been supported by several empirical recent studies (e.g., Allers and Elhorst, 2005; Revelli and Tovmo, 2007; and Schaltegger and Küttel, 2002).

same county as comparison jurisdictions; this approach ensures that the comparison jurisdictions are close enough to be visible but are not limited to neighboring jurisdictions, which might share a district's unobservable traits.[16]

The yardstick competition theory indicates that a jurisdiction responds to the performance of jurisdictions in its comparison group. Therefore, we use as IVs exogenous traits of comparison jurisdictions that influence their performance. More specifically, the IVs are the average percentages of low-income and special education students in comparison school districts.[17] These IVs appear to satisfy the two fundamental requirements for valid IVs. They have a conceptual link with the endogenous explanatory variable, S. There is no reason to think that they are correlated with the error term in equation (10) — that is, with E after controlling for both S and the determinants of e.

Like some other education cost studies (Duncombe and Yinger, 1997, 1998, 2000, 2005; Reschovsky and Imazeki, 1997), we also treat teacher salaries (W) in equation (10) as endogenous. Teachers are the most important input in the education production process, and their wages are usually determined simultaneously with expenditures in the budget process. Our two IVs for W are the log of the annual average wage in comparable private sector jobs and the average share of African American population in comparison districts. The yardstick competition discussed previously justifies the use of the second IV, as several studies show that teacher mobility — and thus salaries to attract and retain them — varies significantly, depending on the district demographics (Hanushek et al., 2004; Lankford et al., 2002). We also explore the validity of all of our IVs for both S and W by subjecting them to overidentification and weak-instrument tests.

3.2. Demand Function

Voters' income and preferences, as well as the price of education (via property taxes) they face, influence their demand for education. Assuming that the decisive median voter's demand function has a constant-elasticity form, we specify community demand for education as a function of the median voter's augmented income (equation (5)), his/her tax price (equation (6)),

---

[16]Massachusetts has 14 counties, compared to 315 municipalities.
[17]The average percentages exclude the value of the district itself. Also, a valid IV does not require the effect on the endogenous variable to be unidirectional (Pearl, 2009, pp. 247–248).

and other variables influencing demand, H. These variables include the shares of population groups that may have differential demands for student performance and the two IVs used in the estimation of the expenditure equation. People who graduated from college and senior citizens (over the age of 65) may have different demands for school performance than other population groups. H also includes the regional district dummy defined the same way as in the expenditure equation. This dummy is intended to see whether institutional structure has any direct significant influence on demand.

$$S = h_4 \left(Y + f_S \frac{A}{\kappa} \left(\frac{V}{\overline{V}} \right) \right)^{\tau} (C_M)^{\gamma} \left(\frac{V}{\overline{V}} \right)^{\sigma} MC^{\eta} e^{-\varphi} H^{\theta} \qquad (11)$$

where h_4 is a constant. We expect the flypaper effect of Chapter 70 aid, f_S, in the demand equation to be different from that in the efficiency equation. τ is the income elasticity of demand whereas σ, η, and φ are price elasticities for different components in tax price. Equation (11) also uses C_M to account for the possibility of a non-constant κ or unobserved cost factors. The parameter of C_M, γ, is the cross-price elasticity of demand for student performance. It measures the responsiveness of demand for student performance, given a change in the price of non-school services. A significant positive or negative elasticity of non-school costs indicates whether municipal services and school quality are substitutes or complements, respectively.

Equations (7) and (8) indicate that MC and e (via MC) are both functions of S, making them endogenous in equation (11). It is, however, impossible to find IVs for these two endogenous variables, because any instrument that is correlated to MC and e is also, by definition, correlated to the dependent variable, S. Instead of searching for instruments, therefore, we solve the demand function for S — a step that leaves only indices of the exogenous components of cost and efficiency on the right side.

More specifically, we substitute equations (7) and (8) into equation (11) and solve for S. After taking logs and using the approximation given earlier, the resulting demand function is

$$\ln S = h_5 + \tau^* f_S \frac{1}{\kappa} \frac{A}{Y} \left(\frac{V}{\overline{V}} \right) \tau^* \ln Y + \sigma^* \ln \left(\frac{V}{\overline{V}} \right) + \gamma^* \ln(C_M)$$
$$+ \eta^* \ln(MC^*) - \varphi^* \ln(e^*) + \theta^* \ln H + \epsilon \qquad (12)$$

where h_5 is a constant and ϵ is the error term. The exogenous indices of cost and efficiency (MC^* and e^*), which can be derived from equations (7) and (8), are

$$MC^* = h_1^* W^\mu N^\lambda \tag{13}$$

$$e^* = h_2^* \left(Y + f_e \frac{A}{\kappa} \left(\frac{V}{\bar{V}} \right) \right)^\alpha \left(\frac{1}{\kappa} \right)^\beta \left(MC^* \frac{V}{\bar{V}} \right)^\psi M^\rho \tag{14}$$

where h_1^* is defined so that MC^* equals 1 for the average district and h_2^* is defined so that e^* equals 1 for the most efficient district.[18] This adjustment of the constant terms does not change the coefficient estimates. The calculations of MC^* and e^* are based on the estimated coefficients from the expenditure equation (equation (10)). The cost index, MC^*, indicates a district's minimum level of cost per pupil to attain the average S compared to the average cost district, holding constant efficiency factors (including property taxes). This index can be used to indicate the level of need for assistance. More specifically, high-need districts are those with high educational costs (Yinger, 2001). A district with a cost index of 2 implies that it costs this district twice as much to achieve the average S as the average cost district, all else equal.

The starred parameters in equation (12) are the ratios of their corresponding unstarred structural parameters in equation (11) to λ^*, where λ^* is equal to $(1 - (\delta - 1)(\eta - \varphi\psi))$. The parameters δ and ψ are already determined from estimating the expenditure equation (equation (10)). For example, $\tau^* = \tau/\lambda^*$. To compute λ^*, we derive the values of η and φ by solving a system of two equations: $\eta^* = \eta/\lambda^*$ and $\varphi^* = \varphi/\lambda^*$ for φ and η as follows:

$$\varphi = \frac{\varphi^*}{[1 + (\delta - 1)(\eta^* - \varphi^*\psi)]} \tag{15}$$

$$\eta = \frac{\eta^* + \eta^*(\delta - 1)\varphi\psi}{(1 + \eta^*(\delta - 1))}. \tag{16}$$

Both the expenditure and demand equations (equations (10) and (12)) are estimated with robust standard errors to address the possibility of heteroskedasticity, and with clustering by school district to account for

---

[18]We could assume that all of the cost factors in the expenditure equation are already accounted for, and what is left in the error term of this equation is unobserved efficiency factors and can be added to equation (14). However, we do not adopt this approach because it shows signs of endogeneity. First, the new efficiency index has a very much higher t-statistic in the demand estimation. Second, the error terms of the efficiency and demand equations are highly correlated (-0.65).

pooling across years.[19] Hypothesis tests for nonlinear structural parameters in the demand equation are conducted with the "delta method" using the STATA *nlcom* command.

4. Data

Educational expenditures and demand in Massachusetts are estimated with data between 2001 and 2006.[20] (See Table 1 for descriptive statistics.) The data were obtained from the Massachusetts Department of Education (MDOE), the Massachusetts Department of Revenue (MDOR), the Massachusetts Executive Office of Labor and Workforce Development (EOLWD), and Census 2000. Specifically, the MDOE provided data on per-pupil operating expenditures (E), the student performance index (S), average teacher salaries, enrollment and student demographics (N), Chapter 70 aid, and regular or regional district types. The MDOR websites provided data on total taxable property values to derive $\bar{V}$. Data on private sector wages are obtained from the EOLWD website. Census 2000 gave us data for median house value, median earnings, the percentages of senior citizens (over the age of 65), African American population, families with school-aged children, people with college education, and owner-occupied houses.

The dependent variable for the expenditure function is total education operating expenditures per pupil (E). Student performance (S) is an equally weighted index of combined test scores for English and mathematics developed by the Massachusetts Department of Education. The test scores are derived from annually organized and required Massachusetts Comprehensive Assessment System (MCAS) tests in English and mathematics for regular

---

[19]One might think that because the indices of cost and efficiency are generated from the expenditure equation, it is necessary to bootstrap standard errors for the demand equation to take into account the randomness due to the estimation of these two indices. We did try this approach. Statistical inference with bootstrap standard errors in the demand equation is, however, not different from that with cluster-robust standard errors. In fact, there is no need for bootstrapping if feasible generalized least squares (FGLS) are used in both equations (Cameron and Trivedi, 1998, p. 44). FGLS is based on an assumption that variances are different for each panel and constant within panel. If the assumption is correct, FGLS is more efficient. If variances are not constant within panel, then FGLS standard errors are inefficient and incorrect. However, cluster-robust standard errors that we use are always correct (though less efficient) in both cases.

[20]The formula to derive per-pupil expenditures has changed since 2006, making data for later years incomparable to those before 2006. Student performance data are not available before 2001.

Table 1   Descriptive statistics (2001–2006).

Variables used in estimation	Mean	Standard deviation	Min.	Max.
Operating expenditures per pupil	8,517	2,116	5,415	22,948
Student performance index	80.70	8.05	45.82	97.74
Average teacher salaries	50,636	6,157	27,094	77,541
Enrollment	3,145	4,605	44	63,024
Percentage of ELL students	1.82	3.94	0	27.80
Percentage of special education students	14.88	3.39	1.50	31.30
Percentage of low-income students	15.07	15.38	0	84.60
Per-capita non-school cost	1,414	975	579	3,243
Dummy variable (= 1 for grade 6–12 districts, = 0 otherwise)	0.06	0.24	0	1
Dummy variable (= 1 for K–12 districts, = 0 otherwise)	0.70	0.46	0	1
Median income	30,904	7,252	6,768	56,557
Chapter 70 aid per pupil	2,601	1,669	348	9,558
State education aid per pupil in 1993	1,155	892	0	4,351
Tax share	0.25	0.12	0.01	0.93
Percentage of families with school-age children	54.75	5.96	40.10	75.00
Percentage of senior citizens (>65 years of age)	13.59	4.38	4.48	36.12
Percentage of owner-occupied housing units	25.25	14.12	2.72	70.98
Percentage of college graduates	35.89	16.40	9.95	83.47
Regional school districts (=1)	0.18	0.38	0	1
Average percentage of special education students in comparison districts	14.88	1.28	11.96	22.83
Average percentage of low-income students in comparison districts	15.07	6.48	4.50	69.60
Average annual salary in comparable private sector	45,808	18,504	5,453	167,523
Average percentage of African American population in comparison districts	1.72	1.14	0.65	11.63

Note: The total number of observations is 1,776 (296 districts in 6 years).

students and from the MCAS Alternate Assessment for severely disabled students. A point value assigned to each performance level on both tests is multiplied by the number of students scoring at each level. The total number of points is then divided by the total number of students tested. The point-based results from the two MCAS tests are then combined into the Composite Performance Index (CPI) for English and mathematics separately.

We employ Bradbury and Zhao's (2009) continuous measure of non-school costs (in per-capita terms) for municipalities in Massachusetts. This cost measure reflects factors that lie outside the control of the municipalities and influence the cost of non-school public services.[21]

5. Estimation Results

Tables 2 and 3 present estimation results of expenditure and demand equations under three specifications. Columns 1 in both of the tables report the base results from estimating equations (10) and (12) for expenditures and demand, respectively. Because we use non-school costs either as an indicator of variation in κ across school districts or a proxy for unobserved non-school costs, columns 2 document the estimates from a specification without non-school costs. We also test the hypothesis that the effects of income and tax price on educational expenditures and demand are different in places with higher non-school costs and in regional districts, and explore whether there exists an interaction between non-school costs and regional districts. The interaction terms are almost never close to significant in both of the expenditure and demand equations. The only interaction that proves to be statistically significant is between non-school costs and regional districts. Columns 3 in Tables 2 and 3 present the estimation results with this interaction.[22] Because the three specifications produce marginally different results for most of the variables, our interpretation will focus on this third, or full, specification.

The expenditure equation is estimated with teacher salary and student performance treated as endogenous. Using the Hansen J statistic, we fail to reject the joint null hypothesis that the IVs are valid (i.e., uncorrelated with the error term). This test provides statistical support for our choice of instruments under the assumption that at least one of them is exogenous.

The first panel of Table 2 shows that the coefficient of student performance is highly significant. Money does matter in raising student performance in Massachusetts, as in other states. Specifically, school districts

---

[21] Variables in Bradbury and Zhao's municipal cost regressions include unemployment rate, population density, percentage of population in poverty, and private jobs per resident. See Bradbury and Zhao (2009) for more detailed discussions. Although Bradbury and Zhao's (2009) non-school cost measure used data in 2000, the authors generously provided us with this variable computed for the period of 2001–2006 using the same approach.

[22] Because there is no district with a non-school cost of 0, we center the non-school cost variable for ease of interpretation. More specifically, $\ln(C_M^{\text{centered}}) = \ln(C_M) - \ln(\overline{C_M})$. Kam and Franzese (2007, p. 97) prove that centering does not change the estimated effects of any variable.

Table 2 Expenditure equation regression results (2001–2006)
(Dependent variable: Log of total operating expenditures per pupil).

	Base	Without logged non-school costs (C_M)	Interacted with regional dummy (RD)
	(1)	(2)	(3)
Cost variables			
Log of student performance	2.519	2.641	2.687
	$(3.55)^{***}$	$(3.59)^{***}$	$(3.59)^{***}$
Log of average teacher salary	0.703	0.642	0.571
	$(2.67)^{***}$	$(2.49)^{**}$	$(1.97)^{**}$
Log of enrollment	−0.235	−0.218	−0.210
	$(-2.84)^{***}$	$(-2.59)^{***}$	$(-2.75)^{***}$
Squared log of enrollment	0.01	0.01	0.01
	$(2.63)^{***}$	$(2.37)^{**}$	$(2.32)^{**}$
Percentage of ELL students	0.008	0.008	0.008
	(1.50)	(1.58)	(1.51)
Percentage of special education students	0.007	0.007	0.008
	$(2.70)^{***}$	$(2.80)^{***}$	$(2.91)^{***}$
Percentage of low-income students	0.011	0.012	0.011
	$(3.14)^{***}$	$(3.23)^{***}$	$(2.96)^{***}$
Dummy variable (= 1 for grade 6–12 districts, = 0 otherwise)	0.033	0.042	0.025
	(0.74)	(0.92)	(0.55)
Dummy variable (= 1 for K–12 districts, = 0 otherwise)	0.169	0.177	0.151
	$(3.30)^{***}$	$(3.43)^{***}$	$(2.89)^{***}$
Efficiency variables			
Chapter 70 aid component of adjusted income	1.650	1.839	1.626
	$(2.66)^{***}$	$(2.90)^{***}$	$(2.50)^{**}$
Log of median income	−0.001	−0.005	−0.005
	(-0.01)	(-0.06)	(-0.06)
Log of tax share	−0.173	−0.190	−0.168
	$(-4.80)^{***}$	$(-5.42)^{***}$	$(-4.40)^{***}$
Percentage of owner-occupied housing units	0.002	0.002	0.002
	$(1.94)^{*}$	$(1.91)^{**}$	(1.32)
Percentage of families with school-age children	−0.002	−0.002	−0.001
	(-0.73)	(-0.69)	(-0.58)
Regional districts (RD) (= 1 for RD and = 0 otherwise)	−0.078	−0.007	−0.074
	$(-1.97)^{**}$	(-0.32)	$(-1.98)^{**}$

(*Continued*)

Table 2 (*Continued*)

	Base	Without logged non-school costs (C_M)	Interacted with regional dummy (RD)
	(1)	(2)	(3)
Other variables			
Log of non-school costs (logged C_M)	0.084		0.222
	$(2.20)^{**}$		$(2.99)^{***}$
Logged $C_M \times RD$			−0.185
			$(-2.30)^{**}$
Number of observations	1,776	1,776	1,776
F-statistics in the first stage			
Log of student performance index	4.74	4.55	4.74
Log of teacher salaries	5.42	5.36	5.59
Hansen J statistic *p*-value			
(overidentification test of all instruments)	0.40	0.47	0.29

Note: All regressions are estimated with year dummies. Estimated with the Fuller-k regression with $k = 4$ using *ivreg2* in STATA. The log of teacher salaries and student performance are treated as endogenous. The instruments for the former are the logged average annual salary in comparable private sector in the district, and the average share of African American population in same-county districts. Student performance is instrumented with the average percentage of low-income and special education students in same-county districts. Robust standard errors (controlling for clustering at district level) are used for hypothesis testing. *T*-statistics are in parentheses. $^{***}p < 0.01$, $^{**}p < 0.05$, $^{*}p < 0.1$.

in Massachusetts must raise spending per pupil by about 2.7 percent to obtain a 1 percent increase in student performance, holding district efficiency constant. This result indicates decreasing returns to quality scale for student performance. This elasticity is higher for cost studies (with different student performance measures) in some states — namely Kansas, Missouri (Duncombe *et al.*, 2008), and New York (Duncombe *et al.*, 2003), but a bit smaller than California (Duncombe and Yinger, 2011b).[23] In addition, a 1 percent increase in average teacher salary is associated with a 0.6 percent increase in spending per pupil to maintain the same student performance.

[23] The student performance elasticity is, in order of increasing magnitude, 0.37 for Missouri, 0.5 for Kansas, 0.75 for New York, and 3 for California.

Most of the other cost variables in Table 2 are highly significant with expected signs. Specifically, a percentage-point increase of 1 in the share of low-income students requires a 1.1 percent rise in the district's per-pupil spending if the same student performance is to be maintained. The coefficient for low-income students in Massachusetts is higher than those found for Kansas and Missouri (Duncombe *et al.*, 2008) and for Texas (Reschovsky and Imazeki, 2003) (0.4, 0.5, and 0.1, respectively). It also costs districts in Massachusetts more to educate special education students; a percentage-point rise of 1 in the share of special education students is associated with a 0.8 percent increase in per-pupil expenditures. It costs K–12 districts more to maintain the same student performance than K–6 districts. We find empirical evidence that there is a significant U-shaped relationship between spending per pupil and student enrollment. Although more students decrease educational expenditures, diseconomies of size start to set in at an enrollment of 36,315. (Only the enrollment of the Boston School District exceeds this threshold.) Given that large school districts with enrollments greater than 10,000 (e.g., Springfield, Worcester, Brockton, or Lowell) are located far apart, this finding suggests that almost all of the school districts in Massachusetts would be able to save if they merged with one or more of their neighboring school districts.

The second section of Table 2 reports evidence that voters in Massachusetts, like voters in other states, respond to income and price incentives associated with school district efficiency. Although the coefficient on median income is insignificant, an increase in Chapter 70 aid is associated with lower district efficiency while tax share and efficiency are positively related. More concretely, tax share is highly significant with a price elasticity of -0.17, which is relatively higher in absolute terms than -0.09 and -0.02 for Missouri and Kansas, respectively (Duncombe *et al.*, 2008). Despite the fiscal dependency of their school districts, local residents in Massachusetts appear to increase their monitoring of school spending when they face a high tax share.

Although the regional district dummy becomes insignificant without non-school costs (column 2), this dummy is significantly negative in the base and full specifications. More specifically, column 3 of Table 2 reports that a regional district with the mean school cost is more efficient and thus incurs significantly lower (7.4 percent) education spending than regular districts. The significantly negative interaction term between the regional dummy and non-school costs indicates that regional districts with higher non-school costs appear to be even more efficient and spend less on education. Together with the cost-related economies of size we found earlier, these findings are in line with the regionalization objectives of enhanced efficiency and cost savings and previous studies on school district consolidation.[24]

Greater efficiency can come from both of the efficiency components. First, regional districts may receive intensified monitoring efforts by residents from two or more member districts, thereby leading to reduced waste. Second, as noted earlier, the allocation of local required contributions among member communities was inequitable or even nonsensical in several instances during our sample years (Massachusetts Department of Elementary and Secondary Education, 2008). Differences in preferences for spending between regional members with the same student characteristics and ability to pay can present a major problem. Also, poor communication between member districts may frustrate local officials and breed distrust and feelings of resentment (Massachusetts Department of Revenue, n.d.). All of these problems may dampen spending on school outputs other than those specified in S — the first component of efficiency.[25]

The results reported in the third section of Table 2 indicate that non-school costs work better as a proxy for unobserved cost factors rather than for the cross-district different shares of property tax levies for schools. Higher non-school costs are associated with a rise of 0.2 or 0.03 percent (= 0.22–0.19) in spending per pupil in regular and regional districts, respectively.

Table 3 reports regression results from the demand equation (equation (12)), and Table 4 documents structural parameters in equation (11). These structural parameters are derived by the formulas after equation (14) that incorporate the results from the expenditure function estimations. Based on column 3 of Table 4, we find an income elasticity of 0.13, which means that greater income induces voters to demand higher school performance. This income elasticity is quite similar to that of 0.15 for California found in Duncombe and Yinger (2011b).

---

[24] For instance, Duncombe and Yinger (2007) find that doubling enrollment cuts operating costs per pupil by 61.7 percent for a 300-pupil district and by 49.6 percent for a 1,500-pupil district.

[25] These problems may be a cause for de-regionalization considerations. For instance, Bridgewater-Raynham is considering de-regionalizing to better accommodate their different spending preferences (Carleton *et al.*, 2009).

Table 3 Demand estimation regression results (2001–2006)
(Dependent variable: Log of student performance index).

	Base	Without logged non-school costs (C_M)	Interacted with regional dummy (RD)
	(1)	(2)	(3)
Income and price variables			
Chapter 70 aid component of adjusted	1.576	1.871	1.917
income	$(2.47)^{**}$	$(2.57)^{**}$	$(2.58)^{**}$
Log of median income	0.082	0.076	0.075
	$(2.09)^{**}$	$(1.96)^{*}$	$(2.01)^{**}$
Log of tax share	−0.265	−0.288	−0.287
	$(-4.05)^{***}$	$(-3.87)^{***}$	$(-3.75)^{***}$
Log of cost index	−0.472	−0.513	−0.504
	$(-6.38)^{***}$	$(-6.33)^{***}$	$(-6.08)^{***}$
Log of efficiency index	1.548	1.547	1.705
	$(4.01)^{***}$	$(3.87)^{***}$	$(3.67)^{***}$
Log of non-school costs	−0.020		−0.034
	$(-1.82)^{*}$		$(-1.92)^{*}$
Other variables			
Regional districts (RD) (= 1 for RD and	−0.068	0.009	−0.079
= 0 otherwise) $C_M \times RD$	$(-1.98)^{**}$	(1.02)	$(-2.03)^{**}$
			−0.249
			$(-2.48)^{**}$
Percentage of college graduates	0.003	0.004	0.003
	$(3.63)^{***}$	$(3.60)^{***}$	$(3.75)^{***}$
Percentage of senior citizens	0.000	0.000	0.000
	(0.02)	(0.07)	(0.18)
Percentage of low-income students in	−0.001	−0.001	−0.001
comparison districts	$(-2.33)^{**}$	$(-2.30)^{**}$	$(-2.13)^{**}$
Percentage of special education students	0.008	0.007	0.007
in comparison districts	(1.48)	(1.37)	(1.22)
Number of observations	1,776	1,776	1,776

Note: All regressions are estimated with year dummies. Robust standard errors (controlling for clustering at district level) are used for hypothesis testing. T-statistics are in parentheses. $^{***}p < 0.01$, $^{**}p < 0.05$, $^{*}p < 0.1$.

The price elasticities of demand are reported in the second section of Table 4. The significant tax share elasticity of −0.52 indicates that like in other states, voters in Massachusetts demand less if they have to pay more in property taxes for an increase in student performance. However, this tax share elasticity is, in absolute terms, relatively larger than −0.21 and −0.014 for New York and California, respectively (Duncombe and Yinger, 2011b;

Table 4 Major structural parameters of the demand equation (11).

	Base	Without logged non-school costs (C_M)	Interacted with regional dummy (RD)
	(1)	(2)	(3)
Income elasticity (τ)	0.13	0.14	0.13
	$(2.35)^{**}$	$(2.26)^{**}$	$(2.30)^{**}$
Flypaper effect and $1/\kappa$ $\left(f_S \frac{1}{\kappa}\right)$	12	13.64	14.26
	$(1.68)^{**}$	$(1.64)^{*}$	$(1.64)^{*}$
Price elasticities			
Tax share (σ)	-0.42	-0.52	-0.52
	$(-3.78)^{***}$	$(-3.58)^{***}$	$(-3.47)^{***}$
Marginal educational cost (η)	-0.75	-0.92	-0.91
	$(-4.62)^{***}$	$(-4.35)^{***}$	$(-4.28)^{***}$
Efficiency (e_f)($-\varphi$)	0.40	0.36	0.33
	$(3.76)^{***}$	$(3.59)^{***}$	$(3.42)^{***}$
Non-school cost (γ)	-0.03		-0.06
	$(-1.86)^{*}$		$(-1.78)^{*}$
Regional school districts (θ_1)	-0.11	0.02	-0.14
	$(-1.96)^{**}$	(1.02)	$(-1.99)^{**}$
$C_M \times RD(\theta_0)$			-0.45
			$(-2.41)^{**}$
Percentage of college graduates (θ_2)	0.006	0.006	0.006
	$(3.21)^{***}$	$(3.10)^{***}$	$(3.19)^{***}$
Percentage of seniors (θ_3)	0.00003	0.0001	0.0003
	(0.02)	(0.07)	(0.18)

Notes: The parameters in this table are derived based on formulas after equation (14). Hypothesis tests are conducted with the "delta method" using the STATA *nlcom* command. $^{***}p < 0.01$, $^{**}p < 0.05$, $^{*}p < 0.1$.

Eom *et al.*, 2014). The panel also reports significant impacts on demand of the other three components of tax price — namely marginal educational cost, efficiency, and non-school cost. The marginal educational cost elasticity of -0.91 implies that voters demand lower student performance when the cost of added performance in their district is relatively high. Also, greater district efficiency is found to lead to higher school quality demand. Interestingly, the significantly negative non-school cost elasticity of demand indicates that school and non-school service qualities are complements. A higher cost for non-school outputs leads to lower schooling demand after controlling for the non-school costs as a proxy for omitted school costs.

Column 3 of Table 4 also shows that regional school districts have lower demand for school quality. Regional districts with higher non-school

Table 5 Changes in state education aid distribution by cost index deciles.

Districts by cost index deciles	Total operating expenditures per pupil in 1993	Rank based on (1) (descending order)	Average state education aid per pupil in 1993	Rank based on (3) (descending order)	Average Chapter 70 aid per pupil in 2006	Rank based on (5) (descending order)
	(1)	(2)	(3)	(4)	(5)	(6)
1st (lowest)	5,111	10	651	9	2,074	7
2nd	5,873	5	638	10	1,809	8
3rd	5,846	6	705	8	1,710	10
4th	6,211	2	817	7	1,793	9
5th	5,644	9	1,163	5	2,474	5
6th	6,321	1	1,015	6	2,163	6
7th	5,710	7	1,556	2	3,051	4
8th	5,659	8	1,343	4	3,128	3
9th	6,160	3	1,493	3	3,171	2
10th (highest)	6,067	4	2,300	1	5,579	1

costs demand even less school quality. Together with the results from the expenditure equation, these results indicate that regional school districts have lower demand for *all* student outputs specified and unspecified in *S*. Finally, college graduates expectedly have a higher demand for their districts' educational performance.

6. Simulation

As noted earlier, the state has substantially increased Chapter 70 aid between 1993 and 2006 (except for a few years). Table 5 shows that the distribution of state aid by cost index deciles has changed remarkably as well.[26] As previously explained, the higher the cost index, the more the district is in greater need for state aid assistance, all else equal. Columns 4 and 6 of this table show that average state aid per pupil became more consistent with the level of need especially among those high-need districts (i.e., those in deciles 7–10) in 2006 than in 1993.[27]

Our focus is on whether such substantial increases in Chapter 70 aid and changes in its distribution have improved student performance, especially

---

[26] As described earlier, the cost index is derived from estimating the fully specified model of the expenditure equation.

[27] Column 2 of Table 5 shows that the level of spending per pupil is not completely consistent with the cost index-based rank and thus may not be a good indicator of need.

among high-need school districts. Increased state aid does not always lead to higher student performance, because it exerts opposing effects on school quality. As previously modeled, Chapter 70 aid can affect student performance directly as an explanatory variable in the demand model (equation (12)) and indirectly through the efficiency index derived from the expenditure equation (equation (10)). More specifically, more Chapter 70 aid can lead to both higher voter demand for student performance and lower performance as a result of aid-induced higher inefficiency. In order to find the combined effect of Chapter 70 aid on school quality, we predict student performance in 2006 using (1) state education aid per pupil in 1993 (the academic year just before MERA came into effect), (2) state aid per pupil in 1993 blown up to the 2006 Chapter 70 aid total,[28] and (3) actual Chapter 70 aid per pupil in 2006. The first scenario shows us what school districts would have achieved in 2006 if they had received the amount of state education aid in 1993. The second simulation predicts districts' student performance if the state had delivered the same amount of state aid as 2006 but with the 1993 distribution. The predicted performance in the first two scenarios is then compared with the third scenario to see how Chapter 70 aid affects student performance.[29]

We adopt the following procedures to predict student performance in those three scenarios with three different values of state aid as described in the preceding paragraph. For each scenario, we first derive the efficiency index with equation (14) using the estimated coefficients in the expenditure model, the state aid term for the corresponding scenario, and actual values of other efficiency factors. We then employ the coefficients estimated from the demand equation (equation (12)) and actual values except for that state aid term and the new efficiency index to predict student performance.[30] These procedures are performed with the fully specified model reported in columns 3 of Tables 3 and 4.[31]

---

[28]Put differently, districts' education aid per pupil in 1993 is bumped up with a constant across the board so that the boosted aid total is equal to the actual Chapter 70 aid total in 2006. Boosting the aid this way does not change its distribution.

[29]We do not use actual performance in 2006 for comparisons because actual values include an error term. In fact, the actual and simulated mean test scores in 2006 by cost decile are highly correlated. For instance, the correlation coefficient in the 10th decile is 0.87. The lowest correlation coefficient in the 8th decile is 0.57, whereas the coefficients in the remaining deciles range between 0.61 and 0.77.

[30]Because the dependent variable of the demand models are in logarithmic form, we adjust the predicted values following the procedures in Wooldridge (2003).

[31]Predictions derived from the base specification are very similar to those reported.

Table 6 Simulated student performance in 2006 by cost index deciles.

Districts by cost index deciles	Mean test scores with actual 1993 state education aid per pupil	Mean test scores with boosted 1993 state education aid per pupil	Mean test scores with actual Chapter 70 aid per pupil	Differences	
	(1)	(2)	(3)	(3) − (1)	(3) − (2)
1st (lowest)	80.72	81.57	88.33	7.61	6.77
2nd	79.52	80.46	87.07	7.55	6.62
3rd	78.43	79.33	86.00	7.57	6.67
4th	77.80	78.74	85.37	7.56	6.63
5th	76.65	78.20	83.87	7.22	5.67
6th	75.49	76.73	82.73	7.24	6.00
7th	74.82	77.02	81.82	7.00	4.80
8th	72.39	74.21	79.29	6.90	5.07
9th	71.86	74.14	78.74	6.88	4.60
10th (highest)	64.86	68.87	69.60	4.75	0.73
Difference between highest and lowest deciles (in percentage points)	15.87	12.69	18.73	−2.86	−6.04

Table 6 reports that actual or boosted 1993 state aid per pupil gives smaller predicted mean test scores by cost index deciles than predicted mean test scores in 2006. This finding suggests that the substantial increase in Chapter 70 aid over the years and changes in its distribution have paid off. If state education aid had remained unchanged since 1993, the mean student performance of all district deciles would have been substantially worse (at least 4.6 percentage points less) than the case of actual Chapter 70 aid in 2006. The higher mean performance reported in column 3 relative to column 2 indicates that the distributional changes in state aid also result in better mean school quality for all district deciles.

This table shows that the lower the cost index decile, the lower the increase in the mean student performance. In other words, although the neediest districts (as reported in Table 5) receive more Chapter 70 aid than lower-need districts, the former on average increase their performance less than the latter. More specifically, relative to the scenario with the 1993 state aid per pupil, actual Chapter 70 aid per pupil in 2006 led to a rise of only

4.8 percentage points in average test scores for the neediest districts in the tenth decile but an improvement of 7.6 percentage points for the lowest decile of districts. The final line of Table 6 shows that changes in Chapter 70 aid appear to widen the mean performance difference between the lowest and highest decile districts (18.7 vs. 15.9 or 12.7). These interesting findings suggest that the increase in inefficiency that in turn lowers performance as a result of higher Chapter 70 aid is much greater among the highest-need districts than that among the lowest-need districts. These relative increases in inefficiency could reflect increases in school quality measures that are not included in our student-performance index but that are valuable to high-need districts. These results are different from the finding in Downes *et al.* (2009) report that the performance of districts with low spending prior to MERA has improved relative to high-spending districts.[32]

7. Conclusion

Estimating the expenditure and demand equations for Massachusetts, we find that fiscally dependent school districts in the state in the second phase of MERA demonstrate common behavioral responses reported in other states. The cost of providing an adequate education incurred by school districts in Massachusetts varies with multiple cost factors. Money is important to raise student performance. It costs more for districts with a relatively greater concentration of disadvantaged students to reach the same level of performance as other districts. In addition, voters respond to income and price incentives. Increases in income lead to both higher demand for school quality and a reduction in monitoring efforts, thus making districts less efficient. Massachusetts voters also monitor district officials more but have lower demand for school quality if they have to pay relatively more in property taxes at the margin. Greater Chapter 70 aid both undermines district efficiency and has a positive impact on voter demand for school quality.

We also find results that are unique in Massachusetts. First, presumably as a proxy for omitted school costs, non-school costs have a significant

---

[32]Following Downes *et al.* (2009), we also simulate test scores for districts in the 1992 highest and lowest spending quartiles. The simulated results are the same. The increase in student performance among districts in the lowest spending quartile is smaller than that among the highest-spending districts. Also, the performance difference in these two groups of districts grows larger as a result of Chapter 70 aid.

positive impact on the spending of fiscally dependent school districts. Also, municipal and educational services seem to be complementary goods to voters in Massachusetts when higher municipal costs are associated with lower demand for schooling services. Second, most regular school districts in the state would benefit from economies of size from regionalization. Also, current regional districts are found to be more efficient and spend less on education than regular ones. Voters in regional districts demand less for all educational outputs. Their low demand is even lower in places with higher non-school costs.

Our simulations show that the substantial rise in Chapter 70 aid and its distributional changes as a result of MERA led to a substantial increase in student performance across all districts. However, Chapter 70 aid induced a greater rise in the performance of the lowest-need districts than that of the neediest districts, and widened the mean performance gap between these two groups of districts. These findings suggest that compared to low-need districts, the relatively smaller rise in the mean performance among high-need districts comes from relatively greater inefficiency induced by higher state education aid, which may reflect the wide range of educational needs in the high-need districts. A further exploration of changes in spending patterns across types of districts is an excellent candidate for further research.

References

Acosta, P. 2010. The "flypaper effect" in presence of spatial interdependence: Evidence from Argentinean municipalities. *Annals of Regional Science* **44**(3): 453–466.

Allers, M. A. and Elhorst, J. P. 2005. Tax mimicking and yardstick competition among local governments in the Netherlands. *International Tax and Public Finance* **12**(4): 493–513.

Andrews, M., Duncombe, W., and Yinger, J. 2002. Revisiting economies of size in American education: Are we any closer to a consensus? *Economics of Education Review* **21**(3): 245–262.

Anthony, P. and Rossman, G. 1994. *The Massachusetts Education Reform Act: What is it and Will it Work?* Educational Resources Information Center.

Ardon, K. and Costrell, R. M. 2001. *Fairness in School Funding: Reformulating Local Aid of Phase Two of Education Reform* (Policy Report). Boston, MA: Massachusetts Executive Office for Administration and Finance.

Barron, D. J., Frug, G. E., and Su, R. T. 2004. *Dispelling the Myth of Home Rule: Local Power in Greater Boston*. Cambridge, MA: Rappaport Institute for Greater Boston.

Bergstrom, T C. and Goodman, R. P. 1973. Private demands for public goods. *American Economic Review* **63**(3): 280–296.

Berry, C. and West, M. 2010. Growing pains: The school consolidation movement and student outcomes. *Journal of Law, Economics, and Organization* **26**(1): 1–29.

Besley, T. and Case, A. C. 1995. Incumbent behavior: Vote-seeking, tax-setting, and yardstick competition. *American Economic Review* **85**(1): 25–45.

Bradbury, K. L. and Zhao, B. 2009. Measuring non-school fiscal disparities among municipalities. *National Tax Journal* **62**(1): 25–56.

Brooks, L. and Phillips, J. H. 2010. An institutional explanation for the stickiness of federal grants. *Journal of Law, Economics, and Organization* **26**(2): 243–264.

Cameron, A. C. and Trivedi, P. K. 1998. *Regression Analysis of Count Data.* Cambridge, UK: Cambridge University Press.

Carleton, S., Lynch, C., and O'Donnell, R. 2009. *School District Consolidation in Massachusetts: Opportunities and Obstacles.* Massachusetts Department of Elementary and Secondary Education.

Dee, T. S. and Levine, J. 2004. The fate of new funding: Evidence from Massachusetts' education finance reforms. *Educational Evaluation and Policy Analysis* **26**(3): 199–215.

Deller, S. C., Maher, C. S., and Lledo, V. 2007. Wisconsin local government, state shared revenues and the illusive flypaper effect. *Journal of Public Budgeting, Accounting & Financial Management* **19**(2): 200–220.

Downes, T. A. 2000. Does fiscal dependency matter? Aid elasticities for dependent and independent school districts. *Economics of Education Review* **19**(4): 417–429.

Downes, T. A. and Pogue, T. 1994. Adjusting school aid formulas for the higher cost of educating disadvantaged students. *National Tax Journal* **47**(1): 89–110.

Downes, T. A., Zabel, J. E., and Ansel, D. 2009. *Incomplete Grade: Massachusetts Education Reform at 15.* Massachusetts Institute for a New Commonwealth.

Duncombe, W. and Yinger, J. 1997. Why is it so hard to help central city schools? *Journal of Policy Analysis and Management* **16**(1): 85–113.

Duncombe, W. and Yinger, J. 1998. School finance reform: Aid formulas and equity objectives. *National Tax Journal* **51**(2): 239–262. [Chapter 12]

Duncombe, W. and Yinger, J. 2000. Financing higher student performance standards: The case of New York State. *Economics of Education Review* **19**(4): 363–386.

Duncombe, W. and Yinger, J. 2005. How much more does a disadvantaged student cost? *Economics of Education Review* **24**(5): 513–532. [Chapter 7]

Duncombe, W. and Yinger, J. 2007. Does school district consolidation cut costs? *Education Finance and Policy*, **2**(4): 341–375. [Chapter 18]

Duncombe, W. and Yinger, J. 2011a. Are education cost functions ready for prime time? An examination of their validity and reliability. *Peabody Journal of Education* **86**(1): 28–57. [Chapter 5]

Duncombe, W. and Yinger, J. 2011b. Making do: State constraints and local responses in California's education finance system. *International Tax and Public Finance* **18**(3): 337–368. [Chapter 10]

Duncombe, W., Lukemeyer, A., and Yinger, J. 2003. Financing an adequate education: A case study of New York. In W. J. Fowler (ed.), *Developments in School Finance: 2001–02*, pp. 129–153. Washington, DC: National Center for Education Statistics.

Duncombe, W., Lukemeyer, A., and Yinger, J. 2008. The No Child Left Behind Act: Have federal funds been left behind? *Public Finance Review* **36**(4): 381–407. [Chapter 6]

Eom, T., Duncombe, W., Nguyen-Hoang, P., and Yinger, J. 2014. The unintended consequences of property tax relief: New York's STAR program. *Education Finance and Policy* **9**(4) (Fall): 446–480. [Chapter 8]

Evans, W. N., Murray, S. E., and Schwab, R. M. 1997. Schoolhouses, courthouses, and statehouses after Serrano. *Journal of Policy Analysis and Management* **16**(1): 10–31.

Fahy, C. 2011. Education funding in Massachusetts: The effects of aid modifications on vertical and horizontal equity. *Journal of Education Finance* **36**(3): 217–243.

Fahy, C. 2012. Fiscal capacity measurement and equity in local contributions to schools: The effects of education finance reform in Massachusetts. *Journal of Education Finance* **37**(4): 317–346.

Golebiewski, J. A. 2011. An overview of the literature measuring education cost differentials. *Peabody Journal of Education* **86**(1): 84–112.

Hahn, J., Hausman, J., and Kuersteiner, G. 2004. Estimation with weak instruments: Accuracy of higher-order bias and MSE approximations. *Econometrics Journal* **7**(1): 272–306.

Hanushek, E. A., Kain, J. F., and Rivkin, S. G. 2004. Why public schools lose teachers. *Journal of Human Resources* **39**(2): 326.

Hines, J. R. and Thaler, R. H. 1995. Anomalies: The flypaper effect. *Journal of Economic Perspectives* **9**(4): 217–226.

Kam, C. D. and Franzese, R. J. 2007. *Modeling and Interpreting Interactive Hypotheses in Regression Analysis.* Ann Arbor: University of Michigan Press.

Lankford, H., Loeb, S., and Wyckoff, J. 2002. Teacher sorting and the plight of urban schools: A descriptive analysis. *Educational Evaluation and Policy Analysis* **24**(1): 37.

Lukemeyer, A. 2004. Financing a constitutional education: Views from the bench. In *Helping Children Left Behind: State Aid and the Pursuit of Educational Equity,* pp. 59–86. Cambridge, MA: MIT Press.

Massachusetts Department of Elementary and Secondary Education. 2008. *Report to the Legislature: Equity Effects of Regional Allocation Methodology on Regional Vocational Technical Schools.* Massachusetts Department of Elementary and Secondary Education.

Massachusetts Department of Revenue. n.d. *Monitoring Regional School Finances.* Division of Local Services, Massachusetts Department of Revenue.

Massachusetts Department of Revenue. 2005. *Levy Limits: A Primer on Proposition 2½.* Boston, MA: Massachusetts Department of Revenue.

Miyares, B. and Skinner, K. 2004. *Mastering the Maze of School Accountability: A Handbook for Massachusetts Schools and Local Association Leaders.* Boston, MA: Massachusetts Teachers Association.

Murillo-Zamorano, L. R. 2004. Economic efficiency and frontier techniques. *Journal of Economic Surveys* **18**(1): 33–77.

Nguyen-Hoang, P. and Yinger, J. 2011. The capitalization of school quality into house values: A review. *Journal of Housing Economics* **20**(1): 30–48. [Chapter 15]

Pearl, J. 2009. *Causality: Models, Reasoning, and Influence.* Cambridge, UK: Cambridge University Press.

Peterson, D. L. 1964. School districts: New England style. *Maine Law Review* **16**: 145–176.

Regional Advisory Commission. 2010. Report of the Regional Advisory Commission. Retrieved from www.mass.gov/governor/regional.

Reschovsky, A. and Imazeki, J. 1997. The development of school finance formulas to guarantee the provision of adequate education to low-income students. *Developments in School Finance,* 123–147.

Reschovsky, A. and Imazeki, J. 2003. Let no child be left behind: Determining the cost of improving student performance. *Public Finance Review* **31**(3): 263–290.

Revelli, F. and Tovmo, P. 2007. Revealed yardstick competition: Local government efficiency patterns in Norway. *Journal of Urban Economics* **62**(1): 121–134.

Schaltegger, C. A. and Küttel, D. 2002. Exit, voice, and mimicking behavior: Evidence from Swiss Cantons. *Public Choice* **113**(1): 1–23.

Storrow, B. 2010. Local school advocates ready to fight any regionalization efforts. Retrieved from www.gazettenet.com/print/270333

U.S. Census Bureau. 2002. *2002 Census of Governments*, Vol. 1(2), Individual State Descriptions. Washington, DC: U.S. Government Printing Office.

Wooldridge, J. M. 2003. *Introductory Econometrics: A Modern Approach*. Cincinnati, OH: South-Western College Publishing.

Yinger, J. 2001. *Fixing New York's State Aid Education Dinosaur: A Proposal* (Policy Brief). Center for Policy Research, Syracuse University.

Chapter 10

Making Do: State Constraints and Local Responses in California's Education Finance System[*]

William Duncombe[‡] and John Yinger[†,§]

*†Departments of Public Administration and
International Affairs and of Economics,
Syracuse University, Syracuse, NY, United States*
§jyinger@maxwell.syr.edu

California's unique education finance system combines general state support for school districts, numerous state categorical aid programs, a restricted local property tax, and two unusual small local revenue sources: a parcel tax and contributions from educational foundations. This paper explores the incentives this system creates for local voters and school officials and estimates the impact of these incentives on education costs, school district efficiency, and the demand for student performance. The paper finds that voters in California respond to the price incentives in this system even though they work through the hard-to-pass parcel tax instead of the property tax; that educational outcomes are strongly influenced by student characteristics and other factors that influence educational costs; that school district efficiency is undermined by the state's current emphasis on categorical instead of unrestricted aid; and that, overall, the education finance system is not well designed to meet the state's educational objectives.

---

[*]This chapter is reproduced from "Making Do: State Constraints and Local Responses in California's Education Finance System," *International Tax and Public Finance*, **18**(3), June 2011, pp. 337–368.
[‡]Deceased.

1. Introduction

California's unique education finance system combines general state support
for school districts, numerous state categorical aid programs, a local
property tax, and two unusual small local revenue sources: a parcel tax and
contributions from educational foundations. The revenue available through
general state support and the property tax is limited by a series of complex
amendments to the California state constitution.[1] We explore the incentives
this system creates for local voters and school officials and estimate the
impact of these incentives on education costs, school district efficiency, and
student performance. We focus on two questions: To what extent does voters'
demand for education influence student-performance outcomes in this highly
centralized system? Do the incentives created by the education finance
system undermine the state's expressed educational objectives? Our analysis
does not consider the impact of California's 2009–2010 financial crisis on its
education finance system.

We begin with an overview of the California education finance system. We
then show how the features of this system can be incorporated into education
demand and cost functions, which can be estimated with school-district
data. The next section describes our data and methodology and presents
our empirical results. We find that despite the restrictions in California's
education finance system, educational outcomes are still influenced by local
demand factors, such as income and tax price. In addition, we find that
educational costs in California vary widely across districts based on student
characteristics and labor market conditions. The final section summarizes
our main results and discusses several ways in which California's education
finance system works against the state's objectives for student performance.

2. Overview of the California Education Finance System

The education finance system in California limits variation in revenue across
districts in two fundamental ways. First, Proposition 13 limits the local
property tax rate to 1 percent of assessed value and restricts the growth in
assessed values for property that does not change hands. Most of the resulting

---

[1]Constitutional amendments set the minimum state funding to support revenue limits but
do not determine the way this funding is allocated. The amount of money per pupil usually
equals the amount from the previous year increased by an inflation factor (which depends
on the circumstances). If state tax revenue is growing sufficiently fast, however, the money
available equals 39.032 percent of state general fund taxes. See Goldfinger (2006).

property tax revenue goes to schools. Second, the *Serrano* court rulings limit differences across districts in general-purpose revenue per pupil, defined as unrestricted state aid plus property taxes.

The initial *Serrano* decision found that California's education finance system was unconstitutional because the funds available for a child's education depended on the wealth in his or her school district. The state responded by designing a new education finance system that specified a revenue limit, that is, an amount of general-purpose revenue, for each district. Subsequent court decisions required differences in general-purpose revenue across districts of less than $100 per pupil (in 1974 dollars) and ruled that the post-*Serrano* education finance system was close enough to satisfy this standard. See Timar (2006).

The Proposition 13 limit is a severe constraint because school districts have no other major sources of revenue. As a result, every school district's revenue is largely determined by state policy makers. The *Serrano* restriction is less binding because it does not apply to state categorical aid, which varies widely across districts, and because the state has met the court's revenue-limit guidelines, so it is now free to implement additional education finance reforms.

3. State and Local Shares

These features lead to an education finance system in which, compared to other states, the state government plays a large role but general-purpose aid plays a small role. Table 1 shows the 2006–2007 local, state, and federal shares of school revenue for California and several comparison states. The state share in California, 60.4 percent, is higher than the share in the average state, 47.6 percent. Table 2 compares types of state education aid in

Table 1   Education funding by level of government, 2006–2007.

	California	United States	Big States	West Coast
State %	60.41%	47.55%	38.96%	58.08%
Local %	29.31%	44.11%	52.95%	33.59%
Federal %	10.27%	8.34%	8.09%	8.33%

Notes: Big states are Illinois, Florida, New York, Pennsylvania, and Texas; West Coast is Washington and Oregon. Local percentage includes all tax revenue collected locally, even if the rate is set by the state.

Source: US Census (2009).

Table 2 Decomposition of state aid to education, 2006–2007.

	California	United States	Big States	West Coast
Formula %	56.45%	66.77%	58.05%	78.14%
Comp. %	3.29%	2.40%	0.09%	1.16%
Sp. Ed. %	7.05%	5.95%	9.09%	5.54%
Voc %	0.01%	0.36%	0.42%	0.00%
Transp. %	1.39%	1.69%	2.57%	3.01%
Other %	29.73%	19.01%	26.23%	12.15%
Payment %	2.07%	3.82%	3.54%	0.00%
Total	100.00%	100.00%	100.00%	100.00%

Notes: Big states are Illinois, Florida, New York, Pennsylvania, and Texas; West Coast is Washington and Oregon. Formula = Unrestricted, formula-driven aid; Comp. = Compensatory categorical aid for "at-risk" students; Sp. Ed. = Categorical aid for special education; Voc. = Categorical aid for vocational education; Transp. = Categorical aid for transportation; Other = Other categorical aid; Payment = Other payments, mainly payments for teacher pensions.

Source: US Census (2009).

California and other states in 2006–2007. This table shows that California, like other large states, provides a relatively small share of its state education aid in general-purpose form compared to the average state.

3.1. *General-purpose Aid*

The distribution formula for general-purpose aid in California is equivalent to a foundation aid formula, which is used in most other states.[2] With foundation aid, a district's aid per pupil equals a spending target, called the foundation amount, minus an expected local contribution (Yinger, 2004).[3]

---

[2]According to Huang (2004, Table B.3), 30 states use a foundation formula for general-purpose aid and 11 other states use a foundation formula in combination with some other type of formula.

[3]In principle, the foundation amount is the spending needed to provide the minimum education level expected by the state. In 12 states aid is "based on a state-determined number of teachers per student or on the expenditures in a real or hypothetical school district" (Huang, 2004, p. 348). (For reviews of this approach, often called costing-out, see Guthrie and Rothstein (1999) and Duncombe and Yinger (2007).) Huang also finds that 22 states set the foundation amount based on "historical data, the state's fiscal situation for that year, and the state's priority for supporting elementary and secondary education compared with other items in the state budget" (p. 348). The remaining foundation states, including California, adjust the foundation amount each year, usually based on inflation and changes in enrollment.

California's revenue limit is analogous to the foundation amount. The details of the revenue-limit calculations in California are complicated (see Goldfinger, 2006).[4] Roughly speaking, each district's limit equals its 1972–1973 spending increased for subsequent changes in state-wide income per capita. These increases are higher in some districts than in others, as the *Serrano* decisions required. Revenue limits are not adjusted for educational costs.[5]

Proposition 13 sets the parameters of the expected local contribution in California's aid formula.[6] It not only sets limits on assessing (a practice used in only a few other states) but also sets the property tax rate. This rate equals the share of the 1 percent maximum local property rate that the state allocates to schools, which varies across school districts and, in some cases, within school districts that contain multiple jurisdictions of other types. This rate (or value-weighted average rate) serves as both the rate in the aid formula and as the actual tax rate.[7] These rules effectively transform "local" revenue into "state" revenue. The property tax checks still are paid to the school district, but the district has little or no say about property tax revenue. Thus, California has one of the most centralized education finance systems in the nation.

Because it has a highly centralized system and the *Serrano* decisions reduced revenue-limit differences across districts, one might think that total revenue has less variation in California than in other states. As shown by Table 3, this is not the case. This table compares the across-district

---

[4]A complex formula determines the revenue limit for each district based on previous spending, an inflation factor, and other variables. District revenue limits are adjusted up or down to equal the total funds available (see note 1). See Goldfinger (2006).

[5]In 24 states, the foundation amount is adjusted for the fact that it costs more to provide education in some districts than in others, either because some districts must pay higher wages to attract teachers of any given quality level or because some districts face extra expenses due to a concentration of disadvantaged students (Huang, 2004, Table B.3).

[6]The expected local contribution in foundation aid is usually a percentage of the local property tax base; hence, the foundation aid program makes up the difference between the revenue a district could raise at a given property tax rate and the amount the district must spend to achieve the expected education level. In many states, the local contribution is a required minimum (Huang, 2004, Table B.4). In other states, it serves only as a place holder in the aid formula.

[7]Twenty-four other states with foundation formulas also limit supplementation by school districts to some degree, and two other states allow supplementation but only with a financial penalty. Most of these restrictions are less severe than those in California. A few states (Alabama, Nevada, Michigan) have total restrictions on supplementation, however, and one state (Hawaii) has no independent school districts (Huang, 2004, Table B.4).

Table 3 Distribution of per pupil school district revenue by level of government in California and New York (2007).

	Total revenue	State revenue	State formula aid	State categorical aid	Federal revenue	Local revenue	Property taxes	State formula aid + Property taxes
California								
Ratio of 95th to 5th	2.5	5.4	32.7	5.1	11.1	10.0	17.5	2.1
Ratio of 75th to 25th	1.3	1.5	1.8	1.7	2.5	2.4	3.2	1.2
95th percentile	$20,128	$11,346	$5,927	$5,884	$2,480	$11,691	$8,961	$10,473
75th percentile	$12,093	$7,200	$4,665	$2,689	$1,190	$5,096	$3,558	$6,654
Median	$10,259	$6,082	$3,945	$1,979	$773	$3,290	$1,999	$5,870
25th percentile	$9,308	$4,823	$2,645	$1,575	$477	$2,154	$1,126	$5,480
5th percentile	$8,165	$2,094	$181	$1,144	$224	$1,163	$513	$5,109
New York								
Ratio of 95th to 5th	2.2	4.5	12.1	2.5	6.6	7.6	9.2	2.7
Ratio of 75th to 25th	1.3	1.8	2.5	1.4	2.4	2.5	2.8	1.4
95th percentile	$29,322	$13,062	$8,996	$4,538	$1,749	$24,407	$22,179	$23,889
75th percentile	$20,650	$10,496	$6,992	$3,525	$1,008	$12,464	$11,453	$15,012
Median	$17,281	$8,385	$5,005	$3,022	$680	$7,288	$6,235	$11,958
25th percentile	$15,350	$5,888	$2,758	$2,527	$423	$4,982	$4,077	$10,494
5th percentile	$13,561	$2,902	$742	$1,812	$263	$3,228	$2,418	$8,753
California median as percent of New York	59.4%	72.5%	78.8%	65.5%	113.6%	45.1%	32.1%	49.1%

Notes: Sample size is 970 districts in California and 683 districts in New York.

Source: US Bureau of Census, Public Elementary-Secondary Education Finance Data, 2006–2007 fiscal year.

variation in revenue in California and New York, which has a highly decentralized education finance system. The amount of revenue is much higher in New York, but in some cases, such as the ratio of the 95th percentile to the 5th percentile, the variation in revenue is higher in California. This higher variation does not show up in basic state aid plus property taxes (the revenue limit in California); instead, it shows up in state categorical aid and federal aid.

3.2. *Categorical Aid*

Table 2 reveals that California devotes more of its education aid budget to categorical aid, which appears in rows 2 though 6, than do many other states. The second row indicates that California devotes somewhat more of its aid budget than do most states to what the Census calls "compensatory" aid programs, which include programs "for 'at risk' or other economically disadvantaged students including migratory children."[8]

The main difference between California and other states shows up in the "other" category (row 6); according to the US Bureau of the Census (2009), this category includes aid for

> bilingual education, gifted and talented programs, food services, debt services, instructional materials, textbooks, computer equipment, library resources, guidance and psychological services, driver education, energy conservation, enrollment increases and losses, health, alcohol and drug abuse, AIDS, child abuse, summer school, pre-kindergarten and early childhood, adult education (excluding vocational), desegregation, private schools, safety and law enforcement, and community services.

California has many categorical aid programs for these purposes (Goldfinger, 2006).[9]

Each categorical aid program puts programmatic constraints and administrative responsibilities on school districts. Thus, heavy reliance on categorical aid gives state lawmakers more control over the allocation of school district budgets, but it also limits local flexibility and innovation and raises the share of resources devoted to bookkeeping. As shown in Table 4, categorical aid made up 27.0 percent of total aid in 2006–2007,

---

[8]These programs place California with 17 other states that combine compensatory categorical aid programs with a foundation aid program that is unadjusted for costs (Huang, 2004).

[9]California's current categorical aid programs are described by the Education Data Partnership at http://www.ed-data.k12.ca.us/articles/article.asp?title=categorical%20aid.

Table 4 Composition of "state–level" school revenue in California, 1994–1995 to 2006–2007.

	Categorical aid	Unrestricted funds	
		Operating aid	Property taxes
1991–92	21.75%	52.85%	25.40%
1992–93	24.07%	49.51%	26.42%
1993–94	21.98%	49.20%	28.82%
1994–95	19.53%	41.74%	38.73%
1995–96	21.34%	43.17%	35.49%
1996–97	24.57%	43.87%	31.57%
1997–98	24.93%	44.43%	30.64%
1998–99	27.04%	42.84%	30.12%
1999–2000	28.53%	41.46%	30.00%
2000–01	29.64%	41.75%	28.61%
2001–02	27.84%	42.02%	30.14%
2002–03	25.53%	41.88%	32.59%
2003–04	23.80%	40.76%	35.44%
2004–05	24.35%	46.94%	28.71%
2005–06	24.38%	47.15%	28.54%
2006–07	27.00%	46.16%	26.84%

Notes: Due to changes in the Census categories, the figures before 2004–2005 are not strictly comparable to those in later years.

Source: US Census, *Public Education Finances,* various years. Available at: http://www.census.gov/govs/www/school.html.

but categorical aid programs are often added or consolidated, and this share has been as high as 29.6 percent.

Although California's "other" categorical aid is not explicitly "compensatory," it may flow disproportionately to districts with more "at-risk" students. Thus, the combination of other and compensatory categorical aid may, to some degree, offset the lack of cost adjustments in California's revenue-limit calculations. This effect appears to be modest, however; Baker and Duncombe (2004) find that per pupil education aid in the poorest quarter of districts was only 12 percent above the aid in the average district in California in 2001, compared to a differential of 24 percent in the average state.[10] Overall, California's unrestricted aid programs do not adjust at all for the high costs of educating disadvantaged students, and its categorical aid programs do not address these costs in a comprehensive manner.[11]

---

[10]For alternative approaches to the link between funding and student disadvantage, see Education Trust (2005) and Rose *et al.* (2003).

3.3. *Sources of Local Revenue*

The property tax is, of course, the main source of local revenue for elementary and secondary education. The first row of Table 5 indicates that California relies as heavily on school property taxes as the average state but less heavily than other big states. In many states, however, some of the school districts are dependent, which means that they are a department of a "parent" government, usually a city. Although a few of these parent governments, such as New York City, have an income tax and/or a sales tax, the vast majority of the revenue they collect comes through the property tax. Moreover, in California, some money is funneled to school districts through counties. Thus a more accurate picture can be seen by adding the rows for the property tax, parent government, and other governments. This sum suggests that California (at 72.7 percent) relies less heavily on the property tax than the average state (82.4 percent).

Table 5 also indicates that taxes other than the property tax make up a small share of local school revenue in California, as in other states. A notable difference between California and other states appears in the last row: 20.3 percent of local revenue in California falls into the "other category," compared to 9.0 percent in the average state. Local revenue sources other than the property tax are described in Table 6. The first column refers to the parcel tax, which is unique to California and which cannot be implemented without a two-thirds vote. In the vast majority of cases, it is levied at a fixed rate per parcel.[12] The parcel tax provided 8.8 percent of local non-property-tax revenue in 2007–2008, compared with 5.6 percent in 1995–1996.[13] Table 6 also shows that "other" sources constitute almost half of local non-property-tax revenue. These other

---

[11] This *ad hoc* approach was retained in the state budget for 2006–2007, which added $350 million in categorical grants directed toward disadvantaged students and English language learners (ELL), along with $50 million in one-time grants to help attract and retain teachers in districts with poorly performing schools (California School Boards Association, 2006).

[12] Using data for all parcel tax votes, we find that the parcel tax is levied at a fixed rate per parcel in 93.8 percent of the cases. Other designs are separate rates for residential and commercial parcels, separate rates for single-unit and multi-unit parcels, and rates based on a parcel's square footage. We are grateful to Eric Brunner for proving us with these data.

[13] Only 208 parcel taxes had been passed by November 2005 (Timar, 2006), only 58 districts had a parcel tax in 2004, and parcel tax revenue was less than $500 per pupil in all but 26 of these districts (Brunner and Sonstelie, 2005).

Table 5   Local revenue for K-12 education, 2006–2007.

	California	United States	Big States	West Coast
Property taxes	67.66%	63.24%	76.61%	75.05%
Other taxes	1.59%	2.79%	1.91%	0.02%
Parent government	3.74%	16.99%	9.14%	0.00%
Other government	1.30%	2.20%	0.58%	2.35%
School lunch	2.78%	2.82%	2.10%	3.41%
Tuition & Transportation	0.27%	0.48%	0.26%	1.55%
Other charges	2.36%	2.50%	1.52%	4.68%
Other revenue	20.29%	8.97%	7.89%	12.94%

Notes: Big states are Illinois, Florida, New York, Pennsylvania, and Texas; West Coast is Washington and Oregon. Other revenue includes rental income, interest on investments, private contributions, reimbursements for previous years.

Source: US Census (2009).

Table 6   Composition of local school revenue other than the property tax in California, 1995–1996 to 2007–2008.

	Parcel tax	Local other sales	Leases and rents	Interest	Fees	Other
1995–96	5.60%	0.70%	8.70%	35.40%	18.60%	31.00%
1996–97	5.50%	0.50%	8.40%	37.10%	18.30%	30.20%
1997–98	5.30%	0.40%	7.80%	36.50%	16.90%	33.10%
1998–99	5.20%	0.30%	7.00%	36.70%	16.80%	34.10%
1999–2000	5.10%	0.50%	6.40%	35.70%	17.20%	35.10%
2000–01	4.50%	0.30%	6.40%	37.00%	16.70%	35.10%
2001–02	6.10%	0.40%	7.70%	25.10%	18.60%	42.10%
2002–03	8.00%	0.30%	7.80%	15.40%	19.70%	48.80%
2003–04	8.00%	2.92%	7.29%	9.81%	17.27%	54.71%
2004–05	9.63%	2.66%	7.24%	12.51%	17.72%	50.24%
2005–06	9.99%	2.31%	6.85%	17.84%	15.62%	47.38%
2006–07	9.14%	1.88%	6.14%	22.07%	16.08%	44.68%
2007–08	8.80%	1.82%	6.28%	20.59%	16.71%	45.80%

Notes: The accounting system changed in 2003–2004, so the numbers starting in this year may not be comparable to the numbers in earlier years.

Source: Unaudited financial data provided by the California Department of Education. Available at http://www.ed-data.k12.ca.us/welcome.asp.

sources are varied, but their main component is donations from educational foundations.[14]

4. Modeling Incentives in the California Education Finance System

Although the California education finance system places severe constraints on school districts, it also creates incentives for local actors to behave in certain ways. We derive and estimates education demand and cost functions that incorporate these incentives.

4.1. *Education Demand Functions*

A household's demand for education quality, like its demand for a private good, is influenced by its income and preferences and by the price of education it faces (Duncombe and Yinger, 1998, 2001). We measure education quality using California's Academic Performance Index, API, which is a weighted average of a district's student test scores on a variety of subjects from grades 2 through 12. The subjects include English language arts, mathematics, history/social science, and science. This index was defined by the 1999 Public Schools Accountability Act and is central to California's school accountability system (CDE, 2006).

Let V stand for the market value of a voter's home and t indicate the effective property tax rate for education, as determined by the state. Moreover, let the parcel tax equal $\$P$ and the taxpayer's contribution to an education foundation equal $\$F$. If Y is a voter's income and Z is spending on everything except public schools, then a California voter's budget constraint is

$$Y = Z + tV + P + F \tag{1}$$

A school district faces a cost function, $C\{S, W, Q\}$, where C is total cost per pupil, S is education quality, W is the price of hiring a teacher of given

---

[14]We compared school-district level data on net giving by education foundations, based on tax return data (Brunner and Sonstelie, 2003), with "other" local revenue; the correlation is 0.86. A $1 increase in net foundation giving per pupil in a district is associated with a $0.73 increase in that district's other local revenue per pupil in 2004 and a $0.89 increase in 2005. These results suggest that, on average, 73 to 89 percent of foundation gifts go directly to the school district. Moreover, a $1 increase in local revenue per pupil is associated with a $0.93 ($0.91) increase in foundation giving per pupil in 2004 (2005), which suggests that about 92 percent of other local revenue per pupil comes from foundations.

quality, and Q is a set of variables describing students in the district, such as total enrollment and the poverty rate. The derivative of this function with respect to S, $\partial C/\partial S$, equals marginal cost, MC. Spending per pupil, E, equals C divided by district efficiency, e. Without loss of generality, this efficiency measure can be scaled to equal one in a fully efficient district and to fall below one in less efficient districts. Cost functions and efficiency are discussed more fully in the next section.

School district revenue comes primarily from property taxes and unrestricted lump-sum state aid, A^U, which add up to a district's revenue limit, R. A district also may receive revenue from categorical aid, A^C; federal aid, A^F; parcel taxes, and educational foundations. Let $\bar{V}$ indicate property value per pupil, N equal the number of parcels per pupil, and $\bar{F}$ equal foundation contributions per pupil. Then the district budget constraint per pupil is

$$E \equiv \frac{C\{S, W, Q\}}{e} = t\bar{V} + A^U + A^C + A^F + NP + \bar{F}$$

$$= R + A^C + A^F + NP + \bar{F} \tag{2}$$

Solving (2) for P, the parcel tax level needed to balance the budget, and substituting the result into (1) yields.

$$Y + \frac{R + A^C + A^F + \bar{F}}{N} = Z + tV + \frac{C\{S, W, Q\}}{e}N + F \tag{3}$$

The left-hand side of this equation is household income augmented by school revenue, or Y^* for short, and the right-hand side is household spending. Tax price, P^*, is what an increment in S costs a voter:

$$P^* \equiv \frac{\partial \text{Spending}}{\partial S} = \frac{dC}{dS}\frac{1}{eN} = \frac{MC}{eN} \tag{4}$$

Equation (4) replicates a result in Brunner (2001), namely, that tax price depends on the inverse of the number of parcels per pupil. A higher N results in a lower price, that is, in a greater ability to spread out the cost of education over many parcels. If school revenue were restricted to state-controlled sources (state aid and property taxes) and a parcel tax, school districts without a parcel tax would be at a corner solution, with no local revenue, and this tax price measure would not necessarily apply. In fact, however, the property tax makes up only 67.7 percent of local revenue (Table 5), and all school districts find themselves at an interior solution, where they are making decisions about how much local revenue to raise. Equation (4) indicates what it would cost voters to raise more local revenue using the broadest source available to them, namely, the parcel tax. Note that P^* depends on MC and e, as well as on N.

Because the parcel tax is a relatively new option that is used by only a few districts, voters may not be aware that it is a possibility and may not respond to it in the same way that they respond to other components of their tax price. We test for voter perceptions by interacting the parcel tax component of tax price, $1/N$, with a measure of voter awareness based on the district's experience with parcel tax votes. We explore three measures of this experience: whether the district has ever had a parcel tax vote, whether a parcel tax vote has received majority support in the district, and whether the district has ever implemented a parcel tax.

District-level demand for S is a function of district-level income, augmented by state aid, and of district-level tax price. More specifically, we specify a demand function by substituting the above expressions for augmented income and tax price into a standard multiplicative form for demand. Because 67 percent of the voters must agree before a parcel tax can be implemented and because higher-income voters are more likely to approve, our measure of voter income is the 33rd percentile of a district's household income distribution. We also add a flypaper effect, f, which allows government revenue to have a different impact on demand than does household income, and include other demand determinants, X.[15] The result:

$$S = K_D \left(Y + f \left(\frac{R + A^C + A^F + \bar{F}}{N} \right) \right)^\theta \left(\frac{MC}{eN} \right)^\mu X^\alpha \qquad (5)$$

where K_D is a constant, θ is the income elasticity of demand, μ is the (negative) price elasticity. For conciseness, (5) is written with single values for θ and μ, but the components of Y^* and P^* may be perceived differently by voters, so we estimate separate elasticities for each component.

Equation (5) contains three endogenous variables: e, MC, and $\bar{F}$. The first two are endogenous because they are functions of S. As discussed more fully below, we address this endogeneity by solving for S and including in the regression cost and efficiency indexes, which are functions of exogenous variables in the expenditure function. We address the endogeneity of $\bar{F}$ using two-stage least squares, 2SLS. To find instruments for $\bar{F}$, we draw on the recent literature on foundation contributions (Brunner and Sonstelie, 2003).

In the standard model, the value of aid to a voter depends on the voter's property tax share, that is, on the voter's share of the money saved by cutting local property taxes (Oates, 1972). Equation (5) shows that in California, this effect works through the parcel tax; a $1 increase in any component of

---

[15] For a review of the literature on the flypaper effect, see Hines and Thaler (1995).

augmented income makes it possible to collect the same amount of revenue after decreasing the parcel tax amount, P, by $\$(1/N)$. This effect, like the more direct tax-price effect, may depend on voter perceptions. As discussed below, we devise a specification that allows us to test whether the parcel-tax component of this term is perceived.

The variables in X fall into two categories. The first includes variables identifying groups that may have relatively high or low demand for student performance on the API.[16] Two variables, the share of the population between 5 and 17 years old and the share of the population above age 64, characterize the age distribution in a district. The signs of these variables are not clear a priori. A high concentration of school age children might indicate that a district has many parents, who are likely to demand relatively high levels of student performance, but it also signals a high cost of education per adult, which might lead to lower demand. Similarly, elderly voters might have a relatively low demand for student performance, because they no longer have children in public schools, but they might also want a good education to keep up the value of their property or to help their grandchildren, particularly since they, like other voters, have a fixed property tax rate. The final variable in this category is the percentage of the students in a district who are African American. White voters, who make up the majority, may lower their support for public schools as the African–American share increases.

Second, we assume that voters' desired level of public output depends in part on output in comparison districts. This notion is called "copycat" behavior by Case *et al.* (1993) and "yardstick competition" by Besley and Case (1995). Case, Hines, and Rosen estimate a structural model of this theory in which output in every jurisdiction is treated as endogenous. In contrast, our focus is on the school-district demand function; instead of adding potentially endogenous output (i.e., student-performance) measures for comparison districts, therefore, we include exogenous characteristics of other districts that affect the level of output they select.

The comparison-district characteristics we include are the share of students in poverty, the share of the student who are African–American, and median house value. The definition of "comparison districts" is critical. The definition should not be so broad as to include districts that are too far away to be known to the district's voters nor so narrow as to include just neighboring districts, which might share the district's unobservable factors.

---

[16]These variables also might pick up the price impacts of unobserved cost factors.

Our approach is to select an intermediate definition: districts in the same labor market area.[17] Hence, each district's values for these three variables are expressed as averages for the district's labor market area, excluding the values for the district itself.

4.2. *The Education Cost and Efficiency Functions*

An education cost function indicates the minimum amount of money a district must spend per pupil to obtain a given level of educational output with given input prices. We measure output using the API. The key input price is teacher salaries.

As shown by previous studies, application of this tool to education requires three principal extensions.[18] First, we observe spending, not cost; any estimation must recognize that spending exceeds cost in an inefficient district. Second, educational costs depend not only on input prices, but also on school and student characteristics. Third, measures of student performance and teachers' salaries are influenced by school district decisions and are therefore must be treated as endogenous in any education cost estimation. In this section, we explain our approach to these extensions. Imazeki's (2008) recent study of California does not address the third extension, but does address the other two, and we also compare our approach to hers.

4.3. *Accounting for Efficiency*

A production activity is defined to be efficient if it uses the minimum resources possible to produce a particular output given current technology and to be inefficient if it uses more than this minimum. Three features of efficiency are critical in the education context. First, a school district is not inefficient if it spends more than other districts with the same output for reasons outside its control. As a result, our analysis controls for factors outside district control, such as the district's labor market environment and the background of its students.

---

[17]We use the definition of labor market area in Rose (2006), which is based on Census place-of-work areas.

[18]Education cost functions have been estimated for Arizona (Downes and Pogue, 1994), Kansas (Duncombe and Johnston, 2004), California (Imazeki, 2008), New York (Duncombe and Yinger, 2005; Duncombe *et al.*, 2003), Texas (Imazeki and Reschovsky, 2004a, 2004b; Gronberg *et al.*, 2004), and Wisconsin (Reschovsky and Imazeki, 2001).

Second, efficiency can only be defined relative to the output selected by the analyst. In the case of a firm with a single output, inefficient firms are those that use machines based on an outmoded technology, pay employees more than the market wage, send executives on expensive junkets, or deviate in other ways from the best available technology for producing that output. Given the nature of these activities, an "inefficient" firm is often said to be "wasteful."

When a firm produces multiple outputs with some sharing of inputs, however, the concept of "inefficiency" depends on the outputs, and "inefficiency" and "waste" may no longer be equivalent. Consider a firm that produces widgets and then produces gadgets from the material left over from widget production. This firm might be inefficient in producing widgets (because a lot of material is left over) and efficient in producing gadgets (because it has so much left-over material). This type of inefficiency has nothing to do with waste; instead, it has to do with the firm's trade-off across the two outputs. Of course, the firm may also be wasteful, but it is not possible to separate these two types of inefficiency in empirical analysis.

Multiple outputs and input sharing are inherent characteristics of public education; the same teachers and classrooms, supported by the same administrators, provide many outputs. These outputs include student performance on standardized tests in English, math, social studies, and science, as well as high-school completion rates and student performance in art, music, athletics, and citizenship. Thus, inefficiency in producing English performance reflects both spending to promote other outputs and the use of outmoded techniques or other forms of waste.

Third, both components of inefficiency are behavioral outcomes that can be modeled. The "waste" component reflects the incentives facing school officials and the incentives that encourage voters to monitor school activities. The "other output" component reflects factors influencing the demand for outputs other than the one specified by the analyst.

Both components of efficiency may be influenced by district income (Duncombe and Yinger, 2001, 2005; Duncombe et al., 2003). First, a higher wage rate has both an income and substitution effect for voter monitoring, which is a type of leisure activity. The income effect leads to more monitoring, the substitution effect to less, so the net impact could be positive or negative. Second, a higher income may encourage voters to push for a broader set of outputs, which lowers efficiency. As in demand equation, income in the efficiency equation is augmented with aid and contributions and has a flypaper effect, now labeled g. These other sources of income have only an income effect for monitoring, not a substitution effect. For all sources of income, the net impact on spending (and the sign of g) depends on the balance of the impact on monitoring and the impact on the demand for other outputs.

Previous studies also suggest that a lower tax price weakens voters' incentives to monitor school officials and boosts their demand for a broader set of objectives (Duncombe and Yinger, 2001). Our analysis of demand indicates that tax-price reflects MC and N.[19] A district with more parcels per pupil has a lower tax price and, all else equal, will be less efficient.

Our approach is to incorporate these hypotheses into a multiplicative efficiency equation. Let γ be the income elasticity of efficiency, δ be the price elasticity of efficiency, and K_e be a constant. Then this equation is

$$e = K_e \left(Y + g \left(\frac{R + A^C + A^F + \bar{F}}{N} \right) \right)^{\gamma} \left(\frac{MC}{N} \right)^{\delta} M^{\lambda} \qquad (6)$$

The above analysis indicates that the signs of both γ and δ could be positive or negative. Determinants of efficiency other than augmented income and tax-price are represented by M. These variables are associated either with the incentives that lead voters to monitor school officials or with the incentives of school officials themselves. The sole (and insignificant) efficiency variable included by Imazeki (2008), a measure of competition based on the number of school districts in a given district's metropolitan area, falls into this category.

Variables linked to voters' incentives in California. We cannot observe voters' monitoring activities directly, but we can observe several factors that might influence monitoring, and hence efficiency. First, we hypothesize that recent migrants are less connected to their community than other voters and hence less likely to engage in monitoring. We test this hypothesis using the share of the population that moved into the school district from outside the county from 1995 to 2000.[20]

---

[19] We exclude the efficiency component of tax price from the efficiency equation. It makes no sense to argue that efficiency is a function of itself.

[20] Migration into a school district might affect educational costs. As discussed below, however, we control for variables linked to migration: the share of students from poor families, the share of students who are English learners, total enrollment, and enrollment change.

Second, voters who expect high performance may enforce their expectations through monitoring. Since 1978, revenue limits have gone up for under-
funded districts at a higher rate than for well-funded districts (Sonstelie
et al., 2000). Voters in districts with real declines in their revenue limits,
usually high-performing districts, may expect their high performance in
previous years to continue, so their monitoring activities may boost efficiency.
Voters in districts with relatively large increases in their revenue limits,
usually low-performing districts, observe higher performance increases than
expected, so their monitoring activities may have a smaller impact on
efficiency. With this type of monitoring, the change in a district's revenue
limit between 1974–1975 and 2004–2005 will have a positive impact on its
spending.[21]

Variables linked to school officials' incentives in California. Revenue limit
changes may also be linked to the incentives facing school district officials. School officials in high revenue/high performance districts may work
especially hard to maintain the performance level in their district despite
the decline in their revenue. Similarly, school officials in low revenue/low
performance districts may be able to use the relatively large increases in
their revenue limits to increase their relative performance even without being
relatively efficient.

The options available to school officials also are influenced by the restrictions linked to the state aid they receive. Unlike the property tax revenue
and aid that make up a district's revenue limit, categorical aid must be spent
on particular programs. The lawmakers who pass categorical aid programs
apparently believe that the restrictions in these programs will foster the
achievement of the state's educational objectives. Goldfinger (2006, p. 177)
reports, for example, that lawmakers think additional unrestricted funds
would lead to higher teacher salaries without boosting student performance.

An alternative view is that school district officials are in the best position
to determine the allocation of funds that maximizes student performance.
The restrictions in categorical aid programs require a school to devote more
resources to red tape; to spend time and energy on programs that may
not boost API; and, if the categorical aid program is underfunded, to shift
money out of general-purpose funds where it may have more impact on API.

---

[21]As in other cases, we cannot formally rule out the possibility that this variable picks
up the impact of cost variables that are correlated with revenue limit changes and that
we cannot observe. Because of our extensive cost controls, however, we believe that an
efficiency interpretation for this variable is more compelling than a cost interpretation.

This view suggests, in other words, that categorical aid will have a smaller impact on student performance, as measured by the API, than would an equal amount of unrestricted aid.

We explore these arguments by including in our expenditure equation a variable measuring the share of state aid that comes in the form of categorical grants. A negative sign for this variable would support the first view, where a positive sign would support the second. Based on our earlier discussion, we assume that voters' monitoring incentives associated with categorical aid are captured by the associated component of augmented income, so that this additional categorical-aid variable captures the incentives of school officials. We cannot test this assumption, however, so we focus on the net impact of categorical aid on efficiency.

4.4. *The Expenditure Equation*

Efficiency cannot be measured directly, but its determinants can be incorporated into the estimation of a cost function (Duncombe and Yinger, 2001). Following standard practice (Downes and Pogue, 1994; Duncombe and Yinger, 1998, 2005; Reschovsky and Imazeki, 2001, 2003), we assume that educational cost depends, in a multiplicative way on teacher salaries, W, and school characteristics, Q, such as enrollment and measures of disadvantage:

$$C = K_C S^\sigma W^\rho Q^\upsilon \tag{7}$$

where K is a constant and σ measures returns to quality scale; $\sigma < 1.0$ indicates increasing returns and $\sigma > 1$ indicates decreasing returns. With this cost function, marginal cost is not constant:

$$MC \equiv \frac{\partial C}{\partial S} = \sigma K_C S^{\sigma-1} W^\rho Q^\upsilon \tag{8}$$

Substituting (6)–(8) into the definition of E in (2), we find that

$$E = K_E (S^{\sigma-\delta(\sigma-1)})(W^\rho Q^\upsilon)^{1-\delta}\left(Y + g\left(\frac{R + A^C + A^F + \bar{F}}{N}\right)\right)^{-\gamma} N^\delta M^{-\lambda} \tag{9}$$

where $K_E = (K_C)^{1-\delta}/(K_e \sigma^\delta)k^*$. Taking logs, using the simplification for Y^* that $\ln\{1 + \alpha\} \approx \alpha$ when α is positive but less than one, and adding a separate flypaper effect for each element of school revenue yields an equation that can be estimated:

$$\ln\{E\} = \ln\{K_E\} + (\sigma - \delta(\sigma - 1))\ln\{S\} + \rho(1 - \delta)\ln\{W\} + \upsilon(1 - \delta)\ln\{Q\}$$

$$- \gamma\ln\{Y\} - \gamma g_1\left(\frac{R}{Y \cdot N}\right) - \gamma g_2\left(\frac{A^C}{Y \cdot N}\right) - \gamma g_3\left(\frac{A^F}{Y \cdot N}\right)$$

$$- \gamma g_4\left(\frac{\bar{F}}{Y \cdot N}\right) + \delta\ln\{N\} - \lambda\ln\{M\} \tag{10}$$

This equation identifies all the parameters in (6) and (8) except the constants, which are not needed to calculate cost and efficiency indexes, and the elasticity of e with respect to MC, which we assume to equal the elasticity of e with respect to another component of P^*, $(1/N)$.[22]

To determine whether voters actually perceive the impact of the parcel tax on the value they receive from state aid, we split all the revenue terms into two parts. In the case of the revenue limit, the two terms included in the expenditure equation are:

$$- \gamma g_{11}\left(\frac{R}{Y}\right) - \gamma g_{12}\left(\frac{R}{Y}\right)\left(\frac{1}{N} - 1\right) \tag{11}$$

If the estimated coefficients of the two terms are equal, then this reduces to the form in (10), which supports the hypothesis that voters perceive the parcel-tax effect. If the coefficient of the second term equals zero, then we can reject the hypothesis that voters recognize the impact of the parcel tax on the value of the aid they receive.

Student characteristics and other fixed inputs. Many studies find that the per-pupil cost of education is higher in school districts with a higher concentration of disadvantaged students (Duncombe and Yinger, 2005). Our analysis looks at the cost impacts of student poverty and the share of students with limited English proficiency. Educational costs are also affected by the share of students with various disabilities. Because there are so many types of disabilities, however, and because school districts have some control over the way student are classified into disability categories, we estimate our models excluding spending for special education. Instead, we include the share of students with severe disabilities in our analysis to determine

---

[22]Since δ, equals minus one multiplied by the coefficient of the tax-share variable, the values of the cost parameters, α and λ, can be determined from the coefficients of the cost variables. The efficiency income elasticity, γ, is the negative of the coefficient of $\ln\{Y\}$. The economies-of-scale parameter, σ, can be found using the coefficient of $\ln\{S\}$ and the estimate of δ.

whether a concentration of students with severe disabilities alters the cost of education for other students.[23]

We also account for cost differences associated with the set of grades served by the school district by including dummy variables for high-school-only and elementary-school-only districts, with unified districts as the omitted category. In addition, we estimate the extent of economies or diseconomies of size. As in previous studies, our equation allows for a U-shaped relationship between district enrollment and per-pupil costs.[24]

Finally, we investigate the impact on spending per pupil of short-run enrollment change, defined as the percent change in enrollment over a three-year period. We estimate the impact of enrollment increases and enrollment decreases separately. Enrollment change is largely outside a district's control, so enrollment change variables can be interpreted as cost factors. Because we also control for total enrollment, the estimated impacts of these variables indicate whether two districts with the same current enrollment and the same student performance will have different costs if one of these districts has experienced a recent enrollment change and the other has not. In the short run, adding several new students to existing classrooms has little impact on the budget and, therefore, lowers spending per pupil. Similarly, taking students out of existing classrooms causes spending per pupil to rise.[25] Thus, we expect that short-run per-pupil costs will decline when enrollment rises and increase when enrollment declines.

Addressing endogeneity. Some unobserved district characteristics may affect both the dependent variable in our cost equation, spending, and a key explanatory variable, API, so we estimate our expenditure equation with 2SLS. The instruments for S are the X variables in the demand

---

[23]Imazeki (2008) addresses the same student characteristics but makes different choices. She estimates her model with a single year of data and averages the free lunch variable over two years. She separates Spanish-speaking and other English learners, includes special education spending, and includes variables for the share of students both in special education (which may be endogenous) and with high-cost disabilities.

[24]Imazeki (2008) uses the same specification for these variables.

[25]Smaller classes might lead to higher student performance (Boozer and Rouse, 2001; Krueger, 1999; Krueger and Whitmore, 2001; Finn *et al.*, 2005). If these short-run class-size changes do affect student performance, then short-run enrollment decline might lower the per-pupil cost of obtaining a given level of student performance. In practice, however, the impact of class size on performance does not appear to be large enough for this to occur.

equation that are associated with the copy-cat (or yardstick competition) theory.[26]

A good instrument also must not be correlated with the error term in the expenditure equation. This type of correlation can arise if the instruments influence comparison districts' choices of outputs other than API and those choices, in turn, are copied (or become a yardstick) for a district's own choices. With our framework, this type of correlation is highly unlikely. The main reason is that copy-cat behavior is unlikely to extend much beyond the API. Not only is the API a very broad measure of student performance (recall all the grades and subjects it covers), but it is also the basis for the state's accountability system and is by far the most publicized measure of district performance in the state. Our instruments are therefore likely to have little or no impact on district spending after controlling for API. In addition, our expenditure equation controls for other measures of student performance through our efficiency variables. In short, our instruments are endogenous only in the unlikely event that they influence unobserved performance measures in a district's comparison districts that are both copied by the district and not captured by our efficiency variables.[27]

Teacher salaries and contributions to local foundations also might be endogenous. Because a school district must compete for teachers with private market alternatives, our instrument for teacher salaries is the log of estimated comparable private wages in the same labor market area (Rose, 2006). Our instruments for education foundation contributions are the ones used for the demand equation.

Calculating MC and e for the demand equation. To estimate the demand function, we begin with (5) and then take the following steps: (1) substitute

---

[26] Our demand results show that these instruments do indeed affect API. Formal first-stage regressions (available upon request) also support the validity of these and other instruments.

[27] One possible, but unlikely channel for such an event arises if a district's unobserved school performance measures not captured by our efficiency variables lead to household migration that alters the comparison- district characteristics that we use as instruments. This possibility can be addressed by restating our instruments as averages for the area including the district; after all, within-area movement of households does not alter area-wide household averages. This approach yields virtually the same results (available upon request) as the approach in the text.

(6) and (8), which define e and MC, into (5); (2) solve the resulting equation for S; (3) introduce separate price elasticities for the three components of tax price (MC, e, and N) and separate flypaper effects for the components of Y^*; (4) take the logarithm of this equation, using the above simplification for Y^*. These steps lead to:

$$\ln\{S\} = \ln\{K^*\} + \theta^* \ln\{Y\} + \theta^* f_1 \frac{R}{Y \cdot N} + \theta^* f_2 \frac{A^C}{Y \cdot N} + \theta^* f_3 \frac{A^F}{Y \cdot N}$$

$$+ \theta^* f_4 \frac{\bar{F}}{Y \cdot N} + \mu_1^* \ln\{C^*\} - \mu_2^* \ln\{e^*\} - \mu_3^* \ln\{N\} + \alpha^* \ln\{X\}$$

$$(12)$$

where K^* is a constant; C^* and e^* contain all the terms in (6) and (8), respectively, except for S; $\theta^* = \theta/(1 - \mu_3(\sigma-1)(1-\delta))$; $\mu_i^* = \mu_i/(1 - \mu_i(\sigma-1))$ $(1 - \delta)$; $\alpha^* = \alpha/(1 - \mu_3(\sigma-1)(1-\delta))$; and f_i is the flypaper effect for the ith component of Y^*.

The terms C^* and e^* are calculated based on the estimated coefficients from (10). Moreover, we can use an analog to (11) to determine whether voters perceive the impact of the parcel tax on the value of state aid.

4.5. *Estimates of the Impact of Incentives in the California Education Finance System Data*

Our models are estimated with data for almost all regular school districts in California in 2003–2004 and 2004–2005.[28] Data from the 2 years are pooled, a dummy variable for 2003–2004 is included in the regression, and the standard errors are adjusted to account for the fact that there are two observations for each school district. Although we have 2 years of data, there is not enough time variation in the explanatory variables to estimate the models with fixed effects. Most of the data were produced by the California Department of Education (CDE) and downloaded from the CDE website. The dependent variable for our expenditure equation is per pupil operating spending minus

---

[28]Because of missing data, the cost and demand models were estimated with 920 school districts in 2005 and 921 in 2004, which is more than 90 percent of the total districts in California.

transportation and special education.[29] The dependent variable for the demand equations is a district's API.[30]

The wage variable in the expenditure equation is a district's minimum teacher salary, which is the only salary variable available to us that is comparable across districts.[31] Student poverty is measured by the share of students eligible for a free lunch, and limited English proficiency is measured by the share of students classified as English learners (EL) based on the Language Census. Our measure of student special needs is the share of students outside a regular classroom at least 80 percent of the time.[32]

Data for the revenue limit in 1975 comes from financial records for that year, and data for revenue from private foundations comes from IRS records.[33] Data on earnings, income, population, housing units, renters, demographics, and employment come from the 2000 Census. We use the 33rd percentile of the household income distribution as the income measure in the demand equation. To emphasize the link between opportunity cost and voter monitoring, we use median earnings in the expenditure equation.[34]

---

[29] This figure is obtained by adding spending in the general fund and in several special revenue funds as defined in the Standard Accounting Code System (SACS). We included personnel compensation (objects 1100–3902), books and supplies (4100–4700), services and other operating expenses (5200–5900), except transfers of direct costs to other funds (5750) and tuition (7110–7143). We excluded pupil transportation, special education, facilities acquisition and construction, facilities rents and leases, and debt service. Our procedure removes all spending labeled "special education," but may not remove some related spending items with a different label, such as special education spending run through county offices of education.

[30] Value-added measures for the API, which must compare scores for the same set of cohorts at different times (Duncombe and Yinger, 2007), are not available.

[31] This variable is missing for about 80 districts. We fill in the remaining districts using the coefficients from a regression (for districts without missing data) of the salary variable on private sector wages in the labor market area (Rose, 2006), county population, and the percent of the district's population in an urban area. This variable with the filled-in observations is treated as endogenous in our 2SLS procedure. An alternative procedure, which yields similar results, is to simply use the predicted value from this regression as the (exogenous) salary variable.

[32] We imputed missing values for this variable using the predicted value from a regression of this variable on the share of enrollment with more severe disabilities, which is defined as the share of disabled students who are not classified as having a "speech or language impairment" or "specific learning disability." We are grateful to Dr. Jay Chambers for providing these data.

[33] We are grateful to Eric Brunner for supplying both these variables.

[34] We obtain similar results using median income in the demand equation or using income instead of earnings in the expenditure equation.

Information on the number of parcels in each school district is not readily available from a centralized source in California. We contacted the auditor-controller or assessor in each county and received data from 28 counties and 507 school districts. We then regressed parcels on the number of housing units, the number of business establishments in the county, and total employment in the district, all expressed in per pupil terms, and used the coefficients from this regression to predict the number of parcels for missing observations.[35]

4.6. *Expenditure Regression: Methods and Results*

Our expenditure equation was first estimated with a simultaneous equations procedure, treating API, teacher salaries, and $\bar{F}$ as endogenous. As indicated earlier, instruments for API are exogenous characteristics of comparison districts, and the instrument for teacher salaries describes labor market conditions. Following Brunner and Sonstelie (2003), who find that foundation contributions are smaller in rural areas and increase less than proportionately with district size, our instruments for $\bar{F}$ are the percentage of the district's population classified as rural and the percentage difference between a district's population and the average population of other districts in the same county. In fact, however, $\bar{F}$ was never significant, regardless of the instruments we used, and it was dropped from the final regressions.

To determine whether voters are aware of the parcel tax, we added an interaction between the parcel-tax component of tax-price and a measure of voter experience with the parcel tax. This interaction was never close to significant for any of our three measure of voter experience. As a result, these interaction terms are not included in the final models in Table 7. Finally, we implemented (11) and discovered that the parcel tax component of every aid term had a coefficient that was insignificant and close to zero. As a result, only the first term in (11) is included in our final regressions.

Table 7 presents OLS, 2SLS, and LIML estimates for our final expenditure equation. A comparison of results using OLS, which is the approach used by

---

[35]The number of parcels per pupil (Y), is regressed on the log of private sector salaries $(X1)$, per pupil housing units $(X1)$, per pupil business establishments in the county $(X2)$, and per pupil private employment in the district $(X3)$. The coefficients (t-statistics) are: $Y = 1.1104(1.69) + 2.3416(23.42)X1 + 0.0382(8.78)X2 - 0.9502(-5.12)X3(R^2 = 0.51)$. The number of private establishments in 2005 is from the Quarterly Census of Employment and Wages (ES202), which is produced by the California Labor Market Information Division.

Table 7 Expenditure equation estimates for California school districts (2003–2004 and 2004–2005).

Variables	OLS		2SLS		Fuller LIML ($\alpha = 1$)	
	Coefficient	t-statistic	Coefficient	t-statistic	Coefficient	t-statistic
Intercept	2.0997*	1.73	−17.8712**	−3.52	−18.6749**	−4.67
Academic Performance Index[a]	0.2992**	1.98	2.6294**	3.78	2.7390**	5.05
Cost variables						
Predicted minimum teacher salaries[b]	0.3079**	5.79	0.9055**	2.14	0.9193**	2.76
Share of free lunch students	−0.0004	−0.87	0.0052**	2.95	0.0054**	3.89
Share of limited English language students	0.0041**	6.98	0.0052**	4.76	0.0052**	6.17
Share of disabled students out of classroom 80% of the time	0.0052	0.67	0.0197**	2.17	0.0204**	2.84
Enrollment[a]	−0.1756**	−7.50	−0.1813**	−5.00	−0.1811**	−6.11
Enrollment squared[c]	0.0087**	5.78	0.0083**	3.57	0.0083**	4.40
Percent 3-year enrollment change if positive	−0.0952**	−4.34	−0.0872**	−3.54	−0.0868**	−3.91
Percent 3-year enrollment change if negative	−0.3417**	−4.21	−0.3688**	−3.23	−0.3699**	−3.96
Elementary district (1 = yes)	−0.0719**	−4.42	−0.2014**	−5.33	−0.2071**	−7.15
High school district (1 = yes)	0.0028	0.10	0.1576	2.34	0.1655**	3.18

Variables Associated with Voters' Incentives						
Median earnings (2000)[a]	0.1832**	5.44	-0.0030	-0.05	-0.0105	-0.21
Revenue limit component of adjusted income	1.0179**	7.54	1.0871**	6.45	1.0900**	8.28
Categorical aid component of adjusted income	-0.4152**	-2.61	-0.4701*	-1.90	-0.4703**	-2.10
Federal aid component of adjusted income	0.8167**	4.42	0.6781**	2.56	0.6717**	3.05
Parcels per pupil (inverse of tax price)[a]	0.0486**	4.44	0.0377**	2.43	0.0373**	3.06
Population migration rate (2000)	0.0022**	3.55	0.0016*	1.83	0.0015**	2.27
Variables Associated with School Officials' Incentives						
Categorical aid as percent of total operating revenue	0.4455**	3.08	0.6779**	3.03	0.6862**	3.80
Other Variables						
Year = 2004 (1 = yes)	0.0010	0.15	0.0803**	3.87	0.0837**	4.49

Notes: The dependent variable is the log of current general fund expenditures; the log of API and minimum salary are treated as endogenous in the second two models; sample size is 1,841; robust standard errors are reported (controlling for clustering at district level in the 2SLS model); a * (**) indicates significance at the two-tailed 10 (5) percent level.
[a] Expressed as natural logarithm.
[b] Square of the log of enrollment.

Imazeki (2008), and 2SLS reveals that a failure to correct for endogeneity biases some coefficients, such as those for API, teacher salaries, and poverty.[36] The API coefficient, for example, goes from 0.30 with OLS to 2.63 with 2SLS. We conducted an over-identification test (Wooldridge, 2003); based on the Hansen J-statistic, we cannot reject the hypothesis that our instruments are exogenous.[37]

Following the advice of Murray (2006), we use the weak-instrument test of Stock and Yogo (2005), which compares a Craff–McDonald F-statistic with Stock and Yogo's critical values associated with different reductions of bias using 2SLS relative to OLS. This comparison indicates that we might have a weak-instrument problem, so, again following Murray (2006), we reestimate our models using the modified limited-information maximum likelihood (LIML) method developed by Fuller (1977).[38] As shown in Table 7, the results are similar to 2SLS, which indicates that weak instruments are not an important source of bias in our case.

Focusing on the LIML results, we find that API is highly significant; its positive sign indicates that higher student performance requires higher spending. Despite the restrictions associated with *Serrano* and Proposition 13, money does matter in California. Using the formula in (10), we find that $\sigma = 2.81$; a 1 percent increase in API requires a 2.81 percent increase in spending per pupil, all else equal. This significant estimate indicates decreasing returns to quality scale for the API.[39]

---

[36]The treatment of endogeneity is not the only difference between our study and Imazeki's, but it seems to make the most difference. Indeed, our OLS estimates for the API, teacher salary, and poverty variables are similar to those estimated by Imazeki. The controls for efficiency also appear to make a substantial difference. One difference not discussed earlier is that Imazeki weights her observations by pupil size. As she points out, this weighting has little impact on the results. The main statistical issue this type of weighting is thought to address, heteroskedasticity, is also addressed with robust standard errors, which are used for all our estimates.

[37]The Hansen J-statistic for the 2SLS model is 2.528 with a *P*-value of 0.2825. This statistic tests for the exogeneity of all instruments assuming that at least one instrument is exogenous. In our case, our instrument for teacher salaries (private wages) appears to be exogenous.

[38]The Craff–Donald F-statistic for the 2SLS model is 9.0; the critical value for the Stock and Yogo (2005) weak-instrument test for a 5 percent relative bias is 11.0. Based on Murray's (2006) recommendation, we implemented the Fuller LIML procedure with parameter values of 1 and 3. We present the former results because the point estimates are "approximately unbiased" (Murray, 2006). Our results with a parameter value of 3 are similar and are available upon request.

[39]We used Wald tests for the statistical significance of the structural parameters. All the structural parameters based on significant regression coefficients in either the expenditure or demand model are also significant themselves.

The second panel of this table presents results for the cost variables, all of which have the expected signs and are statistically significant. Again using formulas in (10), we find that a 1.0 percent increase in the salary required to attract teachers of a given quality leads to a 0.95 percent increase in the spending required to maintain the same API. Per pupil costs are 56.3 percent higher for a student from a poor family than for a student from a non-poor family and 54.5 percent higher for a student with limited English proficiency than for a student proficient in English. In addition, overall costs per pupil rise by 2.1 percent for each 1 percentage point increase in the share of students with a severe handicap. In New York, the extra cost associated with a student from a poor family is higher, 110 percent, (Duncombe and Yinger, 2005), using different indices of student performance and different spending and poverty measures.

The coefficients for the enrollment variables indicate a significant U-shaped relationship between cost per pupil and student enrollment. This type of relationship has been found in many previous studies (Andrews *et al.*, 2002). The minimum cost enrollment implied by these estimates is for a school district with 58,099 which is larger than the comparable estimate for other states. The estimated scale effects are not large, however; in fact, predicted per-pupil spending at the minimum-cost enrollment size is less than 5.5 percent lower than per-pupil spending at an enrollment of 5,000 students or at 700,000 students, which is approximately the size of the state's largest district, Los Angeles. We also find that educational costs decrease with a short-run (3-year) enrollment increase and increase with a short-run enrollment decline. These results support the view that school districts do not instantly adjust their student-teacher ratios in response to short-run enrollment changes, but instead accept the savings in per-pupil costs that arise when their student-teacher ratio temporarily goes up and pay the increase in these costs when this ratio temporarily declines.

School districts in California are high-school, elementary-school, or unified districts. The final two rows in the first panel show that elementary districts have a lower cost per pupil and high school districts a higher cost per pupil than do unified districts, the omitted category. These findings probably reflect the added costs, such as science laboratories, that come with the increased specialization in high schools. Recall, however, that the API weights test scores from elementary, middle, and high- school grades. These estimated cost effects are valid for the API as it is defined, but they might be different for a different weighting scheme.

The third and fourth panels of Table 7 present the results for the efficiency variables. We find that the higher a district's revenue limit, the greater its inefficiency, which suggests that unrestricted resources induce voters to push for types of spending that do not boost API. Federal aid also increases inefficiency, but this effect is only about two-thirds as large. The income variable is not significant, however, so a meaningful flypaper effect cannot be calculated.

We also find that school district efficiency decreases with the number of parcels and the share of recent migrants. Voters appear less likely to monitor if they face a low tax price or if they are recent migrants into a county. The former result, which is small in magnitude, also could reflect added demand for services other than API when the tax price is low.

Categorical aid appears in two of the efficiency variables, categorical aid as a share of total state aid and the categorical aid component of Y^*. The first of these variables is designed to capture the incentives facing school officials and the second is designed to capture the incentives facing voters. The (significant) positive coefficient for the first variable suggests that the restrictions in categorical aid programs pull school officials away from best practices and therefore undermine efficiency. The (significant) negative coefficient for the second variable suggests that categorical aid might encourage monitoring, perhaps through an income effect, and discourage demand for broad set of outcomes, perhaps because of its restrictions. Another possibility is that voters treat categorical aid as if it lowers their income, because underfunded categorical aid programs require contributions from other revenue sources.

We are not confident, however, that the specification of these two variables is precise enough to separate the incentives of school officials and voters. As a result, we focus on the net impact of these two variables on efficiency. We find that at the average values of these two categorical aid variables, a 10 percent increase in categorical aid, holding revenue-limit aid and other factors constant, results in a 1.33 percent decrease in district efficiency. A doubling of categorical aid would decrease district efficiency by 10.88 percent. Although we cannot clearly separate the incentives of voters and school officials, therefore, we can still conclude that a shift away from unrestricted aid toward categorical aid, at least using the programs in 2004–2006, would cause school-district efficiency to decline, probably because the restrictions in these categorical aid programs result in activities that deviate from best practices. In interpreting this result, it is important to re-state that efficiency in this regression is defined in relation to the API. The lesson of this result is that lawmakers can obtain a larger boost in the API for their aid dollars, if they provide those dollars in the form of unrestricted aid instead of categorical aid.[40]

4.7. *Demand Equation: Methods and Results*

Our demand equation is estimated with 2SLS, treating $\bar{F}$ as endogenous. We use the same instruments that appeared in our preliminary expenditure equation, which come from the literature on contributions. As with the expenditure equation, we also explore interactions between the parcel tax component of the tax-price term and voter experience with parcel tax votes and we test whether voters are aware of the impact of the parcel tax on the value of state aid. The interaction between the parcel-tax component of tax price and voter experience with a parcel tax always has a coefficient that is insignificant and close to zero, regardless of which measure of experience was used. As a result, this interaction is not included in the final regressions. Most of the parcel-tax terms for the aid variables are also insignificant, but the parcel-tax term for revenue-limit aid is close to significant in some preliminary regressions. Thus, we retain this term, which is the analog to the second term in (11), for revenue-limit aid.

Table 8 presents the demand results using OLS, 2SLS, and LIML. In this case, the choice of method has little impact on any coefficient except the one for the contributions variable, which is larger but insignificant with a

---

[40] An alternative interpretation is that this result captures the impact of cost factors that are correlated with categorical aid but omitted from our regression, such as the presence of students with special needs, who do receive some categorical grants. In fact, however, we exclude spending on special education from our dependant variable and control for the share of students with severe disabilities, so the impact of the categorical aid share on spending does not reflect a link between categorical aid and the relatively high costs of students with special needs. Moreover, we obtain a similar result for the categorical aid variable when special education spending is included in the dependent variable. This probably reflects two features of the California system. First, as of 1998–1999, when AB62 was passed, California's categorical aid programs for special education are based on a formula in which reimbursement is "not linked to pupils served or services provided," but is instead based on an average share of students in various categories as reported by the US Census (Goldfinger, 2006, p. 103). This change was implemented to ensure that "there are not benefits driving placements" (p. 127). Second, the correlation between our categorical aid variable and various categories of students with special needs, from both the California and Census data, ranges between −0.20 and 0.20, with most correlations close to zero. Moreover, the correlation between our percent categorical variable and the per pupil special education aid variable from the Census is only 0.24.

Table 8 Demand equation estimates California school districts (2003–2004 and 2004–2005).

Variables	OLS		2SLS		Fuller LIML ($\alpha = 1$)	
	Coefficient	t-statistic	Coefficient	t-statistic	Coefficient	t-statistic
Intercept	3.4821**	8.96	3.4978**	8.51	3.4964**	10.37
Augmented Income Variables						
33rd percentile of income distribution[a]	0.1454**	10.72	0.1441**	9.44	0.1442**	11.29
Revenue limit component of adjusted income	0.2860**	2.96	0.2771**	2.63	0.2775**	3.33
Revenue limit component of adjusted income with tax share	0.0984	1.18	0.0986	1.17	0.0986	1.54
Categorical aid component of adjusted Income	-0.0501	-0.99	-0.0558	-1.09	-0.0556	-1.16
Federal aid component of adjusted income	0.0755	0.77	0.0554	0.43	0.0562	0.56
Contributions component of adjusted income	0.6396**	2.98	1.3818	0.67	1.3576	0.87
Tax Price Variables						
Tax share (=inverse of parcels per pupil)[a]	-0.0143**	-2.09	-0.0135*	-1.81	-0.0136**	-2.27
Tax share in majority renter districts	0.0031	1.20	0.0034	1.24	0.0034	1.62
Cost index[a]	-0.1578**	-7.60	-0.1575**	-7.44	-0.1575**	-7.88
Efficiency index[a]	0.0861	1.23	0.0856	1.16	0.0858	1.38

Preference Variables						
Percent of population 5 to 17 years old	-0.0031**	-4.30	-0.0029**	-2.93	-0.0029**	-3.70
Percent of population above age 65	0.0017**	3.16	0.0017**	3.03	0.0017**	3.86
Percent of population that is African American	-0.2064**	-4.19	-0.2045**	-4.10	-0.2045**	-5.62
Elementary district (1 = yes)	0.0158**	3.39	0.0155**	2.82	0.0155**	3.68
High school district (1 = yes)	-0.0364**	-4.56	-0.0352**	-4.12	-0.0352**	-5.22
Copy-Cat Variables (for Comparison Districts)						
Share of free lunch students	-0.0005*	-1.72	-0.0004	-1.36	-0.0004*	-1.70
Percent of population that is African American	-0.0024**	-2.89	-0.0023**	-2.60	-0.0023**	-3.47
Median house value[a]	-0.0227**	-2.66	-0.0229**	-2.74	-0.0229**	-3.30
Other Variables						
Year = 2004 (1 = yes)	-0.0016	-0.12	-0.0017	-0.13	-0.0017	-0.15

Notes: The dependent variable is the log of API; the contributions and efficiency variables are treated as endogenous in the second and third models; sample size is 1,821; robust standard errors are reported (controlling for clustering at district level in the 2SLS model); a * (**) indicates significance at the two-tailed 10 (5) percent level.
[a]Expressed as natural logarithm.

correction for its endogeneity.[41] The 2LSL (and LIML) results in Table 8 pass the J-test for the exogeneity of the instruments, but the weak instrument tests suggest that the coefficients may be biased.[42] Thus, we focus on the LIML results. Overall, we find that despite all the restrictions imposed by *Serrano* and Proposition 13, education demand responds to many of the same incentives in California as in other states.

4.8. *Income Variables*

The first panel of this table presents results for income variables. Like previous studies, we find that household income has a significant impact on demand, with a highly significant income elasticity of 0.15 (based on the formula after (12)). The next four rows refer to the other components of adjusted income. We find that the demand for API increases significantly with only one major revenue source, namely, revenue limit aid. The specification in Table 8 includes the two terms analogous to those in (11). The second term falls just short of significance at the 10 percent level. Thus, we can reject the hypothesis that voter's response to aid depends on their tax price. With no parcel-tax weighting, the estimates in Table 8 imply that a $1 increase in aid has the same impact on demand as a $1.31 of voter income. An alternative model in which the second revenue-limit term is dropped (not presented) yields a similar flypaper effect, namely $1.38. The estimated impacts of state categorical aid and federal aid are insignificant and close to zero. The estimated impact of contributions is much larger, with a flypaper effect of 9.41, but this estimate is not significant.

4.9. *Price Variables*

The second panel of Table 8 presents results for price variables. Again focusing on the LIML results, the tax share associated with the parcel tax is significant, but it has a low price elasticity of −0.014 (based on the

---

[41]The Hansen J-statistic for the 2SLS model is 0.132 with a *P*-value of 0.726. We examined several instruments for contributions. Instrument sets that included features of the income distribution in a district (the share of households above a high income threshold or the ratio of the 75th to the 25th percentile of the income distribution) resulted in a significant coefficient for the contributions variable in the demand regression — but failed the exogeneity test.

[42]The Craff–Donald F-statistic in the 2SLS model is 12.275; the critical value for the Stock and Yogo (2005) weak-instrument test for a 10 percent relative bias is 19.93. As with the expenditure regression, the LIML results are virtually identical with a parameter of 1 (in Table 8) or 3 (available on request).

formula after (12)). Perhaps because of the two-thirds voting requirement, therefore, this parcel-tax-based tax share has a smaller impact on demand than does the property-tax-based tax share in other states (Fisher and Papke, 2000; Duncombe and Yinger, 2001). The second row in this panel tests the hypothesis that the response to this tax price is different for renters and owners. We find that the price elasticity is slightly smaller in majority-renter communities, but this result is not statistically significant.

The other two components of tax price, *MC* and *(1/e)*, have the expected impact on demand, but only the former is statistically significant. The estimated price elasticities for these two components (using the formula after (12)) are −0.22 and −0.10.[43] The result for *MC* indicates that voters are aware of and respond to the high costs of attracting teachers to some districts and of educating disadvantaged students. This result is similar to comparable elasticity estimated for New York (Duncombe and Yinger, 2001).

4.10. *Other Variables*

The next two panels of Table 8 contain results for the preference and copy-cat variables. We find that the demand for API decreases with the share of a district's population that consists of school-aged children and increases with the share that is elderly. The first result indicates that the average adult demands a lower quality of education when the quantity of students he or she must fund goes up. The second result indicates that the elderly have relatively high demand for education when they are protected (as are other taxpayers) from property tax increases. Demand is also significantly lower in districts with a higher concentration of African Americans. This result is consistent with the view that white voters' support for public schools declines as the concentration of African–American students increases.[44]

---

[43] Assuming that all cost factors have been observed, the error term in the expenditure equation can be treated as part of the efficiency index. This approach lead to results that are similar to the ones in Table 9 except that the efficiency variable is much more significant. We have not used this approach here because the error terms in the efficiency and demand equations are highly correlated ($p = -0.66$), so that this alternative efficiency variable is endogenous. No instruments are available to account for this endogeneity because any observable determinant of efficiency is already included in the efficiency equation.

[44] It also might reflect cost factors; because of the legacy of discrimination, school districts with a high share of African Americans might have higher educational costs based on unobserved factors, such as a high share of single-parent families. Some cost studies find that educational costs increase with the share of families that have a single parent, even after controlling for the poverty rate. See Duncombe and Yinger (2001) and Baker and Green (2010).

Table 9   Features of the California education finance system, 2005.

District type	Number of districts	API	Cost index	Efficiency index	Spending per pupil	Revenue-limit aid	State categorical aid
Large central cities	42	683	130	51	$6,978	$4,687	$2,204
Medium cities	108	725	106	53	$6,416	$4,840	$1,339
Urban fringe of large cities	227	735	101	54	$6,195	$4,808	$1,225
Urban fringe of medium cities	147	709	106	50	$6,428	$4,915	$1,206
Small town	48	725	99	48	$6,635	$4,980	$1,100
Rural metro	118	737	94	45	$7,280	$5,083	$1,325
Rural non-metro	230	721	102	49	$6,548	$4,798	$1,197
State average	920	716	110	53	$6,501	$4,796	$1,509

Notes: In this table, spending is total operating spending less transportation and special education. Each entry is an enrollment-weighted average for the districts in the row. Sources of revenue not reported here include federal aid and miscellaneous local revenue, which is described in Table 6. All figures are for 2005.

We also find that the demand for API is significantly lower in high-school districts and significantly higher in elementary-school districts than in unified districts. Voters' response to the relatively high cost of high schools is already captured by our cost index, so this variable indicates that the demand for high-school student performance is lower (and the demand for elementary-school performance is higher) than average demand, even after cost effects are considered. Recall that the API is a weighted average of student test scores in high school and other grades. These results suggest, therefore, that the voters place a lower weight on high-school performance and a higher weight on elementary-school performance than the weights that go into the API, but they also might reflect unobserved demand differences across district types.

Finally, two of the copy-cat variables are significant, namely the median house value and the percent African–American in comparison districts. These results are consistent with the view that voters' demand for API is affected by the demand conditions in comparison districts.

5. Conclusions and Implications

These results shed light on the two questions posed at the beginning. First, despite the extensive centralization in the California education finance system, the factors influencing voters' demand for education have a significant impact on student-performance outcomes in California, as they do in other states. We find that California's voters respond to the price incentives in their education finance system, even though these incentives work through a hard-to-pass parcel tax instead of a property tax. To be specific, the parcel-tax component of tax price has a small but significant impact on voter demand for API and on school district efficiency. The latter result could reflect the impact of tax price on voters' monitoring or on their demand for other education outputs. We also find that the demand for student performance increases with district income; the income elasticity is small (0.15) but significant. Higher-income districts find ways to obtain better student performance.

Second, our results imply that California's education finance system undermines the state's educational objectives in two ways. The first is that it maintains inequities that interfere with the state's 800 API target for all districts. We find that education costs vary widely across school districts in California, because of differences in both the salaries needed to attract high-quality teachers and the share of disadvantaged students. Nevertheless, California's unrestricted aid to school districts is not adjusted for educational costs and its categorical aid programs do not account for these costs in any systematic way.[45] As a result, districts with high concentrations of poor students or of English learners and districts in high-wage labor markets are expected to meet the same API target as other districts without being given the funds they need to do so. Introducing cost adjustments into the revenue-limit calculations or categorical aid programs would boost the fairness of California's education finance system.

These points are summarized in Table 9. The large central cities have by far the highest educational costs in the state but have lower-than-average revenue-limit aid. Thanks to the compensatory nature of many categorical aid programs, these districts have by far the largest categorical aid per pupil.

---

[45]The parcel tax is another source of inequity. This tax is highly regressive and our results indicate that it contributes to variation in student performance across districts.

This added categorical aid is not nearly sufficient, however, to bring the total aid of large cities up to the state average in real terms. Moreover, the poor performance in large cities (as measured by API) cannot be attributed to inefficient behavior on their part; in fact, the efficiency index for large cities is only slightly below the state average.

The second unintended consequence of the current system is that existing categorical aid programs in California come with so many strings attached that they undermine school district efficiency. The California legislature apparently recognizes this problem and has taken some steps to add flexibility to existing categorical aid programs. A law passed in 2009, for example, cuts total categorical aid for school by about 6 percent but also transforms the money allocated for 39 different categorical aid programs,[46] which together account for about one-third of total categorical aid, into unrestricted aid. Our analysis suggests that this added flexibility offsets to some degree the negative impact of these aid cuts on student performance.

Overall, California's education finance system is not well designed to support the state's goals. The distribution of funding does not adequately recognize the across-district variation in educational costs, and policy makers are not aware of the sometimes-perverse incentives this system creates. Policies to address these problems could be informed by analyses of education costs, efficiency, and demand, such as the ones in this paper.

Acknowledgments

This paper is a revised version of Duncombe and Yinger (2006), a report prepared for the Getting Down to Facts project, which was directed by Susanna Loeb of Stanford University and funded by The Bill and Melinda Gates Foundation, the William and Flora Hewlett Foundation, The James Irvine Foundation, and The Stuart Foundation. The views expressed in this paper should not be attributed to anyone except the authors. We are grateful to Julie Anna Golebiewski for excellent research assistance and helpful comments; to Eric Brunner, Jay Chambers, and Jennifer Imazeki for providing us with California data and advice on how to use it; to Susanna Loeb, Phuong Nguyen-Hoang, and two anonymous referees for helpful comments; and to the participants in the Getting Down to Facts project meetings in June and November 2006 for their comments on our work

---

[46]These programs are listed by the California Department of Education at http://www. cde.ca.gov/fg/ac/co/sbx34budgetflexb.asp.

and their helpful presentations on many aspects of the California education finance system.

References

Andrews, M., Duncombe, W., and Yinger, J. 2002. Revisiting economies of size in American education: are we any closer to a consensus? *Economics of Education Review* **21**(3): 245–262.

Baker, B. and Duncombe, W. 2004. Balancing district needs and student needs: the role of economies of scale adjustments and pupil need weights in school finance formulas. *Journal of Education Finance* **29**(3): 195–221.

Baker, B. D. and Green, P. C. 2011. Equal educational opportunity and the distribution to state aid to schools: can or should racial composition be a factor? *Journal of Education Finance* **34**(3): 289–323.

Besley, T. and Case, A. 1995. Incumbent behavior: vote-seeking, tax-setting, and yardstick competition. *The American Economic Review* **85**(1): 25–45.

Boozer, M. and Rouse, C. 2001. Intraschool variation in class size: patterns and implications. *Journal of Urban Economics* **50**(1): 163–189.

Brunner, E. J. 2001. The parcel tax. In J. Sonstelie, P. Richardson (eds.), *School Finance and California's Master Plan for Education*, pp. 89–212. San Francisco: Public Policy Institute of California.

Brunner, E. J. and Sonstelie, J. 2003. School finance reform and voluntary fiscal federalism. *Journal of Public Economics* **87**(9–10): 2157–2185.

Brunner, E. J. and Sonstelie, J. 2005. *California's School Finance Reform: An Experiment in Fiscal Federalism.* Unpublished Manuscript, University of California, Santa Barbara, September.

California Department of Education. (CDE) 2006. *Overview of the Academic Performance Index Base Reports for 2005.* Available at: http://www.cde.ca.gov/ta/ac/ap/index.asp.

California School Boards Association. 2006. *2006–07 K12 Budget Advisory.* August. Available at: http://www.csba.org/co/BudgetAdvisory_FINAL.pdf.

Case, A. C., Hines, J. R., Jr., and Rosen, H. S. 1993. Budget spillovers and fiscal policy interdependence: evidence from the states. *Journal of Public Economics* **53**(3): 285–307.

Downes, T. A. and Pogue, T. F. 1994. Adjusting school aid formulas for the higher cost of educating disadvantaged students. *National Tax Journal* **67**: 89–110.

Duncombe, W. and Johnston, J. 2004. The impacts of school finance reform in Kansas: equity is in the eye of the beholder. In J. Yinger (ed.), *Helping Children Left Behind: State Aid and the Pursuit of Educational Equity*, pp. 147–193. Cambridge: MIT Press.

Duncombe, W. and Yinger, J. 1998. School finance reform: aid formulas and equity objectives. *National Tax Journal* **51**: 239–262. [Chapter 12]

Duncombe, W. and Yinger, J. 2001. Alternative paths to property tax relief. In W. E. Oates (ed.), *Property Taxation and Local Government Finance*, pp. 243–294, Cambridge: Lincoln Institute of Land Policy.

Duncombe, W. and Yinger, J. 2005. How much more does a disadvantaged student cost? *Economics of Education Review* **24**: 513–532. [Chapter 7]

Duncombe, W. and Yinger, J. 2006. *Understanding the Incentives in California's Education Finance System.* Report submitted to the Getting Down to Facts Project, directed by Susanna Loeb, Stanford University. Syracuse University, December.

Duncombe, W. and Yinger, J. 2007. Measurement of cost differentials. In E. Fiske, H. F. Ladd (eds.), *Handbook of Education Finance and Policy*, pp. 238–256, Hillschule: Erlbaum.

Duncombe, W., Lukemeyer, A., and Yinger, J. 2003. Financing an adequate education: the case of New York. In W. J. Fowler (ed.), *Developments in School Finance: 2001–02*, pp. 127–154. Washington: National Center for Education Statistics. [Chapter 9]

Education Trust. 2005. *The Funding Gap 2005*. Available at: http://www2.edtrust. org/NR/rdonlyres/31D276EF-72E1-458A-8C71-E3D262A4C91E/0/FundingGap2005 .pdf.

Finn, J. D., Gerber, S., and Boyd-Zaharias, J. 2005. Small classes in the early grades, academic achievement, and graduating from high school. *Journal of Educational Psychology* **97**(2), 214–223.

Fisher, R. C. and Papke, L. E. 2000. Local government responses to education grants. *National Tax Journal* **53**: 153–168.

Fuller, W. A. 1977. Some properties of a modification of the limited information maximum likelihood estimator. *Econometrica* **45**(4): 939–954.

Goldfinger, P. M. 2006. *Revenues and Revenue Limits: A Guide to School Finance in California*, 2006 Edition, Sacramento: School Services of California, Inc.

Guthrie, J. W., and Rothstein, R. 1999. Enabling 'adequacy' to achieve reality: translating adequacy into state school finance distribution arrangements. In H. F. Ladd, R. Chalk, and J. Hansen (eds.), *Equity and Adequacy in Education Finance: Issues and Perspectives*, pp. 209–259. Washington: National Academy Press.

Gronberg, T., Jansen, D. W., Taylor, L. L., and Booker, K. 2004. *School Outcomes and School Costs: The Cost Function Approach*. Available at: http://www.schoolfunding. info/states/tx/march4%20cost%20study.pdf.

Hines, J. R., Jr. and Thaler, R. H. 1995. The flypaper effect. *Journal of Economic Perspectives* **9**: 217–226.

Huang, Y. 2004. Appendix A: a guide to state operating aid programs for elementary and secondary education. In J. Yinger (ed.), *Helping Children Left Behind: State Aid and the Pursuit of Educational Adequacy*, pp. 331–352. Cambridge: MIT Press. [Chapter 14]

Imazeki, J. 2008. Assessing the costs of adequacy in California public schools: a cost function approach. *Education Finance and Policy* **3**(1): 90–108.

Imazeki, J. and Reschovsky, A. 2004a. School finance reform in Texas: a never ending story? In J. Yinger (ed.), *Helping Children Left Behind: State Aid and the Pursuit of Educational Equity*, pp. 251–281. Cambridge: MIT Press.

Imazeki, J. and Reschovsky, A. 2004b. *Estimating the Costs of Meeting the Texas Educational Accountability Standards*. Available at: http://www.investintexasschools. org/schoolfinancelibrary/studies/files/2005/january/reschovsky_coststudy.doc.

Krueger, A. B. 1999. Experimental estimates of education production functions. *Quarterly Journal of Economics* **114**(2): 497–532.

Krueger, A. B. and Whitmore, D. 2001. The effect of attending a small class in the early grades on college-test taking and middle school test results: evidence from project STAR. *Economic Journal* **111**(468): 1–28.

Murray, M. P. 2006. Avoiding invalid instruments and coping with weak instruments. *Journal of Economic Perspectives* **20**(4): 111–132.

Oates, W. E. 1972. *Fiscal Federalism*. New York: Harcourt Brace Jovanovich.

Reschovsky, A. and Imazeki, J. 2001. Achieving educational adequacy through school finance reform. *Journal of Education Finance* **26**(4): 373–396.

Reschovsky, A. and Imazeki, J. 2003. Let no child be left behind: determining the cost of improving student performance. *Public Finance Review* **31**: 263–290.

Rose, H. 2006. *Teacher Compensation in California.* Paper prepared for the Getting Down to Facts project. Available at: http://irepp.stanford.edu/projects/list-researchers/Rose_teacher%20salaries_050106a.pdf#search=%22Teacher%20Compensation%20in%20California%20Rose%22.

Rose, H., Sonstelie, J., Reinhard, R., and Shermaine, H. 2003. *High Expectations, Modest Means: The Challenge Facing California's Public Schools.* San Francisco: Public Policy Institute of California. Available at: http://www.ppic.org/content/pubs/report/R_1003HRR.pdf.

Sonstelie, J., Brunner, E., and Ardon, K. 2000. *For Better or for Worse? School Finance Reform in California.* San Francisco: Public Policy Institute of California. Available at: http://www.ppic.org/content/pubs/report/R_200JSR.pdf.

Stock, J. H. and Yogo, M. 2005. Testing for weak instruments in IV regression. In D. W. K. Andrews, and J. H. Stock (eds.), *Identification and Inference for Econometric Models: A Festschrift in Honor of Thomas Rothenberg,* pp. 80–108. Cambridge: Cambridge University Press.

Timar, T. 2006. *Financing K-12 Education in California: A System Overview.* Unpublished Manuscript, University of California, Davis, March.

U.S. Bureau of the Census. 2009. *Public Education Finances, 2007.* Available at: http://www.census.gov/govs/school/.

Wooldridge, J. M. 2003. *Introductory Econometrics: A Modern Approach,* 2nd edition, Mason: South-Western/Thomson Learning,

Yinger, J. 2004. State aid and the pursuit of educational equity: An overview. In J. Yinger (ed.), *Helping Children Left Behind: State Aid and the Pursuit of Educational Adequacy,* pp. 3–58. Cambridge: MIT Press. [Chapter 11]

Part 5

State Aid to Education

Chapter 11

State Aid and the Pursuit of Educational Equity: An Overview[*],[†]

John Yinger

Departments of Public Administration and International Affairs and of Economics, Syracuse University, Syracuse, NY, United States

jyinger@maxwell.syr.edu

1. Introduction

In 1971, the California Supreme Court ushered in a new era in education finance by ruling, in *Serrano v. Priest*, that California's system for financing

---

[*]This chapter is reproduced from "State Aid and the Pursuit of Educational Equity: An Overview," in J. Yinger (ed.), *Helping Children Left Behind: State Aid and the Pursuit of Educational Equity*, pp. 3–57. Cambridge, MA: MIT Press, 2004.

[†]This chapter has benefited greatly from the presentations and comments made by the participants in the Conference on State Aid to Education, which was held at the Maxwell School, Syracuse University, in April 2002. Indeed, many of the ideas expressed in this chapter are based on something I learned at this conference, and I am very grateful to the people who participated, including the authors of the other chapters in this volume. I would particularly like to single out the discussants at this conference, Katharine Bradbury, Timothy Gronberg, Robert Inman, Therese McCarty, Robert Schwab, David Sjoquist, Leanna Stiefel, and Robert Strauss, who did a wonderful job of highlighting important issues in the papers presented at the conference and identifying themes that appeared in several of the state reform plans. Moreover, the discussants ran a very informative wrap-up session designed to bring out the key themes of the conference. Other participants, many of whom also made helpful remarks during the conference discussion, are listed in the preface. In addition, I received helpful comments on earlier drafts of this chapter from Julie Cullen, Tom Dee, Bill Duncombe, Peg Goertz, Anna Lukemeyer, Therese McCarty, Jerry Miner, Dick Murnane, and Allan Odden. Although my debt to all of these people is large, none of them should be held responsible for anything I say.

elementary and secondary education violated the state's constitution.[1] Relying heavily on a property tax to finance education was unconstitutional, the court declared, because it made a child's education dependent on the wealth of his or her school district.

Since then, forty-three additional state courts have heard challenges to the constitutionality of the education finance system in their state. Although the legal standards vary from state to state and have shifted over time, seventeen more education finance systems have been declared unconstitutional by state supreme courts since *Serrano v. Priest*.[2] The most recent such decision was in New York in June 2003. In most cases, these court decisions have been followed by significant education finance reforms.

The impact of state courts goes far beyond these eighteen state supreme court decisions. Reforms passed in response to one of these decisions have been upheld by the supreme court in Texas, and further education reform litigation is ongoing in Arizona, California, Connecticut, Kentucky, Massachusetts, Montana, New Hampshire, New Jersey, and West Virginia. State supreme courts also have reversed lower-court decisions rejecting education reform in Idaho, Kansas, North Carolina, and South Carolina, and litigation continues in all of these states.[3] Moreover, the Missouri Supreme Court upheld a reform that was passed in response to a trial court decision,[4]

---

[1] Strictly speaking, the California Supreme Court was responding to a trial court's ruling that even if the facts alleged by the plaintiffs in *Serrano* were true, they did not establish that California's school financing system was unconstitutional. The 1971 *Serrano* decision, referred to as *Serrano I*, overturned this ruling and sent the case back to the trial court for further discussion of the facts. The facts were compelling, however, so the legislature interpreted this ruling as a rejection of the existing system and passed Senate Bill 90, which set up a new system, in 1972. This new system was definitively rejected by the California Supreme Court in 1977 in a decision referred to as *Serrano II* (see Sonstelie, Brunner, and Ardon, 2000). The 1971 decision was based on both the U.S. Constitution and the California constitution. A 1973 U.S. Supreme Court decision in *San Antonio Independent School District v. Rodriguez* effectively overturned that portion of *Serrano I* that was based on the U.S. Constitution but left standing the conclusions based on the state constitution (see Lukemeyer, 2003). Because of this U.S. Supreme Court decision, educational-finance equity is now debated exclusively in state courts.
[2] All significant state court decisions on education finance, including these supreme court decisions and the decisions discussed in the following paragraphs, are summarized in Huang, Lukemeyer and Yinger (2003, with full legal citations).
[3] The North Carolina case is back before the state supreme court.
[4] Before the most recent litigation in Kansas, the state supreme court there also upheld an education finance reform stimulated by a lower-court decision. See Duncombe and Johnston (2003) and Huang *et al.* (2003, Table A.2.)

and trial courts in Alaska and New Mexico have rejected their states' systems for funding school facilities.

State supreme courts have upheld the existing education finance systems in eighteen states, but these decisions have not prevented education finance reform or further litigation in many cases. Among the states in this category, for example, additional lower-court litigation spurred major education finance reforms in Colorado (National Center for Education Statistics, 2001b) and Maryland (Montgomery, 2002), and Michigan (Cullen and Loeb, 2003) passed a major education finance reform without any further court involvement. Moreover, voters in two states, Florida and Oregon, responded to state supreme court decisions upholding the education finance systems in those states by passing an amendment to the education clauses of their state constitutions. The Florida amendment calls for "a uniform, efficient, safe, secure, and high quality system of free public schools," which is one of the strongest equity standards in the nation (Advocacy Center for Children's Education Success with Standards (ACCESS), 2003). Finally, new education finance litigation is pending in Colorado and Florida.

All this litigation and reform reflects, of course, the dramatic disparities in school spending and student performance that divide school districts in most states. In the average state in 2000, for example, low-poverty school districts spent almost $1,000 more per pupil than did high-poverty districts (The Education Trust, 2002). Some evidence on performance gaps is provided in Casserly 2002, which compares 2001 reading and math test scores in large cities, where poverty is concentrated, and the states in which they are located. The gaps in eighth-grade reading and math scores are presented in Tables 1 and 2, respectively.[5] These tables indicate the extent to which large cities lag behind the remainder of their states in bringing eighth-grade students up to a target score on the state's standardized tests. Student performance falls short of the state average in virtually every big city in the United States, and the test score gaps are often very large. In the case of reading, the share of students reaching the target score is almost 70 percent below the state average in St. Louis and more than 40 percent below the state average in eleven other cities. The disparities in math scores are even larger.

---

[5]The figures presented in Tables 1 and 2 include all the big-city school districts in Casserly (2002) that have data on the share of students that passed the reading and math tests required by the state in which they are located. These figures understate the difference in test scores between big cities and the rest of their states because the big cities' results are included in the state averages.

Table 1　Eighth-grade reading test score gaps between big cities and states, 2001.

>60%	St. Louis, Baltimore, Philadelphia
50–59%	New Orleans
40–49%	Milwaukee, Buffalo, Detroit, Providence, Rochester, Denver, Oakland, Newark
30–39%	Boston, Los Angeles, Indianapolis, Minneapolis, Richmond, Fresno, St. Paul, Miami
20–29%	Pittsburgh, Chicago, New York City, Oklahoma City, Dayton, Norfolk
10–19%	Cleveland, Long Beach, Columbus, Atlanta, Dallas, Toledo, Sacramento
0–9%	Austin, Fort Worth, Nashville, Charlotte, San Francisco, Houston, Portland, Greensboro, Seattle
−4–0%	San Diego

Note: Results for cities in Ohio and Tennessee are for ninth-grade scores, and results for Denver, Detroit, St. Louis, and Seattle are for seventh-grade scores.

Source: Casserly 2002.

Table 2　Eighth-grade math test score gaps between big cities and states, 2001.

>70%	Milwaukee, Rochester, Baltimore
60–69%	Philadelphia, Providence, Denver, New Orleans, Newark, St. Louis
50–59%	Buffalo, Dayton, Cleveland, Chicago
40–49%	Indianapolis, Pittsburgh, Oakland, Detroit, Richmond, Los Angeles, Minneapolis, Boston, New York City
30–39%	St. Paul, Toledo, Columbus, Oklahoma City, Fresno, Atlanta
20–29%	Memphis, Miami, Norfolk
10–19%	Dallas, San Diego, Long Beach, Nashville
0–9%	Austin, Fort Worth, Charlotte, Sacramento, Greensboro, Houston
−17–0%	Portland, Seattle, San Francisco

Note: Results for cities in Ohio and Tennessee are for ninth-grade scores, and results for Denver, Detroit, and Seattle are for seventh-grade scores. The results for Detroit refer to scores on 2000 tests.

Source: Casserly 2002.

Milwaukee falls almost 80 percent below its state average in the number of its students reaching the state's target score in math, and twenty-one other cities are more than 40 percent below the averages in their states.

The new state aid programs that were passed in response to the 1971 *Serrano v. Priest* decision (*Serrano I*) and the related 1977 *Serrano v. Priest* decision (*Serrano II*) dramatically reduced the disparities in spending per pupil across school districts in California. In contrast, these programs do not appear to have significantly reduced across-district disparities in student achievement or raised the performance of students in high-poverty urban districts (see Downes, 1992 and Sonstelie, Brunner, and Ardon, 2000).

The same patterns emerge in other states that have implemented reforms. Evans, Murray, and Schwab (1997, 1999) and Murray, Evans, and Schwab (1998) demonstrate that court-induced reforms in state aid reduce per-pupil spending disparities across school districts in the state. These reforms have not had nearly as large an effect on disparities in student performance, however, as they have had on disparities in spending. Indeed, some scholars argue that they have not affected performance disparities at all, and the available evidence indicates that students in many districts, especially high-poverty urban districts, still perform far below the state average even after major school aid reform. Tables 1 and 2 reveal significant test score gaps facing Los Angeles, Oakland, Dallas, and Fort Worth, for example, despite significant education finance reform efforts in California and Texas. There is no agreement, however, about the meaning of this evidence. Some scholars interpret it as a sign that equalization of education financing across districts is ineffective and should not be tried;[6] others, including myself, interpret it as a sign that many existing equalization efforts are flawed and that new approaches are needed.

The persistence of large across-district disparities in educational performance in many states is one of the factors that have pushed state legislatures and education departments toward a new focus on student performance and toward new programs to promote school district accountability. Forty-eight states now require local schools to administer state-selected tests in reading and mathematics (Goertz and Duffy, 2001).[7] A majority of states also require tests in writing, social studies, and science.

These tests are accompanied by various types of accountability systems. Goertz and Duffy (2001) classify accountability systems into three categories: public reporting, locally defined, and state defined.[8] Thirteen states fall into the first category, in which requirements are imposed on school districts to report on various performance measures determined by the state. The second category, which involves only two states, is similar, except that in states in this category, each district selects its own performance measures. State-defined accountability systems, which are found in thirty-three states, set targets for student performance on achievement tests and then reward

---

[6]Fischel (2001), for example, concludes that "court-ordered centralization of school finance and the supposed fiscal disparities that have driven it are largely wrongheaded" (161).

[7]The remaining two states, Iowa and Nebraska, require tests in these two subject areas but allow each district to decide which tests to administer. See Goertz and Duffy (2001).

[8]See also Meyer *et al.* (2002), which provides up-to-date details about states' accountability systems.

districts that meet their targets and/or sanction districts that fall short.[9] These rewards and sanctions obviously constitute a new element of the education finance system.

The book from which this chapter is drawn (Yinger, 2003) provides an overview of the research on state aid to education and a detailed look at state aid reform in five key states: Kansas, Kentucky, Michigan, Texas, and Vermont. The state aid reform efforts in these states are particularly ambitious, and they illustrate the range of recent reform strategies.

To be more specific, Part 1 of Yinger (2003) addresses the general issues involved in state aid reform. Anna Lukemeyer (2003), provides an introduction to the court cases and legal theories at the center of state aid reform efforts over the last thirty years. David Figlio (2003), examines several central conceptual issues in state aid reform, and Thomas Nechyba (2003), explores the effects of state aid reform on residential patterns and other non-educational outcomes and the feedback from these effects to education. Part 2 includes William Duncombe and Jocelyn Johnston (2003), Ann Flanagan and Sheila Murray (2003), Julie Cullen and Susanna Loeb (2003), Jennifer Imazeki and Andrew Reschovsky (2003), and Thomas Downes (2003) on each of the five states mentioned (Kansas, Kentucky, Michigan, Texas, and Vermont, respectively). Yinger (2003) also includes some general reference material: Huang *et al.* (2003) describes significant education finance decisions by state courts, Huang (2003) describes state operating aid programs, and Wang (2003) describes state building aid programs.

This chapter provides some background information regarding the debate about state aid, introduces the key themes that arise in discussions of state aid reform, and presents a guide to the examination of these themes in later chapters. The rest of the chapter is organized in four sections. Section 2 provides background information on some important analytical issues. Section 3 reviews the main choices that a state must make in designing a package for reforming its education aid system. Section 4 discusses a variety of issues that arise in evaluating the effects of aid reform efforts. Section 5 offers some conclusions from the chapter's discussion.

---

[9]This approach has been picked up at the federal level, too. The No Child Left Behind Act of 2001 includes rewards and sanctions for individual school districts based on changes in student performance in the district. See Robelen (2002).

2. Background

Any discussion of state aid to education must build on several key concepts and on an understanding of state aid formulas. These topics are introduced in this section and discussed throughout Yinger (2003), particularly in Lukemeyer (2003) and Figlio (2003).

2.1. *Selecting a Method for Measuring Education and an Equity Standard*

Most scholars agree that any education finance system needs to be based on a method for measuring the education provided by a school district and the selection of an equity standard (see, for example, Berne and Stiefel, 1984, 1999; Monk, 1990). The three most widely discussed methods for measuring education are *spending* per pupil, *real resources* per pupil, and *student performance* based on test scores and perhaps other measures. Spending per pupil is obviously a simple method to work with, but it is widely regarded as unsatisfactory, because it does not recognize that educational costs vary across districts for reasons outside the control of school officials. The other two methods, however, explicitly account for educational costs.

Measuring education using real resources per pupil is a way to account for the fact that teacher wages (and perhaps other input prices) are not the same in every district. Teacher wages vary across districts for two fundamental reasons that are outside the control of school officials.[10] First, it costs more to attract teachers into education from the private sector in high-wage than in low-wage regions. Second, some districts have to pay more than others to attract teachers of a given quality because they have more disadvantaged students or special-needs students, who pose extra challenges in the classroom (see Chambers, 1998; Duncombe, Ruggiero, and Yinger, 1996; Duncombe and Yinger, 1999; Guthrie and Rothstein, 1999; and Odden, 1999).

Educational-performance measures, such as test scores, can, of course, stand on their own without any reference to educational costs. However, incorporating a performance-based method for measuring education into a

---

[10]Wages also vary across districts because of variation in districts' generosity and in teachers' negotiating skills. It obviously is inappropriate for state aid to reflect wage variation from either of these sources, so state aid formulas should make use of wage cost indexes, not actual teacher wages.

state aid formula requires a translation of spending into performance; in other words, such an incorporation must recognize that it costs more to obtain a given level of performance in some districts than in others. This cost variation arises not only because of teacher wage differences but also because districts with more at-risk students must spend more than other districts to obtain the same student performance (Downes and Pogue, 1994b). School districts with a high concentration of poor students, for example, may need lower student-teacher ratios or additional prekindergarten, health, or counseling programs to overcome the disadvantages their students bring to school.[11]

Spending can be translated into performance in a way that accounts for both of these factors using a comprehensive educational-cost index (see Duncombe, Ruggiero, and Yinger, 1996; Duncombe and Yinger, 1997, 1998; Reschovsky and Imazeki, 1998, 2001). As discussed in the next section, it may also be possible to accomplish this step with an aid formula that gives more weight to at-risk students.

Several standards for establishing the equity of an education finance system have been discussed in court opinions and in the academic literature. The most basic standard is educational *adequacy,* which is said to exist when students in every school district receive an education that meets some minimum standard. The impact of this standard depends, of course, on how high it is set, and as is shown throughout Yinger (2003), some states have set a much higher standard than others.

Another key equity standard is *access equality,* defined as a situation in which an increase in taxpayer effort, as measured by the effective property tax rate, has the same impact on per-pupil revenue in every district. This standard was proposed in Coons, Clune, and Sugarman (1970), and it played an important role in the original *Serrano* decision (see Sonstelie, Brunner, and Ardon, 2000). Access equality is similar to, but distinct from, another standard, known as *wealth neutrality,* which is achieved when district wealth and district education are not correlated. These two standards were initially thought to be the same, but Feldstein (1975) demonstrated that they are not. They differ in that one of them, access equality, refers to school districts' budget constraints, and the other, wealth neutrality, refers to the outcome of

---

[11]Evidence that class size affects performance is provided by Krueger (1999, 2003) and Krueger and Whitmore (2001). Evidence that prekindergarten programs can boost performance in later grades for children who are poor or otherwise at risk is provided by Karoly *et al.* (1998).

decisions made by the school district. Any policy that alters school districts' budget constraints will have an impact on what districts decide to do; the magnitude of this impact is difficult to predict, however, and no particular distribution of education across districts can be guaranteed, no matter how education is measured.

A final standard is *equality*, defined as the same education in every school district. Several state supreme courts have used language that appears to set equality as the required constitutional standard. No court, however, has combined an equality standard with a clear statement about how education should be measured or a clear statement about the steps a state must take to achieve this standard.[12]

2.2. *Aid Formulas and Equity Objectives*

The equity objective of an education finance system is defined by one of these equity standards combined with any of these methods for measuring education. Policymakers in a particular state might decide, for example, that they want an education system that achieves an adequate education as measured by real resources per pupil. After describing the two main types of formulas for awarding state educational aid, I show how these types of formulas can be modified to achieve any combination of these equity standards and education measurements.

2.2.1. *Foundation aid*

The most basic type of education-aid formula is called *foundation aid.* This type of formula sets aid per pupil to district i, A_i, equal to a foundation amount of spending per pupil, E^*, which is the same for all districts, minus the amount of money the district can raise at a state-determined minimum tax rate, say t^*. If V_i is property value per pupil in district i, then this amount is t^*V_i, and the aid formula is

$$A_i = E^* - t^*V_i. \qquad (1)$$

---

[12]In addition, Hawaii has a state-run education system, which at least suggests educational equality, and as noted previously, the recent constitutional amendment in Florida explicitly requires "uniform" schools. It is not clear, however, how Florida courts will interpret this requirement.

This standard foundation formula is suited for education as measured by spending per pupil and for an adequacy objective. Specifically, E^* equals the minimally adequate spending per pupil selected by state policymakers.

As shown by Ladd and Yinger (1994), however, this formula can easily be altered to accommodate the other two methods for measuring education. Let W_i be an index of teacher wage costs and C_i be a comprehensive index of educational costs in district i that reflects both wage costs and the extra costs associated with educating disadvantaged students. Then multiplying E^* by W_i is equivalent to measuring education using real resources per pupil, and multiplying E^* by C_i is equivalent to measuring education using student performance.[13] In principle, an equivalent adjustment for the cost impact of student characteristics can be made by giving aid on the basis of "weighted" pupils, such that more disadvantaged students receive higher weight in the funding formula.[14]

This analysis reveals that educational-cost indexes play a critical role in helping education finance systems catch up with the new focus on student performance in the broader debate about education policy. Unless it adjusts for differences in educational costs from district to district, a state education aid program simply is not compatible with performance objectives. Although scholars do not agree on the best method to account for these cost differences, there is widespread agreement that state aid formulas should include cost adjustments.[15] The need for cost indexes was emphasized, for example, in a

---

[13]Hoxby (2001) contrasts "school finance equalization" (SFE) programs, which are defined as programs that link aid to property values, with "categorical" aid programs, which are defined as programs that link aid to student characteristics or other school district characteristics. For example, she specifically defines foundation aid to be a scheme that "is like flat categorical aid *except* that it redistributes among districts based on per-pupil property values, not on sociodemographic characteristics of households" (1194–1195, emphasis in original). She also argues that "categorical aid has been almost entirely replaced by SFE for major redistribution" (1193). As shown in this chapter and as illustrated by the reforms in Kansas, Kentucky, and Texas, however, student characteristics can easily be incorporated in an SFE program, such as foundation aid.

[14]I say "in principle" because many states use pupil weights that are *ad hoc* and not associated with an attempt to estimate an educational cost index. As shown by Duncombe and Yinger (2005), however, the empirical procedures used to obtain a comprehensive cost index can also be used to determine per-pupil weights that result in approximately the same adjustment for the cost impact of student characteristics as does the cost index.

[15]Scholars do agree on several issues regarding cost indexes, however. For example, there is widespread agreement that a cost index should not give districts an incentive to place students in a "special-needs" category (see Duncombe and Johnston, 2003). Similarly, it is generally agreed that a cost index should not reward a district for paying overly generous wages (see Duncombe and Yinger, 1997, 1998).

recent report by the National Research Council's Committee on Education Finance (Ladd and Hansen, 1999). See also Duncombe and Yinger (1999); Guthrie and Rothstein (1999), and Odden (1999).

To design a foundation aid program, a state not only must decide how to measure education, but it also must (1) select a foundation level, (2) select a minimum tax rate for districts, (3) decide whether districts are required to comply with this minimum tax rate, and (4) decide whether to restrict district supplementation of the foundation amount. Selecting the appropriate foundation level corresponds to deciding what level of education the state will regard as adequate. Because a higher foundation level implies a higher budgetary cost, each state must balance the educational benefits of a higher standard against the costs of achieving it.

The higher the minimum tax rate imposed on districts, the higher the local contribution to the education finance system. Thus, one way for a state to lower the burden of local property taxes is to lower t^* and to fund the resulting increases in aid payments required to reach the foundation spending level through state-level taxes. A decision about t^* is therefore one aspect of the broader issue of financing education aid reform, which is discussed in Section 3.4. So long as the districts are required to impose at least the minimum tax rate, all districts will reach the foundation spending level.[16] If districts are not required to tax at the minimum rate, however, many districts receiving a relatively high amount of aid will cut their tax rates below t^* to free up taxpayers' resources for non-school purposes.

The final decision, involving supplementation, is perhaps the most controversial. If *adequacy* is the equity standard, there is no reason to prevent spending beyond the foundation amount by the least-needy districts. To achieve educational *equality* across its districts, however, a state would have to prevent any district from spending more than the foundation amount.[17] Other standards may call for some restrictions on supplementation.

One way to reduce supplementation can be built right into a foundation plan. (Other ways are discussed in Section 3.3.) To be specific, a state can recapture aid from the wealthiest or lowest-cost districts, that is, from the

---

[16]One qualification to this statement is that relatively inefficient districts might not meet a performance target. See Duncombe and Yinger (1998). I return to the link between aid and efficiency in Section 4.4.

[17]This approach would not literally ensure equality by any of the definitions of education, because district budgets can be supplemented with private contributions, which cannot be prohibited by the state. As discussed in Section 4.5.3, such private supplementation has appeared in many districts in California.

districts that have negative aid according to the above formula. Making aid
payments negative, that is, requiring direct payments from low-need school
districts to the state, is not politically feasible and has never been attempted,
but a state can accomplish the same thing by eliminating the property tax
at the district level and turning it into a state tax. As I show in subsequent
sections, a few states have used modified versions of this approach. When a
state property tax is used to finance a foundation program, more property
tax revenue is collected in low-need school districts than is required to fund
their foundation payments. Consequently, shifting to a state property tax
lowers the disposable income of voters in low-need districts below the point
where it was with a local property tax and therefore lowers their desired
level of school spending.[18]

2.2.2. *Guaranteed tax base aid*

The second main type of aid formula is called a district power–equalizing or
guaranteed tax base (GTB) program. This type of formula is derived from
the principle that per-pupil spending in a district, E_i, should depend only
on the effective property tax rate the district is willing to impose, t_i; that is,
$E_i = t_i V^*$, where V^* is a policy parameter selected by the state. Because aid
per pupil, A_i, equals total spending per pupil minus local property taxes per
pupil, $t_i V_i$, this principle leads to the following formula for a GTP program:

$$A_i = E_i \left(1 - V_i/V^*\right). \tag{2}$$

This formula describes a matching grant in which the state's share of
spending per pupil (A_i/E_i) is much higher for low-wealth districts than for
high-wealth districts. The high rate at which the state matches education
spending in low-wealth districts greatly lowers the price of education in those
districts, thereby inducing them to increase their spending on education
substantially.[19] The price of education falls by a smaller amount in middle-
wealth districts, so they have a more modest incentive to raise their education
spending.

From a state's point of view, the key issue in a GTB formula is the
selection of V^*. If V^* is set equal to property value per pupil in the wealthiest

---

[18]State aid that is funded through state taxes other than the property tax also involves
redistribution across districts and may also influence supplementation. I return to this
issue in Section 3.3.

[19]Many studies have demonstrated that school districts respond to this type of price
incentive. For a recent review see Fisher and Papke (2000).

district, then every district in the state except the wealthiest receives some aid through the program, the price subsidy for the poorest districts is very large, and the cost to the state is very high. Lowering V^* lowers the magnitude of the subsidies and the cost to the state.

A state also can use a GTB formula to limit spending by high-wealth districts if it lowers V^* and reclaims funds from districts with negative aid according to the above formula, that is, from the richest districts. As discussed more fully in Section 3.3, an approach of this type, often referred to as "recapture," is included in the reforms enacted in Texas (Imazeki and Reschovsky, 2003) and Vermont (Downes, 2003). A recapture provision in a GTB formula limits spending by high-wealth districts because it confronts these districts with a negative matching rate and hence a higher price of education. If a district's property value per pupil is 50 percent higher than V^*, for example, then its matching rate is $(1 - 1.5) = -0.5$, and it must pay the state an amount equal to half of its total spending. This is equivalent to a 50 percent increase in the price of education, which may easily result in a 20 or 30 percent decrease in school spending in the district (see Fisher and Papke, 2000).

The standard GTB formula is designed for education measured by spending per pupil. As shown by Ladd and Yinger (1994), however, it can easily be adjusted to accommodate either of the other ways of measuring education simply by replacing the 1 in equation (2) with either W_i (for measurement by real resources) or C_i (for measurement by performance). A similar approach, which is used by Texas (Imazeki and Reschovsky, 2003) is to express the GTB formula in terms of weighted pupils, with weights for pupils that reflect the higher costs of educating disadvantaged students. Despite the contradiction between a GTB formula based on spending per pupil and the current focus in other realms of education policy on education performance, however, adjustments of this type are rare.

In principle, a GTB formula also could be adjusted to achieve wealth neutrality. As shown by Feldstein (1975), this would require that the (V_i/V^*) term in equation (2) be raised to a power that reflects the estimated behavioral response to the matching grant provided by the state under the formula.[20] Because a matching grant is a type of price subsidy, this estimated behavioral response is a type of price elasticity. Alternatively, Duncombe

---

[20]Feldstein also demonstrated, no doubt inadvertently, that such behavioral responses are difficult to estimate; in fact, his estimates differ significantly from others in the literature. See Fisher and Papke (2000) and Duncombe and Yinger (1998).

and Yinger (1998) argue that wealth neutrality could be approximated by defining a formula in which the (V_i/V^*) term is raised to a power, say α, and then adjusting α every year until the correlation between district wealth and district education falls below some acceptable threshold.

The recognition that some districts face higher educational costs than others leads not only to a change in the method for measuring education, but also to a reconsideration of the wealth neutrality standard. A student is just as disadvantaged, after all, by living in a district with relatively high costs as he or she is by living in a district with relatively low wealth. So an alternative, more general equity standard is "fiscal" neutrality, which is said to exist when a district's education is not correlated with the balance between its taxing capacity (i.e., wealth) and spending requirements outside its control (i.e., costs). Duncombe and Yinger (1998) show how the GTB approach can be modified to yield this type of neutrality. To be specific, they measure the balance between wealth and costs in a district using the ratio of its property value index (V_i/V^*) to its cost index $(W_i$ or $C_i)$. Fiscal neutrality can then be approximated by replacing the property value index in equation (2) with this ratio and by introducing an adjustable policy parameter, as in the previous paragraph.

Although wealth neutrality is the equity standard that has been set by several state supreme courts and touted by several policymakers, no state has implemented an aid program designed to achieve it, that is, a program that incorporates the adjustments required to account for districts' behavioral responses to the aid formula. Aid programs of this type are simply too complicated to implement. The inconsistency between access equality and a performance-based method for measuring discrimination has been recognized, at least implicitly, by several state supreme courts. In its 1997 decision, *Brigham v. State,* for example, the Vermont Supreme Court calls for access equality but also says that "differences among school districts in terms of size, special educational needs, transportation costs, and other factors will invariably create unavoidable differences in per-pupil expenditures" (p. 22). Nevertheless, Vermont, unlike Texas, does not use a performance-based method for measuring education in its GTB formula, and no state has even considered a performance-based expression of its GTB program's equity objective.

Duncombe and Yinger (1998) also show that GTB formulas are not very good for achieving educational adequacy; even if wealth neutrality or fiscal neutrality is achieved through the implementation of the formula, some districts will decide to levy tax rates that are well below the rate needed to fund any reasonable adequacy target. Moreover, foundation formulas cannot eliminate the correlation between educational outcomes and wealth (or fiscal health) without an extremely high value for the foundation level and a required minimum tax rate. Different aid formulas clearly satisfy different equity objectives.

2.2.3. *Summary*

The foregoing discussion is summarized in Table 3, which indicates the type of aid formula that is required to achieve each possible combination of the three methods for measuring education and the four equity standards presented in Section 2.1. Many of the aid formulas specified in this table have never been tried. As I show in Section 3, however, examples can be found among the states of all the formulas in the first row, and some of these have been combined with restrictions on supplementation that move them toward an equality standard, as in the table's last row. It is not surprising that most of the other formulas in the table have not been tried because, as explained

Table 3   Aid formulas and equity objectives.

| Equity standard | Definition of education | | |
	Spending per pupil	Real resources per pupil	Student performance
Adequacy	Standard foundation formula (with required minimum tax rate)	Foundation formula with foundation level adjusted for resource costs	Foundation formula with foundation level adjusted for educational costs
Access equality	Standard GTB formula	GTB formula with adjustment for resource costs	GTB formula with adjustment for educational costs
Fiscal neutrality	Standard GTB formula with adjustment for behavioral response	GTB formula with adjustments for resource costs and behavioral response	GTB formula with adjustments for educational costs and behavioral response
Equality	Standard foundation formula with prohibition of supplementation	Foundation formula with adjustment for resource costs and no supplementation	Foundation formula with adjustment for educational costs and no supplementation

earlier, they involve complex adjustments either for educational costs or for behavioral responses by school districts or both.

3. Policy Choices in State Aid Reform

With the background presented in the previous section, we can now turn to a discussion of the themes raised by the chapters in this book. The first set of themes, which is considered in this section, involves the policy choices that states must make in reforming their education finance system. The second set of themes, which is considered in the following section, involves an evaluation of existing efforts to reform education finance in the states.

3.1. *What is the Appropriate Aid Formula?*

Perhaps the most fundamental step in any effort to reform education funding is the selection of a formula for awarding a state's educational aid to localities. This selection is usually guided by the legal requirements in court decisions, but of course it also reflects the interests of state policymakers. As discussed in Lukemeyer (2003), many of the early state court decisions in the area of education finance equity focused on access equality. On the basis of these decisions, several states, including California, adopted GTB formulas (Sonstelie, Brunner, and Ardon, 2000). Lukemeyer also points out that several state courts have not distinguished among access equality, wealth neutrality, and equality, so that the signals they are sending about the right aid formula to select are, to say the least, confusing.

Recent state court decisions have emphasized adequacy as the objective of the education finance system. According to the widely cited 1989 Kentucky Supreme Court decision in *Rose v. Council for Better Education,* for example, all students have the constitutional right to "an equal opportunity to an adequate education." The recent decision by New York's highest court in *Campaign for Fiscal Equity v. New York* (2003) also emphasized adequacy. According to this decision, the state must provide "schoolchildren the opportunity for a meaningful high school education, one which prepares them to function productively as civic participants" (slip op. at 15). It is perhaps not surprising, therefore, that all five of the states discussed in Yinger (2003) have based their education finance reforms on a foundation plan.

With or without a court case to guide a state in its choice of a method for financing education, foundation aid formulas are very popular. In fact, forty-one states employ a foundation formula (Huang, 2003, Table B.3).[21] In many cases, therefore, "reform" of a state's education finance system involves passing a significant increase in the foundation level (E^*), instead of coming up with a new funding formula altogether.

Regardless of whether the foundation formula in a state is old or new, the generosity of a reform program based on it is determined largely by the foundation level. The *Rose* decision in Kentucky implicitly called for a high foundation level by ruling that the state constitution required an education system providing each student with a set of seven capacities, such as "sufficient oral and written communication skills to enable students to function in a complex and rapidly changing civilization." Other states have set less ambitious, and hence less costly, standards (see Huang, 2003).

A second key issue in regard to the use of a foundation formula is whether localities are required to impose the minimum property tax rate specified in the formula. As explained earlier, the foundation level of spending in the formula is unlikely to be reached without such a requirement. Although twenty-eight of the states with foundation formulas require a minimum tax rate to be imposed in the state's localities or, equivalently, that localities provide a minimum local share of education costs, the others do not (Huang, 2003, Table B.4).

Only three states, Indiana, Missouri and Wisconsin, rely exclusively on a GTB formula to finance education in the state. However, four of the states considered in Yinger (2003) (Kansas, Kentucky, Texas, and Vermont) combine their foundation programs with a second tier of aid based on a GTB formula. Such an approach is also used in six other states, and Delaware combines flat grants with a GTB-like formula (Huang, 2003, Table B.3). In states that use this type of approach, the foundation aid is given first, and the GTB applies to taxes above the minimum rate in the foundation formula, generally up to some maximum.[22] Such an approach is designed to ensure that a minimum education level is achieved throughout the state via the foundation formula and then to place districts on an equal footing if they want to supplement the foundation level by raising additional taxes.

---

[21] An alternative, earlier classification effort came to a similar conclusion, namely, that 80 percent of the states at the time of the study used a foundation formula (Gold, Smith, and Lawton, 1995).

[22] In Texas, for example, the GTB matching aid is capped at a specified local tax rate, which turns out to be the maximum allowable rate under the state's property tax limitation measure. See Imazeki and Reschovsky (2003).

In other words, it combines the adequacy standard with the access equality standard for supplementation.

This type of approach has been recommended by several scholars (Gess *et al.*, 1996; Odden and Picus, 1992), but on the basis of the results of some simulations, one of those scholars (Odden, 1999) recently changed his mind. These simulations showed that adding a second-tier GTB formula on top of a foundation formula may actually lower the equity of educational outcomes in a state on a variety of measures, despite the large price subsidy it provides to low-wealth districts.[23] This result reflects a point made earlier in this chapter about the tax rate employed in a foundation formula: If districts are not required to tax at this rate at a minimum, many low-wealth districts will decide to set their tax rates below the rate in the formula so that they can free up money for non-school spending.[24] This type of response is clearly evident in states that impose no minimum tax rate on localities.[25] It follows that when a minimum tax rate is imposed, most low-wealth districts are forced to tax at a rate that is above the one that they would select if they were unconstrained. When a GTB plan is added, most low-wealth districts find that the required minimum rate is so far above the one they would otherwise prefer that they do not want to increase their tax rate any further, despite the large price subsidy they stand to receive through the GTB plan. As a result, only districts with property values that are relatively high but still below V^* are affected by the GTB plan; these districts do not feel constrained

---

[23]This may not occur in all cases, of course; that is, some second-tier GTB programs may increase educational equity. The ability of these programs to promote equity is quite limited, however, because, as explained earlier in the chapter, they have little power to influence educational spending in high-need districts unless the required minimum tax rate is set below the rate high-need districts would otherwise select. Note that this limit on equalizing effectiveness does not arise with a stand-alone GTB program, which always increases spending by low-wealth districts. As noted earlier in the chapter, however, this increase in spending is generally not sufficient to bring all low-wealth districts up to any reasonable adequacy standard. Indiana and Missouri address this issue by combining a GTB program with a minimum required local property tax rate. See Huang (2003).

[24]This explanation for Odden's simulation result is mine, not his. He presents the simulation results with no explanation.

[25]A large literature shows that increases in state aid go partly toward reductions in local taxes. See Fisher and Papke (2000). The simulations by Nechyba (2003) show the impact of such a response on the outcomes of state aid reform, and evidence on this issue for New York is provided by Duncombe and Yinger (1998, 2000).

by the requirement of a minimum tax rate and respond to the modest price subsidy they receive from the GTB formula.

This analysis provides a reminder of how important it is to distinguish between access equality and wealth neutrality or any other equity standard based on the distribution of education (however defined) across districts. A second-tier GTB does equalize the ability of all districts in a state to supplement the foundation level of spending, but it does not equalize spending or cost-adjusted spending across districts, because it fails to recognize that the tax rate in low-wealth districts is already far above the level that they would choose if they were unconstrained. In this context, granting access equality is essentially meaningless, because low-wealth districts are not in a position to take advantage of the access they have been given.

When it is used as a second tier on top of a foundation program, therefore, a GTB program is a poor tool for boosting educational spending in an equitable manner. For any equity objective except strict access equality, a better approach is to repeal the GTB program and use the resulting savings to fund a higher foundation level.

3.2. *Should the Formula Account for Student Characteristics and Wage Costs?*

A second key policy choice is whether to bring educational costs into state aid reform. In the terms of Table 3, the issue is whether to shift the measurement of education from spending per pupil to real resources per pupil or to performance. The highest courts in some states, such as New York and Tennessee, have explicitly rejected spending as a way to measure education because it does not account for costs, and many other courts implicitly reject spending by talking about "educational quality" (Lukemeyer, 2003).[26]

Perhaps the clearest signals on educational costs have come from New Jersey. In 1998, for example, the New Jersey Supreme Court ruled, in *Abbott v. Burke* (*Abbott v. Burke V*), that the state was responsible for providing supplementary programs in twenty-eight urban school districts

---

[26]For more on the Tennessee Supreme Court decision and the reforms it generated, see Cohen-Vogel (2001).

to bring student performance in these districts up to an adequate level (Goertz and Edwards, 1999).[27] To be specific, the court required the state to provide these urban schools with whole-school reform, kindergarten, a half day of preschool for three- and four-year-olds, coordination with health programs, and programs to deal with security and technology.[28] Additional requirements for the preschool programs, such as student-teacher ratios, were spelled out in *Abbott v. Burke* in 2000 (*Abbott v. Burke VI*).

All these requirements explicitly recognize that educational costs are higher in urban districts, with their concentration of disadvantaged students, than in others.[29] As the court put it in an earlier decision,

> We have decided this case on the premise that the children of poorer urban districts are as capable as all others; that their deficiencies stem from their socioeconomic status; and that through an effective education and changes in that socioeconomic status, they can perform as well as others. Our constitutional mandate does not allow us to consign poorer children permanently to an inferior

---

[27]The New Jersey court made its first pronouncement on this issue in 1973 when it said, "Although we have dealt with the constitutional problem in terms of dollar input per pupil, we should not be understood to mean that the State may not recognize differences in area costs, or a need for additional dollar input to equip classes of disadvantaged children for the educational opportunity" (*Robinson v. Cahill* [1973], 72). In its 1995 decision, *Campbell County School District v. State*, the Wyoming Supreme Court also explicitly required extra spending for disadvantaged students. See Lukemeyer (2003).

[28]A 2000 trial court decision in North Carolina (*Hoke County v. State*), which is being appealed by the state, also called upon the state to fund prekindergarten programs for all at-risk four-year-olds (ACCESS, 2003). (Recall that the benefits of prekindergarten programs are reviewed in Karoly *et al.*, 1998.) Whole-school reform programs, which attempt to alter many aspect of school life, such as curriculum, management techniques, and parental involvement, are widely used, but evidence concerning their effectiveness in improving educational outcomes is quite mixed. See Ladd and Hansen (1999) and Berends, Bodilly, and Kirby (2002). The New Jersey Supreme Court actually required a particular whole-school reform plan, Success for All, with its extension, Roots and Wings (Goertz and Edwards, 1999). This plan has shown signs of effectiveness in some studies, but few of them were conducted by independent scholars. One recent independent study (Bifulco *et al.*, 2005) finds, for example, that Success for All actually lowers elementary math performance in New York City schools while having no impact on reading. As the National Research Council's Committee on Education Finance puts it, some whole-school reform "[d]esigns have achieved popularity in spite rather than because of strong evidence of effectiveness and replicability" (Ladd and Hansen, 1999, 213). Moreover, whole-school reform programs appear not to work very well when they are imposed on a school instead of being selected by the teachers and administrators at the school (Berends, Bodilly, and Kirby, 2002). Indeed, there is some evidence of this outcome in New Jersey (Hendrie, 2001).

[29]This argument is echoed by New York's highest court in *CFE v. New York* (2003), in which the court says, "[W]e cannot accept the premise that children come to the New York City schools ineducable, unfit to learn" (slip op. at 42–43).

education on the theory that they cannot afford a better one or that they would not benefit from it. (*Abbott v. Burke* [1990] [*Abbott v. Burke II*], 385–386)

The New Jersey court has not recognized, however, that educational costs also may vary across non-urban districts (see Lauver, Ritter, and Goertz, 2001).

These court decisions, along with the growing emphasis on performance in state education policy, appear to have encouraged states to include cost adjustments in their state educational aid formulas. A recent survey finds that "38 states currently distribute some education funds on the basis of poverty" (Carey, 2002, 1), which is a key determinant of educational costs. Of these states, thirteen incorporate district poverty into their main aid formula, eighteen have supplementary aid programs weighted toward districts with poor children, and seven use both of these approaches.[30] Using a slightly broader definition than poverty, the U.S. Census finds that twenty states have categorical "compensatory" programs for "economically disadvantaged" students (Huang, 2003, Table B.2). Aid formulas in several states also reflect other factors known to affect educational costs, such as the cost of living or the share of students with limited English proficiency or with a handicap.[31] For example, thirty-three states have categorical aid programs for handicapped students (Huang, 2003, Table B.2), and only three states (Delaware, Nevada, and South Dakota) have aid programs that ignore educational costs altogether (Huang, 2003, Table B.3).

Adjusting aid formulas for educational costs is difficult, however, and existing methods for doing so range from *ad hoc* cost adjustments in many states to a regression-based comprehensive cost index in Massachusetts during the 1980s (Bradbury *et al.*, 1984). To account for the higher cost of educating poor students, sixteen states use pupil weights, five states make cost-based adjustments to their main aid formula, and twenty-four states use categorical grants; these figures include seven states that combine two

---

[30]Gold, Smith, and Lawton (1995) estimate that two-thirds of U.S. states use an aid formula that contains some form of extra compensation for low-income students. A few states also have cost adjustments in their building aid formula. See Wang (2003, Table C.4).

[31]See Huang (2003, Table B.4) and Carey (2002, Table 1b). One troubling feature of the aid formulas in nine states is that they give more aid to districts with lower student test scores, presumably on the grounds that low test scores reflect a concentration of disadvantaged students (Huang, 2003, Table B.6). Test scores also reflect the quality of education the district provides, however, and such provisions serve to reward incompetent districts. These provisions clearly should be replaced with educational-cost adjustments based on factors outside district control.

of these approaches and leave out the twelve states with no cost-based aid (Huang, 2003, Table B.5). Clearly, no consensus has emerged on the best way to proceed, and existing methods almost certainly understate the variation in educational costs across districts.[32] Carey (2002) finds, for example, that the average state provides 17.2 percent more funding for a poor student than for a non-poor student, whereas existing research suggests that the cost of educating a poor student is at least 100 percent higher than that of educating a non-poor student.[33] Only one state, Maryland, gives every poor student an additional weight this high (Huang, 2003).

All of the reforms reviewed in this book also involve some form of cost adjustment in the state educational aid formula. Kansas, Kentucky, Texas, and Vermont adjust their basic foundation amount for the share of a district's students in poverty, with special needs, or with limited English proficiency, but the adjustments are fairly *ad hoc*. Texas also adjusts for the geographic cost of living. Michigan does not include cost adjustments in its foundation amount but does provide categorical programs with *ad hoc* adjustments for concentrations of poor students or other students with special needs; unfortunately, these programs have never been fully funded and may therefore have relatively little impact on the state educational aid received by high-cost districts (see Cullen and Loeb, 2003).[34]

Perhaps the main issue in these cost adjustments, along with the ones in other states, is their *ad hoc* nature. As a result, existing cost adjustments move states away from the first column in Table 3 toward the third column (usually in the first row), but none of them can be considered fully consistent with a performance-based method for measuring education. Several of the chapters in Yinger (2003) explore alternative, more accurate ways to account for educational costs.[35] Given the emphasis of state education policy on

---

[32]No state currently uses a statistically based adjustment for educational costs. Moreover, the share of the state aid budget that goes to categorical aid programs for economically disadvantaged students (for handicapped students) is only 3.9 percent (6.6 percent) in states with such programs. Only four states spend more than 5 percent of their aid budgets on categorical programs for at-risk students (Huang, 2003, Table B.2).
[33]Carey cites Maryland Commission on Education Finance, Equity, and Excellence (2002); Reschovsky and Imazeki (1998); and Duncombe (2002). In these studies the cost of educating a poor student is between 97 and 159 percent higher than the cost of educating a non-poor student.
[34]Categorical aid programs serve a similar purpose and face a similar restriction in California. See Kramer (2002). See also Carey (2002) and Huang (2003).
[35]An alternative analysis of educational costs in Texas is provided by Alexander *et al.* (2000).

student performance, this is a key issue for scholars and policymakers to pursue.

Cost adjustments in state aid reforms in the five states examined in Yinger (2003) raise two additional issues. First, the reforms in Kansas, Texas, and Vermont include a cost adjustment that raises the foundation level for the smallest districts. Size adjustments also appear in the aid programs of fourteen other states (Huang, 2003, Table B.5). This type of adjustment is not about transportation costs, which are considered separately. Instead, the rationale for this type of adjustment is the well-known result (surveyed in Andrews, Duncombe, and Yinger 2002) that the per-pupil cost of education is higher in very small districts than in medium-sized ones. It is not clear, however, that a cost adjustment is the appropriate response to this finding, because the cost disadvantage of small districts can be eliminated in many cases through district consolidation (Duncombe and Yinger, 2007). If per-pupil costs can be lowered through consolidation, a state is wasting money by rewarding districts that refuse to consolidate.[36] More research is needed to determine the circumstances under which consolidation of school districts is a cost-effective option.

Second, four of the states examined in Yinger (2003), Kansas, Kentucky, Michigan, and Texas, provide more aid to districts with a relatively high concentration of "exceptional" or gifted students. The aid programs in thirty other states follow suit (Huang, 2003, Table B.6). These provisions have nothing to do with ensuring adequacy in student performance. An educational cost adjustment is designed to recognize that some districts must spend more than others to achieve a given level of student performance. Districts with many exceptional students may decide to spend money on special programs for these students, but these districts have to spend *less* than other districts to reach any given performance target. Policymakers and courts may want to encourage the creation of programs for gifted students with provisions such as these, but if they do, they should recognize that these provisions are not cost adjustments and have nothing whatsoever to do with achieving performance objectives.[37]

---

[36] This statement implicitly holds educational quality constant; that is, the issue is whether a consolidation lowers per-pupil costs without cutting educational quality.

[37] As shown in Huang (2003), several states also give more aid to districts that have more highly qualified teachers. This provision is presumably designed to encourage districts to raise their teachers' qualifications. This type of aid never covers the full cost of hiring more qualified teachers, however, and in practice it serves to reward wealthy districts, which can afford to hire highly qualified teachers. In other words, this is another type of anti equalizing aid program.

3.3. *Should Supplementation by Wealthy Districts be Reduced?*

Another key issue facing policymakers is whether education finance reform should reduce the extent to which wealthy (or otherwise low-need) districts supplement the foundation amount specified in the aid formula. The recent emphasis on adequacy in state court decisions indicates that restrictions on supplementation may not be required, but the continuing role of other equity standards in some states, including some that emphasize adequacy, suggests that reductions in supplementation may be called for in many, if not most, cases.[38] In fact, all five of the reform efforts reviewed in Yinger (2003) explicitly restrict supplementation by high-wealth districts to some degree.[39] These limits tend to be complicated and are often politically unpopular, so the debate on supplementation in these states is likely to continue for many years.[40] Moreover, virtually any aid reform plan includes some provisions that reduce this type of supplementation, even if those provisions are not explicitly designed to do so.

States limit supplementation in five ways. The most direct approach is simply to prohibit supplementation or to prohibit it beyond some limit. The Kansas reform, for example, prohibits supplementation beyond the spending level supported by its second-tier GTB program (Duncombe and Johnston, 2003), the Kentucky reform prohibits supplementation beyond 30 percent above the spending level supported by the state's second-tier GTB program (Flanagan and Murray, 2003), and the Michigan reform calls for phased-in provisions that will eventually allow only a limited amount of supplementation even in the wealthiest districts (Cullen and Loeb, 2003).

These limitations on supplementation build on a long tradition of local tax and expenditure limitations, which exist in one form or another in forty-four states, usually with some form of override provision (O'Sullivan,

---

[38] An example of court signals on supplementation is provided by the New Jersey Supreme Court's first education finance decision: "Nor do we say that if the State assumes the cost of providing the constitutionally mandated education, it may not authorize local government to go further and to tax to that further end, provided that such authorization does not become a device for diluting the State's mandated responsibility" (*Robinson v. Cahill* [1973], 72–73).

[39] As indicated in Huang (2003, Table B.4), twenty-eight states restrict supplementation through an explicit tax or expenditure limit, a recapture provision, or some other provision stronger than simply requiring voter approval.

[40] Many scholars have argued in favor of an equality standard, which generally requires restrictions on supplementation. See Kramer (2002) for a recent example.

2001).[41] In fact, all of the states examined in Yinger (2003) except Vermont had school property tax limitations before they implemented their school finance reform plans, and they either replaced their tax limitations with features of the reform plan or, as in Texas, incorporated the tax limitations into their reforms. Five other states with court-mandated school reform also already had school property tax limitations in place before the reforms, and four more states added such limitations after the implementation of a reform ordered by the state supreme court (see Evans, Murray, and Schwab, 2001).[42] The last category includes the well-known case of California, which passed a property tax limitation, Proposition 13, in 1978, after the *Serrano I* and *Serrano II* decisions. This proposition dramatically limited school spending (Sonstelie, Brunner, and Ardon, 2000).

A second approach to limiting supplementation, used by a few states, involves a second-tier GTB program with a recapture provision that raises the price of supplementation in high-wealth districts.[43] This approach does not forbid spending above the foundation level but instead discourages it by making its price very high. As noted earlier in the chapter, a large literature demonstrates that school districts are sensitive to price changes, so this approach can significantly lower spending by low-need districts. Versions of this approach are used by Texas and Vermont.

This approach has two weaknesses, however. First, it is likely to be unpopular in wealthy districts, where voters may resent the extra "tax" that it imposes. Second, the amount of revenue that it recaptures depends on the spending decisions of the high-wealth districts and therefore cannot be known when the state aid budget is determined. These problems are illustrated by the original second-tier GTB formula in Vermont, which applied to all revenue above the foundation amount (Downes, 2003). Vermont collected recaptured funds in an account and then returned them to districts based on the tax rate they imposed and (inversely) on their wealth. No

---

[41] Evidence from Massachusetts (Cutler, Elmendorf, and Zeckhauser, 1999) indicates that the voters most affected by tax limitations are the most likely to take advantage of overrides, if they are available.

[42] Fischel (2001) claims that school finance equalization leads to tax limitations. Evans, Murray, and Schwab (2001) show that this is not the case. Specifically, they identify seven states other than Vermont that have an education finance system reformed in response to a court order but no property tax limitation and nine states that have a tax limitation but have not reformed their school finance systems.

[43] McCarty and Brazer (1990) recommended building recapture into a GTB program. A GTB program can also be designed to recapture funds from districts with a high ratio of wealth to educational costs.

state funds were involved. The key problem with this design was that it left all districts uncertain about the revenue consequences of their tax rate decisions.[44] This uncertainty was eliminated in 2003, when Vermont switched to a more traditional GTB formula (ACCESS, 2003). The recapture provisions in the Texas reforms are less dramatic, primarily because they apply to only 88 (out of 965) school districts in the state (Imazeki and Reschovsky, 2003).[45] Moreover, the Texas provisions give wealthy districts five options for meeting their recapture obligations, thereby eliminating the uncertainty that was present in the original Vermont approach.

Both Texas and Vermont use their second-tier GTB formulas both to promote access equality and to limit supplementation. As explained earlier in the chapter, the promise of access equality is an empty one, and a better approach would be to use a GTB solely to promote the second objective. This requires a relatively low value for V^*, as in Vermont.[46] However, lowering V^*, magnifies the negative matching rates in the wealthiest districts and is therefore likely to increase their opposition to a reform plan. One way to mitigate this opposition would be to multiply the matching rate in equation (2) by a fraction, thereby lowering both the price increase that wealthy districts face and the reduction in supplementation.

The third way for a state to limit supplementation in low-need districts is to transform the property tax into a state tax and use the revenue to finance the foundation plan. As explained in Section 2.2.1, this approach lowers the disposable income of high-wealth districts (or low-cost districts, if a cost adjustment is included in the foundation plan) relative to a foundation plan based on a local property tax. The resulting income effect results in a decline in the desired education spending level, and hence in the level of

---

[44]By refusing to use state funds for this provision, Vermont shifted the budgetary uncertainty from the state to the school districts. However, the state is in a much better position to handle this uncertainty. After all, state officials cannot make a budget without forecasting the revenue from each source, after accounting for the relevant behavioral responses to the tax. The only difference between the GTB revenue source and others is that the forecast must consider the behavioral responses of school districts, instead of the behavioral responses of individuals or firms.
[45]These reforms apply only to a few districts because V^* in the Texas version of equation (2) is set not far below the property value per pupil in the state's richest district. In Vermont, V^* is set near the property value per pupil in the average district.
[46]One possibility is to set V^* in the GTB formula at the wealth level at which foundation aid falls to zero and to use the GTB formula solely to determine recapture from districts with wealth above V^*, not to determine aid for districts with wealth below V^*, all of which receive aid through the foundation program.

supplementation, in those districts. Although not definitive, the available evidence suggests that this approach, which operates through an income effect, is likely to have a smaller impact on supplementation than the GTB approach, which operates through a price effect.

The local property tax was transformed into a state tax as part of education finance reform efforts in Kansas (Duncombe and Johnston, 2003), Michigan (Cullen and Loeb, 2003), and Vermont (Downes, 2003), but the impact of these changes on supplementation was mitigated, if not eliminated, by the details of the transformation. In Kansas, the transformation was accompanied by large increases in state aid funded by other state taxes, primarily the sales tax, so that the current state-set property tax rate is below the prereform local property tax rate except in a few wealthy districts. State aid from other sources also increased in Vermont after the transformation, although to a lesser degree than in Kansas. In Michigan, the transformation was accompanied by a dramatic reduction in the property tax rate, so that the condition required to reduce supplementation, namely, a state tax rate above the prereform local tax rate, does not exist in any district.

The fourth way a state can limit supplementation in low-need districts is by redistributing state aid away from these districts toward high-need districts. This approach faces political obstacles, because it involves cutting the aid of low-need districts, but it is a relatively low-cost way to shift a state's focus away from general school support toward an adequacy standard. It builds on the relationship between state aid and local spending, which is another form of an income effect. According to a large literature, cutting aid to low-need districts lowers their effective income and induces them to choose a lower spending level for education (see Fisher and Papke, 2000). Moreover, extensive empirical evidence indicates that the impact on school spending of a change in state aid is significantly larger than the impact of an equivalent change in voters' disposable income.[47] As a result, the type of redistribution involved in this approach is likely to have a larger impact on supplementation by low-need districts than is state takeover of the property tax, and it might have a larger impact than a GTB plan with recapture.

---

[47]This difference is known as the flypaper effect; money given directly to a school district is more likely to remain in a school district's budget than is a change in income that has exactly the same impact on voters' budget constraints. For a review of the literature on this topic, see Hines and Thaler (1995).

Finally, any state aid reform plan that raises state taxes in high-wealth (or otherwise low-need) districts will reduce supplementation in those districts to some degree. The more progressive the increase in state taxes, the larger this effect is likely to be. The education finance reform undertaken in Kentucky falls into this category; the state financed an increase in its foundation level through a significant increase in state taxes, along with an increase in the required minimum local tax rate (Flanagan and Murray, 2003).[48] This approach, like the previous two, works through income effects; that is, supplementation is reduced because of a decline in the resources available in high-wealth districts. In this case, however, the changes in financing affect voters in high-wealth districts only to the extent that variables predicting which voters experience an increase in taxes, such as their income, are correlated with district wealth. An income tax increase, for example, will lower supplementation in districts that have high wealth because their residents have high incomes and are able to buy expensive houses, but it will not lower supplementation in districts that have poor residents along with a power plant that results in high property wealth per pupil.

This discussion of ways to limit supplementation leads to four main conclusions. First, it is virtually impossible to reform state aid through an expanded foundation aid program without limiting supplementation by low-need districts. The limits on supplementation can be severe, as are those that have been imposed in Kansas, Michigan, and Vermont; moderate, as is that implemented in Texas; or weak, as is that applied in Kentucky. But the only way to increase the foundation spending level, E^*, in equation (1) without limiting supplementation is to pay for the increase entirely through an increase in the required local tax rate, t^*. This approach shifts resources toward the districts with the lowest wealth without influencing districts that are too wealthy to receive funding under the original foundation plan.[49] No existing state aid reform plan has relied exclusively on this approach, although, as noted earlier, it is part of the Kentucky plan.

The literature recognizes that state aid reform can promote educational equity by providing more resources to districts with low student performance (called "leveling up") or by restricting the ability of districts with high student performance to go beyond the provision of basic educational services

---

[48] As shown by Flanagan and Murray (2003), this combination of policies resulted in virtually no change in the state's share of education spending.

[49] Even this approach limits supplementation by districts that received foundation aid under the original plan but do not under the revised plan.

("leveling down"). As the cases considered in this book illustrate, all aid reform plans involve elements of both of these strategies. Scholars disagree, however, on the net impact of the typical reform; that is, they disagree about the impact of reform on spending in the average district or on performance by the average student in the state. Murray, Evans, and Schwab (1998) and Dee (2000) find that the typical reform involves more leveling up, whereas Hoxby (2001) finds that many reform plans, especially the most dramatic, involve more leveling down.[50] According to Hoxby, this outcome reflects the fact that some types of leveling down allow the state to keep its own costs down. As she puts it: "It is expensive to bribe districts that would prefer low spending into spending a lot. It is inexpensive to forbid high spending" (1222).

The analysis presented in Yinger (2003) does not reveal, of course, whether the average reform levels up or levels down, but it does indicate that the choice for policymakers is not whether to reduce supplementation by low-need districts, but instead how much to reduce supplementation using which approach. Some leveling down arises, after all, even when a state uses state taxes to pay for an increase in the foundation spending level. Thus, each state must select the approach to supplementation that best fits the mandates of its courts and its policy objectives.[51]

The second conclusion arising from the discussion of supplementation is that reductions in supplementation by high-wealth districts accompany state aid reforms designed to meet legitimate educational objectives and do not necessarily arise simply from a state's desire to minimize its own costs. It is true, of course, as Hoxby (2001) points out, that a state may be able to minimize how much it must pay to meet an equality standard by explicitly limiting supplementation in high-wealth districts. It is also true, however, that supplementation by high-wealth districts is reduced whenever a state decides, in the name of fairness, to redistribute some of its aid money from

---

[50]For further evidence on this debate, see Downes and Shah (1995); Manwaring and Sheffrin (1995); and Silva and Sonstelie (1995).

[51]Moreover, the long-run consequences of supplementation are poorly understood. Loeb (2001) shows that unlimited supplementation might undermine state voters' support for a high state-funded foundation level. In other words, some limits on supplementation might be needed to sustain adequacy. Even with limits on supplementation, however, the high cost of sustaining a generous foundation aid program may result in waning voter support for state education spending over time. This appears to be the case in Kansas (see Duncombe and Johnston, 2003).

wealthy to poor districts or to pay for a higher foundation amount by turning a local property tax into a state tax.

It is tempting to regard reductions in supplementation as part of education finance reform as somehow punitive or inappropriate because they pull wealthy districts below their preferred level of school spending. In fact, however, the level of spending wealthy districts "prefer" is heavily influenced by the education finance system in place prior to any reform. This preferred level of spending is boosted by state aid, for example, and it is boosted by a state's decision to set an extremely low foundation spending level and thereby to forgo the high state taxes needed to bring foundation spending up to a level courts or education experts regard as adequate. Indeed, this preferred level of spending is even influenced by the way the state draws school district boundaries, which are the principal determinant of a school district's wealth and of the extent to which its students are disadvantaged.[52] As a result, rejecting reductions in supplementation as part of a reform package is equivalent, in many cases, to endorsing the prereform education finance system created by the state.

A better approach to the issue of supplementation would be for a state considering reform to decide on its educational objectives, on constitutional or policy grounds, and then to determine which methods for reducing supplementation by wealthy districts are most consistent with those objectives. The analysis surrounding this determination should recognize that preventing wealthy districts from using their own funds to supplement the state's foundation amount may promote an equality objective but also imposes costs on society in the form of lost educational benefits in those districts.[53] It should also recognize, however, that a state may not be able to meet its constitutional or policy-based equity objectives without removing some of the existing subsidies that wealthy districts receive in the form of state aid or tax relief.

---

[52] As emphasized by Fischel (2001), a school district's wealth also might be influenced by its ability to attract or retain various types of property, a factor that does not reflect decisions by the state.

[53] More formally, a district will not use its own resources for education unless the marginal benefits of doing so exceed the marginal costs. As a result, limits on supplementation impose a net cost whenever they prevent supplementation using local taxes that a district would otherwise choose. Measures of this type of loss are not available for school finance reform, but they are documented for property tax limitations. See Bradbury, Mayer, and Case (2001). Transferring state aid from wealthy to poor districts also lowers educational benefits in wealthy districts, but these losses are presumably offset by increased educational benefits in poor districts.

The third conclusion is that supplementation by wealthy districts can be reduced through a variety of policies, but little is known about the relative impact of different approaches. Explicit limits on supplementation may appear to be the most effective policy, but these limits can be set to permit such high levels of supplementation that they have little impact on behavior. Moreover, inferences about the income and price effects of many policies on school district spending can be made on the basis of related studies, but there is no direct evidence on the extent to which supplementation is reduced by GTB programs with recapture, state takeover of local property taxes, redistribution of existing aid funds, or tax increases to pay for a higher foundation spending level. As indicated earlier in the chapter, my own ranking based on existing indirect evidence is that GTB programs and redistribution of existing aid funds have the largest effects on supplementation, followed by state takeover of the property tax, and then by increases in other state taxes, but more research on this topic is clearly needed.

The fourth conclusion is that the reforms in Kansas, Kentucky, Michigan, and Texas all combine some adjustments of aid amounts for differences in educational costs with some limits on supplementation. In effect, therefore, these reforms bear some resemblance to the entry in the bottom right of Table 3, which involves full cost adjustment and no supplementation. The actual reforms do not go all the way to the system described in that entry, however, because both their cost adjustments and their equalization efforts are incomplete.

3.4. *How Should State Aid Reform Be Financed?*

Another fundamental issue in any school aid reform plan is how to pay for it. This issue has two parts. The first part is the extent to which the burden for funding a state's schools should be shifted from school districts to the state, and the second part is the choice of taxes to fund the state's share of the burden.

The average state provides half of the revenue for elementary and secondary education, but this share varies widely from state to state (see Huang, 2003, Table B.1). Concern about the state's contribution has been central to the education finance debate since *Serrano I* identified the local property tax as a source of educational inequity. Because other local taxes are generally not available to school districts, any funding plan for education that reduces reliance on the local property tax almost inevitably involves an increase in the state's share of educational funding. With one exception, every education funding reform plan discussed in Yinger (2003) both reduces local property taxes and increases the state's share of the funding burden. The exception is the reform in Kentucky, in which the state share of funding was already very high and, as noted previously, both state and local taxes were increased.

In many states that have undertaken reform of their systems for funding education, including Michigan and Vermont, voter dissatisfaction with high property taxes was also a key motivation for the reform. In Michigan, for example, a frustrated legislature decided to eliminate the state's property tax to force the state to design a better education finance system (Cullen and Loeb, 2003). Moreover, concern for high property tax burdens is such a powerful issue in some states that it gets in the way of school aid reform.

Consider the case of New York, which passed a $3 billion School Tax Relief Program (STAR) in 1997. This program takes the form of a state-funded homestead exemption, which exempts homeowners from school property taxes on the first $30,000 of the market value of their home. STAR provides little help, however, for districts with a high concentration of renters, particularly the poor urban districts, which are the neediest school districts in the state (Duncombe and Yinger, 2001).[54] Its cost represents over 20 percent of the state's budget for education aid. With this much money, New York could have implemented a new state aid program that would have gone a long way toward eliminating the educational inequities that are currently under debate after the *CFE v. New York* decision by the state's highest court.[55] This type of aid increase would also provide property tax relief, because aid increases are not fully translated into spending increases, and it could be designed to promote widely recognized educational-equity standards.

The extent of any shift from local to state funding that results from school finance reform is largely controlled through decisions about the parameters of the school aid formula. With a foundation formula, the key issues are the

---

[54] One particularly troubling feature of the STAR program is that it gives a higher property tax exemption to taxpayers in high-wealth counties. I know of no equity standard that can justify this provision. In addition, the STAR program is accompanied by a state-funded credit on the New York City income tax, which goes to both renters and owners. Other cities in the state, however, which also have relatively large renter populations, do not receive any extra payments. See Duncombe and Yinger (2001).

[55] In 1999, New Jersey passed a property tax exemption modeled on the New York plan that used $1 billion in state funds that could have been used to meet the New Jersey Supreme Court's mandate to improve educational equity. See Gray (1999). The New Jersey case is discussed in more detail later in the chapter.

magnitudes of the foundation spending level and of the required minimum local property tax rate. Raising the foundation spending level with the required tax rate held constant raises the state's share of education funding. Moreover, the lower this tax rate for a given foundation level, the higher the state share of education funding must be.[56] If the property tax is turned into a state tax — that is, if the revenue from the property tax is sent directly to the state rather than to the localities — then the decision about the property tax rate determines the share of education revenue that comes from the property tax, instead of from other state taxes.

One implication of this analysis is that a state can minimize the increase in state taxes (or, if the property tax is a state tax, in other state taxes) needed to finance a higher adequacy standard by raising the minimum required property tax rate school districts must charge. With a local property tax, however, a state obviously cannot fully fund reform in this way, because it places the burden for financing reform on the neediest districts. Moreover, any preexisting voter dissatisfaction with the property tax may undermine this approach, regardless of whether the property tax is collected by school districts or the state.

Policymakers also must decide whether to pay for any increase in the state's contribution to education that may result from education finance reform by increasing the state income tax or the state sales tax. This choice raises complex issues of equity and efficiency that will not be addressed here. Suffice it to say that a debate about the best state tax to use to finance a state aid reform plan is an appropriate, and almost inevitable, part of designing such a plan. One interesting example comes from Michigan, where the voters explicitly selected a higher sales tax over a higher income tax as a way to pay for education aid reform in the state (Cullen and Loeb, 2003).

3.5. *Should Aid Reform Be Linked to Accountability?*

A fourth choice that policymakers designing a plan for state aid reform must make is whether state education aid should be linked to an accountability program. As noted earlier, virtually all states have some type of accountability program, and a majority of states have a program that imposes some type of financial rewards and punishments. The courts did not link accountability to state aid reform until fairly recently, but the Kentucky Supreme Court's *Rose* decision in 1989 threw out the state's existing system

---

[56]With a GTB formula, the state's contribution is determined largely by the value of the V^* parameter and by whether the formula includes a recapture provision.

of school governance and brought new visibility to accountability programs. Moreover, the recent state aid reforms in Kentucky, Michigan, and Texas have all been accompanied by accountability programs that include district-level rewards and sanctions.

It is now widely recognized that state aid reform and accountability are inextricably linked (Figlio, 2003). State legislatures are often reluctant to give more money to school districts without assurances that the money will be well spent, and some scholars have found that increases in state aid are likely to undermine school district efficiency (Duncombe and Yinger, 1997, 1998). (In this context, efficiency is a measure of a school district's success in translating inputs into student performance, after accounting for factors outside the district's control, such as concentrated poverty among its students.) Indeed, some scholars have argued that aid increases are unlikely to boost student performance at all, either because their negative impacts on school district efficiency are so large or because additional inputs are unable to influence performance.[57] Because of these concerns it seems reasonable to combine aid increases for needy school districts with accountability programs that preserve the efficiency with which these districts operate and even encourage them to operate with greater efficiency.

The problem is that our knowledge of accountability programs is distressingly limited. Many of the early accountability programs were seriously flawed because they set up rewards based solely on student test scores. Approaches of this sort fail to recognize that poor performance depends both on a school district's efficiency and on cost factors, such as wage rates and student characteristics, that are outside the district's control. An "accountability" system that punishes a district because it contains many disadvantaged students obviously makes no sense.

Unfortunately, however, it is difficult to separate these two causes of poor performance. Some existing accountability programs have made steps in this direction (Clotfelter and Ladd, 1996; Hanushek and Raymond, 2001; Ladd, 2001; Murnane and Levy, 2001), but to some degree all existing programs reward some districts and punish others for factors that are outside the districts' control.[58] These points are nicely summarized by Hansen (2001, 2):

---

[57]This sentence refers, of course, to the debate about whether money matters. For an argument that it does not, see Hanushek (1996, 1997); for arguments that it does, see Ferguson (1991); Ferguson and Ladd (1996); Krueger (1999, 2002); and Krueger and Whitmore (2001).

[58]Even programs that base rewards and punishments on *changes* in average student scores (instead of on levels) run into serious problems. See Ladd and Walsh (2002). Among

Research is just beginning into the reliability and stability of different methods of ranking and rating schools for the purposes of determining rewards and sanctions. Differences in school size and in the size of relevant cohorts of students ... can result in accountability systems with perverse incentives. ... Improperly designed incentives can have serious effects on the morale and motivation of school personnel.

Moreover, there is no compelling evidence on the impact of accountability programs on student performance. One study (Ladd, 1999) finds some evidence consistent with a positive impact on student achievement resulting from Dallas's accountability program, but this study observes only a single year before the program was implemented and cannot rule out the possibility that the observed increases in student performance in later years reflect something unusual about this year, instead of the impact of the account-ability program. Ultimately, accountability programs themselves must be held accountable. If they do not result in higher student performance, then they should be dropped. There is obviously room for more research on this important topic and for experiments with more accountability programs.

The objective of accountability programs is to give school districts incentives to be more efficient, that is, to improve student performance with no increase in resources. An alternative method for promoting this objective is to mandate certain teaching or management practices that, in the opinion of state officials, will result in higher school efficiency. This approach was taken by the New Jersey Supreme Court, which, as noted earlier, required the state to implement a specific whole-school reform program in twenty-eight (later thirty) low-performing urban school districts. Moreover, in its 1989 *Rose* decision, the Kentucky Supreme Court found constitutional violations in school curriculum and governance, as well as in school finance. The subsequent reforms included major changes in curriculum and management (see Flanagan and Murray, 2003).

3.6. *Should Aid Reform Be Linked to School Choice?*

Expanding school choice is another type of policy that is linked to education finance reform in several states. School choice plans, which come in many different forms, give parents alternatives to sending their children to the local

---

other things, these programs, which include the federal No Child Left Behind Act of 2001, punish schools that were efficient in the past and therefore have less room for improvement. Moreover, schools with high costs must spend more than other schools to obtain the same *increase* in student scores, just as they must spend more to attain the same performance target.

public schools in their neighborhood. Choice plans allow parents to send their
children to other schools in the same district or to schools in other districts,
enable the creation of public charter schools subject to fewer restrictions
than existing public schools, or provide vouchers that parents can use to
help send their children to private schools. These plans are intended not
only to provide parents with choices regarding their children's education but
also to promote competition among schools. Some people argue that such
competition will force existing public schools to improve, that is, to become
more efficient (see Nechyba, 2003).

The potential role of school choice in school aid reform is illustrated
by the case of Michigan (Cullen and Loeb, 2003). The school aid reforms
implemented in Michigan in 1994 included strong encouragement of charter
schools, and these reforms were complemented with a new school choice plan
a few years later. Michigan now has about 180 charter schools, three-quarters
of which are run by private, for-profit companies (*New York Times*, 2002).

Charter schools and school choice plans are difficult to evaluate, but
the limited available evidence does not suggest that charter schools provide
significantly better education than other public schools or that competition
from charter schools or choice plans forces public schools to become more
efficient (Gill *et al.*, 2001). Nevertheless, these approaches continue to have
many supporters, and they will undoubtedly continue to be the subject of
further experiments and further research.

School vouchers have not been part of any major school finance reform
plan implemented to date, but vouchers have been used in several places,
including Milwaukee, Cleveland, and Florida. The Florida voucher plan
blends the notions of choice and accountability by making vouchers available
to students in schools rated "failing" by the state (see Figlio, 2003). So far,
however, only a handful of students have made use of the voucher option. A
2002 U.S. Supreme Court decision, *Zelman v. Simmons-Harris*, upheld the
constitutionality of the Cleveland vouchers, which are used primarily to send
children to Catholic schools. As a result, voucher plans may become more
widely used in the future.

The available evidence indicates that some existing voucher programs
have a small positive impact on the performance of participating students,
at least in mathematics, whereas other voucher programs have no impact
on performance at all (Rouse, 1998). This evidence, however, is difficult
to interpret. Rouse (2000) presents some evidence, for example, suggesting
that the Milwaukee voucher program has a small positive effect on math
performance because of smaller class sizes in the private schools attended

by Milwaukee voucher recipients than in the public schools these students would otherwise attend. The cause of this class size difference is not known, however. Voucher proponents might argue that it arises because private schools are more efficient than public schools and can hire more teachers with the money they save. Voucher opponents can counter that these extra teachers could be hired thanks to cost savings associated with a smaller concentration of disadvantaged students in participating private schools than in the public school population as a whole. Moreover, participants in the Cleveland program primarily send their children to Catholic schools because subsidies to these schools from the Catholic Church keep the tuition low enough that the voucher can cover it. Subsidies of this type obviously would not be available in a large voucher program.

3.7. *Should Capital Spending Be Included?*

A final choice for policymakers confronting education aid reform is whether the reform plan should attempt to promote equity in capital spending. With some notable exceptions, most of the court cases have focused on the equity of operating spending in the state, not of capital spending. One important exception can be found in New Jersey, where capital spending was included in the original *Robinson v. Cahill* ruling in 1973 and where the 1997 *Abbott v. Burke* ruling (*Abbott v. Burke IV*) explicitly called for more capital spending in poor urban school districts (Goertz and Edwards, 1999).[59] Capital spending was not included in the initial court cases involving school aid reform in Texas, but in its 1995 decision in *Edgewood Independent School District v. Meno,* known as *Edgewood IV,* the Texas Supreme Court ordered the state to deal with inequity in capital spending among the state's school districts (see Imazeki and Reschovsky, 2003). Moreover, as noted earlier, a recent supreme court decision in Arizona and recent trial court decisions in Alaska and New Mexico declared that these states' systems for funding capital spending are unconstitutional (see Huang *et al.*, 2003).

At one level, it obviously makes no sense to eliminate inequities across districts within a state in operating spending but to allow them in capital spending; after all, both types of spending are crucial for providing education. It is also true, however, that capital spending has a less direct

---

[59]As the New Jersey Court put it in 1973: "The State's obligation includes as well the capital expenditures without which the required educational opportunity could not be provided" (*Robinson v. Cahill* [1973], 72).

connection to student performance than does operating spending and that state formulas for building and operating aid tend to be fundamentally different from one another (Sielke, 2001).

Compared to operating aid, for example, building aid relies much more heavily on matching grants (Wang, 2003). In fact, only six states rely exclusively on lump-sum grants for capital spending, whereas twenty-three states use only matching grants, and nine states use a combination of the two. Regardless of the formula used, many of these grants also require that individual building projects be approved by the state. In contrast, eleven states do not provide any building aid to localities at all, and Hawaii, with its state school system, fully funds school capital spending. Finally, building aid programs are far less likely than operating aid programs to adjust for district property wealth. To be specific, only twenty-five states have at least one building aid program weighted toward low-wealth districts.

Unfortunately, the principles behind and the behavioral consequences of these building aid formulas are not well understood. More work by both policymakers and scholars is clearly needed to shed light on inequities involved in capital spending — and on the best ways to alleviate them.

4. Analyzing the Effects of State Aid Reform

A second set of themes in this book involves the effects of reforms to state education-aid programs. Are court mandates actually implemented? Do state aid reforms eliminate disparities in spending and in student performance? Do these reforms have unintended consequences, and are they undermined or reinforced by behavioral responses unanticipated by policymakers? We now turn to an examination of these questions.

4.1. *To What Extent (and Over What Period) Are Court Mandates Implemented?*

In most cases, state education-aid reform is stimulated by a state supreme court decision. One of the key factors influencing the effectiveness of the eventual reform, therefore, is the process that leads from a court decision to an actual aid reform program. This process appears to depend on the willingness of the state's legislative and executive branches to respond to a court decision that overturns the state's education finance system and on the willingness of the state supreme court to impose specific requirements on the other branches of government in the state. To some degree, of course, the legislative and executive branches must defer to the court on constitutional matters, and courts traditionally have deferred to the other branches of government on matters of educational policy. But despite this general standard of deference, the range of outcomes for this process is amazingly large.

In some states, a relatively weak signal from the courts results in dramatic reform by the legislative and executive branches. Kansas (Duncombe and Johnston, 2003) provides one example of this type of situation. Maryland provides another. In 1994 a trial court in Maryland approved a settlement that called for the state to increase its funding for Baltimore's schools. In 2000, this court ruled that this decree had not been followed and ordered the state to increase its funding to Baltimore. The legislature and governor did not immediately comply with the court's ruling but instead set up a commission to make recommendations for improving the adequacy and equity of education in Maryland. This commission issued its final report in January 2002 and recommended a dramatic increase in state education aid to localities, particularly for schools with high concentrations of poor students, students with special needs, or students with limited English proficiency. A grassroots campaign convinced the legislature to pass legislation based on the commission's recommendations, and these recommendations were signed into law in April of the same year (Montgomery, 2002; Hunter, 2003).

Another common route to state aid reform is a clear state supreme court decision that is taken seriously by the legislative and executive branches. This route is illustrated by Kentucky (Murray and Flanagan, 2003) and Vermont (Downes, 2003). The Vermont case is somewhat unusual in that voter dissatisfaction with high property taxes was reflected in the legislature that was elected right before the state supreme court handed down its decision in 1997 striking down the state's education funding system. As a result, this legislature acted promptly to put a new system in place.

Other states have witnessed a drawn-out tug-of-war between the legislative and executive branches on the one hand and the courts on the other. Texas (Imazeki and Reschovsky, 2003) provides one example of this pattern and Ohio (ACCESS, 2003) provides another.[60] The most dramatic

---

[60]The saga in Ohio recently took a strange new twist. In December 2002, the Ohio State Supreme Court upheld earlier decisions overturning the state's reliance on the property tax, but then in May 2003, it prohibited the trial court from enforcing those decisions. See ACCESS 2003 and Huang *et al.* (2003, Table A.2).

example, however, is undoubtedly New Jersey (Goertz and Edwards, 1999; ACCESS, 2003), which has experienced decades of legislative and executive resistance to reform of the state's school finance system combined with gradual strengthening of requirements imposed on the state by the state's highest court. The original lawsuit challenging the education finance system in New Jersey was filed in 1970, and in 1973 the New Jersey Supreme Court ruled, in *Robinson v. Cahill,* that the state's education finance system did not meet the constitutional requirement in the state for "thorough and efficient" schools. The New Jersey Supreme Court has issued twelve more decisions in the area of education finance since then, and the battle between policymakers and the courts continued into 2003. The legislature responded to the early decisions by increasing the state's share of education funding, but not until *Robinson v. Cahill* in 1976 (*Robinson v. Cahill V*) did the court give tentative approval to a state aid system. Despite this approval, the legislature refused to appropriate money for its own legislation, so the court briefly shut down the schools in the summer of 1976. This action led to a state income tax to fund school aid followed by the reopening of the schools in time for the 1976–1977 school year.

A second round of litigation, known as *Abbott v. Burke,* began when the Education Law Center filed a lawsuit on behalf of the state's urban school districts. After a series of preliminary decisions, the court ruled in favor of the plaintiffs; that is, it required education finance reform. Twice the state passed legislation in an attempt to satisfy the court, and twice the court ruled that the new legislation was still unconstitutional. The court's frustration with state policymakers finally led it to impose specific spending requirements on the state. As noted above, the court ruled, in *Abbott v. Burke V* in 1998 and in *Abbott v. Burke VI* in 2000, that the state was responsible for funding a variety of specific programs in urban schools. The long-standing battle between policymakers and the court appeared to end early in 2002, when the new governor of New Jersey, James McGreevey, dropped the state's opposition to the court orders issued in the *Abbott* decisions and set up a panel to oversee the state's implementation of the requirements the court had imposed (Kocieniewski, 2002).[61]

---

[61]The battle hasn't quite ended. The New Jersey Supreme Court responded to the state's budget crisis of 2002 by granting a one-year delay in the requirement for full implementation of its programmatic requirements. Then, in April 2003, the court required both parties in the suit to participate in mediation concerning state-requested changes in the programmatic requirements imposed by the court. See Huang *et al.* (2003) and ACCESS (2003).

Overall, anyone trying to understand state aid reform in a given state would do well to begin by looking into the role of the state courts in the reform process and the interplay between courts and policy-makers. These factors are, of course, different in every state, but they almost always have a significant impact on the nature of the reform package that is ultimately adopted.

4.2. *Effects on the Equality of Spending*

A key issue in evaluating state aid reform is whether it actually makes school spending more equitable, that is, whether it reduces disparities in spending across school districts, as required by several state supreme court decisions. The case studies in Yinger (2003) examine this issue, and all find that reform does reduce spending disparities, sometimes substantially, but does not lead to complete spending equality.[62] These analyses build on the work of several scholars who have studied the link between aid reform and spending equality using national data.

Murray, Evans, and Schwab (1998) examine data for over 10,000 school districts in forty-six states over the period 1972 to 1992. During this period, eleven of the states studied implemented court-mandated education aid reforms. Murray and her colleagues find that these reforms significantly reduced spending inequality across districts.[63] The precise results vary with the measure of inequality they use, but all measures suggest large reductions in inequality — on the order of 20 to 30 percent. They also find that these reductions in inequality reflect an increase in spending by the districts that spent the least before the reforms combined with no change in spending in the highest-spending districts. Finally, they find that state aid reform is always accompanied by a significant increase in the share of education spending that is financed by the state government.

Evans, Murray, and Schwab (1997, 1999) explore the impact of court-ordered reform on the sources of revenue in various types of school districts. They find that the lowest-income districts (and the districts with the lowest

---

[62] Kramer (2002) provides an alternative look at the impact of state aid reform on spending equity in two of these states, Kentucky and Texas, and in California.

[63] Murray and her colleagues measure "reform" either with a dummy variable that equals one in a year after a court-ordered reform has been implemented or with a variable to measure the number of years since the last implementation of this type. These two approaches yield qualitatively similar results. The text discussion is based on the first approach.

levels of local revenue before reform) raised less money for education after reform but that the cuts in their local revenue were more than offset by their increased state aid.[64] These results imply that the typical reform did not impose a high minimum tax rate on all school districts.

An alternative approach to the impact of state aid reform on spending equity is provided by Hoxby (2001). Instead of treating state aid reform as an event, she develops a framework for classifying state aid systems, using equations similar to (1) and (2), and determines the parameters of the aid systems in every state in 1990. Many other studies have used a similar approach for a single state, but no other study has attempted it for all the states in the nation. This approach allows her to determine how the spending in a school district is affected by the parameters of the state aid system, which differ across states and sometimes across districts within a state, instead of assuming that all state aid reforms have the same effect.

Hoxby finds that per-pupil spending in a school district responds as expected to the parameters of a foundation aid program, and specifically, that it increases with the foundation amount and decreases with the required minimum tax rate.[65] She also finds that spending decreases with the tax price, which is defined as the amount of money a district must raise itself to obtain another dollar of spending per pupil.[66] A standard GTB program lowers the tax price in low-wealth districts, because, as shown earlier, it shifts a share of any spending increase onto the state. Moreover, a GTB program with recapture raises the tax price in high-wealth districts. This result implies, therefore, that a GTB program with recapture will decrease spending where wealth is high and increase it where wealth is low.

---

[64]Using national data for 1990 alone, Dee (2000) essentially replicates a key finding of Evans, Murray, and Schwab (1997). To be specific, he finds that court-mandated reform raises spending in low-spending districts but has little impact on high-spending districts.

[65]Although her theoretical discussion (as well as equation (1)) implies that school district behavior is affected by net aid (the foundation amount minus the required minimum tax rate multiplied by the local tax base), Hoxby estimates separately the effects of the foundation amount and of the required minimum tax rate (and does not, as called for by her theory, interact the tax rate with the local tax base). This approach leads to the following misleading statement: "The introduction of a stringent FA [foundation aid] scheme might increase the foundation tax rate by 30 mills, or 0.030. The coefficient indicates that a 30 mill increase would generate a 6.4 percent fall in per-pupil spending" (1216). In fact, however, a scheme that raises the foundation tax rate without also raising the foundation amount is *anti equalizing*; any scheme that raises net aid will raise spending.

[66]This definition leaves out the voter's tax share, usually measured as the ratio of the median to the mean property value, which is included as part of the price of education in most studies. See Inman (1978); Ladd and Yinger (1991); and Fisher and Papke (2000).

Hoxby summarizes these results by showing the impact of each state's education aid system on various measures of spending equality across districts (compared to a system of local finance alone). She finds that the state aid system increases equality in every state. The magnitude of this increase is particularly large in states with dramatic equalization programs.[67] In other words, state aid reform can increase across-district equity in per-pupil spending, but existing state aid systems also promote such equity, even if they do not reflect a major reform.

Overall, there appears to be a broad consensus that state aid reform can reduce across-district inequality in spending per pupil. As discussed earlier in the chapter, however, different aid reforms are linked to different notions of equity. A reform that raises the foundation spending level, for example, promotes an adequacy objective, and adjusting this spending level for educational costs provides a way to express this objective in performance terms. Moreover, the evidence in Hoxby (2001) suggests that all states engage in some equalization. The key issue for policymakers and courts, therefore, is not whether the state should use education aid to make education spending more equitable; instead, the issue is how it should equalize — and how much.

4.3. *Effects on Equality of Performance*

As discussed earlier, the emphasis in the debate about state aid reform has gradually shifted from spending to student performance. Another key question, therefore, is whether state aid reform leads to an increase in student performance, particularly for districts in which performance is relatively low. This question has proven to be difficult to study, however, and no consensus on the answer has yet emerged. Some insight into the complexity of the topic is provided by case studies in Yinger (2003), each of which investigates, using the best available evidence, the impact of a particular state aid reform on student performance. Although some of the evidence indicates that state aid reform can boost student performance, none of the findings are definitive, and some of them are quite ambiguous. In Texas, for example, evidence from state-designed tests indicates that aid reform boosted the performance of poor students and students from minority groups, but this result is not

---

[67]Hoxby also finds, however, that state aid makes a majority of the poorest districts (those with mean household income or with per-pupil property values below the 20th percentile) worse off in the two states with the most dramatic equalization programs in 1990 (California and New Mexico).

confirmed by the evidence from national tests (Imazeki and Reschovsky, 2003).

As discussed by Figlio (2003), the main problems confronting any national study of the impact of state aid reform on student performance are (1) the enormous diversity in the nature of state aid reform plans and (2) the paucity of national-level student performance data. One study that addresses the first of these problems is Hoxby (2001).[68] Following the methodology she developed to study the impact of state aid reform on spending equality, Hoxby estimates the impact of various state aid parameters on the dropout rate, which is one dimension of student performance. She finds that a higher foundation spending level is associated with a lower dropout rate. A typical foundation program does not, of course, raise spending in high-spending districts. Thus, Hoxby concludes, "equalization improves student achievement the most (perhaps only) in schools that would have very low spending if left to their own devices" (1228).[69]

Overall, the available evidence suggests that complicated reform plans that involve GTB formulas and recapture have complicated impacts on student performance that are difficult to sort out and that may not always correspond to the effects that were expected when the plans were formulated. This is, in effect, another application of the insight provided by Feldstein (1975) many years ago, namely, that one cannot predict the outcomes of a state aid reform without understanding the incentives it creates for school districts and estimating how the districts will respond to those incentives. In contrast, the available evidence is also consistent with the view that foundation plans can boost student performance in low-performing districts.

---

[68] Other relevant studies include Card and Payne (2002); Downes (1992); and Downes and Figlio (2000). These studies and others are reviewed in Evans, Murray, and Schwab (1999).

[69] Hoxby also estimates another model in which the dropout rate is a function of per-pupil spending, and the foundation amount and other state aid parameters are used as instruments to deal with the simultaneity of spending and performance. Because spending is not statistically significant in this model, Hoxby claims that the evidence linking the foundation amount to the dropout rate is "mixed" (1228). However, this alternative model, which she calls an "education production function," is not compelling. In an education production function, performance is a function of inputs and student characteristics (often called "fixed inputs"). Hoxby's approach relies on the strong assumption that spending is a good proxy for inputs purchased by the school, such as teachers, after controlling for student characteristics. Several other variables in the model, including income and the share of the district population over sixty-five years old, are often considered demand variables, and some scholars argue that they do not belong in the regression (Dewey, Husted, and Kenny, 1999). In my view, however, these are efficiency variables, which should be included.

Nevertheless, the precise nature of this impact is still unclear, and more research is needed to determine the impact on performance of various state decisions, such as the foundation spending level, whether districts are required to impose a tax that does not fall below a certain minimum rate, and whether the foundation level is adjusted for educational costs.

4.4. *Effects on School District Efficiency*

School district inefficiency is defined by scholars as a situation in which a school district spends more than necessary to achieve a given student performance. School districts are inefficient when they provide services that make minimal contributions to student performance or when they use outmoded management or teaching techniques.[70] Unlike student performance or school spending, however, school district inefficiency cannot be directly measured, and scholars are just beginning to devise methods for studying it. All existing methods have important limitations, and scholars have not reached a consensus on the best method to use (see Bifulco and Bretschneider, 2001; McCarty and Yaisawarng, 1993).

Using data for New York state, Duncombe and Yinger (1997, 2001) estimate the impact of state aid on school district efficiency and then simulate the impact on efficiency of various state aid reform proposals. They measure efficiency using a technique called "data envelopment analysis," which determines the extent to which each district spends more per pupil than other districts with the same student performance.[71] They also control for education costs; as noted earlier, a district should not be called inefficient if spends more than other districts due to the characteristics of its students or other factors beyond its control.

Duncombe and Yinger (2001) find that a school district's efficiency increases when it receives less aid than districts with which it is likely to compare itself, namely, those that are similar to it in terms of property values and student enrollment, or when it is in a class of districts that receives less aid than other classes. These results suggest that low-aid districts make extra

---

[70]For example, Strauss *et al.* (2000) discuss the efficiency consequences of outmoded procedures for hiring teachers.

[71]The results of this analysis obviously depend on the definition of student performance. Duncombe and Yinger measure performance using the share of students meeting state-determined standards on elementary math and English tests, high school graduation rates, and the share of students that graduate from high school with a Regents diploma, which requires them to pass certain state tests.

efforts to keep up with other, similar districts. In addition, the higher the tax price in a district, that is, the higher the property tax increment voters in the district must pay to increase public services, the higher is district efficiency. This result suggests that voters monitor school districts more carefully when more of their own funds are at stake.

On the basis of these results, Duncombe and Yinger estimate that introducing a foundation aid program with an adjustment for educational costs, which corresponds to the program type described in the top right corner of Table 3, would lower the efficiency of the neediest districts, which are, of course, the districts that receive the biggest increment in aid under such a program.[72] In other words, some of the aid provided to these districts "leaks out" in the form of lower managerial efficiency. In some cases, this leakage is substantial, but it never eliminates the benefits from increased aid. Under the current aid system, the efficiency level is 62.2 percent in New York City, about 53 percent in the downstate small cities and suburbs, 72.5 percent in the upstate "big-three" cities, and about 68 percent in the upstate small cities and suburbs.[73] A cost-adjusted foundation program that set the foundation level at the amount of spending required to reach the median of the current performance distribution and doubled the state aid budget would reduce the efficiency index in New York City, which receives the largest increase in aid under such a reform program, to 49.8 percent, and would reduce the efficiency index in the upstate big-three cities to 62.4 percent. Suburbs and small cities in the state, which would receive aid cuts under such a reform program, would experience small increases in efficiency. Even after the reform, however, the average large city would still be more efficient than the average small city or suburb.

---

[72]Duncombe and Yinger (1998) present simulations of GTB programs that account for the impact of these programs on tax prices and hence on school district efficiency. With a standard GTB program, for example, a low-wealth district receives a high matching rate, which corresponds to a large reduction in its tax price, and therefore becomes much less efficient.

[73]Note that efficiency is lower in the small cities and suburbs than in the large cities. This result reflects the fact that small cities and suburbs provide a wider range of educational programs, some of which, such as music and art programs, make only minimal contributions to the performance objectives specified in footnote 71. This efficiency result undoubtedly would be different if student performance in these programs were included in the performance standards. To the best of my knowledge, however, all existing state accountability systems use performance standards similar to the ones used in Duncombe and Yinger's analysis.

Despite these few attempts to study the link between state aid reform and school district efficiency, the gap between policymakers and academics on this issue is still huge. As noted earlier, policymakers formulating education finance reform programs in Kentucky, Michigan, and Texas took the position that state aid reform needs to be accompanied by programs to boost school district efficiency, especially in high-need districts. Many other states are adopting accountability programs without any explicit link to state aid reform. As also noted earlier in the chapter, however, there is virtually no evidence that accountability programs can boost performance without raising costs, which is the same thing as boosting efficiency. Moreover, no study exists to help policymakers design a state aid reform that will minimize negative impacts on school district efficiency, particularly in the neediest school districts. More research on these topics is urgently needed.

4.5. *Unintended Consequences*

Major state aid reform can influence many outcomes other than school spending and student performance. In other words, state aid reform can have many unintended consequences. Three different types of unintended consequence have been stressed in the literature and are discussed in Yinger (2003): changes in property values, movement to private schools, and increased funding from private educational foundations.

4.5.1. *Impacts on property values*

As many scholars have pointed out, state aid reform can affect property values. More specifically, property values are likely to rise in school districts that receive more state aid because of the reform and to fall in districts that receive less aid. These property value changes may reflect property tax rate cuts that are made possible by reform or reform-induced increases in educational performance, either of which increases the amount people are willing to pay for housing in a given school district. Clear evidence that state aid reform affects property values is provided by Dee (2000) and Hoxby (2001), and Nechyba (2003) simulates the impact of various aid reform plans on property values.[74] Dee finds, for example, that state aid reform has a large, positive, statistically significant impact on property values in school

---

[74]There is also a large literature on the capitalization of property tax rates and school performance without reference to state aid reform. This literature is reviewed in Ross and Yinger (1999). For a recent contribution see Downes and Zabel (2002).

districts with relatively low local school revenues, that is, in the districts
most likely to be aided by the reform.[75] Dee also finds that state aid reform
boosts apartment rents in these districts.

The impact of property tax rates and school quality on house values,
which is known as capitalization, is of interest to policymakers because, as
emphasized by Wyckoff (1995, 2001), it alters the distribution of gains and
losses from state aid reform. People who own property in districts that gain
from reform are winners, and people who own property in districts that lose
from reform are losers. People who move into either type of district in the
future, however, are likely to be unaffected by the reform. If they move into
a district that gained from reform, for example, they will have to pay for
access to this gain in the form of a higher housing price (or a higher rent).
As a result, the winners and losers are a very specific set of people, namely,
those who owned property at the time the reform was announced.

Although the primary purpose of state aid reform is to alter educational
outcomes, a few state supreme courts have also expressed tax equity
objectives for the education finance system. Indeed, the notion of access
equality can be thought of as a form of tax equity. However, the tax equity
standards expressed by courts and policymakers have to do with tax rates
and revenue-raising ability, not with capital gains and losses. One could
argue, following Wyckoff, that capitalization should be considered in any
analysis of tax equity, but it seems unlikely that it actually will be.

Nevertheless, capitalization is an important unintended consequence of
state aid reform, even if the reform does not have any expressed tax
equity objectives. The capital gains and losses potentially generated by a
particular reform plan are likely to influence political support for the plan,

---

[75]Dee (2000) claims that studies of capitalization provide insight into the impact of state
aid reform on school quality. Under the assumption that aid reform does not result in
property tax reductions in poor districts, he interprets reform-induced property value
increases as a sign of an improvement in student performance or in some other dimension
of education that homeowners care about. Unfortunately, however, Dee does not test this
assumption, and the evidence in support of it is mixed, at best. Evans, Murray, and Schwab
(1997, 26) conclude, for example, that "successful litigation will lead the state government
to provide the lowest revenue districts additional state aid of $700 per student 10 years
after reform. These districts reduced local revenue by $190, and thus total revenue rose
by $510." Dee's approach cannot rule out the possibility that property value increases
are due solely to the $190 cut in local revenue. His approach does work, however, for a
foundation-based reform plan that requires a minimum tax rate at or above the rate used
by high-need districts before the reform — as do the reforms implemented in several states.

and they have real fairness consequences that scholars should continue to investigate.[76]

4.5.2. *Movement to private schools*

School aid reform also might have the unintended consequence of encouraging some parents to send their children to private schools.[77] This issue is examined in detail by Nechyba (2003). This type of consequence is, of course, particularly relevant for state aid reform plans that limit supplementation in wealthy districts. Hoxby (2001) estimates that the most extreme reform plans in this category could boost private schooling in the wealthiest districts by as much as three percentage points. Because the national average private school attendance is about 11 percent, this is a fairly large effect. In contrast, Sonstelie, Brunner, and Ardon (2000) do not find a significant increase in private school attendance in California, one of the states with an extremely equalizing aid system.

The potential for increases in private school enrollment as a result of school finance reform is obviously of great interest to policymakers, because it can place a limit on their ability to achieve certain educational equity objectives. If attempts to achieve educational equity through leveling down drive many children from high-income families into private schools, then more equality within the public education system may be attained at the cost of less equality in the elementary and secondary education system taken as a whole. Unfortunately, however, the available evidence on the impact of aid reform on private school attendance is ambiguous, and this topic is certainly worthy of further investigation.

4.5.3. *New funding through private educational foundations*

Another unintended consequence of state aid reform might be the creation of private education foundations in wealthy districts. Because these foundations are private organizations, they are not subject to the same constraints as public schools, and they can, in principle, replace some of the funds that are

---

[76] As noted in Section 3.4, a state aid reform plan must select a method of funding, and the choice of a funding method also has fairness consequences. A few studies investigate the impact of state aid reform on tax incidence. See Cullen and Loeb (2003).

[77] Of course, state aid reform also lowers the incentive of parents in needy districts to send their children to private school. See Nechyba (2003). This type of response is not as important, however, because few parents in needy districts send their children to private schools to begin with.

eliminated in wealthy districts by restrictions on supplementation. On the surface, this appears to be exactly what happened in California. In 1971, the year of the *Serrano I* decision, California had only 6 education foundations; now it has over 500 (Sonstelie, Brunner, and Ardon, 2000). A careful look at these foundations reveals, however, that they have a relatively small impact on education finance in the state. In 1994 they raised only $45 per pupil, on average, and over 90 percent of the students in the state were in districts in which annual contributions were less than $100 per pupil (Sonstelie, Brunner, and Ardon, 2000).

As in the case of increased recourse to private schooling, the creation of private foundations is of concern to policymakers because these foundations can, in principle, undermine educational-equity outcomes. Some educational-equity goals cannot be achieved if restrictions on supplementation through tax revenue are offset by supplementation through private foundations. The available evidence indicates, however, that so far, at least, this type of response to education finance reform has not been large enough to warrant serious concern.

4.6. *General Equilibrium Effects*

Finally, a state aid reform can have complex consequences and feedback effects that are relevant for the reform's objectives. This type of feedback, called a general equilibrium effect by economists, is explored by Nechyba (2003).

As Nechyba makes clear, the most basic type of general equilibrium effect arises from the link between school quality and residential location. Under most circumstances, the only children eligible to attend a particular public school are children who live in the school district in which the school is located. As a result, households compete for housing in desirable school districts, and high-income households generally outbid low-income households for housing in the districts that have the best schools. State aid reform can have a direct impact on this sorting process. By improving schools in low-wealth or high-cost districts or by limiting supplementation in high-wealth or low-cost districts, state aid reform can alter the relative attractiveness of various districts and alter the type of households each district contains. If more high-income households are attracted to a high-poverty district, for example, the poverty concentration in that district will decline, thereby lowering the cost of education. This decrease in educational costs will magnify the initial impact of state aid reform. Nechyba also shows that movement to private schools can have a similar type of feedback effect:

By altering the mix of students in public schools, such movement can alter educational costs.

One important example of a general equilibrium effect, which was first pointed out by Inman (1978) and Inman and Rubinfeld (1979) and which is simulated by Nechyba (2003), arises in the case of a GTB program. Under this type of aid formula, the aid a district receives depends on its tax base, but its tax base, that is, the value of its property, depends on the aid it receives. Low-wealth districts, which receive a large increase in aid when this type of aid formula is implemented, experience a property value increase, which leads, in turn, to a decrease in their aid, thereby undermining the reform effort. The opposite outcome, which also undermines the reform, occurs in high-wealth districts.[78]

Yinger (2020) points out that this type of negative feedback does not arise with a foundation aid program, at least not if the foundation level is set high enough. A foundation plan is insulated from this type of effect because it specifies the amount a district must spend on education. Moreover, under some foundation program designs, capitalization can actually enhance the equalizing impact of the program. This type of enhancement occurs when property value increases in low-wealth districts result in higher local revenues and thereby allow the state to boost the foundation level with no increase in the state aid budget. Yinger also shows that the impact of foundation aid on school district efficiency could result in feedback effects that either enhance or undermine a reform plan's equity objectives.

The general equilibrium issues raised by Nechyba (2003), particularly the link between school quality and residential location, are also important for understanding the impacts of vouchers, which, as pointed out earlier, might be included in future school finance reforms. As Nechyba carefully explains, voucher programs make it possible for many students to attend public or private schools in districts other than the one in which they live. This mobility weakens the link between school quality and property values and alters the way households are sorted across school districts. For example, the introduction of a voucher program might encourage some wealthy families that send their children to private schools to move to previously low-wealth

---

[78]Hoxby (2001) also mentions this type of feedback, along with two others. First, the parameters of an aid reform program are sometimes functions of behavioral outcomes, such as mean per-pupil spending in the state. Second, movement to private schools could lower voter support for state aid or for local property taxes in high-spending districts.

school districts, thereby boosting those districts' school tax revenue and
school performance.

Nechyba (2003) uses simulation techniques to build a strong case for
the view that policymakers and academics need to pay more attention to
the general equilibrium effects of state aid reform. Unfortunately, however,
there is virtually no empirical evidence on the magnitude of these effects.
More work on this topic is clearly needed.

5. Conclusions

State supreme courts, policymakers, and scholars appear to have reached a
consensus that a foundation plan with a foundation level based on a generous
notion of educational adequacy, a required minimum tax rate, and some
kind of educational cost adjustment that provides extra funds for high-
need districts forms the core of an acceptable reform of state education
finance.[79] This emerging consensus still leaves a lot of room for debate,
of course. Exactly how high should the foundation level be? What is a
reasonable minimum tax rate? Should the tax required for funding the reform
be a state tax (to facilitate recapture) or a local tax (to facilitate local
control)? What type of cost adjustment is appropriate? Nevertheless, this
consensus regarding the centrality of a foundation plan narrows the debate
considerably, and a great deal has been learned in recent years about some
of these unresolved issues, such as the features of various approaches to cost
adjustments.

Beyond this emerging consensus on the use of a foundation plan, however,
there is little sign of agreement. Perhaps the most contentious question
is whether a foundation plan is sufficient to achieve educational equity,
particularly in the eyes of state supreme courts. The answer would appear
to be affirmative if a state's supreme court decides that the state can meet
its constitutional obligations simply by providing an adequate education in
every district. In fact, however, few courts have issued a clear-cut ruling of
this type. Instead, many courts have hinted at broader equity objectives
without being clear, or, in some cases, even consistent.[80] Moreover, a

---

[79] For an analysis of this consensus in court cases, see Minorini and Sugarman (1999a);
Rebell (2002); and Lukemeyer (2003); for a view on the scholarly consensus, see Odden
(1999) or Guthrie and Rothstein (1999).

[80] Perhaps the clearest ruling of this type comes from the 1976 *Serrano II* decision by
the California Supreme Court, which affirmed a lower court's ruling that wealth-related
spending could not be more than $100 higher per pupil in any one district than another.

foundation plan could be sufficient to meet a strong equality objective if its foundation level were set high enough. The problem, of course, is that such a high foundation level would require an enormous increase in state aid, and hence in state taxes, or else an extremely high required minimum local tax rate. No state has yet been willing to follow either of these routes.

Hence, many states have decided to move beyond an adequacy standard, usually by turning to limits on local property tax revenues, a GTB formula with recapture, or some other active method to reduce supplementation by high-wealth districts.[81] Although reducing supplementation may cut the increase in state taxes necessary to achieve a strong equality objective, it also may impose a cost on society in the form of poorer education performance in high-wealth districts. The more stringent the limits on supplementation, the higher this cost will be. The challenge facing policymakers is to design a reform plan in which the equity gains resulting from the reform outweigh these costs. Moreover, programs that limit supplementation may push parents in high-wealth districts to send their children to private schools or to set up private educational foundations that provide the supplementation that is not allowed through property taxes. Although the size of such responses does not appear to have been large in the case of existing reforms, they do have the potential to undermine the equity objectives of future aid reform efforts.

A consensus on the reforms that should accompany a new foundation aid program might be easier to achieve through a shift away from the question of how to reduce supplementation to the question of how to share the financial and other burdens imposed by school finance reform. Regardless of the constitutional and/or policy objectives it is designed to achieve, any school finance reform imposes burdens on some state residents. Reforms that raise the minimum required local property tax rate impose a burden on the low-wealth or high-cost districts the plan is presumably most designed to help. A reform plan can also impose a burden on high-wealth or low-cost districts if it includes cuts in their state aid, recapture provisions, state

---

This approach obviously requires severe limits on supplementation. It also does not recognize variation across districts in the cost of providing education; however, categorical aid is not wealth related, so it could, in principle, still be used to offset educational cost differences across districts.

[81]Recall that any increase in state taxes to pay for a higher foundation level reduces supplementation in wealthy districts to some degree. The point here is that many states have selected policies that go beyond this minimal reduction in supplementation. See Huang (2003).

takeover of the property tax, or limitations on their ability to raise local school taxes. And of course, any reform plan that raises state taxes to pay for an increase in state aid imposes burdens on state taxpayers in all school districts; the distribution of these burdens depends on the incidence of the new taxes. Every state needs to find a way for these three (overlapping) groups to share the burden that is perceived to be fair and that meets the state's constitutional requirements.

A related issue is the considerable confusion that still appears to exist about the access equality standard. Some state supreme courts have endorsed access equality, but many of these courts also appear to believe that access equality is the same thing as wealth neutrality or even the same thing as equal outcomes. This is clearly not the case. Access equality refers to the nature of a district's budget constraint, not to any educational outcome. The same type of confusion arises when aid programs add (or scholars recommend) a GTB program as a second tier on top of a foundation plan, then justify this as a way to promote an outcome-based equity standard. In fact, such an approach appears to be a poor tool for promoting any standard of this type, at least in its current forms.

All of the participants in the school aid debate, including courts and policymakers and scholars, appreciate the value of a simple formula, and GTB programs undoubtedly linger because they are based on a simple formula with considerable intuitive appeal. In fact, however, standard GTB programs do not fit with the performance focus of current education policy, revised GTB programs that account for the link between spending and performance are rare, and revised GTB programs that account for the behavioral responses of school districts to the programs are too complicated to be adopted. Thus, GTB programs helped to focus attention on the possibility for state aid reform in the years right after the *Serrano I* decision, but it is not clear what role they can or should play today.

Finally, a key emerging issue is whether to combine state aid reform with an accountability program. Such an approach has great intuitive appeal; the available evidence indicates that state aid increases lead to greater school district inefficiency, and state policymakers want to take steps to ensure that new aid funds are well spent. Unfortunately, however, the available evidence also indicates that existing types of accountability programs are likely to undermine, not enhance, the equity objectives of state aid reform. Programs that set high student performance standards without giving high-cost, low-wealth districts the resources they need to meet these standards are a recipe for these districts to fail. Programs that reward districts on the basis of student test scores without formally and explicitly accounting for the impact on these scores of student characteristics and wage costs, which are not the product of school district actions, inevitably penalize those districts that need help the most. Basing rewards on test score gains appears to be a step in the right direction, but these gains may also be influenced by factors that are outside a district's control. States that are serious about improving the performance of students in high-cost districts should move cautiously on accountability programs until these programs can distinguish between managerial inefficiency and high spending caused by a concentration of disadvantaged students or a high-wage environment.[82]

Federal legislation passed in 2001 declares, through its title, that no child should be left behind. This legislation notwithstanding, the sad truth is that many children are being left behind, particularly in large, poor urban school districts. How can states help these children? Some state policymakers, usually spurred on by state courts, have made considerable progress in reforming the education finance system that contributed to the educational disparities that exist in their state, but many other states, including some that have passed so-called reforms, have not made much progress at all. The studies in Yinger (2003) are designed to build on past experience as a guide to help all states move toward more equitable education finance systems.

References

Advocacy Center for Children's Educational Success with Standards" (ACCESS). 2003. "State-by-State" Page. Available at: http://www.accessednetwork.org.

Alexander, Kern, and Richard Salmon. 1995. *Public School Finance*. Boston: Allyn and Bacon.

Andrews, Matthew, William D. Duncombe, and John Yinger. 2002. Revisiting economies of size in education: Are we any closer to a consensus? *Economics of Education Review* **21**(3) (June): 245–262.

Berends, Mark, Susan J. Bodilly, and Sheila Nataraj Kirby. 2002. *Facing the Challenges of Whole-School Reform: New American Schools after a Decade*. Santa Monica, CA: RAND.

Berne, Robert, and Leanna Stiefel. 1984. *The Measurement of Equity in School Finance: Conceptual, Methodological and Empirical Dimensions*. Baltimore: The Johns Hopkins University Press.

---

[82]The caution also applies to federal legislation, but it obviously was not heeded by the people who wrote the No Child Left Behind Act of 2001. This act devised rewards and penalties that do not account for student characteristics or wage costs.

Berne, Robert, and Leanna Stiefel. 1999. Concepts of school finance equity: 1970 to the present. In *Equity and Adequacy in Education Finance*, ed. H. F. Ladd, R. Chalk and J. S. Hansen, 7–33. Washington, D. C.: National Academy Press.

Bifulco, Robert, William D. Duncombe, and John Yinger. 2005. Does whole-school reform boost student performance: The case of New York city. *Journal of Policy Analysis and Management* 24(1): 47–72.

Bifulco, Robert, and Stuart Bretschneider. 2001. Estimating school efficiency: A comparison of methods using simulated data. *Economics of Education Review* 20(5) (October): 417–429.

Bradbury, Katharine L., Helen F. Ladd, Mark Perrault, Andrew Reschovsky, and John Yinger. 1984. State aid to offset fiscal disparities across communities. *National Tax Journal* 37 (June): 151–170.

Bradbury, Katharine L., Christopher J. Mayer, and Karl E. Case. 2001. Property tax limits, local fiscal behavior, and property values: Evidence from massachusetts under proposition 2 1/2. *Journal of Public Economics* 80: 287–311.

Card, David, and A. Abigail Payne. 2002. School finance reform, the distribution of school spending, and the distribution of student test scores. *Journal of Public Economics* 82 (January): 49–82.

Carey, Kevin. 2002. *State Poverty-Based Education Funding: A Survey of Current Programs and Options for Improvement*. Washington, D.C.: Center on Budget and Policy Priorities.

Casserly, Michael. 2002. *Beating the Odds: A City-by-City Analysis of Student Performance and Achievement Gaps on State Assessments*. Washington, DC: Council of the Great City Schools.

Chambers, Jay G. 1998. Geographic variation in public schools' costs. Working Paper 98–04. U. S. Department of Education, National Center for Education Statistics, Washington, D.C.

Clotfelter, Charles T., and Helen F. Ladd. 1996. Recognizing and rewarding success in public schools. In *Holding Schools Accountable: Performance-Based Reform in Education*, ed. H. F. Ladd, 265–298. Washington, DC: The Brookings Institution.

Cohen-Vogel, Lora Ann. 2001. School finance reform in tennessee: Inching toward adequacy. *Journal of Education Finance* 26(3) (Winter): 297–317.

Coons, John, William H. Clune III, and Stephen D. Sugarman. 1970. *Private Wealth and Public Education*. Cambridge, MA: Harvard University Press.

Cutler, David M., Douglas W. Elmendorf, and Richard Zeckhauser. 1999. Restraining the leviathan: Property tax limitation in massachusetts. *Journal of Public Economics* 71(3): 313–334.

Dee, Thomas. 2000. The capitalization of education finance reforms. *Journal of Law and Economics* 53 (April): 185–214.

Dewey, James, Thomas A. Husted, and Lawrence W. Kenny. 1999. The ineffectiveness of school inputs: A product of misspecification? *Economics of Education Review* 19(1) (February): 27–45.

Downes, Thomas A. 1992. Evaluating the impact of school finance reform on the provision of public education: The California case. *National Tax Journal* 45(4): 405–419.

Downes, Thomas. 2003. School finance reform and school quality: Lessons from Vermont. In *Helping Children Left Behind: State Aid and the Pursuit of Educational Equity*, ed. J. Yinger, J, 283–313. Cambridge, MA: The MIT Press.

Downes, Thomas A., and David N. Figlio. 2000. School finance Reforms, Tax Limits, and Student Performance: Do Reforms Level-Up or Dumb Down? Working Paper, Tufts University, Medford, MA.

Downes, Thomas A., and Thomas F. Pogue. 1994. Adjusting school aid formulas for the higher cost of educating disadvantaged students. *National Tax Journal* **67** (March): 89–110.

Downes, Thomas A., and Mona Shah. 1995. The Effect of School Finance Reform on the Level and Growth of Per Pupil Expenditures. Medford, MA: Tufts University Working Paper No. 95–4. June.

Downes, Thomas A., and Jeffrey E. Zabel. 2002. The impact of school characteristics on house prices: Chicago 1987–1991. *Journal of Urban Economics* **52**(1) (July): 1–25.

Duncombe, William D. 2002. Estimating the Cost of an Adequate Education in New York. Working Paper No. 44, Center for Policy Research, No. 44. The Maxwell School of Citizenship and Public Affairs, Syracuse University, Syracuse, NY.

Duncombe, William, and Jocelyn Johnston. 2003. The impacts of school finance reform in Kansas: Equity is in the eye of the beholder. In *Helping Children Left Behind: State Aid and the Pursuit of Educational Equity*, ed. J. Yinger, 147–194. Cambridge, MA: The MIT Press.

Duncombe, William D., John Ruggiero, and John Yinger. 1996. Alternative approaches to measuring the cost of education. In *Holding Schools Accountable: Performance-Based Reform in Education*, ed. H.F. Ladd, 327–356. Washington, D. C.: The Brookings Institution.

Duncombe, William D., and John Yinger. 1997. Why is it so hard to help central city schools? *Journal of Policy Analysis and Management* **16** (Winter): 85–113.

Duncombe, William D., and John Yinger. 1998. School finance reform: Aid formulas and equity objectives. *National Tax Journal* (June): 239–262. [Chapter 12]

Duncombe, William D., and John Yinger. 1999. Performance standards and educational cost indexes: You can't have one without the other. In *Equity and Adequacy in Education Finance*, ed. H. F. Ladd, R. Chalk, and J. S. Hansen, 260–297. Washington, D.C.: National Academy Press.

Duncombe, William D., and John Yinger. 2000. Financing higher student performance standards: The case of New York State. *Economics of Education Review* **19** (October): 363–386.

Duncombe, William D., and John Yinger. 2001. Alternative paths to property tax relief. In *Property Taxation and Local Government Finance*, ed. W.E. Oates, 243–294. Cambridge, MA: Lincoln Institute of Land Policy.

Duncombe, William D., and John Yinger. 2005. How much more does a disadvantaged student cost? *Economics of Education Review* **24**(5) (October): 513–532. [Chapter 7]

Duncombe, William D., and John Yinger. 2007. Does school district consolidation cut costs? *Education Finance and Policy* **2**(4) (Fall): 341–375. [Chapter 18]

The Education Trust. 2002. *The Funding Gap: Low-Income and Minority Students Receive Fewer Dollars*. Washington, DC: The Education Trust.

Evans, William N., Sheila E. Murray, and Robert M. Schwab. 1997. Schoolhouses, courthouses, and statehouses after Serrano. *Journal of Policy Analysis and Management* **16** (Winter): 10–31.

Evans, William N., Sheila E. Murray, and Robert M. Schwab. 1999. The impact of court-mandated school finance reform. In *Equity and Adequacy in Education Finance: Issues and Perspectives*, ed. H. F. Ladd, R. Chalk and J. S. Hansen, 72–98. Washington, D. C.: National Academy Press.

Evans, William N., Sheila E. Murray, and Robert M. Schwab. 2001. The property tax and education finance, uneasy compromises. In *Property Taxation and Local Government Finance*, ed. W.E. Oates, 209–235. Cambridge, MA: Lincoln Institute of Land Policy.

Feldstein, Martin. 1975. Wealth neutrality and local choice in education. *American Economic Review* **61** (March): 75–89.

Figlio, David N. 2002. Aggregation and accountability. In *No Child Left Behind: What Will it Take?* ed. C. Finn. Washington, D.C.: Thomas B. Fordham Foundation.

Figlio, David N. 2003. Funding and accountability: Some conceptual and technical issues in state aid reform. In *Helping Children Left Behind: State Aid and the Pursuit of Educational Equity*, ed. J. Yinger, 87–110. Cambridge, MA: The MIT Press.

Fischel, William A. 2001. *The Homevoter Hypothesis: How Home Values Influence Local Government Taxation, School Finance, and Land-Use Policies*. Cambridge, MA: Harvard University Press.

Fisher, Ronald C, and Leslie Papke. 2000. Local government responses to education grants. *National Tax Journal* **53** (March): 153–168.

Flanagan, Ann E. and Sheila E. Murray. 2003. A decade of reform: The impact of school reform in Kentucky. In *Helping Children Left Behind: State Aid and the Pursuit of Educational Equity*, ed. J. Yinger, 195–214. Cambridge, MA: The MIT Press.

Gess, Larry R., Paul A. Montello, David L. Sjoquist, and John F. Sears. 1996. Public school finance: a rational response to reform pressures. In *Proceedings of the Eighty-Eighth Annual Conference on Taxation*, ed. L. Ebel, 92–97. Washington, D. C., National Tax Association.

Goertz, Margaret E., and Mark C. Duffy (with Kerstin Carlson Le Floch). 2001. Assessment and accountability systems in the 50 states: 1999–2000. Consortium for Policy Research in Education CPRE Research Report Series RR-046. Philadelphia: University of Pennsylvania.

Goertz, Margaret E., and Malik Edwards. 1999. In search of excellence for all: The courts and New Jersey school finance reform. *Journal of Education Finance* **25**(1) (Summer): 5–31.

Gold, Steven, David Smith, Stephen Lawton. 1995. *Public School Finance Programs in the United States and Canada 1993–1994*. Vol. 1. Albany, NY: American Education Finance Association and the Nelson A. Rockefeller Institute of Government.

Gray, Jerry. 1999. Whitman signs bills cutting property taxes. *The New York Times* April 14, p. B4.

Guthrie, James W., and Richard Rothstein. 1999. Enabling "Adequacy" to achieve reality: translating adequacy into state school finance distribution arrangements, In *Equity and Adequacy in Education Finance: Issues and Perspectives*, ed. H.F. Ladd, R. Chalk and J. Hansen, 209–259. Washington, DC: National Academy Press.

Hanushek, Eric A. 1996. School resources and student performance. In *Does Money Matter? The Effect of School Resources on Student Performance and Adult Success*, ed. G. Burtless, 43–73. Washington, DC: The Brookings Institution.

Hanushek, Eric A. 1997. Accessing the effects of school resources on student performance: An update. *Educational Evaluation and Policy Analysis* **19**(2): 141–164.

Hanushek, Eric A., and Margaret E. Raymond. 2001. The confusing world of educational accountability. *National Tax Journal* **54**(2) (June): 365–384.

Hendrie, Caroline. 2001. N.J.'s 'Whole school' approach found hard for districts. *Education Week*, February 21, p. 12.

Hines, James R., Jr., and Richard H. Thaler. 1995. The flypaper effect. *The Journal of Economic Perspectives* **9** (Fall): 217–226.

Hoxby, Carolyn M. 2001. All school finance equalizations are not created equal. *Quarterly Journal of Economics* **66** (November): 1189–1232.

Huang, Yao. 2003. Appendix B: A guide to state operating aid programs for elementary and secondary education. In *Helping Children Left Behind: State Aid and the Pursuit of Educational Equity*, ed. J. Yinger, 331–352. Cambridge, MA: The MIT Press.

Huang, Yao, Anna Lukemeyer, and John Yinger. 2003. Appendix A: A guide to state court decisions on education finance. In *Helping Children Left Behind: State Aid and the Pursuit of Educational Equity*, ed. J. Yinger, 317–330. Cambridge, MA: The MIT Press.

Hunter, Molly A. 2003. Maryland enacts modern standards-based education finance system: Reforms based on 'Adequacy' cost study and parallel court funding principles. Advocacy Center for Children's Educational Success with Standards.

Imazeki, Jennifer, and Andrew Reschovsky. 2003. School finance reform in Texas: A never-ending story? In *Helping Children Left Behind: State Aid and the Pursuit of Educational Equity*, ed. J. Yinger, 251–282. Cambridge, MA: The MIT Press.

Inman, Robert P. 1978. Optimal fiscal reform of metropolitan schools. *American Economic Review* **68**(1): 107–122.

Inman, Robert P., and David Rubinfeld. 1979. The judicial pursuit of local fiscal equity. *Harvard Law Review* **92**: 1662–1750.

Karoly, Lynn A., Peter W. Greenwood, Susan M. Sohler Everingham, Jill Hoube, M. Rebecca Kilburn, C. Peter Rydell, Matthew R. Sanders, and James R. Chiesa. 1998. *Investing in Our Children: What We Know and Don't Know About the Costs and Benefits of Early Childhood Interventions.* Santa Monica, CA: RAND Corporation.

Kocieniewski, David. 2002. Panel created in new jersey to aid poor school districts. *The New York Times*, February 20, p. B-5.

Kramer, Liz. 2002. Achieving equitable education through the courts: A comparative analysis of three states. *Journal of Law & Education* **31**(1) (January): 1–51.

Krueger, Alan B. 1999. Experimental estimates of education production functions. *Quarterly Journal of Economics* **11**(2): 497–532.

Krueger, Alan B. 2003. Economic considerations and class size. *The Economic Journal* **113**(485) (February): F34–F63.

Krueger, Alan B., and Diane M. Whitmore. 2001. The effect of attending a small class in the early grades on college-test taking and middle school test results: Evidence from project star. *Economic Journal* **11** (January): 1–28.

Ladd, Helen F. 1999. The Dallas school accountability and incentive program: An evaluation of its impacts on student outcomes. *Economics of Education Review* **18**(1) (February): 1–16.

Ladd, Helen F. 2001. School-based educational accountability systems: The promise and the pitfalls. *National Tax Journal* **54**(2) (June): 385–400.

Ladd, Helen F., and Janet S. Hansen. 1999. *Making Money Matter: Financing America's Schools.* Washington, DC: National Academy Press.

Ladd, Helen F., and Randall P. Walsh. 2002. Implementing value-added measures of school effectiveness: getting the incentives right. *Economics of Education Review* **21**(1) (February): 1–17.

Ladd, Helen F., and John Yinger. 1991. *America's Ailing Cities: Fiscal Health and the Design of Urban Policy.* Updated Edition. Baltimore: The John Hopkins University Press.

Ladd, Helen F., and John Yinger. 1994. The case for equalizing aid. *National Tax Journal* **47**(1): 211–224. [Chapter 13]

Lauver, Sherri C, Gary W. Ritter, and Margaret E Goertz. 2001. Caught in the middle: The fate of the non-urban districts in the wake of new jersey's school finance litigation. *Journal of Education Finance* **26** (Part 3) (Winter): 281–296.

Lukemeyer, Anna. 2003. Financing a constitutional education: Views from the bench. In *Helping Children Left Behind: State Aid and the Pursuit of Educational Equity*, ed. J. Yinger, 59–86. Cambridge, MA: The MIT Press.

Manwaring, Robert L., and Steven M. Sheffrin. 1995. The effects of education equalization
    litigation on the levels of funding: An empirical analysis. Working Paper, Department
    of Economics, University of California-Davis, Davis CA.
Maryland Commission on Education Finance, Equity, and Excellence. 2002. *Final Report.*
    Baltimore: Maryland Commission on Education Finance, Equity, and Excellence.
McCarty, Therese A., and Harvey E. Brazer. 1990. On equalizing school expenditures.
    Economics of Education Review **9**(3): 251–264.
McCarty, Therese, and Suthathip Yaisawarng. 1993. Technical efficiency in new jersey
    school districts. In *The Measurement of Productive Efficiency: Techniques and
    Applications*, ed. H. Fried, C. Lovell and S. Schmidt, 197–277. New York: Oxford
    University Press.
Meyer, Lori, Greg F. Orlofsky, Ronald A. Skinner, and Scott Spicer. 2002. The state of
    the states. *Education Week* (Special Report), January 10.
Minorini, Paul A., and Stephen D. Sugarman. 1999. Educational adequacy and the courts:
    The promise and problems of moving to a new paradigm. In *Equity and Adequacy in
    Education Finance: Issues and Perspectives*, ed. H.F. Ladd, R. Chalk and J.S. Hansen,
    175–208. Washington, DC: National Academy Press.
Monk, David H. 1990. *Education Finance: An Economic Approach.* New York: McGraw-
    Hill.
Montgomery, Lori. 2002. Md. Seeks 'Adequacy,' Recasting School Debate. *Washington
    Post*, April 22, p. A01.
Murnane, Richard J., and Frank Levy. 2001. Will standards-based reforms improve the
    education of students of color? *The National Tax Journal* **54** (June): 401–415.
Murray, Sheila A., William N. Evans, and Robert M. Schwab. 1998. Education-finance
    reform and the distribution of educational resources. *American Economic Review*
    88(4): 789–812.
National Center for Education Statistics. 2001. Table 4: Enrollments in Grades K-12 in
    Public Elementary and Secondary Schools, by Region and State, with Projections:
    Fall 1993 to Fall 2011. In *Projections of Education Statistics to 2011*. Washington,
    DC: National Center for Education Statistics, U.S. Department of Education.
Nechyba, Thomas J. Prospects for achieving equity or adequacy in education: The limits
    of state aid in general equilibrium. In *Helping Children Left Behind: State Aid and
    the Pursuit of Educational Equity*, ed. J. Yinger, 111–143. Cambridge, MA: The MIT
    Press.
The New York Times. 2002. Public Schooling for Profit. Editorial. May 26, p. 4–10.
Odden, Allan. 1999. Improving state school finance systems: New realities create need to re-
    engineer school finance structures. CPRE Occasional Paper Series OP-04. Consortium
    for Policy Research in Education, University of Pennsylvania, Philadelphia, PA.
Odden, Allen R., and Lawrence O. Picus. 1992. *School Finance: A Policy Perspective.* New
    York: McGraw Hill.
O'Sullivan, Arthur. 2001. Limitation on local property taxation: The United States
    experience. In *Property Taxation and Local Government Finance*, ed. W.E. Oates,
    177–200. Cambridge, MA: Lincoln Institute of Land Policy.
Reschovsky, Andrew, and Jennifer Imazeki. 1998. The development of school finance
    formulas to guarantee the provision of adequate education to low-income students.
    In *Developments in School Finance, 1997: Does Money Matter?* ed. W.J. Fowler
    Jr., 121–148. Washington, D.C.: U.S. Department of Education, National Center for
    Educational Statistics.
Reschovsky, Andrew, and Jennifer Imazeki. 2001. Achieving educational adequacy through
    school finance reform. *Journal of Education Finance* **26** (Part 4) (Spring): 373–396.

Robelen, Erik W. 2002. ESEA to boost federal role in education. *Education Week*, January 9.

Ross, Stephen L., and John Yinger. 1999. Sorting and voting: A review of the literature on urban public finance. In *Handbook of Urban and Regional Economics Vol. 3, Applied Urban Economics*, ed. E.S. Mills and P. Cheshire, 2001–2060. Amsterdam: North-Holland.

Rouse, Cecilia. 1998. Private school vouchers and student achievement: An evaluation of the Milwaukee parental choice program. *The Quarterly Journal of Economics* **113**(2) (May): 553–602.

Rouse, Cecilia. 2000. School reform in the 21st century: A look at the effect of class size and school vouchers on the academic achievement of minority students. Industrial Relations Section Working Paper #440. Princeton University, Princeton, NJ.

Sielke, Catherine C. 2001. Funding school infrastructure needs across the states. *Journal of Education Finance* **27** (Part 2) (Fall): 653–662.

Silva, Fabio, and Jon Sonstelie. 1995. Did Serrano cause a decline in school spending? *National Tax Journal* **48**(2): 199–215.

Sonstelie, Jon, Eric Brunner, and Kenneth Ardon. 2000. For Better or For Worse? School Finance Reform in California. Public Policy Institute of California, San Francisco, CA.

Strauss, Robert P., Lori R. Bowes, Mindy S Marks, and Mark R. Plesko. 2000. Improving teacher preparation and selection: lessons from the Pennsylvania experience. *Economics of Education Review* **19**: 387–415.

Wang, Wen. 2003. Appendix C: A guide to state building aid formulas for elementary and secondary education. In *Helping Children Left Behind: State Aid and the Pursuit of Educational Equity*, ed. J. Yinger, 335–366. Cambridge, MA: The MIT Press.

Wyckoff, Paul G. 1995. Capitalization, equalization, and intergovernmental aid. *Public Finance Quarterly* **23**(4): 484–508.

Wyckoff, Paul G. 2001. Capitalization and the incidence of school aid. *Journal of Education Finance* **27**(1) (Summer): 585–607.

Yinger, John, editor. 2003. *Helping Children Left Behind: State Aid and the Pursuit of Educational Equity*. Cambridge, MA: The MIT Press.

Yinger, John. 2020. Capitalization and equalization: The feedback effects of foundation aid for schools. In *Poverty and Proficiency: The Cost of and Demand for Local Public Education*, ed. J. Yinger. New Jersey: World Scientific Publishing. [Chapter 14]

Chapter 12

School Finance Reform: Aid Formulas and Equity Objectives[*]

William Duncombe[‡] and John Yinger[†,§]

[†]*Departments of Public Administration and International Affairs and of Economics, Syracuse University, Syracuse, NY, United States*

[§]*jyinger@maxwell.syr.edu*

State education officials have implemented performance standards, but state education aid has not kept up. By focusing on the relationship between spending and property wealth, most existing aid formulas only partially account for cost differences across districts and, thus, fail to fully promote equity in school performance. This paper shows how to estimate comprehensive educational cost indexes that control for school district inefficiency and include them in state aid formulas. It also simulates for New York the impact of several aid formulas on educational performance and evaluates each formula using several equity criteria. The results indicate that outcome-based foundation formulas can achieve adequacy objectives, but that practical policies to promote vertical equity or wealth neutrality do not yet exist.

1. Introduction

School finance equity has been a central issue of educational policy for decades. This paper explores the potential of several school aid formulas to satisfy the most widely discussed equity objectives. For the most part, the

---

[*]This chapter is reproduced from "School Finance Reform: Aid Formulas and Equity Objectives," *National Tax Journal*, **51**(2), June 1998, pp. 239–262.

[‡]Deceased.

school equity debate has focused on the relationship between a school district's expenditure and its property tax wealth. In keeping with the growing emphasis on performance standards in education, states need to refocus their aid formulas toward the achievement of outcome equity objectives. Because educational costs vary widely across districts, an outcome standard is quite different from an expenditure standard. This paper provides one method for estimating comprehensive educational cost indexes and shows how to include them in state aid formulas designed to achieve particular equity goals.

Educational outcomes are influenced by school management and teaching methods as well as by state aid. Many state policies address these other issues. Although questions of school management and teaching reform are beyond its scope, this paper sheds some light on the role of inefficiency in the provision of education services. Inefficiency can prevent a district from reaching minimum outcome standards, even with an outcome-based foundation formula. We illustrate how inefficiency could be taken into account in aid system design without providing incentives for districts to become more inefficient. The analysis is illustrated with detailed school aid simulations for New York state school districts.

2. Aid Formulas and Equity Objectives

Education in the United States is predominantly a local function, but most states fund a large share of local school budgets through intergovernmental aid.[1] Although many categorical aid programs exist, most school aid is distributed through general-purpose aid to support the basic operation of schools. Our focus is on the design of such basic operating aid. In particular, we explain the link between alternative aid formulas and various equity objectives, which are reviewed in Berne and Stiefel (1984) and Monk (1990).

2.1. *Foundation Aid*

The most widely used form of education aid is a foundation grant, which is designed to ensure educational adequacy, defined as a situation in which all districts provide at least some minimum level of education. In its simplest form, a foundation grant provides the difference between the state-selected minimum per pupil spending level, E^*, and the amount of revenue a district

---

[1] In Michigan and Wisconsin, for example, state funding recently increased from about one-third to about two-thirds of local education budgets (Kearney, 1995; Reschovsky, 1994).

can raise at a tax rate that the state decides is fair, t^*. Let V_i stand for the property tax base in district i. Then the district's **expenditure-based foundation grant** per pupil is defined by

$$A_i = E^* - t^* V_i = E^* \left(1 - \frac{V_i}{V^*} \right) = E^*(1 - v_i) \tag{1}$$

where $V^* = E^*/t^*$ is the property value above which a district receives no aid and $v_i = V_i/V^*$. If taken literally, equation (1) implies that districts with tax bases above V^* actually receive negative aid. This formula is usually modified in practice, through minimum aid amounts or hold-harmless clauses, so that all districts receive some aid, thereby reducing the equalizing power of the formula. Moreover, a foundation grant usually is accompanied by a requirement that each district levy a tax rate of at least t^*; otherwise, some districts might not provide the minimum acceptable spending level, E^*. New York and Illinois are notable exceptions; see Miner (1991) and Downes and McGuire (1994).

Even if one accepts the objective of guaranteeing a minimum level of education, traditional foundation grants are flawed because they do not systematically adjust for educational costs. In practice, some state aid formulas include educational cost adjustments (Gold *et al.*, 1992), but these adjustments inevitably are *ad hoc* and incomplete. In other words, they may ensure a minimum level of spending but not of educational outcomes, such as student learning, thereby leaving higher cost districts at lower outcomes than other districts with the same property value. Because outcomes are what parents and voters care about, they are a more appropriate target of equalization. A less central problem with a standard foundation formula is that wealth is an imperfect measure of a school district's revenue-raising capacity. Districts differ in revenue-raising capacity because of (1) differences in income and (2) differences in their ability to export some of their tax burden to non-residents. Because it does not explicitly recognize the role of exporting, wealth is an imperfect measure of revenue-raising capacity.[2]

As shown by Ladd and Yinger (1994), these two problems can be solved through the use of an educational cost index and a more general measure of revenue-raising capacity that accounts for exporting. Suppose educational outcomes in district i can be measured with an index, S_i, and that S^* is

---

[2] Under some circumstances, wealth may be a reasonable approximation of a more general measure. In the case of Minnesota cities, for example, Ladd, Reschovsky, and Yinger (1991) found the correlation between wealth and a general measure of capacity to be 0.92. In New York, however, the correlation is only 0.7.

the minimum acceptable value of this index. Moreover, let C_i be the amount the district must spend to obtain one unit of S, so that $E_i = C_i S_i$ (ignoring efficiency for the moment). Now if, $\bar{C}$ is the cost of S in the average district, then we can redefine E^* as the amount that a district with average costs would have to spend to obtain the minimum acceptable level of educational outcomes, namely, $\bar{C} S^*$. Finally, let R_i be a general measure of district i's revenue-raising capacity.

To bring all districts up to S^* at an acceptable tax burden on their residents, the **outcome-based** foundation formula should be

$$A_i = E^* \left(\frac{C_i}{\bar{C}} - \frac{R_i}{R^*} \right) = E^*(c_i - r_i) \tag{2}$$

where $c_i = C_i/\bar{C}$ is the cost index, $r_i = R_i/R^*$ is a revenue capacity index, and R^* is the revenue-raising capacity (set by state policymakers) at which a district **with average costs** would receive no aid. As with equation (1), raising E^* to an extremely high level would, at great cost, result in an equal educational output in every district, and allowing negative grants would boost the equalizing impact of the program.

As discussed earlier, some school districts are more efficient than others. The consideration of efficiency complicates matters because a district might receive enough resources to achieve S^* given its costs and still fall short because it is inefficient. All else equal, inefficient districts not only must spend more to achieve any given level of S but also are likely to select a lower level of S, because efficiency raises the effective price of educational services. This issue is fundamentally different from the issues of costs and revenue-raising capacity, however, because it is inappropriate to compensate a district for its inefficiency, or for anything else within its control. Even though children are penalized for living in inefficient districts, any state program that gives aid based on inefficiency would undermine a district's incentive to provide education as efficiently as possible.

Our resolution of this issue is to define an efficiency index, k_i, with a maximum value of 1.0 in an efficient district; we then employ a foundation formula that gives each district enough resources to achieve S^* so long as its efficiency index is at or above k^*, a state-determined minimum acceptable level. To be specific, this formula sets $E^* = S^* C_i / k^*$.[3] If eligible for this

---

[3]Strictly speaking, setting k^* is equivalent to altering the base of the cost index. Because the cost index is serving only to translate S^* into its spending equivalent, however, we see no reason to use a cost-index base other than the cost of the average district.

foundation aid, districts with $k_i > k^*$ will receive somewhat more aid than they need to reach S^*, and districts with $k_i < k^*$ will not achieve S^* unless they become more efficient. To protect students in these inefficient districts, the state must place additional requirements on these districts in the form of either management improvements or a higher local sacrifice.

2.2. *Power-Equalizing Aid*

A few states use some form of a "power-equalizing" aid formula, which was popularized by Coons, Clune, and Sugarman (1970). This approach promotes vertical equity in the sense that it lessens disparities in educational outcomes across districts by linking spending to tax effort. Unlike a lump-sum foundation grant, a power-equalizing grant comes in the form of a matching rate, with a higher rate for lower wealth districts. To be specific, an **expenditure-based** power-equalizing grant takes the following form:

$$A_i = E_i \left(1 - \theta \frac{V_i}{\bar{V}}\right) = E_i \left(1 - \frac{V_i}{V^*}\right) = E_i(1 - v_i). \tag{3}$$

This formula differs from the foundation formula (equation (1)) in that it is based on actual spending, E_i, not minimum acceptable spending, E^*. The matching rate, that is, the state's share of total spending, is the expression in parentheses. The local share, which is the local "price" of educational spending, is one minus the state share, or simply v_i. As before, V^* is a policy parameter that indicates the property value at which a district receives no aid. In this case, however, V^* is determined by the size of the aid budget. An equivalent formulation, the first one in equation (3), is that the budget determines a parameter, θ, which is multiplied by the ratio of V_i to the property value in the average district, $\bar{V}$.

A standard power-equalizing grant is designed to help equalize educational spending. As shown by Ladd and Yinger (1994), it can be transformed to help equalize educational outcomes. Moreover, property value can be replaced with a more general measure of revenue-raising capacity. With these two changes, an **outcome-based** power-equalizing grant is

$$A_i = S_i \left(\frac{C_i}{\bar{C}} - \theta \frac{R_i}{\bar{R}}\right) = S_i \left(\frac{C_i}{\bar{C}} - \frac{R_i}{R^*}\right)$$

$$= S_i(c_i - r_i) = E_i \left(1 - \frac{r_i}{c_i}\right). \tag{4}$$

Strictly speaking, equation (4) implies that some districts will receive negative aid. This negative aid can be eliminated by lowering the value of θ

(or, equivalently, raising the value of R^*), which increases the cost of the program, or by placing arbitrary floors on the matching rate, which weakens the program's equalizing impact.

Because it lowers the price of all spending, including wasteful spending, this power-equalizing formula has the disadvantage that it rewards district inefficiency. In principle, this problem can be avoided by basing the grant on spending adjusted for efficiency, not actual spending. Let k_i be a measure of efficiency in district i. Then adjusted spending equals $E_i k_i / k^*$, where, as before, k^* is minimum acceptable efficiency. Unfortunately, this approach is not yet practical because no method for calculating a district's efficiency is well known enough to be acceptable in the calculation of a district's aid amount. Moreover, as shown by Duncombe and Yinger (1997), changes in aid may alter a district's efficiency, so that efficiency and the appropriate aid amount must be simultaneously determined. Solving these problems is beyond the scope of this paper, so we simulate the effects of power-equalizing formulas that have no adjustment for efficiency.

One important equity standard is **wealth neutrality**, which is defined as a situation in which education, measured by spending per pupil or, more appropriately, by educational outcomes, is not correlated with district wealth. As first explained by Feldstein (1975), a standard power-equalizing grant helps equalize educational spending, but it does not lead, except by coincidence, to wealth neutrality. Although it ensures that districts with the same tax rate receive the same revenue, it cannot rule out the possibility that higher wealth districts systematically select higher (or lower) tax rates than low-wealth districts. Moreover, Feldstein showed that this problem could be solved by estimating the relevant behavioral elasticities and incorporating them into a grant formula.

We do not think this is practical. As an alternative, we propose building on the Feldstein intuition by adding a new policy parameter to the standard power-equalizing formula. This parameter alters the impact of wealth on the matching rate, and it can be adjusted over time until wealth neutrality is achieved. This parameter, which we call α, appears in the formula as follows[4]:

$$A_i = E_i(1 - (v_i)^\alpha). \tag{5}$$

[4]The Feldstein approach builds on a quasi-behavioral regression. A detailed comparison of our approach with that of Feldstein using expenditures or outcomes is available from the authors upon request.

For example, if α is set at 1.0 (the standard power-equalizing formula) and the state falls short of wealth neutrality after the formula is implemented, then the next year the value of α would be raised slightly, say, to 1.1. This process would be continued until spending and wealth were not correlated. Eliminating the correlation between spending and wealth does not imply that all districts spend the same amount per pupil. In fact, wide variation in spending within a wealth class, including spending below any definition of adequacy, is consistent with wealth neutrality.

The grant formula in equation (5) focuses on educational spending. The appropriate switch to educational outcomes can be accomplished by applying the Feldstein approach to equation (4) instead of to equation (3). The most straightforward way to do this is to use v_i as a measure of r_i and to insert the policy parameter, now called β, as follows:

$$A_i = E_i \left(1 - \left(\frac{v_i}{c_i} \right)^{\beta} \right). \tag{6}$$

As before, β could be adjusted over time until the correlation between S_i and v_i equaled zero. Once the role of educational costs has been recognized, it does not make sense to limit the notion of "neutrality" to the revenue side of the budget, and a more general equity objective is fiscal-health neutrality, which exists when educational outcomes are not correlated with a district's fiscal health, defined here as v_i/c_i.

3. An Empirical Analysis of Educational Cost, Inefficiency, and Demand for New York State

Our simulations of various aid formulas are based on models of both the costs of producing educational outcomes and community decisions about these outcomes. This section describes our models in general terms and explains how we estimate education cost and demand models for 631 school districts in New York state in 1991.[5] Table 1 provides descriptive statistics.

---

[5] There were 695 school districts in New York in 1991. Due to missing observations, including New York City and Yonkers, the sample was limited to 631 observations. Except for these two notable omissions, the sample appears representative of the major regions in New York State.

Table 1   Descriptive statistics for cost and demand models (New York school districts in 1991, $n = 631$).

Variable	Mean	Standard deviation	Minimum	Maximum
Cost model:				
Dependent variable:				
Log of per pupil expenditures	8.662	0.286	8.060	10.142
Independent variables:				
PEP scores (average percent of students above SRP)	94.243	3.787	64.500	100.000
Percent receiving Regents diploma	40.437	13.072	0.000	75.385
Percent non-dropouts	97.593	1.835	88.100	100.000
Log of teacher salaries	10.108	0.122	9.558	10.461
Log of enrollment	7.377	0.879	4.220	10.741
Percent children in poverty	11.569	7.453	0.258	38.040
Percent female-headed households	8.788	2.712	2.464	34.684
Percent handicapped students	10.638	3.371	1.626	30.680
Percent severely handicapped students	4.488	2.120	0.000	14.570
Persons with limited English proficiency (percent)	0.987	1.272	0.000	11.957
DEA index (percent)[a]	66.462	15.765	19.488	100.000
Estimated efficiency index (percent)[a]	69.050	9.780	45.469	100.000
Demand model:				
Dependent variable:				
Index of educational outcomes	4,914.190	1,547.250	810.710	10,284.810
Independent variables:				
Log of median family income	10.554	0.313	9.960	11.631
Ratio of operating aid to median income	0.039	0.025	0.001	0.178
Ratio of other lump-sum aid to median income	0.006	0.008	0.000	0.082
Ratio of matching aid to median income	0.006	0.005	0.000	0.045
Log of tax share	−0.623	0.464	−2.702	1.071
Log of efficiency index	−0.440	0.261	−1.635	0.000
Percent owner-occupied housing	75.362	10.158	36.499	95.381
Relative percent of adults with college education[b]	0.000	5.737	−17.146	22.800
Instruments:				
District population (thousands)	15.634	21.853	0.544	328.123
Population density	1,093.060	1,998.910	2.051	16,330.980
Percent employees managers/professionals	26.445	9.262	11.972	63.067
City district (1 = yes)	0.092	0.289	0.000	1.000
Hourly manufacturing wage (production workers)	12.146	1.853	7.500	17.965
1990 county population (thousands)	388.939	457.034	5.279	1,321.860

Notes: [a]Efficient districts have an index of 100. This is based on DEA estimates for the three outcome variables listed and per pupil expenditures.
[b]To remove collinearity with income, this variable is the residual from a regression of the percent of adults with a college education on median income.

Sources: New York State Department of Education, Comprehensive Assessment Report, Basic Education Data System and Fiscal Profile, and National Center for Education Statistics, School District Data Book.

3.1. *Cost Model: Theory and Results*

The key step in creating outcome-based aid formulas is estimating cost models for education and using the estimates to construct education cost indexes. Our cost model borrows from the large literature in educational production and public sector costs.[6] Expenditures (E) in a school district depend on the level of outputs (G), such as reading or math classes, the district chooses to provide; the prices (P) that it pays for inputs, such as teachers; and unobserved district characteristics (ε):

$$E = c(G, P, \varepsilon). \tag{7}$$

Bringing outcomes into educational cost functions draws from the long recognized fact that educational outcomes are a function of educational outputs and of "environmental" factors, such as the number of pupils in a district and the share of pupils who live in poverty. In symbols, educational outcomes, S, can be written as follows:

$$S = f(G, N, F, D), \tag{8}$$

where N is the number of pupils in the district, F represents students' family backgrounds, and D represents other student characteristics. Thus, for example, the same G per student might lead to a higher S per student in a middle-sized district than in a very small or a very large one.

Solving equation (8) for G and substituting the result into equation (7) yields a cost function for outcomes:

$$E = g(S, P, N, F, D, \varepsilon). \tag{9}$$

In short, the spending required to provide a given level of student achievement is a function of factor prices, environmental factors, and unobserved district characteristics. A district's relative cost is defined as the extent to which input prices and environmental factors require it to pay more than other districts to receive the same level of S. In terms of equation (9), a cost index is based on the impact of $(P, N, F,$ and $D)$ on E, holding S and ε constant.

---

[6]The literature on education production functions and costs is reviewed in Bridge, Judd, and Moock (1979), Hanushek (1986), Cohn and Geske (1990), and Monk (1990). Several recent production function studies include Ferguson (1991) and Ferguson and Ladd (1996). For research on educational cost functions, see Ratcliffe, Riddle, and Yinger (1990), Downes and Pogue (1994), and Duncombe, Ruggiero, and Yinger (1996).

A district's approved operating expense (AOE) per pupil, which is provided by the New York State Department of Education, is our measure of expenditure. The AOE includes salaries and fringe benefits of teachers and other school staff, other instructional expenditure, and all other non-transportation expenditure related to operation and maintenance of schools. Our input price variable is a teacher salary index. This index adjusts for differences in teacher experience, education, and certification to reflect differences in the cost of teachers of equivalent quality. Because of the potential endogeneity of teachers' salaries, which are set by district administrators, we base this index on salaries of teachers with five or fewer years of experience, and we treat this wage variable as endogenous.[7]

Selecting educational outcomes is clearly difficult and controversial. We began by selecting educational outcome variables that seemed reasonable based on previous literature and that appeared to be valued by voters, as indicated by a correlation with such voter demand variables as income and tax share.[8] These criteria led us to reject average achievement test scores as outcome variables, but supported the use of three other measures. The first is the average percentage of students performing above a standard reference point on Pupil Evaluation Program, (PEP), tests given in New York to all third- and sixth-grade students in reading and math. The second measure is the percentage of students receiving a Regents diploma upon graduation from high school. Regents diplomas are given to students who pass standardized tests given by the state to high school students. The third measure is the percentage of students not dropping out of school before their scheduled graduation, which is the inverse of the dropout rate.

---

[7]Salaries and teacher characteristics are collected in a self-reporting survey called the "Personnel Master File" of the "Basic Education Data System" (BEDS). Salaries were adjusted to control for teacher characteristics, such as years of experience, level of education, type of certification, and tenure. A number of districts were missing information on salary levels. We filled in for these missing observations by assuming that a district had the same average adjusted salary level as other districts of the same type (e.g., suburban or rural) in its county. As instruments for teacher salaries, we use hourly wages for production workers in manufacturing at the county level and 1990 county population.

[8]For a review of earlier studies and discussion of the outcome selection process, see Duncombe, Ruggiero, and Yinger (1996). A variable was considered to be correlated with demand factors if the R-squared of a regression of that variable on those factors was 0.1 or higher. We also checked our selections using factor analysis, which indicated that the variables we identified explained most of the variation in the set of outcome variables in our data set.

These three variables make an appealing package because they reflect a key trade-off that every school district faces in designing its programs, that between bringing up the bottom or raising the top of the achievement distribution.

Since many studies find that expenditure per pupil is a U-shaped function of enrollment, we include a district's enrollment and its square as environmental variables. The studies cited earlier that estimate cost indexes also found that student or family characteristics can be important environmental variables. Thus, our analysis of district costs examines the percentage of children in poverty, the percentage of households with a female single parent, the percentage of children with limited English proficiency, and the percentage of students with severe disabilities (requiring special services out of the regular classroom at least 60 percent of the school day).[9]

We estimate our educational cost model in log-linear form, with the outcome measures, the efficiency index (discussed below), and the price of labor treated as endogenous. The results are reported in Table 2. The specification performs well. The outcome measures all have positive coefficients, as expected; two of the three coefficients are highly significant statistically; and the third has a *t*-statistic of 1.62. The efficiency index has a negative coefficient and is statistically significant; as expected, higher efficiency is associated with lower expenditures. Moreover, five of the seven cost variables have a statistically significant coefficient with the expected sign. The teacher salary variable, child poverty rate, percentage of households that are female-headed, and percentage of students with limited English proficiency are positively related to expenditure and significantly different from zero at least at the ten percent level (with a one-sided test). Both enrollment variables are statistically significant and indicate a U-shaped per pupil expenditure function. The percentage of students with a severe handicap has the expected sign but is not significant, probably because some special education expenditures are not included in AOE.

The cost model in Table 2 is used to construct a comprehensive educational cost index. This index indicates the amount a district must spend, relative to the state average, to obtain a given level of service

---

[9]The source of most of these variables is the *1990 Census* as reported in the "School District Data Book" (Washington, DC: U.S. Bureau of the Census and the National Center for Education Statistics, 1994). The remaining variables come from the New York Department of Education's BEDS.

Table 2 Educational cost and demand model results, New York school Districts, 1991.[a]

Variables	Coefficient	t-Statistic
Cost model:		
Intercept	−4.9550	−1.53
PEP scores (average percent above standard reference point)*	5.1106	2.50
Percent non-dropouts*	4.4757	1.62
Percent receiving Regents diploma*	1.3449	3.19
DEA efficiency index (percent)*	−1.1670	−4.87
Log of teacher salaries*	0.6487	1.57
Log of enrollment	−0.5680	−3.54
Square of log of enrollment	0.0345	3.44
Percent children in poverty	1.0109	3.93
Percent female-headed households	2.2261	3.85
Percent severely handicapped students	0.8584	1.29
Limited English proficiency (percent)	4.0525	2.65
SSE	34.58	
Adjusted R-square	0.31	
Demand model:		
Intercept	−1.2552	−1.45
Log of median family income	0.8947	9.65
Ratio of operating aid to median income	3.4337	2.45
Ratio of other lump-sum aid to median income	3.1814	1.38
Ratio of matching aid to median income	−7.8947	−1.53
Log of tax share	−0.3133	−6.47
Log of DEA efficiency index*	0.4637	2.10
Percent owner-occupied housing	0.2148	1.39
Relative percent of adults with college education	0.1591	0.60
n	631	
SSE	37.05	
Adjusted R-square	0.47	

Notes: [a]Cost and demand models estimated with linear 2SLS regression; variables marked with an asterisk are treated as endogenous. The dependent variables are the logarithms of per pupil operating expenditures in the cost model and the outcome index for the demand model. The outcome index is based on the three outcome variables in the cost model weighted by their regression coefficients.

quality, holding efficiency constant.[10] A district with a high cost index has a high underlying cost of hiring teachers (the opportunity wage), unfavorable environmental factors (such as concentrated student poverty), or both. This index has a range of 74 to 261, with a standard deviation of 19. Seventy-five percent of the districts have indexes below 105, and 75 percent have indexes above 89.

3.2. *Measuring Inefficiency*

One key element of unobserved district characteristics, ε, is school-district inefficiency, which, like relatively high costs, can lead to relatively high spending. Without controlling for inefficiency, cost adjustments in aid formulas may inappropriately reward inefficient as well as higher-cost districts. Our strategy is to measure inefficiency directly, so that our cost indexes — and aid formulas — can be adjusted to avoid this problem.

Our measure of inefficiency is based on data envelopment analysis (DEA). This non-parametric programming technique compares the spending of each district with the spending of other districts that deliver the same quality of public services. In this context, the quality of public services is measured by the S variables included in equation (9). A district's inefficiency is measured by the extent to which it spends more than its comparison districts. This inefficiency can arise either because the district uses too many inputs to produce the output (called technical inefficiency) or because it uses the wrong combination of inputs given output prices (called input-allocative inefficiency). For a more detailed discussion of this DEA measure, see Duncombe, Ruggiero, and Yinger (1996) or Ruggiero (1996). A cost "efficiency" index was constructed for each school district in New York State. This index has a value of one (1.0) for a perfectly "efficient" district. The average "efficiency" score is 0.66, 23 districts (4 percent) have an index of 1.0, and 350 districts (55 percent) have an index below 0.7.

---

[10]To be specific, we multiply regression coefficients by actual district values for each cost factor (and by the state average for outcomes and efficiency) to construct a measure of the expenditure each district must make to provide average quality services given average inefficiency. Similar procedures (without the efficiency variable) are used by Ratcliffe, Riddle, and Yinger (1990), Ladd and Yinger (1991), Downes and Pogue (1994), and Duncombe, Ruggiero, and Yinger (1996). Since the price of labor is treated as endogenous in the cost model, a predicted wage is used to construct the cost index. The predicted wage is based on the predicted value of a first-stage regression between the price of labor and all exogenous and instrumental variables used in the cost model.

The word "efficiency" is in quotation marks here because this DEA measure reflects factors in addition to efficiency. In fact, it reflects any factor that influences the relationship between observed S and E, including unobserved public service outcomes, cost variables, and a district's past decisions about education. Thus, the DEA variable inevitably duplicates some information in the cost model, and including it in the cost equation may cause multicollinearity. In fact, however, the coefficients of most of these variables are estimated with precision (that is, they are statistically significant at conventional levels), so the DEA variable can be included in our cost equation (and, on similar grounds, in our demand equation) to avoid potential bias from the omission of a control for efficiency. Finally, any efficiency measure might be endogenous; some of the same factors that influence decisions about spending might also influence decisions that lead districts to act in an efficient manner. To account for this possibility, we treat our DEA variables as endogenous, with instruments drawn from the public choice literature.[11]

In the aid simulations, we need to calculate the district expenditure associated with a given outcome level. The DEA variable cannot be used directly in this calculation, because the conversion of our simulated outcome, S, into expenditure, E, requires a measure of productive efficiency alone, not an index that may reflect other things. In symbols, $E_i = S_i c_i / k_i$, where k is an efficiency index. To estimate this efficiency index, we regress the DEA measure on the cost factors in equation (9); demand factors (discussed below), which control for omitted educational outcomes; and public choice factors (Duncombe and Yinger, 1997). The efficiency index is the predicted value from this equation, holding cost and demand factors at the state average while allowing public choice factors to vary across districts. The resulting index is rescaled so its highest value is 1.0 (for perfect efficiency). The mean of this efficiency index is higher, and its standard deviation lower, than that of the DEA measure.

---

[11] Identifying instruments for the efficiency index is difficult. While there is a large literature on bureaucratic behavior (Niskanen, 1975; Leibenstein, 1978), there is little associated empirical literature. The bureaucratic models suggest that greater inefficiency will be associated with larger and wealthier school districts, those facing less competition, and those with poorer performance incentives for their employees. Income is already used as an instrument. Our new instruments include total district population and population density, the occupational mix of the district (the percent of total private employees that are managers or professionals), and whether a district faces a budget referendum. City districts in New York do not have to submit any portion of their budget to voter approval.

3.3. *Demand Model: Theory and Results*

One of the issues that arises in estimating equation (9) is that service quality, S, is clearly endogenous; communities make decisions about service quality and spending simultaneously. Moreover, one cannot simulate the impact of a new aid program on educational outcomes without understanding how such outcomes are determined. Thus, a formal analysis of the determinants of the demand for S is central to the objectives of this paper.

We draw on the large literature on the demand for educational outcomes (Inman, 1979; Rubinfeld, 1987; Ladd and Yinger, 1991). In particular, we employ the median voter model, in which a district's demand for educational outcomes, as determined through voting, is a function of the median voter's aggregate income, TY; her tax price, TP; efficiency; and various preference variables, R. Following much of the literature, we specify a constant elasticity demand function:

$$S = TY^{\theta} TP^{\mu} DEA^{\gamma} R^{V}. \tag{10}$$

Our demand model uses an index of the three outcomes discussed previously as the dependent variable (Table 1). The weights for these outcomes are derived directly from the cost model.[12] Preference variables include community characteristics, such as the percentage of adults who graduated from college and the percentage of households living in owner-occupied housing, that might affect voting outcomes.[13]

Following the literature (especially Ladd and Yinger, 1991), we define the tax price, TP, as tax share, τ, multiplied by the marginal expenditure for educational services. We measure τ with the ratio of median housing value to total property value per pupil. Marginal expenditure equals marginal cost divided by the efficiency index to reflect wasted spending. Assuming constant returns to scale with respect to S, average cost equals marginal cost, and the educational cost index from the cost model can be used as a measure of marginal cost. In estimating the demand model, we split marginal

---

[12]Under the assumption of constant costs per unit of output, the coefficients of the cost equation can be interpreted as the weight that voters place on each output variable. The state aid formula requires $S^{*}C_{i}$, to be the amount a district must spend to obtain the outcome level S^{*}. Thus, our outcome index S has to be rescaled. See Duncombe and Yinger (1997) for a proof of the first proposition and an explanation of the scaling process.

[13]Because of a high correlation between the percent of college graduates and median income, we used the residual from a regression of percent college on median income as the college variable.

expenditure into two pieces. The first piece is τ multiplied by the cost index and the second is the DEA index.

Aggregate income (TY) equals the median voter's income plus her share of state aid:

$$TY = Y + \tau A = Y \left(1 + \tau \frac{A}{Y} \right) \tag{11}$$

where Y is median income, A is aid per pupil, and τ is the median voter's tax share. Because the term in parentheses is close to one in value, this form can be approximated using the aid-income index ($\tau A/Y$) in unlogged form. New York, like most states, has several education aid programs; together, they fund about 40 percent of school district budgets. The aid distributed by formula (over 95 percent of the total) can be divided into lump-sum and matching grants. The largest program, basic operating aid, is a lump-sum, non-categorical, foundation-type grant, which constitutes 60 percent of total state aid and provided \$3.05 billion in 1991. We include this grant separately in the demand model since it is closest in design to the general operating aid programs we simulate. In addition, we combine several smaller lump-sum grants into a second aid variable[14] and several matching aid programs into a third aid variable. Because they are not open ended, the matching grants cannot be expressed as an adjustment to the tax price.[15]

We estimate our demand model in log-linear form, with the DEA index treated as endogenous. Based on the form in equation (11), the aid variables are not expressed in natural logarithms. Following standard practice for percentages, neither are the preference variables. The results are in Table 2. The income elasticity for education is estimated to be somewhat below unity, 0.89. Our estimate is higher than that found in most past research

---

[14]The other lump-sum grants include aid for large and small city students with compensatory education needs (PCEN and PSCEN), aid for educationally related support services (ERSSA), Attendance Improvement–Dropout Prevention Aid, and Limited English Proficiency Aid. Since some of these grants are for higher cost students, it was important to include them in the model. In total, these aid programs provided approximately \$0.6 billion in aid in 1991.

[15]Aid programs included in the matching aid variable include Excess Cost Aid and High Cost Aid for handicapped students and High Tax Aid for districts with relatively high tax effort. The two aid types for handicapped students provide aid to districts based on the actual district operating expenditure and a weighted pupil count of handicapped students. While these aid programs are not traditional matching grants, they are not purely lump-sum since they can be affected by district behavior. Matching aid given by New York State for transportation, buildings, and computer equipment is not included in our analysis since we are focusing solely on non-transportation operating expenditure.

(Inman, 1979), possibly due to our controls for costs and efficiency.[16] The elasticity for the operating aid variable is 3.4. This result is consistent with the so-called "flypaper" effect. In the average district, a $1 increase in state aid is associated with a $0.33 increase in educational expenditure, whereas expenditure rises by only $0.10 when district income increases by $1. The other aid variables are not statistically significant.

The price elasticity for education, μ, is estimated to be -0.31, which is in line with past research on education (Inman, 1979). In addition, the coefficient of the DEA index is positive and statistically significant; as expected, higher efficiency lowers the effective price facing the median voter and increases demand for S. The preference variables are positively related to educational outcomes, but are not statistically significant.

4. School Aid Simulations for New York

To evaluate alternative aid formulas on the basis of various equity criteria, we used our results to simulate the choices school districts in New York would make if several different aid formulas were implemented. We are particularly concerned, of course, with their choice of educational outcome, S. While simulations have been performed on individual aid systems (Megdal, 1983; Rothstein, 1992), our paper represents one of the first attempts to assess the implications of different school aid formulas for several equity standards.

4.1. *Simulation Methodology*

The first step in our simulation is to construct the aid formulas presented previously. Since foundation aid is exogenous to local behavior, aid can be allocated prior to estimating districts' behavioral responses. Aid given according to equation (1), for example, depends only on a district's tax base. Power-equalizing aid formulas (equations (5) and (6)) yield matching rates, not aid amounts. All of the aid simulations are adjusted to keep total state spending approximately at the 1991 level of actual state operating aid and other lump-sum aid, namely, $3.65 billion or $2,427 per pupil.[17]

---

[16]When we estimate a median voter model without the cost index or the efficiency index, the income elasticity drops to 0.5. This result is consistent with the predictions of Schwab and Zampelli (1987), who highlight the potential downward bias in the income elasticity when costs are omitted from the tax price.

[17]For the aid systems without negative aid or for all power-equalizing aid systems, an iterative process was used to adjust V^* (or R^*) to reach approximate budget neutrality. Aid budgets were kept within three percent of the original state operating budget in 1991.

To simulate service outcomes under different aid formulas, the coefficients of the demand regression (Table 2) are multiplied by actual district data for median income, tax price, efficiency, matching aid, and preference variables. In addition, we include the estimated residual in the simulation to pick up district-specific effects not captured by our demand model. For each foundation plan, the new aid-income ratio is multiplied by the operating aid elasticity to simulate the income effect of the grant. The aid ratio for other lump-sum aid is set to zero because we want to simulate the distribution of all general lump-sum aid through one foundation formula. For power-equalizing grants, the aid-income ratios for both lump-sum aid variables are set to zero, which is equivalent to eliminating lump-sum aid, and the estimated price elasticity is used to simulate the effects of the new matching rate. These steps yield a simulated value of S for each grant formula. The value of E is found by multiplying S by the cost index and dividing it by the estimated efficiency index, k (not the DEA index). The estimated matching aid amount is found by multiplying E by the matching rate.

We carry out simulations (a) comparing lump-sum (foundation) and matching (power-equalizing) grants (b) with and without negative aid and (c) based on expenditure or outcome as the object of equalization. Outcome-based formulas are constructed using both property wealth and revenue-raising capacity. Foundation formulas are tested for three different foundation levels: the 25th, 50th, and 75th percentiles of the 1991 expenditure or outcome distribution. These foundation levels correspond to E^* (for expenditure) or S^* (for outcome) in the aid formulas. The foundation formulas also set k^*, the minimum acceptable efficiency level, at the 75th percentile of the current efficiency distribution, as defined by k, not by the DEA measure. Power-equalizing formulas are constructed for seven values of α in equation (5) (or β in equation (6)) to determine how much the standard power-equalizing matching rate formula needs to be dampened or accentuated to achieve wealth (or fiscal-health) neutrality. For comparative purposes, we also include the simplest of all aid plans — a flat grant per pupil. If an aid plan does not do much better at equalizing than a flat grant, then the costs associated with implementing a more complex aid system are probably not worth it.

4.2. Simulation Results

The distribution of aid for various aid formulas is presented in Table 3. Three themes emerge from this table. First, systems that allow for negative aid permit more redistribution than those that do not. For example, the aid

Table 3 Distribution of aid by type of aid system[a] New York school districts in 1991 percentiles of the aid distribution.

Aid system	95th Percentile	75th Percentile	Median	25th Percentile	5th Percentile
Present aid system	$4,135	$3,545	$3,066	$2,106	$921
Foundation plans:					
Expenditure based:					
Negative aid					
$E^* = $ 25th percentile	$3,891	$3,560	$3,153	$2,024	−$1,761
$E^* = $ median	$4,248	$3,837	$3,331	$1,926	−$2,786
$E^* = $ 75th percentile	$5,081	$4,481	$3,744	$1,697	−$5,169
No negative aid					
$E^* = $ 25th percentile	$3,790	$3,421	$2,967	$1,707	$0
$E^* = $ median	$4,084	$3,609	$3,026	$1,406	$0
$E^* = $ 75th percentile	$4,740	$4,010	$3,112	$619	$0
Outcome based (using property values):					
Negative aid					
$S^* = $ 25th percentile	$4,206	$3,302	$2,540	$1,430	−$1,852
$S^* = $ median	$5,081	$3,728	$2,814	$1,009	−$4,117
$S^* = $ 75th percentile	$6,044	$4,311	$3,112	$567	−$7,095
No negative aid					
$S^* = $ 25th percentile	$4,074	$3,025	$2,334	$1,027	$0
$S^* = $ median	$4,690	$3,308	$2,239	$0	$0
$S^* = $ 75th percentile	$5,324	$3,402	$2,005	$0	$0
Outcome based (using revenue raising capacity):					
Negative aid					
$S^* = $ 25th percentile	$4,293	$3,287	$2,650	$1,678	−$453
$S^* = $ median	$5,179	$3,867	$2,958	$1,524	−$1,937
$S^* = $ 75th percentile	$6,180	$4,444	$3,277	$1,335	−$3,540
No negative aid					
$S^* = $ 25th percentile	$4,219	$3,189	$2,540	$1,503	$0
$S^* = $ median	$4,986	$3,578	$2,630	$1,048	$0
$S^* = $ 75th percentile	$5,762	$3,938	$2,615	$307	$0
Power-equalizing plans[b]:					
Expenditure based:					
Negative aid	$5,850	$4,359	$3,459	$2,114	−$5,428
No negative aid	$5,033	$3,752	$2,906	$1,058	$0
Outcome based (using property values):					
Negative aid	$5,993	$4,242	$3,272	$1,876	−$5,288
No negative aid	$5,269	$3,610	$2,696	$732	$0
Outcome based (using revenue raising capacity):					
Negative aid	$6,942	$4,343	$3,325	$2,208	−$2,674
No negative aid	$6,399	$3,949	$2,894	$1,654	$0

Notes: [a]All plans are adjusted to have approximately the same budget as 1991 operating and other lump-sum aid — $3.65 billion.
[b]For comparison purposes, the value of α (or β) is held at one; see the text.

per pupil received by the five percent of districts deemed most needy by a
particular formula is up to $700 higher with negative aid than without it.
Second, for foundation plans, increasing the value of E^* (or of S^*) raises
the extent of redistribution, but the impact of such an increase is greater if
there is negative aid. Third, in both foundation and power-equalizing plans,
switching from an expenditure-based to an outcome-based formula tends
to increase redistribution. For example, the neediest districts receive about
$1,000 more per pupil with the most generous outcome-based foundation
plans than with the comparable expenditure-based plan. This table hides
another feature of these simulations, namely, that aid to specific districts may
be quite different in two plans with similar implications for redistribution.

To explore the impacts of the various plans in more detail. Tables 4
through 7 show how each plan performs according to five different equity
standards. Tables 4 and 5 present results for foundation plans (with and
without negative aid), and Tables 6 and 7 present results for power-equalizing
plans (with and without negative aid). The absolute equity standard in the
first two columns is the share of the outcome gap below an absolute standard
closed by each aid plan. The first column sets the absolute standard at the
current median S, and the second sets it at the current 25th percentile
of S. The outcome gap is defined as the weighted average difference, across
districts with outcomes below the absolute standard, between the actual
district outcome and the absolute standard. In this definition, the weights
reflect the number of students in each district. We calculate the gap for our
new aid formulas and the gap for actual aid formulas in 1991 and estimate
the percent of the existing gap that would be closed by the new formulas.
Thus, the entries in these two columns indicate how far each aid formula
goes toward bringing all students up to the stated absolute standard.

In addition, these tables use the Gini coefficient (column 3) as a vertical
equity standard, the elasticity of outcomes with respect to property wealth
(column 4) as a measure of wealth neutrality, and the elasticity of outcomes
with respect to fiscal health (column 5) as a measure of fiscal-health
neutrality. A higher percentage indicates a higher ranking for the two
absolute standards, whereas a value closer to zero indicates a higher ranking
for the other three standards.

4.2.1. *Absolute standards*

Which aid systems do the best job of boosting students in poor or high-cost
districts above some minimum educational standard? As shown in Tables 4
and 5, the clear winners in this case are the plans explicitly designed to meet

Table 4 Equity comparisons for different foundation formulas with negative aid, New York school districts, 1991.[a]

Aid system	Absolute standard		Relative standard	Fiscal neutrality[b]	
	Percent of outcome gap closed minimum outcome set at		Gini coefficient (outcome index)	Elasticity of outcomes and property wealth	Elasticity of outcomes and fiscal health
	Median	25th percentile			
Present aid distribution	0%	0%	0.203	0.147	0.259
Flat grant	−4%	−1%	0.200	0.235	0.317
Expenditure based:					
No minimum t^*					
$E^* =$ 25th percentile	8%	14%	0.182	0.124	0.218
$E^* =$ median	11%	16%	0.178	0.096	0.194
$E^* =$ 75th percentile	16%	22%	0.173	0.033	0.138
Minimum t^*					
$E^* =$ 25th percentile	22%	36%	0.166	0.098	0.169
$E^* =$ median	34%	48%	0.153	0.054	0.122
$E^* =$ 75th percentile	60%	75%	0.123	−0.048	0.011
Outcome based (using property value):					
No minimum t^*					
$S^* =$ 25th percentile	17%	42%	0.162	0.133	0.200
$S^* =$ median	27%	52%	0.149	0.072	0.139
$S^* =$ 75th percentile	35%	63%	0.140	0.006	0.073
Minimum t^*					
$S^* =$ 25th percentile	43%	84%	0.134	0.114	0.152
$S^* =$ median	74%	98%	0.103	0.021	0.038
$S^* =$ 75th percentile	95%	100%	0.081	−0.074	−0.078
Outcome based (using revenue raising capacity):					
No minimum t^*					
$S^* =$ 25th percentile	13%	36%	0.165	0.163	0.195
$S^* =$ median	20%	44%	0.154	0.120	0.131
$S^* =$ 75th percentile	28%	50%	0.145	0.072	0.062
Minimum t^*					
$S^* =$ 25th percentile	41%	83%	0.135	0.142	0.149
$S^* =$ median	73%	99%	0.103	0.060	0.037
$S^* =$ 75th percentile	95%	100%	0.080	−0.028	−0.073

Notes: [a] All grants require approximately the same state budget to fund as the aid system in 1991 — $3.65 billion.
[b] The fiscal health index used in the fiscal neutrality calculation uses a general measure of revenue raising capacity.

this objective, namely, outcome-based foundation plans that both set S^* high enough and require a minimum t^*. If S^* is set at least as high as the standard that policymakers are trying to meet and districts are required to set t^* high enough to fund this outcome, then at least 70 percent of the outcome gap

Table 5 Equity comparisons for different foundation formulas without negative aid, New York school districts, 1991.[a]

	Absolute standard		Relative standard	Fiscal neutrality[b]	
	Percent of outcome gap closed minimum outcome set at		Gini coefficient (outcome index)	Elasticity of outcomes and property wealth	Elasticity of outcomes and fiscal health
Aid system	Median	25th percentile			
Present aid distribution	0%	0%	0.203	0.147	0.259
Flat grant	−4%	−1%	0.200	0.235	0.317
Expenditure based:					
No minimum t^*					
$E^* =$ 25th percentile	6%	11%	0.183	0.147	0.235
$E^* =$ median	8%	13%	0.181	0.133	0.222
$E^* =$ 75th percentile	10%	15%	0.178	0.105	0.195
Minimum t^*					
$E^* =$ 25th percentile	21%	36%	0.170	0.167	0.216
$E^* =$ median	35%	48%	0.160	0.167	0.199
$E^* =$ 75th percentile	64%	77%	0.141	0.189	0.177
Outcome based (using property value):					
No minimum t^*					
$S^* =$ 25th percentile	13%	39%	0.165	0.159	0.221
$S^* =$ median	18%	45%	0.158	0.135	0.192
$S^* =$ 75th percentile	21%	49%	0.155	0.118	0.170
Minimum t^*					
$S^* =$ 25th percentile	41%	84%	0.140	0.191	0.206
$S^* =$ median	75%	99%	0.124	0.224	0.182
$S^* =$ 75th percentile	98%	100%	0.133	0.307	0.211
Outcome based (using revenue raising capacity):					
No minimum t^*					
$S^* =$ 25th percentile	11%	34%	0.167	0.175	0.211
$S^* =$ median	15%	39%	0.160	0.152	0.172
$S^* =$ 75th percentile	18%	42%	0.156	0.132	0.137
Minimum t^*					
$S^* =$ 25th percentile	41%	83%	0.136	0.160	0.173
$S^* =$ median	74%	99%	0.113	0.124	0.125
$S^* =$ 75th percentile	97%	100%	0.110	0.112	0.126

Notes: [a]All grants require approximately the same state budget to fund as the aid system in 1991 — $3.65 billion.
[b]The fiscal health index used in the fiscal neutrality calculation uses a general measure of revenue raising capacity.

is closed, regardless of whether there is negative aid. The entire outcome gap is not closed because some of the districts with low values of S are relatively inefficient. Thus, students in these districts are penalized because of the inefficiency of their school district. One way the state could avoid

Table 6 Equity comparisons for different power-equalizing formulas with negative aid, New York school districts, 1991.[a]

Aid system	Absolute standard		Relative standard	Fiscal neutrality[b]	
	Percent of outcome gap closed minimum outcome set at		Gini coefficient (outcome index)	Elasticity of outcomes and property wealth	Elasticity of outcomes and fiscal health
	Median	25th percentile			
Present aid distribution	0%	0%	0.204	0.147	0.259
Flat grant	−4%	−1%	0.201	0.235	0.317
Expenditure based:[c]					
$\alpha = 0.7$	13%	18%	0.183	0.084	0.184
$\alpha = 0.8$	16%	21%	0.179	0.053	0.157
$\alpha = 0.9$	19%	23%	0.177	0.022	0.130
$\alpha = 1.0$	21%	26%	0.175	−0.009	0.103
$\alpha = 1.1$	24%	28%	0.173	−0.041	0.076
$\alpha = 1.15$	26%	29%	0.173	−0.056	0.063
$\alpha = 1.4$	32%	35%	0.171	−0.135	−0.004
Outcome based (using property value):[d]					
$\beta = 0.7$	19%	33%	0.169	0.090	0.169
$\beta = 0.8$	23%	38%	0.164	0.059	0.140
$\beta = 0.9$	27%	44%	0.160	0.029	0.111
$\beta = 1.0$	31%	49%	0.156	−0.002	0.082
$\beta = 1.1$	36%	52%	0.152	−0.032	0.053
$\beta = 1.15$	38%	54%	0.151	−0.048	0.038
$\beta = 1.3$	44%	59%	0.146	−0.093	−0.005
Outcome based (using revenue raising capacity):[d]					
$\beta = 0.7$	13%	23%	0.173	0.160	0.152
$\beta = 0.8$	16%	27%	0.168	0.139	0.121
$\beta = 0.9$	20%	31%	0.164	0.118	0.089
$\beta = 1.0$	23%	35%	0.159	0.098	0.058
$\beta = 1.1$	26%	39%	0.156	0.077	0.027
$\beta = 1.15$	28%	41%	0.154	0.068	0.011
$\beta = 1.2$	30%	43%	0.151	0.056	−0.005

Notes: [a] All grants require approximately the same state budget to fund as the aid system in 1991 — $3.65 billion.
[b] The fiscal health index used in the fiscal neutrality calculation uses a general measure of revenue raising capacity.
[c] The role of α is defined in equation (5).
[d] The role of β is defined in equation (6).

this problem would be to set the inefficiency standard, k^*, at the minimum efficiency level of all districts. This approach would not provide incentives for districts to be inefficient, and it would require either a substantial increase in either state aid or t^*.

While expenditure-based foundation plans are certainly an improvement over the present system in New York or a simple flat grant per pupil,

Table 7 Equity comparisons for different power-equalizing formulas without negative aid, New York school districts, 1991.[a]

	Absolute standard		Relative standard	Fiscal neutrality[b]	
	Percent of outcome gap closed minimum outcome set at		Gini coefficient (Outcome index)	Elasticity of outcomes and property wealth	Elasticity of outcomes and fiscal health
Aid system	Median	25th percentile			
Present aid distribution	0%	0%	0.204	0.147	0.259
Flat grant	−4%	−1%	0.201	0.235	0.317
Expenditure based[c]:					
$\alpha = 0.7$	9%	14%	0.184	0.134	0.219
$\alpha = 0.8$	11%	16%	0.182	0.120	0.206
$\alpha = 0.9$	12%	17%	0.179	0.107	0.194
$\alpha = 1.0$	14%	18%	0.178	0.095	0.183
$\alpha = 1.1$	15%	19%	0.176	0.084	0.172
$\alpha = 1.15$	16%	20%	0.175	0.074	0.161
$\alpha = 3.25$	20%	23%	0.177	−0.058	0.027
Outcome based (using property value)[d]:					
$\beta = 0.7$	14%	29%	0.172	0.137	0.205
$\beta = 0.8$	17%	33%	0.169	0.123	0.190
$\beta = 0.9$	19%	37%	0.165	0.110	0.177
$\beta = 1.0$	21%	40%	0.162	0.099	0.164
$\beta = 1.1$	23%	43%	0.160	0.088	0.152
$\beta = 1.15$	25%	45%	0.158	0.079	0.142
$\beta = 3.25$	30%	59%	0.160	−0.002	0.036
Outcome based (using revenue raising capacity)[d]:					
$\beta = 0.7$	10%	21%	0.172	0.177	0.177
$\beta = 0.8$	13%	24%	0.168	0.165	0.156
$\beta = 0.9$	15%	28%	0.165	0.153	0.137
$\beta = 1.0$	17%	30%	0.162	0.143	0.119
$\beta = 1.1$	18%	33%	0.160	0.132	0.101
$\beta = 1.15$	20%	35%	0.158	0.123	0.085
$\beta = 2.00$	27%	45%	0.151	0.066	−0.022

Notes: [a]All grants require approximately the same state budget to fund as the aid system in 1991 — $3.65 billion.
[b]The fiscal health index used in the fiscal neutrality calculation uses a general measure of revenue raising capacity.
[c]The role of α is defined in equation (5).
[d]The role of β is defined in equation (6).

they do not close as much of the outcome gap as an outcome-based foundation because they neglect high-cost, low-outcome districts. In fact, these aid systems close between 30 and 40 percent less of the outcome gap. Expenditure-based plans bring approximately the same number of districts above an outcome-based adequacy standard as do otherwise comparable outcome-based plans, but their impact is primarily on low-cost districts currently just below the standard. Even with a high expenditure standard (E^* = 75th percentile) and a required local tax rate, 25 percent of the outcome gap below the 25th percentile would remain after aid distribution. By comparison, this outcome gap would be eliminated entirely under the two outcome-based plans. This finding is particularly important because most existing foundation plans account principally for wealth differences across districts with few adjustments for cost differences.

Plans with a required minimum tax rate promote adequacy because they force needy school districts to raise their tax effort. For an outcome-based foundation plan (using a more general capacity measure), where the standard is set at the current median outcome, 80 percent of districts with outcomes presently below the standard would be forced to impose a higher tax rate than the median voter would select. For the median of these districts, the required tax rate would be twice the desired level. Even with required minimum tax rates, however, school tax rates in districts with low fiscal health are slightly lower, on average, than in other districts. If one accepts the property tax rate as a suitable measure of effort, taxpayers in these "unhealthy" districts are not being asked to make a greater effort than are other taxpayers.

Without a minimum t^*, we find, somewhat surprisingly, that power-equalizing formulas designed to achieve fiscal neutrality with respect to fiscal health close slightly more of the outcome gap below the median than do outcome-based foundation plans (Table 6). Thirty to forty-four percent of the outcome gap below the median level of S^* is closed under power equalization (with negative aid) compared to between 28 and 35 percent for the most redistributive outcome-based foundation plans (S^* = 75th percentile). This finding reflects the well-known fact that the price effect in a matching grant makes it more powerful than a lump-sum grant in raising expenditures and outcomes. Thus, the high matching rates in low-capacity districts are more effective in raising outcomes than are the large amounts of aid in foundation formulas. However, these matching plans are much less effective at targeting aid to districts with the worst current educational outcomes; outcome-based foundation plans close more of the gap below the 25th percentile than do power-equalizing grants.

4.2.2. *Vertical equity*

We measure vertical equity with the Gini coefficient. Several other measures of vertical equity are available (Berne and Stiefel, 1984), including the coefficient of variation and several range measures; they all yield similar results.

The current aid system, with a Gini coefficient of 0.203, is no more equalizing than a flat grant per pupil for every district. Assuming no restrictions on local tax rates, most aid plans result in a Gini between 0.14 and 0.19, which indicates more equity than the current system. Eliminating negative aid causes a small decrease in equity in most cases. Tables 4 and 5 indicate, for example, that the Gini for an outcome-based foundation plan (when S^* is set at the 75th percentile) goes from 0.14 to 0.155 when negative aid is disallowed. Moving from an expenditure-based to an outcome-based aid system improves equity, with Gini coefficients dropping by 10 to 20 percent.

Under outcome-based foundation plans, requiring a minimum tax rate significantly improves vertical equity, with Gini coefficients falling to as low as 0.08 (when $S^* = $ 75th percentile). This large improvement in equity is achieved because most of the outcome gap below S^* is closed. For example, with an S^* set at the 50th percentile (and negative aid), 73 percent of the outcome gap is closed and there is little variation in S, let alone inequity. As noted earlier, most of this boost in equity is due to forced local spending by low-capacity/high-cost districts rather than to the intergovernmental aid itself.

4.2.3. *Fiscal neutrality*

We measure fiscal neutrality by the elasticity (at the mean) of the simulated service outcomes relative to either property wealth or fiscal health. The elasticity of the present (1991) aid distribution is 0.147 with respect to wealth and 0.259 with respect to fiscal health. In other words, a 1 percent increase in a district's property wealth (fiscal health) is associated with a 0.147 percent (0.259 percent) increase in S. A flat per pupil aid system would increase both elasticities — and thereby move the system away from neutrality.

Not surprisingly, power-equalizing grants with negative aid do particularly well by these standards (Table 6). For an unadjusted (α or $\beta = 1$) power-equalizing grant, elasticities range from -0.01 to 0.1 for wealth and from 0.06 to 0.1 for fiscal condition. Expenditure- and outcome-based power-equalizing grants based on wealth both come close to wealth neutrality (as indicated by the very small negative elasticity), but do not achieve fiscal-health neutrality. Outcome-based power-equalizing grants based on a general measure of capacity come closer to fiscal-health neutrality, but do not get all the way there unless β is set at approximately 1.2.

Table 7 shows that power-equalizing grants have a difficult time achieving fiscal neutrality without negative aid. In order for wealth and fiscal-health elasticities to approximate zero, α (or β) must be set at 2.0 or above. Thus, standard formulas must be altered dramatically to come close to neutrality in either sense. Moreover, the more one boosts the matching rate for the lowest wealth (or fiscal-health) districts, the more redistribution occurs among districts that receive aid, but the fewer districts receive aid (to keep the budget constant). As a result, some states may find it impossible to obtain wealth or fiscal-health neutrality without negative aid. Despite their origins, realistic power-equalizing systems (that is, those without negative aid) actually prove to be a difficult way to achieve fiscal neutrality.

Foundation formulas vary significantly in their impact on fiscal neutrality (Tables 4 and 5). Increasing the redistributive power of the grant by raising S^* lowers the elasticities for all types of foundation formulas with negative aid. Forcing districts below S^* to assess a minimum tax rate lowers the elasticities still further, particularly when S^* is set at a high level. For example, with S^* set at the 75th percentile, elasticities with respect to wealth and fiscal health are actually negative for outcome-based aid formulas. The results change dramatically when negative aid is not permitted. Elasticities remain at 0.10 or above for all aid systems and elasticities actually go up with S^* in some cases when a minimum t^* is imposed. In general, similar expenditure- and outcome-based foundation formulas have roughly equivalent impacts on wealth or fiscal-health neutrality.

5. Conclusions

Expenditure-based foundation grants, which are used by over 80 percent of states, do not perform well by either absolute or vertical equity standards — even when a minimum t^* is imposed. By controlling for costs in an *ad hoc* fashion, the typical foundation formula does not provide sufficient aid to high-cost districts, and therefore leaves many students below any reasonable standard for educational outcomes. The resulting wide disparities also show up in higher Gini coefficients or in other measures of vertical equity. By shifting to performance standards for local schools, states have implicitly recognized the role of input and environmental cost factors, so it is particularly troubling that they continue to rely so heavily on aid formulas that only partially account for these factors, if at all. Moreover, there appears to be a growing emphasis on absolute outcome standards, often called educational adequacy (Clune, 1993). State policymakers need to understand that expenditure-based foundation grants do not and indeed cannot assure that educational adequacy is achieved.

Outcome-based foundation plans cannot be implemented without addressing several difficult issues, such as deciding which educational outputs and environmental cost factors to consider and selecting a way to control for district efficiency. We provide one method for addressing these issues that attempts to find a balance between the precision required by scholars and the simplicity required for actual implementation. Our simulations of the impacts of the resulting outcome-based plans indicate that such plans can be an effective tool for promoting educational adequacy, at least when they include a required minimum tax rate. Indeed, by requiring contributions from local taxpayers, these plans can bring the vast majority of districts up to any educational outcome standard policymakers select. The districts that remain below the standard are relatively inefficient.[18]

The majority of states with foundation plans do require minimum tax rates, but states tempted to drop this requirement (or states considering the adoption of an outcome-based foundation plan without it) should recognize that it is essential to the goal of educational adequacy. Without a required minimum tax rate, many districts will spend below a relatively modest adequacy standard (in this paper, the 25th percentile of the current distribution) even if the foundation level is set very high. Of course, states can minimize the impact of a required minimum tax rate on needy districts by boosting the state budget. Without an extremely generous state plan, however, a significant increase in the tax rate in many districts is necessary, at least in New York, to meet any reasonable adequacy standard. Our simulations for New York also indicate that foundation plans with negative aid and a required minimum tax rate promote vertical equity and fiscal neutrality, at least if the foundation level is set high enough. Indeed, if the outcome foundation level is set at the 75th percentile of the current distribution, the two outcome-based foundation plans have the lowest Gini coefficients of all plans and are close to fiscal neutrality.

---

[18]One uncertainty regarding the impact of equalizing grants is whether increased aid for poor districts leads to more inefficiency. Our results from a related study (Duncombe and Yinger, 1997) indicate that the most generous foundation plans actually raise efficiency in the average district, and in the central-city districts, which receive the largest increases in aid, inefficiency increases by at most 15 percent.

We also find, not surprisingly, that power-equalizing grants with negative aid are particularly effective at achieving fiscal-health (or wealth) neutrality, even without boosting their power beyond that in the standard formula. Thus, policymakers concerned with wealth neutrality should continue to consider power-equalizing grants. However, a child is just as disadvantaged by poor education associated with high costs as by poor education associated with low wealth, and it is difficult to justify a neutrality objective that ignores the role of costs. Thus, we believe that fiscal-health neutrality is a more general and more appealing objective than is wealth neutrality. As it turns out, outcome-based power-equalizing grants with negative aid can be effective in promoting fiscal-health neutrality. Such grants cannot be implemented, of course, without overcoming the same challenges that face outcome-based foundation plans. Power-equalizing grants do not do as well in promoting educational adequacy. They have a stronger carrot for low-outcome districts than do foundation plans because they involve a matching rate, and hence have a price effect, but they do not have the same stick in the form of a required minimum tax rate. Without this stick, many districts fall below any reasonable minimum standard even with the most generous power-equalizing formula.

Overall, if policymakers and courts are prepared to focus on outcome-based equity standards, aid formulas are available to help them move toward these goals. Adequacy goals can be achieved with an outcome-based foundation plan that includes a required minimum tax rate. Fiscal neutrality or vertical equity goals can be achieved either with a power-equalizing plan that includes negative aid or with a foundation plan that includes a minimum tax rate combined with a very high outcome target and negative aid. Only the second of these routes will result both in fiscal neutrality and in educational adequacy for high-cost, low-wealth districts.

The problem, of course, is that change in an education finance system seldom comes easily. A required high minimum tax rate, negative aid, or a significant increase in the state budget all imply a greater state role in education finance, and the political fallout from this reduction in local control is likely to be compounded by the inevitable conflict between winners and losers under any new aid system. Moreover, required minimum tax rates are bound to be unpopular, and moving to an outcome-based aid system requires the introduction of new and potentially controversial measures of outcomes, costs, and efficiency. In light of these formidable political hurdles, it is small wonder that states have made so little progress in improving the equity of educational outcomes.

Acknowledgments

The authors have benefitted from discussions with Eric Hanushek, Michael Wolkoff, Jerry Miner, and John Ruggiero and from the comments of two anonymous reviewers.

References

Berne, Robert and Leanna Stiefel. 1984. *The Measurement of Equity in School Finance.* Baltimore: Johns Hopkins University Press.

Bridge, R. Gary, Charles Judd, and Peter Moock. 1979. *The Determinants of Educational Outcomes: The Impact of Families, Peers, Teachers and Schools.* Cambridge, MA: Ballinger Publishing Company.

Clune, William. 1993. The shift from equity to adequacy in school finance. *The World and* **18**(9): 389–405.

Cohn, Elchanan and Terry Geske. 1990. *The Economics of Education.* 3rd edition. New York: Pergamon Press.

Coons, John, William Clune, and Stephen Sugarman. 1970. *Private Wealth and Public Education.* Cambridge, MA: Harvard University Press.

Downes, Thomas and Therese McGuire. 1994. Alternative solutions to Illinois' school finance dilemma: A policy brief. *State Tax Notes* 415–419.

Downes, Thomas and Thomas Pogue. 1994. Adjusting school aid formulas for the higher cost of educating disadvantaged students. *National Tax Journal* **47**(1): 89–110.

Duncombe, William D., John Ruggiero, and John Yinger. 1996. Alternative approaches to measuring the cost of education. In Helen F. Ladd (ed.), *Holding Schools Accountable: Performance-Based Reform in Education,* Washington, DC: The Brookings Institution Press.

Duncombe, William D. and John Yinger. 1997. Why is it so hard to help central city schools? *Journal of Policy Analysis and Management* **16**(1): 85–113.

Feldstein, Martin. 1975. Wealth neutrality and local choice in public education. *American Economic Review* **61**(1): 75–89.

Ferguson, Ronald. 1991. Paying for public education: new evidence on how and why money matters. *Harvard Journal on Legislation* **28**(2): 465–498.

Ferguson, Ronald and Helen F. Ladd. 1996. Additional evidence on how and why money matters: a production function analysis of Alabama schools. In Helen F. Ladd (ed.), *Holding Schools Accountable: Performance-Based Reform in Education,* Washington, DC: Brookings Institution Press.

Gold, Steven, David Smith, Stephen Lawton, and Andrea C. Hyary. 1992. *Public School Finance Programs of the United States and Canada, 1990–91.* Albany, NY: The Nelson A. Rockefeller Institute of Government.

Hanushek, Eric. 1986. The economics of schooling: production and efficiency in public schools." *Journal of Economic Literature* **24**(3): 1141–1177.

Inman, Robert. 1979. The fiscal performance of local governments: an interpretative review. In Peter Mieszkowski and Mahlon Straszheim (ed.), *Current Issues in Urban Economics,* Baltimore: The Johns Hopkins University Press.

Kearney, C. Philip. 1995. Reducing local school property taxes: recent experiences in Michigan. *Journal of Education Finance* **21**(1): 165–85.

Ladd, Helen F. and John Yinger. 1991. *America's Ailing Cities: Fiscal Health and the Design of Urban Policy.* Baltimore: The Johns Hopkins University Press.

Ladd, Helen F. and John Yinger. 1994. The case for equalizing aid. *National Tax Journal* **47**(1): 211–224. [Chapter 13]

Ladd, Helen F., Andrew Reschovsky, and John Yinger. 1991. City fiscal condition and state equalizing aid: the case of Minnesota. In *Proceedings of the Eighty-Fourth Annual Conference on Taxation.* Columbus: National Tax Association-Tax Institute of America.

Leibenstein, Harvey. 1978. On the basic proposition of X-efficiency theory. *American Economic Review* **68**(2): 328–332.

Megdal, Sharon B. 1983. Equalization of expenditures and the demand for local public education: the case of New Jersey. *Public Finance Quarterly* **11**(3): 365–376.

Miner, Jerry. 1991. A decade of New York state aid to local schools. Metropolitan Studies Program Occasional Paper No. 141. Syracuse: Center for Policy Research, The Maxwell School, Syracuse University.

Monk, David. 1990. *Educational Finance: An Economic Approach.* New York: McGraw-Hill Publishing Company.

Niskanen, William A. 1975. Bureaucrats and politicians. *Journal of Law and Economics* **18**(3): 617–643.

Ratcliffe, Kerri, Bruce Riddle, and John Yinger. 1990. The fiscal condition of school districts in Nebraska: Is small beautiful? *Economics of Education Review* **9**(1): 81–99.

Reschovsky, Andrew. 1994. A Wisconsin property tax primer. *State Tax Notes* **5**: 1735–1743.

Rothstein, Paul. 1992. The demand for education with 'power equalizing' aid: estimation and simulation. *Journal of Public Economics* **49**(2): 135–62.

Rubinfeld, Daniel. 1987. The economics of the local public sector. In Alan Auerbach and Martin Feldstein (eds.), *Handbook of Public Economics*, vol. 2, New York: Elsevier Science Publishers.

Ruggiero, John. 1996. Efficiency of educational production: An analysis of New York school districts. *Review of Economics and Statistics* **78**(3): 499–509.

Schwab, Robert and Ernest Zampelli. 1987. Disentangling the demand function from the production function for local public services: The case of public safety. *Journal of Public Economics* **33**(2): 245–60.

Chapter 13

The Case for Equalizing Aid[*]

Helen F. Ladd[†] and John Yinger[‡,§]

[†]*Sanford School of Public Policy, Duke University,*
Durham, North Carolina
[‡]*Departments of Public Administration and*
International Affairs and of Economics,
Syracuse University, Syracuse, NY, United States
[§]*jyinger@maxwell.syr.edu*

Equalizing aid can be used by the federal government to equalize fiscal outcomes or resources among subnational governments, or by states to equalize outcomes or resources among local governments. Although equalizing aid can sometimes be justified in part on efficiency grounds, we focus on its primary function, namely, to achieve equity objectives.[1] The equity objective of a donor government can take many forms. The central theme of this paper is that the appropriate design for an equalizing aid program depends on the form of this objective.

Intergovernmental aid is not, of course, the only tool higher-level governments can use to assist poor or troubled lower-level governments. State governments, for example, can achieve equity objectives by altering the fiscal arrangements within which local governments operate. A state could take over from local governments the financing of certain services, such as

---

[*]This chapter is reproduced from "The Case for Equalizing Aid," *National Tax Journal,* **47**(1), March 1994, pp. 211–224.
[1]For a discussion of some of the efficiency arguments in favor of equalizing aid, see Ladd and Yinger (1991) and Oates and Schwab (1988). For some efficiency arguments against equalizing aid, see Oakland (1994).

social services, that place large burdens on a few jurisdictions,[2] or, to counter
fiscal disparities in education financing, a state could encourage the merger
of school districts. Hence, intergovernmental aid should be viewed as only
one tool, and not always the best tool, to achieve fiscal equity.

We place equity objectives into two classes: categorical equity, which
relates to public sector spending, either on specific functions or on all
functions, and distributional equity, which is aimed at equalizing the real
incomes of local residents. In the following discussion, we focus on state
aid to local governments.[3] For simplicity of presentation, we assume that
local governments have access to only one local revenue source, a local
property tax, and recognize that the local tax base *per capita* varies across
jurisdictions.

Many of the specifics of what follows are well known to public finance
experts. Our contributions are as follows: to incorporate cost considerations
into the various aid formulas, to highlight the similarities and differences
among formulas in a common framework, to highlight the role of capitalization in the discussion of equalizing real incomes, and to argue that equalizing
aid is a valuable policy tool under some circumstances.

As we use the term, a local government's public service costs indicate
how much a jurisdiction must spend to provide a given package of public
services at a given quality level. These costs reflect both the cost of inputs
and the harshness of the environment for providing public services.[4] Local
governments that must pay more to attract employees from the private sector
obviously have higher public service costs than other governments, all else
equal.[5] Moreover, as first pointed out by Bradford, Malt, and Oates (1969),
a jurisdiction with a harsh environment must pay more, all else equal, to
obtain the same service quality. Extensive old housing, for example, raises
the cost of fire protection, and a concentration of poor or disadvantaged
residents raises the cost of most local public services.

---

[2] Around 1970, for example, many states moved the responsibility for welfare services from
the city to the county or state level. See Ladd and Yinger (1991).

[3] For an analysis of the extent of equalization in existing state aid to local governments,
see Yinger and Ladd (1989).

[4] The fact that household characteristics may influence the environment for providing
public services leads to an important efficiency argument for equalizing grants, namely, to
offset the externality imposed on jurisdictions when low-cost individuals leave. See Oates
and Schwab (1988).

[5] Note that actual public wages are a poor measure of costs because they are influenced
by local officials. Cost measures — and hence aid formulas — should be based on factors
outside the control of local officials. For more on this issue, see Ladd and Yinger (1991).

In practice, costs can be derived from the coefficients of input and environmental cost factors in a multivariate regression analysis of local public spending that controls for income, price, and taste variation across jurisdictions.[6] To facilitate their inclusion in an equalizing aid formula, these estimated costs are best expressed in index form, with the index equal to one in a jurisdiction with average costs. To avoid giving inappropriate incentives to recipient jurisdictions, the cost factors included in this index should be largely, if not totally, outside the control of local public officials.

1. Categorical Equity Arguments for Equalizing Aid

The most fundamental equity argument for equalizing aid is categorical equity, which exists when all citizens have fair access to public services that are thought to be particularly important to their opportunities in life.[7] Although policy makers at any higher level of government may have categorical equity objectives, the attainment of categorical equity is particularly important to states, each of which bears the primary responsibility for its system of local governments and the resulting distribution of local public services. This section presents several possible categorical equity objectives for a donor government (that is, several possible definitions of fair access), and describes the grants needed to achieve them.[8]

1.1. *Ensuring a Minimum Outcome*

One widely applied categorical equity standard requires that all citizens (or students) have access to a minimum quality of public services. This standard

---

[6]For examples of this procedure, see Bradbury *et al.* (1984), Ratcliffe, Riddle, and Yinger (1990), Ladd and Yinger (1991), and Ladd, Reschovsky, and Yinger (1991). Oakland (1994) states that because "spending is not a valid measure of output ... the coefficients produced by spending studies measure handicap only if actual budget policy compensates exactly for the handicap." This argument is not correct. The regression-based method is rigorous and requires no such assumption. See Yinger and Ladd (1991, Chapter 10).

[7]Oakland (1994) discounts categorical equity objectives (except, apparently, in the case of education) because he sees no reason to think that public services are worth more to people than are private goods and services. We find categorical equity worthwhile not only because certain public services, such as education and public safety, are important to a person's opportunities, but also because a person cannot directly select the level of public services he or she receives.

[8]If many citizens believe in any of these equity objectives (or the one in the next section), then there is an efficiency gain to equalizing grants that parallels each equity objective. This is an application of the well-known theory of efficiency-improving redistribution (Hochman and Rogers, 1969). See also Ladd and Doolittle (1982).

can be applied to an individual public service, such as education or public safety, or to local public services in general.

The most direct way to achieve this standard is with a foundation grant, which ensures that each jurisdiction can reach some minimum level of spending *per capita*, labeled E^*, if it is willing to levy a property tax rate, labeled t^*, that is considered to be a fair minimum.[9] Both the minimum level of spending and the minimum fair tax rate are policy parameters that must be set by public officials.

With this approach, the state grant *per capita* to jurisdiction j, A_j, equals the minimum spending minus the local revenue that can be raised at the fair tax rate. If V_j is the property tax base *per capita* in jurisdiction j, then the foundation formula is

$$A_j = E^* - t^* V_j. \tag{1}$$

An alternative version of this formula highlights the fact that a foundation grant is a block grant, which means that it does not vary with a jurisdiction's chosen spending level, and that it is larger for jurisdictions with relatively small tax bases.[10] If V^* is defined as the tax base at which A_j equals zero, it follows immediately that $E^* = t^* V^*$ or $t^* = E^*/V^*$. Substituting this result into equation (1) yields

$$A_j = E^* \left(1 - \frac{V_j}{V^*} \right). \tag{2}$$

Note that negative grants are not allowed; jurisdictions with tax bases above V^* receive no aid.

---

[9]The issue of property tax capitalization, which is discussed at length in a later section, is not relevant here. The minimum service objective (along with most of the other categorical equity objectives) includes a statement about the share of a jurisdiction's tax base that represents a fair contribution to the provision of the relevant public services. The fact that a jurisdiction's property tax base may reflect the tax rate that it actually selects has nothing to do with selection of this share. One might object, however, to the use of the property tax base as a measure of a jurisdiction's capacity to raise revenue, because it reflects the jurisdiction's actual tax decisions. This problem can be solved by using a more general measure of revenue-raising capacity, which is discussed in footnote 14.

[10]Grants inversely related to a jurisdiction's tax base also may have efficiency consequences. Oakland (1994) argues that they may either offset distortions that arise when location decisions are based on tax or service levels or lower efficiency by lowering interjurisdictional variation in service-tax packages. Others have argued that these grants undercut a jurisdiction's incentive to attract more property. Because broad economic and social forces have a much larger influence on a city's tax base than anything the city can do, we do not find this argument compelling. See Ladd and Yinger (1991).

This approach easily can be extended to include public service costs. In this case, the first policy parameter is the minimum acceptable service quality, S^*; C_j is a cost index for jurisdiction j; and state aid is the difference between the spending needed to achieve S^*, namely S^*C_j, and local revenue at the fair tax rate. In practice, S^* can be set equal to the minimum acceptable spending in a community with average costs, that is, with $C_j = 1$. In symbols,

$$A_j = S^*C_j - t^*V_j. \tag{3}$$

Now redefine V^* to be the tax base at which state aid would equal zero assuming a cost index equal to unity, so that $t^* = S^*/V^*$ and

$$A_j = S^* \left(C_j - \frac{V_j}{V^*} \right). \tag{4}$$

This formula describes a block grant that depends both on a jurisdiction's costs and tax base. Remember that the cost index, C_j, is defined as a jurisdictions's costs relative to the average jurisdiction; hence the terms in brackets are both expressed in relative terms.

A foundation grant makes it possible for a jurisdiction to provide the minimum acceptable service level at the fair minimum tax rate. It does not guarantee, however, that a community actually will provide this level unless it is accompanied by the requirement that the jurisdiction levy at least the minimum tax rate, t^*, to support the relevant service or services.[11]

1.2. *Easing the Burden of Providing Standard-Quality Public Services*

Sometimes a donor government is unwilling to require local governments to provide a specific service level on the grounds that local governments should be free to make their own decisions. Nevertheless, because some jurisdictions are fiscally disadvantaged relative to others and some service or services are viewed as particularly important, the donor government may want, without imposing a spending requirement, to help equalize the ease with which jurisdictions can achieve a specified service level. Fiscal disadvantages arise from two sources: below-average capacity to raise revenue, as measured

---

[11] An equivalent requirement is that the jurisdiction spend at least S^*C_j on the service. Note that if t^* is defined as the minimum tax rate required for a jurisdiction to be eligible for the program, instead of the minimum tax rate permitted, then some low-spending jurisdictions might choose not to participate in the grant program at all.

by V_j, and above-average costs of providing the standard service quality, as measured by C_j. Hence, to successfully ease the burden of providing standard-quality public services, the donor government should give more aid to jurisdictions that have larger fiscal disadvantages, measured by what we call the *need-capacity gap*.[12] This approach makes it possible for all jurisdictions to move toward standard-quality services at a standard tax rate.

To be specific, we define a jurisdiction's need-capacity gap as the difference between its *expenditure need* and its *revenue-raising capacity*, all defined in *per capita* terms. Expenditure need is the amount of money required for the jurisdiction to provide the standard-quality services and is calculated as the standardized service quality, S', multiplied by the jurisdiction's cost index, C_j.[13]

Revenue-raising capacity is the amount of money a jurisdiction could raise at a standard tax rate given its own tax base, which equals the standard tax rate, t', multiplied by V_j.[14] The need-capacity gap indicates the extent to which the revenue the jurisdiction can raise at a standard tax rate falls short of the amount it must spend to provide standard-quality public services. The meaning of "standard" must be set by policy makers; that is, S' and t' are policy parameters.

Once the need-capacity gap has been defined, the natural grant system is to close a certain portion of the gap in each jurisdiction. In symbols,

$$A_j = a + b\, G_j = a + b\, (S'C_j - t'V_j), \tag{5}$$

where a and b are policy parameters that define the aid program. Defining G' as the gap at which aid equals zero, we find that $a = -bG'$. Substituting this result into equation (5) yields:

$$A_j = b(G_j - G') = b(S'C_j - t'V_j - G'). \tag{6}$$

---

[12]Grants of this type were implemented by the state of Massachusetts in 1980. See Bradbury *et al.* (1984). Grants of this type also are described in Ratcliffe, Riddle and Yinger (1990) and Ladd, Reschovsky, and Yinger (1991).

[13]In some cases, a measure of expenditure need also must account for differences across jurisdictions in service responsibilities. See Ladd and Yinger (1991).

[14]An alternative approach to revenue-raising capacity is given by Ladd and Yinger (1991). In this approach, a jurisdiction's capacity is the amount it could raise at a standard tax burden on its residents. Ladd and Yinger show how this measure of capacity depends on a jurisdiction's income and its ability to export tax burdens to non-residents. This approach is more complicated to implement, however, largely because export ratios are difficult to estimate, and it appears to be highly correlated with the tax-base approach used in the text. In Minnesota, for example, the correlation between the two approaches across municipalities is 0.92. See Ladd, Reschovsky, and Yinger (1991).

As before, negative aid is not allowed, so jurisdictions with a gap less than G' receive no aid.

Foundation grants are a special case of this formula, in which b is set equal to one (that is, the entire gap is closed); S' is set at the minimum acceptable level of services, S^*; t' is set at what is believed to be the minimum fair tax rate, t^*; and G' is set to zero (that is, jurisdictions that can afford the minimum service quality at the fair tax rate receive no aid).

The more general form in equation (6) allows a grant program to close only part of the gap between expenditure need and revenue-raising capacity and to give some aid to jurisdictions that have negative need-capacity gaps. With b less than one and without a requirement that each jurisdiction impose at least the standard tax rate, t', the grant program helps jurisdictions move toward the selected service level at a fair tax rate, but neither fully funds the move to this outcome nor requires it. Moreover, the amount appropriated for the grant program determines the extent of equalization. In general, there is an inverse relationship between b and the program's budget, holding G' constant; raising G', that is, excluding more jurisdictions from aid, increases the value of b that can be achieved for a given budget.[15]

1.3. *Ensuring Equal Service for a Given Sacrifice*

Another widely discussed categorical equity objective is to ensure that every jurisdiction willing to make a certain level of sacrifice will receive the same level of public services, regardless of its own tax base. In this context, "sacrifice" is defined as the effective property tax rate.[16] Grants to achieve this objective are called "power-equalizing" grants. In 1991–1992, eight states used some form of power-equalizing grant, usually with severe restrictions, to help finance local education (Gold *et al.*, 1992).

---

[15]These claims can easily be proven by substituting the formula for aid *per capita*, equation (6), into the program's budget constraint and rearranging the terms. This budget constraint can be written as follows:

$$B = \sum_{j=1}^{j} N_j A_j$$

where B is the total budget for the program, J is the number of jurisdictions that receive aid, and N_j is the population of jurisdiction j.

[16]This notion of sacrifice is not without problems. Jurisdictions may have other sources of revenue, for example. Philosophical objections to this notion also can be raised. See Feldstein (1975).

In equation form, this objective is to set

$$E_j = t_j \hat{V} \tag{7}$$

where $\hat{V}$ is a policy parameter. Since local revenue equals $t_j V_j$ and state aid equals the difference between spending and local revenue, this formula leads directly to

$$A_j = E_j - L_j = t_j(\hat{V} - V_j). \tag{8}$$

Now solving equation (7) for t_j and substituting the result into equation (8) yields

$$A_j = E_j \left(1 - \frac{V_j}{\hat{V}}\right). \tag{9}$$

This equation defines a matching grant in which the state's share of total spending, which is the term in brackets, is higher for jurisdictions with lower tax bases. Note that when the two policy parameters, V^* and $\hat{V}$, are equal, the term in brackets is the same as for a foundation formula, but this term is multiplied by actual spending in equation (9), not by the state-determined minimum spending as in equation (2). With a power-equalizing formula, in other words, a jurisdiction's aid depends both on the spending level it selects and on the divergence between its tax base and the tax base designated by policy makers.

Note also that the policy parameters in equations (9) and (2) need not be the same. The derivation of equation (9) does not assume that power-equalizing grants go only to a subset of jurisdictions. Thus, if $\hat{V}$ is set at any level below the tax base of the richest jurisdiction, the formula implies that some jurisdictions will have negative matching rates, an outcome that usually is politically unacceptable.[17] Negative matching rates can be eliminated by raising $\hat{V}$, but this action would increase the cost of the program. Instead, power-equalizing grants, as implemented, virtually always override the formula to assure a minimum amount of aid for each jurisdiction and thereby limit the extent of equalization relative to equation (9).

This type of grant also can be modified to account for a jurisdiction's costs.[18] In particular, the defining equation can be restated to say that

[17] An experiment with negative matching rates was attempted by the state of Maine but was quickly overturned by a referendum.
[18] This point was made, although not implemented, by Feldstein (1975, p. 77): "expenditure per pupil could be modified to reflect local differences in input prices or student abilities."

service quality, or real spending, will depend only on sacrifice. In symbols,

$$\frac{E_j}{C_j} = S_j = t_j \hat{V}. \tag{10}$$

Following the same steps as before, this equation leads to the grant formula

$$A_j = S_j \left(C_j - \frac{V_j}{\hat{V}} \right). \tag{11}$$

Now the matching rate, that is, the state's share of total spending, depends on a jurisdictions's cost index as well as its tax base. Equation (11) differs from the cost-adjusted foundation formula, equation (4), because it is based on a jurisdiction's actual real spending (or service quality), not on a fixed minimum real spending.

1.4. *Wealth Neutrality*

In some of the early school finance cases, courts ruled that the wealth of the local school district should be viewed as a "suspect category," which constitutionally cannot serve as the basis for differences in the quality of education services, often measured by per pupil spending, available to pupils across the state.[19] These rulings express another possible equity objective, called wealth neutrality, which requires that variation across districts in per pupil spending, or preferably in school service levels, be uncorrelated with variation in the per pupil property tax base, a measure of wealth. Wealth neutrality could be an objective for other public services as well.

One way to achieve this outcome is to redefine school districts so that they all have the same tax base per pupil. By eliminating variation in district tax bases, this non-aid approach would assure that any remaining variation in spending or service levels was uncorrelated with district wealth.[20] Given the obvious political difficulties of redrawing district boundaries, the challenge is to design an intergovernmental aid formula that achieves the same goal.

By assuring that every jurisdiction, regardless of the size of its tax base, can generate the same revenue *per capita* (or per pupil) as the district

---

[19]In the 1973 Texas case of *Rodriguez v. San Antonio*, the U.S. Supreme Court, in a 5–4 decision, held that education was not a fundamental right and that school district wealth was not a suspect category under the United States Constitution. See Odden and Picus (1992, p. 27). Rulings by state courts have not been so definitive. For more on these issues, see Reschovsky (1994).

[20]An extreme version of this approach is to provide schools at the state level, as is done in Hawaii.

with base V^*, power-equalizing grants appear at first to generate wealth neutrality. As pointed out by Feldstein (1975), however, this statement is not generally true. Although higher matching rates for lower-wealth jurisdictions are likely to push a system toward wealth neutrality, they also may induce lower-wealth jurisdictions to select lower (or higher) tax rates than high-wealth jurisdictions, so that a correlation between service outcomes and wealth remains despite the rule imposed by equation (7).

Feldstein (1975) also shows that, assuming a particular algebraic form for the demand for education, a wealth-neutralizing matching grant is defined by

$$A_j = E_j(1 - kV_j^{\beta_w/\beta_p}), \tag{12}$$

where k is a scale parameter, which roughly corresponds to $1/\hat{V}$ in equation (9) and which determines the overall level of spending; β_w is the elasticity of spending with respect to wealth; and β_p is the (negative) elasticity of spending with respect to price.[21] As in equation (9), the term in brackets defines a matching rate. Comparing equations (9) and (12) reveals that a power-equalizing grant is wealth-neutral only when the two elasticities in equation (12) are equal in absolute value. If they are not equal, a jurisdiction's response to the matching grant, which is determined by the price elasticity, does not exactly offset the existing impact of its wealth on service demand.

Feldstein (1975) estimates that the required exponent for V_j in this formula equals about 0.33 for cities and towns in Massachusetts in 1970. According to this estimate, the implicit unitary exponent on wealth in the power-equalizing formula, equation (9), is too large, in the sense that it leads to a negative correlation between wealth and spending. Feldstein's estimated price elasticity is, however, much greater in absolute value than the price elasticity estimated by most other studies of local spending.[22] With a more widely accepted value for this parameter, one might conclude that

---

[21] Feldstein's demand function expresses the log of spending as a function of the log of wealth, the log of price (as determined by the matching rate), and the log of other variables, which may be correlated with wealth. The elasticity of spending with respect to wealth includes the direct elasticity for the wealth variable and the indirect elasticity for all other variables that affect demand and are correlated with wealth. In principle, a weaker form of wealth neutrality could be achieved with the Feldstein approach if the components of the wealth elasticity are confined to variables that are thought to be systematically, not incidentally, related to wealth.

[22] Feldstein's estimate price elasticity is -1.0. Most estimates for education fall between -0.1 and -0.5. See Inman (1979) and Bergstrom, Rubinfeld, and Shapiro (1982).

the implicit exponent in a power-equalizing formula is about right or even too small to generate wealth neutrality.

The Feldstein (1975) formula is general enough to encompass public service costs. Cost factors that are uncorrelated with wealth do not influence the formula at all; if costs are uncorrelated with wealth across school districts, achieving wealth neutrality with respect to spending implies achieving wealth neutrality with respect to service quality. Moreover, so long as all cost variables that are correlated with wealth are included in the empirical analysis, and therefore influence the estimate of β_w, equation (12) leads to wealth neutrality with respect to service quality.[23]

Another way to achieve wealth neutrality would be to equalize voters' budget constraints in all jurisdictions. A constraint-equalizing grant program would consist of lump-sum grants to offset income differences across districts and matching grants to offset tax-price differences.[24] This approach has the advantage over the Feldstein (1975) approach that it does not require the incorporation of estimated elasticities into the grant formula. It costs the state more than the Feldstein approach, however, because it uses block grants instead of relying exclusively on matching grants. Given the low price elasticities found by most studies, however, the cost difference might not be too large.[25]

---

[23] As it turns out, Feldstein's equations contain no cost variables, so substituting his estimated elasticities into his formula will not yield wealth neutrality with respect to service quality, given that many other studies have found that cost factors influence education. See Hanushek (1986) or Ratcliffe, Riddle, and Yinger (1990).

[24] The precise forms of the block grant and matching grant can be found from the median voter's budget constraint. In a standard model, the block grant equals the difference between the target income (a policy parameter) and the median voter's actual income divided by the median voter's tax share (which is her house value divided by house value *per capita* in the jurisdiction). Assuming constant costs in the production of service quality, the matching rate equals the jurisdiction's cost index divided by the median voter's tax share and by the target tax price (another policy parameter). For a derivation of this type of grant in a more complex model, see Yinger (1986). Strictly speaking, this approach raises two new issues. First, it removes all systematic correlation between wealth and service outcomes, but not literally all correlation, as does the Feldstein approach. Preference differences that are correlated with wealth, for example, still might influence outcomes. Second, it assumes that it is appropriate to base grants on a majority rule (or median-voter) framework even if actual decisions diverge from what the median voter would choose. Moreover, it assumes that the median voter can be identified as the person with median income and median preferences. The conditions under which this is true are stated by Bergstrom and Goodman (1973).

[25] In addition, this approach achieves only the weaker form of wealth neutrality described in the previous footnote, which may or may not satisfy courts in school equity cases.

In conclusion, no state has attempted to implement a program that would literally be wealth-neutral. Foundation and power-equalization programs move toward this objective, at least if implemented in pure form, but they cannot achieve it. Programs that could achieve wealth neutrality are either too complicated, in the sense that they must be based on estimated elasticities, or too expensive, in the sense that they involve extensive redistribution, to be politically feasible — at least so far.

1.5. *Ensuring Equal Outcomes*

An even stronger equity objective than wealth neutrality is complete equality in service levels. This objective is based on the view that certain public services (education, police, or fire, for example) are so important to a person's life chances that all citizens should have equal access to them, regardless of their circumstances or the circumstances of their community.[26]

None of the plans described so far meets this objective. If they are implemented without limits and loopholes, they all move toward it, but none of them achieves full equality of outcomes. A foundation grant places no limit on the spending by rich districts; power-equalizing grants do not even achieve wealth neutrality, which is a necessary condition for equal outcomes; and wealth-neutral grants do not eliminate spending variation that is uncorrelated with wealth.

The only way we know of to meet this objective through grants is to use a foundation plan that requires each jurisdiction to set its tax rate exactly at t^*.[27] However, attempts to restrict the school tax rates of wealthy jurisdictions have proved to be unpopular and could, as emphasized by Reschovsky (1994), encourage wealthy taxpayers to send their children to private schools.[28] In principle, these political problems could be avoided

---

[26] Reschovsky (1994) points out that several state courts appear to be requiring this objective for education.

[27] One way to achieve this objective without a grant is for a state to take over provision of the service, and then to provide the same service level in each community. In Hawaii, for example, education is provided at the state level and, in principle, the same level of education could be (but undoubtedly is not) provided in each school. Another way is for the state to "take over" the local property tax. See Giertz and McGuire (1992). In Kansas, for example, every district must levy the same state-determined property tax rate and return any revenue above a certain amount to the state. Districts also can supplement their revenue with an additional local levy, although this option is scheduled to phase out. See Myers (1992).

[28] A description of a debate over restrictions on the tax levy for high-wealth districts can be found in a case entitled "Funding Schools in Washington State" in Gomez-Ibanez and Kalt (1990).

if the "minimum acceptable level" were set above the spending that any jurisdiction would select, but this approach would run into another political problem: its prohibitive expense.

1.6. *The Case for Equalizing Grants*

In our judgement, a strong case can be made for equalizing grants to achieve categorical equity, although the appropriate form of the grants depends on the circumstances. According to their constitutions, many state governments are explicitly responsible for the character of the system that provides elementary and secondary education (see Reschovsky, 1994). We believe that a state's most fundamental responsibility in education is to ensure that every student receives a minimum acceptable level of educational services. Thus, we agree with Reschovsky (1994) that the best grant program for education is a "complete" foundation plan with a required minimum tax rate, with costs in the formula, and, we would add, with a relatively high minimum service quality.

Compared to ensuring a minimum acceptable education, the objectives of equal service per unit sacrifice, of wealth neutrality, or of equal outcomes are stronger in the sense that they require adjustments by all districts, including those that would provide high-quality education without additional assistance. However, controversy surrounding these stronger objectives inevitably leads to compromises that severely limit the extent of equalization. Some people support programs to promote equal service per unit sacrifice or wealth neutrality because those programs allow some variation in service quality even at low levels of wealth and thereby enhance choice for parents.[29] We believe that this extra choice comes at a high equity cost imposed on the students who consequently receive inadequate services. Thus, we prefer a complete foundation plan to the most widely discussed alternative, a power-equalizing grant, as well as to wealth-neutral or equal-outcome grants, and we strongly prefer a complete foundation plan to power-equalizing grants as they are typically implemented with no consideration of costs, with hold harmless clauses, and with a minimum amount of aid to each district.

---

[29] Oakland (1994) criticizes equalizing aid programs for diminishing efficiency-enhancing variation in public service outcomes. However, efficiency does not require variation in outcomes associated with income or wealth; instead, it requires that communities with different preferences at any given level of income or wealth be allowed to make different choices.

Although state constitutions do not specifically mention local services other than education, this case for a complete foundation plan also can be extended to other key local public services, such as public safety. Outside of education, however, the minimum acceptable service quality may prove to be difficult for state officials to define, and a practical alternative to a foundation plan is a plan based on the need-capacity gap. This approach makes it possible to give more help to the jurisdictions that face the most severe constraints in providing these services, but it does not literally require a minimum service level. Moreover, unlike a foundation plan, this approach has the practical advantage that, holding constant the state's budget, the number of jurisdictions receiving aid (and hence the political support for the program) can be increased by lowering the extent to which state aid actually closes measured need-capacity gaps. Because the state may want to treat other local services, such as social services, the same way it treats public safety, a grant program based on the need-capacity gap also might be appropriate for all local spending.

2. Equalizing Real Incomes Through Equalizing Aid

Another possible objective for an equalizing grant program is to make more equal the distribution of households' real incomes. Although more direct methods able, a possible role remains for equalizing grants. This role arises because low-income people cannot directly select the level of public services or taxes in their jurisdiction, and indeed may not have enough votes or political power to influence their jurisdiction's choices. If a jurisdiction in which a low-income household lives provides a service level that is far below what the household prefers, federal or state resources might have a larger impact on the household's utility if they were devoted to increasing the quality of public services than if they were devoted to transfers that directly increase the household's income. This possibility is magnified if local services are characterized by non-rivalry in consumption. Moreover, if the local tax system is regressive, so that tax reductions yield the greatest benefits to people at the bottom of the income distribution, intergovernmental grants that lead to reduced local taxes also might be worth more to low-income people than higher transfers. These are theoretical arguments; we know of no empirical work that determines whether these conditions are met.

Even if these conditions are satisfied, however, the potential of intergovernmental aid programs to boost the real incomes of low-income households may be limited by capitalization, which arises when local service quality and local tax rates affect property values.[30] In the presence of capitalization, which has been documented by many empirical studies,[31] increases in real income associated with higher service quality or lower taxes may be partially or totally offset by higher rents or housing prices.[32]

To be more specific, full capitalization implies that the benefits to tenants from grant-induced increases in service quality are canceled by rent increases and that the benefits to homeowners are confined to people who currently own property in the community. Homeowners who arrive in the future must pay a higher price to enter the community and therefore are no better off as a result of the improved services. With capitalization, therefore, an equalizing grant program appears likely to help many current low-income homeowners and current landlords (some of whom may have low incomes), but appears unlikely to help low-income renters or future low-income homeowners.

Moreover, the existence of capitalization undercuts to some degree an implicit premise in the basic objective of equalizing real incomes, namely that a person's real income depends in part on the service quality and tax rate in the jurisdiction where she lives.[33] If all households are mobile, every household with a given set of skills and preferences can achieve the same real income. Hence, because of compensation in the form of lower housing prices, low-income households who live in jurisdictions with poor public services or high taxes already are no worse off than low-income households who live in jurisdictions with excellent services or low taxes.

For two reasons, however, this capitalization argument neither completely invalidates the premise that real incomes depend on public service quality nor completely eliminates the possibility of using intergovernmental grants to equalize real incomes. The first reason is that age, disability, poverty,

---

[30]For more detailed discussions of this issue, see Yinger (1986) or Wyckoff (1992).

[31]For a review of existing studies with a focus on tax capitalization, see Yinger *et al.* (1988).

[32]Although the impact of public service quality on rents is not literally an example of "capitalization," because it does not involve an asset price, it generally is included in the concept of capitalization. In addition, note that when many urban areas are considered, service quality or tax differences also could be partially or fully offset by wage differences. Moreover, one cannot get around capitalization by giving higher transfers to individuals in low-service or high-tax jurisdictions. Any program in which benefits depend on residence runs into the problem of capitalization.

[33]A similar point is made by Oakland (1994). In discussing differences resulting from higher wage costs, he says: "To equalize for these premia would be to doubly compensate individuals for disamenities."

and discrimination reduce the mobility of many low-income people.[34] With barriers to mobility, differences in service quality or tax rates need not be fully reflected in housing prices.

The second reason is that even if low-income people are mobile, the impact of grants on housing prices depends on the solution to a complex general equilibrium problem, which does not always yield offsetting housing price changes. A general treatment of this problem is not available, but this point can be illustrated by examining several special cases.

Suppose, for example, that all low-income people live in central cities with poor public services, that these central cities contain only low-income people, and that all of these central cities receive equalizing grants. Because capitalization reflects competition among households of a given type for housing in communities with different public service levels, there is nothing to capitalize in this case. Hence, the real incomes of all low-income households are depressed by the fact that they receive low-quality public services, and raising the quality of public services in all these central cities boosts the real incomes of all low-income households without having any impact on prices. In other words, if a grant program raises service quality in every jurisdiction where low-income people live, a capitalization effect does not arise, and capitalization has no impact either on the validity of the objective or on the ability of grants to achieve it.

Wyckoff (1992) analyzes an alternative case in which there are two communities and three income classes. One community (call it the central city) contains all low-income households, the other (call it the suburb) contains all high-income households, and both contain some of the middle-income households. In this case, capitalization reflects the service demands of the middle-income households who are the households at the moving margin. Raising service quality in the central city therefore boosts the price of housing enough to keep middle-income households in equilibrium, that is, enough to offset middle-income households' valuation of the increment in service quality. This change in housing price could be higher than, lower than, or equal to the value of the public service increment to low-income households. It follows that the real income of low-income households could go down, go up, or be unchanged by equalizing grants. Wyckoff also shows that if the central city contains "a large fraction of the population of the metropolitan area, most of the relative price changes between housing prices in the two

---

[34] Racial and ethnic discrimination continues to be a severe barrier to mobility. For a review of evidence from the 1989 Housing Discrimination Study, see Yinger (1993).

communities necessary to restore middle class indifference are accomplished by price changes in the" suburb (p. 22). In this case, intergovernmental aid has the desired effect; that is, it raises the real income of low-income households.

We conclude that capitalization weakens, but does not eliminate, the case for using intergovernmental grants to equalize real incomes. Further research is needed to determine the extent to which capitalization offsets the redistributional benefits of these grants.

3. Conclusions

Both state governments and the federal government have a long history of attempting to meet equity objectives through intergovernmental grants. The key step in designing an equalizing grant program is deciding on the form of this equity objective. Many different categorical equity objectives, including the guarantee of a minimum service quality and wealth neutrality, can be attained with an appropriately designed equalizing aid program, and under some circumstances equalizing grants can make a contribution to a fairer distribution of real incomes. Moreover, because all relevant equity objectives are concerned with service quality, not spending as such, grant formulas to achieve them must account for public service costs. Although few grant programs account for costs in a systematic way, methods for doing so are readily available.

Different equity objectives and grant programs are appropriate under different circumstances. In our judgement, a complete foundation plan, that is, a foundation plan that requires a minimum tax rate, accounts for costs, and sets a relatively high minimum service level, is appropriate for elementary and secondary education. For police, fire, and other local services, grants based on the need-capacity gap provide a flexible way to focus aid on the jurisdictions that, through no fault of their own, need help the most.

References

Bergstrom, Theodore C. and Robert Goodman. 1973. Private demand for public goods. *American Economic Review* **53** (June): 280–296.

Bergstrom, Theodore C., Daniel L. Rubinfeld, and Perry Shapiro. 1982. Micro-based estimates of demand functions for local school expenditures. *Econometrica* **50** (September): 1183–1205.

Bradbury, Katharine L., Helen F. Ladd, Mark Perrault, Andrew Reschovsky, and John Yinger. 1984. State aid to offset fiscal disparities across communities. *National Tax Journal* **37** (June): 151–170.

Bradford, David F., R. A. Malt, and Wallace E. Oates. 1969. The rising cost of local public services: some evidence and reflections. *National Tax Journal* **22** (June): 185–202.

Feldstein, Martin S. 1975. Wealth neutrality and local choice in public education. *American Economic Review* **65** (March): 75–89.

Giertz, J. Fred and Therese J. McGuire. 1992. Regional and state-wide property tax base sharing for education. In *Proceedings of the 85th Annual Conference of the National Tax Association — Tax Institute of America*, pp. 190–194.

Gold, Steven, David Smith, Stephen Lawton, and Andrea C. Hyary. 1992. *Public School Finance Programs of the United States and Canada*. Albany, NY: The Nelson A. Rockefeller Institute of Government.

Gomez-Ibanez, Jose A. and Joseph P. Kalt. 1990. *Cases in Microeconomics*. Englewood Cliffs, NJ: Prentice-Hall.

Hanushek, Eric. 1986. The economics of schooling. 1986. *Journal of Economic Literature* **24** (September): 1141–1175.

Hochman, H. M. and J. D. Rogers. 1969. Pareto optimal redistribution. *American Economic Review* **59** (September): 542–557.

Inman, Robert P. 1979. The fiscal performance of local governments: an interpretative review. In P. Mieszkowski and M. Straszheim (eds.), *Current Issues in Urban Economics*, pp. 270–321. Baltimore: Johns Hopkins University Press.

Ladd, Helen F. and Frederick C. Doolittle. 1982. Which level of government should assist poor people? *National Tax Journal* **35** (September): 323–336.

Ladd, Helen F. and John Yinger. 1991. *America's Ailing Cities: Fiscal Health and the Design of Urban Policy*. Updated ed. Baltimore: Johns Hopkins Press.

Ladd, Helen F., Andrew Reschovsky, and John Yinger. 1991. City fiscal condition and state equalizing aid: the case of Minnesota. In *Proceedings of the 84th Annual Conference of the National Tax Association — Tax Institute of America*.

Myers, Will S. 1992. Local government implications of recent trends in state education finance. In *Proceedings of the 85th Annual Conference of the National Tax Association — Tax Institute of America*, pp. 184–189.

Oakland, William. 1994. Fiscal equalization: an empty box? *National Tax Journal* **47**(1) (March).

Oates, Wallace E. and Robert Schwab. 1988. Economic competition among jurisdictions: efficiency enhancing or distortion inducing? *Journal of Public Economics* **35** 333–354.

Odden, Allan R. and Lawrence O. Picus. 1992. *School Finance: A Policy Perspective*. New York. McGraw-Hill.

Ratcliffe, Kerri, Bruce Riddle, and John Yinger. 1990. The fiscal condition of school districts in Nebraska: is small beautiful? *Economics of Education Review* (January), pp. 81–99. [Chapter 26]

Reschovsky, Andrew. 1994. Fiscal equalization and school finance. *National Tax Journal* **47**(1) (March).

Wyckoff, Paul Gary. 1992. Capitalization, equalization, and intergovernmental aid. Unpublished Manuscript.

Yinger, John. 1993. Access denied, access constrained: results and implications of the 1989 housing discrimination study. In M. Fix and R. Struyk (eds.), *Clear and Convincing Evidence: Measurement of Discrimination in America*, pp. 69–112. Washington, DC: The Urban Institute Press.

Yinger, John. 1986. On fiscal disparities across cities. *Journal of Urban Economics* **19** (May): 316–337.

Yinger, John and Helen F. Ladd. 1989. The determinants of state assistance to central cities. *National Tax Journal* **62**(December): 413–428.

Yinger, John, Axel Boersch-Supan, Howard S. Bloom, and Helen F. Ladd. 1988. *Property Taxes and House Values: The Theory and Estimation of Intrajurisdictional Property Tax Capitalization*. New York: Academic Press.

Chapter 14

Capitalization and Equalization: The Feedback Effects of Foundation Aid for Schools*

John Yinger

*Departments of Public Administration and
International Affairs and of Economics,
Syracuse University, Syracuse, NY, United States*
jyinger@maxwell.syr.edu

1. Introduction

Many states have tried to help poor school districts, sometimes at the behest of a court ruling, by turning to a more equalizing state aid formula. In this context, an equalizing formula is one in which higher property values result in lower aid. One scholarly criticism of this approach is that it is self-defeating; increased state aid to a school district will, if it is effective, raise school quality and thereby increase property values in that district, which will, in turn, lead to decreased state aid. This chapter examines this type of feedback loop in the case of a foundation aid formula, which is the type of formula used by about three-quarters of the states.[1]

The chapter begins with a brief review of the feedback arguments in the literature. Then we turn to the algebra of foundation formulas. On the basis of this algebra, we then analyze two cases: increased equalization holding the

---

*This chapter is a lightly edited version of John Yinger, 2012, "Capitalization and Equalization: The Feedback Effects of Foundation Aid for Schools," Center for Policy Research Working Paper, Syracuse University.
[1]The analysis in this chapter does not apply, for example, to power-equalizing aid (also called guaranteed-tax-base aid).

state-aid budget constant, and increased equalization funded by an increase in state aid. We show that first-order feedback effects do not exist with foundation aid, but that a variety of second-order feedbacks are worthy of more scholarly attention. Surprisingly, however, these second-order feedback effects could work in either direction; it is possible, in other words, that the feedback through capitalization could enhance the goals of the equalizing aid program instead of undermining them.

2. Previous Studies on Property-Value Feedback

Scholars have long recognized that the capitalization of property tax rates and public service levels into house values has important implications for the distributional consequences of many state policies, including state aid to education. See Yinger (1986), Ladd and Yinger (1994), Oakland (1994), Wyckoff (1995, 2001), and Dee (2000). Although these scholars disagree about the magnitude of this feedback effect, they agree that policies providing new resources for a jurisdiction will raise property values and rents there. These increases will, to some degree, offset the benefits from the new resources for renters and for people who move into the jurisdiction in the future. In the extreme case of full capitalization, renters and future owners will not gain from these policies at all.

A few scholars have pointed out that feedback effects through capitalization also are relevant when one is concerned about the distribution of educational performance across jurisdictions, instead of about the distribution of income or wealth. See Walker (1998) and Hoxby (2001). To be specific, suppose a jurisdiction receives an increase in state aid as part of a state aid reform. If this aid increase is effective, it will result in higher educational performance in the district and this higher performance will be capitalized into house values. Because most redistributive aid formulas are based on property values, among other things, this capitalization will lead to a reduction in the initial aid increase, and hence will undermine the program's performance impact. As Hoxby (2001) puts it

> the consequences of an SFE [school finance equalization] can be capitalized. Because households will choose among residences within the state, the price of housing will fall in districts that pay more into the scheme than they get out of it, and vice versa. Since net aid is a negative function of property values, capitalization of an SFE will partially undo it. Put another way, the basis of redistribution is *endogenous* to the consequences of the redistribution scheme (p. 1205).

In this chapter, I analyze this type of feedback effect in the case of a foundation aid program, which is one of the school finance equalization programs considered by Hoxby.

3. The Algebra of Foundation Aid Formulas

A foundation formula is designed to ensure that all school districts can afford to provide a certain level of spending per pupil, called the "foundation" level, if they levy a certain minimum property tax rate. We call this minimum the "required" property tax rate because it is the rate that state policy makers require before a school district is guaranteed to be able to afford the state-determined foundation spending level. In addition, most states that use a foundation aid formula actually require each district receiving aid to levy a tax rate no lower than this minimum. Throughout this chapter, I assume that this rate is, indeed, a required minimum. This is an effective tax rate in the sense that it is expressed as a percentage of the market value of a district's property. Thus, aid to a district equals the foundation level minus the revenue the district can raise itself at the required minimum tax rate. Districts that can fully fund the foundation spending level with the property taxes they raise at the required minimum tax rate receive no aid from the state.

In symbols, let A_i be the aid per pupil received by school district i, let V_i be school district i's property value per pupil, let E^* be the foundation spending level, and let t^* be the required minimum property tax rate. Then a foundation formula can be written as follows:

$$
\begin{aligned}
A_i &= E^* - t^*V_i \quad &&\text{if } E^* - t^*V_i > 0 \\
&= 0 \quad &&\text{if } E^* - t^*V_i \leq 0.
\end{aligned}
\tag{1}
$$

One crucial implication of a foundation formula is that changes in the policy parameters in the formula, or in the state-wide distribution of V_i, can alter the set of districts that receive aid. One way to think about this is to define V^* as the property value per pupil below which a district receives aid. Setting A_i equal to zero, the above formula implies that

$$
V^* = \frac{E^*}{t^*}
\tag{2}
$$

Thus, increasing E^* or decreasing t^* raises the property value below which a district receives aid.

The overall state-aid budget plays an important role in our analysis. Let N stand for the total number of pupils in the state, B stand for the state-aid budget per pupil, N_i stand for the number of pupils in district i, and I^* stand for the set of districts that receive aid. Then the total state aid budget equals $(B)(N)$, the state aid given to district i equals $A_i N_i$, and the state aid budget must satisfy

$$
(B)(N) = \sum_{I^*} N_i A_i
$$

$$
= \sum_{I^*} N_i (E^* - t^* V_i)
$$

$$
= E^* \sum_{I^*} N_i - t^* \sum_{I^*} N_i V_i. \tag{3}
$$

This formula can be simplified by defining N^* as the number of students in districts receiving aid, $\bar{V}^*$ as the total property value per pupil in those districts, and B^* as the aid per pupil in those districts. With these definitions,

$$
B^* = B\left(\frac{N}{N^*}\right) = E^* - t^* V^*. \tag{4}
$$

4. Feedback Effects for a No-Cost Increase in Equalization

The first question to ask is whether a no-cost increase in equalization, defined by a \$1.00 increase in E^* holding B constant, is undermined by feedback effects through property values.

4.1. *No Change in the Set of Districts Receiving Aid*

Suppose to begin that this change in E^* does not alter the set of school districts that receive aid.[2] This need not be the case, of course. A change in E^* might alter V^* or the V_i's or both, and therefore might either push some districts receiving aid into the no-aid group or might result in new districts becoming eligible for aid. Nevertheless, this assumption will be approximately true in many cases and is a good place to start our analysis. Note that this assumption implies that N^* does not change.

---

[2]The analysis in this chapter assumes that state aid changes do not lead to a change in the number of pupils in any district. The impact of aid on school district efficiency is also not considered.

Now let a subscript "1" indicate the initial situation and a subscript "2" indicate the situation after the change in E^*. Then the budget equation with a \$1 increase in E^* holding B and I^* constant can be written as follows:

$$E^* \sum_{I^*} N_i - t_1^* \sum_{I^*} V_{i1} N_i = (B)(N) = (E^* + 1) \sum_{I^*} N_i - t_2^* \sum_{I^*} V_{i2} N_i. \quad (5)$$

Solving this equation for t_2^*, we find that

$$t_2^* = \frac{1 + t_1^* \bar{V}_1^*}{\bar{V}_2^*} \quad (6)$$

Note that this case almost certainly involves an increase in t^*. The state is setting a higher E^* without coming up with any more money. As a result the increase in E^* must be financed by higher local tax rates. With no change in $\bar{V}^*$, for example, equation (6) implies that the tax rate increases by $(1/\bar{V}^*)$. Moreover, the change in $\bar{V}^*$ is likely to be negative. Any district willing to finance a \$1 increase in spending by raising its property taxes would already have done so. Any district spending the minimum allowable, namely E^*, must believe that the benefits of an increase in spending are not worth the property tax costs. By forcing such an increase, therefore, the new aid policy moves the district to a less desirable outcome and therefore lowers its property values.

The change in state aid for an individual district can now be found from equations (1) and (6):

$$A_{i2} - A_{i1} = (E_1^* + 1) - t_t^* V_{i2} - (E^* - t_1^* V_{i1})$$
$$= 1 - t_2^* V_{i2} + t_1^* V_{i1}$$
$$= 1 - \left(\frac{1 + t_1^* \bar{V}_1^*}{\bar{V}_2^*} \right) V_{i2} + t_1^* V_{i1}. \quad (7)$$

This result leads to a fundamental insight about equalization: If $V_{i1} = \bar{V}_1^*$ and $V_{i2} = \bar{V}_2^*$, then an increase in E^* does not alter the aid to district i at all. Any change in property value in this district is exactly offset by a change in t^*. Regardless of the extent of capitalization, in other words, an increase in E^* that does not change the set of districts receiving aid also does not change the aid received by a district with the average property value for recipient districts both before and after the change. If, for example, all recipient districts have the same initial property value and experience the same capitalization, then there is absolutely no feedback from this capitalization to the amount of aid they receive.

This result does not imply, of course, that increasing the degree of equalization, holding B constant, leaves aid unchanged for every district in a heterogeneous set. To analyze this case, we begin with the observation that the property value increase in response to an increase in state aid equals the present value of the stream of net benefits that flow from this extra aid. These benefits could take the form of increased public services or lower property taxes. The precise form of these benefits, which depends on the household utility function, among other things, cannot be determined without simulations, which are not attempted here. For now, it is appropriate to approximate this relationship by assuming that a $1 change in aid per capita leads to a $\$\alpha$ change in a district's average property value. In symbols,

$$\Delta V_i = \alpha \Delta A_i \tag{8}$$

With this formulation, property values do not change in a district in which the change in aid is zero. This formulation implicitly assumes that a district receiving no change in aid, which is, as shown above, a district with average property values before and after the increase in equalization, is either already spending more than $(E^* + 1)$ with a property tax rate above t_2^*, so that it is not affected by the increase in the required minimum tax rate, or else is just indifferent to a $1 increase in E combined with the tax increase needed to finance it. This may be true, at least approximately, in many cases. However, if E^* is far above the value the district would choose on its own if it received the same amount of aid with no strings, then the required increase in E is probably worth less to the voters than the property taxes needed to finance it.

Equation (8) also implies that $\bar{V}_2^* = \bar{V}_1^*$. This is true because the difference between these two average values depends on the sum of the population-weighted aid changes across recipient districts. Because the total aid budget does not change, this sum equals zero.

Substituting equation (8) into (7) and recognizing that $\bar{V}_2^* = \bar{V}_1^*$, we find that

$$\Delta A_i = \frac{\bar{V}_1^* - V_{i1}}{\bar{V}_1^* + \alpha \left(1 + t_1^* \bar{V}_1^*\right)} \tag{9}$$

This equation obviously implies that

$$\begin{aligned}
\Delta A_i &> 0 &&\text{if } V_{i1} < \bar{V}_1^* \\
&= 0 &&\text{if } V_{i1} = \bar{V}_1^* \\
&< 0 &&\text{if } V_{i1} > \bar{V}_1^*.
\end{aligned} \tag{10}$$

In this case, therefore, the increase in equalization works exactly as one would expect; among the set of districts receiving aid, it increases aid to the poorest districts and decreases aid to the richest districts. If α equals zero, which means there is no capitalization, the change in aid in a district equals $(1 - V_{i1}/\bar{V}_1^*)$. Differentiating equation (9) with respect to α also reveals that an increase in capitalization lowers the extent of aid redistribution; that is, the higher the value of the α, the smaller the absolute value of the change in aid at any given value of V_{i1}.

The question is: Does this decline in the extent of aid redistribution have a feedback effect onto educational performance, that is, does it undermine the equalizing objective of the program? The answer depends on the generosity of the aid program. If E^* is set above the level of spending that a district would provide if it received the state aid with no strings, which is equivalent to saying that t^* is above the tax rate the district would freely select, then capitalization has no impact on educational spending or performance. Spending is E^*, and the performance in each district is the performance purchased with E^*, with or without capitalization. To put in another way, with a high foundation level capitalization affects the tax payments of homeowners, and in particular increases their taxes if they become wealthier, but has no impact on the education that children receive.

If the aid program is not very generous, however, so that E^* is below the level the district would spend with no strings on its state aid, then capitalization does have an impact on educational performance. For districts with property values below $\bar{V}_1^*$, capitalization results in a decrease in aid and hence in a decrease in educational spending. The opposite is true for districts with property values above $\bar{V}_1^*$. The first of these responses does undermine equalization among the poorest districts. However, if E^* is set so that it constrains only the districts with property values below $\bar{V}_1^*$, the effect of capitalization is to magnify the desired education spending increases, not to undermine them.

4.2. *Change in the Set of Districts Receiving Aid*

Now let us consider the possibility that an increase in E^* alters the set of districts eligible for aid. An increase in E^* raises t^*, and therefore lowers V^*. It follows that the only possible change in the set of districts is that the highest-value districts among those receiving aid will drop out of the recipient pool. Recall, however, that an increase in E^* also cuts the aid to these districts, which results in a drop in their property values. Moreover, if the increase in t^* is binding for these districts, then the increase in E^*

is likely to be worth less to them than the tax cost, thereby driving down their values even more. So the question is: Are there districts with values near V^* who experience such a small drop in their own V that the drop in V^* overtakes them and makes them ineligible for aid? It seems reasonable to suppose that the set of districts that meet this condition is small, but it may not be empty. The only way to sort this out is through simulations.

If some districts drop out of the recipient pool, the money available to the other districts goes up. This means that t^* can go back down a bit (and V^* back up). Two outcomes are possible. First, there might just be more redistribution to the new, smaller set of recipient districts. This is not likely to be a large effect because any district that drops out is receiving very little aid per pupil and is likely to have a very small share of the total pupils in districts receiving aid. Second, there might be some kind of cycling in and out of the set of recipient districts — a type of disequilibrium — as districts with V below the V^* based on the initial recipient pool find themselves with V above the adjusted V^* that holds after some districts drop out of this pool. Only simulation can determine whether this type of outcome is possible.

5. Feedback Effects for a State-Financed Increase in Equalization

Another important case to consider is an increase in equalization that is fully funded by the state government. This case can be analyzed by assuming that E^* goes up by \$1 and that the state aid budget increases enough to pay for this increase in the districts initially receiving aid, namely, by $\$N^*$.

5.1. *No Change in the Set of Districts Receiving Aid*

As before, let us begin with the case in which the increased equalization does not alter the set of districts receiving aid. In this case, we can determine the new minimum tax rate as follows:

$$E^*N^* - t_1^*\bar{V}_1^*N^* + N^* = (E^* + 1)\,N^* - t_2^*\bar{V}_2^*N^* \tag{11}$$

Solving this equation for t_2^* yields

$$t_2^* = t_1^*\left(\frac{\bar{V}_1^*}{\bar{V}_2^*}\right) \tag{12}$$

This result allows us to solve for the change in a district's aid.

$$A_{i2} - A_{i1} = (E^* + 1) - t_2^* V_{i2} - (E^* - t_1^* V_{i1})$$

$$= 1 - t_1^* \left(V_{i2} \left(\frac{\bar{V}_1^*}{\bar{V}_2^*} \right) - V_{i1} \right). \tag{13}$$

Not surprisingly, the aid change for an "average" district is no longer zero. Specifically, if $V_{i1} = \bar{V}_1^*$ and $V_{i2} = \bar{V}_1^*$, then the state-funded increase in E^* increases the aid to district i by exactly \$1, regardless of the extent of capitalization. This \$1 increase is, of course, exactly what is intended. Thus, with the example given earlier, namely a set of identical recipient districts, there is still no feedback from this capitalization to the amount of aid the districts receive; \$E$ grows by exactly \$1, at the state's expense, regardless of the extent of capitalization.

Now suppose, as before, that capitalization follows the form in equation (8). Substituting this formula into the state's budget constraint implies that

$$\bar{V}_2^* = \bar{V}_1^* + \alpha \tag{14}$$

When combined with equation (7), this result implies that

$$\Delta A_i = \frac{\bar{V}_1^* + \alpha \left(1 + t_1^* V_{i1} \right)}{\bar{V}_1^* + \alpha \left(1 + t_1^* \bar{V}_1^* \right)} \tag{15}$$

This equation implies that the change in aid per pupil is always positive. If there is no capitalization, aid per pupil obviously goes up by \$1 in every district. With capitalization, however,

$$\begin{aligned} \Delta A_i &< 1 \quad \text{if } V_{i1} < \bar{V}_1^* \\ &= 1 \quad \text{if } V_{i1} = \bar{V}_1^* \\ &> 1 \quad \text{if } V_{i1} > \bar{V}_1^*. \end{aligned} \tag{16}$$

This result reflects that fact that any decline in t^* has a larger positive impact, in terms of aid per pupil, on districts with higher wealth. Moreover, it is obviously an anti-equalizing result. Whenever there is capitalization, an increase in E^* combined with a decrease in t^* leads to higher aid increases in wealthier districts than in poorer districts (among those receiving aid), which is a type of negative feedback from capitalization. Moreover, this effect increases with the degree of capitalization, as measured by α.

5.2. *Change in the Set of Districts Receiving Aid*

Because aid increases for all districts and the required minimum tax rate declines, the net benefits from education services increase in every district and capitalization drives up property values everywhere. The decline in t^* also boosts V^*, that maximum property value at which a district can receive aid. These factors lead to a "race" between the property-value increase in the highest-value recipient districts value and the increase in V^*. If a district "wins" it is no longer eligible for aid. If all districts "lose," they all continue to receive aid despite the increases in their property values.

If one or more districts is removed from the set of eligible districts, the type of cycling problem described earlier could arise. Once a district loses aid, its average property value could decline back to its pre-aid-change level so that the district becomes eligible for aid again. As before, the foundation aid program might not have an equilibrium allocation.

In addition, any increase in V^* might "capture" more districts for the recipient pool. Any increase in the pool spreads the available resources more thinly and thereby undermines equalization to a small degree. This type of effect also could lead to another type of cycle. As new districts are brought in, t^* must rise to balance the state's budget, which implies that V^* must drop, and the new districts might no longer be eligible.

6. Feedback Effects for a Partially State-Financed Increase in Equalization

A final case to consider is one in which the state budget increases by $\$N$, enough to finance a $\$1$ increase in E in every district currently receiving aid, and the minimum required tax rate is held constant at t_1^*. This case blends the previous two in the sense that it involves a higher contribution to education by both the state and school districts.

6.1. *No Change in the Set of Districts Receiving Aid*

In this case, t^* is held constant and we must solve for ΔE^* using the state budget constraint. To be specific:

$$E^* N^* - t_1^* \bar{V}_1^* + N^* = \left(E^* + \Delta E^*\right) N^* - t_1^* \bar{V}_2^* N^* \tag{17}$$

This equation implies that

$$\Delta E^* = 1 + t_1^* \left(\bar{V}_2^* - \bar{V}_1^* \right) \tag{18}$$

In addition, equation (7) implies that the change in aid is given by

$$\begin{aligned} \Delta A_i &= \Delta E^* - t_1^* \left(V_{i2} - V_{i1} \right) \\ &= 1 + t_1^* \left[\left(\bar{V}_2^* - \bar{V}_1^* \right) - \left(V_{i2} - V_{i1} \right) \right] \\ &= 1 + t_1^* \left[\left(\bar{V}_2^* - V_{i2} \right) - \left(\bar{V}_1^* - V_{i1} \right) \right] \end{aligned} \tag{19}$$

As in the previous case, ΔA_i equals 1 for a district with average values (among the set of recipient districts) before and after the change. However, if we now add equation (8), we find that ΔA_i equals 1 for **every** district, regardless of its initial property value and regardless of the degree of capitalization!

The difference between this case and the last one is that capitalization no longer alters the minimum required tax rate, which is held fixed by policy makers. Instead, by increasing districts' property tax base at a fixed minimum tax rate, and thereby increasing the contribution each recipient district is expected to make out of its own funds, capitalization requires the state government to increase E^* in order to make sure that its budget is all used up. In other words, capitalization simply finances an increase in E^* beyond the $1 increase in the previous case. Far from undermining equalization, therefore, capitalization increases educational spending in the recipient districts. Moreover, this increase is accomplished without any redistribution among the recipient districts, at least not when equation (8) holds.

6.2. *Change in the Set of Districts Receiving Aid*

Because this case does not change t^* or V^*, it does not pull any new districts into the recipient set. However, some recipient districts could experience an increase in property values sufficient to make them ineligible for aid. Once a district is removed from the eligible set, of course, the drop in aid it experiences will result in a decline in its property values so that it "falls" back into this set. This is another example of a cycling or disequilibrium problem. Simulations would have to be conducted to determine the likelihood of this type of problem.

7. Conclusions

The punchline of all this is that capitalization has several types of feedback effects when equalization is boosted:

It redistributes aid among districts that initially receive it, as it lowers both the "reward" to the lower-wealth districts and "penalty" to higher-wealth districts in this set.

It could alter the set of districts receiving aid, although this is far from certain. If it does, then it could either boost (no-cost case) or thin out (state-sponsored case) the aid to the original recipients. Moreover, it could result in a lack of equilibrium in the set of districts that receive aid, with a few districts receiving aid one year but not the next. This possibility does not appear likely, however. Overall, the magnitude of these effects is unclear without simulation, but they do not appear likely to be large.

Finally, it appears that the impact of capitalization on educational outcomes (through the feedback on aid amounts) can be minimized by keeping E^*, the foundation spending level in the aid formula, reasonably high — at least as high as the spending poor districts would select if their property tax rate were not constrained by the aid program. Similarly, the negative distributional consequences of feedback can be minimized by making the tax rate in the foundation formula, t^*, a required minimum tax rate and by keeping this rate at or above the value already selected by low-wealth districts.

References

Dee, Thomas S. 2000. The capitalization of education finance reforms. *Law and Economics* **43**(1): 185–214.

Hoxby, Caroline M. 2001. All school finance equalizations are not created equal. *Quarterly Journal of Economics* **116**(4): 1189–1232.

Ladd, Helen F. and John Yinger. 1994. The case for equalizing aid. *National Tax Journal* **47**(1): 211–224. [Chapter 13]

Oakland, William H. 1994. Fiscal equalization: an empty box? *National Tax Journal* **47**(1): 199–210.

Walker, Craig. 1998. A theoretical and empirical model of the demand for local public education services recognizing the effects of capitalization and closed-end matching grants. Unpublished Ph.D Dissertation, Southern Methodist University.

Wyckoff, Paul Gary. 1995. Capitalization, equalization, and intergovernmental aid. *Public Finance Quarterly* **23**(4): 484–508.

Wyckoff, Paul Gary. 2001. Capitalization and the incidence of school aid. *Journal of Education Finance* **27**(1): 585–607.

Yinger, John. 1986. On fiscal disparities across cities. *Journal of Urban Economics* **19**(3): 316–337.

Part 6
School Quality and Property Values

Chapter 15

The Capitalization of School Quality into House Values: A Review[*]

Phuong Nguyen-Hoang[†] and John Yinger[‡,§]

[†]*Public Policy Center and School of Urban and Regional Planning,*
University of Iowa, Iowa City, IA 52242, United States
[‡]*Departments of Public Administration and*
International Affairs and of Economics,
Syracuse University, Syracuse, NY, United States
[§]*jyinger@maxwell.syr.edu*

This paper provides a comprehensive review of empirical studies on the capitalization of school quality into house values that have appeared since 1999. We explore their methodological innovations and capitalization results. Most studies find significant capitalization especially for educational outputs, although the magnitudes are smaller for studies with fixed-effects estimation strategies. These studies find that house values rise by below 4% for a one-standard deviation increase in student test scores. Although major conceptual and estimation challenges remain, much progress has been made on this topic.

1. Introduction

House values provide a window into household demand for public services, including public school quality. Starting with Oates (1969), many scholars have explored the impact of school quality and local property taxes on house values, using a wide range of methods and data sets. This literature has expanded significantly in recent years as measures of student performance on standardized tests, which are key indicators of school quality, have become

---

[*]This chapter is reproduced from "The Capitalization of School Quality into House Values: A Review." *Journal of Housing Economics*, **20**(1), March 2011, pp. 30–48.

more widely available. Studies published before 1999 are reviewed in Ross and Yinger (1999), but a comprehensive survey of the studies published since then is not available.[1] This paper is designed to fill this gap. We explore methodological innovations in the recent literature and ask whether recent studies consistently find a significant impact of school quality on house values.

This paper proceeds as follows. Section 2 provides a conceptual framework for thinking about school quality capitalization. Section 3 presents a methodological review of 50 capitalization studies and their results. Section 4 concludes the paper with suggestions for future research.

2. Conceptual Framework

This section develops a conceptual framework for public service capitalization and discusses the implications of this framework for empirical work on the topic.

2.1. Bidding and Sorting

As presented in Ross and Yinger (1999), the standard model of school quality capitalization builds on five central assumptions. First, households fall into distinct income-taste classes, and households in a class are assumed to have identical demand for housing, school quality, and other goods. Second, mobile households can move at no cost across jurisdictions until households of the same class obtain the same utility level, leading to an equilibrium in which no household has an incentive to move. Third, only residents in a jurisdiction can benefit from school services provided there, and the same services are received by all households in a given jurisdiction. Fourth, an urban area has many communities with fixed boundaries that offer different school qualities and effective property tax rates. Fifth, all households are homeowners.

A household's budget constraint requires income to equal spending.

$$Y = Z + PH + tV = Z + PH + t\frac{PH}{r} = Z + PH + t^*PH$$
$$= Z + PH(1 + t^*) \tag{1}$$

---

[1]Recent views of the "hedonics" literature, which addresses the relationship between house values and amenities in general, include Chin and Chau (2003), Guilfoyle (2000), and Taylor (2008). These reviews, however, do not focus on school quality capitalization. Gibbons and Machin (2008) review some of this literature, but do not provide a comprehensive coverage of issues and articles.

where Y is the household's income; Z is a numeraire good; H is units of housing services, which are sold at price P; t is the effective property tax rate, which is equal to [(nominal tax rate $\times$ assessed values)/market (or sales) values]; V is the market value of a house and equal to PH/r, where r is the appropriate discount rate; and $t^* = t/r$.

The household's problem is to determine how much to pay for H given the quality of local public services, S, and the effective tax rate, t. This problem can be specified by determining the maximum price a household will pay for housing associated with a given S, holding their utility constant. More technically, the household problem is defined by solving (1) for P and maximizing the result with respect to H and Z subject to a utility constraint. Or, maximize

$$P = \frac{Y - Z}{H(1 + t^*)} \tag{2}$$

subject to

$$U(Z, H, S) = U^0(Y) \tag{3}$$

where U^0 is the utility achieved by households with income Y.

Now we can use the envelope theorem and the first-order condition of this problem with respect to Z to derive the well-known result:

$$P_S = \frac{U_S/U_Z}{H(1 + t^*)} = \frac{MB}{H(1 + t^*)} \tag{4}$$

where U_S/U_Z indicates the marginal rate of substitution between S and Z, which is the marginal benefit from S in dollar terms, MB. Equation (4) is a differential equation with a solution, $P\{S\}$, which depends on the form of the utility function. Let $\hat{P}$ stand for the before-tax price of housing. Then using well-known results about property tax capitalization and the above formula for housing price, V, we can write[2]:

$$V = \frac{PH}{r} = \frac{\hat{P}\{S\}H}{r + \beta t} = \frac{\hat{P}\{S\}H}{r\left(1 + \frac{\beta}{r}t\right)} \tag{5}$$

where β is the degree of property tax capitalization. Using the approximation $\ln(1 + \epsilon) \approx \epsilon$ when ϵ is close to 0, taking the log of equation (5) and adding

---

[2]The property tax capitalization formula can be derived by applying the envelope theorem to the above household maximization problem and using the initial condition that the before-tax and after-tax prices of housing are equal when $t = 0$. See Ross and Yinger (1999).

a constant, κ, and error term, ϵ, produces an estimation equation.[3]

$$\ln V = \kappa + \alpha \ln \widehat{P}\{S\} + \varphi \ln H - \left(\frac{\beta}{r}\right) t + \epsilon \tag{6}$$

The principal theoretical problem with equation (6) is that it applies to a single household type. Houses are sold to many household types, however, and the implicit parameters in the $\widehat{P}$ function, can vary from one household type to another. This issue can be resolved by turning to the Rosen (1974) framework and to the concept of household sorting. In this framework, equation (6) is the bid function for a single household type, and the housing price or value function we observe in the market is the envelope of the underlying household bid functions. Households sort according to the slopes of their bid functions, such that households with steeper bid function for S (that is, a higher ratio of MB to H) win the competition for housing in the jurisdictions where the level of S is highest. Thus, movement along the bid-function envelope reflects both change in bids as S changes and changes in household types due to sorting.

Although the logic of a bid-function envelope is well known, only a few studies have attempted to derive this envelope. Epple (1987) considers the case of a utility function equal to

$$U_i = \sum_j \theta \left(X_j - \alpha_{ij}\right) + Z \tag{7}$$

where X is a housing attribute, Z is still a numeraire good, θ and α are preference parameters, and i and j index households and housing attributes, respectively. He assumes the distributions of X and α are normal and shows that the resulting bid-function envelope, $P\{X\}$, is

$$P\{X\} = \beta_0 + \sum_j \beta_{1j} X_j + \sum_j \beta_{2j}(X_j)^2 + \sum_j \sum_{j'} \beta_{3jj'} X_j X_{j'} \tag{8}$$

In this equation, the βs are functions of the θs and of the parameters of the α and X distributions. This formulation could be applied to housing if all public service and structural traits were brought into the X vector.

Yinger (2015) derives bid-function envelopes under the assumptions that the service and housing demand functions take the constant-elasticity form; that sorting is determined by bid-function slopes (as in the standard

---

[3]Note that $\ln r$ is included in κ.

theorem discussed above); and that the equilibrium relationship between the service level, S, and the bid-function slope, ψ, can be approximated by $S = (\sigma_1 + \sigma_2 \psi)^{\sigma_3}$. Three easy-to estimate special cases of this envelope arise when the price elasticity of demand for housing is minus one and σ_3 equals one. Let μ be the price elasticity of demand for S and C be a constant, then these cases, which can be introduced into equation (6), are

$$\ln\{\widehat{P}\} = C + \left(\frac{\sigma_1}{\sigma_2}\right)\left(\frac{1}{S}\right) + \left(\frac{1}{\sigma_2}\right)\ln\{S\} \quad \text{(if } \mu = -0.5\text{)}, \tag{9a}$$

$$\ln\{\widehat{P}\} = C - \left(\frac{\sigma_1}{\sigma_2}\right)\ln\{S\} + \left(\frac{1}{\sigma_2}\right)S \quad \text{(if } \mu = -1.0\text{)}, \tag{9b}$$

$$\ln\{\widehat{P}\} = C - \left(\frac{\sigma_1}{\sigma_2}\right)S + \left(\frac{1}{\sigma_2}\right)S^2 \quad \text{(if } \mu = -\infty\text{)}. \tag{9c}$$

These results can be extended to applications involving more than one S. Moreover, the last of these cases is equivalent to the Epple envelope except that it does not contain interaction terms.

Perhaps the main lesson from these derivations is that the bid-function envelope is unlikely to be characterized by a linear relationship (even in logarithms) between V and S. Indeed, the simplest form, which approximates both Epple and the third case above, is to regress $\ln\{V\}$ on a quadratic specification of S. Although service-capitalization studies inevitably estimate the envelope (because the underlying bid-functions are not observed), few of these studies (see below) use this quadratic form or any other two-variable specification for S. Although more research on the appropriate form for the envelope is clearly needed, it seems safe to conclude that most studies use forms more appropriate for bid functions than for bid-function envelopes.

Studies by Epple and Sieg (1999) and Epple *et al.* (2001) are important exceptions to this conclusion. These studies derive bid-functions that vary with household income and with a preference parameter in the utility function and then use equilibrium conditions for housing prices at jurisdiction boundaries to simultaneously set housing prices and allocate household across jurisdictions. Although these studies do not literally specify and estimate a bid-function envelope, they provide an equivalent procedure. The Epple *et al.* study also takes another step by not only incorporating sorting into the estimating procedure, but also by simultaneously estimating sorting and the determination of S through majority rule based on the people who sort into each community.

These two path-breaking studies set the standard for a comprehensive treatment of sorting, but they also have limitations.[4] They require specific assumptions about the form of the utility function and characterize household heterogeneity using income and one utility-function parameter. Also, they combine school quality and the crime rate into a single index of public service quality (with one estimated weight) and make use of jurisdiction-level data. Although these limitations could, in principle, be addressed, the approach in these studies seems unlikely to gain wide acceptance in the school-capitalization literature because it involves an elaborate estimating procedure and does not yield an intuitively appealing measure of public service capitalization.

According to the Rosen framework, a household sets its marginal willingness to pay for school quality equal to the "implicit price" of school quality, which is the slope of the bid-function envelope. Because the envelope is nonlinear, implicit prices vary across households. This framework leads to Rosen's second step, which is to regress the quantity of S selected by a household on the implicit price it faces (treated as endogenous), its income, and other demand variables. This approach indicates each household's marginal willingness to pay for S. Several studies have estimated Rosen's second step for measures of school quality, but this step is not covered in this review.

Before leaving this topic, it is important to point out that some studies mistakenly interpret the results of a regression of V on S, Rosen's first step, as an indication of the marginal willingness to pay for S. In other words, these studies interpret the derivative of V with respect to S as a measure of the extent to which a household's bid would increase if the level of S went up by one unit. In fact, however, the Rosen framework makes it clear that movement along the bid-function envelope reflects two factors: marginal willingness to pay for S and the change in bid-function slopes caused by household sorting. Marginal willingness to pay is not directly

---

[4]Bayer et al. (2007) also address sorting by developing a discrete model of location choice that incorporates sorting directly into the estimating procedure. Although a hedonic equation is estimated as part of this procedure, the hedonic itself does not account for sorting. Indeed, this hedonic is estimated in linear form, which, as shown in the text, is not compatible with sorting. Bayer et al. also argue (p. 620) that "there is likely to be only a slight difference between the mean preferences estimated in the heterogeneous sorting model and the coefficients of the hedonic price regression." In the Rosen framework with heterogeneous preferences, however, the hedonic function does not coincide, even approximately, with any of the underlying bid functions.

observed. Unless the functional form explicitly identifies the underlying demand parameters, as in Epple (1987) and Yinger (2010), the coefficient of S in a capitalization equation cannot be used to measure marginal willingness to pay.

Nevertheless, school quality cannot have an impact on the envelope unless households value it. As a result, the significance of various school quality measures provides important information about household preferences for school quality. Moreover, the impact of school quality on house values is an important topic in its own right, regardless of whether or not it yields a measure of willingness to pay. Regressions of V on S help explain, for example, why housing prices are higher in some places than others, and they provide information for state officials and voters who may want to know how much property values change in response to changes in school quality.

In short, this review interprets studies of school quality capitalization as estimates of a bid-function envelope. Even though these estimates cannot be translated into measures of willingness to pay, at least not without further analysis, they provide important information about the nature of housing markets and of federal systems in various countries, especially in the United States.

2.2. *Methodological Issues*

This section discusses methodological issues for each term in a bid-function envelope.

2.2.1. *Functional forms of $\widehat{P}\{S\}$*

The first challenge is that the theoretical literature provides limited guidance for the functional form of $\widehat{P}\{S\}$ in the presence of household heterogeneity. As shown above, Epple (1987) and Yinger (2015) derive functional forms consistent with sorting under certain assumptions, but other studies have not followed this route. Instead, several studies investigate the performance of various functional forms in the hedonic model in general, instead of focusing on $\widehat{P}\{S\}$. They usually do so by comparing the linear, logarithmic, and Box–Cox (1964) specifications. The existing empirical evidence is inconclusive about which functional form is the most appropriate. Specifically, Box–Cox tests in Halvorsen and Pollakowski (1981) lead to the rejection of the three most commonly used specifications, namely linear, log-linear and linear-log. Cropper *et al.* (1988) argue that linear Box–Cox functions perform best in either correctly specified or possibly misspecified models, whereas quadratic semi-log specifications out perform the linear Box–Cox specification in Rasmussen and Zuehlke (1990). Halstead *et al.* (1997) find that the double-log specification performs best while Huh and Kwak (1997) show that the Box–Cox functional form is the best hedonic price specification for data in Seoul, Korea.

Note that, with the exception of Rasmussen and Zuehlke (1990), these studies all miss the lesson expressed earlier, namely that one-variable specifications for S are unlikely to be consistent with sorting. This lesson is supported by Rasmussen and Zuehlke's rejection of a Box–Cox in favor of a quadratic specification. Moreover, Yinger (2015) shows that the Box–Cox, log, and semi-log specifications are all inconsistent with sorting, at least given constant-elasticity demand functions for S and H. Overall, the inconclusive and sometimes contradictory results in these studies remind us that more research is still needed to guide the choice of functional forms in empirical studies of school quality capitalization. At this point, it seems reasonable to recommend that capitalization studies should at least examine a specification including S and S^2, which is consistent with Epple's (1987) and with Yinger's third special case in equation (9c).[5]

2.2.2. *School vs. neighborhood effects*

Good schools are correlated with other public services and with neighborhood amenities, such as crime rates, air quality, and proximity to employment or to shopping centers.[6] As a result, the estimating equation should really be based on $\widehat{P}\{S, N\}$, where N stands for other public services and neighborhood amenities. One possibility is to estimate an equation of the form:

$$\ln V = \kappa + \alpha_1 S + \alpha_2 S^2 + \gamma_1 N + \gamma_1 N^2 + \varphi \ln H - \left(\frac{\beta}{r}\right) t + \epsilon \qquad (10)$$

An unbiased estimate of the αs in equation (10) calls for controls for all appropriate N variables correlated with S and V. However, most studies

---

[5]Another approach is to estimate the hedonic model non-parametrically (i.e., without specifying a functional form). See Heckman *et al.* (2010).

[6]One might note that the definitions of neighborhood can vary from one study to another. For instance, neighborhoods in Clapp *et al.* (2008) are census tracts. In Bogart and Cromwell (2000), a neighborhood is like a catchment area because each neighborhood is associated with an elementary school. Ries and Somerville (2010) use the definition by the British Columbia Assessment Authority in Vancouver, Canada.

face limitations on data availability and hence may be subject to bias from omitted service or neighborhood variables.

One possible response to this problem is to use instrumental variable (IV) estimation, as in Downes and Zabel (2002) and Gibbons and Machin (2003). If a valid instrument or instruments could be found, two stage least squares (2SLS) estimation could be used to obtain an unbiased estimate of the desired α coefficients. Despite its theoretical lure, however, the IV approach is not without challenges. Valid IVs must be both correlated with the endogenous explanatory variables S and S^2, and exogenous in equation (10). These two conditions are not readily met in practice, and as Murray (2006) puts it, the dark cloud of invalidity hanging over IV estimation never goes entirely away.

A more common strategy is to employ fixed-effects estimation. Many types of fixed-effects approaches appear in the literature. As summarized in Table 1, they can be differentiated both by the geographic level of the fixed effects and by whether multiple years of data are available.

Several studies have made use of boundary fixed effects (BFE)[7] what was popularized in Black (1999).[8] The BFE design identifies segments of (usually elementary) school attendance-zone boundaries and defines a fixed effect for the houses sold within a narrow band on either side of each segment. The set of such fixed effects is then included in the hedonic regression to control for the unobserved neighborhood variables shared by people on either side of the boundary. This approach cannot be expected to account for all unobserved neighborhood traits. Gibbons *et al.* (2009) argue, for example, that discontinuity in house prices across zone boundaries could arise from different directional outlooks, omitted geographical features (e.g., a major road or rail station), or other location-specific amenities. Moreover, many existing studies use elementary attendance zones, which have many segments, and thereby ignore variation in high-school assignments. Estimates of elementary school capitalization could be biased downward when households on either side of the border do not share a high school. Nevertheless, the use of BFE is a creative way to lower the likely magnitude of omitted variable bias.

The BFE approach raises several challenging methodological issues. When used for attendance zone borders as in column 4 of Table 1, this

---

[7]Although it is sometimes called the boundary discontinuity approach, BFE is different from the traditional regression discontinuity approach adopted by Cellini *et al.* (2010).

[8]The borders approach was first adopted in Gill (1983) and Cushing (1984).

Table 1 Fixed effects in school quality capitalization studies.

Time dimension	Level of fixed effects				
	District or attendance zone (1)	Neighborhood[a] (2)	School district border (3)	Attendance zone border (4)	House (5)
One-year	n.a.	Controls for unobserved neighborhood traits; can only pick up the impact of within-district variation in S	Controls for unobserved neighborhood traits shared across district boundary; requires strong assumptions about similarity across border; cuts observations; does not account for sorting (e.g., Crone)	Controls for unobserved neighborhood traits shared across zone boundary; can only pick up the impact of within-district variation in elementary S; requires control for within-district variation in high school S; cuts observations; does not account for sorting (e.g., Leech and Campos)	n.a.
Multi-year	Controls for unobserved district (zone) traits; identifies effect based on time-variation in S or changes in district (zone) boundaries (e.g., Reback, Dills)	Controls for unobserved neighborhood traits; identifies effect based on time-variation in S (e.g., Clapp et al.)	Controls for unobserved neighborhood trends shared across district boundary; requires strong assumptions about similarity across border; cuts observations; does not account for sorting (e.g., Dhar and Ross)	Controls for unobserved neighborhood trends shared across zone boundary; can only pick up the impact of within-district variation in elementary S; requires control for within-district variation in high school S; cuts observations; does not account for sorting (e.g., Black, Kane et al., Bayer et al.)	Controls for all time-invariant variables; identifies all coefficients based on time variation; selection problem (e.g., Figlio and Lucas, Ries and Somerville)

Notes: [a] Although studies may have different definitions of neighborhoods, the boundaries of a neighborhood meant in this table are smaller than attendance zones.

approach by construction eliminates all across-district variation in S.[9] Therefore, scholars interested in across-district capitalization need another approach. Also, two potential sources of bias can undermine this approach. First, the notion that neighborhood traits are shared is more compelling if the neighborhood is small, that is, if the band defining the BFE is small. As a result, this approach calls for dropping observations that are far from a boundary. Non-random dropping of observations is always a concern, and in this case it raises the possibility of bias because neighborhoods near attendance-zone boundaries may differ from other neighborhoods for a variety of reasons. One possibility, discussed by Cheshire and Sheppard (2004) and Zahirovic-Herbert and Turnbull (2008), is that households living close to a boundary place a lower weight on across-zone differences in school quality than other households because they believe that these boundaries might change, as they occasionally do.

The second issue, which is discussed by Kane *et al.* (2006) and Bayer *et al.* (2007), is that boundaries often lead to sorting, so that neighborhoods on either side of a school attendance zone (or school district) boundary may contain people with different preferences for public services. This difference may not only lead to differences in bids for shared neighborhood traits on the two sides of the border, but may also lead, in the long run, to differences in neighborhood traits, such as average housing quality or the existence of neighborhood parks. As Kane *et al.* (2006, p. 194) put it, these differences could arise even if "houses and neighborhoods are very similar on either side of a school border *when the boundary is originally drawn*" [italics in the original]. The implication of this across-border heterogeneity is that border fixed effects do not adequately control for unobservable neighborhood factors. They neither account for the possibility that bids for the same neighborhood traits may be different on either side of the border nor capture difference in neighborhood traits that may arise over time due to sorting.

Bayer *et al.*'s (2007) solution to this problem is to include neighborhood income and education, measured separately on each side of the border, as control variables. These variables are highly significant in their hedonic regression, and their inclusion significantly lowers the estimated impact of school quality on house values. Bayer *et al.* interpret these demographic variables as direct measures of neighborhood quality, which is the second issue discussed above. They conclude, therefore, that a failure to measure

---

[9]The terms "across-" or "within-district" include studies at other levels of analysis than school districts.

neighborhood quality differences that arise from sorting leads to an over-statement of school quality's impact on house values.

We find this to be a helpful solution, but two other interpretations of their results cannot be ruled out. First, income and education are clearly demand variables, that is, they belong in the demand functions for school quality and housing. In the Rosen framework, the bid-function envelope, unlike the underlying bid functions, should not contain any demand variables. Indeed, including demand variables in the envelope can lead to the classic endogeneity bias discussed earlier, which arises because households' simultaneously select housing price and school quality, both of which depend on these demand variables. This point has been emphasized by several authors. After identifying a set of hedonic studies that include these variables, for example, Butler (1982, 1, fn. 1) writes that "income and other demander characteristics were intended as proxies for neighborhood quality. However, since the data used were aggregated to the 'neighborhood' level, it is impossible to separate the function of, for example, income as a neighborhood quality proxy from its role as a characteristic of demanders in that neighborhood."

Because neighborhood income and education are difficult for a home buyer to observe, we believe that these variables are unlikely to be direct measures of neighborhood traits that home buyers care about, and neither Bayer *et al.* nor any other study provides evidence that home buyers directly consider these variables in making their bids. Even if they are not literally neighborhood traits themselves, however, the logic of sorting indicates that these variables are likely to be correlated both with neighborhood traits that people care about and with bids on these traits in different locations. Let N stand for these neighborhood traits and Y stand for demographic factors, then this logic implies that

$$N = a + bY + e \tag{11}$$

In this equation, the error term, e, reflects the extent to which income measures reflect underlying demand instead of N. Now if the hedonic takes the form of equation (10), leaving off the N^2 term for simplicity, the insertion of Y from equation (11) into equation (10) as a control variable leads to

$$\ln V = \left(\kappa + \frac{\gamma_1 a}{b}\right) + \alpha_1 S + \alpha_2 S^2 + \gamma_1 \left(\frac{N - a - e}{b}\right)$$
$$+ \varphi \ln H - \left(\frac{\beta}{r}\right) t + \left(\epsilon + \frac{\gamma_1 e}{b}\right) \tag{12}$$

Because e is correlated with S and H, this equation suffers from endogeneity bias. This bias disappears only when $e = 0$, that is, when Y is a direct measure of all the sorting-related neighborhood traits that home buyers care about.

Another issue that arises with the Bayer *et al.* approach, which is not intrinsic to their method but instead arises because of their particular specification, is that the omission of the S^2 term combined with the inclusion of Y (and other demographics) may lead to a biased estimate of α_1, that is, of average service capitalization. As discussed earlier, the S^2 term or its equivalent appears in all formally derived envelope specifications that are consistent with sorting. The sign of α_2 is expected to be positive; indeed, Yinger (2015) shows that a positive sign for this coefficient supports the hypothesis that households sort according to the slopes of their bid functions. Moreover, a high value for Y is associated with a steep bid function, so the omission of S_2 is likely to bias upward the coefficient of Y and may lead to an understatement of service capitalization.

Alternative approaches, which solve the first of these two bias sources but not the second, are provided by Clapp *et al.* (2008) and Dhar and Ross (2010), both of which use data for house sales in Connecticut in several years. School district boundaries, which are coincident with town boundaries in the Connecticut sample, almost never change so anticipated changes should not be an issue. Clapp *et al.* control for unobserved neighborhood traits, including those associated with sorting together, with census tract fixed effects. (See column 2 and row 2 of Table 1.) With this approach, which does not require any observations to be dropped, the coefficient of S (school district quality) is identified based on variation in S over time. Clapp *et al.* find, as do Bayer *et al.*, that the coefficient of S declines significantly when small-neighborhood demographic variables are included, and they obtain the same result with their fixed effects.

By bringing in school district boundary fixed effects (column 3 and row 2 of Table 1), Dhar and Ross compare difference (across boundaries) in the difference of property values (over time) with difference (across boundaries) in the difference of school quality (over time). With this difference-in-differences approach, they find that small capitalization effects come from unobserved school quality, rather than from uncertainty over school district attendance borders. Overall, although both of these studies focus on school district quality instead of within-district school quality as in Bayer *et al.*, their findings suggest that uncertainty over school attendance boundaries may not be a major source of bias. Because they both do not include S^2

(or its equivalent for another envelope specification), however, these studies cannot rule out the second source of bias.

In short, Kane *et al.* and Bayer *et al.* provide important evidence that hedonic equations must account for sorting. The Bayer *et al.* solution to this problem, namely to include small-neighborhood demographics as control variables, is a good first step, but runs into some difficult problems of interpretation and specification. Clapp *et al.* and Dhar and Ross provide better solutions which are available only with a panel of house sales over more than one year. As implemented, however, both of these studies appear to estimate reduced-form specifications that do not recognize the impact of sorting on school-quality capitalization.

Clapp *et al.* is an example of a fixed-effects strategy made possible by more than one year of data. As shown in Table 1, a variety of other such strategies are available. These strategies face several challenges.[10] First, the fixed effects identification of capitalization is based only on changes in school quality over time. If the school quality exhibits little temporal variation, its effect on house prices cannot be determined with precision. Second, the inclusion of fixed effects typically reduces variation arising from unobservables, thereby increasing the relative importance of any measurement error in the data (Clapp *et al.*, 2008). In fact, studies find that school quality measures tend to show a significant component of random variation across years (Kane and Staiger, 2002a; Ries and Somerville, 2010). This measurement error in test scores may bias downwards the effect of school quality on house values in a fixed effects model (Brasington and Haurin, 2006).[11]

A few studies, including Figlio and Lucas (2004) and Ries and Somerville (2010), have access to a panel of house sales over time that is large enough to identify a sample of double sales. These data make it possible to use house-specific fixed effects (the bottom right cell of Table 1) and thereby to control for all time-invariant house and neighborhood traits. As pointed out by Downes and Zabel (2002), this approach may suffer from selection bias if houses that sell more than once are systematically different from

---

[10]Gujarati (2002), for instance, presents cautionary notes on possible problems plaguing the fixed effects model: loss of degrees of freedom, multicollinearity, failure to estimate time-invariant variables of interest, and inaccuracy of the classical assumption of the error term.

[11]The capitalization effect is also downwards biased when households perceive short-term score changes as random fluctuations and thus do not value them (Brasington and Haurin, 2006).

other houses, but with a large sample and sufficient time variation in school quality, it can lead to particularly compelling results.

2.2.3. *Spatial interactions*

Omitted neighborhood variables are a major focus of cross-section capitalization studies that employ hedonic models with spatial interaction effects.[12] These studies adopt either (or both) spatial lag or spatial error models modified from equation (10) as follows[13]:

$$\ln V = \kappa + \rho W \ln V + \alpha_1 S + \gamma_1 N + \varphi \ln H - \left(\frac{\beta}{r}\right) t + u, \qquad (13)$$

$$\ln V = \kappa + \alpha_1 S + \gamma_1 N + \varphi \ln H - \left(\frac{\beta}{r}\right) t + \epsilon \qquad (14)$$

where $\epsilon = \phi W + u$ and u is a random error term with mean equal to 0 and variance–covariance matrix $\sigma^2 I$. In both of these equations, W is a $n \times n$ spatial weights matrix indicating the inter-dependence of the nearby houses in the sample.[14] "Nearby" houses could be defined as houses that share a common border or are within a certain distance of each other. The spatial lag model, equation (13), assumes that the price for a given house is dependent on the prices, not only the characteristics, of surrounding houses (Sedgley *et al.*, 2008). The spatial error model, equation (14), is specified on the assumption that houses located near one another have similar unobservable attributes. In other words, the spatial error model deals with the issue of omitted neighborhood quality variables as one of efficiency.

Although the literature on spatial econometrics has developed substantially over the past thirty years (Anselin, 2010), few school quality capitalization studies have made use of spatial hedonic models because they raise conceptual and empirical issues that fall outside the scope of traditional

---

[12]The recent literature on spatial econometrics has expanded into panel data settings and attempted to explore both temporal (or serial) and spatial correlation in an integrated spatiotemporal framework (e.g., Baltagi *et al.* (2007), Elhorst (2008), LeSage and Pace (2004)).

[13]None of these studies, however, specify the quadratic specification of S or N as in equation (10).

[14]The specification of this weights matrix represents a potential weakness of spatial econometric models. Economic theory provides little guidance on how to specify the spatial weights matrix W (Leenders, 2002). Also, the accuracy of parameter estimates is very sensitive to the specification of the weights matrix (Pįez *et al.*, 2008; Stakhovych and Bijmolt, 2009).

capitalization studies. There is no agreement, for example, on the best model to specify spatial interaction effects.[15] In addition, even if the true data generation process is a spatial lag model, then scholars do not agree about the extent to which the estimate of school quality capitalization will be biased if spatial lags are ignored or about the extent to which a spatial lag model addresses omitted variable bias. Brasington and Haurin (2006) argue that the spatial lag model can account for omitted variables bias because the spatial lag term "acts like a highly localized dummy variable capturing highly localized influences common to just the nearest neighbors of each house." However, Pace and LeSage (2010) show that the presence of spatial lags magnifies conventional omitted variables bias, and that spatial hedonic models produce estimates with bias similar to the conventional omitted variable case. In other words, the spatial lag model does not eliminate omitted variable bias.

Another problem is that the spatially lagged dependent variable should also be treated as endogenous because it implies simultaneous interaction (Fingleton and Le Gallo, 2008). In fact, Anselin (2003, 316) proves that the spatially lagged dependent variable is correlated with u and is therefore endogenous even when u is iid. However, only a few recent studies have attempted to estimate a spatial hedonic model with both spatial and non-spatial endogenous variables.[16]

Scholars usually use either 2SLS or maximum likelihood approaches to estimate spatial hedonic models. Fingleton and Le Gallo's (2010) simulations show that 2SLS estimations perform much better in terms of bias and root mean square error than an OLS estimator. Maximum likelihood can address

---

[15]More general models of spatial interactions, which have been used in other contexts, have not yet been applied to school capitalization. More specifically, Kelejian–Prucha's (1998) model combines both of the spatial lag and spatial error specifications. The spatial Durbin model that was introduced by Anselin (1988) has a spatially lagged dependent variable ($W \ln V$) and spatially lagged explanatory variables. The most general spatial econometric model is Manski's (1993) model with the spatially lagged dependent variable, spatially lagged independent variables and spatially autocorrelated error terms. Of these models, the spatial Durbin model advocated by LeSage and Pace (2009) proves to be superior because it gives unbiased estimates even if the true data generation process is a spatial lag, spatial error or Kelejian-Prucha model (Elhorst, 2010). Given a multitude of spatial econometric models, a recommended approach for school-quality capitalization studies is comparing these models following the steps laid out in Elhorst (2010).

[16]Anselin and Lozano-Gracia (2009) and Fingleton and Le Gallo (2008) are among the first studies that implement spatial two stage least squares estimation for spatial hedonic models with spatial and non-spatial endogenous variables.

the endogeneity of spatial and non-spatial variables. However, Fingleton and Le Gallo (2008, 320) note that it is difficult, if not impossible, to implement maximum likelihood of a model with a spatial error process and endogenous variables. Also, maximum likelihood in spatial analysis can produce consistent and efficient estimates only when the full model including the functional form and the error distribution of the endogenous variables conditional on exogenous variables is assumed to be known in advance (McMillen, 2010). This assumption with little guidance from economic theory can be arbitrary and must be examined on a case-by-case basis (Wooldridge, 2002).

2.2.4. *Housing characteristics*

Equation (10) indicates that housing characteristics influence house prices. The effect of school quality on house values can be separated from that of housing characteristics using either, or both, of the following methods. The first method is a direct inclusion of standard explanatory variables such as square footage, age, number of bathrooms, bedrooms, presence of garage and/or basement, and air conditioning. Although Atkinson and Crocker (1987) stress the importance of including an extensive set of housing characteristics to avoid bias in parameters of interest including the coefficient of school quality, the availability of data could be a determinant of how many housing characteristics researchers include in their studies.

However extensive the list of housing controls, the direct inclusion method does not account for unobserved time-invariant housing characteristics, which are a potential source of bias. The second method, namely the use of fixed effects with repeat sales data, can address this issue. This approach, however, does not deal with potential bias caused by time-varying unobservables, including renovations or additions (Ries and Somerville, 2010).

2.2.5. *Effective tax rates*[17]

As shown by equation (5), property tax rates are capitalized into house values. A large literature, reviewed in Yinger *et al.* (1988) and Ross and Yinger (1999), finds evidence that, all else equal, higher effective property tax rates lead to lower house values, which is evidence of property tax

---

[17]Effective tax rates can be subsumed under neighborhood characteristics. However, we consider them separately because they enter into equation (10) as a key independent variable but as succeeding discussions indicate, often get improperly treated.

capitalization. For our purposes, the key issue is that property taxes are correlated with school quality, so unbiased estimates of school quality capitalization require controls for property tax rates.

Effective tax rates are equivalent to nominal rates with accurate assessments.[18] When these rates are not identical due to inaccurate or out-of-date assessment, two modeling issues concerning property tax rates warrant discussions. First, effective tax rates, not nominal tax rates, are capitalized into property values. Second, it may be necessary to treat the effective property tax rate, t, as endogenous. This step is not necessary if assessment errors are random or houses are accurately re-assessed upon sale for studies with individual sales price,[19] but long lags between reassessment result in higher assessment/sales ratios, and hence higher effective tax rates, in neighborhoods with slow value growth than in neighborhoods with high value growth. Under these circumstances, unobserved factors that result in higher V also result in lower t, which is a form of endogeneity. Scholars should therefore examine assessment practices when determining how to treat the property tax variables.

2.3. Measurement Issues

Estimation results from equation (10) also depend on the data for house values and school quality.

2.3.1. Measures of house values

School quality capitalization studies have employed many different measures of house values, including aggregate values, median or average house values, house price indexes, owner-reported house values, advertised house prices, and actual sales prices.

Aggregate or median house values are widely available and can prove useful at the school district level. However, employing these types of data can produce biased parameter estimates as a result of their failure to effectively control for new housing developments and housing quality. In contrast, house

---

[18] Effective and nominal tax rates are in fact the same when the 100% assessment ratio of assessed values to market value is mandated.

[19] Even with accurate assessments upon sale, studies that use a tax jurisdiction's median or average house values with long lags between reassessment may still need to treat effective tax rates as endogenous. It is because only a proportion of houses are sold in a year in a tax jurisdiction; therefore, the mean or average effective rate of this jurisdiction may be distorted by the houses that are unsold and not re-assessed in that year.

indexes are better at controlling for housing quality and comprehensive in representing houses of all types. There is, however, still considerable disagreement on the best approach to constructing the index.[20]

Some studies use data on individual houses even without data on actual sales prices. Owner-reported house values provide an example, but homeowners tend to overvalue their home between 5.1 (Kiel and Zabel, 1999) and 6% (Goodman and Ittner, 1992). Advertised house prices provide another approach. Although they can sometimes be better in cases in which *reported* transaction prices are subject to understatement for reduced tax payments (Gravel *et al.*, 2006), advertised house prices may behave differently from actual sales ones, and no study has provided a careful comparison.

Actual sales prices are preferred to these other measures, of course, when they are available. As shown below, studies with sales data far outnumber those employing other types of house value measures. Repeat sales data have the additional advantage that they make it possible to control for time-invariant unobservables. However, repeat sales data may not provide a complete coverage of housing types changing hands within a sample time period. As previously mentioned, the data might be subject to selection bias whereby houses that sell for more than once could be systematically different from others. Also, the reliability of repeat sales data is contingent upon an assumption that all housing structural characteristics have remained constant over time. The longer the time frame, the more likely it is that a house has had substantial structural changes.

2.3.2. *Dimensions of school quality*

The key explanatory variable in a school quality capitalization study is a measure of school quality. Dimensions of school quality fall into three types: school inputs, school outputs, and other related factors. School inputs can be student–teacher ratios, teacher salary, and per pupil spending. School inputs can be incorporated in the hedonic model without or with school outputs. Inputs (mostly spending) may be used as a proxy for school quality when measures of school outputs, which are preferred, are not available. In cases where both spending and outputs (e.g., test scores) are included, the estimated coefficient of spending is open to interpretation.

---

[20]Bourassa *et al.* (2006) provide a comparison of strengths and weaknesses of several approaches to the construction of the house price index.

Because spending in this case can be a proxy for other unspecified outputs, the coefficient represents, holding test scores constant, parental concern either about spending or about unspecified outputs that are correlated with spending.

School output measures can be student standardized test scores, test score-based school grades (as in Figlio and Lucas (2004)), or dropout rates. Either levels of, or gains in, these measures can be used as key explanatory variables in school quality capitalization studies. The rationale for value-added measures of school quality is that households may care about value added rather than about levels of school achievement (Brasington and Haurin, 2006). The value-added approach has two major problems. First, value-added measures provide noisy signals about student performance, particularly in small school districts (Kane and Staiger, 2002b). Second, the approach needs test score information for the same cohorts in different grades, which is not usually available.

A few studies tend to focus on secondary measures of school inputs or outputs. They are related either to school spending such as education finance reform (Dee, 2000), or to school outputs, such as school schedules (Clauretie and Neill, 2000) or investments in school facilities (Cellini *et al.*, 2010). Clapp *et al.* (2008) treat student demographics as school inputs.

3. School Quality Capitalization Studies Since 1999

Our review covers a comprehensive list of empirical[21] journal articles since 1999. The studies we select to review incorporate a measure of school quality as a key explanatory variable for residential housing values. Therefore, we do not review studies that look primarily into property tax capitalization,[22] the capitalization into housing prices of environmental amenities such as proximity to open space (Anderson and West, 2006), of neighborhood characteristics such as crime, water quality (Leggett and Bockstael, 2000), or access to public parks (Lall and Lundberg, 2007), or of school district consolidation (Brasington, 2004; Hu and Yinger, 2008). We did an extensive keyword search for school quality capitalization articles on all major academic databases, and also followed references in these articles. Fifty studies we select for review cover a wide range of geographic areas

---

[21]The emphasis on empirical studies excludes simulation papers such as Nechyba (2003).
[22]Recent property tax capitalization studies are Bohanon and Keil (2000), Bradbury *et al.* (2001), Dachis *et al.* (2009), and Lang and Jian (2004).

from the United States (36), the United Kingdom (6), France (2), Norway (2), Australia (1), Canada (1), New Zealand (1), and Singapore (1) (see column 1 of Table 2).

Based on the conceptual framework, we will use the following review criteria regarding estimation methodologies adopted by school capitalization studies and their results:

(1) What functional forms do the studies use?
(2) What principal methodological approaches are used to isolate the effect of school quality from that of neighborhood qualities?
(3) How are house values are measured and how are housing characteristics treated?
(4) How are effective tax rates controlled for?
(5) What are the results regarding the degree of capitalization for various school quality measures?

Table 2 presents the summary of the answers to these questions.

3.1. *Functional Forms*

Clapp *et al.* (2008) argue that the log-linear form is "standard in the literature," and a large majority of reviewed studies employ this form (see column 2 of Table 2). A few studies adopt the Box–Cox functional form, either as the main functional form (Cheshire and Sheppard, 2004; Crone, 2006), or as a sensitivity check (Clark and Herrin, 2000). Similarly, several studies use linear forms (Barrow and Rouse, 2004; Fingleton, 2006). While Dee's (2000) tests of the linear model produce results similar to those of the log-linear form, Chin and Foong (2006) find that the log-linear form has a greater explanatory power as compared with the linear form. Our view is that using $\ln\{V\}$ as the dependent variable is the most reasonable procedure on both conceptual and empirical grounds, but we do not think that there is a strong case for linear, log, or Box–Cox specifications of the explanatory variables in a bid-function envelope. Instead, the existing evidence points to a quadratic specification or to other two-variable specifications. Using data for house sales in the Cleveland area in 2000, for example, Yinger (2015) shows that a quadratic specification is preferred to a linear one, and that for a measure of high school quality, the first specification in equation (9a) above, which assumes that the price elasticity of demand for this variable is -0.5, is preferred to the quadratic specification. Additional work on these specification issues is clearly warranted.

Table 2   Summary of school quality capitalization studies since 1999.

Studies	Data (1)	Functional forms (2)	Neighborhood effects (3)	Housing data and characteristics (4)	Effective tax rates (5)	Measures of school quality (6)	Results (7)
Ries and Somerville (2010)	P (Canada) NH: 87,381 NS: 87 ND: 1	LL	FE	PI; HD	TI as a single district	TS	Yes for high-value houses
Yinger (2015)	C (Ohio) NH: 22,880	Nonlinear	DN	SP; HD	TE	TS	Yes
Cellini et al. (2010)	P (California) NH: 15,151	LL	FE, IV[a]	MA; HD	TN	O[c]	Yes
Chiodo et al. (2010)	P (Missouri) NH: 38,676 NS: 121 ND: 15	Nonlinear	FE	SP; HD	TN	TS, VA	Yes
Dhar and Ross (2010)	P (Connecticut) NH: 68,288	LL	FE	SP; HD	TE	TS	Yes
Fack and Grenet (2010)	P (Paris, France) NH: 124,608	LL	FE	SP; HD	TI as a single municipality	TS	Yes
Brasington and Haurin (2009)	C (Ohio) ND:123 NH: 26,502	LL	SH	SP; HI	TE	O[d]	Yes
Dougherty et al. (2009)	P (Connecticut) NH: 8.736	LL	FE	SP; HD	TI as a single district	TS	Yes
Gibbons et al. (2009)	P (UK) NH: 138,132	LL	FE	SP; HI by matching	TN	TS, VA	Yes

Hilber and Mayer (2009)	P (Massachusetts) ND: 208	LL	IV, FE	PI; HI by FE	TE	TS, PE	Yes but depending on housing supply elasticities
Seo and Simons (2009)	P (Ohio) ND: 30 NH: 12,462	LL	SH, FE	SP; HI	TE	TS, PE, SG, VA	TS and SG
Zahirovic-Herbert and Turnbull (2009)	P (Louisiana) ND: 1 NH: 9821	LL	FE	SP; HD	TI as a single district	TS, O^e	Yes for O
Clapp *et al.* (2008)	P (Connecticut) NH: 356,829	LL	FE	SP; HI by FE	TE	TS	Yes
Davidoff and Leigh (2008)	P (Australia) NH: 580	LL	FE	SP; HD	NA	TS	Yes
Fiva and Kirkeboen (2008)	P (Oslo, Norway) NH: 79,322	LL	FE	SP; HI by FE	TI by FE	TS	Yes
Machin and Salvanes (2008)	P (Oslo, Norway) NH: 15495	LL	FE	SP; HD	NA	SG	Yes
Mathur (2008)	P (Washington) NH: 119,645	LL	DN	SP; HD	TN	PE	Yes for high-quality houses
Rehm and Filippova (2008)	P (New Zealand) NH: 10,187	LL	FE	SP; HD	NA	O^f	Yes
Sedgley *et al.* (2008)	C (Maryland) NH: 3164	LL	SH	SP; HD	NA	TS	Yes but not for all measures
Zahirovic-Herbert and Turnbull (2008)	P (Louisiana) NH: 6465 ND: 1	LL	FE	SP; HD	TI by a single district	TS, SG	Yes but depending on housing supply elasticities

(*Continued*)

Table 2 (*Continued*)

Studies	Data (1)	Functional forms (2)	Neighborhood effects (3)	Housing data and characteristics (4)	Effective tax rates (5)	Measures of school quality (6)	Results (7)
Bayer et al. (2007).	P (California) NH: 242,1000 NS: 195	LL	FE	SP, OR; HD	TI by FE	TS	Yes
Owusu-Edusei et al. (2007).	P (S. Carolina) NH: 3732	LL	DN	SP; HD	NA	TS, O^g	Yes
Brasington and Haurin (2006)	C (Ohio) NH: 77578 ND: 310	LL	FE, SH	SP; HD	TE	TS, PE, VA	Yes for TS, PE
Chin and Foong (2006)	P (Singapore) NH: 12,790	L, LL	DN	SP; HD	NA	O^g	Yes
Crone (2006)	C (Pennsylvania) NH: 3,150 ND: 21	LL, BC	FE	SP; HD	TN	TS, PE	Yes for TS
Fingleton (2006)	C (UK) ND: 353	L	SH	MA; No	NA	TS	Yes
Gibbons and Machin (2006)	P (UK) NH: 106,717	LL	FE, IV	SP; No	No	TS	Yes
Gravel et al. (2006)	P (Paris, France) NH: 8200	BC	DN	AP; HD	TN	TS, ST	Yes
Kane et al. (2006)	P (N. Carolina) NH: 89,793	LL	FE	SP; HD	TI by FE	TS	Yes
Reback (2005)	P (Minnesota) ND: 383	LL	FE	MA; HD	TI by FE	TS	Yes

Barrow and Rouse (2004)	P (United States) ND: 9076	L	FE	AV; HD	TN	PE	Yes
Cheshire and Sheppard (2004)	C (Reading, UK) NH: 490 NS: 1	BC	DN	SP; HD	No	TS	Yes but depending on housing supply elasticities
Dills (2004)	P (Texas) ND: 428	LL	FE	AV; HI by FE	TN	TS, VA	Yes for only one measure
Figlio and Lucas (2004)	P (Florida) NH: 73782 NS: 481	LL	FE	SP; HI by FE	TI by FE	TS, SG	Yes
Gibbons and Machin (2003)	P (England, UK) NH: 8067	LL	IV[b]	MA; HD	TI	TS	Yes
Kane *et al.* (2003)	P (N. Carolina) NH: 86,865	LL	FE	SP; HD	TI by FE	TS, SG, VA	Yes for TS
Leech and Campos (2003)	C (Coventry, UK) NH: 248	LL	FE	AP; HD	No	O[f]	Yes
Rosenthal (2003)	P (England) NH: 150,000 NS: 2000	LL	IV, FE	SP; HD	TI by FE	TS	Yes
Brasington (2002)	C (Ohio) NH: 26,979	LL	DN	SP; HD	TN	TS	Yes but weaker at urban edge
Brunner *et al.* (2002).	P (California) NH: 94,233 ND: 40	LL	FE	SP; HD	TI by adjusting house prices	TS, PE	Yes

(Continued)

Table 2 (*Continued*)

Studies	Data (1)	Functional forms (2)	Neighborhood effects (3)	Housing data and characteristics (4)	Effective tax rates (5)	Measures of school quality (6)	Results (7)
Downes and Zabel (2002)	P (Chicago) NH: 743	LL	IV, FE	OR; HD	TN	TS, PE, VA	Yes for TS
Brasington (2001)	C (Ohio) NH: 44,255 ND: 140	LL	DN	SP; HD	TN	TS	Yes but weaker in large communities
Weimer and Wolkoff (2001)	C (New York) NH: 1,193 ND: 23	LL, DL	IV, FE	SP; HD	TE	TS	Yes
Bogart and Cromwell (2000)	P (Ohio) NH: 4463 NS: 1	LL	FE	SP; HD	TI by FE	TS	Yes
Clark and Herrin (2000)	P (California) NH: 6837	LL, tested with BC	FE	SP; HD	TN	$O^{f,h}$	Yes
Clauretie and Neill (2000)	P (Nevada) NH: 8,912 ND: 1	LL	DN	SP; HD	TI as a single district	TS, O^i	Yes for O
Dee (2000)	C (United States) ND: 10,476	LL, tested with L	FE	MA; No	No	O^j	Yes
Mitchell (2000)	C (Oklahoma) NH: 367	LL	DN	SP; HD	No	TS	Yes

Black (1999)	P (Massachusetts) NH: 22679 ND: 39	LL	FE	SP; HD	TN	TS, PE, ST	Yes
Brasington (1999)	C (Ohio) NH: 27,440	LL	SH	SP; HD	TN	TS, PE	Yes

Abbreviations:

Column (1): C: Cross-sectional; P: Panel or pooled cross-sectional; NH: Number of houses or house sales transactions; NS: Number of schools; ND: Number of school districts.

Column (2): LL: Log-linear; L: Linear; BC: Box–Cox; DL: Double-log.

Column (3): IV: Instrumental variables; FE: Fixed-effects approach; SH: Spatial hedonics; DN: Direct inclusion of neighboring characteristics if not using one of the above.

Column (4): SP: Sale prices; MA: median or average sale prices; PI: house price indexes; OR: owner-reported values; AV: aggregate house values; AP: Advertised house prices.

HD: Direct inclusion of housing characteristics; HI: Indirect control for housing characteristics;

Column (5): TE: Effective tax rates; TN: Nominal tax rates; TI: Indirect control for tax rates; NA: either without available information or irrelevance for the study's geographic area.

Column (6): TS: Test scores; SG: Test score-based school/district grades; PE: Per-pupil expenditures; VA: Value-added test scores; ST: Student–teacher ratios; O: Others.

Other Notes:

[a] Combined with the regression discontinuity approach.

[b] Combined with the kernel-based semi-parametric estimation technique.

[c] School facility investments identified by school bond referenda passed or failed by narrow margins.

[d] This study estimates an education production function in which the dependent variable of test scores is regressed on three components: parental inputs, peer effects and school inputs.

[e] Variables indicating an improvement in a categorical ranking of school performance.

[f] No measure of school quality but a set of dummy variables indicating school zones to which a house is assigned.

[g] Proximity to (good) schools.

[h] An extensive list of school inputs and outputs including dropout rates.

[i] School-year schedules.

[j] Education finance reforms.

3.2. School vs. Neighborhood Effects

We found four major approaches to the challenge of accounting for neighborhood characteristics: direct inclusion of neighborhood characteristics, instrumental variables, fixed effects, and spatial econometrics (see column 3 of Table 2). While the first method controls for observed neighborhood characteristics, the latter three are intended to address estimation bias caused by omitted variables. Some studies use more than one of these approaches.

3.2.1. Direct inclusion of neighborhood characteristics

School quality capitalization studies generally include in their model as many observed measures of neighborhood quality as possible. Studies vary considerably, however, in the nature and quantity of neighborhood quality variables. Yinger (2015) seems to incorporate the largest number of neighborhood characteristics, including crime rates, ethnic composition, and air quality, along with distance to a hazardous waste site, to a public housing project, and to a lake. Several studies, including Chin and Foong (2006), Chiodo et al. (2010), Mathur (2008), and Yinger (2015) draw on urban economics to specify a commuting variable, such as distance to a central business district. Other variables with fewer empirical applications are heavy traffic (Bogart and Cromwell, 2000), and an employment deprivation index in Cheshire and Sheppard (2004).

Many studies control for student demographics in public schools, which are a type of neighborhood variable[23] but also could be a measure of school quality as perceived by some parents. Variables in this category include proportions of minority students (African Americans, Hispanics, or Native Americans) (Downes and Zabel, 2002; Zahirovic-Herbert and Turnbull, 2008) and of economically disadvantaged students such as students with low-incomes, limited English proficiency (Zahirovic-Herbert and Turnbull, 2008) or special needs (Dills, 2004). Instead of student characteristics, some studies include population demographics for the neighborhood such as shares of

---

[23] In certain instances, student demographics are not a good indicator of the neighborhood's socio-economic status (SES). For example, Edward Hill in his comment following Kane et al.'s (2003) on their use of percent African-American students as a SES proxy points out that Charlotte, a major city in their dataset, has a sizable middle-class African-American community. Also, some studies such as Clapp et al. (2008) and Zahirovic-Herbert and Turnbull (2009) include variables indicating both school attributes and neighborhood qualities.

African Americans (or whites) (Bayer *et al.*, 2007; Clauretie and Neill, 2000; Kane *et al.*, 2006), and levels of education (Black, 1999; Brasington and Haurin, 2006; Reback, 2005; Barrow and Rouse, 2004).

Some studies include median or mean household income as a proxy for residential housing demand or as a neighborhood amenity (Bayer *et al.*, 2007; Davidoff and Leigh, 2008; Hilber and Mayer, 2009; Kane *et al.*, 2003). As earlier discussed in greater detail, we believe that income does influence housing demand and thus is unlikely to be exogenous in the bid-function envelope, and that it is unlikely to be a good proxy for actual measures of neighborhood characteristics.

Owusu-Edusei *et al.* (2007) and Reback (2005) include median house value as an amenity variable. As discussed in succeeding sections, median house value in the neighborhood should be considered as endogenous (Weimer and Wolkoff, 2001), because unobservable factors can affect both the log of individual house prices, which is the dependent variable, and median house values.

3.2.2. *Instrumental variables*

Several studies treat neighborhood or school qualities as endogenous and employ instrumental variables (IVs) to eliminate endogeneity bias. Despite the authors' attempts to find strong and valid instruments, the strength and validity of their IVs are debatable.

3.2.2.1. IVs for neighborhood effects

Weimer and Wolkoff (2001) use median house value as a measure of neighborhood quality, but recognize that this variable is likely to be endogenous. As a result, they estimate their model using an IV approach with ten neighborhood characteristics as instruments. These instruments indicate both traits of the people in a neighborhood (e.g., median household income, educational attainment of the median household, percent of households that are Hispanic, non-white, and in poverty) and physical neighborhood traits (e.g., percent vacant units, percent units which are group homes). We do not find these instruments compelling. As discussed earlier, sorting makes demand characteristics endogenous.

3.2.2.2. IVs for school quality

Several other studies employ the IV approach to eliminate bias from a correlation between school quality and omitted variables. Some of the instruments in these studies are clever, but it is difficult to find sets of instruments that are clearly exogenous. Gibbons and Machin (2006) use as an IV the "beacon" status designation for schools exhibiting high teaching standards and models of good practice. However, this variable reflects school decisions and therefore could be linked to the same unobservable factors as test scores (their measures of school quality). Gibbons and Machin (2003) instrument school performance with school type and school admissions age-range dummies. These instruments are questionable because they may directly affect households' housing bids. Downes and Zabel (2002) employ the proportion of the tax base that is residential, per pupil assessed value, the proportion renting, and the proportion of the population that is school aged as instruments for nominal tax rates, per-pupil expenditures and test scores. One cannot rule out the possibility, however, that these variables directly affect the owners' assessment of their house values as the dependent variable. In fact, one of their instruments, the school-aged population, was included as an explanatory variable by Zahirovic-Herbert and Turnbull (2008).

We find instruments in Rosenthal (2003) to be more convincing. Rosenthal instruments for school quality using the recent occurrence(s) of an external school inspection. The school has to be inspected at least once in a four-year cycle. The occurrence and timings of these inspections are therefore independent of unobserved neighborhood factors.

Hilber and Mayer (2009) and Brunner et al. (2002) include both test scores and school spending in their regressions but instrument only for school spending, perhaps because school spending is of primary interest in these studies. This approach appears to be a step in the right direction, but it is unlikely to fully eliminate endogeneity bias.

3.2.3. *Fixed effects*

The third way to control for the correlation of school quality and unobserved neighborhood characteristics is the use of fixed effects. First, the boundary fixed effects, or BFE, approach in Black (1999) identifies attendance-zone boundaries for local elementary schools, divides these boundaries into segments, and defines a fixed effect for the houses on either side of each segment. This approach has been extended in subsequent studies. Fack and Grenet (2010) develop a matching procedure in which a reference transaction is derived by computing the weighted geometric mean of the prices of all housing sale transactions that took place in the same year but on the other side of the common attendance boundary. Gibbons et al. (2009) employ several BFE-based model extensions including matching as in Fack and

Grenet (2010), incorporating within-boundary variation, and controlling for distance-to-boundary trends.

The conceptual framework presented earlier points to two potential sources of bias in the BFE approach. Bayer *et al.* (2007) and Kane *et al.* (2006) conduct tests to see whether observed housing and neighborhood characteristics shift discontinuously at the school boundaries. The results indicate that houses and households on the high-and low-scoring side of school boundaries have different characteristics, as one would expect when households sort on the basis of school characteristics. Dhar and Ross (2010) find that bias associated with across-border neighborhood quality differences ranges from 6 percent to 8 percent points. Bayer *et al.* (2007) respond to this possibility by including in their regressions household demographic characteristics such as median household income. However, as discussed earlier, these characteristics are determinants of the demand for public services, and are likely to be endogenous. As a result, we do not find this to be a compelling solution to the problems associated with household sorting.

An important decision in using the BFE approach is how to determine the sample size. Table 3 indicates that most studies choose to select all sales within some distance to the closest boundary instead of relying on inter-property distance. The table also shows that the maximum boundary distance is 2000 feet in most studies, and several of them compare their empirical results from different sample sizes. Sometimes, catchment area boundaries may present difficulty increasing subsamples. For instance, Chiodo *et al.* (2010) can only look at houses within a 0.1 mile buffer to the nearest boundary because wider boundaries would encompass some attendance zones almost entirely. Regardless of how the sample is selected, the loss of sample size is potentially a weakness of the BFE approach.[24]

A few studies adopt variants of the fixed-effects estimation. In the first variant, a set of dummy variables indicating school zones to which a house is assigned are included *without* school quality measures such as test scores (Leech and Campos, 2003; Rehm and Filippova, 2008). A major weakness of this approach is that it cannot determine which dimensions of school quality influence house values.

The second variant relies on a policy change whereby some houses are reassigned to a different catchment area while others stay in the same area as before. This "natural experiment" allows for difference-in-differences (DID)

---

[24]The standard errors of the school quality variable(s) in the reviewed studies with the BFE design are quite stable with different sample sizes, though.

Table 3 Maximum boundary and inter-property distance.

	Maximum distance to the closest boundary	Distance between property pairs
Ries and Somerville (2010)	250, 350, and 500 m (or 820, 1148, 1640 feet)	
Chiodo *et al.* (2010)	0.1 mile (or 528 feet)	
Dhar and Ross (2010)	1000,1500, and 2500 feet	
Dougherty *et al.* (2009)	800 feet	
Gibbons *et al.* (2009)	500[a] m	725[a] m (or 2378 feet)
Zahirovic-Herbert and Turnbull (2009)	0.3 mile (or 1584 feet)	
Davidoff and Leigh (2008)	200, 500, and 600 m (or 656, 1640, or 1969 feet)	
Fack and Grenet (2010)	250, 300 and 350 m	
Machin and Salvanes (2008)	500 m (or 1640 feet)	
Bayer *et al.* (2007)	0.2 mile (or 1056 feet)	
Crone (2006)	0.5 mile (or 2640 feet)	
Gibbons and Machin (2006)		500[a] m (or 1640 feet)
Kane *et al.* (2006)	500, 1000, and 2000 feet	
Gibbons and Machin (2003)	0.25 km (or 1378 feet)	
Kane *et al.* (2003)	500, 1000, and 2000 feet	
Black (1999)	0.15, 0.2, and 0.35 mile (or 792, 1056, and 1848 feet)	

Note: [a]Mean values.

estimation. The DID estimator measures the degree of capitalization by comparing the before-after mean difference in house prices between houses reassigned to a new catchment zone and those that have long belonged to this zone. The DID estimator can be specified with or without performance measures. Bogart and Cromwell (2000) and Ries and Somerville (2010) take advantage of this DID approach for changes in attendance zones in Shaker Heights, Ohio and Vancouver, British Columbia respectively.

Other papers in the literature adopt a more traditional fixed effects approach at various levels of analysis. More specifically, fixed effects are used at the census tract level (Clapp *et al.*, 2008), school district level (Barrow and Rouse, 2004; Dills, 2004; Reback, 2005), school catchment areas (Fiva and Kirkeboen, 2008), county level (Rosenthal, 2003), or state level (Dee, 2000). One of the earlier discussed concerns over the use of fixed effects is the increased importance of any measurement error in the data, especially test scores. To address this concern, Clapp *et al.* (2008), Gibbons and Machin (2003), and Kane *et al.* (2003) use multiple-year moving averages of district attributes.

3.2.4. *Other estimation techniques*

A few papers with cross-sectional data construct spatial econometric estimation models, mostly spatial lag and/or spatial error models.[25] The former approach is designed to address bias; the latter is designed to deal with efficiency. Most studies compare estimates from different spatial econometric models with the baseline OLS results. Comparing the results from the county fixed effects and spatial lag models, Brasington and Haurin (2006) find that the effect of test scores on house prices hardly changes at all between the two models. Not surprisingly, the OLS and spatial error models in Brasington (1999) yield similar results for a wide range of school quality measures. Sedgley *et al.* (2008) find that the key school quality measure is statistically significant in a spatial lag model, but not in a spatial error model. Brasington and Haurin (2009) and Fingleton (2006) show that less restricted models (namely the Kelejian–Prucha's or spatial Durbin models respectively) perform better with their datasets than the spatial lag and spatial error ones. This finding suggests that future school quality capitalization studies might consider exploring a variety of spatial econometric specifications including less restrictive models.

In terms of estimation approaches, the studies authored by Brasington together with Seo and Simons (2009) adopt maximum likelihood estimation without diagnostic tests to see if this estimator is appropriate. Sedgley *et al.* (2008) choose 2SLS estimation with instruments for the spatially lagged dependent variable over maximum likelihood as a result of their diagnostic tests of the error structure. Fingleton (2006) presents estimation results from both maximum likelihood and 2SLS estimations. Finally, as earlier noted, the estimates from spatial hedonic models may be sensitive to weights matrix specifications; only Brasington and Haurin (2009) and Sedgley *et al.* (2008) claim that their results are robust to changes in the weights matrix, W.

Cellini *et al.* (2010) is the only study that employs the regression discontinuity to examine the effects of school facility investments on property values. Their strategy is to compare districts that barely passed a proposed bond issue (the "treatment group") with others that barely rejected a bond measure (the "control group").

---

[25]Gibbons and Machin (2003) adopt a variant of spatial modeling in which regressions are made on transformed data that reflect deviations from spatially weighted means of the variables in the hedonic model. As pointed out by an anonymous referee, their approach is equivalent to a BFE method combined with a spatial smoother.

3.3. *House Value Measures and Treatment of Housing Characteristics*

Column 4 of Table 2 documents that an overwhelming majority of studies employ actual sales prices. The use of mean or average house values is also popular among aggregate studies, especially those at the school district level in the United States. A few studies adopt one of the remaining four types of house value data, namely house price indexes, owner-reported values, aggregate values, and advertised prices. Because owner-reported house prices are probably not a highly accurate indicator of true market values, Downes and Zabel (2002) attempt to minimize the resulting bias by including length of tenure as an independent variable in their hedonic regression. They argue that this approach leads to bias only in the constant term, not in the coefficients of the explanatory variables.

This column also reports on methods to control for housing characteristics in hedonic models. As discussed in the conceptual framework, direct inclusion of housing covariates and fixed effects with repeat sales data are two common approaches to isolate the school quality effect from that of housing characteristics. The number of house characteristics included in hedonic pricing models varies substantially from one study to another. Omitted variable bias is a concern in studies, such as Mitchell (2000), without either house-level fixed effects or extensive housing characteristics.

The fixed-effects approach with repeat house sales data obviates the need to control for a long list of housing covariates. In fact, the repeat sales data studies, such as Bogart and Cromwell (2000) and Figlio and Lucas (2004), do not include the structural characteristics of housing in their models. The exclusion of housing covariates is based on the assumption that few houses have undergone major renovations during the sample period. A couple of papers attempt to address this assumption. For instance, Ries and Somerville (2010) delete houses with major structural changes from their data set using building permits. Figlio and Lucas (2004) find that their model is robust to the inclusion of housing changes proxied by building permits.

3.4. *Effective Tax Rates*

The conceptual framework emphasizes the need to properly control for property taxes. Property tax rates generally receive less attention in the studies we review (see column 5 of Table 2). A few studies (e.g., Clapp *et al.*, 2008; Hilber and Mayer, 2009) incorporate effective property tax rates; several studies, however, employ nominal tax rates. While some of the latter studies claim that these nominal rates are identical or at least close to effective tax rates as a result of assessment requirements (Crone, 2006; Mitchell, 2000), others make no mention of the link to effective rates (Gravel *et al.*, 2006; Mathur, 2008).[26] Studies may use nominal tax rates because effective rates are not available (Downes and Zabel, 2002).

Some studies employ the fixed-effects approach to account for property taxes. For instance, Kane *et al.* (2006) control for tax rate differences with fixed effects for taxing jurisdictions. Moreover, the articles that look at school quality capitalization in a single school district do not include property tax rates (Ries and Somerville, 2010; Zahirovic-Herbert and Turnbull, 2008). Houses in the same school district or tax jurisdiction have the same nominal tax rates, of course, but may have differential effective tax rates due to inaccurate assessments. As earlier indicated, unless assessment errors are not correlated with unobserved factors in the hedonic model, the omission of effective tax rates may be a source of bias.

Studies with repeat sales data, e.g., Figlio and Lucas (2004), use fixed effects at the household level to account for variation in effective tax rates across houses at a point in time. This approach is based on the assumption that houses are accurately re-assessed upon sale (i.e., re-assessed values reflect market values). If this assumption does not hold, this fixed-effects approach cannot account for variation in effective tax rates across houses that may arise over time as market values diverge from assessments. An improvement in a neighborhood's school quality leads to an increase in property values there which, if assessments are held constant, leads to a decline in the effective property tax rate. The net change in house values in this neighborhood therefore reflects the capitalization of both the school quality increase and the correlated effective tax rate decrease. Therefore, studies with repeat sales data still need to explore assessment practices to determine whether household fixed effects are sufficient to control for effective property tax rates.

3.5. *Results*

The capitalization of school outputs into house values has received greater research interest than that of school inputs and other related dimensions

---

[26]This is also the case with Ohio data studies (co-)authored by Brasington. However, nominal tax rates appear to be close to effective rates in Ohio due to assessment requirements.

of school quality (such as education finance reform, school schedules, investments in school facilities, or student demographics). See column 6 of Table 2. The following review focuses on the estimation results of the capitalization of major school inputs and outputs into house prices.[27] While existing studies provide less consistent and difficult-to-interpret evidence on the capitalization effect of school inputs, the evidence concerning educational outputs appears to be relatively strong and consistent.

3.5.1. *Capitalization of school inputs*

A major input measure is per-pupil expenditures. As the conceptual framework noted, school expenditures can be incorporated together with student performance or as a proxy for it. Following the former approach, Downes and Zabel (2002) find that expenditures do not have any effect on property values. Other studies using this approach do find an effect of expenditures, however. Per-pupil expenditures have a positive and significant relationship with house prices in 16 of Brasington and Haurin's (2006) 21 regressions. Dhar and Ross (2010), Hilber and Mayer (2009), and Brunner *et al.* (2002) find the positive capitalization of school expenditures into property values. Particularly, Brunner *et al.* (2002) present a large effect of reform-induced spending per pupil in which a one-dollar rise in spending per pupil results approximately in a six-dollar increase in the price of a home, all else equal. Black (1999) finds that a $500 increase in per-pupil expenditures leads to a 2.2% increase in house prices. Barrow and Rouse (2004) find that more spending as a result of increased state aid is reflected in greater housing values. Mathur (2008) reports positive and negative effects of spending per pupil on house prices depending on housing types and quality.

In sum, many of the school quality capitalization studies find evidence on positive effects of school spending on house values, controlling for student performance. However, there are two caveats. First, as we discussed in preceding sections, many of these studies do not completely addressed concerns over estimation bias. Second, there is no way to tell whether the results indicate parental valuation of spending itself or of unspecified outputs that are correlated with spending.

---

[27]Inputs such as teacher salary, student-teacher ratios are not reviewed because few papers investigate them (Black, 1999; Brasington, 1999; Seo and Simons, 2009).We also do not review school outputs such as dropout rates, or their distant aspects, namely school-year schedules, school facility investments, etc. See Column 6 of Table 2 for further detail.

3.5.2. *Capitalization of school outputs*

The outputs representing school quality used in the reviewed studies are mostly test scores, score-based school grades, or the change in these outputs (commonly known as value added). Column 7 in Table 2 indicates that almost all studies find a positive relationship between a certain measure of test scores and residential property value. Generally, the effect of test scores on house values in cross-sectional studies is larger than that in studies with fixed effects. All else being equal, an increase in test scores by one-standard deviation raises house prices by 7.1 percent or 9.8 percent in Brasington and Haurin (2006) and Cheshire and Sheppard (2004), respectively.[28],[29] Many of the studies using fixed effects with elementary test scores report smaller levels of capitalization for a one-standard deviation increase in the test scores, ranging from 1.8 percent in Bayer *et al.* (2007), to 1.9 percent in Dougherty *et al.* (2009), and to 2.1 percent in Black (1999).[30] Small (or, below 4 percent) capitalization effects are also found in studies using secondary test scores such as Clapp *et al.* (2008), Dhar and Ross (2010), Davidoff and Leigh (2008), and Fiva and Kirkeboen (2008).

The capitalization results of these studies have three implications. First, although the studies use different test score measures, they provide markedly similar results. Second, small capitalization effects can be found not only in studies with the BFE design but in those with traditional fixed effects. Clapp *et al.* (2008) and Fiva and Kirkeboen (2008) are of the second type. Third, most of the studies with small capitalization effects focus on elementary school quality only and therefore do not provide a comprehensive measure of the capitalization of school district quality.[31] Moreover, Kane *et al.* (2003) shows that the magnitude of the coefficient on elementary test scores goes

---

[28]The magnitude for Cheshire and Sheppard is interpolated by Gibbons and Machin (2008).

[29]Not all studies report the degree of capitalization by a one-standard deviation change in test scores. Nor is it straightforward to derive comparable results. Of these studies, Rosenthal (2003) provides compelling evidence estimated with potentially valid IVs that an extra five percentage points on secondary school exam pass rates in England can add about £450 to the average house price in the locality.

[30]An exception is Kane *et al.* (2006), who find that a one-standard deviation increase in a school's mean test score is associated with a 10 percent rise in house value.

[31]It is usually the case that catchment areas for secondary schools are larger than those for elementary schools. For instance, there are only two middle-high school attendance zones relative to 14 elementary school zones in the West Hartford Public School District in Connecticut explored in Dougherty *et al.* (2009).

down when fixed effects for high schools are added. Yinger (2015) finds from his estimations with both elementary and high school quality variables that high school quality, measured as the share of students who enter 12th grade and subsequently pass all five of the Ohio state 12th grade tests, has a large and significant impact on house values. All else equal, house values increase about 30 percent from the district with the lowest passing rate (5 percent) to the district with the highest passing rate (77 percent).

A few papers look into the effect of test score-based school grading (part of a state's accountability system) on house values. Finding no effect of state school grading on house values, Kane *et al.* (2003) suggest that residents have already learned which schools are low-performing so that the state reports provide no new information. As discussed earlier, this study includes mean income as an independent variable, which does not appear to us to be appropriate. The results in Zahirovic-Herbert and Turnbull (2008) and Figlio and Lucas (2004) are more compelling. Zahirovic-Herbert and Turnbull create two dummies for school grade changes: one for an improvement in school grades and the other for a decline. They present evidence that while declining schools make houses more difficult to sell, only school improvement is positively capitalized into property values. Figlio and Lucas report strong evidence of elementary school grades capitalized into property values. A school's receipt of grade "A" is estimated to lead to a 19.5% increase in property values relative to "B"-graded schools. The effect of school grades on house prices in Figlio and Lucas is robust to a variety of sensitivity checks, and independent of other student achievement measures, namely test scores, or suspension rates.[32]

While most of the studies use a measure of average student performance, some studies use value-added measures. Brasington and Haurin (2006) and Downes and Zabel (2002) did not find capitalization for the value-added measures of school quality in district-level models. Downes and Zabel do not consider the value-added model as the best one.[33] Kane *et al.* (2006) also presents no-capitalization evidence for value-added test scores. In contrast, the study of schools in the United Kingdom by Gibbons *et al.* (2009) finds that the school quality capitalization effect is the same in value-added and level specifications.

---

[32]Figlio and Lucas (2004) did not report the effect of test scores on property values, though.
[33]Of the standard log-linear, first-difference, and value-added models, they claim the first-difference model to be the best.

4. Conclusions

This paper has provided a review of school quality capitalization studies that have appeared since 1999. These studies have made substantial contributions to the literature. First, they provide us with extensive evidence that school quality — a public service output — is capitalized into property values in many geographical areas in eight countries. Almost all of the reviewed studies find evidence that school quality, especially as measured by test scores, is capitalized into house values. In most cases, cross-sectional studies find a larger degree of capitalization than studies with fixed effects. Moreover, despite different data and fixed effects strategies, these studies provide remarkably similar results, namely that house values rise by 1–4% for a one-standard-deviation increase in student test scores. Some studies find that homebuyers also care about score-based school grades (as in the two compelling studies by Figlio and Lucas (2004) and Zahirovic-Herbert and Turnbull (2008)), but no US-based study finds support for the capitalization of value-added measures of student performance. Evidence about the capitalization of school inputs into house values is less consistent and more difficult to interpret. Additional research with a range of output measures is needed to distinguish between the possibilities that home buyers care about inputs (controlling for one key test score) and that they care about several school outputs in addition to test scores.

Second, scholars have made substantial progress towards obtaining unbiased estimates of school quality capitalization effects by adopting advanced estimation strategies such as use of instrumental variables, boundary fixed effects, or spatial econometrics. Major methodological challenges, however, remain. The first challenge is the functional form of the hedonic equation. Although most of the studies we review adopt the log-linear functional form, few of them provide conceptual support for their choice or conduct robustness checks against other functional forms. Yinger (2015) derives and estimates quadratic and similar functional forms in which school quality appears in two terms, not one. These forms are supported by specification tests. We believe that a strong conceptual case can be made for two-term specifications, but future research on hedonic functional forms is clearly warranted.

The second methodological challenge is how to isolate the impact of school quality on property values from that of neighborhood qualities. A popular approach is to use IV regression. One advantage of this approach is that it can be employed at any level of analysis. Unfortunately, however, it is difficult to find variables that are strongly correlated only with school quality measures but not with the error term of the hedonic equation. As a matter of fact, all of the IVs (except for those in Rosenthal (2003)) in the studies reviewed here are likely to be endogenous.

Another popular approach to isolate the effect of school quality on house values is the use of fixed effects, especially the BFE design. Despite its popularity, however, this approach may be subject to bias from across-boundary neighborhood quality differences as a result of sorting. Bayer *et al.* (2007) address this problem by introducing neighborhood demographics as control variables. These controls may themselves be endogenous, however, and further research on this topic is needed. Another promising approach to sorting is provided by Dhar and Ross (2010), who combine difference-in-differences and boundary fixed effects.

Finally, this literature would benefit from more attention to the implications of residential sorting. Existing studies, which have focused on estimating a single coefficient for school quality capitalization, could benefit from a switch to functional forms that explicitly incorporate sorting, such as the quadratic forms derived by Epple (1987) and Yinger (2015). The question is not only whether school quality affects house values, but also whether school-capitalization studies can detect the sorting process that allocates households with a high marginal willingness to pay for education to some jurisdictions and households with a low marginal willingness to pay to others.

References

Anderson, Soren T. and West, Sarah E. 2006. Open space, residential property values, and spatial context. *Regional Science and Urban Economics* **36**(6): 773–789.

Anselin, Luc, 1988. *Spatial Econometrics: Methods and Models.* Kluwer Academic Publishers, Dordrecht.

Anselin, Luc, 2003. Spatial econometrics. In Baltagi, Badi H. (ed.), *A Companion to Theoretical Econometrics.* pp. 310–330, Wiley-Blackwell.

Anselin, Luc, 2010. Thirty years of spatial econometrics. *Papers in Regional Science* **89**(1): 3–25.

Anselin, Luc and Lozano-Gracia, Nancy, 2009. Errors in variables and spatial effects in hedonic house price models of ambient air quality. In Arbia, Giuseppe, Baltagi, Badi H. (eds.), *Spatial Econometrics: Methods and Applications.* pp. 5–34, Physica-Verlag.

Atkinson, Scott E. and Crocker, Thomas D. 1987. A Bayesian approach to assessing the robustness of hedonic property value studies. *Journal of Applied Econometrics* **2**: 27–45.

Baltagi, Badi H., Song, Seuck Heun, Jung, Byoung Cheol, and Koh, Won, 2007. Testing for serial correlation, spatial autocorrelation and random effects using panel data. *Journal of Econometrics* **140**(1): 5–51.

Barrow, Lisa and Rouse, Cecilia Elena, 2004. Using market valuation to assess public school spending. *Journal of Public Economics* **88**(9): 1747–1769.

Bayer, Patrick, Ferreira, Fernando, and McMillan, Robert, 2007. A unified framework for measuring preferences for schools and neighborhoods. *Journal of Political Economy* **115**(4): 588–638.

Black, Sandra E. 1999. Do better schools matter? Parental valuation of elementary education. *Quarterly Journal of Economics* **114**(2): 577–599.

Bogart, William T. and Cromwell, Brian A. 2000. How much is a neighborhood school worth? *Journal of Urban Economics* **47**(2): 280–305.

Bohanon, Cecil and Keil, Stanley R. 2000. Property tax changes: a case study of a small open region. *Regional Analysis & Policy* **30**(2): 39–53.

Bourassa, Steven C., Hoesli, Martin, and Sun, Jian, 2006. A simple alternative house price index method. *Journal of Housing Economics* **15**(1): 80–97.

Box, George E.P. and Cox, David R. 1964. An analysis of transformations. *Journal of the Royal Statistical Society: Series B* **26**(2): 211–252.

Bradbury, Katharine L., Mayer, Christopher J., and Case, Karl E. 2001. Property tax limits, local fiscal behavior, and property values: evidence from Massachusetts under Proposition 2 1/2. *Journal of Public Economics* **80**(2): 287–311.

Brasington, David M. 1999. Which measures of school quality does the housing market value? Spatial and non-spatial evidence. *Journal of Real Estate Research* **18**(3): 395–413.

Brasington, David M. 2001. Capitalization and community size. *Journal of Urban Economics* **50**(3): 385–395.

Brasington, David M. 2002. Edge versus center: finding common ground in the capitalization debate. *Journal of Urban Economics* **52**(3): 524–541.

Brasington, David M. 2004. House prices and the structure of local government: an application of spatial statistics. *Journal of Real Estate Finance and Economics* **29**(2): 211–231.

Brasington, David M. and Haurin, Donald R. 2006. Educational outcomes and house values: a test of the value-added approach. *Journal of Regional Science* **46**(2): 245–268.

Brasington, David M. and Haurin, Donald R. 2009. Parents, peers, or school inputs: which components of school outcomes are capitalized into house value? *Regional Science and Urban Economics* **39**(5): 523–529.

Brunner, Eric J., Murdoch, James, and Thayer, Mark 2002. School finance reform and housing values: evidence from the Los Angeles metropolitan area. *Public Finance and Management* **2**(4): 535–565.

Butler, Richard V. 1982. The specification of hedonic indexes for urban housing. *Land Economics* **58**(1): 96–108.

Cellini, Stephanie R., Ferreira, Fernando, and Rothstein, Jesse M. 2010. The value of school facility investments: evidence from a dynamic regression discontinuity design. *Quarterly Journal of Economics* **125**(1): 215–261.

Cheshire, Paul and Sheppard, Stephen 2004. Capitalising the value of free schools: the impact of supply characteristics and uncertainty. *Economic Journal* **114**(499): 397–424.

Chin, Hoong C. and Foong, Kok W. 2006. Influence of school accessibility on housing values. *Journal of Urban Planning and Development* **132**(3): 120–129.

Chin, T.L. and Chau, K.W. 2003. A critical review of literature on the hedonic price model. *International Journal for Housing and Its Applications* **27**(2): 145–165.

Chiodo, Abbigail J., Hernandez-Murillo, Ruben, and Owyang, Michael T. 2010. Nonlinear effects of school quality on house prices. *Federal Reserve Bank of St. Louis Review* **92**(3): 185–204.

Clapp, John M., Nanda, Anupam, and Ross, Stephen L. 2008. Which school attributes matter? The influence of school district performance and demographic composition on property values. *Journal of Urban Economics* **63**(2): 451–466.

Clark, David E. and Herrin, William E. 2000. The impact of public school attributes on home sale prices in California. *Growth and Change* **31**(3): 385–407.

Clauretie, Terrence M. and Neill, Helen R. 2000. Year-round school schedules and residential property values. *Journal of Real Estate Finance and Economics* **20**(3): 311–322.

Crone, Theodore, 2006. Capitalization of the quality of local public schools: What do home buyers value? Working Paper. *Federal Reserve Bank of Philadelphia*.

Cropper, Maureen L., Deck, Leland B., and McConnell, Kenneth E. 1988. On the choice of functional form for hedonic price functions. *Review of Economics and Statistics* **70**(4): 668–675.

Cushing, Brian J. 1984. Capitalization of interjurisdictional fiscal differentials: an alternative approach. *Journal of Urban Economics* **15**(3): 317–326.

Dachis, Ben, Duranton, Gilles, and Turner, Matthew A. 2009. The effects of land transfer taxes on real estate markets: Evidence from a natural experiment in Toronto. Working Paper.

Davidoff, Ian and Leigh, Andrew, 2008. How much do public schools really cost? Estimating the relationship between house prices and school quality. *Economic Record* **84**(265): 193–206.

Dee, Thomas S. 2000. The capitalization of education finance reforms. *Journal of Law and Economics* **43**(1): 185–214.

Dhar, Paramita and Ross, Stephen L. 2010. School quality and property values: re-examining the boundary approach. Working Paper. Department of Economics, University of Connecticut.

Dills, Angela K. 2004. Do parents value changes in test scores? High stakes testing in Texas. *Contributions to Economic Analysis & Policy* **3**(1): 1–32.

Dougherty, Jack, Harrelson, Jeffrey, Maloney, Laura, Murphy, Drew, Smith, Russell, Snow, Michael, and Zannoni, Diane, 2009. School choice in suburbia: test scores, race, and housing markets. *American Journal of Education* **115**(4): 523–548.

Downes, Thomas A. and Zabel, Jeffrey E. 2002. The impact of school characteristics on house prices: Chicago 1987–1991. *Journal of Urban Economics* **52**(1): 1–25.

Elhorst, Paul J. 2008. Serial and spatial autocorrelation. *Economics Letters* **100**(3): 422–424.

Elhorst, Paul J. 2010. Applied spatial econometrics: raising the bar. *Spatial Economic Analysis* **5**(1): 9–28.

Epple, Dennis, 1987. Hedonic prices and implicit markets: estimating demand and supply functions for differentiated products. *Journal of Political Economy* **95**(1): 59–80.

Epple, Dennis, Romer, Thomas, and Sieg, Holger, 2001. Interjurisdictional sorting and majority rule: an empirical analysis. *Econometrica* **69**(6): 1437–1465.

Epple, Dennis and Sieg, Holger, 1999. Estimating equilibrium models of local jurisdictions. *Journal of Political Economy* **107**(4): 645–681.

Fack, Gabrielle and Grenet, Julien, 2010. When do better schools raise housing prices? Evidence from Paris public and private schools. *Journal of Public Economics* **94**(1): 59–77.

Figlio, David N. and Lucas, Maurice E. 2004. What's in a grade? School report cards and the housing market. *American Economic Review* **94**(3): 591–604.

Fingleton, Bernard, 2006. A cross-sectional analysis of residential property prices: the effects of income, commuting, schooling, the housing stock and spatial interaction in the English regions. *Papers in Regional Science* **85**(3): 339–361.

Fingleton, Bernard and Le Gallo, Julie, 2008. Estimating spatial models with endogenous variables, a spatial lag and spatially dependent disturbances: finite sample properties. *Papers in Regional Science* **87**(3): 319–339.

Fingleton, Bernard and Le Gallo, Julie, 2010. Endogeneity in a spatial context: properties of estimators. In Paez, Antonio, Le Gallo, Jullie, Buliung, Ron N., Dall'erba, Sandy (eds.), *Progress in Spatial Analysis: Methods and Applications*. pp. 59–73, Springer.

Fiva, Jon H. and Kirkeboen, Lars J. 2008. Does the housing market react to new information on school quality? CESIFO Working Paper No. 2299.

Gibbons, Stephen and Machin, Stephen, 2003. Valuing English primary schools. *Journal of Urban Economics* **53**(2): 197–219.

Gibbons, Stephen and Machin, Stephen, 2006. Paying for primary schools: admission constraints, school popularity or congestion? *Economic Journal* **116**(510): 77–92.

Gibbons, Stephen and Machin, Stephen, 2008. Valuing school quality, better transport, and lower crime: evidence from house prices. *Oxford Review of Economic Policy* **24**(1): 99–199.

Gibbons, Stephen, Machin, Stephen, and Silva, Olmo. 2009. Valuing school quality using boundary discontinuities. Working Paper. Spatial Economics Research Centre.

Gill, Leroy H. 1983. Changes in city and suburban house prices during a period of expected school desegregation. *Southern Economic Journal* **50**(1): 169–184.

Goodman, John L. and Ittner, John B. 1992. The accuracy of home owners' estimates of house value. *Journal of Housing Economics* **2**(4): 339–357.

Gravel, Nicolas, Michelangeli, Alessandra, and Trannoy, Alain, 2006. Measuring the social value of local public goods: an empirical analysis within Paris metropolitan area. *Applied Economics* **38**(16): 1945–1961.

Guilfoyle, Jeffrey P. 2000. The effect of property taxes on home value. *Journal of Real Estate Literature* **8**(2): 111–130.

Gujarati, Damodar, 2002. Basic Econometrics, fourth ed. McGraw-Hill, Irwin.

Halstead, John M., Bouvier, Rachel A., and Hansen, Bruce E. 1997. On the issue of functional form choice in hedonic price functions: further evidence. *Environmental Management* **21**(5): 759–765.

Halvorsen, Robert and Pollakowski, Henry O. 1981. Choice of functional form for hedonic price equations. *Journal of Urban Economics* **10**(1): 37–49.

Heckman, James J., Matzkin, Rosa, and Nesheim, Lars, 2010. Nonparametric identification and estimation of nonadditive hedonic models. *Econometrica* **78**(5): 1569–1591.

Hilber, Christian A.L. and Mayer, Christopher J. 2009. Why do households without children support local public schools? Linking house price capitalization to school spending. *Journal of Urban Economics* **65**(1): 74–90.

Hu, Yue and Yinger, John, 2008. The impact of school district consolidation on housing prices. *National Tax Journal* **61**(4): 609–633.

Huh, Serim and Kwak, Seung-Jun, 1997. The choice of functional form and variables in the hedonic price model in Seoul. *Urban Studies* **34**(7): 989–998.

Kane, Thomas J., Riegg, Stephanie K., and Staiger, Douglas O. 2006. School quality, neighborhoods, and housing prices. *American Law and Economics Review* **8**(2): 183–212.

Kane, Thomas J. and Staiger, Douglas O. 2002a. Volatility in school test scores: implications for test-based accountability systems. *Brookings Papers on Education Policy* (5): 235–283.

Kane, Thomas J. and Staiger, Douglas O. 2002b. The promise and pitfalls of using imprecise school accountability measures. *Journal of Economic Perspectives* **16**(4): 91–114.

Kane, Thomas J., Staiger, Douglas O., and Samms, Gavin, 2003. School accountability ratings and housing values. *Brookings–Wharton Papers on Urban Affairs* **4**: 83–137.

Kelejian, Harry H. and Prucha, Ingmar R. 1998. A generalized spatial two-stage least squares procedure for estimating a spatial autoregressive model with autoregressive disturbances. *Journal of Real Estate Finance and Economics* **17**(1): 99–121.

Kiel, Katherine A. and Zabel, Jeffrey E. 1999. The accuracy of owner-provided house values: the 1978–1991 American housing survey. *Real Estate Economics* **27**(2): 263–266.

Lall, Somik V. and Lundberg, Mattias, 2007. What are public services worth, and to whom? Non-parametric estimation of capitalization in Pune. *Journal of Housing Economics* **17**(1): 34–64.

Lang, Kevin and Jian, Tianlun, 2004. Property taxes and property values: evidence from Proposition 2 1/2. *Journal of Urban Economics* **55**(3): 439–457.

Leech, Dennis and Campos, Erick, 2003. Is comprehensive education really free? A case-study of the effects of secondary school admissions policies on house prices in one local area. *Journal of the Royal Statistical Society: Series A* **166**(1): 135–154.

Leenders, Roger Th.A.J. 2002. Modeling social influence through network autocorrelation: constructing the weight matrix. *Social Networks* **24**(1): 21–47.

Leggett, Christopher and Bockstael, Nancy E. 2000. Evidence of the effects of water quality on residential land prices. *Journal of Environmental Economics and Management* **39**(2): 121–144.

LeSage, James P. and Pace, Kelley R. (eds.) 2004. Advances in Econometrics: Spatial and Spatiotemporal Econometrics, vol. 18. Elsevier Science.

LeSage, James P. and Pace, Kelley R. 2009. Introduction to Spatial Econometrics. Taylor & Francis, Boca Raton.

Machin, Stephen and Salvanes, Kjell G. 2008. Valuing School Choice and Social Interactions: Evidence From an Admissions Reform. Working Paper. Centre for the Economics of Education, London School of Economics.

Manski, Charles F. 1993. Identification of endogenous social effects: the reflection problem. *Review of Economic Studies* **60**(3): 531–542.

Mathur, Shishir, 2008. Impact of transportation and other jurisdictional-level infrastructure and services on housing prices. *Journal of Urban Planning and Development* **134**(1): 32–41.

McMillen, Daniel P. 2010. Issues in spatial data analysis. *Journal of Regional Science* **50**(1): 119–141.

Mitchell, David M. 2000. School quality and housing values. *Journal of Economics* **26**(1): 53–70.

Murray, Michael P. 2006. Avoiding invalid instruments and coping with weak instruments. *Journal of Economic Perspectives* **20**(4): 111–132.

Nechyba, Thomas, 2003. School finance, spatial income segregation, and the nature of communities. *Journal of Urban Economics* **54**(1): 61–88.

Oates, Wallace E. 1969. The effects of property taxes and local public spending on property values: an empirical study of tax capitalization and the Tiebout hypothesis. *Journal of Political Economy* **77**(6): 957–971.

Owusu-Edusei, Kwame, Espey, Molly, and Lin, Huiyan, 2007. Does close count? School proximity, school quality, and residential property values. *Journal of Agricultural and Applied Economics* **39**(1): 211–221.

Pace, Kelly R. and LeSage, James P. 2010. Omitted variable biases of OLS and spatial lag models. In Paez, Antonio, Le Gallo, Jullie, Buliung, Ron N., Dall'erba, Sandy (eds.), *Progress in Spatial Analysis: Methods and Applications*, pp. 17–28, Springer.

Pijez, A., Scott, D.M., and Volz, E. 2008. Weight matrices for social influence analysis: an investigation of measurement errors and their effect on model identification and estimation quality. *Social Networks* **30**(4): 309–317.

Rasmussen, David W. and Zuehlke, Thomas W. 1990. On the choice of functional form for hedonic price functions. *Applied Economics* **22**(4): 431–438.

Reback, Randall, 2005. House prices and the provision of local public services: capitalization under school choice programs. *Journal of Urban Economics* **57**(2): 275–301.

Rehm, Michael and Filippova, Olga, 2008. The impact of geographically defined school zones on house prices in New Zealand. *International Journal of Housing Markets and Analysis* **1**(4): 313–336.

Ries, John and Somerville, Tsur, 2010. School quality and residential values: evidence from Vancouver zoning. *Review of Economics and Statistics* **92**(4): 928–944.

Rosen, Sherwin, 1974. Hedonic prices and implicit markets: product differentiation in pure competition. *Journal of Political Economy* **82**(1): 34–55.

Rosenthal, Leslie, 2003. The value of secondary school quality. *Oxford Bulletin of Economics and Statistics* **65**(3): 329–355.

Ross, Stephen and Yinger, John, 1999. Sorting and voting: a review of the literature on urban public finance. In Cheshire, Paul., Mills, Edwin. S. (eds.), *Handbook of Urban and Regional Economics*, vol. 3. pp. 2001–2060, North Holland.

Sedgley, Norman H., Williams, Nancy A., and Derrick, Frederick W. 2008. The effect of educational test scores on house prices in a model with spatial dependence. *Journal of Housing Economics* **17**(2): 191–200.

Seo, Youngme and Simons, Robert, 2009. The effect of school quality on residential sales price. *Journal of Real Estate Research* **31**(3): 307–327.

Stakhovych, Stanislav and Bijmolt, Tammo H.A. 2009. Specification of spatial models: a simulation study on weights matrices. *Papers in Regional Science* **88**(2): 389–408.

Taylor, Laura, 2008. Theoretical foundations and empirical developments in hedonic modeling. In Baranzini, Andrea, Ramirez, José, Schaerer, Caroline, Thalmann, Philippe (eds.), *Hedonic Methods in Housing Markets: Pricing Environmental Amenities and Segregation.* pp. 15–37, Springer: New York.

Weimer, David L. and Wolkoff, Michael J. 2001. School performance and housing values: using non-contiguous district and incorporation boundaries to identify school effects. *National Tax Journal* **54**(2): 231–254.

Wooldridge, Jeffrey M. 2002. *Econometric Analysis of Cross Section and Panel Data.* MIT Press, Cambridge, MA.

Yinger, John. 2015. Hedonic markets and sorting equilibria: bid-function envelopes for public services and neighborhood amenities. *Journal of Urban Economics* **86** (March): 9–25.

Yinger, John, Bloom, Howard S., Boersch-Supan, Axel, and Ladd, Helen F. 1988. *Property Taxes and House Values: The Theory and Estimation of Intrajurisdictional Property Tax Capitalization.* Harcourt Brace Jovanovich Academic Press.

Zahirovic-Herbert, Velma and Turnbull, Geoffrey, 2008. School quality, house prices and liquidity. *Journal of Real Estate Finance and Economics* **37**(2): 113–130.

Zahirovic-Herbert, Velma and Turnbull, Geoffrey, 2009. Public school reform, expectations, and capitalization: what signals quality to homebuyers? *Southern Economic Journal* **75**(4): 1094–1113.

Chapter 16

The Impact of State Aid Reform on Property Values: A Case Study of Maryland's Bridge to Excellence in Public Schools Act[*]

Il Hwan Chung[†], William Duncombe[§], and John Yinger[‡,¶]

[†]*Department of Public Administration, College of Social Sciences,*
Sungkyunkwan University, South Korea
[‡]*Departments of Public Administration and*
International Affairs and of Economics,
Syracuse University, Syracuse, NY, United States
[¶]*jyinger@maxwell.syr.edu*

A major feature of the school finance landscape over the last two decades has been the reform of state school finance systems. Using the case of Maryland's Bridge to Excellence in Public Schools Act, this paper extends the current literature by developing a conceptual framework for residential bidding and sorting and using it to estimate housing market responses to the Maryland state aid reform. With repeat-sales data and many control variables, we find that an increase of $1,000 in current state aid per pupil induced by the reform is associated with an increase of 5 percent to 13 percent in property values. Moreover, within a district the property-value increases are greater in higher-income tracts, where the demand for school quality is likely to be greater.

1. Introduction

A major feature of the school finance landscape over the last two decades has been the reform of state school finance systems in a number of states,

---

[*]This chapter is reproduced from "The Impact of State Aid Reform on Property Values: A Case Study of Maryland's Bridge to Excellence in Public Schools Act," *Education Finance and Policy*, **13**(3), Summer 2018, pp. 369–394.
[§]Deceased.

often prompted by state court decisions. Most of these reforms have involved changes in the state school aid system to improve educational equity or adequacy. Along these lines, the State of Maryland initiated a significant school finance reform without direct judicial prodding, which resulted in the implementation of the Bridge to Excellence in Public Schools Act of 2002 (Senate Bill 856). The financing system for public education in Maryland changed substantially beginning in fiscal year (FY) 2004, and the act was fully phased in by FY 2008. This reform required an additional $1.3 billion above the amount that local school districts would have received from the state under the previous state aid formula, an increase of approximately 75 percent between FY 2002 and FY 2008.

One potentially important unintended effect of school finance reform is on residential bidding and sorting (e.g., Dee, 2000; Hoxby, 2001; Roy, 2004). Because households decide jointly where to live and where to send their children to school, people can respond to any educational reforms affecting property tax rates and the quality of schools by moving to another school district (Aaronson, 1999) or placing their children in private schools (Hoxby, 2001). In turn, this residential sorting can affect the property tax base of school districts and the student composition of schools, which could substantially undermine or amplify the intended impacts of reforms. Increases in housing prices in some locations due to education finance reform, for example, give capital gains to current homeowners but increase housing costs for renters (Wyckoff, 1995, 2001; Dee, 2000; Yinger, 2004). Thus, understanding the impacts of reform on residential sorting is important for assessing the longer-term equity impacts of school aid reforms.

This paper extends the current literature by developing a conceptual framework for residential bidding and sorting and using it to estimate housing market responses to the state aid reform. On the national-level analysis, Dee (2000) finds the capitalization of education finance reforms but state-level analyses reveal the heterogeneous impacts of reforms (e.g., California in Brunner, Murdoch, and Thayer, 2002; Michigan in Chakrabarti and Roy, 2015; and Vermont in Downes, 2010). Significant redistribution of aid in Maryland provides a unique opportunity to examine the complex impact of education finance reform on property values. To be specific, this paper uses panel data for individual house sales, which allows us to identify repeat sales, and differences out time-invariant fixed effects at each house, thereby minimizing problems associated with omitted variables. We also add the series of control variables explaining the different trajectories of housing prices over time. We find that an increase of $1,000 in current state aid per pupil induced by the reform is associated with an increase of 5 percent to 10 percent in property values. Because educational costs vary across school districts, $1,000 of aid will not go as far in some districts as in others. We find that an increase of $1,000 in cost-adjusted state aid per pupil is associated with an increase of 11 percent to 14 percent in housing prices, which suggests that home buyers are aware of these cost differences.

The underlying assumption for identifying the effect of school finance reform is that the trend of housing prices in a district before the reform continues into subsequent years, after controlling for heterogeneous housing market trends in neighborhoods with different income levels. Subsequently, changes in this trend after reform can be interpreted as being a result of the reform's effects. To determine whether our findings hold up under alternative assumptions, we also estimate the model with census tract time-trend variables with all sales data, instead of just with repeat sales. Both approaches yield results similar to those from our baseline model.

The rest of the paper is structured as follows. The next section reviews the literature on the impact of education finance reform on property values. We then provide an overview of the Maryland school finance system and its state aid reform in Section 3. Section 4 introduces our conceptual framework. We then present the empirical strategy and data sources used in the analysis. Finally, the last section provides results and policy implications from the empirical analysis.

2. Literature Review

Studies on the impact of education finance reform on property values have been conducted using reduced form estimates (e.g., Guilfoyle, 1998; Dee, 2000; Hoxby, 2001; Brunner, Murdoch, and Thayer, 2002; Roy, 2004; Downes, 2010) or simulation models designed to capture the general equilibrium effects (e.g., Nechyba, 2004; Epple and Ferreyra, 2008; Ferreya, 2009).

In the earliest empirical study, Dee (2000) investigates the impact of state aid reforms on median housing prices at the school district level using national data. By treating all education finance reforms as a single event, he finds that median housing values increase by 11–20 percent in the poorest school districts, which receive the largest aid increases.[1] Other studies explore diverse state responses to education reforms (Hoxby, 2001; Downes, 2010). Empirical studies with a focus on a single state have documented that the capitalization effect of education finance reform varies depending on the characteristics of the reform (Guilfoyle, 1998; Brunner, Murdoch, and Thayer, 2002; Downes, 2010; Chakrabarti and Roy, 2015).

For example, using house-level data, Brunner, Murdoch, and Thayer (2002) investigate the impact of school finance reform on property values in California. They examine whether reform-induced changes in school spending are capitalized, whether equalization of resources between school districts leads to equalization of housing price differences, and whether spending and housing price convergence works through leveling up or leveling down. They find that a $1 increase in spending per pupil is associated with a $6 increase in property value. Guilfoyle (1998) investigates the impact of state aid reform on property values in Michigan using two samples of housing prices: the median housing price at the district level and the individual housing price with repeated sales data. With dual sales data, he estimates that a $100 increase in per pupil spending increases house prices by 0.51 percent, and a decrease of $1 in annual property taxes raises housing prices by a $4.23. Chakrabarti and Roy (2015) also find a positive relation between Michigan school finance reform and school district property values.

By contrast, Downes (2010) investigates the impact of school finance reform in Vermont (Act 60) on housing price by using individual property sales data. He takes advantage of repeat sales data to avoid possible bias caused by the correlation between neighborhood quality and state aid. He finds little evidence for capitalization of school finance reform.

3. Maryland's Education Finance Reform

Prior to school finance reform, the education finance system in Maryland relied more heavily on local revenue sources than did the vast majority of states. In 2001, for example, the national average for the share of revenue from state governments was 49.9 percent, whereas in Maryland the state government provided only 37.3 percent. Local governments provided

---

[1]Hoxby (2001) estimates the impacts of parameters in school finance reform schemes on property values, but she does not estimate the overall impact on property values of specific reform plans. Some studies also look at the general relation between state aid and housing prices (Barrow and Rouse, 2004; Hilber, Lyytikäinen, and Vermeulen, 2011).

56.8 percent of total funding in Maryland; only two states, Connecticut and Nebraska, had a higher local government revenue share (Huang, 2004). This financing arrangement led to wide variation in local funding for education and undoubtedly contributed to disparities in education quality across school districts.

In 1999, the Commission on Education Finance, Equity and Excellence (Thornton Commission) was created under Chapter 601 Laws of Maryland. Its task was to restructure the state's education finance system. Based on the recommendation from the Thornton Commission, the legislature passed Chapter 288 in 2002, commonly called the Bridge to Excellence in Public Schools Act, or BTE. It changed dramatically the components of Maryland's education financing system starting in 2004.[2] The legislation eliminated or phased out twenty-seven aid programs and consolidated them into four broad categories: (1) the Foundation Program; (2) three programs for special needs students; (3) a general matching grant to encourage local tax effort; and (4) several other types of aid programs for non-instructional purposes.

Table 1 summarizes differences between the main state aid programs on several key features before and after the implementation of BTE. One of the biggest changes in the state aid formula involves the foundation amount, which increased 31 percent, from $4,291 to $5,634 per pupil (in 2003 dollars), when fully phased in. In addition, school districts with a large share of low-income students are major beneficiaries of BTE because the new state aid formula provides more funding for these students. The additional state aid per low-income pupil was $1,073 under the previous formula but rose to $6,197 under BTE. With regard to limited English proficiency (LEP) students, $1,350 in additional state aid per pupil was provided under the old formula, compared with $5,634 with BTE. Moreover, the additional aid for a pupil requiring special education rose from $774 per pupil to $4,169 per pupil under the new formula.

Finally, a form of matching grant called a guaranteed tax base (GTB) program was included in BTE to encourage tax effort in districts with below average wealth. However, it restricts the maximum amount of aid a district can receive to 20 percent of per pupil foundation amount. Moreover, scholars

---

[2]BTE provides "bridge funding" in FY 2003 between the old and new systems, which was financed with a 34-cent increase in the tobacco tax. Up to $64.7 million among the $80.5 million is distributed "in a way that is proportionate to the amount of funding that the school systems would have received in fiscal 2003 under Senate Bill 856 if the phase-in of the new financing system had started in fiscal 2003" (Maryland Department of Legislative Services 2002, pp. 15–16).

Table 1 Major differences in State Aid Schemes before and after reform.

Foundation program	Pre-reform	Post-reform
Foundation amount	$4,291 in $2003	$5,634 in $2003
GCEI	No	Yes
Minimum state aid	No	15% of foundation amount
Special Needs Students		
Special education	Ad hoc	Weight of 0.74* per pupil foundation
Compensatory	25% of per pupil foundation amount	Weight of 1.10* per pupil foundation
LEP	$1,350 per pupil	Weights of 1.00* per pupil foundation
Guaranteed Tax Base Program	None	Only if less than 80% avg. wealth per pupil and only for the local tax effort above that required in the foundation program; no more than 20% of per pupil foundation amount

Note: LEP = limited English proficiency students.

Source: Authors' calculations based on Maryland State Department of Education and Maryland Department of Legislative Services (2002).

have shown that add-on guaranteed tax base programs of this sort have little impact on school district behavior (Yinger, 2004).

Figure 1 and Table 2 summarize the impact of state aid reform on different types of districts. School districts with larger concentrations of students from poor families receive a larger increase, and more rapid growth, state aid than did other types of district.

4. Conceptual Framework

This paper draws on the literature concerning hedonic regressions and their application to housing.[3] In the standard model, households bid for housing in different jurisdictions based on public services levels and local tax rates, and compete for entry into the jurisdictions with the best public services. Observed housing prices (the hedonic envelope) equal the

---

[3]Hedonic studies, which build on Rosen (1974), are reviewed in Taylor (2008); the relevant literature in local public finance is reviewed in Ross and Yinger (1999). The connections between these two literatures are explored in Yinger (2015).

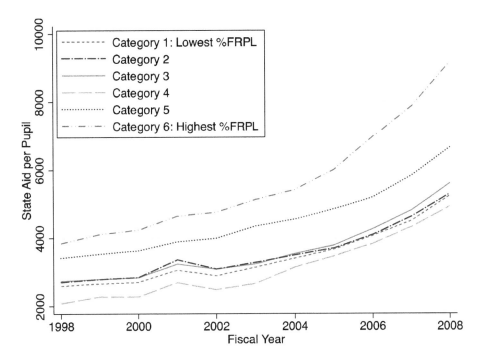

Figure 1 State aid per pupil at different level of share of FRPL students.

Note: Adjusted to 2005 dollars using the Implicit Price Deflator for State and Local Government Purchases (IPD). State aid is measured as the current state aid per pupil without the state contribution to teacher retirement cost. FRPL = free or reduced-price lunch eligible.

Source: Author's calculation based on data from Maryland State Department of Education.

Table 2 Average characteristics of school districts by FRPL% for change in per pupil state aid.

Quintile	Percentage FRPL-eligible students	Change in state aid per pupil ($)	Change in state aid per pupil ($)	Percent change in state aid per pupil (%)	Percent change in state aid per pupil (%)	Median household income
	FY2001	FY02–FY08	FY03–FY08	FY02–FY08	FY03–FY08	FY2001
Group 1	10.4%	$2,100	$1,842	66.7%	54.1%	$66,898
Group 2	16.1%	$2,014	$1,789	61.5%	51.1%	$57,231
Group 3	22.0%	$2,356	$2,063	72.7%	58.3%	$58,226
Group 4	30.8%	$2,255	$1,782	84.6%	56.8%	$43,221
Group 5	40.5%	$2,300	$2,098	52.8%	46.1%	$36,540
Group 6	52.3%	$4,022	$3,737	78.4%	69.0%	$36,181

Notes: Quintiles are based on percentage of free or reduced-price lunch eligible students. State aid per pupil includes the current state aid without the state contribution to retirement cost and inflation is adjusted with Implicit Price Deflator on the basis of 2005 dollars.
FRPL = free or reduced-price lunch eligible.

bids of the households who win this competition in each jurisdiction. Moreover, the households with the steepest bid functions, that is, with the largest willingness to pay for an increment in public services, win the competition for housing in the locations where the public services are the best. The same logic applies to neighborhood amenities.

A hedonic equation for public services or neighborhood amenities should have a nonlinear specification. Consider the case in which a household's willingness to pay for housing services (on the vertical axis) increases linearly with public service quality (on the horizontal axis). These bid functions have different slopes for different household types — a steeper slope indicates a greater willingness to pay for service-quality improvement. Now consider a service level, S^*, at which the bid functions of household type A and household type B cross, and suppose that household type A has the steeper function. Under these circumstances, the (flatter) bid function for household type B will be higher to the left of S^* and the (steeper) bid function for household type A will be higher to the right. A house seller obviously wants to sell to the household that bids the most, so sellers to the left of S^* (that is, in jurisdictions with relatively low public service quality) will sell to household type B and sellers to the right will sell to type A. This behavior results in a nonlinear hedonic envelope. Panel (a) of Figure 2 illustrates a nonlinear envelope with nonlinear bid functions. With many household types, the bid-function envelope can be approximated with a quadratic specification.[4]

An extensive empirical literature (reviewed in Nguyen-Hoang and Yinger, 2011) estimates the impact of school quality on house values. Virtually all of these studies confirm that housing prices are higher in school districts (or school attendance zones) with higher-quality schools. This literature includes studies that investigate the impact of a change in school outcomes on the change in house values. Figlio and Lucas (2004), for example, estimate how much house values change when the local elementary school receives a failing grade from Florida's school accountability program. Bogin and Nguyen-Hoang (2014) extend this analysis to consider the impact on house values in Charlottesville of a failing grade in the federal No Child Left Behind accountability system. Drawing on the conceptual literature, these

---

[4]Yinger (2015) derives a more general version of this approach based on constant elasticity demand functions for public services and housing. He shows that the quadratic case corresponds to the assumption that the price elasticity of demand for public services is infinite, which corresponds in turn to a public service demand curve that is horizontal. He also shows that a linear specification for the hedonic is inconsistent with the standard sorting theorem.

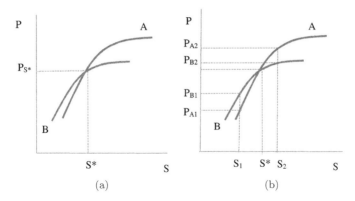

Figure 2 Conceptual framework: Impact of state aid reform on property values. (a) Sorting pre-reform. (b) Impact of state aid reform on property values with re-sorting.

Note: The x-axis is school quality and y-axis is the bidding price for two income taste groups (A and B). Specifically, S_1 indicates school quality at a community during pre-reform years and S_2 represents school quality at a community during post-reform years. P_{ij} refers to the price that income taste group i bids at time j ($i =$ A, B and $j = 1$ during pre-reform years or $j = 2$ during post-reform years). Note that there is another round of adjustments to reach equilibrium because the re-sorting expands the set of locations for group A even though its population does not change.

two studies recognize that the impact of a failing grade on house values operates through two channels. First, the types of households attracted to the neighborhood before the announcement of the failing grade may bid less for housing because of the negative information about the local school provided by this announcement. Second, the announcement may change the types of households moving into the neighborhood, and these households may have different bids for school quality than the households living there before the announcement. As shown by Bogin and Nguyen-Hoang, the second possibility implies that the observed change in house values after a failing grade is announced may understate how much the original residents are willing to pay to have a non-failing school.

This paper also draws on another branch of local public finance, namely, the specification and estimation of cost functions and demand functions for local public education.[5] The key findings from this literature on which we draw are (1) the cost of education in a school district depends on several

---

[5]The literature on cost functions is reviewed in Duncombe and Yinger (2001 and 2011); studies of the impact of state aid on the demand for local services are reviewed in Fisher and Papke (2000); other aspects of this demand are examined in Duncombe and Yinger (1998, 2011) and Nguyen-Hoang and Yinger (2014).

student traits, including the poverty level and the share of students who speak English as a second language; (2) the demand for education increases with income and decreases with tax price; and (3) increases in state aid induce voters to demand some combination of school quality improvements and local property tax cuts.

This literature implies that BTE could affect house values through three channels. First, the additional aid provided by BTE loosens a district's budget constraint and allows voters to select a school service–tax package more to their liking. People moving into the district who have school-quality demands similar to the voters already in the district will therefore bid more for housing there than they would have before BTE.

Because BTE does not have the same impact in every school district, it also could lead to a new pattern of household sorting.[6] Re-sorting caused by BTE leads to the second and third channels for possible house-value impacts. The second channel is the one discussed by Figlio and Lucas (2004) and Bogin and Nguyen-Hoang (2014), namely, that the people moving into a district after BTE is implemented may have different demands for education than the people moving in before BTE. This channel is illustrated in panel (b) of Figure 2. A district with a relatively large BTE-induced increase in school quality, from S_1 to S_2, for example, might attract new residents with a higher demand for school quality than the pre-BTE residents. In this case, the change in house values (P_{B1} to P_{A2}) will reflect not only the BTE-induced improvement in school quality (P_{B1} to P_{B2}) as seen by the original type of households, but also the increase in bids for housing associated with the BTE-induced shift to homebuyers with a higher demand for school quality (P_{B2} to P_{A2}). The third channel is that changes in the types of students in a district, which also might result from re-sorting, may change educational costs.[7] A BTE-induced increase in school quality might attract higher-income residents, for example, thereby lowering the share of neighborhood residents in poverty and lowering the cost of education in the district. This decrease in the cost of education will lead, in turn, to a higher

---

[6] Any re-sorting will be associated with BTE-induced changes in school quality — not with BTE-induced changes in school property taxes. Ross and Yinger (1999) show that property tax differences across communities are capitalized into house values but do not result in sorting because all households are willing to pay $1 for a $1 lower property-tax payment.

[7] Changes in sorting might also lead to changes in housing characteristics, such as the addition of new rooms when richer households move in. However, we only observe changes in housing characteristics between sales, which, by definition, are made by the pre-BTE buyer, not the post-BTE buyer.

demand for school quality. To the best of our knowledge, this channel has not been recognized in previous research.

It is not possible to estimate the impact of BTE on house values through each of these channels. Moreover, it is not possible to distinguish between changes in school characteristics that are induced by BTE from changes in school characteristics that have other causes, such as demographic trends within the state. Our strategy, therefore, is to focus on the impact of BTE through the first channel by controlling for observable changes in school and neighborhood characteristics. This strategy cannot shed light on the second two channels, but it has the virtue that it minimizes potential bias in estimating the first channel caused by a correlation between changes in a school district's state aid and district or neighborhood changes that have nothing to do with BTE.

5. Empirical Strategy

Consider the following simple hedonic model to explain house price, V, in a panel setting. Let X stand for housing characteristics, N stand for neighborhood amenities, D_d be a fixed effect for school district or school-district type d, and R_t be a binary variable that equals 1 in years after school finance reform and zero before. Reform takes place in year t^*. The term $(t - t^*)$ defines the post-reform time trend. In this specification, the post-reform shifts in both the intercept and the time trend are estimated for each d. Moreover, let μ be unobservable time-invariant house factors, v be unobservable neighborhood effects, and ϵ be a random error. Then a hedonic model for house h in neighborhood type j at time t that accounts for district-type-specific trends with a possible shift after reform is[8]:

$$\ln\{V_{hjtd}\} = \sum_i \alpha_i X_{iht} + \sum_k \beta_k N_{kht} + \sum_d \gamma_d D_{dh} + \sum_d \delta_{dt} D_{dh}$$

$$+ \sum_d \gamma'_d R_t D_{dh} + \sum_d \delta'_d R_t (t - t^*) D_{dh} + \mu_h + v_{jht} + \varepsilon_{ht}. \quad (1)$$

This model is difficult to estimate without bias because it requires many Xs and many Ns and key house-specific factors and neighborhood amenities may not be observed. With double-sales data, however, we can estimate

---

[8]For simplicity, equation 1 expresses the N variables in linear form — following the earlier discussion, however, our equation actually uses a quadratic form for these variables when they are continuous. For readability, the h subscript is omitted from the time variables.

a different version of the model that is much simpler and that greatly minimizes the potential for omitted variable bias. Our main versions of this model assume that the variables in X and N are constant over time (as are their coefficients). However, we also present results that add time-varying controls for these variables.

Now suppose we observe house h selling at two different times, t and t', where $t' > t$. Then differencing equation (1) eliminates time invariant variables: the Xs, the Ns, the first term with district fixed effects, and the house fixed effect.[9] The result is

$$\ln\left\{\frac{V_{hjt'd}}{V_{hjtd}}\right\} = \sum_d \gamma'_d (R_{t'} - R_t) D_{dh} + \sum_d \delta_d (t' - t) D_{dh}$$

$$\sum_d \delta'_d [R_{t'}(t' - t^*) - R_t(t - t^*)] D_{dh}$$

$$+ (\upsilon_{jht'} - \upsilon_{jht}) + (\varepsilon_{ht'} - \varepsilon_{ht}). \tag{2}$$

We define neighborhood types based on census tract income. The resulting neighborhood-income-by-year fixed effects ensure that our estimates of the impacts of BTE control for underlying housing market trends that may differ for neighborhoods at different income levels (Glaeser, Gottlieb, and Tobio, 2012). These controls are particularly important in our sample, which includes the recession years of 2001 and 2002. Our sample does not include the housing market crash, which began in 2008 but nevertheless controls for housing market trends leading up to that event. In other words, the identification strategy in our interrupted time analysis is not simply to assume that the trend of housing prices within school districts prior to the reform provides a valid counterfactual for what would have happened to housing prices within school districts had state aid reform not been implemented. Instead, we recognize that different types of neighborhoods might experience different housing price trends after reform for reasons that are separate from but correlated with changes in state education aid reform (Morgan and Winship, 2007). These fixed effects minimize the bias from this possibility.

Equation (2) applies to cases in which both sales occur before reform ($R_{t'} = R_t = 0$), both sales occur after reform ($R_{t'} = R_t = 1$), or the first sale occurs before reform and the second one occurs after ($R_t = 0; R_{t'} = 1$).

---

[9]Without the assumption that Ns and Xs are constant over time, a differenced version of our model includes the changes in N and X. In cases of houses being sold more than three times, we used each pair of repeated sales.

As a result, all double sales observations can be used, regardless of whether they straddle the reform. In the first and second case the first term, $[(R_{t'} - R_t)D_{hd}]$, drops out, and in the first case the third term, $([R_{t'}(t' - t^*) - R_t(t - t^*)]D_{hd})$, drops out.[10]

We estimate equation (2) for two different school district definitions. First, we follow Chakrabarti and Roy (2015), henceforth CR, by defining categories of districts based on a pre-reform trait that is related to the magnitude of the reform in a district, and hence to the expected impact on property values. In the Michigan case analyzed by CR, the reform was designed to bring per pupil spending up to $6,000 in all districts, with a grandfather clause for districts spending more than that amount already. As a result, CR based their analysis on quintiles of the pre-reform per pupil spending distribution, which define the reform-based change in spending. They expected (and found) larger impacts in the lowest quintile, where the impacts of the reform were largest. However, it is not appropriate for us to define district types based on pre-reform spending levels because, in the Maryland case, the change in spending induced by the reform is not exogenous. We can, however, take advantage of the fact that one of the main features of Maryland's reformed education aid formula was a large increase in the weight placed on pupils eligible for a free or reduced-price lunch (FRPL). Hence, the pre-reform share of FRPL-eligible students predicts the magnitude of the aid change in a given district, and we define district types based on this share (see Figure 1). Because of the link between the pre-reform FRPL share and the state aid change, we expect that the impact of the reform as estimated by equation (2) will be larger in districts with a higher pre-reform FRPL share.

Second, we estimate equation (2) with d as a school-district indicator; that is, we estimate the pre-reform and post-reform time trends separately for each district. This approach has the advantage of allowing for a different price impact from BTE in each district, not just in a type of district. A district's γ' coefficient indicates how much the district's property values shift when the reform is initiated. A district's δ' coefficient indicates the change in the

---

[10]The growth rate can be estimated with months as the unit of time (instead of years) but is written here with the year indicator to simplify the notation. If months are used, then double sales within a single year can be included, even though the district-based variables all equal zero for these observations. It increases the number of observations that can be used in the analysis, but some care needs to be taken in using sales data within a year because it is possible that repeated sales data within a year might just reflect changes in the property records, not actual sales of houses.

slope of a district's time trend during the post-reform years. A district's δ coefficient captures the underlying time trend for each district. To identify the impact of BTE with this approach, we estimate a second-stage regression to determine whether the estimated changes in the path of house values in a district after the implementation of BTE are correlated with the aid changes associated with this reform. This change in house value in a given district in year t' equals $\gamma'_d + \delta'_d(t' - t^*)$. We estimate a regression with this change in house value as the dependent variable and with the change in aid as the explanatory variable. We also explore the extent to which this dependent variable can be explained by reform-induced changes in student test scores and tax rates or by reform-induced changes in sorting outcomes, as measured by changes in household incomes.[11]

6. Data

We have ten years of data on residential sales (1998 to 2007) and housing characteristics from two different databases produced by the Maryland State Department of Assessments and Taxation (SDAT): Real Property Sales File (RPSF) and Computer Assisted Mass Appraisal (CAMA). House sale prices come from the RPSF.[12] After data cleaning, we have 772,566 sales records from 603,258 houses. This leads to 314,395 repeat sales records for 144,955 houses.

School district variables are used in the second step of our analysis, which links the predicted change in housing price (compared with pre-reform trend) with the change in school district traits. School districts in Maryland are coterminous with counties. Total state aid per pupil (from Maryland Department of Education) includes aid recorded in any school district fund, including current expenses fund, food service fund, school construction fund, and debt service fund. Current state aid refers to state aid recorded only in the current expenses fund without the state's contribution

---

[11] Aside from the tobacco tax mentioned in footnote 2, the BTE reforms were funded by state general revenue, which comes largely from income and sales taxes. The connection between these taxes is not very salient, so the effect on household bids is likely to be small. Nevertheless, both of our methods net out any tax-related changes. Method 1 nets them out by expressing results relative to type-1 districts. Method 2 nets them out by including neighborhood income-by-year fixed effects.

[12] Appendix Table A.1 summarizes our data-filtering process.

to teacher retirements. Student performance measures include dropout rates, and passing rates in Reading and Math for third and fifth grades from the Maryland School Assessment (MSA) and the Maryland School Performance Assessment Program (MSPAP).

One possible limitation that arises when using student test scores is that to conform to the requirements of No Child Left Behind, Maryland changed its tests in 2003 from MSPAP (school-based reporting system and essay exams) to MSA (multiple choice, short-answer questions, and individual student reporting system). We estimate Cronbach's alpha to check the reliability of measurement in each test score over our sample period (1997–2007).[13] The results show that Cronbach's alphas are 0.96 and 0.98 in third and fifth grade reading, respectively, and 0.95 and 0.97 in third and fifth grade math, respectively. Because an alpha of 0.70 or higher is sufficient for modest reliability (Nunnally and Bernstein, 1994), these results provide evidence that the test does not substantially change during our sample period.

The effective tax rate (ETR) in each county is the product of the county's nominal tax rate and average assessment to sales ratios in residential properties drawn from Assessment Ratio Surveys in SDAT. Following Clapp, Nanda, and Ross (2008), the final property tax variable equals $\log\{r + \text{ETR}\}$, where the discount rate (r) is 0.03, which is the standard rate in the literature.[14]

A variety of amenities and disamenities variables are included in the analysis. Data on the crime rate at the school district level come from the Uniform Crime Reporting Program in the Federal Bureau of Investigation, measuring the total and violent crime rates per 100,000 inhabitants. In addition, Geographic Information System software was used to bring in other neighborhood characteristics. Table 3 describes the summary statistics for repeated sales data in our baseline model. Appendix Tables A.2 and A.3 list and define our school district variables and our neighborhood amenities or disamenities.

---

[13]Cronbach's alpha is one of the common statistics for test construction and use. It mainly checks the reliability of tests based on split-half reliability concepts (Cronbach, 1951; Cortina, 1993).

[14]We do not know the assessment for an individual house, so we cannot examine the capitalization of within-district variation in the effective tax rate, as in Yinger *et al.* (1988).

Table 3 Summary statistics for sales price difference and variables used in hedonic analysis for repeated sales data.

Variables	Mean	Standard deviation	Min	Max
Difference in sales price	113110	110763.9	−3509000	4837132
House characteristics				
Story	4.8	3.07	0	13
Square feet	1,608	719	1	22,932
Good condition	0.0045	0.067	0	1
Age	33.3	23.79	3	316
Rail station	0.245	0.43	0	1
Change in state aid per pupil ($1,000)				
Unadjusted	1.09	0.87	−0.43	3.58
Cost-Adjusted	0.49	0.335	−0.84	1.52
Percent change in state aid per pupil				
Unadjusted	36.06	26.4	−12.88	104.2
Cost-adjusted	27.9	21.13	−3.48	101.6
Neighborhood characteristics				
%Hispanic	0.069	0.065	0.0008	0.207
%Black	0.304	0.228	0.002	0.889
%LEP	0.035	0.03	0	0.102
%FRPL	0.259	0.137	0.06	0.778
%Special	0.118	0.017	0.084	0.186
Crime rate	4027.1	1723	1619	11657

Note: FRPL = free or reduced-price lunch eligible; LEP = limited English proficiency.

7. Empirical Results

Our empirical strategy leads to two estimating methods. The first method implements equation (2) with school district types defined by FRPL share. The second method implements this equation with a separate impact of BTE for each school district, and then estimates the link between housing trend shifts and state aid.

7.1. *Method 1*

The results for the first method are presented in Table 4. This method estimates equation (2) with six district classes defined by the share of FRPL-eligible students. We omit class 1 so that the coefficients measure differences from the lowest-FRPL districts. BTE substantially changed the aid formula starting in FY2004, so property that was sold after September 2003 was considered to be affected by state aid reform. Both columns in this table indicate that in the districts with the highest share of FRPL-eligible

Table 4   Impact of State aid reform on property values.

Change in	(1)	(2)
Group 2*Reform	−0.0150	−0.0205
	(0.0131)	(0.0130)
Group 3*Reform	0.0179	0.0092
	(0.0134)	(0.0093)
Group 4*Reform	−0.0382**	−0.0502***
	(0.0126)	(0.0114)
Group 5*Reform	−0.0098	0.0051
	(0.0248)	(0.0222)
Group 6*Reform	−0.0721**	−0.0699***
	(0.0222)	(0.0164)
Group 2*Reform*Trend	0.0130	0.0106
	(0.0109)	(0.0113)
Group 3*Reform*Trend	0.0132	0.0024
	(0.0147)	(0.0142)
Group 4*Reform*Trend	0.0348**	0.0265*
	(0.0098)	(0.0097)
Group 5*Reform*Trend	0.0300**	0.0068
	(0.0106)	(0.0123)
Group 6*Reform*Trend	0.0614***	0.0513***
	(0.0098)	(0.0106)
Group 2*Trend	−0.0020	0.0003
	(0.0067)	(0.0057)
Group 3*Trend	−0.0062	−0.0045
	(0.0092)	(0.0078)
Group 4*Trend	−0.0303**	−0.0189**
	(0.0091)	(0.0057)
Group 5*Trend	−0.0170	−0.0132
	(0.0130)	(0.0099)
Group 6*Trend	−0.0464***	−0.0402***
	(0.0095)	(0.0066)
Reform	0.1487***	0.0897***
	(0.0155)	(0.0111)
Trend	0.0772***	0.0713***
	(0.0054)	(0.0050)
Reform*trend	0.0128	0.0066
	(0.0081)	(0.0119)
Housing and neighborhood characteristics[a]	Yes	Yes
Income level/year fixed effect	No	Yes
R^2	0.864	0.876
N	157,859	157,859

Note: [a]Housing and neighborhood characteristics include all control variables used in Table 3.
**$p < 0.05$; ***$p < 0.01$.

students, housing prices shifted downward relative to those in the lowest-FRPL districts in the year BTE was implemented but then grew significantly faster in later years.[15] These effects are highly significant. The downward shift is slightly smaller and the increase in the trend is slightly greater when the neighborhood income-by-year fixed effects are included (column 2). The same pattern exists for houses in district class 4, which received a larger boost in state aid than did the districts in class 5 (see Figure 1), although the effects are smaller than the ones for class 6. The effects are not significant for districts with other FRPL shares.

These results appear to indicate either uncertainty about the impacts of the reform or some type of adjustment costs at the time of BTE implementation in September 2003, with a drop in housing prices of almost 7 percent in the highest-FRPL districts relative to those in the lowest-FRPL districts. This drop was quickly reversed, however, and, based on the results in column 2, it had disappeared by the end of 2004. By September 2007, housing prices in these districts were 13 percent above the class-1 baseline (see Figure 3). In short, the post-reform housing price increases were highest in the districts with the highest concentrations of FRPL-eligible students, which are precisely the districts where BTE is predicted to have the greatest impact. Neither this figure nor any of our other results predicts, of course, what happened after 2007.

7.2. *Method 2*

Table 5 shows regression results based on equation (2) with separate estimates for each school district in Maryland. All regressions are estimated with standard errors clustered at the school district level. This is the first stage of our second method, which allows for heterogeneous effects of reform on property values at the school district level. Because our empirical specification is the differenced version of a hedonic model with repeat-sales data, neighborhood and housing traits are included in the model as changes during the repeat sales period. The inclusion of neighborhood variables changes the interpretation of the estimated impact of state aid reform as a whole on property values. Because state aid reform may change sorting, controlling for variables (such as the crime rate, which may be influenced

---

[15]Prices and price trends shifted upward in all district classes relative to the pre-reform trend. Following our theoretical predictions, we focus on changes relative to the lowest-FRPL districts.

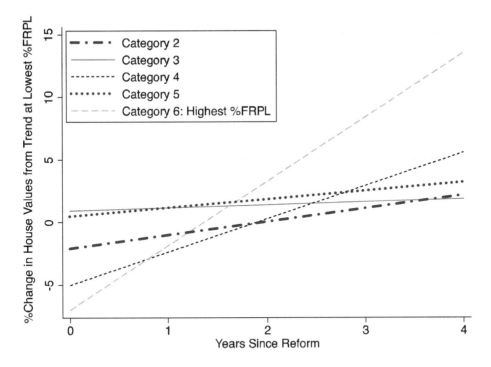

Figure 3 Impact of state aid reforms on housing values.

Note: The graph is based on the results from the second column of Table 4. FRPL = free or reduced-price lunch eligible.

by sorting) implies that we may not be capturing all impacts of state aid reform. Coefficients in this hedonic model should be interpreted as partial effects of aid reform after controlling for possible changes in sorting that the reform induced.

In the first column of Table 5, the coefficients indicate each school district's γ', which measures how much property values in the district shift after BTE was implemented compared to the pre-reform trend. For example, BTE increased property values in the Howard and Calvert districts by 8.2 percent and 10.3 percent, respectively. In contrast, the reform lowered property values by about 7.5 percent in the Allegany school district. The third column of Table 5 provides the impact of reform on the change in the time trend in housing prices after controlling for time-varying housing traits and neighborhood characteristics. For example, the Allegany and Calvert school districts had positive, statistically significant changes in their trends; the rate of increase in property values rose by 6.0 and 5.0 percentage points, respectively, after the reform compared to prereform trend. All housing and neighborhood variables are in change form. To capture the nonlinearity in

Table 5 Impact of state aid reform on property values using repeat sales data with time variant controls.

School district	District's intercept shift after the reform	District's time trend	Change in the slope of a district's time	Control variables: housing and neighborhood	
Allegany	−0.0746***	0.0518***	0.0599***	Story	−0.0180
Anne Arundel	0.0825***	0.0925***	0.028***	Square feet	0.00012***
Baltimore city	0.0123	0.1315***	0.0077	Good cond	−0.078***
Baltimore county	0.0514***	0.0951***	0.0461***	Age	−0.00016
Calvert	0.1029***	0.0706***	0.0504***	Brick	−0.1093***
Caroline	0.1198***	0.0635***	0.0298***	Rail Station	−0.0255*
Carroll	0.0781***	0.0785***	0.0199***	%Hispanic	2.015
Cecil	0.0326***	0.0779***	0.0228**	%Black	−1.688
Charles	0.0617***	0.1073***	0.081***	%LEP	−0.3817
Dorchester	0.0767***	0.0884***	0.0082	%FRPL	0.2074
Frederick	0.1083***	0.0857***	0.0085	%Special	0.6857
Garrett	0.069***	0.0654***	−0.0084	$(\%\text{Hisp})^2$	−3.8339
Harford	0.057***	0.0674***	0.0589***	$(\%\text{Black})^2$	−0.4534
Howard	0.0824***	0.0928***	0.0263***	$(\%\text{LEP})^2$	11.593**
Kent	0.0412***	0.0852***	−0.0018	$(\%\text{FRPL})^2$	−0.8189***
Montgomery	0.0923***	0.1134***	−0.0179	$(\%\text{Special})^2$	−1.631
Prince Georges	0.0384***	0.0778***	0.0438***	Crime	4.20E−06
Queen Anne	0.0566***	0.093***	−0.0046	$(\text{Crime})^2$	−7.70E−10
Somerset	0.0781***	0.048***	0.0781***		
St Mary	0.0351**	0.0712***	0.0261**		
Talbot	0.0477***	0.0894***	−0.0183*		
Washington	0.1102***	0.0802***	0.0233**		
Wicomico	0.0096	0.069***	0.0397***		
Worcester	0.0277***	0.1122***	−0.0443***		

Notes: Dependent variable is change in the log of housing price, compared to pre-reform trend. Equation is estimated with ordinary least squares (no constant term) and standard errors clustered at the school district level. Specification is based on equation 2 with repeat sales data. The number of observations is 157,859. R^2 is 0.878. Districts are sorted by median household income, low to high. All housing and neighborhood variables are in change form. The quadratic terms are the change in the square of the variable. FRPL = free or reduced-price lunch eligible; LEP = limited English proficiency.
$^*p < 0.10$; $^{**}p < 0.05$; $^{***}p < 0.01$.

the hedonic, we include the change in the level and the change in the square of each variable.[16]

---

[16]The quadratic form is not used for the *Rail station* variable because it is a dichotomous variable representing whether the closest rail station is located less than five miles away from the property (and appears or disappears between sales).

The second step with this method is to investigate the relationship between the change in house value associated with education finance reform and the change in state aid at the district level. This step addresses the question: Did the BTE aid changes lead to changes in house values? Each school district has its own coefficients derived from empirical specification 2, which allows us to provide the predicted reform-induced change in house value at the school district level for each post-reform year. Each district's predicted change in the log of housing price, which equals $\gamma'_d + \delta'_d(t' - t^*)$, is regressed on the district's change in state aid between time t' and t^*.[17] The measure of the change in state aid used in the analysis should reflect the change in state aid that bidders in the housing market are most apt to perceive. Because little is known about these perceptions, we examined several aid measures. We find that absolute and percent change measures in per pupil spending yield qualitatively similar results and, for conciseness, focus on the former.

Table 6 presents results of ordinary least squares (OLS) regressions of predicted change in property values on the change in state aid. To account for heteroskedasticity and autocorrelation in the second step, we use Newey–West standard errors. Except for the quadratic term in columns 3 and 6, the regression coefficients are all positive and significant at the 1 percent level. These results support the hypothesis that post-reform changes in property values reflect the changes in state aid associated with BTE. To be specific, results from the first column of Table 6 indicate that an increase of $1,000 in current state aid per pupil is associated with an increase of about 5.1 percent in property values. Because different districts face different educational costs, homebuyers may recognize that aid does not go as far in some districts as in others. The results in Table 6 (columns 4, 5, and 6) support this view — when changes in state aid are adjusted for educational cost differences, the coefficients are even larger.[18] An increase of $1,000 in cost-adjusted state

---

[17]We use pre-reform pupil measures when calculating state aid per pupil. For example, change in state aid per pupil between FY 2003 and FY 2007 is measured as the difference between (aid for FY 2007/enrollment for FY 2003) and (aid for FY 2003/enrollment for FY 2003). Thus, we are able to exclude any possible effects of re-sorting that reform induced (due to change in enrollment or education cost) on housing price. This allows us to estimate the impact of change in the state aid formula on housing prices.

[18]Cost-adjusted state aid refers to Geographic Cost Education Index (GCEI)-adjusted state aid per pupil. The calculation process was as follows: first, current inflation-adjusted state aid was divided by the GCEI for the state of Maryland (developed by Duncombe and Goldhaber, 2003, 2009). Then, aid per pupil was generated using weights that had been used in Maryland school finance reform for special education, LEP, and FRPL-eligible students. To be specific, the weights of students with special needs (e.g., special education, LEP, and FRPL) are 1.16, 1.10, and 1, respectively.

Table 6 Results of a regression between predicted change in housing prices and change in state aid per pupil.

	(1)	(2)	(3)	(4)	(5)	(6)
Change in state aid	0.051*** (0.01)	0.046*** (0.009)	0.105** (0.052)	0.113*** (0.029)	0.038*** (0.011)	0.02 (0.17)
Change in (state aid)²			−0.0048 (0.0046)			0.0165 (0.03)
Measure of state aid change	Absolute change in state aid per pupil	Ln (absolute change in state aid per pupil)	Absolute change in state aid per pupil	Absolute change in cost-adjusted state aid per pupil	Ln (absolute change in cost-adjusted state aid per pupil)	Absolute change in cost-adjusted state aid per pupil
N	120	117	120	120	117	120
Adj R²	0.244	0.198	0.265	0.174	0.126	0.181

Notes: Dependent variable is predicted change in the log of housing price, compared to pre-reform trend from results in Table 5. The unit for the absolute change in state aid per pupil ($) is rescaled to $1,000. Equation is estimated with pooled ordinary least squares with Newey–West standard errors.

** $p < 0.05$; *** $p < 0.01$.

aid per pupil is associated with a 11.3 percent increase in housing prices in column 4.

Homebuyers may be more attuned to changes in school quality and property tax rates than they are the associated changes in state aid. Table 7 looks into this possibility with both the linear and the quadratic form. We find that the state aid coefficients are still positive and statistically significant

Table 7 Results of a regression between predicted change in housing prices and change in school district characteristics.

	(1)	(2)	(3)	(4)
Change in state aid	0.065*** (0.011)	0.147*** (0.037)	0.078* (0.046)	−0.1426 (0.15)
Change in test score for 3rd grade	0.0022 (0.0014)	0.0027* (0.001)	0.001 (0.003)	0.0011 (0.0023)
Change in test score for 5th grade	−0.0045*** (0.002)	−0.0046*** (0.0016)	−0.009 (0.006)	−0.012** (0.006)
Change in dropout rate	−0.002 (0.009)	0.0056 (0.01)	0.018 (0.03)	0.0085 (0.022)
Change in effective tax rate	0.031 (0.347)	0.0237 (0.361)	−0.29 (0.46)	−0.597 (0.493)
Quadratic Form (All terms are squared)				
Change in (state aid)^2			−0.0014 (0.004)	0.0461* (0.0245)
Change in (test score for 3rd grade)^2			−0.000014 (0.000029)	−0.00001 (0.00002)
Change in (test score for 5th grade)^2			0.000045 (0.00004)	0.0008* (0.00005)
Change in (dropout rate)^2			−0.0014 (0.0021)	0.0051* (0.002)
Observations	120	120	120	120
Measure of State Aid	State aid per pupil	Cost-adjusted state aid per pupil	State aid per pupil	Cost-adjusted state aid per pupil
Adjusted R^2	0.188	0.145	0.349	0.418

Notes: Dependent variable is predicted change in the log of housing price, compared to pre-reform trend from results in Table 5. Equation is estimated with a pooled ordinary least squares and Newey–West standard errors. The unit for the absolute change in state aid per pupil ($) is rescaled to $1,000.
*$p < 0.10$; **$p < 0.05$; ***$p < 0.01$.

after controlling for changes in student performance and the effective tax rate. Specifically, when a school district (i.e., the school district receiving the median level of state aid prior to the reform) receives a $1,000 increase in state aid per pupil through state aid reform, its property values increase by about 6.5 percent to 7.8 percent (columns 1 and 3 in Table 7). Cost-adjusted aid (column 2) has an even larger effect. The variables for change in student performance and tax rate have mixed findings. These results suggest that voters interpret aid changes as a reasonably complete summary of the impact of reform. The exception is that an increase in the test scores for fifth graders has a small negative and significant impact on house values, which is not the expected sign.

These impacts of state aid provide similar estimates from previous studies. For instance, Dee (2000) shows that state aid reform leads to an 11 percent to 20 percent increase in median housing prices, and Guilfoyle (1998) provides evidence that a $1,000 increase in per pupil spending is associated with a 5.1 percent increase in housing prices. In absolute dollar terms, our results imply that a $1 increase in state aid per pupil leads to an increase in median housing price (in 2000) of approximately $8 to $17. In a similar vein, Barrow and Rouse (2004) estimate that a $1 increase in state aid per pupil is associated with a $30 increase in housing prices, and Brunner, Murdoch, and Thayer (2002) find that housing prices increase by $6 for every $1 increase in spending per pupil.

8. Heterogeneous Impacts Caused by Sorting

As discussed earlier, the sorting of households across locations could result in heterogeneous impacts of an education finance reform on housing prices. The school districts in Maryland are not homogeneous, and even within a given district, higher-income households might place more value on educational improvements than do lower-income households. As a result, BTE might lead to a greater increase in housing prices in high-income neighborhoods than in low-income neighborhoods in the same district.

An additional complication arises in Maryland, however, because the impact of BTE on housing prices depends on homebuyers' perceptions about the way additional state aid would be used. Because education finance reform is designed to help low-performing students, households may expect that the additional aid their district receives will go to the lowest-performing elementary schools in the district. The lowest-performing elementary schools tend to be located in low-income neighborhoods, so this possibility can lead to the opposite prediction from the one in the previous paragraph — namely, that the impact of an aid increase could be smaller in high-income neighborhoods because people buying housing in those neighborhoods do not expect much of the aid to be directed toward the associated elementary schools.

Table 8 shows the relationship between our estimate of the reform-induced change in housing price and household median income during pre-reform

Table 8 Results of relation between predicted change in housing prices and household demands at the census tract level.

	(1)	(2)	(3)	(4)	(5)	(6)	(7)
Change in state aid per pupil	0.0463*** (0.0050)	0.0419*** (0.0059)	0.0341*** (0.0062)	0.0362*** (0.0061)	0.0385*** (0.0060)	0.0418*** (0.0055)	0.0357*** (0.0049)
Interaction with state aid							
Median income	0.0127*** (0.0030)						0.0357*** (0.0049)
High school		0.0010 (0.0008)					0.0178** (0.0054)
Bachelor			−0.0001 (0.0004)				−0.0015 (0.0012)
English				−0.0002 (0.0005)			−0.0013* (0.0006)
Old					−0.0034*** (0.0008)		0.0006 (0.0005)
Child						0.0028** (0.0011)	−0.0038* (0.0018)
Median income	−0.0075*** (0.0022)						−0.0004 (0.0021)
High school		0.0002 (0.0007)					−0.0044 (0.0038)
Bachelor			−0.0008** (0.0003)				0.0049*** (0.0013)
English				0.0014*** (0.0003)			−0.0021*** (0.0006)
Old					−0.0004 (0.0006)		−0.0001 (0.0004)
Child						0.0007 (0.0008)	0.0005 (0.0014)
Observations	4,386	4,386	4,386	4,386	4,386	4,386	4,386
R²	0.1411	0.1292	0.1566	0.1359	0.1463	0.1404	0.2234

Notes: Dependent variable is predicted change in housing price after the reform at the census tract level. Equation is estimated with ordinary least squares, and cluster standard errors in the district level are in parentheses. All demand variables are recorded as mean-centered variables. The unit of median income is rescaled to $10,000.
*$p < 0.10$; **$p < 0.05$; ***$p < 0.01$.

years. The dependent variable is based on a regression like the one in Table 4, except that the shifts in the intercept and trend are estimated for each census tract, not for each school district. The explanatory variables in column 1 include tract median income and an interaction between the district-level change in state aid per pupil and tract income. In other words, this regression determines whether the impact of higher state aid on house values in a census tract depends on that tract's median income. The other columns provide the same type of test for other variables that might influence the demand for education, such as education, age, and family composition. The last column includes all of these variables and their interactions with the change in state aid.

The key result in Table 8 is that the impact of higher state aid on property values is higher in high-income census tracts, even within the same school district. This effect persists when other demand variables are included. The last column also indicates that the impact of aid increases with education (at least up to a high school degree). These results suggest that pre-reform sorting influences the property-value impacts of school finance reform, and that people buying housing expect the benefits of higher aid will be spread throughout a school district.

9. Robustness Checks

Several robustness checks are presented in an online appendix that can be accessed on *Education Finance and Policy*'s Web site at www. mitpressjournals.org/doi/suppl/10.1162/edfp_a_00230. To begin, we used our first method to see if the effects of reforms were anticipated. Second, we conducted a separate analysis using our second method with just the school districts in the Baltimore metropolitan area. A hedonic equation represents the sorting equilibrium for the households competing against each other for housing in a given urban area, so using an entire state, even a relatively small one like Maryland, might produce misleading results. Third, we added a quadratic term to the trends in equation (2). Fourth, we reestimated equation (2) with all sales, not just repeat sales. Each of these robustness checks supports our conclusion that the relatively large increases in state aid to education in some school districts associated with BTE resulted in relatively large increases in house values in those school districts.

10. Conclusions and Discussion

One major feature of the U.S. education system is disparities in funding across school districts. Many states have made efforts to reduce these funding gaps through education finance reforms. This study contributes to the debate by examining the unintended impact of Maryland state aid reform on property values.

Our approach is to use repeat-sales data to isolate the impact of education finance reform on property values over time in the intercept and slope of housing prices in affected school districts. This approach minimizes the problem of omitted variable bias, which is a key challenge in the hedonics literature. We find that all school districts except Allegany have a positive intercept shift, and the change in slope of the time trend is positive in most districts. In the second step, we explore the link between the reform-induced change in housing price and the change in state aid. We find a strong association between these two variables, even after controlling for changes in student performance and in the property tax rate. Homebuyers appear to recognize that state aid reform will boost student performance. In addition, we extend the results by determining the extent to which changes in cost-adjusted aid influences property values. The positive relationship between these two variables implies that homeowners recognize that high poverty levels lead to the need for additional state aid.

Our main conclusion is that homebuyers are aware of major reforms to state education aid, believe that an increase in aid associated with such a reform will lead to a better service-tax package, and, as a result, bid more for housing in locations with relatively large aid increases. Moreover, homeowners appear to be aware that what matters is cost-adjusted aid, not simply dollars of aid per pupil. In the long run, when the aid reforms are not fresh in homebuyers' minds, the impact of aid on house values may diminish and be replaced by the impact of changes in school quality and tax rates. Within our sample period, however, the impacts of aid dominate.

Post-reform house-value increases represent some combination of higher bids by households similar to the ones who lived in districts with aid increases before the reform was passed, a replacement of those households with others who place a higher value on the post-reform school-tax package, and changes in bids due to changes in education costs associated with reform-induced

household re-sorting. We focus on the first of these components. We find
that reform-induced changes in property values in a given district are higher
in high-income tracts than in low-income tracts. We interpret this result
as a reflection of the demand for education — high-income households
are willing to pay more than low-income households for the school quality
improvements expected from higher education aid. A full analysis of all
three components of house-value increases remains a challenge for future
research.

Our results, with a focus on Maryland education finance reform, are
similar to previous case studies in California, Texas, and Michigan, but not
one in Vermont. Downes (2010) argues that the unique result in Vermont
could be due to the prominence of vacation homes or expectations of
overturning reform. Understanding the heterogeneous effect of the reform
at the state level is a task for future research.

A secondary conclusion of this paper, as discussed by Wyckoff (1995,
2001) and Yinger (2004), is that capitalization of state aid reform leads to
winners and losers with regard to changes in property wealth across school
districts. Those who own property in school districts with large increases
in state aid, for example, will experience an increase in their housing price
compared with those who own property in districts with small increases.
These wealth changes affect people who own homes at the time of the reform,
but not people who buy homes in the future, because they must pay a higher
price to enter a district in which reform has improved school performance.
Although we do not examine effects on renters, they are also likely to
have to pay more to live in a district with reform-induced educational
improvements. Of course, these effects are secondary to the main purpose
of the reform, which is to help children, but they may make it difficult
for some low-income families to afford housing in newly improved school
districts.

Acknowledgments

The authors are grateful for comments from participants in presentations
at the annual meetings of both the Association for Education Finance
and Policy and the Association for Public Policy Analysis and Management, from the editors, and from two anonymous referees. Bill Duncombe
passed away in May 2013, before the final revisions on this paper were

carried out. However, Bill played a critical role in designing this project and preparing the original draft, and his insights appear throughout the paper.

Appendix A: Data Description

Appendix Table A.1 presents the data-filtering process conducted in order to eliminate house sales observations that may be inaccurate. Our initial sales data about houses from 1998 to 2007 is 796,887. When combining two datasets (e.g., CAMA and RPSF) using account information on the property, the matching rate is 99.78 percent.

To clean the dataset of inaccurate observations, we eliminated sales with the following procedure. Because neighborhood amenities will be attached to houses based on their geographic location (e.g., latitude and longitude), 229 sales of houses that could not be projected on the map were dropped. Sales records are dropped (7,221 sales records) if sales of houses are repeated within a six-month period because it could simply reflect the transition

Table A.1   Data filtering process.

Items	Number of observations
Raw data set (arm's length sales data, land use of residential, townhouse, and townhouse condominium)	796,887
Dropped one of sales if sales of houses repeated within the 6-month period	7,221
Dropped samples when houses are boat slips, mobile homes, or rental dwellings	16,006
Dropped samples when houses cannot be projected on the map	229
Dropped samples when sales price < $20,000 or >$5,000,000[a]	865
All sales data after data filtering process[b]	772,566
Dropped non-repeated sales data	458,171
Repeat sales after data filtering process[c]	314,395

Notes: [a]To check any possible bias arising from omission of sales data with extreme value, several versions of the dataset were utilized in the analysis. The results show a consistent pattern.
[b]Total number of houses is 603,258.
[c]Total number of houses is 144,955.

Table A.2 Variables for neighborhood amenities/disamenities.

Name	Description	Data source
Boat ramp	Dichotomous variable equals one if distance to nearest boat ramp is less than 0.25 miles, otherwise zero	MDSHA
BWI airport	Dichotomous variable equals one if distance to nearest BWI airport road is less than 10 miles, otherwise zero	MDSHA
Commuter/subway/metro station	Dichotomous variable equals one if distance to nearest station is less than 5 miles, otherwise zero	MDSHA
Court	Dichotomous variable equals one if distance to nearest court is less than 0.25 miles, otherwise zero	MDSHA
Environmental hazard	Dichotomous variable equals one if distance to nearest environmental hazard is less than 1 miles, otherwise zero	EPA
Fire station	Dichotomous variable equals one if distance to nearest post office is less than 0.25 miles, otherwise zero	MDSHA
Golf course	Dichotomous variable equals one if distance to nearest golf course is less than 0.25 miles, otherwise zero	MDSHA
Government office	Dichotomous variable equals one if distance to nearest government office is less than 0.25 miles, otherwise zero	MDSHA
Highway	Dichotomous variable equals one if distance to nearest highway road is less than 0.25 miles, otherwise zero	MDSHA
Historic site	Dichotomous variable equals one if distance to nearest boat ramp is less than 0.25 miles, otherwise zero	MDSHA
Hospital	Dichotomous variable equals one if distance to nearest hospital road is less than 0.25 miles, otherwise zero	MDSHA
Small airport (landing strip)	Dichotomous variable equals one if distance to nearest small airport is less than 1 miles, otherwise zero	MDSHA
Library	Dichotomous variable equals one if distance to nearest library is less than 0.25 miles, otherwise zero	MDSHA

(Continued)

Table A.2 (*Continued*)

Name	Description	Data source
Museum	Dichotomous variable equals one if distance to nearest museum road is less than 0.25 miles, otherwise zero	MDSHA
Park	Dichotomous variable equals one if distance to nearest park is less than 0.25 miles, otherwise zero	MDP
Park & ride	Dichotomous variable equals one if distance to nearest park & ride is less than 0.25 miles, otherwise zero	MDSHA
Police station	Dichotomous variable equals one if distance to nearest police station is less than 0.25 miles, otherwise zero	MDSHA
Post office	Dichotomous variable equals one if distance to nearest post office is less than 0.25 miles, otherwise zero	MDSHA
Prison	Dichotomous variable equals one if distance to nearest prison is less than 0.25 miles, otherwise zero	MDSHA
Railroad	Dichotomous variable equals one if distance to nearest railroad is less than 0.25 miles, otherwise zero	MDSHA
Shopping center	Dichotomous variable equals one if distance to nearest shopping center is less than 1 miles, otherwise zero	MDSHA
Total crime rate	Total crime rate per 100,000 inhabitants	FBI
Town hall	Dichotomous variable equals one if distance to nearest town hall is less than 0.25 miles, otherwise zero	MDSHA
Water	Dichotomous variable equals one if distance to nearest lake or sea is less than 0.25 miles, otherwise zero	MDP
Distance to BWI airport	Distance to nearest BWI airport if less than 10 miles	MDSHA
Distance to boat ramp	Distance to nearest boat ramp if less than 0.25 mile	MDSHA

(*Continued*)

Table A.2 (*Continued*)

Name	Description	Data source
Distance to commuter/subway/metro stations	Distance to nearest station if less than 5 miles	MDSHA
Distance to highway	Distance to nearest highway if less than 1 mile	MDP
Distance to water	Distance to nearest lake or sea if less than 0.25 mile	MDP

Notes: All variables about distance between amenities and houses are measured in meters. Distances between houses and amenities are calculated on the basis of the *Near* function and *Distance* function in ArcGIS 9.3. *Near* function identifies the nearest amenities from house and *Distance* function calculates the straight-line distance between two points such as houses and amenities. When amenities variables are described as point variables in the map, distance between amenities and house is calculated along a straight line between two points. On the other hand, when amenities variables are represented as a line features such as a river or a set of line features for polygons such as parks, then the distance between amenities and house is calculated along a straight line to the nearest point on the line features. MDP = Maryland Department of Planning; MDSHA = Maryland State Highway Administration.

of a sale record and not the actual sale. Sales of houses that are boat slips, rental dwellings, or mobile homes are dropped because this paper focuses on residential property (16,006 sales records). Like Zabel and Guignet (2012), who use the same source of property value data in Maryland, we exclude houses for which the sales price is lower than \$20,000 or higher than \$5,000,000. This results in another 865 sale records being dropped from the base dataset.[19] In total, approximately 24,000 sales are dropped from the dataset.

As a result of this cleaning process, we have total sales records of 772,566 from 603,258 houses. When focusing on only repeated sales data, there are 314,395 repeated sales records, from samples of 144,955 houses.

---

[19]However, cleaning a dataset based on the dependent variables could generate biased estimates. To check any possible bias arising from omission of sales data with extreme value, several versions of the dataset were utilized in the analysis. The use of different versions of the data does not change the main results.

Table A.3 School district characteristics.

Variables	Definition	Data source
Total state aid per pupil	All types of funds (e.g., current expenses, food service, school construction, and debt service) divided by total enrollment in a school district	MSDE
Current state aid per pupil	The current expenses fund without the state's contribution to teacher retirements, divided by total enrollment in a school district	MSDE
Effective tax rate	Nominal school district tax rates are multiplied by average assessment ratios in residential properties	MSDAT
Dropout rates	The share of dropouts in school district i	MSDE
3rd grade elementary passing rate	The share passing in Reading and Math for third grade from MSA and MSPAP in school district i	MSDE
5th grade elementary passing rate	The share passing in Reading and Math for fifth grade from MSA and MSPAP in school district i	MSDE
High school passing rate	The share passing in English 2, Government, Algebra, and Biology from High School Assessment in school district i	MSDE
African American	The share of African American students in a school district	MSDE
Hispanic	The share of Hispanic students within a school district	MSDE
Free and reduced-price lunch eligible	The share of students eligible for free or reduced-price lunch programs within a school district	MSDE
Special education	The share of students with special education within a school district	MSDE
Limited English proficiency	The share of students with limited English proficiency within a school district	MSDE

Notes: To check any possible bias arising from omission of sales data with extreme value, several versions of the dataset were utilized in the analysis. The results show a consistent pattern. MSA = Maryland School Assessment; MSDAT = Maryland State Department of Assessments and Taxation; MSDE = Maryland State Department of Education; MSPAP = Maryland School Performance Assessment Program.

References

Aaronson, Daniel. 1999. The effect of school finance reform on population heterogeneity. *National Tax Journal* **52**(1): 5–30.

Barrow, Lisa. and Cecilia Elena Rouse. 2004. Using market valuation to assess public school spending. *Journal of Public Economics* **88**(9): 1747–1769.

Bogin, Alexander. and Phuong Nguyen-Hoang. 2014. Property left behind: The unintended consequences of a No Child Left Behind "failing" school designation. *Journal of Regional Science* **54**(5): 788–805.

Brunner, Eric J., James Murdoch, and Mark Thayer. 2002. School finance reform and housing values: Evidence from Los Angeles. *Public Finance and Management* **2**(4): 535–565.

Chakrabarti, Rajashri. and Joydeep Roy. 2015. Housing markets and residential segregation: Impacts of the Michigan school finance reform on inter-and intra-district sorting. *Journal of Public Economics* **122**: 110–132.

Clapp, John M., Anupam Nanda, and Stephen L. Ross. 2008. Which school attributes matter? The influence of school district performance and demographic composition on property values. *Journal of Urban Economics* **63**(2): 451–466.

Cortina, Jose M. 1993. What is coefficient alpha? An examination of theory and applications. *Journal of Applied Psychology* **78**(1): 98–104. doi:10.1037/0021-9010.78.1.98.

Cronbach, Lee J. 1951. Coefficient alpha and the internal structure of tests. *Psychometrika* **16**(3): 297–334.

Dee, Thomas S. 2000. The capitalization of education finance reforms. *Journal of Law & Economics* **43**(1): 185–214.

Downes, Thomas S. 2010. Centralization of school finance and property values: Lessons from Vermont. Working Paper No. WP10RTDI. Cambridge, MA: Lincoln Institute of Land Policy.

Duncombe, William. and Dan Goldhaber. 2003. *Adjusting for Geographic Differences in the Cost of Educational Provision in Maryland.* Available http://dlslibrary.state.md.us/publications/exec/msde/agdcepm_2003.pdf. Accessed 10 December 2017.

Duncombe, William. and Dan Goldhaber. 2009. *Adjusting for Geographic Differences in the Cost of Educational Provision in Maryland: Revisions to the Original Report.* Available https://maryland associationofcounties.files.wordpress.com/2015/10/2009-update.pdf. Accessed 18 December 2017.

Duncombe, William. and John Yinger. 1998. School finance reform: Aid formulas and equity objectives. *National Tax Journal* **51**(2): 239–262. [Chapter 15]

Duncombe, William. and John Yinger. 2001. Alternative paths to property tax relief. In W. E. Oates (ed.), *Property Taxation and Local Government Finance*, pp. 243–294. Cambridge, MA: Lincoln Institute of Land Policy.

Duncombe, William. and John Yinger. 2011. Making do: State constraints and local responses in California's education finance system. *International Tax and Public Finance* **18**(3): 337–368. [Chapter 10]

Epple, Dennis. and Maria Marta Ferreyra. 2008. School finance reform: Assessing general equilibrium effects. *Journal of Public Economics* **92**(5–6): 1326–1351.

Ferreyra, Maria Marta. 2009. An empirical framework for large-scale policy analysis, with an application to school finance reform in Michigan. *American Economic Journal: Economic Policy* **1**(1): 147–180.

Figlio, David N. and Maurice E. Lucas. 2004. What's in a grade? School report cards and the housing market. *American Economic Review* **94**(3): 591–604.

Fisher, Ronald C. and Leslie E. Papke. 2000. Local government responses to education grants. *National Tax Journal* **53**(3): 153–168.

Glaeser, Edward L., Joshua D. Gottlieb, and Kristina Tobio. 2012. Housing booms and city centers. *American Economic Review* **102**(3): 127–133.

Guilfoyle, Jeffrey P. 1998. The incidence and housing market effects of Michigan's 1994 school finance reforms. *Proceedings: Annual Conference on Taxation and Minutes of the Annual Meeting of the National Tax Association* **91**: 223–229.

Hilber, Christian A. L., Teemu Lyytikäinen, and Wouter Vermeulen. 2011. Capitalization of central government grants into local house prices: Panel data evidence from England. *Regional Science and Urban Economics* **41**(4): 394–406.

Hoxby, Caroline M. 2001. All school finance equalizations are not created equal. *Quarterly Journal of Economics* **116**(4): 1189–1231.

Huang, Yao. 2004. A guide to state operating aid programs for elementary and secondary education. In John Yinger (ed.), *Helping Children Left Behind: State Aid and the Pursuit of Educational Equity*, pp. 331–349. Cambridge, MA: MIT Press.

Maryland Department of Legislative Services 2002. *The Bridge to Excellence in Public Schools Act of 2002: Its Origins, Components, and Future.* Available http://dlslibrary.state.md.us/publications/opa/i/cefee_2002_pres.pdf. Accessed 20 December 2017.

Morgan, Stephen L. and Christopher Winship. 2007. *Counterfactuals and Causal Inference: Methods and Principles for Social Research.* New York: Cambridge University Press.

Nechyba, Thomas J. 2004. Prospects for achieving equity or adequacy in education: The limits of state aid in general equilibrium. In John Yinger (ed.), *Helping Children Left Behind: State Aid and the Pursuit of Educational Equity*, pp. 111–143. Cambridge, MA: MIT Press.

Nguyen-Hoang, Phuong. and John Yinger. 2011. The capitalization of school quality into house values: A review. *Journal of Housing Economics* **20**(1): 30–48. [Chapter 15]

Nguyen-Hoang, Phuong. and John Yinger. 2014. Education finance reform, local behavior, and student performance in Massachusetts. *Journal of Education Finance* **39**(4): 297–322. [Chapter 9]

Nunnally, Jum C. and Ira H. Bernstein. 1994. *Psychometric Theory*, 3rd edition, New York: McGraw-Hill, Inc.

Rosen, Sherwin. 1974. Hedonic prices and implicit markets: Product differentiation in pure competition. *Journal of Political Economy* **82**(1): 34–55.

Ross, Stephen. and John Yinger. 1999. Sorting and voting: A review of the literature on urban public finance. In Paul Cheshire and Edwin S. Mills (eds.), *Handbook of Regional and Urban Economics*, pp. 2001–2060. New York: Elsevier North-Holland.

Roy, Joydeep. 2004. *Effect of a School Finance Reform on Housing and Residential Segregation: Evidence from Proposal A in Michigan.* Available at http://dx.doi.org/10.2139/ssrn.630122. Accessed 13 December 2016.

Taylor, Laura O. 2008. Theoretical foundations and empirical developments in hedonic modeling. In Andrea Baranzini, José Ramirez, Caroline Schaerer, and Philippe Thalmann (eds.), *Hedonic Methods in Housing Markets*, pp. 15–37. New York: Springer.

Wyckoff, Paul Gary. 1995. Capitalization, equalization, and intergovernmental aid. *Public Finance Review* **23**(4): 484–508.

Wyckoff, Paul Gary. 2001. Capitalization and the incidence of school aid. *Journal of Education Finance* **27**(1): 585–607.

Yinger, John. 2004. State aid and the pursuit of educational equity: An overview. In John Yinger (ed.), *Helping Children Left Behind: State Aid and the Pursuit of Educational Equity*, pp. 3–57. Cambridge, MA: MIT Press. [Chapter 11]

Yinger, John. 2015. Hedonic markets and sorting equilibria: bid-function envelopes for public services and neighborhood amenities. *Journal of Urban Economics* **86**(March): 9–25.

Yinger, John, Howard S. Bloom, Axel Börsch-Supan, and Helen F. Ladd. 1988. *Property Taxes and House Values: The Theory and Estimation of Intrajurisdictional Property Tax Capitalization.* San Diego: Academic Press.

Zabel, Jeffrey. and Dennis Guignet. 2012. A hedonic analysis of the impact of LUST sites on house prices in Frederick, Baltimore, and Baltimore City counties. *Resource and Energy Economics* **34**: 549–564.

Part 7
School District Consolidation

Chapter 17

School District Consolidation: The Benefits and Costs*,[†]

William Duncombe[§] and John Yinger[‡,¶]

[‡]*Departments of Public Administration and
International Affairs and of Economics,
Syracuse University, Syracuse, NY, United States*

[¶]*jyinger@maxwell.syr.edu*

School district consolidation is a striking phenomenon. According to the National Center for Education Statistics, 117,108 school districts provided elementary and secondary education in 1939–1940. By 2006–2007, the number of districts had dropped to 13,862, a decline of 88 percent. The rate of consolidation has slowed in recent years, but at least a few districts consolidate every year in many states.

Most state governments have policies that influence school district consolidation. The most common form of policy is a state aid program designed to encourage district reorganization, typically in the form of consolidation, by providing additional money for operations or capital projects during the transition to the new form of organization.

The aid bonus from consolidation can be quite large. In New York, consolidating districts may receive an increase in their basic operating aid of up to 40 percent for five years, with declining increases for an additional

*This chapter is reproduced from "The Benefits and Costs of School District Consolidation: What Recent Research Reveals about Potential Cost Savings," *The School Administrator*, **67**(5), May 2010, pp. 10–17.

[†]http://www.aasa.org/SchoolAdministratorArticle.aspx?id=13218

[§]Deceased.

John Yinger (left) and William Duncombe, both professors at Syracuse University's Maxwell School of Citizenship and Public Affairs, have studied the economics of size in public education. Photo by Candi Patterson/Center for Policy Research, Syracuse University.

nine years. On top of this aid, consolidating districts also may receive a 30 percent increase in building aid for projects initiated within 10 years of consolidation.

In many cases, however, state aid policies concerning consolidation are contradictory. In fact, about a third of the states, including some that offer consolidation bonuses, use operating aid formulas that compensate school districts for sparsity (low population density) or for small scale and thereby discourage consolidation, according to Yao Huang, a contributor to *Helping Children Left Behind: State Aid and the Pursuit of Educational Equity*.

So what do states do? Some recent research provides guidance for superintendents and school leaders, especially those facing consolidation.

1. Expected Savings

The main justification for school district consolidation has long been that it is a way to cut costs. These cost savings arise, the argument goes, because the provision of education is characterized by economies of size, which exist whenever the cost of education per pupil declines as the number of pupils goes up. In this context, the cost of education is not the same as education spending but is instead the amount a school district would have to spend to obtain a given level of performance, as measured by test scores, graduation rates and perhaps other output measures.

To put it another way, economies of size exist if spending on education per pupil declines as the number of pupils goes up, controlling for school district performance. Because consolidation creates larger school districts, it results in lower costs per pupil whenever economies of size exist.

Economies of size could arise for many reasons, which we discuss in "Does School District Consolidation Cut Costs?" in the fall 2007 issue of *Education Finance and Policy.*

First, the services provided to each student by certain education professionals may not diminish in quality as the number of students increases, at least over some range. All districts require a superintendent and a school board, for example, and the same central administration may be able to serve a significant range of enrollment with little change in total costs.

Second, education requires certain physical capital, such as a heating system and science laboratories, which require a certain scale to operate efficiently and therefore have a high cost per pupil in small districts.

Third, larger districts may be able to employ more specialized teachers, putting them in a better position to provide the wide range of courses required by state accountability systems and expected today by students and parents.

Finally, teachers in larger districts have more colleagues on which to draw for advice and discussion, interactions that presumably lead to improved effectiveness.

2. Mixed Signals

Although these arguments make a lot of sense, some factors cut in the other direction. First, consolidated school districts usually make use of larger schools, which implies that average transportation distance must increase. As a result, consolidation might increase a district's transportation spending per pupil.

Second, consolidating districts may level up salaries and benefits to those of the most generous participating district, thereby raising personnel costs.

Third, administrators and teachers may have a more positive attitude toward work in smaller schools, which tend to have more flexible rules and procedures.

Finally, students may be more motivated and parents may find it more comfortable to interact with teachers in smaller districts, which tend to have a greater community feel. These reactions and closer student-faculty relationships may result in higher student performance at any given spending level.

Overall, the net impact of consolidation on education costs per pupil is not clear a priori. Some factors indicate consolidation is likely to tap into economies of size and thereby lower these costs, but other factors suggest consolidation might actually cause costs per pupil to rise. As a result, we now turn to empirical studies of consolidation, which can determine whether the net impact of consolidation on costs per pupil is positive or negative.

3. Empirical Evidence

A large body of literature has investigated the relationship between cost per pupil and district enrollment, controlling for school performance. Although these studies cover many locations and use various methodologies, most lead to the same conclusion that emerged from a study, "Revisiting Economies of Size in American Education: Are We Any Closer to a Consensus?" in the June 2002 issue of *Economics of Education Review:* "Sizeable potential cost savings may exist by moving from a very small district ... to a district with 2,000 to 4,000 pupils, both in instructional and administrative costs."

These studies estimate economies of size across all school districts and therefore do not look directly at the cost impact of consolidation. Another approach is provided by the two of us in our *Education Finance and Policy* article in 2007 — namely, to see how costs per pupil change when districts consolidate. This study is based on all the rural school districts in New York state between 1985 and 1997.

During this period, 12 pairs of these districts consolidated. These consolidating districts had enrollments ranging from 250 to 1,990. To isolate the impact of consolidation, the costs in consolidating districts can be compared both with their own costs before consolidation and with the cost of similar districts that did not consolidate. The analysis controls for a variety of district characteristics, including two measures of student performance, namely the percentage of students achieving minimum competency on the state's elementary school math and reading tests and the percentage of students receiving a Regents diploma, which requires passing a set of demanding exams in high school. The second performance variable is important in New York because one argument for consolidation is that it facilitates the offering of special classes to support the Regents exams.

This study explores both operating and capital spending. To account for the extreme "lumpiness" of capital spending, it is averaged over a four-year period.

This study finds strong evidence of economies of size in operating spending but not in capital spending. More specifically, annual operating spending per pupil declines by 61.7 percent when two 300-pupil districts merge and by 49.6 percent when two 1,500-pupil districts merge. The savings are particularly large for the subcategories of instruction and administration, but the study finds no economies — or diseconomies — of size for student transportation.

4. Transition Costs

These results for economies of size are only half the story, however. This study also finds that consolidation involves transition costs not associated with enrollment. Both overall operating spending and operating spending subcategories exhibit a large upward shift in per pupil costs at the time of consolidation, followed by a gradual decline in per pupil costs in the following years. These extra costs appear to disappear after about 10 years. This study also finds large adjustment costs in capital spending, which appear to phase out even more slowly.

To some degree, these adjustment costs offset the cost savings associated with consolidation-induced enrollment increases. Over a 30-year period, the net annual savings after accounting for adjustment costs fall to 43.7 percent for a consolidation of two 300-pupil districts and to 29.6 percent for the consolidation of two 1,500-pupil districts. The savings are smaller with a 10-year horizon because the adjustment costs have not yet phased out.

These results are summarized in the table at right, which replicates data from our study appearing in *Education Finance and Policy* in 2007.

The large adjustment costs in capital spending identified by this study are difficult to interpret. They appear to reflect capital spending encouraged by the building-aid increases associated with consolidation. It is not clear, however, whether these capital spending increases lead to improvements in student performance in the future (that is, outside the sample period of the study) or whether they represent capital spending that does not have a student-performance payoff.

5. Non-Cost Effects

When deciding whether to encourage consolidation, state policymakers may want to consider several factors other than cost savings. To some degree, consolidation may break parents' valued connections with existing schools, result in higher transportation costs for parents and students, or raise costs for improving school outcomes other than the test score measures included in existing studies.

Because consolidation requires the consent of voters in all the consolidating districts, consolidation will not take place unless a majority of voters perceive the net benefits outweigh the costs. Nevertheless, the net benefits of consolidation to voters still could be far below the cost savings to the districts themselves.

Some evidence on these issues comes from two recent studies of the impact of consolidation on housing prices. These studies estimate whether people are willing to pay more for housing in a district after it consolidates. Using data from Ohio, David Brasington, writing in the September 2004 issue of *The Journal of Real Estate Finance and Economics,* found that, after controlling for student performance and property tax rates, consolidation lowers property values by about $3,000 on average.

This result appears puzzling at first. If consolidation lowers property values, why do voters support it? In fact, however, the cost savings from consolidation are translated into either higher student performance or lower property tax rates, so this result simply indicates the cost savings from consolidation must be at least $3,000 per household to offset the apparent losses from consolidation associated with less local control, lessened accessibility of teachers and school administrators, higher parental and student transportation costs, or other unidentified negative effects.

Another study of rural school districts in New York state by Yue Hu and John Yinger, "The Impact of School District Consolidation on Housing Prices" in the December 2008 issue of *National Tax Journal,* yielded results consistent with Brasington's. These results indicate consolidation boosts house values and rents by about 25 percent in very small school districts and that this effect declines with district enrollment.

When two 1,500-student school districts merge, the housing-price impact is only about 6 percent, and consolidation has no impact on housing prices in districts with roughly 1,700 or more students. This declining impact matches the declining economies of size estimated by our own study. Moreover, these results are consistent with Brasington's because they do not control for student performance or property tax rate, but instead estimate the net impact of consolidation, including both its impact on school costs and its impact on other things that households value.

Both studies state that the net impact of consolidation is lower than the cost savings, which means, on balance, households place a negative value on the effects of consolidation other than the cost savings. The net impact of consolidation is still positive for small districts, but this impact is not nearly as large as the cost savings alone.

Two additional findings from the Hu and Yinger study are worth mentioning. First, they found roughly a third of consolidation's positive impact on housing prices is due to the aid bonus that consolidating districts receive in New York. In the smallest school districts, consolidation would boost housing prices even without this aid increase, but the housing-price impact of consolidation would be negative for two 1,500-student districts if they did not receive additional state aid.

Second, the impact of consolidation on housing prices declines as house value and rent increase and is actually negative in the wealthiest neighborhoods. The negative value placed on the impact of consolidation outside the school budget apparently is greater (in absolute value) for households in neighborhoods with relatively expensive housing, predominantly higher-income households, than for households where house values and rents are relatively low. In short, consolidation is popular with the average household in small rural school districts in New York state, but it is not popular among households with relatively valuable housing.

6. Policy Implications

These results have several implications for public policy. The first and most important implication is that states are likely to save money in the provision of elementary and secondary education by encouraging their smallest districts, specifically those with fewer than 1,500 pupils, to consolidate with one of their neighboring districts. These cost savings come from economies of size, which are only partially offset by adjustment costs associated with consolidation.

Geographic barriers or other concerns may rule out consolidation under some circumstances, but the potential savings for small districts are substantial. Indeed, school districts with 1,500 students might be able to cut their cost per pupil by 30 percent through consolidation. These costs savings may not translate into lower spending, of course, if the consolidation leads to higher student performance for these small districts, but performance increases of this type are also a clear gain for society.

One final point for perspective is that even though consolidation-induced cost savings may be large for an individual district, they are inevitably small for the state as a whole because only the smallest districts in the state are involved.

Second, consolidation appears to have significant effects beyond cost savings for school districts. On the one hand, households, particularly those with high incomes, appear to value the features of smaller districts, such as better access to teachers and lower transportation costs. From society's point of view, therefore, the cost savings from consolidation are offset to some degree by the losses households experience outside the school budget. These losses do not eliminate the case for consolidation, but they do indicate the case for consolidation is stronger when a district has 500 or 1,000 pupils than when it has 1,500 pupils.

The existing property-value studies do not indicate exactly which features of consolidation are negatively valued by households, but they do show that negatively valued features exist. Further research is needed to identify what these features are and to determine the enrollment size at which consolidation no longer makes sense. This enrollment size might vary, of course, across states or across circumstances.

The third lesson is that states would be well served by rethinking their aid programs that are linked to consolidation. Our 2007 study found evidence that capital costs shift upward substantially after consolidation, probably because of increased state aid. Some of this capital spending may be justified, but states should be careful to monitor such spending carefully and to direct post-consolidation building aid toward cost-effective projects that are part of a long-run plan.

The 2008 research finding by Hu and Yinger concerning state aid provides another key caution. Increases in housing prices associated with consolidation-based aid bonuses should not be interpreted as evidence that consolidation produces positive net benefits. Extra aid obviously benefits the residents of a newly consolidated district, but this benefit represents a transfer from state taxpayers and does not reflect cost savings. Without this state-aid effect, the net benefits of consolidation are positive only for the smallest districts. In fact, strong evidence for positive net benefits from consolidation, and hence for state intervention, only exists for districts with enrollments below about 1,000 pupils.

As a fourth lesson, states need to recognize that increased aid for school districts with small scale or high sparsity rewards districts for not consolidating. It makes no sense for states to encourage consolidation through one set of programs while discouraging it through others. It might make sense to compensate a district for the relatively high costs associated with a small scale if it is impossible for that district to consolidate. To account for this possibility, an aid program would have to identify factors that make consolidation impossible and limit sparsity aid bonuses to districts to which these factors apply.

7. Equity Grounds

Finally, this research indicates policymakers sometimes may confront a situation in which consolidation makes sense on equity grounds but does not result in decreased costs from society's point of view. A small, poor district would undoubtedly experience a decline in cost per pupil if it merged with a richer neighbor. Moreover, the increase in the average property tax base from such a merger would lower the property tax burden on this district's residents. As a result, this type of consolidation would improve the fairness of the education finance system in the state.

However, a consolidation of this type is unlikely to take place. First, the high-income residents of the neighboring district may not perceive any net benefits from consolidation, even if they are small enough for economies of size to kick in. As shown in the research by Hu and Yinger, high-income residents tend to lose from the effects of consolidation other than school cost savings.

In addition, Brasington's study shows that voters in a high-income district are unlikely to approve consolidation with a low-income district because this type of consolidation would increase their property tax burden, even holding spending per pupil constant.

If consolidation is deemed to be desirable on equity grounds, therefore, state aid bonuses may be needed to convince high-income voters to go along. Hu and Yinger suggest these aid bonuses add to the perceived benefits of consolidation as reflected in housing prices and might be sufficient to induce voters in the richer district to approve consolidation.

8. Advantageous Factors

Debates about school district consolidation often involve a great deal of heat and not much light. Recent research can bring some light to bear on this issue by identifying the circumstances under which consolidation can take advantage of economies of size, by identifying the adjustment costs that may accompany consolidation, by measuring the value that voters place on the non-cost impact of consolidation, and by identifying the circumstances under which consolidation is likely to be accepted by voters.

Because consolidation involves small school districts, it cannot generate large cost savings at the state level, but under some circumstances it can result in large cost savings for individual districts or enhance the fairness of a state's education finance system.

References

Andrews, Matthew, William D. Dancombe, and John Yinger. 2002. "Revisiting economics of size in American education: Are we any closer to a consensus?" *Economics of Education Review* **21**(3) (June): 245–262.

Brasington, David H. 2004. "House prices and the structure of local government: An application of spatial statistics." *Journal of Real Estate Finance and Economics* **29**(2)(September): 211–231.

Duncombe, William D, and John Yinger, 2007. "Does school district consolidation cut costs?" *Education Finance and Policy* **2**(4) (Fall): 341–375. [Chapter 18]

Hoang, Yao. 2004. "Appendix B: A guide to state operating programs for elementary and secondary education." In J. Yinger (ed.), *Helping Children Left Behind: State A.d and the Pursuit of Educational Equity*, pp. 331–351. Cambridge, MA: MIT Press.

Hu, Yue, and John Yinger. 2008. "The impact of school district consolidation on housing prices." *National Tax Journal* **41**(4) (December): 609–633.

National Center for Education Statistics. 2014. *Digest of Education Statistics,* Table 214.10. Available at https://nces.ed.gov/programs/digest/d17/tables/dt17-214-10-asp. Accessed on 19 October 2019.

Chapter 18

Does School District Consolidation Cut Costs?*

William Duncombe[‡] and John Yinger[†,§]

[†]*Departments of Public Administration and
International Affairs and of Economics,
Syracuse University, Syracuse, NY, United States*
[§]*jyinger@maxwell.syr.edu*

Consolidation has dramatically reduced the number of school districts in the United States. Using data from rural school districts in New York, this article provides the first direct estimation of consolidation's cost impacts. We find economies of size in operating spending: all else equal, doubling enrollment cuts operating costs per pupil by 61.7 percent for a 300-pupil district and by 49.6 percent for a 1,500-pupil district. Consolidation also involves large adjustment costs, however. These adjustment costs, which are particularly large for capital spending, lower net cost savings to 31.5 percent and 14.4 percent for a 300-pupil and a 1,500-pupil district, respectively. Overall, consolidation makes fiscal sense, particularly for very small districts, but states should avoid subsidizing unwarranted capital projects.

1. Introduction

School district consolidation represents one of the most dramatic changes in education governance and management in the United States in the

---

*This chapter is reproduced from "Does School District Consolidation Cut Costs?" *Education Finance and Policy*, **2**(4), 2007(Fall), pp. 341–375.
[‡]Deceased.

last 100 years. Over 100,000 school districts have been eliminated through consolidation since 1938, a drop of almost 90 percent (National Center for Education Statistics, 2006, Table 84). This trend continues throughout the country, largely because consolidation is widely regarded as a way for school districts to cut costs. Using a unique panel data set for rural school districts in New York State, this article asks whether consolidation leads to significant cost savings, controlling for student performance. This analysis complements recent research on the causes of consolidation (Brasington, 1999, 2003; Gordon and Knight, 2006).

Although the pace of school district consolidation has slowed since the 1970s, some states still provide incentives to consolidate. New York and several other states have aid programs designed to encourage district "reorganization," typically in the form of consolidation (NCES, 2001). Some other states encourage consolidation through their building or transportation aid formulas (Haller and Monk, 1988). In contrast, about one-third of states use operating aid formulas that compensate school districts for sparsity or small scale (Huang, 2004) and thereby discourage consolidation. Although scholars do not agree on the cost impacts of consolidation, it is likely to remain on the education policy agenda in many states, particularly when school districts are under pressure to cut costs and raise student performance. As Haller and Monk (1988, p. 479) put it, "The modern reform movement is likely to prompt additional school district reorganization efforts, despite its virtual silence on the question of size."

This article begins with a discussion of the concept of economies of size and its link to school district consolidation. The third section provides a review of the cost function literature and evaluates existing evidence on economies of size in education. In the fourth section, we present the first formal evaluation of school district consolidation, including the first look at economies of size in capital spending. This evaluation is based on a panel of rural school districts in New York, some of which consolidated during the sample period, 1985–1997.

2. Economies of Size and the Effects of Consolidation

By altering the size of participating districts, consolidation could raise or lower per pupil costs. In this section we define economies of size and discuss the possible linkages between these economies and consolidation.

2.1. *Defining Economies of Size*

Economies of scale are said to arise when the cost per unit declines as the number of units goes up. In some contexts, the notion of a unit is straightforward; one could ask, for example, how the cost per widget changes with the number of widgets produced. In education, however, several different "units" could be defined, including the number of students, the quality of the services (as measured, say, by student performance), or the scope of educational services.[1]

As in most empirical research on economies of scale in education, the focus here is on economies of size, which refer to the relationship between per pupil expenditure and total enrollment, all else equal. This relationship can be estimated from an education cost function, which controls for output (that is, student performance), input prices, and other variables. Economies (diseconomies) of size exist if the estimated elasticity of education costs per pupil with respect to enrollment is less than (greater than) zero.

2.2. *Potential Sources of Economics of Size*

Tholkes (1991) and Pratten (1991) identify five potential sources of long-run economies of size that seem especially pertinent to education.

1. *Indivisibilities*: Economies of size may exist because the services provided to each student by certain education professionals do not diminish in quality as the number of students increases, at least over some range. For example, all districts require a central administration, namely, a superintendent and school board, and the same central administration may be able to serve a significant range of enrollment. Moreover, teachers may provide a public good over some range of enrollment because they may be able to teach up to, say, fifteen students without a significant drop in the quality of education they provide.[2]

---

[1]See Duncombe and Yinger (1993) for a discussion of the relationship among these three definitions of scale.

[2]Estimates of the effect of class size below fifteen students are hard to come by because classes of that size are not usually observed. For example, Krueger (1999) finds that a shift from twenty-two to fifteen students has significant performance benefits but does not observe the impact of even smaller class sizes. See also Ferguson and Ladd (1996).

2. *Increased dimension*: The traditional long-run concept of economies of scale focuses on savings associated with larger units of capital. Larger plants may be able to produce output at a lower average cost, because they can employ more specialized equipment, for example. In education, the logical plant is the school, and equipment includes the heating plant, communications system, and specialized facilities, such as science or computer labs.
3. *Specialization*: Economies of size might arise if larger schools are able to employ more specialized labor, such as science or math teachers. This possibility may provide a particularly compelling justification for consolidation in an era of rising standards, with its call for more demanding and specialized classes at the high school level (Haller and Monk, 1988).
4. *Price benefits of scale*: Large districts may be able to take advantage of the price benefits of scale by negotiating bulk purchases of supplies and equipment or by using their monopsony power to impose lower wages on their employees (Wasylenko, 1977).
5. *Learning and innovation*: If the cost of implementing innovations in curriculum or management declines with experience, a larger district may be able to implement such innovations at lower cost. In addition, teachers may be more productive in a large school because they can draw on the experience of many colleagues.

2.3. *Potential Sources of Diseconomies of Size*

The existence of economies of size in education has been challenged by recent studies on the effects of large schools on student performance (Fowler and Walberg, 1991; Lee and Smith, 1997). This research focuses on schools rather than districts and on production rather than cost functions. The distinction between school and district size is important in urban districts, but in rural areas the sizes of the district and the high school are highly correlated. These studies claim that the potential cost savings from consolidation are seldom realized and that larger schools have a learning environment that hurts student performance. The research on effective schools provides additional evidence that moderate-sized schools are more successful than large schools at retaining students through high school (Figlio and Stone, 1999; Witte, 1996).

Five potential sources of diseconomies of scale have been cited in this literature (Guthrie, 1979; Howley, 1996; Lee and Smith, 1997).

1. *Higher transportation costs*: One potential source of higher costs for larger districts is transportation. To the extent that consolidating districts make use of larger schools, average transportation distance must increase, as must travel time for students (Kenny, 1982).
2. *Labor relations effects*: According to Tholkes (1991, p. 510), "The labor relations scale effect, caused by seniority hiring within certification areas and by change in comparison groups for collective negotiations, could be a major source of diseconomies of scale." The potential monopsony power of large districts may be counteracted by the increased likelihood of an active teachers' union because larger districts are easier to organize. Stronger unions may also prevent staff layoffs and thereby eliminate a major source of cost savings from consolidation.
3. *Lower staff motivation and effort*: Administrators and teachers may have a more positive attitude toward work in smaller schools, which tend to involve less formalization of rules and procedures, that is, more flexibility (Cotton, 1996). Smaller organizations are also "flatter" organizations with fewer layers of middle management between the teacher or principal and the superintendent, encouraging more input from all school personnel.
4. *Lower student motivation and effort*: Students in smaller schools may be more apt to participate in extracurricular school activities (Cotton, 1996). Moreover, the employees in smaller schools are more likely to know students by name and to identify and assist students at risk of dropping out. Thus students in smaller schools may have a greater sense of belonging to the school community, a more positive attitude toward school, and a higher motivation to learn (Cotton, 1996; Barker and Gump, 1964).
5. *Lower parental involvement*: Parental contributions to educational production may be facilitated by parental participation in school activities and contacts with teachers and administrators. The role of parents is linked to economies of size whenever parents find participation less rewarding or personal contacts more difficult in larger districts.

3. Research on Economies of Size and Consolidation

The vast majority of evidence on economies of size and, by inference, on consolidation has come from the estimation of education cost functions using data on operating or total spending. Literature reviews on this topic have highlighted some of the methodological differences among studies, including differences in outcome and resource-price measures, whether student performance is treated as an endogenous variable, and whether controls are included for unobserved factors, such as inefficiency (Andrews *et al.*, 2002; Fox, 1981). Despite the variety of measures used and geographic areas examined in these studies, a surprising consensus emerges: "Sizeable potential cost savings may exist by moving from a very small district ... to a district with 2000–4000 pupils, both in instructional and administrative costs" (Andrews *et al.*, 2002, p. 255).

While cross-sectional spending regressions can provide evidence of potential cost savings from consolidation, a more direct and compelling approach is to apply longitudinal methods to a sample of school districts in which some consolidation occurred. No formal evaluations of this type have been conducted, however. Existing case studies (Weast, 1997; Benton, 1992) focus on only one school district, have no control group or do not use statistical controls, and have limited pre- and post-consolidation data. A case study by Streifel *et al.* (1991) compares pre- and post-consolidation finance data in a national sample of nineteen school districts but does not include controls for student achievement, teacher salaries, or changing student composition. Thus, as emphasized by Howley (1996, p. 25): "The lack of pre- and post-consolidation studies means that we have no solid information about the accrual of benefits alleged to depend on school closures and consolidation."

4. Evaluation of School District Consolidation in New York

New York State provides an excellent setting for an evaluation of consolidation. First, New York actively promotes the consolidation of small districts by providing "reorganization aid." Specifically, New York contributes up to an additional 40 percent in formula operating aid ("Incentive Operating Aid") to consolidated districts for five years. This aid is then phased out slowly over another nine years. "Incentive Building Aid" provides up to an additional 30 percent in building aid for capital projects that are committed within ten years of reorganization (New York State Education Department, 2006). Reorganization aid totaled over $30 million in 2006.[3] Second, New York, like many other states, still has a large number of small rural districts, and

---

[3]The Incentive Operating Aid subsidy of 40 percent is for consolidations after July 1993. From 1983 until 1993, the incentive aid was 20 percent of basic operating aid. Capital projects may be reimbursed under Incentive Building Aid past ten years as long as the project is approved within ten years of consolidation. Some consolidating districts still receive building subsidies twenty years after consolidation. A number of districts that were

consolidation continues to take place in the state. We examine twelve pairs of districts that consolidated from 1987 to 1995.[4] See Table 1.

4.1. *Evaluation Design*

To estimate the impact of consolidation on education costs, we begin with the standard formulation of an education cost function (Downes and Pogue, 1994; Duncombe and Yinger, 2000, 2001; Reschovsky and Imazeki, 2001; Imazeki and Reschovsky, 2004):

$$E = f(S, P, N, M, Z), \tag{1}$$

where E is school spending per pupil; S is school performance; P is input prices; N is enrollment; M is environmental cost factors, which are fixed inputs outside the control of school officials; and Z is a set of factors that influence school district inefficiency.[5] This cost function can be applied to total spending, to operating or capital spending, or to functional subcategories of spending, such as administration, instruction, or transportation. This approach can account for more than one measure of school performance, and it can shed light on the costs associated with all of a district's activities, including counseling, health, transportation, and administration.

In our data set, which is described below, S is measured using student test scores and the dropout rate, P is measured with teacher salaries, and M is measured by the characteristics of the students in a school district, such as the share who live in poverty. Because we observe spending, not cost, our analysis also must consider school district inefficiency, defined as spending any more than necessary, given input and environmental costs, to provide a given level of performance. Thus inefficiency is tied to the performance variables included in the regression. A school district is inefficient if it provides activities that do not boost performance as measured by the

---

receiving reorganization building aid in 1981 were still receiving this aid in 1997. Most of these districts consolidated before 1979.

[4]During this period, three elementary school districts, each with fewer than one hundred students, merged with much larger K-12 districts. We do not consider these districts in our analysis. Eight consolidations have occurred in New York since the latest one in our data. Although a few of these consolidations took place in our sample period, we do not include them (and we drop the districts involved) because we want to observe at least two years of data after consolidation.

[5]Total enrollment is our measure of district size; in our sample of districts, this variable is highly correlated with an alternative measure, average daily membership.

Table 1 New York school districts consolidating between 1987 and 1995.

District pair	Year of consolidation	Enrollment[a]	District pair	Year of consolidation	Enrollment[a]
Bolivar	1995	690	Dannemora	1989	250
Richburg		380	Saranac		1,360
Bolivar-Richburg		1,070	Saranac-Dannemora		1,610
Cobleskill	1994	1,860	Broadalbin	1988	970
Richmondville		390	Perth		620
Cobleskill-Richmondville		2,250	Broadalbin-Perth		1,590
Cohocton	1994	250	Cherry Valley	1988	480
Wayland		1,640	Springfield		250
Wayland-Cohocton		1,890	Cherry Valley-Springfield		730
Savona	1993	420	Jasper	1988	490
Campbell		710	Troupsburg		250
Campbell-Savona		1,130	Jasper-Troupsburg		740
Cuba	1992	1,010	Draper	1987	1,990
Rushford		310	Mohonasen		920
Cuba-Rushford		1,320	Mohonasen-Draper		2,910
Mount Upton	1991	270	Edwards	1987	290
Gilbertsville		260	Knox Memorial		420
Gilbertsville-Mount Upton		530	Edwards-Knox		710

Notes: [a]Enrollment in the year before consolidation.

variables in S, even if those activities are worthwhile in some other sense, or if it pays overly generous wages, hires too many administrators, or uses outmoded teaching methods. Inefficiency cannot be observed directly; we control for it by including a set of school district characteristics, Z, that influence the extent to which the behavior of teachers and school administrators is monitored by parents and voters (Duncombe and Yinger, 2001, 2007).[6]

To estimate this model, we assemble pre- and post-consolidation data for all consolidating districts and for a comparison group in the years 1985–1997. Because all the consolidating districts are rural, the comparison group consists of other rural districts.[7] All of these districts, consolidating and comparison, are "upstate," that is, not in the New York City region. Following most previous studies, we specify equation 1 in log-linear form.[8]

We face four major methodological challenges. This section describes our basic approach; robustness checks are presented with the results. First, we need to specify the cost impact of consolidation. A key component of this impact is picked up, of course, by the population variable, N.[9] Consolidated districts are, by definition, larger than the separate districts that consolidate, and the cost impact of the resulting increase in enrollment can be determined from the coefficients of the enrollment variables. We use a quadratic specification for $\ln(N)$; that is, we include $\ln(N)$ and $[\ln(N)]^2$. This specification makes it possible to determine if cost per pupil reaches a maximum or minimum at some enrollment level.

In addition, consolidation might result in adjustment costs that fade over time or some other type of spending shock. To account for this possibility, we include a post-consolidation dummy variable and time trend for each

---

[6]Unobserved determinants of school district efficiency are an unlikely source of bias in our regressions because they are largely captured by district fixed effects and time trends, which are discussed below. For a review of approaches to efficiency in a cost model, see Duncombe and Yinger (2007).

[7]Two consolidating districts, Draper and Mohonasen, were classified as "upstate suburban districts" by the New York State Department of Education. However, these districts lie on the edge of a small urban area, Schenectady, and are quite rural in character.

[8]Some studies, such as Gyimah-Brempong and Gyapong (1991), use a general trans-log specification, but this approach is not practical with the sample size available for this study.

[9]For any given district size, the size of schools may affect student performance and costs. It is not appropriate to include school size in a cost model, however, because it reflects endogenous administrative decisions that influence efficiency, not exogenous factors that influence costs.

consolidating district pair.[10] This approach not only yields an estimate of the average adjustment costs, it also allows for the possibility that some districts are more efficient than others in making the adjustments associated with consolidation.

Second, unobserved factors influencing the consolidation decision (and hence N) might also influence spending per pupil, so our estimated coefficients could be subject to endogeneity bias if these unobserved factors are not taken into account. To address this problem, we estimate our model with district-specific fixed effects and time trends. This well-known approach accounts for all unobservable factors that vary linearly over time and therefore eliminates the possibility of bias from these factors, even if they are correlated with consolidation.[11]

To preserve all pre-consolidation information, we retain each district as a separate observation even after it consolidates. Once a district has consolidated, however, we assign it the characteristics of the combined district as a whole. This approach requires an adjustment in the district fixed effects variables to account for consolidation. Because the post-consolidation dependent variable combines spending per pupil for the two districts, the fixed effect for each original district (a) is diluted and (b) has an impact on the dependent variable for post-consolidation observations of its partner district. After consolidation, therefore, each district's fixed effect is weighted by that district's share of total enrollment in the combined district just before the consolidation and is switched on for each consolidating district and its partner.[12] These two steps are also applied to the district-specific time trend.

District fixed effects and time trends provide extensive protection against endogeneity bias but cannot protect against factors that influence both spending and the decision to consolidate and that vary in a nonlinear way over time. In the case of New York State, such factors are unlikely to play a major role. According to the rules in New York, consolidation is a process,

---

[10]We specify these variables so that one coefficient provides the state average post-consolidation shift and one provides the state average post-consolidation trend. See the technical appendix.

[11]The role of fixed effects is discussed in Heckman *et al.* (1999); Bloom (1984) provides an example involving both fixed effects and time trends.

[12]Formal definitions of district fixed effects and trends are in the technical appendix. Our method requires the (possibly incorrect) assumption that the weight assigned to each partner in a consolidating pair does not vary over time; once consolidation has occurred, we observe only characteristics of the consolidated district.

not an event (University of the State of New York, n.d.). Districts considering consolidation must first ask the New York State Department of Education for an analysis of this step, along with a recommendation. Once this analysis and recommendation have been prepared, the districts must negotiate with the state about the aid involved and decide whether to proceed. If they do, they must present the consolidation option to the voters and cannot consolidate without the approval of a majority of the voters in each participating district. As a result, consolidation generally cannot be completed for two or three years from the time the state is brought into the discussion. In this setting, short-term fluctuations in the relative social or economic position of a district are unlikely to have an impact on the consolidation decision, and controlling for district fixed effects and time trends provides adequate insurance against selection bias. One possible exception involves a change in district leadership. A new superintendent might push for consolidation even when his or her predecessor did not think it was a good idea. Thus we control for a change in superintendent within the last two years.

The third methodological challenge is that S, P, and possibly state aid (one of the variables in Z) are influenced by the actions of school officials and are therefore endogenous. The endogeneity of S and P is explored in previous cost studies. The state aid variable used in our capital cost model is endogenous for three main reasons. First, it includes at least one important aid program, building aid, which uses a matching formula.[13] Second, building aid in New York is project based, which means that a district must submit a capital project to the state for approval and funding. Third, as indicated above, New York increases both operating and building aid for districts that consolidate, so aid may also be endogenous if the above steps do not adequately address the endogeneity of the consolidation decision. We avoid this problem in our operating aid regressions by using an operating aid variable that does not include the extra operating aid associated with consolidation. The impact of this extra aid is picked up by our post-consolidation fixed effects and time trends.

We address the endogeneity of S, P, and (in the capital regression) aid using two-stage least squares. Following well-known rules, we select instruments for this procedure that (1) make conceptual sense, (2) help to explain the endogenous explanatory variables, and (3) do not have a significant direct

---

[13] New York uses a closed-ended matching formula, and we do not know if a given district has used up its eligibility for matching funds. Thus we prefer the model with total funding, but models with the matching rate as an explanatory variable yield similar results.

impact on the dependent variable. To meet the first two rules, we considered determinants of the demand for education as instruments for S, determinants of local labor market conditions as instruments for P, and factors influencing state aid as instruments for the aid variable. In addition, we conducted an overidentification test (Wooldridge, 2003) to determine whether our final set of instruments was exogenous, and we implemented the Bound et al. (1995) procedure to check for weak instruments.[14]

The best-known education demand variables are district income, state aid, and tax price. However, income, tax base (the denominator of tax price), and state aid are also determinants of school district efficiency (Duncombe and Yinger, 2000, 2001). In particular, they influence voters' incentives to monitor school officials and voters' preferences for a broad range of educational outcomes, not just basic test scores as identified by S. As a result, these variables violate the third rule listed above and are not legitimate instruments. To identify alternative instruments, we draw on the "copycat" theory of Case et al. (1993), which suggests that voters' desired level of student performance depends in part on what similar districts are able to accomplish. Unlike Case, Hines, and Rosen, however, we are not estimating a structural model of this behavior, so we cannot literally use (potentially endogenous) performance measures for similar districts. Instead, we select instruments from the set of exogenous variables that influence performance in adjacent districts. The amount a district must pay to attract and retain teachers of a given quality depends on conditions in the local private labor market (Ondrich et al., 2007). Variables measuring private wages and employment conditions are therefore used as instruments for teacher wages.

For the operating cost models, the final set of instruments includes the log of average values of per pupil income and per pupil operating aid in adjacent

---

[14]The Bound et al. (1995) procedure is not specified for a model with as many endogenous variables as ours. Neither is the alternative procedure by Stock and Yogo (2005). Thus we examined various combinations of the instruments and used the set that produced the highest partial F test for most endogenous variables. The F statistics for our final runs indicate that we have strong instruments in most cases. For most endogenous variables, the F statistics are all above 15. The one exception is the PEP test variable, for which the F statistics are between 6.4 and 7.9. Operating, instructional, teaching, and capital spending all pass the overidentification test at the 5 percent confidence level. Administration and transportation spending do not pass this test using the instruments we selected for operating spending. When one of the instruments from this list is dropped, however, these models pass the overidentification test and yield results that are virtually the same as those presented in the text.

districts and the log of average private sector wages, the log of average manufacturing wages, the unemployment rate, and the ratio of employment to students in the district's county. The capital spending model uses the same instruments plus average per pupil property value in adjacent districts, lagged three years.

The final methodological challenge is that capital spending is lumpy, so capital spending in a given year is not a good indication of a district's long-term expected annual capital spending. Indeed, capital spending often exhibits a large "spike" somewhere between two and eight years after the consolidation took place. Consolidation is not the whole story, however, because capital spending takes the form of a spike in non-consolidating districts, too. To focus on expected long-term spending, we define the dependent variable in our capital cost regression as a district's four-year average capital spending. We can calculate this variable for every year in our panel, because our data on spending, unlike our data for most explanatory variables, goes back until 1977. The dependent variable for a 1985 observation (the first year in our panel) therefore is based on the four-year average from 1982 through 1985. To reflect the fact that capital deteriorates over time, we used a 2 percent annual depreciation rate to adjust capital spending.

The use of four-year average capital spending necessitates three other changes in our cost model for capital spending. First, we also average the enrollment variable over the same four-year period. This step makes it possible to interpret the coefficient of the enrollment variables as describing the impact of a long-run shift in enrollment on a district's expected long-run annual capital spending. Second, state aid for capital spending in New York State is largely project-based aid, so the time series for state aid is almost as lumpy as the series for capital spending. To smooth out the state-aid data, that is, to translate it into a long-run measure, we also use a district's four-year average state aid as an (endogenous) explanatory variable.[15] Third, the use of a four- year average for capital spending requires a change in the district-specific fixed effects and time trends (including those for the period after consolidation).[16]

---

[15]The property value variable is also defined as a four-year average. The averaging procedure for the dependent variable does not require any change in other explanatory variables because trends in these variables are accounted for by the district-specific time trends.

[16]Details are presented in the technical appendix.

4.2. *Data and Measures*

Our data set covers the years 1985–1997. To ensure at least two years of data before or after each consolidation, we focus on the twelve consolidations that occurred from 1987 to 1995. Approximately 190 other rural districts serve as a comparison group.[17] Our main data sources are the New York State Education Department and the New York State Comptroller.[18]

Our approach requires data on student performance. Previous research on New York has identified two performance measures that are correlated with voter preferences and linked to state accountability programs: the percent of students achieving minimum competency on elementary school math and reading tests (PEP tests) and the percent of students receiving a Regents diploma, which requires passing a set of demanding exams in high school (Duncombe *et al.*, 1996; Duncombe and Yinger, 2000, 2001).[19] Accounting for the second variable is particularly important in New York, where one argument for consolidation is that it facilitates the offering of special classes to support the Regents exams.

For our price variable, we use information on the average salary for teachers with one through five years of experience, which is a better indicator of the cost of attracting teachers than a measure of salaries for more experienced teachers. To control for teacher quality differences, we regressed actual salaries on teacher education and experience, and then constructed a predicted wage for teachers with average experience and education.

Environmental variables identified in past research include the share of students in a district in poverty, from a single-parent family, with limited English proficiency, with special needs, or in high school. Our environmental variables are the percentage of students receiving a subsidized lunch, a well-known proxy for poverty, and the percentage of students in secondary grades.

---

[17] New York State classifies school districts into different region and district types, such as "downstate suburb" or "upstate rural." The upstate rural designation applies generally to non-city districts in a county that is not part of a metropolitan area. During our sample period, 216 non-consolidating districts were classified as rural; because of missing data, however, only 188 districts were used as the comparison group.

[18] Our data come from the *School District Fiscal Profile,* the *Comprehensive Assessment Report,* the *Personnel Master File,* and the *Institutional Master File* published by the State Education Department. Spending, federal aid, income, and property value data come from *The Special Report on Municipal Affairs* from the New York State Comptroller.

[19] Another important performance measure is the graduation rate. An imperfect measure of this rate is available for New York; including it in our analysis has little impact on the results.

District fixed effects and trend variables control for unobserved student and family characteristics, at least to the extent that they follow a linear time trend.

To capture efficiency in the cost model, we include income per pupil, tax base per pupil, and state operating aid per pupil divided by total income, which we call the state aid ratio.[20]

4.3. *Empirical Results*

4.3.1. *Descriptive analysis*

The first two columns of Tables 2 and 3 compare the characteristics of consolidating districts in 1985, before they consolidated, with the characteristics of non-consolidating rural districts in the same year.[21] On the financial side (Table 2), consolidating districts spent less in every category except for central administration, for which the difference is not statistically significant. They also have less local revenue and more state aid than non-consolidating districts and pay somewhat lower salaries. In contrast, consolidating districts spent more than other districts in 1997. The shift in capital spending is particularly striking; consolidating districts were spending three times as much per pupil in 1997, despite considerably lower spending per pupil in 1985. Hence the cost advantages of consolidation, if any, are not visible in the aggregate figures.

Turning to Table 3, we find that in 1985 consolidating districts had fewer pupils per administrator, lower property wealth, smaller total enrollment, smaller schools, fewer schools, and a lower percentage of students going to college. For example, 50 percent of consolidating districts had only one school before consolidation, but no one-school districts remained after consolidation. Table 3 also suggests that consolidation has at best modest

---

[20]Standard theory calls for median income instead of income per pupil, but these two variables are highly correlated. Standard theory also indicates that the income term should be median income plus the product of state aid per pupil and tax price. Our specification for the aid variable is designed to approximate this additive income term. See Duncombe and Yinger (2000, 2001).

[21]We filled in data in a few districts when we had a plausible method for doing so. Thus, for example, we occasionally filled in poverty with the average values for the previous and succeeding years and filled in teacher salaries with the average for similar districts in the same county. We did not fill in missing data on test scores.

Table 2 Comparison of per pupil spending and revenue for consolidating and other rural school districts in New York in 1985 and 1997.

Expenditure/Revenue category (Inflation-adjusted dollars)[a]	1985		1997	
	Districts that have consolidated ($)	Rural districts not consolidating ($)	Districts that have consolidated ($)	Rural districts not consolidating ($)
Aggregate spending:				
Total	6,699	7,447*	13,463	11,360*
Total without capital (w/debt service)	6,527	7,196*	10,585	10,392
Operating (all but capital and debt)	6,147	6,706*	9,311	9,659
Capital spending	272	397**	3,167	1,065*
Spending by function:				
Instructional	4,114	4,472*	6,678	6,818
Teaching	2,393	2,583*	5,481	5,637
Non-instructional	2,306	2,630*	5,800	3,906*
Operating and maintenance	728	894*	3,673	1,603*
Central administration	304	301	541	629
Transportation	487	608*	719	737
Total revenue per pupil				
Local	2,203	3,124*	2,674	4,635*
Federal	310	326	512	456
State	4,381	3,975**	7,440	5,514*
Operating aid	3,837	2,777*	3,561	2,985*
Reorganization aid	0	3	764	7*
Building aid	230	173	517	408
Transportation aid	444	423	573	464*
Average teacher salaries				
1–5 years of experience	22,694	24,265**	32,357	32,961
11–15 years of experience	31,918	35,346*	40,724	41,768
21–25 years of experience	40,177	42,126*	54,651	56,627

Notes: Twelve pairs of districts that consolidated between 1987 and 1995 are used in the calculation; 188 rural districts not consolidating from 1985 to 1997 are used for comparison.
[a] Adjusted using the fixed weighted GNP price deflator for state and local government purchases published by the U.S. Bureau of Economic Analysis (with 2002 dollars as the base).
*statistically significant at 5%; **statistically significant at 10%.

effects on student performance. Differences between consolidating and non-consolidating districts were not significant in 1985, except for a lower college-going rate in consolidating districts. The pattern in 1997 is similar, with only one significant difference — namely, a smaller failure rate on the math PEP

Table 3 Class sizes, fiscal capacity, student characteristics, and outcomes for consolidating and other rural school districts in New York in 1985 and 1997.

District characteristic	1985		1997	
	Districts that have consolidated	Rural districts not consolidating	Districts that have consolidated	Rural districts not consolidating
Staffing ratios				
Pupils per teacher	15.1	15.6	15.3	13.9*
Pupils per school administrator	358.0	423.9**	472.9	441.6
Fiscal capacity (adjusted for inflation)[a]				
Property wealth per pupil (thousands)	$118,326	$174,693*	$175,032	$306,229**
Income per pupil	$33,243	$35,376	$43,026	$47,539
School size and number				
Median elementary school enrollment[b]	407.0	444.0	431.7	457.9
Median high school enrollment[b]	427.3	532.3*	541.0	512.2
Number of schools	1.7	2.3*	3.2	2.3*
Percent of districts with one school	0.5	0.3**	0.0	0.3*
Student characteristics				
Enrollment	703	1061*	1469	1108*
Subsidized lunch (percent)	32.2	29.5	24.4	25.4
Percent secondary students	48.5	49.3	46.4	46.2
Student outcomes				
Percent of students below minimum competency on PEP tests (third and sixth grades)				
Math	11.0	11.3	0.2	0.6*
Reading	10.9	10.0	5.3	5.9
Dropout rate (%)	3.7	3.7	2.3	2.3
College-going rate (%)	17.2	22.0*	31.1	35.1
Percent receiving Regents diploma	44.6	48.4	43.6	45.8

Notes: Twelve pairs of districts that consolidated between 1987 and 1995 are used in the calculation; 188 rural districts not consolidating from 1985 to 1997 are used for comparison.
[a]Adjusted using the fixed weighted GNP price deflator for state and local government purchases published by the U.S. Bureau of Economic Analysis (with 2002 dollars as the base).
[b]For districts with only one school, the school was counted as both a high school and an elementary school in calculating school size.
*statistically significant at 5%; **statistically significant at 10%.

tests for consolidating districts. These differences are consistent with the
view that consolidation boosts performance, but the differences are small
in magnitude. Table 3 also does not support the view that consolidation
increases the number of more demanding Regents courses and hence the
number of students receiving Regents diplomas.

Table 4 shows that, almost across the board, inflation-adjusted expenditure per pupil, revenue per pupil, and average teacher salaries are higher
after consolidation than before. The only exception is state operating aid.
However, a similar pattern emerges in non-consolidating districts.[22] Table 4
also shows that capital and maintenance expenditures rise more rapidly after
consolidation than before, but operating spending, along with associated
spending on teaching and central administration, grows more slowly.

4.3.2. *Cost regression results*

The cost models were estimated using two-stage least squares (2SLS). Student outcomes and teacher salaries were treated as endogenous in all models;
the state aid ratio was also treated as endogenous in the capital spending
model. Separate regressions were estimated for operating expenditure, capital expenditure, and selected functional subcategories of expenditure that do
not involve substantial capital spending. Table 5 presents detailed results for
operating and capital spending per pupil. Regressions for functional spending
subcategories include the same explanatory variables (and instruments) as
the operating spending model.

Because the regressions include district-specific fixed effects and time
trends, the estimated coefficients are identified only by nonlinear variation
in the explanatory variables. Thanks to the large nonlinear changes in
enrollment caused by consolidation, this methodology is ideal for estimating
the enrollment coefficients and other consolidation cost effects, but it also
implies that the coefficients of other variables do not provide compelling
tests of the impact of these variables on education costs. In other words,
the district-specific fixed effects and time trends undermine our ability to
estimate precisely the impact of the non-enrollment variables in order to
minimize the possibility of bias in the coefficients of the consolidation-related
variables.

---

[22]One possible explanation is that New York experienced a rapid increase in special
education spending during this period (Lankford and Wyckoff, 1996).

Table 4 Comparison of per pupil spending and revenue for consolidating districts in New York before and after consolidation.

Expenditure/Revenue category	Inflation-adjusted dollars[a]		Annual percent change (inflation adjusted)[a]	
	Districts before consolidation ($)	Districts after consolidation ($)	Districts before consolidation	Districts after consolidation
Aggregate spending				
Total	8,648	13,280*	8.3	13.1
Total without capital (with debt service)	8,193	11,241*	7.3	7.9
Operating (all but capital and debt)	7,518	8,864*	6.7	1.8*
Capital spending	643	2,408*	66.3	162.3*
Spending by function				
Instructional	5,155	6,332	7.5	2.3*
Teaching	3,386	4,769	11.1	5.0*
Non-instructional	3,005	4,940*	10.1	21.6**
Operating and maintenance	1,047	2,858*	24.9	60.6*
Central administration	464	507	14.9	2.8*
Transportation	601	682	8.8	6.0
Total revenue per pupil				
Local	2,338	2,545*	5.4	1.5*
Federal	350	434*	4.5	7.5
State	5,657	8,288	7.3	10.3
Operating aid	4,592	3,647*	16.6	−0.1*
Reorganization aid	0	673*	n/a	n/a
Building aid	253	316**	17.7	27.6
Transportation aid	437	497*	7.5	12.4
Average teacher salaries				
1–5 years of experience	26,369	32,221*	6.0	2.1*
11–15 years of experience	35,777	41,514*	5.3	1.4*
21–25 years of experience	44,894	53,830*	5.6	2.3

Notes: These calculations are based on the twelve pairs of districts that consolidated between 1987 and 1995.
[a] Adjusted using the fixed weighted GNP price deflator for state and local government purchases published by the U.S. Bureau of Economic Analysis (with 2002 dollars as the base).
*statistically significant at 5%; **statistically significant at 10%.

Table 5   Cost regression results for rural school districts in New York, 1985–1997.

Variable	Operating		Capital	
	Coefficient	t-statistic	Coefficient	t-statistic
Intercept	10.9811	5.27	−24.56679	−2.21
Log of enrollment	**−1.6307**	**−3.28**		
Square of log of enrollment	**0.0587**	**1.79**		
Consolidation intercept change (average)	**0.5157**	**8.75**		
Consolidation time trend change (average)	**−0.0142**	**−4.54**	**0.08190**	**2.15**
Outcomes				
Percent of students below minimum competency on PEP tests (third and sixth grades)	−0.0076	−0.69	−0.12227	−1.32
Percent of graduates receiving Regents diploma	0.0009	0.57	−0.02922	−1.27
Log of teacher salaries (1–5 years)	0.7293	2.60	0.76713	0.34
Other cost factors				
Percent secondary students	0.00007	0.04	−0.69998	−0.24
Percent receiving subsidized lunch	0.00004	0.07	−0.00338	−0.67
Efficiency factors				
State aid ratio[a]	−0.2241	−0.72	1.46611	0.12
Log of property values	0.0227	0.67	−1.212E-03	−0.08
Log of average income	−0.1459	−2.16	0.12930	0.44
Superintendent change in last two years (1 = yes)	0.0062	1.37	−0.03288	−0.56
Sample size	2,734		2,721	

Notes: Estimated using linear 2SLS regression with district fixed effects and trend variables. Student outcomes, state aid, and teacher salaries are treated as endogenous. The dependent variable for the operating cost model is the log of real per pupil spending. The dependent variable for the capital cost model is the four-year average of the log of real per pupil capital spending adjusted for depreciation using a 2% annual rate.
[a]State aid for the operating cost model is real per pupil operating aid (without supplements for consolidation) divided by average income. For the capital cost model, the four-year average of total real state aid per pupil is divided by average income in that year.

In the operating cost regression, the first column of Table 5, the teacher salary variable has the expected sign and magnitude, 0.73, and is statistically significant. The estimated coefficients of the outcome variables and the other cost variables are small and statistically insignificant, however. Because these variables are significant with the expected signs in other analyses using New York data in this period (Duncombe and Yinger, 2000, 2001), we interpret these results as an indication that it is difficult to identify the effects of these variables in a model that contains fixed effects and time trends. We also find that efficiency increases with district income, the opposite of findings in previous studies. The other efficiency variables are insignificant. A change in superintendent increases spending, but this effect is not significant at conventional levels. In the case of capital costs, the district fixed effects and time trends remove so much variation that we cannot identify the impacts of any outcome, cost, or efficiency variables. See the last two columns of Table 5.

4.3.3. *Estimated economies of size*

The coefficients of the enrollment variables in the first column of Table 5 are significant statistically and indicate large economies of size in operating spending.[23] The positive coefficient on the second enrollment variable indicates that these economies diminish with size, but this effect is small and strong economies of size persist throughout the enrollment range in our sample. We find no economies of size in capital spending, however; indeed, the coefficient and its *t*-statistic are close to zero, so we have dropped the enrollment variables from the capital regression in column 2. [24]

Table 6 presents the coefficients of the enrollment variables for various categories of spending. We dropped the second enrollment variable, the square of log enrollment, if it were not statistically significant at the 10 percent level, which was true in every case except overall operating spending. We find that economies of size arise not only for operating spending but also for instructional spending (and its teaching subcategory) and administration. We do not find significant economies of size for transportation.[25]

The estimated economies of size are illustrated in the last three columns of Table 6. These columns indicate the economies of size associated with three hypothetical consolidations, corresponding roughly to the types of consolidations in our data (see Table 1). Our estimates imply that operating

---

[23] Other studies of New York school districts find smaller economies of size, probably because they combine urban and rural districts. Estimates in Duncombe and Yinger (2001), for example, imply operating cost savings of 13 percent for a change in enrollment from three hundred to six hundred.

[24] Dropping the enrollment variable also has little impact on other coefficients in the regression.

[25] We also estimated a three-stage least squares (3SLS) model for instruction, administration, and transportation, to account for the possibility that errors are correlated across equations; the enrollment coefficients are very close to those in Table 6.

Table 6   Coefficients of enrollment variables and implied economies of size, New York school rural districts, 1985–1997.

Expenditure category	Regression coefficients		Economies of size		
	ln(Enrollment)	[ln(Enrollment)]^2	From 300 pupils to 600 pupils	From 900 pupils to 1,800 pupils	From 1,500 pupils to 3,000 pupils
Spending by object					
Operating (all but capital)	−1.6307	0.0587	−61.7%	−53.5%	−49.6%
(*t*-statistic)	(−3.28)	(−1.79)			
Capital spending	—	—	0.0%	0.0%	0.0%
(*t*-statistic)					
Spending by function					
Instructional	−0.8368		−44.0%	−44.0%	−44.0%
(*t*-statistic)	(−4.22)				
Teaching	−0.8445		−44.3%	−44.3%	−44.3%
(*t*-statistic)	(−4.11)				
Non-instructional					
Central administration	−1.1202		−54.0%	−54.0%	−54.0%
(*t*-statistic)	(−3.38)				
Transportation	−0.4678		−27.7%	−27.7%	−27.7%
(*t*-statistic)	(−1.26)				

cost per pupil declines by 61.7 percent when two 300-pupil districts merge, but the cost savings drop to 49.6 percent when two 1,500-pupil districts merge.

Results for the functional spending categories indicate savings of 44 to 54 percent in instruction, teaching, and administration for any consolidation that doubles student enrollment. These results support the view that there is publicness in the provision of classroom instruction and in administration. The (insignificant) result for transportation indicates much smaller savings — 27.7 percent — for this enrollment change.

4.3.4. *Estimated non-enrollment cost impacts of consolidation*

The district-specific fixed effects and time trends for each consolidating pair measure the cost impacts of consolidation that are not associated with enrollment. The mean values of these coefficients (and associated t-statistics) are presented in the first two columns of Table 7. Both operating spending and the spending subcategories exhibit the same significant pattern: a large upward shift in per pupil costs at the time of consolidation, followed by a gradual decline in per pupil costs in the following years. In the case of administration and transportation, these upward shifts declined to zero by ten years, which is the maximum period we observe after a consolidation. In the case of operating, instruction, and teaching, however, the net shift is still positive after ten years.

The last two columns of Table 7 indicate the average annual impact of these post-consolidation cost shifts.[26] These effects are calculated with both a ten-year and a thirty-year horizon. Because the ten-year horizon corresponds to the longest post-consolidation period that we can observe, we have no evidence about adjustment costs after ten years, and the thirty-year calculations assume that adjustment costs drop to zero starting in the eleventh year. Roughly speaking, therefore, the ten-year and thirty-year calculations provide upper and lower bounds, respectively, for the average

---

[26]To derive the formula for these impacts, start with the present value (PV) of real spending E discounted at rate r. The percentage change in PV (or the associated annuity) with adjustment costs equal to n_y percent in year y is

$$\Delta PV_n = \frac{PV_n - PV_o}{PV_o} = \frac{E\sum \frac{(1+n_y)}{(1+r)^y} - E\sum \frac{1}{(1+r)^y}}{E\sum \frac{1}{(1+r)^y}} = \frac{\sum \frac{(1+n_y)}{(1+r)^y}}{\sum \frac{1}{(1+r)^y}} - 1.$$

Table 7 Non-enrollment cost effects of consolidation, New York rural school districts.

	Regression coefficients		Non-enrollment cost effects[a]	
	Average intercept (t-statistic)	Average trend (t-statistic)	Ten-year horizon	Thirty-year horizon[b]
Spending by object				
Total[c]	n/a	n/a	55.93%	28.17%
Operating spending	0.5157	−0.0142	55.91%	28.08%
(t-statistic)	(8.75)	(−4.54)		
Capital spending	—	0.082	56.07%	28.17%
(t-statistic)		(2.15)		
Spending by function				
Instructional	0.5092	−0.0136	55.33%	27.79%
(t-statistic)	(5.93)	(−3.41)		
Teaching	0.4969	−0.0094	56.73%	28.49%
(t-statistic)	(5.58)	(−2.32)		
Non-instructional				
Central administration	0.5196	−0.0526	30.07%	15.11%
(t-statistic)	(4.09)	(7.92)		
Transportation	0.3887	−0.0379	22.29%	11.20%
(t-statistic)	(2.66)	(−4.26)		

Notes: [a]The non-enrollment effects are calculated by first adding the average intercept coefficient and the product of the average time trend coefficient and the number of years after consolidation. Because the dependent variable is in logarithms, this sum is exponentiated to obtain the percent change in costs in a given year. These changes are calculated for each year, and the present value is calculated for the selected time horizon and discount rate using the formula in footnote 26. The discount rate is set at 5 percent.
[b]The non-enrollment cost impacts of consolidation are assumed to end after ten years, which is the maximum number of years after consolidation observed in our data. This approach understates these effects if they linger beyond this time.
[c]The estimate of the total effect is a weighted average of the effects for capital and operating separately, with the weights based on the expenditure share for capital (9.2 percent) and operating (90.8 percent) for non-consolidating districts in 1997.

annual adjustment costs of consolidation over the long run. To put it another way, assuming that the adjustment costs phase out after ten years, instead of simply disappearing, would result in average annual adjustment costs between these two estimates.[27]

---

[27]Simple extrapolation of our results implies that capital adjustment costs continue to grow after ten years. Although this type of growth is implausible, extrapolating our operating and capital results for the thirty-year cost calculations would lower the savings to 27 percent for the first hypothetical consolidation in Table 8 and to 12 percent for the third.

Our estimates indicate large adjustment costs associated with consolidation. With a ten-year horizon, adjustment costs equal 56 percent for both operating and capital spending. They also exceed 55 percent for instructional spending and teaching but are much smaller for administration (30.1 percent) and transportation (22.3 percent). With a thirty-year horizon, these annual adjustment costs are cut in half.

The capital-cost regression in Table 5 holds current student performance constant, but it does not control for future student performance. Consequently, the short-run non-enrollment cost increases we estimate could result in long-run performance increases. One possibility is that consolidation and the aid that accompanies it encourage districts to speed up the capital projects that they would have taken anyway. Indeed, districts have a strong incentive to speed up their capital projects: in order to receive consolidation-based building aid, districts must have capital projects approved within ten years after consolidation. To the extent that the non-enrollment capital cost increases that we estimate reflect this type of speeding up, they will be partially offset by capital cost decreases in the future. From society's point of view, the present value of future cost savings will not fully offset short-run cost increases, but they will offset them to some degree.

A related possibility is that districts take advantage of the opportunities for capital planning and state aid increases that accompany consolidation to undertake capital projects that boost student performance in the long run. Our regressions are not designed to study this type of effect. These regressions estimate the relationship between capital spending over a four-year period and student performance at the end of that period, but, as explained earlier, they include district-specific fixed effects and time trends, so the performance coefficients are based only on nonlinear variation in the performance variables.

4.3.5. *Net cost impacts of consolidation*

Table 8 combines the enrollment effects in Table 6 and the non-enrollment effects in Table 7. Capital costs are weighted at their share of spending in non-consolidating districts in 1997 — 9.2 percent. With this weighting, economies of size in operating spending result in overall annual cost savings of 56.0 percent, 48.6 percent, and 45.1 percent for the three hypothetical consolidations in Table 8 (row 1). Combining the enrollment and non-enrollment cost effects requires a multiplicative, not an additive, formula. More specifically, if economies of size cut costs by x percent and adjustment

Table 8   Net cost changes from consolidation, New York school rural districts, 1985–1997.

	Type of consolidation		
	From 300 pupils to 600 pupils	From 900 pupils to 1,800 pupils	From 1,500 pupils to 3,000 pupils
Total spending			
Enrollment Effects Only	−56.04%	−48.60%	−45.07%
Enrollment plus			
non-enrollment			
Cost effects of consolidation			
Ten-year horizon	−31.45%	−19.84%	−14.35%
Thirty-year horizon	−43.69%	−34.15%	−29.64%
Operating spending			
Enrollment effects only	−61.72%	−53.52%	−49.64%
Enrollment plus			
non-enrollment			
Cost effects of consolidation			
Ten-year horizon	−40.31%	−27.53%	−21.48%
Thirty-year horizon	−50.97%	−40.47%	−35.50%
Capital spending			
Enrollment effects only	0.00%	0.00%	0.00%
Enrollment plus			
non-enrollment			
Cost effects of consolidation			
Ten-year horizon	56.07%	56.07%	56.07%
Thirty-year horizon	28.17%	28.17%	28.17%

costs raise costs by y percent, then the net percentage change in costs equals $[(1-x)(1 + y) - 1]$.[28]

With a ten-year horizon, the net cost savings for the three hypothetical consolidations are 31.5, 19.8, and 14.4, respectively (row 2). The annual cost savings are roughly 14 percentage points higher for our calculations with a thirty-year horizon (row 3). The remaining rows show the net cost impacts of consolidation for operating and capital costs separately.

---

[28] Adding economies of size that lower spending by e percent per year to the formula in note 26 leads to the percent change in PV (or the associated annuity) due to consolidation:

$$\Delta PV_c = \frac{PV_c - PV_o}{PV_o} = \frac{E(1 - e)\sum \frac{(1+n_y)}{(1+r)^y} - E\sum \frac{1}{(1+r)^y}}{E\sum \frac{1}{(1+r)^y}} = (1 - e)(1 + \Delta PV_n) - 1.$$

4.4. *Robustness Checks*

We also estimate several alternative models to address possible weaknesses in our basic approach. These models address concerns about the identification of economies of size, the matching of consolidating and non-consolidating districts, and the possible endogeneity of the consolidation variables despite the steps described earlier.

The enrollment changes and other adjustments that accompany consolidation arise at the same time, so it may be difficult to separate their impacts on education costs. Moreover, our district fixed effects and time trends imply that we estimate the enrollment coefficients based solely on nonlinear changes in enrollment. The most obvious such change is the one associated with consolidation. If enrollment in non-consolidating districts does not have much nonlinear variation over time and the consolidation decision is endogenous, then our procedure might lead to misleading estimates of economies of size. To address these possibilities, we interact the enrollment variable (or variables if a squared term is included) in each regression with the consolidation variable to determine whether estimated economies of size are different in consolidating and non-consolidating districts.[29] This interaction term is never close to statistically significant. This result indicates that we can estimate economies of size based on nonlinear enrollment change in non-consolidating districts, and it suggests that neither collinearity nor endogeneity leads to a different estimate of economies of size in districts that consolidate.

As demonstrated by the large literature on matching, a comparison of treated observations with observations that are unlikely ever to be treated can lead to inaccurate estimates of the treatment effect, at least when this effect varies across observations (Heckman *et al.*, 1999). Our second robustness check is designed to address the possibility by first estimating a logit model of the consolidation decision. As shown in Efron (1988), this model expresses the probability of consolidation in year t, given that it has not happened before t, as a function of the exogenous variables in our cost equation. This model yields a propensity score for each district in each year, defined as the predicted probability that the district will be consolidated in

---

[29] We also estimated models with a dummy variable for the year before consolidation. It was never significant, which suggests that we are not missing a pre-consolidation shock.

that year.[30] Then, following the advice of Cobb-Clark and Crossley (2003, p. 508), we "inspect the distribution of propensity scores and impose the common support condition (by trimming the data)."[31] More specifically, we first find the lowest propensity score for any consolidating district in the year it consolidates. Then we drop every non-consolidating district with a propensity score below this value in every year.

The results are presented in the second column of Table 9. We find that trimming the sample has little impact on estimated economies of size for spending on operating expenses, instruction, teaching, and administration, although it does eliminate the significance of the squared term in the operating regression. In the case of transportation spending, the enrollment coefficient with the trimmed sample is almost 60 percent above the baseline result in the first column and is now statistically significant. These results suggest that non-comparability of the consolidating and non-consolidating samples is not a problem in most cases but might lead to an understatement of economies of size in transportation.

Finally, despite the institutional constraints on consolidation and the steps we have taken to address endogeneity, we cannot formally rule out the possibility that our estimates are biased by unobservable factors that influence both consolidation (and hence enrollment) and nonlinear variation in spending. We address this problem using a control function.[32] As explained by Todd (2006, p. 31), "Control function estimators explicitly recognize that non-random selection in the program (i.e., consolidation) gives rise to an endogeneity problem in the model and try to obtain unbiased parameter estimates by modeling the source of the endogeneity."

---

[30] Our logit model yields the P_{it}, which is the probability that district i will consolidate in year t given that it did not consolidate before t. The propensity to be consolidated in year t, Q_{it}, equals

$$Q_{it} = P_{i1} + \sum_{t=2}^{T} P_{it} \prod_{s=1}^{t=1} (1 - P_{is}).$$

[31] This is, of course, the simplest possible matching procedure. We cannot implement other matching methods, such as propensity-score matching, because some of our observations combine and remain in the sample. We did implement another simple test for heterogeneous impact of consolidation, namely, to interact the consolidation dummy with district characteristics, such as income and property value. No interaction term was significant at the 5 percent level.

[32] We cannot use standard IV methods; consolidation cannot be replaced by a predicted value because it is built into the structure of our fixed effects and time trends. Moreover, we cannot use the Ziliak and Kniesner (1998) IV method for panel data, because it applies to observations that drop out of the sample at a point in time (due, in their case, to unemployment).

Table 9 Coefficients of enrollment variables using alternative samples and models.

Type of spending	Full sample	Trimmed sample based on propensity scores[a]	Full sample model with control function[b]
Operating			
ln(enrollment)	−1.6307	−1.5895	−1.5416
	(−3.28)	(2.10)	(−3.22)
[ln(enrollment)]^2	0.0587	0.0543	0.0545
	(1.79)	(1.09)	(1.68)
Instructional			
ln(enrollment)	−0.8368	−0.8366	−0.7808
	(−4.22)	(−4.34)	(−4.62)
Teaching			
ln(enrollment)	−0.8445	−0.8173	−0.7791
	(−4.11)	(−4.41)	(−4.51)
Administration			
ln(enrollment)	−1.1202	−0.9984	−1.1776
	(−3.38)	(−2.63)	(−4.12)
Transportation			
ln(enrollment)	−0.4678	−0.7406	−0.6548
	(−1.26)	(−2.98)	(−2.65)

Notes: [a]These estimates exclude the seventeen non-consolidating districts with a propensity score that falls below the minimum observed for consolidating districts in the year of consolidation. The propensity scores are obtained from a logit model that includes all exogenous variables from the cost model (except fixed effects and time trends) as explanatory variables.
[b]This model includes as an explanatory variable the propensity score derived from a logit model of the consolidation decision. It explains the decision to consolidate in a given year as a function of the years since the last consolidation in the county, the district's three-year change in enrollment, the aid ratio in districts with similar enrollment, and the instruments used in the operating spending model.

In our case, we estimate another logit model of a district's decision to consolidate in a given year. Then, following the approach described in Heckman and Navarro-Lozano (2004), we include the propensity to be consolidated, as defined earlier, from this model as an explanatory variable in our cost equation.[33] As Heckman and Navarro-Lozano (p. 36) point out, "The control function approach is more general than the matching approach," because it addresses both comparability and endogeneity, and is

---

[33]This propensity score is not significant at the 5 percent level in any of our regressions. Heckman and Navarro-Lozano show (p. 34) that the control function can be approximated by a polynomial in the propensity score. The square of the propensity score is also never significant, and adding it has little impact on our results.

therefore more general, but considerably more complicated, than our simple trimming method.

The control function approach requires a model of the participation decision and identifying restrictions. Drawing on the literature on the decision to consolidate (Brasington, 1999, 2003; Gordon and Knight, 2009), we model consolidation as a function of the history of consolidation in nearby districts, recent social changes in the district, and the environment in which the district operates. More specifically, our logit model estimates the probability of consolidation in a given year as a function of the number of years since the previous consolidation in the same county, the preceding three-year change in the district's enrollment, the total state aid ratio in districts with similar enrollment, and the instruments identified for our cost regression.[34] Because the first three variables are not in the cost regression, they provide the identifying restrictions needed for the control function approach to work.

As shown in the last column of Table 9, the control-function approach leads to virtually the same enrollment coefficients as the baseline model for overall operating spending and for spending on instruction, teaching, and administration. Adding a control function does alter the results for transportation, however. Compared with the baseline model, the control-function model indicates much larger economies of size, which are significant at the 1 percent level. Although these results are not presented in Table 9, we also find that switching to the control-function approach has little impact on estimates of the non-enrollment cost impact of consolidation. The largest impact by far is on transportation, for which the average intercept goes up from 0.389 to 0.445 and the average trend coefficient goes from −0.038 to −0.041.

Overall, our robustness checks provide further evidence for both large economies of scale and large adjustment costs associated with consolidation. Moreover, for all operating spending categories except transportation, our baseline model appears to use reasonably comparable treatment and control groups and to adequately control for the endogeneity of the consolidation decision. These robustness checks in Table 9 also indicate, however, that the baseline model understates both the magnitude and significance of

---

[34]This model is supported by the data. The years since a consolidation in the county have a significant negative impact on consolidation, for example, and the pseudo R-squared of the model is 0.52. The results for the control-function version of the cost model are not highly sensitive to the variables included in this logit model.

economies of size in transportation. In fact, the control function approach indicates that, with a ten-year horizon, doubling enrollment will result in a 36.5 percent decline in transportation costs per pupil due to economies of size and a net decline of 22.3 percent after non-enrollment adjustment costs are taken into account.

5. Conclusions and Policy Implications

Because of significant economies of size, consolidation clearly cuts operating costs for small, rural school districts in New York. Although consolidation also results in large adjustment costs in operating spending, these adjustment costs phase out and are not large enough to eliminate the savings due to economies of size. The operating cost savings are largest when consolidation combines two very small districts, but even two 1,500-pupil districts can cut their operating costs by at least 20 percent through consolidation.

We do not find economies of size in capital spending. Moreover, we find that consolidation results in large adjustment costs in capital spending, costs that grow throughout our sample period. These adjustment costs are clearly worthy of further investigation. To what extent do they decline after the ten-year post-consolidation period in our data? To what extent are they encouraged by the large aid increases that accompany consolidation? To what extent do they boost student performance (and therefore lower costs) in the future?

These results do not provide a complete benefit-cost analysis of consolidation because they do not consider losses in consumer surplus associated with fewer districts to choose from (Bradford and Oates, 1974), changes in transportation costs for students and their parents, or changes in the costs of providing educational outcomes other than those measured by the test scores in our analysis.[35] Because consolidation in New York requires the consent of voters in each consolidating district, we presume that benefits to voters are perceived to outweigh costs in every district that consolidates with another.[36] In other words, costs we do not measure, if they exist, must

---

[35]Consumer surplus losses may be offset by declines in tax price. An analysis of this issue based on demand functions estimated by Duncombe and Yinger (2001) finds this to be true in the average consolidating district in New York. This analysis is available from the authors on request.

[36]This logic is also central to analyses of the fiscal incentives that lead to consolidation (Brasington, 1999, 2003; Gordon and Knight, 2009) and to Fisher and Wassmer's (1998) analysis of the number of school districts in a metropolitan area.

not be large enough to overcome cost savings, at least in the perceptions of voters.

Some evidence on this point comes from another recent study of rural school districts in New York (Hu and Yinger, 2008), which estimates whether people are willing to pay more for housing in a district after it consolidates with another district. The study finds that the impact of consolidation on house values is quite large, about 25 percent, in very small districts but declines with enrollment to about 6 percent in a district with an enrollment of 1,500. These results suggest that home buyers perceive the economies of size associated with consolidation.[37] They also indicate that up to at least 1,500 pupils, the perceived advantages of consolidation outweigh the perceived disadvantages, which could include larger private transportation costs or a loss of consumer surplus. Further exploration of these other issues clearly is warranted.

The key policy question, of course, is whether states should encourage school district consolidation. After all, state education departments have played a central role in encouraging and sometimes financially supporting school district consolidation (Haller and Monk, 1988). New York backs up its commitment to consolidation with a sizable long-term subsidy to consolidating governments, on the order of $30 million per year.

Our results indicate that financial support for consolidation is warranted, particularly for small districts, because a state can lower the overall cost of education by taking advantage of economies of size. Although rural school districts face substantial adjustment costs when they consolidate, economies of size more than offset these costs. Our estimates indicate overall cost savings between 14 and 44 percent, depending on the sizes of the consolidating districts and the time horizon. Rural school districts in New York appear to be reasonably representative of rural districts nationwide, but formal studies of consolidation in other states would be valuable.

We also find that capital costs shift upward substantially after consolidation, in part, perhaps, because of increased state aid. The key lesson for state policy makers, we believe, is that they should carefully monitor post-consolidation capital spending. They need to make certain that consolidation and the state aid given to support it do not result in capital projects that are not cost effective. This is a difficult task, to say the least, because the

---

[37] In estimating the determinants of consolidation, Gordon and Knight (2009) find evidence that voters in Iowa also perceive economies of size, but only up to an enrollment of 250 students.

relationship between capital spending and long-run student performance is poorly understood, but state officials should monitor capital projects based on the best available knowledge about this relationship.

Acknowledgments

The authors acknowledge the valuable assistance with the education data of Richard Glasheen and Ron Danforth at the New York State Education Department, as well as the research assistance provided by Matthew Andrews. Comments by Dan Black, Thomas Downes, William Fowler, Duke Kao, Jan Ondrich, Steve Ross, Lori Taylor, Doug Wolf, two anonymous referees, and participants in seminars at Georgia State University and Michigan State University have also been very helpful.

Technical Appendix

1. *District-specific Variables in a Model of Consolidation*

Definitions

Let superscripts define variables and subscripts define observations. Also, let E = spending per pupil; X = explanatory variables; D^i = dummy for district i; i^* = consolidation partner for district i; C = consolidation dummy ($= 1$ for district i in year t if district i is consolidated with another district in year t and $= 0$ otherwise); w = district weight ($=$ district's share of total enrollment in its consolidated district in the year before consolidation and $= 0$ for districts that do not consolidate); t = time ($1985 = 1$); t^* = value of t in the year before consolidation ($= 0$ in districts that do not consolidate); N = number of districts; and M = number of districts that consolidate. Note that if district i consolidates, $w_i + w_{i*} = 1$.

2. *District-specific Fixed Effects and Time Trends*

Define

$$F1^i = \text{district fixed effect}$$
$$= D^i(1 - c) + w_i C(D^i + D^{i*}); \quad i = 1, N,$$

and

$$T1^i = \text{district time trend}$$
$$= (F1^i)(t); \quad i = 1, N.$$

3. Post-consolidation Fixed Effects and Time Trends

Let $j = j$th consolidating pair; $j_1 = $ value of i for first district in pair j; and $j_2 = $ value of i for second district in pair j. Now define

$$F2^j = C(D_1^j + D_2^j); \quad j = 1, M/2$$

and

$$T2^j = C(D_1^j + D_2^j)(t - t^*); \quad j = 1, M/2.$$

To estimate the average value of the pair effects, define $F2^* = C$ and $T2^* = C(t - t^*)$. Now drop one post-consolidation district-pair effect and time trend and replace them with $F2^*$ and $T2^*$. Then redefine the district-pair effects and trends as follows:

$$F2^{*j} = F2^j - \frac{2C}{M}; \quad j = 1, M/2$$

$$T2^{*j} = T2^j - \frac{2C(t - t^*)}{M}; \quad j = 1, M/2$$

With these variables, the coefficients of $F2^*$ and $T2^*$ are average effects, and their standard errors are the appropriate standard errors for the average effects.

4. District-specific Variables for Capital Spending

The use of average or long-term capital spending fundamentally alters the district-specific variables, which now pick up the role of unobserved factors in different time periods. To account for this, we express the district fixed effects and time trends as averages, too.

Specifically,

$$F1^i = \frac{1}{4} \sum_{t'=t-3}^{t} [D^i(1 - C_{it'}) + w_i C_{it'}(D^i + D^{i*})]\frac{1}{(1+d)^{t-t'}}; \quad i = 1, N,$$

where d is a depreciation rate for capital, which is also used to define average spending. Also,

$$T1^i = \frac{1}{4} \sum_{t'=t-3}^{t} [D^i(1 - C_{it'}) + u_i C_{it'}(D^i + D^{i'})]\frac{t'}{(1+d)^{t-t'}}; \quad i = 1, N.$$

The post-consolidation variables, as before, apply to pairs of consolidating districts:

$$F2^j = \frac{1}{4} \sum_{t'=t-3}^{t} [C_{it'}(D^{j1} + D^{j2})] \frac{1}{(1+d)^{t-t'}}; \quad j = 1, M/2$$

$$T2^j = \frac{1}{4} \sum_{t'=t-3}^{t} [C_{it'}(D^{j1} + D^{j2})] \frac{t'-t^*}{(1+d)^{t-t'}}; \quad j = 1, M/2.$$

In addition,

$$F2^* = \frac{1}{4} \sum_{t'=t-3}^{t} \frac{C_{it'}}{(1+d)^{t-t'}}$$

$$T2^* = \frac{1}{4} \sum_{t'=t-3}^{t} \frac{C_{it'}(t'-t^*)}{(1+d)^{t-t'}}$$

and

$$F2^{*j} = F2^j - \frac{2}{4M} \sum_{t'=t-3}^{t} \frac{C_{it'}}{(1+d)^{t-t'}}; \quad j = 2, M/2$$

$$T2^{*j} = T2^j - \frac{2}{4M} \sum_{t'=t-3}^{t} C_{it'} \left(\frac{t'-t^*}{(1+d)^{t-t'}} \right); \quad j = 2, M/2.$$

When the sets $F2^{*j}$ and $T2^{*j}$ are included, the coefficients of $F2^*$ and $T2^*$ yield the average post-consolidation shift and time trend, respectively, with the appropriate standard errors.

References

Andrews, Matthew, William Duncombe, and John Yinger. 2002. Revisiting economies of size in American education: Are we any closer to a consensus? *Economics of Education Review* **21**: 245–62.

Barker, R. G., and P. V. Gump. 1964. *Big School, Small School: High School Size and Student Behavior*. Stanford, CA: Stanford University Press.

Benton, Davis. 1992. A consolidation success story. *American School Board Journal* **179**: 4–43.

Bloom, Howard S. 1984. Estimating the effects of job-training programs using longitudinal data: Ashenfelter's findings reconsidered. *Journal of Human Resources* **14**: 544–56.

Bound, John, David A. Jaeger, and Regina Baker. 1995. Problems with instrumental variables estimation when the correlation between the instruments and the endogenous explanatory variables is weak. *Journal of the American Statistical Association* **90**: 443–50.

Bradford, David F., and Wallace E. Oates. 1974. Suburban exploitation of central cities and government structure. In H. M. Hochman and G. B. Peterson (eds.), *Redistribution Through Public Choice*, pp. 43–92. New York: Columbia University Press.

Brasington, David M. 1999. Joint provision of public goods: The consolidation of school districts. *Journal of Public Economics* **73**: 373–93.

Brasington, David M. 2003. Size and school district consolidation: Do opposites attract? *Economica* **70**: 673–90.

Case, Anne C., James R. Hines, Jr., and Harvey S. Rosen. 1993. Budget spillovers and fiscal policy interdependence: Evidence from the states. *Journal of Public Economics* **53**(3): 285–307.

Cobb-Clark, Deborah A., and Thomas Crossley. 2003. Econometrics for evaluations: An introduction to recent developments. *Economic Record* **79**: 491–511.

Cotton, Kathleen. 1996. *Affective and Social Benefits of Small-Scale Schooling.* Eric Digest No. ED401088. Available www.ericdigests.org/1997-2/small.htm. Accessed 31 May 2007.

Downes, Thomas A., and Thomas F. Pogue. 1994. Adjusting school aid formulas for the higher cost of educating disadvantaged students. *National Tax Journal* **47**: 89–110.

Duncombe, William, John Ruggiero, and John Yinger. 1996. Alternative approaches to measuring the cost of education. In H. F. Ladd (ed.), *Holding Schools Accountable: Performance-Based Reform in Education,* pp. 327–56. Washington, DC: Brookings Institution.

Duncombe, William, and John Yinger. 1993. An analysis of returns to scale in public production, with an application to fire protection. *Journal of Public Economics* **52**: 49–72.

Duncombe, William, and John Yinger. 2000. Financing higher performance standards: The case of New York State. *Economics of Education Review* **19**: 363–86.

Duncombe, William, and John Yinger. 2001. Alternative paths to property tax relief. In W. E. Oates (ed.), *Property Taxation and Local Government Finance,* pp. 243–94. Cambridge, MA: Lincoln Institute of Land Policy.

Duncombe, William, and John Yinger. 2008. Measurement of cost differentials. In E. Fiske and H. F. Ladd (eds.), *Handbook of Research in Education Finance and Policy,* Sec. 3, Chap. 3. Mahwah, NJ: Laurence Erlbaum Associates.

Efron, Bradley. 1988. Logistic regression, survival analysis, and the Kaplan-Meier curve. *Journal of the American Statistical Association* **83**(402): 414–25.

Ferguson, Ronald F., and Helen F. Ladd. 1996. Additional evidence on how and why money matters: A production function analysis of Alabama schools. In H. F. Ladd (ed.), *Holding Schools Accountable: Performance-Based Reform in Education,* pp. 265–98. Washington, DC: Brookings Institution.

Figlio, David N., and Joe A. Stone. 1999. Are private schools really better? In S. W. Polachek (ed.), *Research in Labor Economics,* vol. 18, pp. 115–40. Stamford, CT: JAI Press.

Fisher, Ronald C., and Robert W. Wassmer. 1998. Economic influences on the structure of local government in U.S. metropolitan areas. *Journal of Urban Economics* **43**: 444–71.

Fowler, William, and Herbert J. Walberg. 1991. School size, characteristics, and outcomes. *Educational Evaluation and Policy Analysis* **13**: 189–202.

Fox, W. F. 1981. Reviewing economies of size in education. *Journal of Educational Finance* **6**: 273–96.

Gordon, Nora, and Brian Knight. 2009. A spatial merger estimator with an application to school district consolidation. *Journal of Public Economics* **93**(5–6) (June): 752–65.

Guthrie, James W. 1979. Organization scale and school success. *Educational Evaluation and Policy Analysis* **1**: 17–27.

Gyimah-Brempong, Kwabena, and Anthony O. Gyapong. 1991. Production of education: Are socioeconomic characteristics important factors? *Eastern Economic Journal* **17**: 507–521.

Haller, Emil J., and David H. Monk. 1988. New reforms, old reforms, and the consolidation of small rural schools. *Educational Administration Quarterly* **24**: 470–483.

Heckman, James J., Robert J. LaLonde, and Jeffrey A. Smith. 1999. The economics and econometrics of active labor market programs. In O. C. Ashenfelter and D. Card (eds.), *Handbook of Labor Economics*, vol. 3A, pp. 1865–2097. Amsterdam: Elsevier.

Heckman, James, and Salvador Navarro-Lozano. 2004. Using matching, instrumental variables, and control functions to estimate economic choice models. *Review of Economics and Statistics* **86**: 30–57.

Howley, Craig. 1996. *The Academic Effectiveness of Small-Scale Schooling (an Update).* Eric Digest No. 372897. Available www.ericdigests.org/1995-1/small.htm. Accessed 31 May 2007.

Hu, Yue, and John Yinger. 2008. The impact of school district consolidation on housing values. *National Tax Journal* **61**(4) (December). [Chapter 24]

Huang, Yao. 2004. Appendix B: A guide to state operating aid programs for elementary and secondary education. In John Yinger (ed.), *Helping Children Left Behind: State Aid and the Pursuit of Educational Equity*, pp. 331–52. Cambridge, MA: MIT Press.

Imazeki, Jennifer, and Andrew Reschovsky. 2004. School finance reform in Texas: A never-ending story? In John Yinger (ed.), *Helping Children Left Behind: State Aid and the Pursuit of Educational Equity*, pp. 251–82. Cambridge, MA: MIT Press.

Kenny, Lawrence. 1982. Economies of scale in schooling. *Economics of Education Review* **2**(1): 1–24.

Krueger, Alan B. 1999. Experimental estimates of education production functions. *Quarterly Journal of Economics* **64**: 497–532.

Lankford, Hamilton, and James Wyckoff. 1996. The allocation of resources to special education and regular instruction. In H. F. Ladd (ed.), *Holding Schools Accountable: Performance-Based Reform in Education,* pp. 221–257. Washington, DC: Brookings Institution.

Lee, Valerie, E., and Julia B. Smith. 1997. High school size: Which works best and for whom? *Educational Evaluation and Policy Analysis* **19**(3): 205–227.

National Center for Education Statistics (NCES). 2001. *Public School Finance Programs of the United States and Canada: 1998–99.* Washington, DC: U.S. Department of Education, National Center for Education Statistics.

National Center for Education Statistics (NCES). 2006. *Digest of Education Statistics: 2005.* Available www.nces.ed.gov/programs/digest/d05/tables-2.asp. Accessed 15 May 2007.

New York State Education Department. 2006. *State Aid to Schools: A Primer.* Fiscal Analysis Unit, New York State Education Department, Albany, NY. Available www.oms.nysed.gov/faru/Primer/Primer06_07/Primer06-07A.pdf Accessed 4 June 2007.

Ondrich, Jan, Emily Pas, and John Yinger. 2007. The determinants of teacher attrition in upstate New York. *Public Finance Review.* In press.

Pratten, Cliff. 1991. *The Competitiveness of Small Firms.* Department of Applied Economics Occasional Papers, No. 57. Cambridge, UK: Cambridge University Press.

Reschovsky, Andrew, and Jennifer Imazeki. 2001. Achieving educational adequacy through school finance reform. *Journal of Education Finance* **24**(4): 373–96.

Stock, James H., and Motohiro Yogo. 2005. Testing for weak instruments in linear IV regression. In D. W. K. Andrews and J. H. Stock (eds.), *Identification and Inference for Econometric Models: Essays in Honor of Thomas J. Rothenberg*, pp. 80–108. Cambridge: Cambridge University Press.

Streifel, James S., George Foldesy, and David Holman. 1991. The financial effects of consolidation. *Journal of Research in Rural Education* **7**: 13–20.

Tholkes, Robert J. 1991. Economies of scale in rural school district reorganization. *Journal of Education Finance* **16**: 497–514.

Todd, Petra E. 2006. Evaluating Social Programs with Endogenous Program Placement and Selection of the Treated. Working paper, University of Pennsylvania. Available athena.sas.upenn.edu/∼ petra/papers/hae.pdf. Accessed 31 May 2007.

University of the State of New York. n.d. A *Guide to the Reorganization of School Districts in New York State*. Available www.emsc.nysed.gov/mgtserv/sch_distjorg/ GuideToReorganizationOfSchoolDistricts.htm. Accessed 31 May 2007.

Wasylenko, Michael. 1977. Some evidence of the elasticity of supply of policemen and firefighters. *Urban Affairs Quarterly* **12**: 365–379.

Weast, Jerry D. 1997. When bigger can be better. *School Administrator* **54**: 38–43.

Witte, John F. 1996. School choice and student performance. In H. F. Ladd (ed.), *Holding Schools Accountable: Performance-Based Reform in Education*, pp. 149–176. Washington, DC: Brookings Institution.

Wooldridge, Jeffrey M. 2003. *Introductory Econometrics: A Modern Approach*, 2nd edition, Cincinnati, OH: South-Western College.

Ziliak, James P., and Thomas J. Kniesner. 1998. The importance of sample attrition in life cycle labor supply estimation. *Journal of Human Resources* **33**(2): 507–530.

Chapter 19

How Does School District Consolidation Affect Property Values? A Case Study of New York*

William Duncombe[§], John Yinger[†,¶] and Pengju Zhang[‡]

[†]*Departments of Public Administration and
International Affairs and of Economics,
Syracuse University, Syracuse, NY, United States*
[‡]*School of Public Affairs and Administration,
Rutgers University–Newark, Newark, NJ 07103, United States*
[¶]*jyinger@maxwell.syr.edu*

This article explores the impact of school district consolidation on house values based on house sales in upstate New York State from 2000 to 2012. By combining propensity score matching (PSM) and double-sales data to compare house value changes in consolidating and comparable school districts, we find that, except in one relatively large district, consolidation has a negative impact on house values during the years right after it occurs and that this effect then fades away and is eventually reversed. This pattern suggests that it takes time either for the advantages of consolidation to be apparent or for the people who prefer consolidated districts to move in. Finally, as in previous studies, the long-run impacts of consolidation on house values are positive in census tracts that initially have low incomes, but negative in high-income census tracts, where parents may have a relatively large willingness to retain the non-budgetary advantages of small districts.

*This chapter is reproduced from "How Does School District Consolidation Affect Property Values: A Case Study of New York," *Public Finance Review*, **44**(1), 2016, pp. 52–79.
[§]Deceased.

Over the past century, the many small school districts that were established as this nation was settled have gradually been consolidated, and the number of districts has been cut by almost 90 percent (National Center for Education Statistics [NCES] 2006, 2011). Despite this dramatic change, many states still contain several school districts with enrollment below 500 pupils, which are good candidates for consolidation. The principal justification for consolidation is economies of scale in the provision of public education, which have been documented by many studies (Andrews *et al.*, 2002; Duncombe and Yinger, 2007). School district consolidation, however, may also have negative impacts on education quality by affecting student motivation, parental involvement in schools, or parental access to teachers. Moreover, the cost and quality of public schools may influence the attraction of a community to potential residents and thereby affect local property values (Nguyen-Hoang and Yinger, 2011). This article combines these two issues by examining the impact of consolidation on housing prices, that is, by determining whether the market value of single-family houses goes up or down when consolidation occurs. Building on previous research by Brasington (2004) and Hu and Yinger (2008), we examine the impact of recent consolidations on housing prices in New York State.

An investigation into the property value impact of consolidation provides information about the way home buyers view consolidation and therefore contributes to the debate about state policies that affect school district size. Despite extensive consolidation in the past, some states still provide incentives to consolidate. Several states, including New York, have aid programs to encourage district "reorganization," which usually means consolidation (NCES, 2001). Transportation or building aid formulas also encourage consolidation in some cases (Haller and Monk, 1988). Surprisingly, however, these pro-consolidation policies may be accompanied by policies that discourage consolidation, such as operating aid formulas that compensate school districts for small enrollment or for small enrollment per square mile (Huang, 2004).

This article reviews the literature on consolidation, with a focus on the impact of consolidation on property values, describes the data and methods we employ, and presents the results from our estimation. A final section presents our conclusions.

1. Literature Review

In principle, consolidation enables school districts to benefit from economies of scale, obtain new aid from state government, and provide students with more course options. According to the New York State Department of Education (NYSED, 2013b), more than thirty school district consolidations have taken place in New York State since 1980. Regardless of potential cost savings, however, school district consolidation is sometimes difficult to achieve. Consolidation may increase travel time for students and therefore impose additional transportation costs on households (Kenny, 1982). Residents may fear a loss of local identity or worry that their own community is not compatible with potential partner districts (NYSED, 2013a). Moreover, high-income households are less likely to support consolidation, perhaps because they place a high value on personal contact with teachers or good access to schools and school activities (Duncombe and Yinger, 2007; Hu and Yinger, 2008). In addition, students in larger school districts may have weaker connections to the school community, a less positive attitude toward school, and a lower motivation to learn (Barker and Gump, 1964; Cotton, 1996; Duncombe and Yinger, 2007). Finally, consolidation may raise concerns about representation on the Board of Education or about whether the new district will operate as expected (NYSED, 2013a). These possibilities help to explain why some consolidation propositions failed to pass in New York, even when the districts involved are relatively comparable.

Several scholars have written about the determinants of consolidation (Brasington, 1999, 2003; Gordon and Knight, 2009) and about the impacts of consolidation on the cost of education (Andrews *et al.*, 2002; Duncombe and Yinger, 2007). This literature indicates that districts with widely disparate characteristics, such as property values, are unlikely to choose to consolidate. Brasington (2003, 687) also finds that "greater differences in income and racial composition discourage consolidation." When two small districts do consolidate, however, they are likely to experience some adjustment costs but to save money overall because of economies of scale. Duncombe and Yinger find that these economies are considerably smaller in percentage terms for two consolidating districts with 1,500 pupils each than for two 500-pupil districts.

Recent articles by Brasington (2004) and Hu and Yinger (2008) explore the property value impact of consolidation. Property value impacts reflect cost savings but also raise additional issues because they may reflect parental concerns that do not appear in school districts' budgets, such as parental access to teachers or the time parents and students spend getting to school. Indeed, Brasington finds that once one controls for changes in student test scores and property tax rates, consolidation has a negative impact on property values.

Hu and Yinger (2008) provide an accounting of the channels through which consolidation affects house values. The first broad channel reflects changes in the quality of local public services. Consolidation leads to increases in state aid to education and, due to economies of scale, it leads to a decline in the marginal cost of public services. Both of these impacts give voters an incentive to demand higher school quality. The impact of each additional unit of school quality on house value is weighted by the difference between the marginal benefits it provides and the taxes it requires. The second broad channel reflects changes in the cost of providing existing school services. This channel has four parts. First, consolidation may raise the cost of off-budget services, such as parental access to teachers or the time it takes students to get to school. Second, consolidation may lead to economies of scale, which means that it may result in a lower cost per pupil to provide the same level of school services. Third, consolidation may involve adjustment costs, such as re-organizing staff or re-designing bus routes. Fourth, consolidation brings in state aid. The first and third parts are likely to have a negative impact on house values, whereas the second and fourth are likely to have a positive impact.

The empirical work by Hu and Yinger (2008), which is based on census tracts in New York State, finds that the impact of consolidation on house values depends on the enrollment change associated with consolidation. As expected from the literature on economies of scale, the property value impacts are largest for the smallest consolidating districts, and positive impacts fade out once a district size of about 1,000 pupils is reached. Hu and Yinger also show that all the impacts of consolidation on property values are weighted by house value. This theoretical prediction is upheld in their empirical work, which finds that consolidation has a strong positive impact on house values in census tracts with low average house values and a strong negative impact where average house value is high.

One final lesson from previous studies is that one must be careful to recognize that changes in property values over time may reflect both changes in the value people place on the school services they receive in each district and changes in household sorting across school districts (Figlio and Lucas, 2004, Bogin and Nguyen–Hoang, 2014, Nguyen-Hoang and Yinger, 2011). Households that strongly prefer the access to teachers they receive in a small district, for example, may leave a school district when it consolidates. As a result, changes in house values when a district consolidates reflect some combination of changes in the willingness to pay of people with the same income and preferences as those originally in the community and changes in the types of people who decide to move there. One way to estimate the impact of consolidation on housing prices is to use a sample of house sales over time to estimate a hedonic regression with house value as the dependent variable and with an indicator variable equal to one in districts where consolidation has occurred. The most obvious problem with this approach is that the decision to consolidate may be influenced by unobserved factors that also influence house value. Brasington (2004) addresses this problem using spatial statistics; Hu and Yinger (2008) use an instrumental variables procedure. An alternative approach to this endogeneity problem, which is used in this article, is to focus on the change in price for houses that sell twice. This difference-in-difference approach compares the change in housing prices in districts that consolidate between sales to the change in housing prices in districts that did not consolidate. As a result, all time-invariant factors that influence the decision to consolidate are differenced out. This approach does not account for time-varying factors that might influence consolidation, but, as discussed in detail by Duncombe and Yinger (2007), consolidation is a long process in New York State and short-run changes are unlikely to influence the consolidation decision.

A limitation of these studies is that the districts that consolidate and the houses they contain may be systematically different from other districts (and their houses). Under these circumstances, a comparison of house sales in treatment (i.e., consolidating) and control (non-consolidating) districts may yield biased results whenever the impact of consolidation depends on district or house traits. This problem can be addressed using a propensity score matching (PSM) estimator, which accounts for the possibility that the impact of consolidation depends on district and house characteristics. With this approach, the first step is to estimate a series of propensity score regressions, which predict the probability that a house sale with certain housing and district traits will be in a district that consolidates. When combined with a weighting scheme, each regression can then be used to select a comparison sample, that is, a set of observations in districts that did not consolidate that are otherwise equivalent to the observations in consolidating districts. Each comparison sample can then be examined with a series of balancing tests to determine whether the distributions of the explanatory variables are similar in "treatment" and "comparison" samples. If they are, then the possibility of bias from an interaction between "treatment" and explanatory variables is minimal. Details of our differencing and matching procedures are presented subsequently.

2. Data and Measures

The data used in this analysis come from two sources. Property sales information and housing characteristics were provided by the New York Office of Real Property Services (ORPS) in the New York State Department of Taxation and Finance (NYDTF). Data from 2000 to 2012 are available in the "Sales" database, which includes 10 years of parcel-level property sales information for the state.[1] Property transfer reports are filed with the County Clerk and forwarded to NYDTF. The Sales database includes information on property location, class, sales date, and sales price. We include in this analysis only arm's-length transactions of one- to three-unit family homes, constructed for year-round residence with a sales price greater than $10,000.

Information from the sales database was merged with the detailed parcel-level data included in the Real Property System (RPS) database. The RPS collects information from local assessors on a number of parcel characteristics. For this analysis, we use information on the characteristics of residential owner-occupied parcels in 2003. We selected 2003 for two reasons. First, two pairs of districts consolidated in 2004, so this base year gives us the pretreatment information we need to implement PSM. Second, we have complete parcel-level data for 2003. These data include measures of quality/condition, size, and the availability of special features for each house. Quality measures include an assessment of the overall physical condition of the residence (including interior and exterior walls, foundation, kitchen, baths, heating, plumbing, and electrical systems).[2] A second quality measure is an assessment of the construction grade of the house, which refers to the quality of the material and workmanship used to construct the house. Additional variables include the number of square feet of living area in a house, the number of bedrooms, and the number of full bathrooms.

---

[1]Information on the sales database is available from NYDTF online, Accessed 10 December 2013, http://www.tax.ny.gov/research/property/assess/sales/localoff.htm.

[2]More information on the house characteristics used in this analysis can be found in the Assessor's Manual produced by NYDTFe available online, Accessed 10 December 2013, http://www.tax.ny.gov/research/property/assess/manuals/assersmanual.htm.

Special housing features in the data set include whether the house has a full basement, central air conditioning, or a fireplace. Finally, the data set contains an estimate of the house age at the time of sale.[3]

We also collected information about the demographics and socioeconomic status of residents in the 2000 census tract of each house sale. Specifically, our data set includes measures of age, race and ethnicity, gender, poverty, income distribution, distribution of house values, educational attainment, enrollment in public schools, employment by industry and occupation, and unemployment. In short, we have housing sales information from 2000 to April 2012, along with housing characteristics data and census tract information before 2004 when the first consolidation in our data set occurred. We merge the three data sets together by assigning house characteristics in 2003 and census tract information in 2000 to the dual-sale houses we observe. We assume that the houses and neighborhoods in our sample have not experienced much change during the sample period — except for a common time trend and, in some cases, consolidation.

3. Method

Compared with traditional regression analysis, matching methods have two key advantages for our study. First, matching methods introduce some of the advantages of a randomized experiment into a study based on observational data. Second, matching methods reduce the sensitivity of results to model-based and inherently untestable assumptions (Stuart and Rubin, 2007). Matching methods and regression-based model adjustments are not mutually exclusive, however. In fact, many scholars argue that the best approach is often to combine the two methods by conducting regression adjustment on balanced samples (Heckman *et al.* 1997; Abadie and Imbens, 2006; Ho *et al.*, 2007). The logic behind this combined empirical strategy is that the matching methods make it possible to reduce large covariate bias between the treated and control groups, and the traditional regression methods can be used to adjust for any residual bias and to increase efficiency (Stuart and Rubin, 2007).

---

[3]Information on the RPS data comes from NYDTF available online, Accessed 10 December 2013, http://www.tax.ny.gov/research/property/assess/rps/index.htm.

3.1. *Selection Problems and Sample Selection*

Between 2000 and 2012, three sets of districts consolidated in New York State.[4] The three sets of districts include Canisteo Central School District (CSD; 921 students) annexing Greenwood CSD (429 students) in 2004, Eastport Unified School District (UFSD; 1,042 students) annexing South Manor UFSD (936 students) and Eastport-South Manor Central High School District (1,159 students) in 2004, and the North Colonie CSD (5,646 students) annexing the Maplewood Common School District (147 students) in 2008. These districts are geographically dispersed across the state (Albany County, Steuben County, and Suffolk County). The combined districts ranged in size (at the time of consolidation) from 1,250 to 5,793 students.

For three reasons, the sample of parcels in the consolidating districts included in this analysis is not likely to be representative of the rest of the state. First, since relatively few districts in New York consolidate, despite generous financial incentives from the state, districts that do consolidate are not likely to be typical even of small districts in the state. Brasington (1999) found that differences in the student population increased the probability of consolidation, while differences in property values per pupil decreased this probability. Gordon and Knight (2009) found that increasing heterogeneity in the share of adults with a college degree and in district spending are negatively associated with the decision to merge. Second, only a small subset of houses experienced two sales from 2000 to 2012, which implies that these houses may not be representative of houses in the state. Third, we limit our sample in consolidating districts to only those with a sale before and after consolidation. As a result, this study should be regarded as a case study about the impact on house values of three specific consolidations, not as a study about the impact of consolidation in general.

Another methodological challenge is that districts with certain unobserved housing or neighborhood traits may be more likely than others to consolidate. These types of unobservable factors might lead to biased estimates of the effects of consolidation on housing prices. To address this problem, we use dual sales data to estimate a difference-in-difference regression. This approach accounts for time-invariant unobservable factors, but does not rule out the possibility of bias from changes in unobserved traits that are correlated with consolidation.

---

[4]In all three cases, one district annexed the other district/districts, but voters in all districts approved. For more information on consolidation, see the NYSED (2013a).

In addition, we used PSM to select a comparison group that is as similar as possible to the treatment group in terms of observable characteristics. Several steps are involved in finding a comparison group with PSM.[5] First, a set of "confounding" variables need to be identified; these variables should be related to both the treatment (the decision to buy/sell a house in a consolidating district) and the dependent variable (property value change). We selected a set of housing characteristics and neighborhood characteristics that are likely to be related to housing prices. These variables include income, property values, racial heterogeneity among enrolled students, and parental educational attainment, which have been found to be related to district consolidation decisions.[6] Model selection was based on both improving the fit of the model and finding a sample that meets the common support criteria.[7] As part of the process of finding a balanced sample, we explored the use of squared and interaction terms. Table 1 describes the variables used in the final PSM regression model.

The results of the PSM logistic regression are reported in Table 2. Parcels in consolidating districts are more apt to be younger, to be in bad condition, to have a higher grade of construction material, to be larger in terms of square feet and the number of bedrooms and bathrooms, and to have central air-conditioning. These homes are less apt to have a full basement and a fireplace, on average. Among census tract variables, the percent of adults with a BA or higher, the share of the population is younger than twenty years old, and the share of owner-occupied houses have a nonlinear relationship with the probability of being in a consolidating district (an inverted U-shape). The child poverty rate and percent of adults in profession or managerial occupations are negatively related to consolidation, while the share of low value houses (less than $50,000) and the share of employment in government are negatively related.

---

[5]For more on PSM, see Guo and Fraser (2010); Steiner and Cook (2013); Heinrich *et al.* (2010); Caliendo and Kopeinig (2005); and Becker and Ichino (2002).

[6]We also estimate a propensity score model that includes local revenue effort (= local revenues divided by property value), since it may be related to the impacts of consolidation. This approach leads to a sample of 482 observations and to a significant impact estimate (−7.25 percent, significant at the 1 percent level), but this sample fails one key balancing test.

[7]See Heinrich *et al.* (2010) and Caliendo and Kopeinig (2008) for more on strategies for variable selection. Models with variables measuring differences between districts and their neighbors in demographics, fiscal capacity, and student need explained more than 90 percent of the probability that a parcel was in a consolidating district, but led to little overlap in propensity scores between treatment and comparison groups.

W.D. Duncombe, J. Yinger & P. Zhang

Table 1 Summary statistics for sales price difference and variables used in propensity score model.

Variables	Mean	Standard deviation	Minimum	Maximum
Difference in sales price adjusted for inflation	18,960.65	63,963.01	−7,820,259	2,858,065
2003 House characteristics				
Overall condition is good (yes-1)	0.004	0.062	0.000	1.000
Overall condition is poor (yes-1)	0.105	0.306	0.000	1.000
Grade A (yes-1)	0.004	0.060	0.000	1.000
Grade B (yes-1)	0.087	0.281	0.000	1.000
Full basement (yes-1)	0.727	0.445	0.000	1.000
Central air conditioning (yes-1)	0.187	0.391	0.000	8.000
Number of full bathrooms	1.403	0.590	0.000	11.000
Number of bedrooms	3.035	0.808	0.000	16.000
No fireplace (yes-1)	0.579	0.494	0.000	1.000
Age	48.721	36.103	0.000	312.000
Square feet	1,600.492	603.702	0.000	14,460.0
2000 Census tract variables				
Percent of adults with a BA or higher	28.615	14.380	4.600	91.600
Poverty rate for persons under 19	9.212	8.213	0.000	65.800
Percent of families with income below $20k	9.960	6.913	0.000	61.300
Percent of houses with value below $50k	6.224	10.580	0.000	82.500
Percent owner occupied house	74.745	14.730	3.200	98.300
Percent of employment in government	6.206	4.047	0.000	26.344
Percent of professional occupations	38.055	11.046	9.648	75.544
Percent of population under 20	13.026	2.329	0.100	36.700
Percent of white in enrolled students	93.132	7.311	15.043	100.000
Number of observations	64,483			

Source: New York State Department of Taxation and Finance, *Online Sales Report* and *Real Property System* database; U.S. Bureau of the Census, 2000 *Census of Population and Housing*. Data on house characteristics from the RPS was available for 2003.

Table 2   Logistic regression results for propensity score model.

Variables	Coefficient	Standard error	p value
House characteristics			
Overall condition is good (yes-1)	−2.0129	0.4917	0.0000
Overall condition is poor (yes-1)	0.6523	1.0486	0.5340
Grade A (yes-1)	0.3793	1.3389	0.7770
Grade B (yes-1)	0.9324	0.2641	0.0000
Full basement (yes-1)	−0.3046	0.1463	0.0370
Central air conditioning (yes-1)	0.4895	0.1561	0.0020
Number of full bathrooms	0.0896	0.1366	0.5120
Number of bedrooms	0.0875	0.1019	0.3900
No fireplace (yes-1)	0.4351	0.1505	0.0040
Age	−0.0065	0.0027	0.0160
Square feet	0.0007	0.0003	0.0170
Square feet squared	0.0000	0.0000	0.1420
2000 Census tract variables			
Percent of adults with a BA or higher	0.7135	0.0498	0.0000
Percent of adults with a BA or higher squared	−0.0066	0.0006	0.0000
Poverty rate for persons under 19	−0.2349	0.0287	0.0000
Percent of families with income below $20k	0.0020	0.0305	0.9470
Percent of houses with value below $50k	0.1403	0.0109	0.0000
Percent owner occupied house	0.3990	0.0581	0.0000
Percent owner occupied house squared	−0.0031	0.0004	0.0000
Percent of employment in government	0.2899	0.0144	0.0000
Percent professional occupations	−0.3091	0.0212	0.0000
Percent of population under 20	2.5835	0.4417	0.0000
Percent of population under 20 squared	−0.1220	0.0193	0.0000
Percent of white in enrolled students	−0.0505	0.0216	0.0190
Constant	−31.9117	3.3604	0.0000
Number of observations	64,483		
Pseudo R^2	0.4373		
Likelihood ratio (x^2)	1,637.75		

Note: Dependent variable is whether district consolidated or not between 2000 and 2012.

The PSM model was then used to develop propensity scores for a parcel being in a consolidating district. We first limit the sample to the area of common support by removing observations outside the region where the propensity scores of treatment and control observations overlap. This step reduced the number of dual sales by 10 percent in consolidating districts and by 5.8 percent in non-consolidating districts. With this trimmed sample, we identified comparison groups using several matching strategies.[8]

---

[8]We conduct the matching using the STATA program "psmatch2" developed by Leuven and Sianesi (2003) and explained by Guo and Fraser (2010).

We focus on the results from a one-to-one nearest neighbor match without replacement because it best meets the balancing tests.[9] The matches are limited to a caliper around the propensity score for the treatment group member.[10] The result is a sample of 271 treatment and 271 comparison parcels.[11] Interestingly, more than half of the houses in this sample represent repeat sales in the consolidating districts in Albany or their matching partners in other areas. The unequal distribution of the sample reinforces the conclusion that our study cannot be interpreted as a general treatment of the impact of consolidation. We return to this issue when discussing our results.

The final step in developing a matching sample is checking the balance between the treatment and comparison parcels. The simplest approach is to compare mean values for each variable in the two groups. If the matched sample is balanced, we should not see any statistically significant differences in the variables in the propensity score model or in the propensity score. As indicated in Table 3, this is the case for this matched sample. It is also important to check whether the difference between treatment and comparison group values (bias) is below some acceptable level. A simple test is to compare the standardized bias (difference in means divided by standard deviation of the respective X variable). One standard that is used is that this bias should be below 0.25 (a quarter of a standard deviation).[12] As indicated in Table 3, none of the confounding variables or the propensity

---

[9]We also tried one-to-one nearest neighbor matching with replacement, which resulted in a reduction of 40 observations. The new sample passed the standardized bias test but not the t-test; results based on it indicate that consolidation, on average, lowered housing price by 2.98 percent (significant at 6.3 percent level) — a result that is similar to the one in Table 4.

[10]Guo and Fraser (2010) recommend using a caliper of 0.25 standard deviations for the log of the odds ratio from the logistic regression ($\log(P/1 - P)$, where P is the propensity score). We set a tougher standard by limiting matches to within 0.15 standard deviations.

[11]We deleted a few (thirteen observations) outliers because they experienced large changes in housing traits. For example, some of them installed central air-conditioning system during the time between the first sale and the second sale; some expanded the square feet of living area; and some "unreasonably" experienced more than a 50 percent price change within one month.

[12]See Ho *et al.* (2007) and Stuart and Rubin (2008) for a discussion of this approach. Ho *et al.* (2007) are critical of using hypothesis testing to check balance and prefer quantile-quantile (QQ) plots. This alternative test could be attempted in future research.

Table 3 Test for balance of sample 1 (one-to-one nearest neighbor match).

	Full sample				Sample 1			
	Mean in districts			Standard	Mean in districts			Standard
	Consolidation	No consolidation	t-test (p value)	mean difference	Consolidation	No consolidation	t-test (p value)	mean difference
2003 House characteristics								
Overall condition good (yes-1)	0.018	0.093	0.000	−0.2580	0.018	0.044	0.085	−0.1486
Overall condition poor (yes-1)	0.004	0.004	0.953	−0.0036	0.004	0.000	0.318	0.0861
Grade A (yes-1)	0.004	0.003	0.915	0.0065	0.004	0.000	0.318	0.0861
Grade B (yes-1)	0.062	0.085	0.167	−0.0834	0.063	0.077	0.502	−0.0578
Full basement (yes-1)	0.703	0.722	0.471	−0.0435	0.712	0.779	0.076	−0.1529
Central air conditioning (yes-1)	0.355	0.191	0.000	0.4161	0.362	0.354	0.858	0.0154
Number of full bathrooms	1.471	1.402	0.052	0.1174	1.480	1.483	0.951	−0.0053
Number of bedrooms	3.083	3.043	0.393	0.0515	3.092	3.037	0.408	0.0713
No fireplace (yes-1)	0.601	0.576	0.385	0.0524	0.598	0.550	0.260	0.0971
Age	43.562	48.173	0.032	−0.1294	43.288	44.487	0.609	−0.0440
Square feet	1,657.300	1,600.000	0.113	0.0955	1,659.200	1,703.300	0.438	−0.0668
Square feet squared (000)	3,200	2,900	0.156	0.0856	3,200	3,300	0.520	−0.0555
2000 Census tract variables								
% adults with BA or higher	36.256	28.547	0.000	0.5877	36.646	36.028	0.464	0.0631
% adults with BA or higher sq.	1412.800	987.060	0.000	0.4767	1434.600	1398.700	0.547	0.0518
Pov. rate for persons under 19	4.144	8.292	0.000	−0.6239	3.912	4.103	0.653	−0.0387
% families with income <$20k	6.631	9.314	0.000	−0.4629	6.390	6.300	0.821	0.0195
% houses with value <$50k	4.557	5.991	0.021	−0.1391	3.743	5.699	0.074	−0.1543
% owner occupied houses	71.612	75.707	0.000	−0.3202	71.515	72.968	0.201	−0.1102
% owner occupied houses sq.	5,281.200	5,895.200	0.000	−0.3389	5,269.600	5,516.800	0.128	−0.1312
% of employment in government	14.934	6.332	0.000	2.1088	15.098	15.834	0.102	−0.1408
% professional occupations	43.395	38.120	0.000	0.5145	43.668	43.441	0.762	0.0261
% population under 20	11.468	12.830	0.000	−0.6741	11.435	11.555	0.302	−0.0889
% population under 20 sq.	133.430	168.680	0.000	−0.6984	132.630	135.300	0.324	−0.0850
% white in enrolled students	92.245	93.858	0.000	−0.2918	92.124	92.426	0.358	−0.0791
Propensity score	0.164	0.004	0.000	5.9403	0.1667	0.16727	0.9600	−0.0043
Number of observations	276	57,768			271	271		

Note: The full sample was limited to the area of common support before the matching was done. Sample 1 is based on 1: 1 nearest neighbor matching within a caliper set at 0.15 standard deviation of the log of the odds ratio. Sampling is done without replacement.

score have a standardized bias above 0.25. So our matched sample passed this test, as well.[13]

3.2. *Regression Models*

To estimate the impact of consolidation on housing prices, we must first decide on the best way to set the date of a particular consolidation. For most districts, three official dates are associated with consolidation: (1) the date of the advisory referendum or filing of petitions, (2) the date of the official referendum on reorganization in each consolidating district, and (3) the actual date of consolidation. While advisory votes are common, they do not take place in all cases of consolidation and their results are non-binding. Instead, we think that the date of the official referendum or the start of the first school year in the consolidated districts are likely to frame the time when home owners of the district become aware that reorganization is taking place. However, for the three consolidating districts in this article, we find big time difference between these two dates ranging from six to eight months. Due to the time gap, we decided to use the date of the official referendum on reorganization as the start of consolidation.[14]

With a well-matched sample, it is possible to determine the average effect of the treatment on the treated (ATT) by comparing the means of the treatment and comparison groups. Since our impact measure is the change in house sale price before and after consolidation, this would be equivalent to

---

[13]Another test suggested by Sianesi (2004) and Caliendo and Kopeinig (2008) is to determine whether the pseudo-R^2 and likelihood ratio χ^2 statistic for the propensity score regression are significantly smaller for the matched sample than for the sample as a whole. We implemented this test using the Stata "pstest" program of Leuven and Sianesi (2003). Compared to the full sample, the pseudo-R^2 for the matched sample decreases from 0.419 to 0.068 and the likelihood ratio χ^2 declines from 1,466.9 to 51 but is still significant. The matched sample also passes this test with 1:5 nearest-neighbor matching and kernel matching but not with Mahalanobis matching. Because these results are ambiguous and this test has no obvious advantages over others, we rely on the balancing tests presented in the text.

[14]We prefer the date of the official referendum as the consolidation date for two reasons. First, residents are likely to know about the reorganization plan by the date of the referendum. Second, if we use the start of the first school year after consolidation, house sales during the time gap will become first sales instead of second sales, thereby reducing our sample size and potentially introducing measurement error. Nevertheless, changing the start date to the beginning of the first academic year for the consolidation (July 1) serves as a robustness check. With this change, our sample has forty-seven fewer observations but the results are similar; for example, consolidation decreases housing prices by 3.6 percent, on average (significant at the 4.5 percent level).

a difference-in-difference method (Guo and Fraser, 2010; Heinrich, Maffioli, and Vazquez, 2010). While this approach has the potential to control for time-invariant unobservable differences across treatment and comparison, this comparison has some limitations in our case. Under the classic difference-in-difference comparison, the treatment is applied at the same time to all treatment group members and the pre- and post-observations are made at the same time. Neither of these conditions is met in this study. Not all the districts consolidated at the same time, and very few of the house sales in our sample occurred on the same day.

To account for these timing differences, we developed a regression model for the matched sample. The dependent variable is the change in the log of house value. We calculated the months between the first sale and the starting date in our sample (1 January 2000), and between the second sale and the starting date. One control variable is the difference in months between these two measures (D) and a second is the difference in the squares of these two measures (D^2). If t_2 represents the time for the second sale, t_1 the time for the first sale, and t_0 represents the starting date (1 January 2000), then these measures can be represented as

$$D = (t_2 - t_0) - (t_1 - t_0) = (t_2 - t_1)$$
$$D^2 = (t_2 - t_0)^2 - (t_1 - t_0)^2. \tag{1}$$

The second measure captures not only the time difference between the first and second sales but also where these sales fall relative to the beginning of the decade. Given recent changes in the housing market, it is important to control for the point in the decade when the sales occur.

Because the effects of consolidation on property values may take time to emerge, we also need to account for where the second sale occurred relative to date of consolidation. We devised measures similar to those in equation (1) to capture the difference in months between the second sale and the date of consolidation (M) and the square of this measure (M^2). If t_c represents the date of consolidation, then these measures can be represented as

$$M = (t_2\_t_0) - (t_c - t_0) = (t_2 - t_c)$$
$$M^2 = (t_2 - t_c)^2. \tag{2}$$

As discussed earlier, Hu and Yinger (2008) found that the impact of consolidation varies across districts and census tracts. Specifically, they found that the positive effects of consolidation on property values decline with enrollment and that the impact is the highest in low-property-value tracts. Given that the North Colonie CSD in Albany has substantially greater pre-consolidation enrollment than all other six consolidating school districts, we hypothesize that the impact of consolidation on property values is smaller in this district than elsewhere. To test this hypothesis, we interact the dichotomous variable for whether the district has consolidated (C) with a dummy variable for the large North Colonie CSD (L). We also test the Hu/Yinger finding that the property value impact of consolidation is smaller in wealthier census tracts by interacting C with the average income in the census tract (I). In both cases, interactions with M and M^2 are included in the specification, as well. The two major models for the change in the log of property values (DV) can be represented as

$$DV = \alpha_0 + \alpha_1 D + \alpha_2 D^2 + \alpha_3 C + \alpha_4 M + \alpha_5 M^2 + \alpha_6 (CL)$$
$$+ \alpha_7 (ML) + \alpha_8 (M^2 L)$$
$$DV = \beta_0 + \beta_1 D + \beta_2 D^2 + \beta_3 C + \beta_4 M + \beta_5 M^2 + \beta_6 (CI)$$
$$+ \beta_7 (MI) + \beta_8 (M^2 I). \tag{3}$$

We also estimate models with both interaction sets to see if these two effects can be separated.

4. Impact Estimates

Table 4 presents impact estimates with several different specifications. Model 1 just includes the consolidation dummy (C) and the measures capturing the months between first and second sale (D and D^2). The coefficient of this dummy is negative and significant at the 9.5 percent level. It indicates that, on average, consolidation lowers house values by about 2.6 percent during our sample period. (The change in the log of house value is approximately equal to a percentage change.) The results for model 2 indicate that this change is not constant over time. Although the coefficients of the two timing variables, M and M^2, are not statistically significant, their magnitudes suggest that house values decline in the years right after consolidation, but then start to increase after about two and a half years. By around five years (sixty-one months) after consolidation, house values have returned to their initial values and then increase beyond that point. These results are illustrated by the solid line in panel A of Figure 1.

Model 3 adds interactions between C, D, and D^2 and a dummy for the North Colonie CSD.[15] Although the first interaction term is only

---

[15] A model containing interactions with district enrollment leads to similar results.

Table 4 Regression for percentage change in sales price after consolidation (based on comparison group selected with a one-to-one nearest neighbor match).

Policy-related variable	Model 1	Model 2	Model 3[a]	Model 4[b]
Consolidation	−0.0256	0.0049	0.1209	−0.0106
	(0.095)	(0.875)	(0.152)	(0.704)
Months since consolidation		−0.0028	−0.0249	−0.0011
		(0.359)	(0.003)	(0.627)
Months since consolidation squared		4.59E-05	0.0004	5.49E-06
		(0.465)	(0.003)	(0.895)
Large school district-consolidation			−0.1464	
interaction			(0.095)	
Large school district-months since			0.0265	
consolidation interaction			(0.002)	
Large school district-months since			−0.0004	
consolidation interaction square			(0.002)	
Income-consolidation interaction				−0.1378
				(0.236)
Income-months since consolidation				0.0254
interaction				(0.013)
Income-months since consolidation				−0.0005
interaction squared				(0.004)
R^2	0.4318	0.4333	0.4586	0.4489

Notes: Dependent variable is change in log of sales price. Sample size is 529. Estimated with ordinary least squares (OLS) regression with robust standard errors. Significance levels are in parentheses. All regression models include as control variables the propensity score, the difference in months between first and second sale, and the difference in months between first and second sales squared.
[a]The large school district indicates the North Colonie CSD in Albany, which has 5,464 students before consolidation, much larger than 772 students, the average pre-consolidation enrollment level of all other school districts in our sample. The coefficients of three interaction terms for that large school district are −0.0256, 0.0016, and −0.0000, respectively; none of them is significant.
[b]The income variable is demeaned in order to make the results of model 4 comparable to those of other models.

significant at the 9.5 percent level, the other two terms (and the three terms taken together) are highly significant. Moreover, the introduction of these interaction terms leads to significant coefficients for two of the three original variables and for the set (the first three rows). Indeed, as shown by the dotted line in panel A of Figure 1, consolidation has a striking effect on house values in the six districts other than North Colonie. The initial impact of consolidation is positive (12.1 percent) but not statistically significant. From that point on, however, the pattern in model 2 arises, but in much stronger

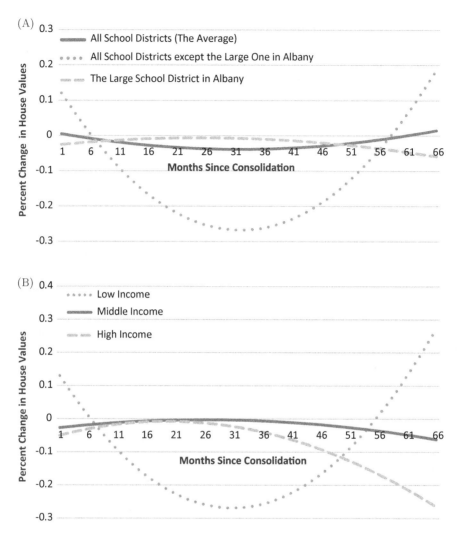

Figure 1   Change in property values after consolidation. Panel A: By school district size. Panel B: By census tract income (adjusted model 4).

form. The estimated net effect of consolidation on house values in the six districts equals zero after about six months and then becomes negative and significant, reaching −26.8 percent after thirty-one months. At this point, the impact turns around, gets back to zero in fifty-seven months, and then becomes positive. At the largest post-consolidation period observed in the data, sixty-five months, the impact of consolidation is positive, as in Hu and Yinger (2008), but this impact, 18.7 percent, is not quite significant. In short, consolidation leads to a significant decline in house values for the first two and half years, but this decline is then reversed and disappears by five years after consolidation takes place.

We believe that these results probably reflect two effects. First, people may be skeptical about consolidation, but then come to appreciate its cost savings and the broader sets of high school courses that tend to accompany it. Second, people who dislike consolidation may leave consolidating districts and be replaced by people who prefer it or who are willing to pay more to get it. We look for signs of sorting in the form of changes in the composition of local residents in consolidating districts, but substantial differences in demographic and economic characteristics across consolidating and non-consolidating areas have not appeared recently. One plausible explanation is that it may take a while for sorting to be noticeable.[16] These effects do not arise in North Colonie because the consolidation we observe there represents a small change in district enrollment and because North Colonie was already so large before consolidation that further cost savings from economies of scale probably were not possible.

Model 4 in Table 4 adds interactions between initial tract average household income and the three consolidation variables in model 2. Two of these interaction terms (and the three together) are statistically significant. The resulting pattern, illustrated in panel B of Figure 1, shows that the impact of consolidation over time is heavily influenced by tract income. Indeed, the solid line in panel A of Figure 1 is magnified in low-income tracts, moderated in middle-income tracts, and reversed in high-income tracts. In the case of low-income tracts, the decline in house values at thirty months for low-income tracts, −26.9 percent, and the increase in house values at sixty-five months, 27.5 percent, are both statistically significant. Moreover, the decline in house values at sixty-five months in high-income tracts, 26.4 percent, is significant, as well. Changes in house values over time are not significant in middle-income tracts.

These income results are consistent with the findings of earlier studies but add a time path. As in Hu and Yinger, the ultimate impact of consolidation

---

[16]We test for sorting by examining whether the composition of residents in consolidating districts has changed, compared with both non-consolidating districts during the same time and consolidating districts in earlier periods. We find more adults with a bachelor's degree or higher, fewer families with an income less than $20,000, a lower poverty rate for persons younger than nineteen, and a bigger percentage of owner-occupied houses in consolidating areas in 2006 to 2010 American Community Survey (ACS) data than in the 2000 census data. But significant differences in census traits are not found across consolidating and non-consolidating districts in the 2006 to 2010 ACS data set.

is to raise house values in low-income tracts and to lower house values in high-income tracts. We also find, however, that the impact of consolidation on house values in low-income tracts is negative at first and only becomes positive after about five years. Moreover, the impact in high-income tracts is minimal at first but eventually becomes significantly negative. As discussed earlier, these patterns reflect some combination of changing views about consolidation as it is experienced and changes in the type of households living in consolidated districts. One possibility is that people in low-income tracts are particularly skeptical about consolidation at first but then come to appreciate its costs savings, whereas high-income people do not expect much from consolidation but eventually become discouraged by the loss of contact with teachers or by some other change that accompanies it. These finding also could reflect changes in the types of people who move into a district once it has consolidated.

We also estimated models that included interactions with both the dummy for North Colonie and initial tract income. Because North Colonie has a relatively high income, however, we were unable to separate these two sets of interactions. In other words, none of the interaction terms is significant in this specification. Thus, we cannot determine whether our results reflect variation in enrollment, variation in initial income, or some combination of the two. Additional research with larger data sets is needed to separate the impacts of these two factors.

5. Robustness Checks

We also examine the sensitivity of our results to differences in the sample, estimation method, and matching algorithm.[17,18] Tables 5 and 6 compare

---

[17] A reviewer suggested that a weighted repeat sales index might be inappropriate when it is based on a small sample size. Given that we just have 529 observations in the balanced sample, we conduct a robustness check based on housing price per square foot. The average house area is 1,669 square feet, and school district consolidation decreases housing price per square foot by $1.68 or by $2,803 (=(1.68)*(1669)) overall. This is consistent with results based on price alone.

[18] A reviewer also suggested that our results might be biased by the inclusion of real estate-owned (REO) properties and foreclosure sales. A decline in price for these houses cannot be simply attributed to a change in the demographics of their community or to residents' perceptions about consolidation. We find that only six houses (1.13 percent of our sample) are in the category "conditional government sale" in which distressed sales are likely to fall. After eliminating these six cases, the consolidation coefficient becomes -0.029 (p-value $= 0.056$), suggesting that houses in this category have little impact on our results.

Table 5   Estimated impacts of consolidation on sales prices with different methodologies.

	1:1 NN matching	1:1 NN matching (neighboring counties)	Propensity score weighted regression on full sample	1:5 NN matching
Panel A: Model 1				
Policy-related variables	Model 1	Model 1	Model 1	Model 1
Consolidation dummy variable	−0.0256 (0.095)	−0.0342 (0.025)	−0.0300 (0.022)	−0.0174 (0.193)
R^2	0.4318	0.4622	0.3075	0.3503
Panel B: Model 2				
Policy-related variables	Model 2	Model 2	Model 2	Model 2
Consolidation dummy variable	−0.0106 (0.704)	−0.0192 (0.488)	−0.0065 (0.839)	0.0034 (0.905)
Months since consolidation	−0.0011 (0.627)	−0.0007 (0.757)	−0.0021 (0.404)	−0.0023 (0.309)
Months since consolidation squared	5.49E-06 (0.895)	−5.05E-06 (0.903)	2.10E-05 (0.627)	3.14E-05 (0.444)
Income-consolidation interaction	−0.1378 (0.236)	−0.1485 (0.204)	−0.2017 (0.100)	−0.1566 (0.163)
Income-months since consolidation interaction	0.0254 (0.013)	0.0257 (0.012)	0.0284 (0.004)	0.0283 (0.003)
Income-months since consolidation interaction squared	−0.0005 (0.004)	−0.0005 (0.004)	−0.0006 (0.000)	−0.0006 (0.000)
R^2	0.4489	0.4817	0.3255	0.3637

Note: Significance levels are in parentheses. NN stands for "nearest neighbor."

estimation results based on our main strategy and three alternatives.[19] We first check whether the results change significantly if we confine the comparison group to the county in which the consolidation occurred or to

---

[19] Following Dinardo (2002), we also calculate both average treatment effects (ATE) and average treatment effects on the treated (ATT) on the full sample; the estimated effects of consolidation are −4.1 percent and −6.5 percent, respectively. Since this approach is sensitive to extreme low or high values of the propensity score (PS), we also estimate our model after deleting observations with a PS below 0.1 or above 0.9. The estimated effects are −7.9 percent and −6.5 percent. These results are consistent with those in the text, but assume, incorrectly in our case, that all consolidations happen at the same time.

Table 6 Distribution of predicted change in sales price after consolidation (results for model 4 with a different sample, weighting method, and matching algorithm).

Distribution	1:1 NN matching model (percentage)	1:1 NN matching (neighboring counties) model 4 (percentage)	Propensity score weighted regression on full sample model 4 (percentage)	1:5 NN matching model 4 (percentage)
Mean	−3.11	−4.18	−3.80	−2.04
5th	−7.34	−8.82	−9.67	−6.91
10th	−6.40	−7.85	−7.52	−5.40
25th	−5.12	−6.28	−5.83	−4.28
Median	−3.53	−4.53	−4.08	−2.83
75th	−1.92	−2.82	−2.65	−1.17
90th	1.35	0.16	−0.83	−2.94
95th	3.73	2.39	1.78	6.32

Note: Predicted percentage change in the sales price between the second and first sale in consolidating districts minus what it would have predicted without consolidation. This accounts for time between the second sale and date of consolidation.

that county's neighbors. The comparison group for the two consolidated school districts in Albany, North Colonie CSD and Maplewood CSD, for example, consists of houses that have sold twice between 2000 and 2012 in Albany, Columbia, Greene, Montgomery, Rensselaer, Saratoga, Schenectady, and Schoharie Counties. By restricting the sample to neighboring regions, we eliminate potential biases from unobserved factors that vary across regions of the state.

The second alternative is to include propensity scores as weights in a weighted regression model (Steiner and Cook, 2013; Guo and Fraser, 2010). The advantage of this approach is that we are able to use all treatment and comparison observations in the area of common support. The disadvantage is that results can be sensitive to outliers (i.e., propensity scores close to zero). Finally, because impact estimates with PSM can also be sensitive to the matching algorithm, we also looked at several other matching strategies, and some of them passed balancing tests. In the sample selected by one to five nearest neighbor matching, for example, none of the variables is significantly different between the treatment group and the control groups.[20]

---

[20]The five closest comparison group observations within the caliper (0.15 standard deviations) are matched with each treatment group member. The final sample was 764 comparison group members and 271 treatment group members. This matching was done with replacement using the "psmatch2" Stata program developed by Leuven and Sianesi (2003).

Panel A of Table 5 indicates that model 1, with just one consolidation variable, yields similar results for all four methods. The range in estimated coefficients is -0.0174 to -0.0342 and two of the estimates are significant at the 5 percent level. Panel B makes the same comparisons based on model 4 in Table 4. The magnitudes and significance of the variables are similar across the four columns of this panel.

As a final check, we looked at the distribution of predicted sales prices changes from model 4 using these different methodologies. As shown in Table 6, the results are quite similar. The median predicted house value change, for example, ranges from -2.83 percent (the fourth column) to -4.53 percent (the second column).

6. Conclusion

This article explores the impact of school district consolidation on house values using a sample of house sales in New York State from 2000 to 2012. During this period, three sets of districts consolidated. We use PSM to identify house sales that are comparable to the sales in these districts and then use double-sales data to compare house value changes in consolidating and comparable districts.

We find that, on average, consolidation has a small negative impact on house values, at least outside of districts that are relatively large before consolidation. This average impact reflects a downward trend in house values right after consolidation combined with a positive trend starting two and a half years later. After five years, house values have returned to their pre-consolidation level and then begin to rise above house values in comparable districts. These results suggest that it takes a while either for the advantages of consolidation to be apparent or for the people who prefer consolidated districts to move in. Finally, the long-run impacts of consolidation on house values are positive in low-income tracts, but negative in high-income census tracts, where parents may have a relatively large willingness to pay for the access to teachers and other non-budgetary advantages of small districts.

Our results reveal a clear time pattern of consolidation-induced changes in house values. This pattern appears to reflect some combination of learning about the consequences of consolidation and differences in the preference of households who move into districts before and after they consolidate. With the data available to us, however, we cannot test these hypotheses about the pattern of house value effects or separate the impact on this pattern of initial district enrollment and of initial neighborhood income. These are topics for future research.

Authors' Note

William Duncombe passed away in May 2013; he was a full partner in preparing previous drafts of this article. We are grateful for helpful comments from Jim Follain, Amy Ellen Schwartz, Leanna Stiefel, participants in a session at the Association for Education Finance and Policy annual conference in March 2012, participants in a session at the Association for Budgeting and Financial Management annual conference in October 2012, participants in the Maxwell Research Symposium ("Housing Issues in the 21st Century") at Syracuse University in September 2012, and an anonymous referee.

Declaration of Conflicting Interests

The author(s) declared no potential conflicts of interest with respect to the research, authorship, and/or publication of this article.

Funding

The author(s) received no financial support for the research, authorship, and/or publication of this article.

References

Abadie, Alberto and Guido Imbens. 2006. Large sample properties of matching estimators for average treatment effects. *Econometrica* **74**: 235–67.

Andrews, Matthew, William D. Duncombe, and John Yinger. 2002. Revisiting economies of size in American education: are we any closer to a consensus? *Economics of Education Review* **21**: 245–62.

Barker, R. G. and P. V. Gump. 1964. *Big School, Small School: High School Size and Student Behavior*. Stanford, CA: Stanford University Press.

Becker, Sascha O. and Andrea Ichino. 2002. Estimation of average treatment effects based on propensity scores. *The Stata Journal* **2**: 358–377.

Bogin, Alexander and Phuong Nguyen-Hoang. 2014. Property left behind: An unintended Consequence of a No Child Left Behind "Falling" school designation. *Journal of Regional Science* **54**(5)(November): 788–805.

Brasington, David M. 1999. Joint provision of public goods: the consolidation of school districts. *Journal of Public Economics* **73**: 373–93.

Brasington, David M. 2003. Size and school district consolidation: do opposites attract? *Economica* **70**: 673–90.

Brasington, David M. 2004. House prices and the structure of local government: an application of spatial statistics. *Journal of Real Estate Finance and Economics* **29**: 211–31.

Caliendo, Marco and Sabine Kopeinig. 2008. Some practical guidance for the implementation of propensity score matching. *Journal of Economic Surveys* **22**(1) (February): 31–72.

Cotton, Kathleen. 1996. Affective and social benefits of small-scale schooling. *Eric Digest* No. ED401088. www.ericdigests.org/1997-2/small.htm. Accessed on December 11, 2013.

Dinardo, John. 2002. Propensity score reweighting and changes in wage distributions. Unpublished Paper. http://www-personal.umich.edu/~jdinardo/bztalk5.pdf. Accessed on January 31, 2013.

Duncombe, William D. and John Yinger. 2007. Does school district consolidation cut costs? *Education Finance and Policy* **2**: 341–375. [Chapter 18]

Figlio, David N. and Maurice E. Lucas. 2004. What's in a grade? School report cards and the housing market. *American Economic Review* **94**: 591–604.

Gordon, Nora and Brian Knight. 2009. A spatial merger estimator with an application to school district consolidation. *Journal of Public Economics* **93**: 752–765.

Guo, Shenyang and Mark Fraser. 2010. *Propensity Score Analysis: Statistical Methods and Applications.* Thousand Oaks, CA: Sage.

Haller, Emil J. and David H. Monk. 1988. New reforms, old reforms, and the consolidation of small rural schools. *Educational Administration Quarterly* **24**: 470–483.

Heckman, James, Hidehiko Ichimura and Petra Todd. 1997. Matching as an econometric evaluation estimator: evidence from evaluating a job training programme. *Review of Economic Studies* **64**: 605–654.

Heinrich, Carolyn, Alessandro Maffioli and Gonzalo Vazquez. 2010. A primer for applying propensity–score matching. Technical Notes No. IDB–TN–161, InterAmerican Development Bank.

Ho, Daniel E., Kosuke Imai, Gary King and Elizabeth A. Stuart. 2007. Matching as nonparametric preprocessing for reducing model dependence in parametric causal inference. *Political Analysis* **15**: 199–236.

Hu, Yue and John Yinger. 2008. The impact of school district consolidation on housing prices. *National Tax Journal* **61**: 609–634.

Huang, Yao. 2004. Appendix B: a guide to state operating aid programs for elementary and secondary education. In John Yinger (ed.), *Helping Children Left Behind: State Aid and the Pursuit of Educational Equity*, 331–352. Cambridge, MA: MIT Press.

Kenny, Lawrence. 1982. Economies of scale in schooling. *Economics of Education Review* **2**: 1–24.

Leuven, Edwin, and Barbara Sianesi. 2003. PSMATCH2: stata module to perform full mahalanobis and propensity score matching, common support graphing, and covariate imbalance testing. http://ideas.repec.org/c/boc/bocode/s432001.html. Accessed on January 31, 2013.

NCES (National Center for Education Statistics). 2001. *Public School Finance Programs of the United States and Canada: 1998–99.* Washington, DC: U.S. Department of Education, NCES.

NCES (National Center for Education Statistics). 2006. *Digest of Education Statistics, 2005.* http://www.nces.ed.gov/programs/digest/d05/tables_2.asp. Accessed on January 31, 2013.

NCES (National Center for Education Statistics). 2011. *Numbers and Types of Public Elementary and Secondary Local Education Agencies from the Common Core of Data: School Year 2009–10.* Washington, DC: U.S. Department of Education, NCES.

Nguyen–Hoang, Phuong and John Yinger. 2011. The capitalization of school quality into house values: a review. *Journal of Housing Economics* **20**: 30–48. [Chapter 15]

NYSED (New York State Education Department). 2013a. *Guide to the Reorganization of School Districts in New York State.* http://www.p12.nysed.gov/mgtserv/sch_dist_org/GuideToReorganizationOfSchool-Districts.htm. Accessed on February 19, 2014.

NYSED (New York State Education Department). 2013b. *Reorganization Incentive Aid Chart, 07/2013.* https://stateaid.nysed.gov/build/xls_docs/ReorgIncVal.xls. Accessed on December 1, 2013.

Sianesi, Barbara. 2004. An evaluation of the swedish system of active labor market programs in the 1990s. *The Review of Economics and Statistics* **86**: 133–55.

Steiner, Peter and David Cook. 2013. Matching and propensity scores. In Todd D. Little (ed.), The *Oxford Handbook of Quantitative Methods*, Vol. 1, New York, NY: Oxford University Press.

Stuart, Elizabeth A. and Donald B. Rubin. 2007. Best practices in quasiexperimental designs: matching methods for causal inference. In Jason Osborne (ed.), *Best Practices in Quantitative Social Science*, pp. 155–176. Thousand Oaks, CA: Sage.

Stuart, Elizabeth A. and Donald B. Rubin. 2008. Matching with multiple control groups and adjusting for group differences. *Journal of Educational and Behavioral Statistics* **33**: 279–306.

Part 8

School Infrastructure

Chapter 20

School District Responses to Matching Aid Programs for Capital Facilities: A Case Study of New York's Building Aid Program[*]

Wen Wang[‡], William Duncombe[‡] and John Yinger[†,§]

[†]*Departments of Public Administration and International Affairs and of Economics, Syracuse University, Syracuse, NY*

[§]*jyinger@maxwell.syr.edu*

States are financing a larger share of capital investment by school districts but little is known about how districts respond to facility aid programs. Our paper addresses this gap in the literature by examining how a short-term increase in the matching rate for the Building Aid program in New York affected district capital investment decisions. We estimate a capital investment model and find that most districts are responsive to price incentives but that price responsiveness is related to the fiscal health and urban location of the district. Drawing on these results, we provide recommendations for the design of capital investment aid programs to increase their effectiveness in supporting high-need urban districts.

1. Introduction

Public school enrollment in grades pre-K through 12 increased by 25 percent from 1985–2008 (National Center for Education Statistics (NCES), 2010). This enrollment growth combined with class-size reduction programs has led to large and growing school facility needs (U.S. Government Accountability Office (GAO), 1995; Crampton and Thompson, 2001). Indeed, NCES (2000)

---

[*]This chapter is reproduced from School district responses to matching aid programs for capital facilities: a case study of New York's building aid program, *National Tax Journal*, **64**(3) September 2011, pp. 759–794.
[‡]Deceased.

estimated that $127 billion is needed for school construction and renovation. Despite this need, state governments provide considerably less financial support to school districts for capital investment than for school operating expenses (Sielke, 2001; Wang and Duncombe, 2009), and in many states the quality of school facilities varies widely across districts (GAO, 1995). School spending grew rapidly over the 1995–2004 decade (Filardo *et al.*, 2006), but the scale and scope of facility needs are so large that more funding for school construction and renovation is still needed. Moreover, the disparity in school facility spending documented by GAO in 1995 has not yet been alleviated. This paper adds to the debate on revising state funding for school facilities by developing a model of school districts' capital investment decisions and using it to estimate districts' responses to an open-ended matching grant for school facilities in New York state.

New York is a particularly appropriate location for this type of analysis for several reasons. First, the Building Aid program is an open-ended matching grant, which provides an opportunity to examine districts' investment responses to tax price changes. Moreover, New York increased the matching rate by 10 percentage points in 1 July 1998, and then removed this increase after 1 July 2000. These policy changes provide an additional source of variation to help identify districts' responses to tax price changes. Third, the design of this aid program has remained relatively stable for three decades which makes it easier to isolate school district price responses from program changes. Finally, the availability of a long time-series of capital investment information in New York (1977–2008) makes it possible to account for the lumpiness of capital spending by small governments.

We find that capital investment decisions by school districts are indeed influenced by the state matching rate, but that this impact is much lower in urban districts with poor fiscal health. In fact, some urban districts responded very little even to generous price incentives. We also examine factors other than tax price that may influence districts' capital investment decisions.

The next section reviews the literature on building aid programs and state and local capital investment decisions. We then describe, in Section 3, the Building Aid program in New York. Section 4 presents a model designed to capture the long time frame and lumpiness that characterize capital investment decisions. In Section 5 we discuss empirical methods, data sources, and the measures used to estimate our model. Section 6 presents the results from our regression analysis of school-district capital investment and examines the robustness of our estimates. We conclude with a discussion of the implications of our research for the design of state aid programs to support school facility investment as well as some suggestions for future research.

2. Literature on Building Aid and Capital Investment

Historically, funding for school infrastructure has been a local responsibility (GAO, 1995). Most school districts issue long-term general obligation bonds to finance capital investment, and local property tax revenues are used to cover debt service payments (Plummer, 2006). Many states provide considerably less financial support for capital investment by districts than for operating expenses (Sielke, 2001), which has resulted in significant disparities across districts in their ability to fund school infrastructure. As a consequence, school finance systems have increasingly been challenged as inconsistent with the state's constitution (Plummer, 2006; Sciarra, Bell, and Kenyon, 2006), and successful court cases are associated with significant increases in capital funding (Filardo *et al.*, 2006). In response to law suits, 20 states have reformed their school facilities funding schemes, and courts in Alaska, New Jersey, Ohio, and elsewhere have specifically determined that adequate facilities are an important component of the state's constitutional responsibility.[1] Equitable funding of school facilities is likely to be a continuing aspect of school finance litigation (Crampton, Thompson, and Vesely, 2004) and states will be under increasing pressure to cover a larger share of the cost of school construction and renovation.

Most research on state school facilities aid has concentrated on describing the design and funding of these assistance programs (Honeyman, 1990; Sielke, 2001; Wang and Duncombe, 2009). In addition, the government financial management literature contains studies both on capital (facility) planning processes and documents (Earthman, 2000; Association of School Business Officials, 1999), and on capital financing mechanisms, particularly long-term debt.[2]

---

[1]See "Facilities: Overview." National Access Network, http://www.schoolfunding.info/policy/facilities/facilities.php3 for a more detailed description of litigation on school facilities funding.

[2]The empirical research on capital finance has concentrated on debt finance, including determinants of bond yields, credit ratings (Ammar *et al.*, 2001; Johnson and Kriz, 2005), and long-term debt burdens (Brecher, Richwerger, and Wagner, 2003; Hildreth and Miller, 2002).

Several scholars have examined the macroeconomic impacts of public infrastructure investments.[3] Existing studies of state and local capital spending decisions include Holtz-Eakin and Rosen (1989, 1993) and Bruce et al. (2007).[4] Holtz-Eakin and Rosen develop and test a model of capital spending based on forward-looking, rational decision makers for a sample of communities in New Jersey. They find support for this model in some areas, but not others.

Research on financing school facilities includes several studies of California (Brunner and Rueben, 2001; Balsdon, Brunner, and Rueben, 2003; and Brunner, 2006). Balsdon, Brunner, and Rueben (2003) develop a theoretical model of voter demand for capital investment that accounts for the long life of capital assets and possible agenda setting by school boards. They estimate a capital spending equation that accounts for the tax price for local voters, the value of the existing capital stock, other revenue sources including general and categorical state aid, and several other price and demand variables. They find that capital investment responds inversely to the local tax price. Because all school districts receive a 50 percent state match on local capital spending (Brunner, 2006), it is not possible in California to examine how districts respond to variation in the matching rate.

Cromwell (1991) examines the impact of federal matching grants on maintenance and new investment in urban mass transit systems. As expected, he finds that local maintenance spending is inversely related to the state and federal government matching rate. Moreover, he finds that private operators are much more likely than their public-sector counterparts to spend money on maintenance partly because generous federal grants for new capital induce local governments to substitute away from maintenance toward new investment.

3. New York's Building Aid Program

State government financing of school facilities is a relatively recent development in most states. As late as 1993–1994, 14 states had no formal program

---

[3]The literature on public capital investment has generally focused on the impact of tax policy on private investment (Jorgenson, 1974; Hall and Jorgenson, 1967; Gravelle, 1982; Hubbard, 1998) and the relationship between government investment in infrastructure and economic growth and productivity (Gramlich, 1994; Holtz-Eakin, 1994; Hulten and Schwab, 1991, 1993; Munnell, 1992).

[4]Bruce et al. (2007) examine state highway spending using a simultaneous-equations model in which each state's spending is influenced by the spending of its neighbors. They find evidence of positive spillovers across state boundaries.

to assist districts in financing school facilities, and many existing state programs were small (Sielke, 2001). New York's Building Aid program is unique in its longevity, stability, and size. The program has been in effect since the 1960s, and its major components have remained roughly the same for three decades, including over 50 percent state funding, on average.

School facilities aid programs are typically formula grants, which require project approval by a State Education Department or building authority. Most are designed as open-ended matching grants (20 states) that limit the size of the project (Wang, 2004). A much smaller share are either closed-ended matching grants (three states), lump-sum grants (six states), or some combination of matching and lump-sum grants (nine states). Most of these formulas are wealth-equalized (or use some fiscal capacity adjustments), but only a few states adjust for cost factors, such as enrollment growth, district need, or geographic cost differences.

New York's Building Aid program has many of the features of the typical program. It is an open-ended wealth-equalized matching grant, at a rate that averages roughly 50 percent, but can vary widely depending on the conditions discussed below. It requires state project approval and places limits on the maximum funding for a given project. Building Aid is available for instructional buildings costing more than $10,000 and for school bus garages. No administrative buildings are eligible. The Facilities Planning Unit of the New York State Education Department (SED) must approve the project after the school district school board of education has voted for it (Zedalis, 2003). New York's Building Aid program funds major renovations but does not fund routine maintenance. In fact, 93 percent of major building projects from 1984–2002 were for renovation of existing buildings. The generous funding associated with the Building Aid program and lack of funding for maintenance may provide an incentive for districts to underinvest in maintenance.

Once the project is approved by SED, the amount of Building Aid is calculated using a Building Aid formula (Education Priorities Panel, 2002), which can be represented as

$$Aid_i = \sum_{j=1} [\min(C_{ij}, MCA_{ij}) \times AR_i]$$

$$MCA_{ij} = BAU_{ij} \times CCI_{ij} \times RCI_i$$

$$AR_i = 1 - \left[\frac{FV_i/N_i}{FV/N} \times 0.51 \right] \tag{1}$$

where i represents a district, j represents a project, Aid = the amount of building aid, C = actual project cost, MCA = Maximum Cost Allowance determined by the SED, AR = the state aid ratio, BAU = Building Aid Units, CCI = Construction Cost Index, RCI = Regional Cost Index, FV = full property value, N = average daily attendance in the district,[5] and $\overline{FV/N}$ = average full value per pupil in the State. For district i and project j, aid is determined as the product of the state aid ratio and the minimum of the actual project cost and the MCA.

MCA is determined using several methods[6] but typically is the product of a measure of capacity for different types of schools (BAU),[7] an estimate of the base cost per BAU adjusted for inflation (CCI),[8] and a cost adjustment reflecting regional variation in construction costs (RCI).[9] According to a SED survey of new schools built in the state (excluding New York City), an average of 22 percent of construction costs were not eligible for reimbursement by the state because they exceeded the MCA (Campaign for Fiscal Equity, 2004).

The final multiplier in the Building Aid formula is the wealth-equalized Building Aid Ratio (AR), which is based on a district's full property value per pupil relative to the state average in a given year (Zedalis, 2003). The state share of expenditure equals 49 percent for districts of average wealth, and can range from zero to 95 percent. For projects approved before 1998, a district automatically received the highest aid ratio it was entitled to in any year since 1982. For projects approved between 1 July 1998 and 30 June 2000,

---

[5]Specifically, resident-weighted average daily attendance, which includes only students that are residents of the school district, is used as the measure of attendance (SED, 2001).

[6]Methods for calculating MCA differ depending on how special education students are included in the calculation, on the level of education and whether special education programs are attached or detached from the school. Districts are eligible for full funding for major contracts (general construction, heating and ventilating, plumbing, and electrical), but only for 20 percent of incidental expenses (site purchase, site development, original equipment, furnishings, machinery or apparatus, and professional fees). For a complete description of the aid formula, and facilities planning and approval process, see "Facilities Planning," State Education Department, Albany, NY, http://www.emsc.nysed.gov/facplan.

[7]BAU was originally designed to reflect building capacity, but now reflects building type (Education Priorities Panel, 2002).

[8]The base cost per Building Aid Unit is determined by the SED and gets adjusted by the Construction Cost Index issued for the month that the construction contract for the specific project was executed (Zedilas, 2003). The CCI is a "New York State Labor Department index, which represents the cost of labor and materials," (Thurnau, 2004, p. 9).

[9]The RCI is calculated by dividing the county composite labor rate for three construction-related industries by the median statewide labor rate ("2007–2008 State Aid Handbook." State Education Department, Albany, New York, https://stateaid.nysed.gov/publications/handbooks/hndbk07.htm).

an additional 10 percentage points were added to the aid ratio, with a maximum of 95 percent.[10] After 1 July 2000, districts were given the choice between the current aid ratio plus 10 percentage points or its highest aid ratio since 1982 without the 10-percentage-point boost.[11] According the New York State Comptroller, "The additional 10 percent building aid incentive appears to have been a victim of its own success. It spurred such growth in local building projects that the State's reaction was to largely eliminate the incentive for all projects approved after July 1, 2000 ⋯ " (McCall, 2001, p. 7).

Once SED has approved a capital project, it (and the associated debt) must be approved by voters of the district either during a regular budget referendum or in a special referendum.[12] Voter approval is not required in the "big five" school districts (New York City, Buffalo, Rochester, Syracuse, and Yonkers), which are fiscally dependent on the city government.

School districts are potentially constrained not only by voter approval but also by limits on general obligation debt as a share of property value. The debt limit is generally more constraining for city districts (particularly large cities) than for suburban and rural districts. Suburban and rural districts can deduct state building aid in calculating total debt, while city districts cannot. The big five city governments have nearly the same overall debt limit to fund all municipal services, as suburban and rural school districts only have to fund education facilities (SED, 2002). Small city districts can also temporarily exceed the debt limit if authorized by 60 percent of the district's voters, whereas large cities do not have this option.[13]

---

[10]Governor Pataki proposed this increase in Building Aid in his Executive Budget as part of a package of school aid increases and a school property tax relief plan (New York State Division of the Budget, 1998). New York experienced a rapid increase in state revenues during the late 1990s, driven primarily by soaring stock prices on Wall Street.

[11]This change has resulted in four times more districts than before, 292 of 680 districts, using their current year aid ratio for capital construction approved since 2000 (SED, 2002).

[12]Between 2000–2008, over 90 percent of districts passed their budget referenda, on average, with the lowest passing rate being 85 percent. SED does not maintain information on budget referenda votes before 2000 or maintain information on separate bond referenda.

[13]The debt limits of small city districts and the big five districts are contained in Article 8 of the New York State Constitution. The debt limit of small city school districts, which have territory that is partially or wholly within the limits of a city having a population of less than 125,000, is 5 percent of the average full property value of the last five years' tax rolls. New York City has a limit of 10 percent of the five-year average for full value, and the Big Four cities are limited to 9 percent. The debt limit for other suburban and rural school districts is defined in Section 104.00 of New York's Local Finance Law. Their limit is 10 percent of the full value of the most recent tax roll (SED, 2002).

4. A Model of School District Capital Investment

This section derives a theoretical capital investment model that can be estimated using linear regression methods. Our model builds on the models of Holtz-Eakin and Rosen (1989, 1993) and Balsdon, Brunner, and Reuben (2003) by accounting for the lumpy nature of capital investment and recognizing the derived nature of demand for school facilities. We begin with a standard identity linking new investment (I^n) and replacement investment (I^r) (Jorgenson, 1974; Gravelle, 1982),

$$I_t = (1 - \lambda)(K_t^* - K_{t-1}) + vK_{t-1}, \tag{2}$$

where $I^n(1 - \lambda)(K^* - K_{t-1})$ and $I^r = vK_{t-1}$. New capital investment (I^n) is assumed to be equal to a fixed share, $(1 - \lambda)$, of the gap between the optimal capital stock, K^*, and the actual capital stock last year, K_{t-1}. The replacement of the capital stock (I^r) is assumed to be equal to a fixed share, v, of last year's capital stock. These investment and stock variables are all measured in units of physical capital per pupil. If information is available on K_{t-1}, then (2) can be re-arranged to express total capital investment as a function of the optimal capital stock and the parameters λ and v, or

$$I_t + (1 - \lambda - v)K_{t-1} = (1 - \lambda)K_t^*. \tag{3}$$

The optimal capital stock is a school district's desired capital input, given its decisions about target levels of school performance and the production function its faces. Thus, we begin by deriving an expression for K_t^* under the assumption that a school district minimizes the cost of producing any given level of school performance. However, school districts, like other public organizations, may face constraints on salaries, working conditions (such as limits to production hours per day), and factor substitution (such as class size requirements) that result in deviations from cost-minimizing choices. As a result, we also introduce measures of political and institutional constraints.

We begin with a standard cost-minimization problem assuming that intermediate school outputs, G, such as geometry lessons, are produced with a Cobb-Douglas technology in which b_1 is the exponent on the labor input (L), b_2 is the exponent on the capital input (K), and $\beta = b_1 + b_2$. Note that β can be interpreted as a measure of technical returns to scale in educational production (Duncombe and Yinger, 1993). The derived demand for capital can be represented as

$$K^* = aP_K^{(-b_1/\beta)}P_L^{(b_1/\beta)}G^{(1/\beta)} \tag{4}$$

where P_K is the price of capital, P_L is the price of labor, and a is a constant.

Since parents and voters are interested in the outcomes from education (S), such as student performance on tests and graduation rates, we follow the education production function literature by modeling S as a function of school outputs (G) and non-school factors, such as enrollment size (N) and the share of disadvantaged students (Z). For simplicity, we assume that the production function for S has the constant elasticity form,

$$S = a'G^{\rho}N^{(-\alpha)}Z^{(-\varphi)} \qquad (5)$$

where a' is a constant, α and φ are elasticities measuring the impact of N and Z on student performance (given G), and ρ is the elasticity capturing differences between technical economies of scale and economies of quality scale (Duncombe and Yinger, 1993).

In addition, we recognize that from the perspective of a school district in New York, the price of capital has two components. First, borrowing from the investment literature, we express the annual rental price of capital for a school district as[14]

$$P_k = q(d + r) \qquad (6)$$

where q is the purchase price of a capital asset, d is the depreciation rate, and r is the real interest rate. The purchase price of capital is potentially a function of the price of land and construction costs in an area. The depreciation rate depends on the useful life of the asset and the level of maintenance. The real interest rate facing a district typically varies with the credit rating a district receives, which is often directly related to the district's economy and finances (Ammar *et al.*, 2001). Second, an open-ended matching grant reduces the tax price of capital to a school district because the local share (LS) of capital spending equals ($1-AR$), where AR is the "aid ratio" or state share. In most states with matching grants, including New York, LS is a function of the district's relative property wealth.

Now combining (4) and (5) and introducing the LS as part of the price of capital we obtain

$$K^* = a''P_K^{(-b_1/\beta)}LS^{\gamma(-b_1/\beta)}P_L^{(b_1/\beta)}S^{[1/(\rho\beta)]}N^{[\alpha/(\rho\beta)]}Z^{[\varphi/(\rho\beta)]} \qquad (7)$$

where a'' is a constant (which includes both a and a'), γ measures the extent to which districts respond differently to LS than to the rental price of capital,

---

[14]The investment literature looks at the effect of the corporate income tax on the price of capital and the level of investment (Gravelle, 1982). Since this is not an issue for local governments, such as school districts, the price without taxes is used.

and $\rho\beta$ captures economies of quality scale.[15] Note that the price elasticity of demand for capital is negative and the cross-price elasticity of demand for capital in response to a change in the price of labor (P_L) is positive, which indicates that capital and labor are substitutes when there are only two inputs. Finally, we can translate the demand for physical capital, K^*, into the demand for annual capital spending, KE^*, by multiplying both sides of (7) by P_k. The result is

$$KE^* = a''P_K^{(-b_2/\beta)}LS^{\gamma(-b_1/\beta)}P_L^{(b_1/\beta)}S^{[1/(\rho\beta)]}N^{[\alpha/(\rho\beta)]}Z^{[\varphi/(\rho\beta)]}. \qquad (8)$$

Equation (8) expresses capital demand as a function of S. Measures of S are often available for cross-sectional analysis or short times series, but consistent measures of S are usually not available over longer periods of time because of changes in performance assessment instruments. This data limitation is particularly binding for a model of capital demand decisions, which are made over a long time horizon. As a result, we follow an alternative approach, namely, to develop a model of the demand for S and then to substitute that model into (8).

Assuming a simple median voter model and a constant elasticity demand function (Balsdon, Brunner, and Rueben, 2003), the median voter's demand for S is

$$S = cTY^\phi TP^\mu T^\theta \qquad (9)$$

where c is a constant, TY is voter income augmented by state aid, TP is the tax price for public education, and T represents voter preference variables. Measures of T that appear in the literature include the age distribution, the religious affiliation, and the educational attainment of the population.

Expressions for TY and TP can be obtained from the standard median voter framework (Rubenfeld, 1987; Ladd and Yinger, 1991). Let Y be the median voter's income, V be the median voter's house value, $\bar{V}$ be the district's property value per pupil, and A be lump-sum state aid. Then,

$$TY = Y + \kappa(V/\bar{V})A. \qquad (10)$$

In this expression, state aid reduces the need for local taxes, so its impact on the demand for S is weighted by $V/\bar{V}$, which is the share of local taxes paid by the median voter. In addition, many scholars have found that the

---

[15]Duncombe and Yinger (1993) state that economies of quality scale exist when a one unit increase in final outcomes (e.g., student test score performance) is associated with a decline in average costs, defined as costs per unit of outcome (e.g., cost per test score point).

impact of aid on the demand for S is larger than the impact of an equivalent change in income; this so-called flypaper effect is indicated by κ.

The variable TP is defined as the amount the median voter must pay for another unit of S. It depends on the marginal resource cost of S, MC, and on tax share, or

$$TP = MC(V/\bar{V}). \tag{11}$$

Note that MC is the derivative of the education cost function (as derived from a Cobb-Douglas production function) with respect to S, or

$$MC = a^* P_K^{(b_2/\beta)} P_L^{(b_1/\beta)} S^{[1/(\rho\beta)-1]} N^{[\alpha/\rho\beta)]} Z^{[\varphi/(\rho\beta)]} \tag{12}$$

where a^* is a constant. Substituting (9)–(12) into (8) results in

$$KE^* = a^{**} P_K^{(1+\mu/\varepsilon)(b_2/\beta)} LS^{\gamma(-b_1/\beta)} P_L^{(1+\mu/\varepsilon)(b_1/\beta)} N^{(1+\mu/\varepsilon)[\alpha/(\rho\beta)]}$$
$$\times Z^{(1+\mu/\varepsilon)[\varphi/(\rho\beta)]} (V/\bar{V})^{(\mu/\varepsilon)} \times [Y + \kappa(V/\bar{V})A]^{(\phi/\varepsilon)} T^{(\theta/\varepsilon)} \tag{13}$$

where $\varepsilon = [\rho\beta - (1-\rho\beta)\mu]$ and a^{**} is a constant.[16]

In (3), $(1-\lambda)$ is the share of the gap between the existing and the optimal capital stock funded this year and captures the adjustment process, which may vary across districts based on political and institutional constraints. Districts facing tighter legal limits on the maximum level of outstanding debt (D), for example, may require more time to adjust. Because most capital investments are long-term and expensive, school districts with more stable management (M) might be more apt to make capital investments. One of the major challenges confronting large central city school districts is the frequent turnover of superintendents. Districts experiencing a rapid increase in enrollment (R) may have difficulty increasing school facilities at the same rate as their growth in need. Assuming a multiplicative function for the factors potentially affecting the adjustment process, multiplying both sides of (3) by the price of capital, and substituting into (13) results in our final equation,

$$IE_t + (1-\lambda-v)KE_{t-1} = \{a^{**} P_K^{(1+\mu/\varepsilon)(b_2/\beta)} LS^{\gamma(-b_1/\beta)} P_L^{(1+\mu/\varepsilon)(b_1/\beta)}$$
$$\times N^{(1+\mu/\varepsilon)[\alpha/(\rho\beta)]} Z^{(1+\mu/\varepsilon)[\varphi/(\rho\beta)]} (V/\bar{V})^{(\mu/\varepsilon)} [Y + \kappa(V/\bar{V})A]^{(\phi/\varepsilon)} T^{(\theta/\varepsilon)}\}$$
$$\times [D^{\pi_1} M^{\pi_2} R^{\pi_3}] \tag{14}$$

---

[16]Identifying the structural parameters in (13) requires some assumption about returns to quality scale ($\rho\beta$) in education and technical returns to scale (β) (Duncombe and Yinger, 1993).

where IE_t and KE_t are new and replacement investment spending, respectively, and π indicates a parameter for one of the adjustment variables. Our empirical model is expressed in linear form by taking the natural log of (14).

5. Data Sources and Measures

This paper analyzes the determinants of school district capital investments by estimating (14) using an extensive data set on New York school districts. In this section, we discuss our data sources and measures. Table 1 presents descriptive statistics for the variables used in the empirical model. All financial variables are deflated using the consumer price index for all urban consumers (CPI-U).

The long-term nature of capital investments implies that an empirical examination of capital investment should involve an extended time series. For this paper, we assembled a 19-year panel data set for approximately 634 school districts in New York state.[17] As discussed below, the capital stock estimate was constructed for the time period 1990–2008, which allows for eight years of capital investment information before the 10 percentage point increase in state aid ratio in 1998 and eight years after this incentive was removed in 2000.

The process of planning for capital construction, applying for Building Aid, getting voter approval, and issuing municipal bonds is time consuming and is likely to take several years to complete. Thus, changes in the aid ratio in the Building Aid program (or changes in any other independent variable) are likely to take several years before they are reflected in capital spending.[18] We try various lags for the independent variables ranging from two to four years and, as reported below, do not find that these variations cause large differences in the results. For the final model we use a three-year lag for our independent variables (1987–2005). The sample includes 25 districts

---

[17]Approximately, 35 districts were dropped from the sample because they had missing data, had fewer than eight teachers, or served only special student populations. In addition, we dropped New York City because capital spending information was not available from the New York State Office of the State Comptroller (OSC). In addition, the implementation of the Building Aid program in New York City has been different than in other districts in the state (Education Priorities Panel, 2002).

[18]This conclusion is based on our discussions with the staff of the Facilities Planning Unit of the New York State Education Department.

Table 1 Descriptive statistics for variables used in capital investment model (New York school districts in 2005).

Variable	Mean	Standard deviation	Minimum	Maximum
Estimated value of per pupil capital stock (2008)	14,428	8,051	1,702	75,116
Per pupil capital spending (2008)	1,035	1,515	22	12,058
Cost variables				
Local capital share (all districts)	33.21	24.97	5.00	90.00
Annual county construction wages	36,430	6,691	20,468	48,708
Teacher salary (one to five years of experience)	36,125	5,574	20,567	54,128
Enrollment	2,639	3,326	43	41,412
Share of students receiving subsidized lunch (%)	30.21	19.92	0.00	86.39
Demand variables				
Local tax share (median house values divided by per pupil property values)	3.50	1.27	0.13	7.94
Estimated market property values per pupil	63,678	190,693	5,574	3,628,453
Income per pupil (adjusted gross income)	146,600	145,154	28,602	1,961,096
Operating aid ratio (operating aid divided by income and multiplied by local tax share)	0.1070	0.1010	0.0001	0.1590
Need/capacity index (index of student poverty divided by index of property values)	3.01	3.07	0.00	24.71
Share of African American students (%)	5.49	11.35	0.00	81.33
Share of all African American students who live in a district that has a majority African American population (%)	0.55	6.33	0.00	81.33
Adjustment variables				
Debt limit variable (dummy variable equals 1 if the ratio of statutory debt limit relative to property values is below 0.07)	0.099	0.298	0.000	1.000
Enrollment change in last five years (%)	−0.0229	0.0979	−0.4273	0.5685
Change of superintendent (=1 if in last three years)	0.19	0.39	0.00	1.00
Consolidated school district (=1 if year after consolidation)	0.04	0.19	0.00	1.00

Notes: The sample size (n) is 649. The sample does not include New York City, districts with fewer than eight teachers, and districts serving special needs populations. All financial variables are inflation-adjusted and expressed in 2000$ using the consumer price index for urban consumers (CPI-U).

that are the product of reorganization (consolidation or annexation) during the sample period. To maintain a balanced panel we combined the information for the consolidating districts before consolidation to create one observation throughout the sample period.

5.1. *Estimate of the Capital Stock*

To construct the dependent variable $[IE_t + (1 - \lambda - v)KE_{t-1}]$, we added capital spending in the current year (IE_t) and an estimate of the value of the capital stock in the previous year (KE_{t-1}) multiplied by an assumed value for $(1 - \lambda - v)$. We do not have a direct measure of the value of the capital stock, but we do have data on capital spending starting in 1977, so we assume a baseline depreciation rate (d) of 2 percent based the depreciation rate calculated by the U.S. Bureau of Economic Analysis for government educational buildings[19] and construct KE_{t-1} as the sum of depreciated capital investment over the previous 10 years. We examine the sensitivity of the model to values for d ranging from 1 to 3 percent and values for $(1-\lambda-v)$ ranging from 0.6 to 1.4; as reported below, the results are not sensitive to these values. Ten years may not be adequate time to accurately capture relative capital stock differences across districts. We also estimate a capital stock measure using 15 years of capital spending data. Capital spending is reported in annual financial reports submitted by school districts to the New York Office of the State Comptroller (OSC, 2007). Capital expenditures include spending on facilities, land, and equipment.[20]

5.2. *Price Variables*

The key price variable considered in our analysis is the share of capital spending financed through local property taxes (LS). LS equals one minus the state aid ratio, which is 49 percent in a district with average property values. State aid ratios are reported annually in the detailed *State Aid Files*

---

[19]See U.S. Bureau of Economic Analysis, "BEA Depreciation Estimates," Bureau of Economic Analysis, Washington, DC, http://www.bea.gov/National/FA2004/Tablecandtext. pdf).

[20]Capital spending includes all types of capital investments including those not funded by Building Aid (e.g., administrative buildings and some athletic facilities). Investment in facilities is generally recorded in the capital projects fund. We use a composite measure of capital expenditures developed by the New York Office of the State Comptroller as part of their *Special Report on Municipal Affairs* (OSC, 2007).

maintained by SED.[21] School districts that consolidated are entitled to additional Building Aid (Reorganization Building Aid) of 25 percent (if the consolidation was before FY 1983) or 30 percent (if it was after FY1983) as long as the state aid ratio does not exceed 95 percent. The aid is available for projects for which the "general construction contract" is signed within ten years from the date the consolidation goes into effect (SED, 2007).[22]

The input factor prices considered in this analysis are the price of capital and teacher salaries. We use a measure of the price of capital (P_K) similar to that used by Balsdon, Brunner, and Reuben (2003), namely, the annual wage rate for construction workers (at the county level) based on the data from the New York State Department of Labor. The annual wage for construction workers captures most of the variation across school districts in the price of capital because most capital spending is for renovations of existing buildings and we expect there is little variation in depreciation rates and interest rates on municipal bonds across school districts (see (6)).[23]

The major labor prices (P_L) affecting school district costs are teacher salaries. To ensure comparability across districts, we use data on individual teachers with one to five years of experience to predict what teachers' salaries would be in each district if teachers had average experience and

---

[21]SED's *State Aid Files* are the working files used by SED to calculate formula aid. Besides the aid districts receive by program, they include all the factors used in aid calculations, such as the state aid ratios used in the calculation of Building Aid, adjusted gross income, and the share of students receiving free or subsidized school lunch. The *State Aid Files* are not published but are available from SED upon request.

[22]We have information on school consolidations dating back to 1980. It is possible that some districts consolidated between 1977–1980 and their increased Building Aid is not reflected in the local capital shares we used. Given that there were only two district consolidations from 1980–1984, we do not expect that very many districts fall into this category.

[23]We do not anticipate substantial differences in depreciation rates across districts in New York, because the Building Aid program provides strong incentives to under-invest in routine maintenance (SED, 2002). The principal factor affecting differences across districts in interest rates for municipal bonds is the credit rating on the bond issue. There are not large variations across districts in their credit rating, because New York has strong state restrictions on the type of debt districts can issue and provides strong security for bond holders through aid intercept provisions (Zedalis, 2003). In principle, capital prices also depend on the cost of land, which varies widely across districts. In fact, however, most capital spending is for renovations of existing buildings and even new construction generally takes place on land already owned by a school district, so that real estate prices have little impact on capital spending (even if they do affect opportunity costs!). Based on the capital project database maintained by SED, 98 percent of the school buildings in 2002 were built before 1984 and over 93 percent of major building construction projects from 1984–2002 were for renovation of existing buildings.

education.[24] Since teacher salaries are potentially set simultaneously with district spending as part of the annual budgeting process, this variable may be endogenous. We estimate the regression model with 2SLS and test several different instruments, all of which are related to comparable private sector wages[25] County population was found to be the strongest instrument based on weak instrument tests (Stock and Yogo, 2005).

The tax share variable is the ratio of the district's median house value to full property value per pupil $(V/\bar{V})$. District property values are an estimate of full market value ("equalized value") developed by the New York Office of Real Property Services (ORPS) and reported by OSC (2007). Median house values are constructed from detailed house-level information collected by ORPS as part of its Real Property System (RPS) database.[26] RPS data is only available from 1999–2008. In order to construct the tax share variable, median house values for other years were predicted using a regression on district per pupil income, county per capita income, and the share of county personal income in transfer payments. This model explained a high share of the variation $(R^2 = 0.85)$ in median house values.[27]

5.3. Augmented Income

Measures of income and state aid are available from SED in the *State Aid Files*. Income (Y) is measured as adjusted gross income per pupil in a district and is calculated from personal income tax returns for SED by the New York Department of Taxation and Finance. For the state aid variable,

---

[24]In the 2006–2007 academic year, 25 percent of teachers had total experience between one and five years. See "New York State Education Department, "Information, Reporting and Technology Services Experience Distributions For Classroom Teachers 2006–2007," http://www.p12.nysed.gov/irs/pmf/2006-07/2007_Stat-17.pdf.

[25]Ideally, we would use a measure of comparable private wages as an instrument. While Taylor and Fowler (2006) have developed a comparable wage index (CWI) for the NCES, it is only available from 1999–2005. To select possible instruments we looked at variables that were strongly correlated with the CWI including county population (0.75) and average county private sector wages (0.86).

[26]Property classes used in the calculation include one-family, two-family, and three family residential housing, rural residence with acreage, mobile homes, and multiple residences (condominiums).

[27]The RPS database is discussed on the ORPS website; see "Offices of Real Property Tax Services." New York State Department of Taxation and Finance, www.orps.state.ny.us. The regression coefficients (and robust standard errors in parentheses) are: log median house value $= -3.455 + 0.594$ (0.028) log of per pupil income $+ 0.827$ (0.045) log of county per capita income $- 0.023$ (0.0019) share of county personal income in transfer payments $(n = 7136)$, (adjusted R-squared $= 0.85$).

we use Operating Aid, which is a general purpose foundation aid program accounting for approximately 50 percent of total formula aid. The design of the Operating Aid Program remained fairly stable during the sample period. The aid ratio is calculated by dividing operating aid by income and multiplying by the tax share $(A/Y)(V/\bar{V})$.[28]

5.4. *Student Variables*

Several student measures are included to capture differences in education costs and in preferences for education services. The enrollment variable (N) is the fall enrollment count from the OSC database (OSC, 2007). Poverty (Z) is measured by the percentage of students in a district receiving a subsidized lunch. Differences in the racial composition of districts, measured by the percentage of African American students, are included to capture possible differences in white residents' support for public schools (T). To allow for the possibility that this effect may be different in districts where the majority of residents are African American, we include an interaction term between percent African American students and whether a majority of the district's population was African American. Population data come from the 1990 and 2000 *Census of Population*.[29] Student demographics are available from SED in either the *State Aid File* or in the *Institutional Master File* collected from each district on an annual basis.[30]

5.5. *Factors Affecting the Adjustment Process*

To capture the relative constraint from the debt limit (D), we divided a district's total debt limit by the total market value of its property.[31]

---

[28]To keep the estimating equation log-linear, we approximate the log of TY by splitting it into the log of Y and (unlogged) per pupil operating aid divided by per pupil income and multiplied by the tax share.

[29]See U.S Census Bureau, http://www.census.gov. Four districts had a majority African American population in 1990 and five districts had a majority African American population in 2000. For the one district that changed between these years, we assumed that there was a linear transition in the share African American population between 1990–2000, which implies that this district became majority African American in 1994.

[30]The *Institutional Master File* (IMF) is data collected by SED from surveys of school principals and central office administrators. It provides information on student and teacher demographics. The IMF data are not published but are available from SED upon request.

[31]The total amount of constitutional and statutory debt limits is available from the New York Office of the State Comptroller for all districts except for the four large central city districts that are fiscally dependent, where the debt limit is 9 percent for all municipal debt. Assuming that half of the debt limit in the dependent cities is used for school facilities, we multiplied 4.5 percent by the five-year average of full property value to obtain the approximate total debt limits in these cities.

This ratio is 10 percent for most districts but lower for city districts. To capture those districts facing a particularly tight debt limit, we use a dummy variable defined to equal one if the ratio of debt limit to property value is 7 percent or less (which is approximately the 10th percentile for all districts). We approximate the stability of district management (M) using a dummy variable indicating whether there was a change in the district superintendent in the last three years. Enrollment change (R) is the percent change in enrollment over the last five years. New York state provides both operating and capital incentives for districts to consolidate. We modified the local share to reflect the additional Building Aid available to consolidated districts (see above). We also included a dummy variable that equals one in a consolidating district after it consolidates to capture the possible effects of increased Operating Aid on capital investment decisions.

6. Empirical Analysis

6.1. *Descriptive Results*

Figure 1 and Table 2 compare variable means using categories developed by SED to indicate the ratio of student needs to resource capacity.[32] The lowest capital spending in the past 20 years has been in the large central cities and other high-need urban/suburban districts (where "high-need" is short for "high need/resource capacity index" (Table 2)). During the first half of the 1990s, large cities had higher capital spending than other high-need urban/suburban districts, but after 1995 this pattern reversed with large cities generally having the lowest capital spending (Figure 1). High-need rural districts have spent by far the most on capital — around 32 percent higher than average-need districts and 60 percent more than high-need urban/suburban districts (Table 2). While high rural capital spending is expected considering the low required local contribution rate (a local share of less than 20 percent), the lower capital spending in high-need urban/suburban districts occurs despite an almost equally low local

---

[32]SED's "Need-to-Resource-Capacity Index" is calculated as the ratio of a standardized measure of student poverty and resource capacity (average of income and property wealth indexes). The numerator is measured using a weighted average of the two-year average of the subsidized lunch rate for 2001 and 2002 and the 2000 Census child poverty rate. The denominator is a fiscal capacity measure used by New York called the combined wealth ratio (CWR), which is an average of an income index and property wealth index (centered around the state average) and was measured for 2001 (SED, 2010).

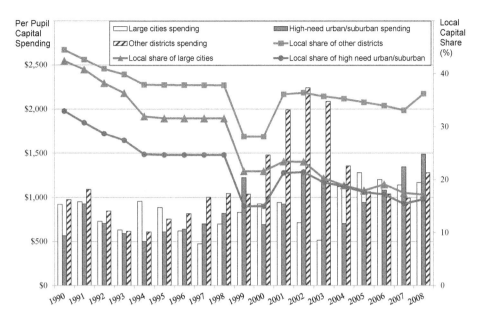

Figure 1 Comparison of capital spending and local share between large cities, other high need urban districts and other districts in New York.

contribution rate (a local capital share averaging 25 percent). While the local capital share is over twice as high in the low-need districts as in the high-need urban/suburban districts, they spend 15 to 20 percent more per pupil on capital.

Figure 1 and Table 3 highlight differences by type of district in the response to the 10 percentage point changes in the state aid ratio in 1999 and 2000. Capital spending after 2000 went up by a modest 20 percent in the four large cities (Buffalo, Rochester, Syracuse, and Yonkers) and by 55 percent in other high-need urban/suburban districts compared to the period before 1999. By contrast, it more than doubled in the other districts, on average. The slower growth in capital spending in the high-need urban districts occurred despite a much larger percentage decrease in the local capital share in these districts, especially in the large cities. These results are consistent with early findings of SED regarding diverging patterns in capital investment across district types:

> During the incentives, rates of capital construction in the high need urban or suburban districts, the Big Four, and New York City lagged behind those of other need/resource categories. On the whole districts in these categories did increase the rate of capital construction while the incentives were in effect, but not by as much as the other districts (SED, 2002, p. 20).

Table 2 Comparison of Means (1987–2005) by Need/Resource-Capacity Category.

Variable	Large cities	High-need urban/Suburban	High-need rural	Average-need	Low-need
Estimated value of per pupil capital stock (2008)	7,124	7,488	11,921	9,009	8,685
Per pupil capital spending (2008)	784	795	1,334	1,030	1,056
Cost variables					
Local capital share (all districts)	31.74	25.07	21.95	33.15	68.74
Annual county construction wages	39,364	36,021	29,640	34,017	42,101
Teacher salary (one to five years of experience)	36,131	34,749	31,905	34,137	39,944
Enrollment	30,768	4,954	1,145	2,591	2,658
Share of students receiving subsidized lunch (%)	74.18	57.18	43.87	24.07	6.00
Demand Variables					
Local tax share	5.09	4.51	2.99	3.51	3.53
Estimated market property values per pupil	21,252	20,653	20,429	30,700	122,012
Income per pupil (adjusted gross income)	88,993	86,403	59,162	100,977	270,072
Operating aid ratio	0.1909	0.1834	0.2125	0.1147	0.0205
Need/capacity index	7.77	5.60	4.99	1.93	0.17
Share of African American students (%)	44.40	23.20	1.83	4.15	3.83
Share of all African American students who live in a majority African American district (%)	0.0000	7.2453	0.0000	0.3747	0.0000
Adjustment variables					
Debt limit variable	1.0000	0.6667	0.0749	0.0687	0.0158
Enrollment change (last five years)	0.0239	−0.0002	−0.0230	0.0102	0.0656
Change of superintendent (=1 if in last three years)	0.2632	0.2066	0.1912	0.1786	0.1613
Consolidated school district (=1 if year after consolidation)	0.0000	0.0000	0.0500	0.0249	0.0000

Notes: Sample size (n) is 12,042 (634 districts). The sample does not include New York City, districts with fewer than eight teachers, and districts serving special needs populations. All financial variables are inflation-adjusted and expressed in 2000$ using the consumer price index for urban consumers (CPI-U). Need/resource-capacity categories were developed by the New York State Education Department and were based on a ratio of student poverty and an index of income and property values (combined wealth ratio). Large cities include Buffalo, Rochester, Syracuse, and Yonkers.

Table 3   Comparison of means before and after the 10 percentage point reduction in the local capital share.

Variable	1990–1998	2001–2005	Percent change
Capital variables			
Estimate of value of capital stock	6,596	12,232	85.45*
Large cities	5,979	7,747	29.58*
Other high-need urban/suburban	6,041	8,396	38.99*
High-need rural	8,143	15,874	94.94*
Other districts	6,112	11,330	85.36*
Per pupil capital spending	844	1,690	100.16*
Large cities	762	914	19.83
Other high-need urban/suburban	675	1,047	55.07*
High-need rural	1,031	2,163	109.81*
Other districts	794	1,585	99.67*
Cost variables			
Local capital share	38.05	34.26	−9.96*
Large cities	35.11	20.78	−40.81*
Other high-need urban/suburban	26.86	19.64	−26.88*
High-need rural	22.47	18.42	−18.02*
Other districts	44.27	40.77	−7.91*
Annual county construction wages	33,719	36,426	8.03*
Teacher salary	35,261	35,926	1.88*
Enrollment (thousands)	2,522	2,653	5.20
Share of students receiving subsidized lunch	27.65	29.01	4.91*
Demand Variables			
Local tax share	3.16	3.56	12.66*
Property values per pupil	46,072	54,362	17.99*
Income per pupil	118,396	138,949	17.36*
Operating aid ratio	0.1150	0.1170	1.74
Need/capacity index	2.6451	2.6915	1.76
Share of African American students (%)	4.6597	5.3269	14.32*
Share of all African American students who live in a majority African American district (%)	57.65	57.93	0.49
Adjustment variables			
Debt limit variable	0.10	0.10	2.12
Enrollment change (last five years)	0.042	−0.006	−113.99*
Change of superintendent (=1 if in last three years)	0.1691	0.2051	21.27*
Consolidated school district (=1 if year after consolidation)	0.02	0.04	66.98*

Notes: Sample size (*n*) averages 638 per year. The sample does not include New York City, districts with fewer than 8 teachers, and districts serving special needs populations. All financial variables are inflation-adjusted and expressed in 2000$ using the consumer price index for urban consumers (CPI-U). Need/resource-capacity categories were developed by the New York State Education Department and were based on a on a ratio of student poverty and an index of income and property values (combined wealth ratio). Large cities include Buffalo, Rochester, Syracuse, and Yonkers. Asterisks denote statistically significant difference in means at 5% level.

The SED report suggests that the lower investment in cities and other high-need urban districts may be due to stricter debt limits, fiscal dependent status (for the five largest cities),[33] and reluctance by districts in fiscal stress to commit to large projects when state aid levels are uncertain. In the next section, we formally examine some of these explanations.

6.2. *Empirical Methodology*

Our log-linear specification of (14) addresses a wide range of factors likely to affect school facility investment decisions, but our results could be biased if these decisions are also influenced by unobserved time-invariant district characteristics. To account for this possibility, we include school-district fixed effects in the model. As discussed in the previous section, teacher salaries could be endogenous, so we estimate the regression model with 2SLS using county population as an instrument.[34]

To account for potential biases in the standard errors we have taken two steps. First, we include year fixed effects to remove statewide factors that do not vary across districts (such as general economic growth) but may be correlated over time.[35] Second, we use the method developed by Newey and West (1987) for estimating heteroskedasticity-and autocorrelation-consistent (HAC) standard errors (Baum, Schaffer, and Stillman, 2007).[36]

---

[33]Fiscally dependent school districts in New York can determine the allocation of the budget and select capital projects, but the city council and mayor control the overall size of the budget and the level of debt that is issued. School districts have to compete with other municipal functions in capital funding and debt issuance decisions of the municipal government.

[34]The model was estimated with xtivreg2 in STATA (Schaffer, 2005). The weak instrument test involves comparing Kleibergen-Paap rk statistic to critical values established by Stock and Yogo (2005). While this comparison is not technically correct given non-i.i.d. errors, Baum, Schaffer, and Stillman (2007) argue that this is a reasonable approximation. The Kleibergen-Paap rk statistic is over 35 in all of the models and well above any critical values established by Stock and Yogo (2005).

[35]An alternative approach to controlling for changes in state economic conditions is to include measures of the state economy directly in the model instead of year fixed effects. We estimated Models 1–3 (Table 4) by dropping the year fixed effects and including instead state averages of per capita gross state product, per capita personal income, the unemployment rate, and level of total employment. The coefficients on the local share variables are similar to those reported in Table 4 and are statistically significant. These estimates are available from the authors upon request.

[36]The Newey West estimation involves specifying the maximum lag to be considered in the autocorrelation structure. Newey and West (1987) recommend calculating the

6.3. *Results of Capital Investment Models*

The descriptive results suggest that all school districts except some high-need urban/suburban districts respond to the incentives in New York's Building Aid program. Other factors that influence school district investment decisions also change over time (Table 3), however, so we estimate our multivariate model, a log-linear version of (14) to isolate the impacts of this program. Our baseline estimates construct the capital stock variable using a 2 percent depreciation rate and an adjustment factor of 1.

Table 4 presents the results for versions of (14), each with a different specification for the local capital share term, *LS*. Model 1 assumes that the local capital share elasticity is the same for all districts. Model 2 allows for possible differences in the investment response to changes in the local capital share between high-need urban/suburban districts and other districts. We measure this by interacting *LS* with a dummy variable for whether a district is a high-need urban/suburban district. Model 3 also examines whether the price response is different for the four large central city districts by including a *LS* interaction variable for these districts as well as an interaction variable for other high-need urban/suburban districts.[37]

The main results of interest are the elasticities of a district's capital stock with respect to the local capital share (*LS*) in the Building Aid formula. In Model 1, the local capital share elasticity is −0.39, which indicates that a one percent increase in the local share is associated with a decrease of 0.39 percent in the value of the capital stock. Using Model 2, this elasticity is −0.42 for most districts, but drops to approximately zero (−0.023) for high-need urban/suburban districts. In other words, high-need urban/suburban districts respond very little, on average, to the price incentives provided in

---

maximum lag using $4(n/100)^{(2/9)} = 4(19/100)^{(2/9)} = 2.76$; others have suggested using $n^{(1/4)} = 19^{(1/4)} \approx 2$ (Wooldridge, 2003). We experimented with one-year to three-year lags and found that the estimates were not very sensitive to this variation; we used a two-year lag in the models presented in Tables 4 to 6. Because one of the variables, the tax share, has as its numerator a predicted value from a regression (median house value), it is possible that the standard errors are biased. We checked this by calculating bootstrapped robust standard errors (100 repetitions). The procedure, xtivreg2 (or xtivreg), does not include an option to calculate bootstrapped HAC standard errors. We are reporting HAC standard errors because they are higher for all variables.

[37] In model 3, the *LS* interaction variable for other high-need urban/suburban districts excludes the four large cities (Buffalo, Rochester, Syracuse, and Yonkers).

Table 4 Regression results for capital investment models (New York school districts).

	Models		
Explanatory variable	1	2	3
Cost variables			
Local capital share (all districts)	−0.394***	−0.426***	−0.426***
	(11.94)	(−12.35)	(−12.34)
Local capital share (high-need urban/suburban districts)		0.403***	0.408***
		(6.43)	(6.20)
Local capital share (four large central cities)			0.371**
			(2.28)
Annual construction wages	0.120	0.068	0.068
	(0.87)	(0.55)	(0.55)
Teacher salary	1.798	2.394*	2.397*
	(1.32)	(1.73)	(1.73)
Enrollment	0.892*	0.824**	0.829*
	(1.91)	(1.74)	(1.74)
Enrollment squared	−0.075**	−0.076*	−0.077**
	(−2.36)	(−2.35)	(−2.36)
Share of students receiving subsidized lunch (%)	−0.001	0.000	0.000
	(−0.60)	(−0.51)	(−0.50)
Demand Variables			
Local tax share	−0.186***	−0.171***	−0.171***
	(−3.64)	(−3.27)	(−3.27)
Income per pupil	0.216***	0.155**	0.155**
	(3.47)	(2.39)	(2.39)
Operating aid ratio	0.193	0.301	0.298
	(1.03)	(1.56)	(1.54)
Share of African American students (%)	−0.010***	−0.007**	−0.007**
	(−3.50)	(−2.39)	(−2.40)
Share of all African American students who live in a majority African American district (%)	0.006**	0.004*	0.004*
	(2.49)	(1.80)	(1.80)
Adjustment variables			
Debt limit variable	−0.110**	−0.087	−0.086
	(−1.97)	(−1.53)	(−1.52)
Enrollment change (last five years)	0.270***	0.259**	0.260**
	(2.67)	(2.50)	(2.50)

(Continued)

Table 4   (*Continued*)

| | Models | | |
Explanatory variable	1	2	3
Change of superintendent (=1 if in last	−0.025*	−0.028**	−0.028**
three years)	(−1.95)	(−2.16)	(−2.16)
Consolidated school district	0.279***	0.227**	0.227**
(=1 if year after consolidation)	(3.11)	(2.43)	(2.43)
Prob > F	0.00	0.01	0.00
RMSE	0.44	0.44	0.44

Notes: Sample size is 12,042 (634 districts). The sample does not include New York City, districts with fewer than eight teachers, and districts serving special needs populations. The dependent variable is the estimated value of the capital stock from 1990–2008. The independent variables are lagged three years (1987–2005). All financial variables are inflation-adjusted and expressed in 2000$ using the consumer price index for urban consumers (CPI-U). All variables except for the operating aid ratio, enrollment change, subsidized lunch, share of African American students, and dichotomous variables are expressed in natural logs. The model is estimated with linear 2SLS (with teacher salaries treated as an endogenous variable) with district and year fixed effects. z-statistics (in parentheses) are based on robust HAC standard errors. Asterisks denote statistical significance at the 1% (***), 5% (**), and 10% (*) levels.

the Building Aid program. The results for Model 3 indicate that large cities are also unresponsive to these price incentives.[38]

The finding of a significantly lower price response to changes in the local share in high-need urban/suburban districts than in other districts is compelling because we control for other factors that might lead to lower capital spending in these districts. They might, for example, have lower debt limits and thus face more binding constraints in issuing debt for capital projects. The results in Table 4 are consistent with this possibility; to be specific, districts with low relative debt limits, which include 100 percent of the large cities and 67 percent of the other high-need urban/suburban districts (Table 2), have lower capital investment than other districts. The magnitude of this effect is between 8 and 11 percent, but it is statistically significant only in Model 1.

---

[38]The sum of the coefficients for the local capital share and the interaction with high-need urban/suburban districts in Models 2 and 3 are not statistically significant from zero based on a Wald test. The same is true for the sum of the local capital share and the interaction with large city districts in Model 3. There is not a statistically significant difference between the coefficients on the interaction variable for the large central cities and the interaction variable for other high-need urban/suburban districts in Model 3.

These high-need urban/suburban districts also might have lower capital investment due to higher construction prices or higher costs in general for providing education. On average, the county construction wages are the highest in the low-need districts and large cities and lowest in the high-need rural districts (Table 2). Table 4 reveals, however, that the capital price elasticity is not statistically significant.[39] As expected, we find that the coefficient on the teacher salary variable is positive and statistically significant at the 10 percent level in Models 2 and 3.

To allow for a possible nonlinear relationship between enrollment and the value of the capital stock, we include a quadratic term in the model.[40] We find that growth in enrollment is positively related to value of the capital stock up to an enrollment of between 220 and 380 students, and negatively related thereafter. Given that over 95 percent of districts have enrollment of over 300 students, this elasticity is negative for most districts. The enrollment elasticity is approximately equal to -0.30 in a district of average size but reaches -0.80 in the largest districts.

We expect lower capital investment in districts that have lower demand for education due to lower income, state aid, tax prices, and preference factors. We find a positive and statistically significant income elasticity ($\phi = 0.20$) and negative and statistically significant tax share elasticity ($\mu = -0.22$).[41] Given that high-need urban/suburban districts tend to have lower income and higher tax shares than average-need or low-need districts, these results help explain the patterns in Table 2. We also find that the

---

[39] This result probably reflects the high correlation between the capital price variable, which is based on county construction wages, and both teacher salaries and the instrument used for teacher salaries, county population. When the labor price is dropped, the coefficient on the construction wage becomes statistically significant.

[40] We examined possible nonlinear relationship for all of the continuous variables in the model. Enrollment is the only variable that is statistically significant at the 10 percent level in all models. The quadratic terms for local tax share and construction wage were significant in some models. We examine the results of the model with both of these variables in quadratic form as part of the sensitivity analysis (Table 6).

[41] The tax share elasticity is similar to that found in other education demand studies (Fisher and Papke, 2000). Assuming constant technical returns to scale ($\beta = 1$) and using an estimate of economies of quality scale ($\rho\beta = 1.4$) from another study (Duncombe, Lukemeyer, and Yinger, 2008), it is possible to calculate the structural parameters for the other cost variables in the model. Using the estimates in Model 2, ε is calculated to be 1.31. For the demand parameters, the structural parameter is equal to the reported coefficient multiplied by ε. For example, the income elasticity (ϕ) is equal to the reported coefficient on income (0.155) multiplied by 1.311.

operating aid ratio has a positive impact on capital investment but this effect is not statistically significant.

In addition, we find that the share of African American students has a statistically significant and negative relationship with capital investment in most districts. Because African Americans constitute a small share of the population in most districts, this result suggests that whites' willingness to support capital spending declines as the minority share increases. When African Americans represent the majority of population, however, demand for capital spending appears unrelated to the share of African American students.[42]

High-need urban districts may also face other challenges that reduce their rate of adjustment between desired and actual capital stocks. We find that a recent change in superintendents is associated with 2.8 percent lower capital investment; high-need urban/suburban districts are much more likely to experience superintendent changes. We also find that enrollment increases in the last five years are positively related to capital investment. The low-need districts and large cities have had the highest five-year enrollment growth on average from 1997–2005, while high-need rural districts have experienced enrollment declines on average (Table 2). Finally, we find that there is a substantial increase (23 percent) in the value of a district's capital stock after consolidation, even after accounting for the higher price subsidy that consolidating districts receive.

6.4. *Local Response and District Fiscal Health*

The key conclusion from Table 4 is that high-need urban districts have not responded to the price incentives in the Building Aid program, controlling for a number of other factors that may affect their price response. These results are even more striking given that the state has paid between 70 percent and 80 percent of their reimbursable facility cost during this time period. For the large upstate central cities, the state aid ratio has typically been above 90 percent. We now explore further the relationship between district fiscal health and price response to Building Aid.

The classification of fiscal health developed by SED, which they call "need/resource-capacity categories," was developed using data for

---

[42]The sum of the coefficients on percent African American students and the interaction term with the dichotomous variable for majority African American population is not statistically significant from zero, based on a Wald test.

2000–2002. Their fiscal health measure is the ratio of student poverty to district fiscal capacity. Districts above the 70th percentile on this ratio are identified as high need; those between the 20th and 70th percentile are identified as average need, and those under the 20th percentile are identified as low need. SED separates districts into urban and rural using information on both enrollment and pupil density. To incorporate fiscal health into our analysis, we calculate the ratio of student poverty to property value per pupil for all the years in our sample.[43] This measure, which is centered on the state average, is similar to the SED measure. A higher value for this need/capacity index indicates worse fiscal health. This index ranges from 7.8 in the large central cities to 0.17 in the low need districts (Table 2). In Table 5, we present results for capital investment models that include the local capital share variable and the interaction between this variable and the need/capacity index (Model 4). (The models in this table also include the uninteracted need/capacity index in place of the student lunch variable.) Model 5 also includes a variable for the local share-need/capacity interaction in urban districts (using the SED definition of "urban"). In both Models 4 and 5, the coefficients of the local share-need/capacity interaction variables are positive and statistically significant. These results indicate that the local response to the price incentives in the Building Aid program is lower in districts in poor fiscal health than in other districts. Model 5 indicates that for any given value of the need/capacity index, the fiscal response is lower in urban districts than in non-urban districts. Coefficients for the other variables in Models 4 and 5 are similar to those in Models 1–3.

At the bottom of Table 5, we present the estimated local capital share elasticities by type of district. We group the three large upstate cities (Buffalo, Rochester, and Syracuse) as one group because their need/capacity index is much higher (approximately 15) than for Yonkers (2.2). On average the elasticity is similar to those estimated in Models 1–3, approximately −0.40. The average elasticity for most types of districts is similar between Models 4 and 5. The exception is for urban districts. The difference is particularly striking for the large upstate cities, where the estimated elasticity is −0.148 in Model 4 and approximately zero in Model 5. For other high-need urban districts, 25 percent are estimated to have elasticities below −0.2 and 10 percent have an estimated elasticity below −0.1. Over 90 percent of rural districts have below-average fiscal health, but rural districts have a

---

[43] More comprehensive measures of fiscal health (Ladd and Yinger, 1991) are not feasible with our approach.

Table 5 Regression results for capital investment models with interaction terms with local capital share variable and need/resource capacity index (New York school Districts).

Explanatory variable	Models	
	4	5
Cost variables		
Local capital share (all districts)	−0.508***	−0.490***
Local capital share interacted with need/capacity index and district type		
All districts	0.025***	0.020**
Urban districts		0.014**
Annual construction wages	0.076	0.077
Teacher salary	2.073	2.169*
Enrollment	0.898*	0.962**
Enrollment squared	−0.080**	−0.084***
Demand Variables		
Local tax share	−0.176***	−0.178***
Income per pupil	0.215***	0.216***
Operating aid ratio	0.207	0.180
Need/resource capacity index	−0.075***	−0.07***
Share of African American students (%)	−0.009***	−0.010***
Share of all African American students who live in a majority African American district (%)	0.005**	0.005**
Adjustment variables		
Debt limit variable	−0.104*	−0.112*
Enrollment change (last five years)	0.281***	0.284***
Change of superintendent (= 1 if in last three years)	−0.026**	−0.027**
Consolidated school district (= 1 if year after consolidation)	0.250***	0.260***
Average elasticity for change in local share	−0.398	−0.405
Three large upstate central cities	−0.148	−0.002
Other high-need urban/suburban	−0.329	−0.251
High-need rural	−0.366	−0.376
Average-need	−0.451	−0.436
Low-need	−0.504	−0.484
Prob > F	0.00	0.00
MSE	0.44	0.44

Notes: Sample size is 12,042 (634 districts). The sample does not include New York City, districts with fewer than eight teachers, and districts serving special needs populations. The dependent variable is the estimated value of the capital stock from 1990–2008. The independent variables are lagged three years (1987–2005). All financial variables are inflation-adjusted and expressed in 2000$ using the consumer price index for urban consumers (CPI-U). All variables except for the operating aid ratio, enrollment change, subsidized lunch, share of African American students, and dichotomous variables are expressed in natural logs. The models are estimated with linear 2SLS (with teacher salaries treated as an endogenous variable) with district and year fixed effects. Asterisks denote statistical significance at the 1% (***), 5% (**), and 10% (*) levels.

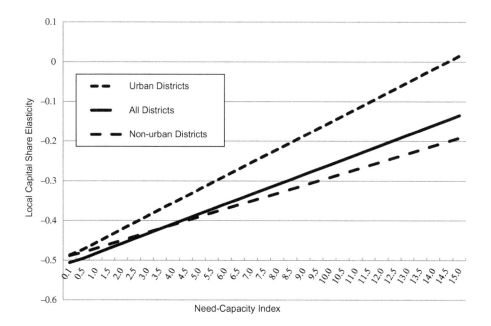

Figure 2   Estimated capital share elasticity by need-capacity index and district type.

Note: The estimates for urban and non-urban districts are based on Model 5 and for all districts based on Model 4.

much higher response to matching aid incentives than do urban districts with the same need/capacity index. Figure 2 illustrates the estimated local share elasticities based on coefficients in Models 4 and 5. The average value for the need/capacity index is 3 and the median is 2.2. For the district in average fiscal health, we find that there is very little difference in the local share elasticity (less than 0.04) between urban and non-urban districts. However, for districts with a need/capacity index above 10 (90th percentile for high-need urban districts and 95th percentile for high-need rural districts), the price response in urban districts is estimated to be half of that in rural districts.

6.5. *Robustness Checks*

We also explored several alternative models based on different choices about measures and model specification. As indicated previously, the estimate of the capital stock requires assumptions about the depreciation rate and adjustment factor. Table 6 presents results for two alternative depreciation rates and levels for the adjustment factor (top two panels). Even with substantial differences in assumptions about these factors, the estimated

Table 6 Sensitivity analysis of local capital share elasticity with different assumptions about the capital stock, laos of independent variables, and model specifications.

	All districts	Three large upstate cities	Other high-need urban/suburban	High-need rural	Average-need	Low-need
Baseline (depreciation = 2%, adjustment factor = 1)	−0.405	−0.002	−0.251	−0.376	−0.436	−0.484
Depreciation (adjustment factor =1)						
1%	−0.418	0.000	−0.250	−0.371	−0.435	−0.486
3%	−0.420	−0.004	−0.251	−0.381	−0.436	−0.483
Adjustment factor (depreciation = 2%)						
0.6	−0.404	−0.006	−0.240	−0.376	−0.418	−0.458
1.4	−0.427	0.000	−0.256	−0.377	−0.445	−0.498
Different lags of independent variables						
2-year lag	−0.398	0.067	−0.220	−0.318	−0.422	−0.493
4-year lag	−0.389	−0.037	−0.240	−0.375	−0.399	−0.429
Multi-year average used to calculate need/resource capacity index						
2-year average	−0.397	0.050	−0.220	−0.367	−0.412	−0.455
3-year average	−0.380	0.052	−0.194	−0.365	−0.392	−0.427
Other Model Specifications						
Quadratic price variables	−0.407	−0.001	−0.241	−0.372	−0.422	−0.466
Property values used instead of tax share	−0.434	−0.002	−0.263	−0.387	−0.452	−0.503
Value of capital stock as RHS variable[1]	−0.468	0.265	−0.137	−0.510	−0.477	−0.503
Capital stock based on 15 years rather than 10	−0.246	0.065	−0.122	−0.209	−0.259	−0.298

Notes: Based on Model 5 in Table 5. The sample does not include New York City, districts with fewer than eight teachers, and districts serving special needs populations. The dependent variable is the estimated value of the capital stock (from 1990–2008) unless otherwise specified. The independent variables are lagged three years (1987–2005) unless indicated otherwise. The capital stock is estimated with a depreciation rate of 2 percent and an adjustment factor of 1 unless indicated otherwise. All financial variables are inflation-adjusted and expressed in 2000$ using the consumer price index for urban consumers (CPI-U). All variables except for operating aid ratio, enrollment change, subsidized lunch, share of African American students, and dichotomous variables are expressed in natural logs. The models are estimated with linear 2SLS (with teacher salaries treated as an endogenous variable) with district and year fixed effects.

(1) The dependent variable is capital spending per pupil. Estimates include the interaction between local share and fiscal health for urban districts only because the coefficient for all districts was not statistically significant. All independent variables are lagged two years.

elasticities are similar to those in baseline model. We also estimated elasticities when the capital stock measure is based on 15 years of past capital spending rather than 10 (last line of Table 6). While the elasticities in this case show a similar pattern across districts, they are much lower. This result may be partly due to the loss of five years of data (1987–1992), which included both an expansion and a recession.

Based on our conversations with SED staff, our baseline model assumes that capital investment decisions are made three years after a change in key independent variables, such as the local capital share. When we relax this assumption and look at lags of two years or four years (third panel in Table 6), the estimated elasticities are similar to the baseline. The fiscal health measure we developed uses contemporaneous data. We also looked at models in which the school lunch index and property value index are based on two-year or three-year moving averages (fourth panel in Table 6) and also found similar elasticities.

We also looked at several alternative specifications of the model.[44] We included quadratic terms for the continuous variables and interactions between the other continuous variables with the local share.[45] The only variables for which the quadratic terms were significant at the 10 percent level in some models were the construction wage and teacher salaries. Including these quadratic terms had little impact on the elasticity estimates. The numerator of the tax share variable is the predicted median house value from a regression based on 10 years of data (1998–2008). This coefficient could be biased if the coefficients in the regression model do not apply to the previous decade (1987–1997). Given that the tax share is not the main

---

[44]One alternative we examined was whether the local response was related to enrollment changes in the district, by interacting the local capital share variable with a dichotomous variable for whether the district had declining enrollment over the previous five years. We found that the interaction term was statistically significant and positive but very small. We also interacted the local share with the five-year enrollment change variable and the interaction was statistically insignificant. These results imply that district response to the local share is not greatly influenced by whether the district had experienced recent enrollment declines.

[45]We estimated a translog cost model with quadratics for continuous variables and interaction terms between independent variables, and found that the vast majority of coefficients were statistically insignificant. It is likely that collinearity is one of the major reasons for the imprecise estimates. To avoid collinearity problems, we have taken a more systematic approach to making the model more general by testing quadratics for all of the continuous variables and looking at interaction terms, which have a meaningful interpretation.

policy variable of interest in this paper, we estimated a model using district property value per pupil instead of tax share and found little impact on the capital share elasticities.

Finally, we looked at an alternative specification of the model in which the capital stock in the previous year is included as a right-side variable and per pupil capital spending is the dependent variable. This is the approach used by Balsdon, Brunner, and Rueben (2003). Based on (14), moving the previous year's capital stock to the right side requires a nonlinear estimator. Instead, we assumed for simplicity that the log of the capital stock can be included as an additive term to the existing log-linear model.[46] As might be expected, the local share elasticity with respect to capital spending is somewhat larger than the elasticity for the capital stock. Our main result still holds, however, as the urban high-need districts still have lower price responses than other districts. Indeed, the estimated elasticity is actually positive (but insignificant) for the three large upstate cities.

7. Summary and Conclusions

Despite the significant growth in state financial support for school infrastructure in the last decade, relatively little research has examined the determinants of capital investment decisions by school districts. The objective of this paper is to help fill this gap by providing an empirical analysis of school district capital investment in New York.

New York's Building Aid program is a categorical grant, which requires project approval by the SED. The grant distribution is by an open-ended matching formula, although the state imposes ceilings on the maximum size of the project to limit the burden on the state budget. The grant is wealth equalized and adjusted for construction costs in different regions of the state. The 10-percentage-point increase in the state matching aid ratio in 1998–2000 provides a natural experiment for examining how districts respond to different tax price reductions. While many districts (particularly the high-need rural districts) significantly increased capital spending after this price change, the high-need urban/suburban districts expanded capital spending at a much lower rate than other districts despite very large price reductions.

---

[46]This model includes the interaction between the local share and fiscal health measures for urban districts only because the coefficient for all districts was not statistically significant. All independent variables are lagged two years.

To empirically examine these differential price responses, we first develop a theoretical model of capital investment that incorporates variables from a capital demand equation and a general education demand equation. The dependent variable for this model is an estimate of the value of the capital stock. The capital investment model was estimated using a 19-year panel for the majority of school districts in New York state. The results of the model generally fit theoretical expectations and we find an inelastic but statistically significant response of capital investment decisions to the local capital share. For high-need urban/suburban districts, however, this price elasticity is much smaller than in other districts, after controlling for other determinants of capital investment. We estimate that this lower price response is the principal reason that the value of the capital stock in the high-need urban/suburban districts is approximately two-thirds of the state average and half of that in high-need rural districts in 2005. These results suggest that the budgetary problems of high-need urban/suburban districts are so severe that they are unwilling to undertake new capital projects even when virtually all the cost will be picked up by the state government. The lack of capital investment by high-need urban/suburban districts in New York is of concern because of recent evidence indicating that a larger capital stock is associated with higher student performance and property values (Jones and Zimmer, 2001; Cellini, Ferreira, and Rothstein, 2010).[47]

These results pose a major dilemma for state policy makers in New York. The capital stock in large, high-need urban districts still lags behind that in other districts, but the ability of policy makers to eliminate this inequity through price incentives appears to be quite limited. Moreover, our finding of a weak relationship between capital investment and Operating Aid suggest that increasing general-purpose foundation aid is unlikely to result in significant capital investment. Given that New York's Building Aid program is unusually generous, our results suggest that the price response facilities aid programs in most other states are unlikely to be effective in stimulating capital investment in high-need urban/suburban districts.

Other approaches, such as full state funding or loosening of debt limits need to be explored. Earlier studies (Wang and Duncombe, 2009) provide suggestive evidence that the type of building-aid formula used by a state may affect the level of inequality in capital investment. State policymakers should

---

[47]However, Gronberg, Jansen, and Taylor (2011) find that educational costs increase with the value of a district's capital stock. This result suggests that a larger capital stock may result in lower student performance.

explore other methods of funding school facilities, such as the adoption of lump-sum capital aid programs, rather than relying predominantly on matching aid. In addition, long-term capital planning requirements for school districts and the development of capital project priorities by state education departments (as in Florida and West Virginia) might help to reduce inequality in capital facilities and ensure that the most-needed projects have first claim on state funds. The fact that rural districts in New York significantly increased capital investments over the last decade relative to other districts even though many were experiencing significant enrollment declines suggests that the targeting of Building Aid in New York could be improved.

An important area for future research is the examination in other states of the impact of political and management factors on decisions about capital investment in high-need urban districts compared to other districts. Are the lower elasticities we found for these districts in New York driven by specific fiscal and institutional constraints unique to New York state, or does the same pattern emerge in other states as well?

Acknowledgments

We appreciate helpful suggestions from Amy Ellen Schwartz on an earlier draft of the paper. Comments from the editors, George Zodrow and William Gentry, and several anonymous reviewers are gratefully acknowledged. Charles Szuberla and his staff in the Facilities Management Unit in the New York State Education Department provided access to facilities data and invaluable help in understanding the Building Aid program and the process of facilities funding in New York state.

References

Ammar, Salwa, William Duncombe, Yilin Hou, Bernard Jump, and Ronald Wright. 2001. Using fuzzy rule-based systems to evaluate overall financial performance of governments: an enhancement to the bond rating process. *Public Budgeting and Finance* **21**(4): 91–110.

Association of School Business Officials International. 1999. *Financing School Facilities.* Association of School Business Officials International, Reston, VA.

Balsdon, Ed, Eric J. Brunner, and Kim Rueben. 2003. Private demands for public capital: evidence from school board referenda. *Journal of Urban Economics* **54**(3): 610–638.

Baum, Christopher, Mark Schaffer, and Steven Stillman. 2007. Enhanced routines for instrumental variables/GMM estimation and testing. *Stata Journal* **7**(4): 465–506.

Brecher, Charles, Kurt Richwerger, and Marcia Van Wagner. 2003. An approach to measuring the affordability of state debt. *Public Budgeting and Finance* **23**(4): 65–85.

Bruce, Donald, Deborah A. Carroll, John A. Deskins, and Jonathan C. Rork. 2007. Road to ruin? A spatial analysis of state highway spending. *Public Budgeting and Finance* **27**(4): 66–85.

Brunner, Eric J. 2006. Financing school facilities in California. Institute for Research on Education Policy and Practice, Stanford University, Stanford, CA.

Brunner, Eric J., and Kim Reuben. 2001. Financing new school construction and modernization: evidence from California. *National Tax Journal* **54**(3): 527–539.

Campaign for Fiscal Equity. 2004. *Making the Right to a Sound Basic Education a Reality: Final Report of the Sound Basic Education Task Force, Part II: Building Aid Reform, Adequate Facilities for All.* Campaign for Fiscal Equity, New York, NY.

Cellini, Stephanie R., Fernando Ferreira, and Jesse Rothstein. 2010. The value of school facilities: evidence from a dynamic regression discontinuity design. *Quarterly Journal of Economics* **125**(1): 215–261.

Crampton, Faith, and David Thompson. 2001. Creating and sustaining school capacity in the twenty-first century: funding a physical environment conducive to student learning. *Journal of Education Finance* **27**(2): 633–652.

Crampton, Faith E., David C. Thompson, and Randall S. Vesely. 2004. The forgotten side of school finance equity: the role of infrastructure funding in student success. *National Association of Secondary School Principals Bulletin* **88**(640): 29–52.

Cromwell, Brian A. 1991. Public sector maintenance: the case of local mass-transit. *National Tax Journal* **44**(2): 199–212.

Duncombe, William, Anna Lukemeyer, and John Yinger. 2008. Dollars without sense: the mismatch between the no child left behind act accountability system and Title I funding. In Kahlenberg, Richard (ed.), *Improving on No Child Left Behind: Getting Education Reform Back on Track*, 19–101. The Century Foundation Press, New York, NY.

Duncombe, William, and John Yinger. 1993. An analysis of returns to scale in public production with an application to fire protection. *Journal of Public Economics* **52**(1): 49–72.

Earthman, Glen. 2000. *Planning Educational Facilities for the Next Century.* Association of School Business Officials International, Reston, VA.

Education Priorities Panel. 2002. *Castles in the Sand: Why School Overcrowding Remains a Problem in NYC.* Education Priorities Panel, New York, NY.

Filardo, Mary, Jeffrey Vincent, Ping Sung, and Travis Stein. 2006. Growth and disparity: a decade of U.S. public school construction. Building Educational Success Together, Washington, DC.

Fisher, Ronald, and Leslie Papke. 2000. Local government responses to education grants. *National Tax Journal* **53**(1): 153–168.

Gramlich, Edward M. 1994. Infrastructure investment: a review essay. *Journal of Economic Literature* **37**(3): 1176–1196.

Gravelle, Jane. 1982. Effects of the 1981 depreciation revisions on the taxation of income from business capital. *National Tax Journal* **35**(1): 1–20.

Gronberg, Timothy J., Dennis W. Jansen, and Lori L. Taylor. 2011. The impact of facilities on the cost of education. *National Tax Journal* **64**(1): 193–218.

Hall, Robert, and Dale Jorgenson. 1967. Tax policy and investment behavior. *American Economic Review* **57**(3): 391–414.

Hildreth, W. Bartley, and Gerald Miller. 2002. Debt and the local economy: problems in benchmarking local government debt affordability. *Public Budgeting and Finance* **22**(4): 99–113.

Holtz-Eakin, Douglas. 1994. Public sector capital and the productivity puzzle. *Review of Economics and Statistics* **76**(1): 12–21.

Holtz-Eakin, Douglas, and Harvey Rosen. 1989. The 'rationality' of municipal capital spending: evidence from New Jersey. *Regional Science and Urban Economics* **19**(3): 517–536.

Holtz-Eakin, Douglas, and Harvey Rosen. 1993. Municipal construction spending: an empirical examination. *Economics and Politics* **5**(1): 61–84.

Honeyman, David. 1990. School facilities and state mechanisms that support school construction: a report from the fifty states. *Journal of Education Finance* **16**(2): 247–272.

Hubbard, R. Glenn. 1998. Capital-market imperfections and investment. *Journal of Economic Literature* **36**(1): 193–225.

Hulten, Charles, and Robert Schwab. 1991. Is there too little public capital? Infrastructure and economic growth. American Enterprise Institute Discussion Paper. American Enterprise Institute, Washington, DC.

Hulten, Charles, and Robert Schwab. 1993. Infrastructure spending: where do we go from here? *National Tax Journal* **46**(3): 261–273.

Johnson, Craig, and Kenneth Kriz. 2005. Fiscal institutions, credit ratings, and borrowing costs. *Public Budgeting and Finance* **25**(1): 84–103.

Jones, John T., and Ron W. Zimmer. 2001. Examining the impact of capital on academic achievement. *Economics of Education Review* **20**(6): 577–588.

Jorgenson, Dale. 1974. investment and production: a review. In Intriligator, Michael D., and David A. Kendrick (eds.), *Frontiers of Quantitative Economics, Volume 2*, 341–366. North-Holland, Amsterdam, Netherlands.

Ladd, Helen F., and John Yinger. 1991. *America's Ailing Cities: Fiscal Health and Design of Urban Policy.* The John Hopkins University Press, Baltimore, MD.

McCall, H. Carl. 2001. School construction and building aid: an on-again, off-again priority. Office of the State Comptroller, Albany, NY.

Munnell, Alicia. 1992. Infrastructure investment and economic growth. *Journal of Economic Perspectives* **6**(4): 189–198.

National Center for Education Statistics. 2000. *Condition of America's Public School Facilities: 1999.* NCES 2000–032. Office of Educational Research and Improvement, U.S. Department of Education, Washington, DC.

National Center for Education Statistics. 2010. *The Condition of Education 2010.* NCES 2010–028. U.S. Government Printing Office, Washington, DC.

New York Office of the State Comptroller. 2007. *Special Report on Municipal Affairs.* Office of the State Comptroller, Albany, NY.

New York State Division of the Budget. 1998. 1998–99 executive budget. New York State Division of the Budget, Albany, NY.

Newey, Whitney K., and Kenneth D. West. 1987. A simple, positive semi-definite, heteroskedasticity and autocorrelation consistent covariance matrix. *Econometrica* **55**(3): 703–708.

Plummer, Elizabeth. 2006. The effects of state funding on property tax rates and school construction. *Economics of Education Review* **25**(5): 532–542.

Rubinfeld, Daniel L. 1987. The economies of the local public sector. In Auerbach, Alan J., and Martin Feldstein (eds.), *Handbook of Public Economics*, vol. 2, pp. 571–639. North-Holland, Amsterdam, Netherlands.

Schaffer, Mark E. 2005. XTIVREG2: stata module to perform extended IV/2SLS, GMM and AC/HAC, LIML and k-class regression for panel data models. Statistical Software Components S456501, Revised edition. Boston College Department of Economics, Chestnut Hill, MA.

Sciarra, David, Koren Bell, and Susan Kenyon. 2006. Safe and adequate: using litigation to address inadequate K–12 school facilities. Education Law Center, Newark, NJ.

Sielke, Catherine. 2001. Funding school infrastructure needs across the states. *Journal of Education Finance* **27**(2): 653–662.

State Education Department. 2001. Analysis of school finances in New York state school districts. New York State Education Department, Albany, NY, http://www.oms.nysed.gov/faru/Analysis/99-00/Text99_00Analysis.html.

State Education Department. 2002. School district responses to building aid incentives. Research Monograph. New York State Education Department, Albany, NY.

State Education Department. 2007. State formula aid and entitlements for schools in New York state (as amended by Chapters of the Laws of 2007). New York State Education Department, Albany, NY.

State Education Department. 2010. Definitions of need/resource-capacity categories of New York state school districts. *New York State Board of Regents Proposal on State Aid to School Districts for School Year 2010–2011.* New York State Education Department, Albany, NY.

Stock, James H. and Motohiro Yogo. 2005. Testing for weak instruments in linear IV regression. In Andrews, Donald W. K., and James H. Stock (eds.), *Identification and Inference for Econometric Models: Essays in Honor of Thomas Rothenberg,* 80–108. Cambridge University Press, Cambridge, UK.

Taylor, Lori, and William Fowler, Jr. 2006. *A Comparative Wage Approach to Geographic Cost Adjustment.* U.S. Department of Education, Washington, DC.

Thurnau, Carl T. 2004. State building aid for public school districts and BOCES. Memorandum. Office of Facilities Planning, New York State Education Department, Albany, NY.

U.S. Government Accountability Office. 1995. *School Facilities: Condition of America's Schools.* GAO/HEHS-95-61. U.S. Government Accountability Office, Washington DC.

Wang, Wen. 2004. Appendix C, a guide to state building aid programs for elementary and secondary education. In Yinger, John (ed.), *Helping Children Left Behind: State Aid and the Pursuit of Educational Equity,* pp. 353–366. MIT Press, Cambridge, MA.

Wang, Wen, and William Duncombe. 2009. School facilities funding and capital outlay distribution in the states. *Journal of Education Finance* **34**(3): 324–350.

Wooldridge, Jeffrey M. 2003. *Introductory Econometrics: A Modern Approach.* South-Western College Publishing, Florence, KY.

Zedalis, Patricia. 2003. *New York State Aid to School Districts for Construction.* New York State Education Department, Albany, NY.

Chapter 21

Still Unknown: The Impact of School Capital on Student Performance[*]

John Yinger

Departments of Public Administration and
International Affairs and of Economics,
Syracuse University, Syracuse, NY, United States
jyinger@maxwell.syr.edu

One of the great unanswered questions in education finance is whether the quantity and quality of school capital — buildings, classrooms, laboratories, and so on — has an impact on student performance.

Gronberg, Jansen, and Taylor (henceforth GJT) estimate educational cost functions using data from Texas and claim that, if anything, school capital, also called infrastructure, raises educational costs holding student performance constant.[1] This claim leads them to reject the possibility that "infrastructure inequalities lead to academic disadvantages" (p. 207).

This conclusion is not warranted. Despite their careful estimation techniques, GJT misinterpret their findings. Their main result is that total costs (or costs per pupil) increase with the amount of school capital, holding student performance constant. The link between infrastructure inequalities and academic disadvantages refers, however, to a different question, namely, whether an increase in school capital leads to an increase student performance. GJT do not provide an answer to this question.

---

[*]This chapter is reproduced from "Still Unknown: The Impact of School Capital on Student Performance." It's Elementary Column, Posted at http://cpr.maxwell.syr.edu/efap/about_efap/ie/Dec12.pdf. December 2012.
[1]Timothy J. Gronberg, Dennis W. Jansen, and Lori L. Taylor. 2011. "The Impact of Facilities on the Cost of Education." *National Tax Journal* **64**(1), (March): 193–218.

This chapter explains where GJT went wrong. It is drawn from a column that is somewhat more technical than my usual column, because it involves long-run and short-run cost curves, but these concepts should be familiar to anyone who has taken a class in microeconomics.

In the case of public schools, a short-run cost curve indicates the relationship between student performance and educational costs, holding school capital constant. School capital is altered much less frequently than the number of teachers or other school inputs, so it often makes sense to consider school capital as fixed in the short run and to explore educational costs under this assumption. A long-run cost curve does not hold school capital constant. Instead, a long-run cost curve indicates the relationship between student performance and educational costs when school capital is adjusted to the lowest-cost level for each level of student performance.

These cost curves are usually illustrated as average cost curves, that is, as costs per unit of quantity, which in this case is cost per unit of student performance. The issue here is not cost per pupil. A school district's costs per pupil may depend, of course, on its enrollment, and several of my earlier columns have addressed this issue.[2] The concepts at issue in this column, however, hold the number of pupils constant and average over the units of student performance.

Figure 1 illustrates what these types of cost curves look like.[3] Student performance is on the horizontal axis and average cost is on the vertical axis. Several short-run cost curves, each at a different level of school capital, are illustrated. The long-run cost curve is the set of lowest points on the short-run curves, that is, it is the set of points that describe the lowest possible cost at each level of student performance. Recall that the long-run curve can be interpreted as the curve that applies once school districts have adjusted to the quantity of school capital that is optimal for the student performance they wish to achieve.

GJT do not plot average cost curves. Instead they plot the relationship between the capital stock per pupil and total cost per pupil.[4] The

---

[2]See the August and September "It's Elementary" columns from 2007, for example. [Available at: http://cpr.maxwell.syr.edu/efap/about_efap/Its_elementary.html.]

[3]For readers with some background in economics, this figure is derived from a constant-elasticity-of-substitution production function in the case of decreasing returns to quality scale. The points in the text also apply with other production functions or scale assumptions.

[4]See Figure 1 in Timothy J. Gronberg, Dennis W. Jansen, and Lori L. Taylor. 2011. "The Impact of Facilities on the Cost of Education." *National Tax Journal* **64**(1), (March): 193–218.

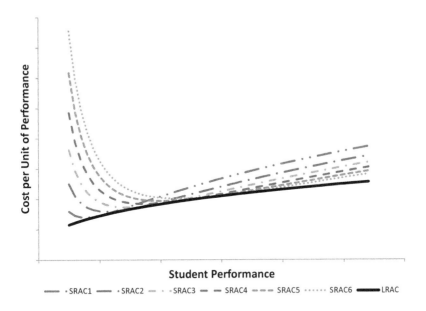

Figure 1   An example of short- and long-run average cost curves.

assumptions that lead to Figure 1 can be used to replicate this type of plot. The result is given in Figure 2. This figure presents capital stock per pupil and total cost per pupil for different values of student performance, Q1 to Q7. The thicker line does not hold student performance constant, but instead shows the long-run relationship between capital stock and performance when the capital stock is set at the optimal value for each level of student performance.

Figure 2 makes it clear that for a given level of student performance, costs decline with the capital stock if the capital stock is too low (that is, below its optimal level) and costs increase with the capital stock when the capital stock is too high. This figure also makes it clear that a district cannot obtain a higher student performance in the long run without spending more on school capital. The figure in GJT holds student performance constant at the state-wide average, so it corresponds to one of the short-run curves in this figure.

GJT interpret their figure as an indication of "gross overutilization of capital relative to an efficient allocation" (p. 205). This interpretation is not correct. Because they hold school performance constant at the mean value in the sample, they are simply tracing out one of the constant-performance curves in Figure 2, such as the one associated with quantity Q2, which looks a lot like their figure. In fact, however, school districts provide different quantities of education and therefore fall on different curves. All districts

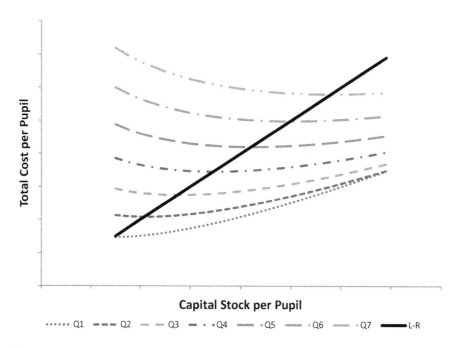

Figure 2   The relationship between capital stock per pupil and total cost per pupil.

could fall on or close to the long-run curve in my Figure 2, along which cost increases with capital stock even though there is no overutilization of capital. Thus, the GJT figure does not show that districts are using too much school capital; instead, it only shows what it would cost if a district provided the state-wide average student performance using more capital than necessary.

GJT go on to say that "the estimates provide no evidence that increases in facilities capital will help districts to reduce the costs associated with maintaining or improving the test score performance of their students, or that infrastructure inequalities lead to academic disadvantages" (p. 207). These claims are overstated, if not incorrect. Consider a district producing a student performance that is above the point where its short-run cost curve (i.e., the short-run cost curve associated with its school capital) touches the long-run cost curve. Figure 1 shows that this district can lower its costs by increasing its school capital. As just discussed, this point is also made in Figure 2: At a given level of student performance, increasing school capital lowers costs for a district with a capital stock that is below the optimal (—long-run) value for that performance level. GJT only plot a school-capital/total-cost curve for one level of student performance; at other levels of student performance, this curve could have a very different shape.

Moreover, the results in GJT are consistent with the possibility that higher "facilities capital," which is the term they use, results in higher student performance, which implies, of course that they are consistent with the possibility that infrastructure inequalities lead to academic disadvantages. As shown in Figure 2, a positive long-run relationship between facilities capital and cost arises even when no inefficiency exists — a model that is perfectly consistent with the GJT results. In other words, perfectly efficient districts (i.e., those on the long-run curve) have to spend more on facilities capital to obtain higher student performance. Thus, it is premature to conclude that infrastructure inequalities do not lead to academic disadvantages.

GJT could resolve this issue by finding the long-run cost curve associated with the short-run cost curves they estimate. This type of calculation has appeared in non-school cost studies that use methods similar to those of GJT. An estimate of this type would make it possible to determine the extent to which some districts deviate from the lowest-cost level of school capital for their student performance level and the extent to which some districts have levels of school capital that are below the optimal value for the student performance that the State of Texas would like them to provide. Neither of these questions can be answered with the information provided by GJT.

In short, despite the claims of GJT, we still do not know the extent to which increases in school capital lead to increases in student performance. Moreover, we still cannot reject — or prove — the hypothesis that infrastructure gaps contribute to gaps in student performance.

Appendices

Present Value and Discounting, with Applications to Local Public Finance

John Yinger

*Departments of Public Administration and
International Affairs and of Economics,
Syracuse University, Syracuse, NY, United States*
jyinger@maxwell.syr.edu

1. Introduction

This appendix reviews the concepts of present value and discounting and explains how these concepts can be applied to property assessment, mortgages, annuities and pensions, and bonds — including municipal bonds. The concepts are illustrated with numerous examples. The concepts of inflation, uncertainty, and risk are briefly considered at the end.

2. Compound Interest

Suppose I put $100 in a savings account on January 1 and it earns interest at a 3 percent rate per year. For now, suppose that this interest is paid all at once at the end of the year. Then if I do not withdraw any money, at the end of the year my account will contain ($100 + 0.03 × $100) = $100 × (1.03) = $103. (The symbol " × " indicates multiplication.)

Now consider what happens if another year is added to the analysis. At a 3 percent interest rate, $100 in my account turns into $103 at the end of the first year. This $103 turn into $100×(1.03)×(1.03) = $100×(1.03)^2 = $100×(1.0609) = $106.09 at the end of the second year. This bank account involves a concept known as ***compound interest***. In the second year, interest is paid not only on the original $100, but also on the $3 of interest received in the second year — a concept known as compounding.

These concepts can be expressed in a general way. Let V_0 be the initial value of an investment (such as my savings account), and let i be the rate of return on this investment (such as the 3 percent interest on my savings account). Then the value of the account at time y is

$$V_y = V_0 \times (1+i)^y \tag{1}$$

Note that y and i both refer to the interval that determines compounding. If the return is compounded once a year, then y indicates years and i indicates the annual interest rate. If the return is compounded every month, then y stands for month and i is the monthly interest rate, which is the annual interest rate divided by 12.

The frequency of compounding makes a small difference, which grows over time. Consider $100 invested in two different savings accounts, both of which have a 6 percent annual interest rate but one of which compounds once a year and the other compounds monthly. At the end of the first year, the first account contains $100\times(1.06) = \$106$, whereas the second contains $100\times(1+.06/12)^{12} = \$106.17$. (The "/" indicates "divided by.") A third account with a 6 percent rate and daily compounding would contain $100\times(1+.06/365)^{365} = \$106.18$. If these three accounts are held for 5 years, their values are $133.82, $134.89, and $134.98, respectively.

3. Present Value and Discounting

Now suppose someone asks me what I would be willing to pay today to receive $103 at the end of the year. This question defines the concept of **present value**, which is what an amount received in the future is worth to me today. The answer is contained in the above expression; if $100 received today turns into $103 in a year, then the receipt of $103 a year from now is worth $103/1.03 = \$100$ today. In this example, in other words, the present value of $103 received a year from now is $100.

We can also ask about the present value of funds received at the end of 2 years. The present value of $106.09 received in 2 years is $106.09/[(1.03)^2] = \$100$. With an interest rate of 3 percent, in other words, I would be equally happy with $100 received now, $103 received a year from now, or $106.09 received 2 years from now.

To write down a general form for these concepts, let FV stand for future value, PV stand for present value. Then we can write down an alternative version of equation (1) and use it to define present value

$$FV_y = PV \times (1+i)^y \tag{2}$$

and

$$PV = \frac{FV_y}{(1+i)^y} \tag{3}$$

With equation (3), we can translate the value of our investment in time period y into a value today, that is, into a present value. As in the case of equation (1), these results apply to any time period for compounding, so long as y and i are defined by the same unit of time.

Wait a minute, you might say, what if I do not want to wait for 2 years to get my money? In the above example, how can $106.09 received in 2 years possibly be as valuable to me as $100 received today? The answer lies in the interest rate, which actually has two meanings, not just one. The first meaning is the return on a particular account. In this example, I receive 3 percent interest on my savings account. The second meaning is the **opportunity cost** of tying up my money in one activity or investment instead of another.

Suppose I could also invest my money in a stock market account that I expect will yield a return of 6 percent per year. (The notion of risk is ignored here, but considered in Section 9.) Then the opportunity cost of placing my money in my savings account is 6 percent, the return I give up, not 3 percent, the return I receive in that account. With this alternative investment possibility, $106.09 received in 2 years is not worth $100 to me today. Instead, it is only worth $106.09/[(1.06)^2] = $94.42.

Thus, it is appropriate to use equation (1) or (2) to calculate the future values of an investment that yields return i, but to use equation (3) to calculate present value based on the return on one's best investment, say r, which may not be the same as i. In symbols,

$$PV = \frac{FV_y}{(1+r)^y} \tag{4}$$

For example, with an opportunity cost rate of r, the present value of V_0 invested at i percent for y time periods is

$$PV = \frac{V_0 \times (1+i)^y}{(1+r)^y} \tag{5}$$

Equation (4) is useful because it allow us to observe returns received in different years in the future and translate them into a common metric, namely present value. For example, we can compare on investment with returns at annual rate of 6.25 percent for 3 years with another investment that has returns at an annual rate of 6 percent for 4 years. If the opportunity cost rate, r, equals 5 percent, then the PV per dollar invested equals $(1.0625)^3/[(1.05)^3] = 1.0361$ for the first investment and $(1.06)^4/[(1.05)^4] = 1.0386$ for the second. Even though the second investment has a smaller annual return, the fact that it produces an above-opportunity-cost return for one more year makes it the better investment of the two.

Finally, it is possible to define an individual's opportunity cost rate, also called **discount rate**, in an even more general way as the value an individual places on future consumption relative to current consumption. A person with a high discount rate values current consumption far more than future consumption, whereas a person with a low discount rate receives roughly equal satisfaction from consumption today and consumption in the future. A high discount rate, that is, a high value for r in equation (5), leads people to reject investments unless they have a high rate of return, but many investments would be worthwhile for a person whose discount rate is low.

Present value and discounting are also crucial tools in governmental calculations, such as benefit-cost analysis. The objective of a benefit-cost study is to find the course of action with the highest present value of net benefits. A key difference with this application compared to a calculation for an individual is that the present value of social benefits and costs, as in a benefit-cost analysis, should make use of a **social discount rate**, not an individual discount rate. The Council of Economic Advisers provides an excellent discussion of the factors to consider in selecting a social discount.[1]

4. Property Assessment

As discussed in Chapter 1, an assessor's job is to estimate the market value of each property in his or her jurisdiction. In the case of owner-occupied housing, house sales are fairly frequent, and the assessor can estimate the market value of a house that did not sell by observing the price of similar houses in similar neighborhoods. Apartment buildings and stores do not sell very often, however, so this method cannot be used. An alternative method,

---

[1]Council of Economic Advisers, Discounting for Public Policy: Theory and Recent Evidence on the Merits of Updating the Discount Rate, Issue Brief, January 2017. Available at: https://obamawhitehouse.archives.gov/sites/default/files/page/files/201701_cea_discounting_issue_brief.pdf

called the income method, builds on the simple idea that an apartment building or a store is an asset and its price, like the price of any asset, is equal to the present value of the perceived net benefits from owning it. Thus, an assessor collects information on current rents or sales (along with expected changes in those amounts in the future), and then determines the present value of the expected stream of benefits, which is the market value of the property.

Suppose R is the expected net rental income for an apartment building and r is the appropriate discount rate, which is the return the landlord could earn on an alternative investment. Then the value of the building, V, is the sum of the present values of the expected rental income in future years

$$V = \frac{R}{(1+r)} + \frac{R}{(1+r)^2} + \frac{R}{(1+r)^3} + \frac{R}{(1+r)^4} + \cdots \tag{6}$$

Fortunately, this equation can be simplified. Let L stand for the expected lifetime of the building. Divide both sides of equation (6) by $(1 + r)$ and subtract the resulting equation from (6). The subtraction problem is

$$V = \frac{R}{(1+r)} + \frac{R}{(1+r)^2} + \frac{R}{(1+r)^3} + \cdots + \frac{R}{(1+r)^L}$$

$$-\frac{V}{1+r} = -\frac{R}{(1+r)^2} - \frac{R}{(1+r)^3} - \cdots - \frac{R}{(1+r)^L} - \frac{R}{(1+r)^{L+1}} \tag{7}$$

On the right side, the stacked terms cancel each other and equation (7) simplifies to:

$$V\left(1 - \frac{1}{(1+r)}\right) = V\left(\frac{r}{(1+r)}\right) = \frac{R}{(1+r)} + \frac{R}{(1+r)^{L+1}} \tag{8}$$

Solving equation (8) for V yields

$$V = \left(\frac{R}{r}\right)\left(1 + \frac{1}{(1+r)^L}\right) \tag{9}$$

Finally, because the lifetime of housing is long, the expression $[1/((1+r)^L)]$ is close to zero. With $r = 0.05$ and $L = 100$, for example, this term equals 0.0076. Thus, equation (9) is approximately equal to

$$V = \left(\frac{R}{r}\right) \tag{10}$$

In this equation, the denominator, r, is often called the *capitalization rate*. It is the rate that transforms an annual flow, in this case R, into an asset value or capital value.

Straightforward extensions of this analysis can bring in both the costs of owning a property and growth over time in rental income. The costs of running an apartment building include maintenance, depreciation, and property taxes. Suppose these three costs are expected to total c percent of V every year. (Chapter 3 provides further analysis of the impact of property taxes on property values.) Then the expected net benefits of owning the apartment are $(R - cV)$, instead of R. Replacing R in the numerator of equation (9) with $(R - cV)$ results in

$$V = \left(\frac{R - cV}{r}\right) \tag{11}$$

Solving this equation for leads too

$$V = \left(\frac{R}{r + c}\right) \tag{12}$$

In short, an assessor can account for costs with a simple extension of the capitalization rate, which is now $(r + c)$.

Accounting for expected real growth in R is a bit more complicated, but this step also leads to a simple adjustment in the capitalization rate. Suppose $R_y = R_0(1+a)^y$, where R_0 is the current rental income, a is the annual real growth rate, and y is a year indicator. In this case, equation (6) becomes

$$V = R_0\frac{(1 + a)}{(1 + r)} + R_0\frac{(1 + a)^2}{(1 + r)^2} + R_0\frac{(1 + a)^3}{(1 + r)^3} + R_0\frac{(1 + a)^4}{(1 + r)^4} + \cdots \tag{13}$$

Now multiplying both sides of equation (13) by $(1 +a)/(1 +r)$ and following the same steps as before leads to

$$V = \left(\frac{R_0}{r - a}\right) \tag{14}$$

In short, with some information on rents and apartment costs and an estimate of future growth in rental income, an assessor can calculate the market value of an apartment building. As discussed in Section 8, this approach can also accommodate inflationary growth in rents.

5. Mortgages

For the purpose of these notes, a mortgage is a contract in which a lender writes a large check to a homeowner in exchange for a promise from the homeowner to make monthly payments for a certain period of time. These payments include interest at a certain rate on the outstanding balance of the loan. In practice, of course, mortgages come in many forms and are used for many purposes. Some mortgages have variable interest rates, for example, homeowners often take out mortgages to fund home improvements, and businesses often take out mortgages to purchase equipment or real estate. Moreover, when mortgage interest rates decline, many homeowners take out a new mortgage (at the new low rates) to pay off their old mortgage (which has a high rate). This is called refinancing. I am not going to consider these possibilities here. Instead, I will analyze a standard, fixed-rate, home-purchase mortgage.

It is also worth pointing out that once a mortgage has been issued, it is an asset that can be bought and sold. A lender who issues a mortgage may sell it to another lender or to an institution that specializes in buying and repackaging mortgages for investors. Selling a mortgage is equivalent to selling the right to receive the monthly payments that are associated with it. These issues are beyond the scope of these notes, which simply explain the logic of a standard mortgage.

To analyze a mortgage, we need to define some terms.

- M_0 is the amount of the mortgage, that is, the size of the check the lender writes to the homeowner;
- m is the contractual monthly interest rate, which is the annual rate divided by 12;
- P is the size of the monthly payment; and
- Y is the term of the loan, that is, the number of months it takes to pay it off.

Now the key to analyzing a mortgage is to recognize that the amount that is still owed on the mortgage gradually declines over time, until it reaches zero at the end of year Y. The amount of the loan can be thought of as the amount that is owed at the initiation of the mortgage, which is why we call this amount M_0. Now let M_y be the amount that is still owed at the end of month y, where y goes from 1 to Y. For a 30-year mortgage, for example, y goes from 1 to $12 \times 30 = 360$. To find a formula for M_y, we have to recognize (a) that the borrower owes interest at the end of each period based on the outstanding balance at the beginning of the period and (b) that the borrower makes a payment equal to P.

With these points in mind, we can write

$$M_1 = M_0(1+m) - P \tag{15}$$

The first term on the right side indicates the initial balance and the interest owed on it and the second term indicates the borrower's payment. (To keep the equation simple, the $\times$ sign indicating that M_0 is multiplied by $(1+m)$

is implicit in (15) and in the equations that follow.) Part of the payment covers the interest that is due at the end of the first period (mM_0) and the rest goes to reducing the loan balance. After the first payment, therefore, the balance declines by ($P - mM_0$).

Following the same logic, we can write down an expression for the outstanding balance at the end of month 2

$$M_2 = M_1(1 + m) - P \tag{16}$$

In the second period, therefore, the mortgage balance declines by ($P - mM_1$). Because M_1 is smaller than M_0, the interest portion is smaller and the decline in the balance is larger in the second period than in the first. Over the lifetime of a mortgage, the share of the payment that goes to interest gradually declines and the share that goes to reducing principal gradually rises.

Now we can substitute equation (15) into equation (16) to obtain

$$M_2 = M_1(1 + m) - P = [M_0(1 + m) - P](1 + m) - P$$
$$= M_0(1 + m)^2 - P(1 + m) - P \tag{17}$$

One more time

$$M_3 = M_2(1 + m) - P = [M_0(1 + m)^2 - P(1 + m) - P](1 + m) - P$$
$$= M_0(1 + m)^3 - P(1 + m)^2 - P(1 + m) - P \tag{18}$$

This process can easily be generalized to obtain a formula for the balance remaining at the end of any period, y. To be specific

$$M_y = M_0(1 + m)^y - P(1 + m)^{y-1} - P(1 + m)^{y-2}$$
$$- P(1 + m)^{y-3} - \cdots - P \tag{19}$$

The series of dots indicates the set of terms that we have not written out — all the terms with exponents between $y-3$ and 1. The number of these terms obviously depends on the value of y we are looking at. With $y = 10$, for example, there are six terms in this set.

Two more steps lead to the formula for a mortgage. The first step is to use a little algebraic magic. We can re-write equation (19) as follows:

$$M_y = M_0(1 + m)^y - P \times S \tag{20}$$

where

$$S = (1 + m)^{y-1} + (1 + m)^{y-2} + (1 + m)^{y-3} + \cdots + 1 \tag{21}$$

A sum of this type can be re-arranged so that only a few terms remain. To see how, first multiply S by $(1+m)$ to obtain

$$S(1 + m) = (1 + m)^y + (1 + m)^{y-1} + (1 + m)^{y-2} + \cdots + (1 + m) \quad (22)$$

Now if we subtract equation (21) from equation (22) we find that all the middle terms in the string cancel out and what remains is

$$S(1 + m) - S = (1 + m)^y - 1 \quad (23)$$

With just a little bit of algebra, this expression can be solved for S

$$S = \frac{(1 + m)^y - 1}{m} \quad (24)$$

Substituting equation (24) back into (20) results in

$$M_y = M_0(1 + m)^y - P\left(\frac{(1 + m)^y - 1}{m}\right) \quad (25)$$

The second step is to recognize that the balance due at the end of month Y has to be zero. In other words, the mortgage has to be fully paid off at the end of its term! So when we evaluate equation (25) at the value of $y = Y$, the left side has to equal zero. In symbols

$$M_Y = 0 = M_0(1 + m)^Y - P\left(\frac{(1 + m)^Y - 1}{m}\right)$$

or $\qquad\qquad\qquad\qquad\qquad\qquad\qquad\qquad\qquad\qquad\qquad (26)$

$$P\left(\frac{(1 + m)^Y - 1}{m}\right) = M_0(1 + m)^Y$$

The final steps just involve re-arranging this result to figure out how the payment, P, depends on the mortgage amount, M_0; the interest rate, m, and the term, Y. We want to multiply both sides of equation (26) by m and divide both sides by $(1 + m)^Y$. Remember that $1/(1 + m)^Y = (1 + m)^{-Y}$. These steps lead to

$$P = \left(\frac{m}{1 - (1 + m)^{-Y}}\right) M_0 \quad (27)$$

In short, in a fixed-rate mortgage contract, the payment is proportional to the mortgage amount, and the proportion, which is shown in equation (27), depends on the mortgage's interest rate and term.

This is a useful equation to know. If you ever borrow money with a fixed-rate loan, you can use equation (27) to see if the lender accurately calculated the monthly payment! Suppose you are taking out a mortgage of $200,000 to buy your dream house. If you have a 30-year mortgage at a 5 percent annual interest rate, then your monthly payment will be

$$\left(\frac{.05/12}{1 - [1 + (.05/12)]^{-(30 \times 12)}}\right) \times \$200,000 = \$1,073.64$$

Finally, note that you can also use this formula to figure out the mortgage you can afford (M_0) for a given monthly payment, P, and given mortgage characteristics, m and Y.

Lenders sometimes offer borrowers a choice between option A, a mortgage with a relatively high interest rate, and option B, a mortgage with a relatively low interest rate combined with "points" paid up front. In this context, a point is 1 percent of the mortgage amount, M_0. Because the points in option B are paid at the beginning of the mortgage, their impact is felt no matter how long one lives in the house. In contrast, the lower interest rates in option B do not yield any benefit unless a person lives in the house for a long time. Let us say that people who expect to move in the near future have a short time horizon. People with a short time horizon experience the costs of option B (points up front) but not the benefits (a long stream of lower interest rates). The same is true for people with a high discount rate, because the long-term benefits of a lower rate are heavily discounted. Both of these groups should pick option A. For people with a long time horizon and a low discount rate, that is, people who expect to be in the house for the long haul, the benefits from a long stream of lower interest rates outweighs the cost of the up-front points. These people should pick option B.

6. Annuities and Pensions

An annuity is a payment stream supported by an initial fund. The most important type of annuity is a pension. For many pensions, a person contributes money into a fund during their working life and then draws a pension payment — an annuity — from the fund after they retire. Annuities do not have to be pensions, however.

It is not correct to calculate the annuity by dividing the fund by the number of pay periods because the fund earns interest along the way. As a result, the payments are actually larger than the fund divided by the number of periods.

An annuity is designed so that the fund will be exhausted at the end of the expected number of pay periods. We have to use the qualifier "expected" here because an annuity generally continues even if the expected number of periods is exceeded. In the case of a pension, for example, the pension payment will be calculated on the basis of an expected lifetime, but will continue even if a person lives longer than expected. The people who set up annuities must account for this type of uncertainty, but we are not going to do that here. Instead, we will just refer to an expected number of pay periods.

As it turns out, except for the uncertainty about timing, a pension is just the inverse of a mortgage. You will be happy to know that we do not have to do any new algebra! An annuity is designed so that the fund is exhausted at the end of the expected number of pay periods — just like a mortgage is paid off at the end of its term. Moreover, an annuity must account for interest received from the amount that remains in the fund — just like a mortgage must account for interest payments on the amount that is still owed.

So let F be the amount of money in a fund supporting an annuity. This money is given to a fund administrator by a retiree (or another investor) to invest in exchange for a promise to pay the retiree an annuity of $\$A$ per month for a period of L months. Suppose g is the interest rate that the fund administrator expects to earn on this fund. Then plugging these terms into equation (27) we find that

$$A = \left(\frac{g}{1 - (1+g)^{-L}} \right) F \tag{28}$$

In some cases, an investor or potential retiree might want to know how large the fund has to be to support a given annuity. The answer to this question (which is analogous to the question of how large a mortgage one can afford at a given payment) can be found by re-arranging equation (28)

$$F = \left(\frac{1 - (1+g)^{-L}}{g} \right) A \tag{29}$$

If you want a pension of $\$2,000$ per month for 25 years and you expect the investments from the fund to earn a 6 percent return per year, then the required fund is

$$\left(\frac{1 - [1 + (.06/12)]^{-(25 \times 12)}}{.06/12} \right) \times \$2,000 = \$2,185,987.92$$

You will have to save up!

Pension planners have to conduct calculations such as this one to ensure that a pension fund will have enough money in it when a person retires to cover promised pensions. The pension fund may receive contributions both from an employee and an employer, and the amount in the fund obviously depends on the size of these contributions, along with the growth in the employee's wages during her working life.

7. Bonds

A bond is an example of a "certificate of indebtedness." A person who buys a bond (from a corporation or a municipal government, for example) receives the legal assurance that she will receive a stream of payments from the institution that issued the bond. Thus, a bond is a form of investment with a particular pattern of returns for the person who buys it. A bond is, of course, quite different from a stock. A person who buys a stock becomes one of the owners of a company, with the right to vote on certain matters and the right to receive dividend payments, which are much less predictable than bond interest payments. The holder of a bond has no ownership rights.

A bond is similar to a mortgage; the person who buys the bond is like the lender and the institution issuing the bond is like the borrower. Local governments issue bonds, for example, to raise funds for infrastructure projects, such as bridges or schools. Moreover bonds, like mortgages, come in many different forms, including forms with variable interest rates and bonds that can be redeemed before the maturity date. These notes just examine basic, fixed-rate bonds.

However, bonds have one characteristic that makes them quite different from a mortgage, namely that the payments do not alter the principal, that is, they do not alter the amount upon which the interest is calculated. As a result, bonds retain a principal amount at the end of the contract, the maturity date; this principal amount must be repaid to the investor.

More specifically, three characteristics are associated with each bond. They are as follows:

(1) the face value, F, (also called the par value or the redemption value or the value at maturity), which is the amount upon which the interest payments are calculated;
(2) the coupon rate, c, which indicates the interest to be paid as a percentage of F; and
(3) the years to maturity, N, which is the number of years during which the investor is entitled to receive interest and also the number of years until the bond can be redeemed.

As an aside, bonds are generally used to cover the cost of a project and they are generally issued in sets with different maturities. More specifically, they are usually issued in serial form, which means that some of the bonds in a set have a maturity of 1 year ($N = 1$), others have $N = 2$, and so on all the way up to the highest selected maturity, say N^*. This approach eases the repayment burden on the issuer. If each maturity up to N^* has the same number of bonds, then the issuer will only have to pay back a share equal to $1/N^*$ of its bonds each year.

The key to understanding bonds is to think about what an investor would pay for a bond that has a certain face value, F, coupon rate, c, and maturity, N. The answer is that an investor will pay the present value of the stream of benefits from owning the bond. Any good investor knows about present value! Suppose an investor has an alternative, similar investment, perhaps a U.S. Treasury Bill, that offers an interest rate r. Then r is the opportunity cost of investing in bonds, and the investor's willingness to pay is the present value of the benefits from holding the bond discounted at rate r.

The present value of a bond is not the same thing as its face value. In fact, these two "values" may be quite different. To see why, we have to recognize that the present value of benefits from owning a bond consists of an interest payment of cF per year and a redemption payment of F in year N. (In practice, interest payments are often made twice a year; if you want to account for this you just need to express everything in "half years" instead of years, with an interest rate of $c/2$, where c is the annual interest rate.) Thus, the present value of a bond, and hence its market price, is

$$P = \frac{cF}{(1+r)} + \frac{cF}{(1+r)^2} + \cdots + \frac{cF}{(1+r)^N} + \frac{F}{(1+r)^N} \tag{30}$$

Note that the last term in this expression does not have c in it; this term is the present value received by the investor when the issuer of the bond returns the face value to the investor, which is called redemption. Note also that this expression, like an earlier one, has a series of dots, which indicate the terms for interest received between years 2 and N.

This expression can be simplified using the same algebraic trick that led to equation (24). Define the sum of all the terms on the right side with cF in the numerator as C, for coupon payments. Then subtract C from $C \times (1+r)$ and solve the result for C. Replacing all the cF terms with this expression for C leads to

$$P = \left(\frac{1 - (1+r)^{-N}}{r} \right) cF + \frac{F}{(1+r)^N}$$

$$= F \left(c \left(\frac{1 - (1+r)^{-N}}{r} \right) + \left(\frac{1}{(1+r)^N} \right) \right) \tag{31}$$

So there is the echo of the mortgage formula in the price of a bond! Again, the difference is that the principal in the bond does not decline in absolute terms (although it does decline in present value!) and is repaid in year N. The price of a bond thus reflects the present value of the coupon payments (the first term in equation (31)) plus the present value of the redemption amount (the second term). If the coupon rate on the bond, c, equals the opportunity-cost rate, r, then equation (31) implies that the price, P, equals the face value, F.

In the second line of equation (31) we can see that P is proportional to F. If this proportion is greater than 1, the bond is said to sell at a premium. If it is less than one, the bond is said to sell at a discount. Consider a bond with $F = \$5{,}000$; $c = 4$ percent, and $N = 20$ for investors with an opportunity cost rate of 6 percent. Then the amount this investor will bid on the bond, P, is

$$\$5{,}000 \times \left(.04 \times \left(\frac{1 - 1.06^{-20}}{.06} \right) + \left(\frac{1}{1.06^{20}} \right) \right) = \$3{,}853.01$$

This bond is priced at a discount ($\$3{,}853.01 < \$5{,}000$) because the rate of return it offers is below the opportunity cost rate. Investors will not buy the bond unless it yields a capital gain, that is, unless the redemption value they receive in year 20 is considerably greater than the price they have to pay.

Sometimes an investor who owns a bond wants to sell it at a given price. In this case, P is known but the rate of return on the bond is not. (This contrasts with the preceding discussion, in which the opportunity cost to investing a bond, r, was known, but the price was not.) This changes the way we use equation (31), because r can now be interpreted as the rate of return on a bond with price P, face value F, coupon rate C, and maturity N. This rate is called the **internal rate of return**. When comparing bonds (or other assets) an investor wants to select the bonds with the highest internal rate of return.

The problem is that equation (31) is highly nonlinear and cannot easily be solved for r. Fortunately, however, finding the internal rate of return is such a common problem that most calculators and spreadsheet programs include a function that calculates r once P, F, c, and N have been entered.

Some municipal bonds push the issuer's payments into the future. This approach lowers the tax burden of repayments in the short run, but raises this burden in the long run. However, the design of a bond does not alter the present value of the associated repayments.

A zero-coupon bond, for example, sets the coupon rate, c, equal to zero. In this case equation (31) indicates that the price of the bond is

$$\text{Zero-coupon bond:} \quad P = \frac{F}{(1 + r)^N} \tag{32}$$

This type of bond provides all of its return to investors in the form of capital gains, not interest. Capital gains are indicated by the difference between F and P, so the price of a zero-coupon bond obviously has to be heavily discounted, that is, P must be far below F, or else no investor would buy it.

Another type of bond that has been used by some local governments to shift repayments into the future is a capital appreciation bond (CAB), also called a compound interest bond. With this type of bond, the interest payments are placed in a fund and reinvested at the coupon rate. The investor claims the money in this fund, along with the face value, at the maturity date. Thus, all returns to this investment are received in year N and discounted by $(1+r)^N$. The payment into the fund each year is cF. The first payment grows to $cF(1+c)^{N-1}$ by the time the bond matures; the second payment grows to $cF(1+c)^{N-2}$; the last payment of cF is paid in year N and does not grow. Let Z be the sum of these accumulated amounts in year N. Then the same algebraic steps that led to equation (24) imply that $Z = cF[(1+c)^N - 1]/c = F[(1+c)^N - 1]$. The price of the bond equals the present value of $(F + Z)$ in year N or

$$\text{Capital appreciation bond:} \quad P = \frac{F + F\left((1+c)^N - 1\right)}{(1+r)^N} = F\left(\frac{(1+c)^N}{(1+r)^N}\right)$$

$$(33)$$

When $c = r$, the price of a capital appreciation bond equals its face value. Moreover, a CAB is similar to a zero-coupon bond in that the CAB interest rate, c, is algebraically equivalent to the implicit annual capital gains rate in a zero-coupon bond. To put it another way, a zero-coupon bond will sell for the same amount as a CAB if the capital gains reflected in its face value equal the accumulated interest for the CAB, that is, if its face value equals the CAB face value multiplied by $(1 + c)^N$.

To compare these three types of municipal bonds, suppose a school district wants to raise \$50,000 to put an addition onto one of its schools. Suppose, as well, that the opportunity cost rate and the coupon rate are set at 5 percent; in this case, equation (31) indicates that standard bonds will sell for their face value. As a result, a 10-year serial issue of \$5,000 bonds will sell for exactly the amount of money the municipality requires. Equation (33) indicates that CABs will also sell for their face value, so a 10-year serial issue of \$5,000 CABs will also raise the required funds. In the case of zero-coupon bonds, equation (33) indicates that a 10-year serial issue cannot raise \$50,000 unless the bonds have a face value that exceeds \$5,000. More specifically, for a 10-year serial issue, the required face value on zero-coupon bonds is \$6,475.23. (Equation (33) shows the relationship

Table 1   A comparison of payments on three types of municipal bond.

	Standard		Zero-coupon		Capital appreciation	
Year	Actual	Present value	Actual	Present value	Actual	Present value
1	$7,500.00	$7,142.86	$6,475.23	$6,166.88	$5,250.00	$5,000.00
2	$7,250.00	$6,575.96	$6,475.23	$5,873.22	$5,512.50	$5,000.00
3	$7,000.00	$6,046.86	$6,475.23	$5,593.55	$5,788.13	$5,000.00
4	$6,750.00	$5,553.24	$6,475.23	$5,327.19	$6,077.53	$5,000.00
5	$6,500.00	$5,092.92	$6,475.23	$5,073.51	$6,381.41	$5,000.00
6	$6,250.00	$4,663.85	$6,475.23	$4,831.92	$6,700.48	$5,000.00
7	$6,000.00	$4,264.09	$6,475.23	$4,601.82	$7,035.50	$5,000.00
8	$5,750.00	$3,891.83	$6,475.23	$4,382.69	$7,387.28	$5,000.00
9	$5,500.00	$3,545.35	$6,475.23	$4,173.99	$7,756.64	$5,000.00
10	$5,250.00	$3,223.04	$6,475.23	$3,975.23	$8,144.47	$5,000.00
Total	$63,750.00	$50,000.00	$64,752.29	$50,000.00	$66,033.94	$50,000.00

Notes: The coupon rate and opportunity cost are set at 5 percent. This table presents the total payments on bonds of all maturities in each year. The face values of the standard and capital appreciation bonds are $5,000; the face values of the zero-coupon bonds are $6,475.23. Following equations (31) and (33), the standard and capital appreciation bonds sell for $5,000, whereas, according to equation (32), the zero-coupon bonds sell for amounts between $4,761.91 (1-year maturity) and $3,069.57 (10-year maturity).

between P and F for a single maturity. This figure is the value of F needed to generate prices that sum up to $50,000 with a 10-year serial issue.)

Table 1 presents a municipality's payments associated with these three types of bonds. For each bond type, the first column gives the actual payments a municipality must make in the form of interest or principal payments in each year. Each of these bond issues yields a 5 percent return to investors, so with an opportunity-cost rate of 5 percent, the present value of the total payments for each bond issue is the same, namely, $50,000. The actual payments are highest for the CAB and lowest for the standard bond. The purpose of a bond issue is to spread out the payment stream over time. With a serial issue that has the same number of bonds of each maturity, as in Table 1, the actual payments are the most even with a zero-coupon bond, whereas the payments in present value terms are smoothest with a CAB. The payment stream associated with a standard bond issue declines over time and requires the lowest total payments. (These statements are also true when $c \neq r$, although in that case the present values of the payments on a CAB are not constant over time.) Another way to put it is that a CAB does the best job pushing the municipality's actual payments into the future, but does not lower the present value of the burden on taxpayers compared to either of the other options.

Although they do not lower the present value of the debt repayment burden, zero-coupon bonds and CABs may help municipalities address other problems. Both zero-coupon bonds and CABs postpone an investor's returns until the maturity date, and may therefore appeal to investors who want to shift some of their income into the future for tax purposes. Moreover, the return provided in the future by a zero-coupon bond takes the form of capital gains, whereas the return provided by a CAB is largely in the form of interest payments. These two types of bonds may therefore appeal to investors with different income tax situations. These considerations may lead some investors to be willing to pay more for some types of bonds, which is the same as accepting a lower return and hence placing a lower burden on the municipality. Although the possibility of a lower return is appealing in principle, a municipality should hire a reputable bond adviser before issuing bonds designed to appeal to a particular class of investor!

In addition, some municipalities face statutory debt limits, which usually refer to the sum of the face values on their outstanding debt. As shown earlier, a zero-coupon bond cannot command the same price (that is, raise the same amount of money) as a standard bond or a CAB unless it has a higher face value. As a result, municipalities nearing a debt limit can be expected to avoid zero-coupon bonds.

A rarer (and more dubious) type of bond is a perpetuity. The holder of this type of bond is entitled to receive interest payments indefinitely, which is equivalent to having an infinite number of years until maturity.[2] Because $[1/(1+r)^\infty] = [(1+r)^{-\infty}] = 0$, equation (31) indicates that the price of this type of bond is

$$\text{Perpetuity:} \quad P = \frac{cF}{r} \tag{34}$$

The ratio of price to face value in this case obviously depends directly on the coupon rate, because the bond can never be redeemed. The bond sells at a premium if $c > r$, that is, if it yields a return greater than the investor's discount rate, and it sells at a discount if $c < r$. In either case, the outcome is that the annual interest from the bond, cF, equals the annual interest that could be earned with the same amount of money invested in an alternative asset, rP.

---

[2] Perpetuities do not exist in the United States. However, some municipal bonds were issued in 1868 by villages in New York State (since incorporated into New York City) with maturities up to 279 years. See Jo Craven McGinty, "That's What You Call Investing for the Long Term," *The New York Times*, 13 February 2009.

8. Inflation

Inflation is a general increase in prices, holding product quality constant. Prices usually increase by at least 2 percent per year and sometimes increase much more. The U.S. Bureau of Labor Statistics collects data on prices and calculates various price indexes relative to some base year, such as the well-known Consumer Price Index. This index is a relative price level multiplied by 100 to make it more readable. A price index of 110, for example, indicates that prices are 10 percent higher than they were in the base year. Actual dollars received are called nominal dollars. Dividing nominal dollars by the price index (without the 100 scalar) yields real dollars for a given base year. When people think about benefits to be received in the future, therefore, they recognize that a given amount of money received in the future will not go as far as the same amount of money received today. To put it another way, dollars will have lower purchasing power in the future.

Because inflation affects the purchasing power of money received in the future, it becomes part of the discount rate. Suppose my discount rate is 5 percent without considering inflation. Then suppose that I expect the rate of inflation to be 3 percent. Under these circumstances, I no longer consider $105 received at the end of the year to be equivalent to $100 received now, because I know that the purchasing power of a dollar has declined. In fact, I need $105×1.03 = $108.15 to feel that I have an equivalent amount.

The no-inflation discount rate is also known as a **real** discount rate, whereas the rate that incorporates inflation is called a **nominal** discount rate. Interest rates that are observed in the market place are all nominal interest rates because they incorporate the inflation expectations of market participants. In the above example, the real discount rate is 5 percent and the nominal discount rate is $[(1 + .05) \times (1 + .03) - 1] = [(1.05) \times (1.03) - 1] = .0815 = 8.15$ percent. A simpler way to calculate the nominal interest rate, which is an approximation to this exact formula, is simply to add the expected rate of inflation to the no-inflation discount rate. To continue the example, the approximate nominal discount rate is 5 percent + 3 percent = 8 percent.

When thinking about inflation it is important to be consistent, that is, to make certain that the dollar amounts and the discount rates are both in either nominal or real terms. It makes no sense to use a nominal discount rate to find the present value of a real return. The examples given above express everything in nominal terms. A nominal return of $108.15 has a present value of $100 when the nominal discount rate is 8.15 percent. It is also possible to obtain the same answer using real values. We can assume that the beginning of the year is the base year, so a nominal value of \$108.15 equals a real value of \$108.15/1.03 = \$105. Now using a real discount rate of 5 percent, the present value of \$105 is \$100. Because we observe nominal rates, not real rates, in the market place, we would have to calculate the real discount rate to follow this approach. Using the approximation in the previous paragraph, the real discount rate is 8 percent − 3 percent = 5 percent.

To write down a general form for this real/nominal relationship, let i_R be the real interest rate, i_N be the nominal interest rate, and p be the anticipated rate of inflation. Then

$$i_N = (1 + i_R)(1 + p) - 1 = i_R + i_R p + p \tag{35}$$

and

$$i_R = \left(\frac{1 + i_N}{1 + p}\right) - 1 = \frac{i_N - p}{1 + p} \tag{36}$$

Because i_R and p are both small numbers, their product is very small, and these equations are sometimes approximated as $i_N = (i_R + p)$ and $i_R = (i_N - p)$.

The assessor formula in Section 3, equation (15), is consistent so long as r is a nominal interest rate and the growth rate in rents, a, includes the expected magnitudes of both real and inflationary growth. The issue of consistency is also important in benefit-cost analysis. If the benefits and costs are expressed in real terms, i.e., if they are not inflated, then a real discount rate must be used. In other words, an estimate of anticipated inflation must be subtracted from the nominal discount rate. If the benefits and costs are inflated over time, then this subtraction is not needed. Unfortunately, many benefit-cost studies avoid making assumptions about future inflation by expressing the benefits and costs in real terms and selecting a nominal interest rate. This approach is not correct, and it leads to the inappropriate rejection of some projects with short-term costs and long-term benefits.

9. Risk and Uncertainty

The financial transactions examined in these notes are all designed with a view toward the future, which cannot, of course, be predicted with perfect accuracy. A homebuyer may or may not default on her mortgage loan. A retiree may live much longer than expected when her pension was designed. A company or a public agency may go bankrupt and be unable to pay off its bondholders. In common parlance, the future is uncertain and financial transactions involve risks. (Following the work of economist Frank Knight, some scholars define these terms in a different way: risk arises when the probabilities of various outcomes are known, even if the outcomes themselves are not, whereas uncertainty refers to cases in which even the underlying probabilities are not known. In these notes, I stick to the more conventional definitions.)

The presence of risk and uncertainty lead to two new central concepts in the analysis of financial transactions. The first concept is **expected value**. The expected value of a financial transaction is the sum across possible outcomes of the probability of an outcome multiplied by its present value. In the case of a mortgage, for example, a default results in a loss of interest payments and to a foreclosure process that might be expensive but that eventually transfers the ownership of the house from the borrower to the lender. The net benefit to the lender could be positive or negative, depending on the magnitude of their costs and the value of the house on which they foreclose. The expected value of mortgage returns in year y is the probability of a default multiplied by the present value of the net benefits from default plus the probability of no default multiplied by the present value of the mortgage payments. The concept of expected value therefore makes it possible to introduce a range of outcomes with known probabilities into the analysis of financial transactions, but it can lead to some pretty complicated algebra! You may be relieved to learn that this type of algebra is beyond the scope of these notes.

The second key concept is **risk aversion**, which is said to exist when a person prefers a (relatively) certain set of outcomes with a given expected value to a (relatively) uncertain set of outcomes with the same expected value. Consider an investor who is trying to decide between buying one set if mortgages with a relatively low mortgage rate and a relatively low probability of default and buying another set of mortgages with a relatively high mortgage rate and a relatively high probability of default. Suppose the expected values of the two investments are the same because the high interest rate on the second investment compensates for the high risk of default. An investor who is risk averse will always prefer the first investment to the second.

Scholars and financial analysts have developed elaborate mathematical tools to account for risk in financial transactions. These tools go way beyond simple algebra and are way beyond the scope of these notes.

The concept of risk aversion also leads to three important ideas about financial markets. First, the widespread presence of risk aversion in a market implies that risky assets will not attract investors unless they offer a higher return than offered by low-risk assets with returns that have the same expected value. In other words, investors have to be compensated for risk.

Second, risk-averse investors often seek to minimize their risk by diversifying their portfolio. In this context, a diversified portfolio is one that contains a series of investments with returns that are not highly correlated with each other, so that bad outcomes for one investment are unlikely to be accompanied by bad returns for another. If you are risk averse, you should think about diversifying your portfolio!

Third, because many investors are risk-averse, they are willing to pay something for a financial agreement that insures them against certain kinds of financial risks. As a result, modern financial markets contain institutions that specialize in accepting risk or, to put it another way, that specialize in providing this type of insurance. The expansion of this type of institution in the mortgage market, along with the lack of regulation of such institutions, contributed to the financial crisis of 2008. This subject is beyond the scope of this appendix.

The State and Local Lunch Group*

John Yinger

Departments of Public Administration and International Affairs and
of Economics, Syracuse University, Syracuse, NY, United States
jyinger@maxwell.syr.edu

This appendix describes the many remarkable colleagues I was fortunate enough to work with at the start of my career as a scholar of state and local public finance. Let me begin with Helen (Sunny) Ladd and Howard Bloom.

The three of us met in August 1976. The Department of City and Regional Planning (CRP) in Harvard's Graduate School of Design had just hired Sunny and Howard and me as assistant professors. We were given the task of preparing a class in state and local public finance, so we spent August working on that assignment. Sunny stayed one more year at Wellesley before she came to Harvard, but Howard and I started teaching that class right away. I cannot remember the exact scheduling, but Sunny and Howard and I taught that class many times at CRP. We also taught it after the 1980 merger of CRP into the Kennedy School of Government (KSG) up until

---

*This appendix was originally prepared for presentation at a symposium called "Education Policy and the Public Interest: Celebrating the Scholarship of Helen 'Sunny' Ladd." This symposium was held at Duke University on May 19, 2017. The first two paragraphs have been edited to account for the new context. The original first paragraph was: "Everybody here knows how wonderful Sunny Ladd is. I have known her longer than most of you, however, so I would like to take this opportunity to tell you a little bit about Sunny as a young scholar." To avoid embarrassing Sunny, I left out the last three paragraphs of my prepared remarks, which touted her amazingly productive career after she moved to Duke, and I added a new final paragraph.

1986 when we all left for other jobs. As I recall, Sunny continued to teach this course at Duke, Howard continued to teach it at NYU (before he moved on to the Manpower Demonstration Research Corporation), and I taught it for 31 years in a row at the Maxwell School at Syracuse.

This collegial and intellectually stimulating collaboration on course preparation turned the three of us into great friends and led to an on-going conversation about research on state and local public finance. Moreover, we discovered that quite a few other young scholars in the Boston area were also interested in this broad topic. Kathy Bradbury was one of these scholars. She was my colleague from 1974 to 1976 as a post-doc at the Poverty Institute at the University of Wisconsin and had just started a job at the Boston Federal Reserve Bank. Andy Reschovsky, who was hired by the economics department at Tufts University in 1978, was another.

I don't remember how it got started, but at some point this group of five, along with various other young scholars, started meeting informally at lunch to discuss state and local public finance. This was the beginning of the State and Local Lunch Group (SLLG). This group became more formal in 1983, when Sunny was appointed to the first of several Massachusetts state commissions on state aid to localities. According to Sunny's vita, her first appointment was to the Massachusetts Local Aid Study Group, which was a task force to advise the Massachusetts Secretary of Administration and Finance on local aid issues. Then in 1985, she was appointed as a member of the Chairman's Economic Policy and Tax and Advisory Group for the Massachusetts Legislature's Joint Committee on Taxation and to the Governor's Special Commission Relative to the Current Local Aid Distribution Formula. The other core members of SLLG volunteered to help Sunny prepare the analysis she would need for these appointments. Mark Perrault, who was recommended to us by one of Andy's acquaintances, also joined this team. Mark worked for the Joint Committee on Taxation and had access to the data we needed.

This collaboration resulted in reports to various governmental bodies, a new state aid formula for Massachusetts, and a 1984 article in the *National Tax Journal* (*NTJ*) called "State Aid to Offset Fiscal Disparities across Communities," with Kathy, Sunny, Mark, Andy, and me as co-authors. Many of the ideas in this article showed up in Sunny's and my 1989 book, *America's Ailing Cities*, and in many post-SLLG research projects by the article's authors. These projects include, for example, Kathy's research on education finance in Massachusetts and Andy's research on education finance in Texas. They also include a series of articles on education costs and demand in New York and a few other states that I published with my late colleague, Bill Duncombe, and, more recently, with my former Ph.D. student Phuong Nguyen-Hoang. Incidentally, Phuong was a masters' student at Duke and took microeconomics from Sunny.

The ability of SLLG to promote successful collaborations is also demonstrated by a long series of other projects co-authored by various combinations of the core SLLG participants. These projects are illustrated in Figure 1. Kathy and Sunny kicked off this series with two articles in the *New England Economic Review* (NEER) in 1982 on Proposition 2 ¹/₂, the 1980 property tax limitation in Massachusetts. Later the same year, a collaboration between Howard and Sunny appeared in the *Journal of Urban Economics* (*JUE*) ("Property Tax Revaluation and Tax Levy Growth"). Kathy and Sunny went on to publish two more articles in *NEER* and one in the *NTJ*, all on city revenue-raising capacity. An article by Kathy and me appeared in the *NEER* in 1984 ("Making Ends Meet: Boston's Fiscal Situation in the 1980s"). Then, in 1988, Howard, Sunny, and I published a book on property tax capitalization (*Property Taxes and House Values*). Axel Boersch-Supan, our colleague at KSG, was a co-author of this book. Sunny and I also published articles on state aid to cities in in *NTJ* in 1989 and 1994, and Sunny, Andy, and I published an article in the 1992 *NTA Proceedings* on our state aid project for the Minnesota Legislature.

1. Bradbury and Ladd, 1982, 1985, 1987; 1988
2. Bloom and Ladd, 1982
3. Bradbury, 1984
4. Bradbury and Yinger
5. Yinger *et al.*, 1984
6. Ladd and Yinger, 1989, 1991; Yinger and Ladd, 1989, 1994
7. Ladd *et al.*, 1992
8. Bifulco, 2006; Bifulco and Ladd, 2006, 2007
9. Bradbury and Zhao, 2009; Zhao and Bradbury, 2009
10. Bifulco *et al.*, 2009a; 2009b
11. Bifulco *et al.*, 2014

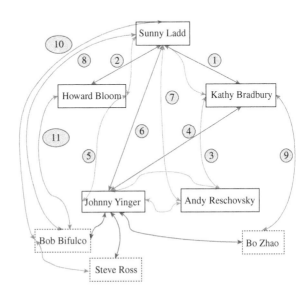

Figure 1 Scholarly collaborations that grew out of the state and local lunch group.

More evidence of collaboration through SLLG comes from a HUD-funded project on city fiscal health in which Kathy, Sunny, and I were joined by Ron Ferguson and Avis Vidal, who were, like Sunny and me, junior faculty members at KSG. Articles linked to this project include three of the articles by Kathy and Sunny that were mentioned above (Bradbury and Ladd, 1985, 1987; Bradbury and Ladd, 1988); three more articles on city fiscal distress by Kathy in *NEER*; a 1986 book chapter by Sunny and Ron ("Measuring the Fiscal Capacity of U.S. Cities"); and, ultimately, Sunny's and my 1989 book. As the preface to that book makes clear, Kathy, Ron, and Avis made important contributions not only through our joint project and related publications, but also through their extensive comments on the book manuscript.

Further testimony to the collegial nature of the interactions among SLLG participants appears in the footnotes of the participants' sole-authored articles. For example, Sunny's 1982 *NTJ* article on tax limits thanks Howard and me; my 1982 article in the *Journal of Political Economy* on capitalization and household sorting across communities cites Howard, Kathy, and Sunny; and my 1986 article in *JUE* on fiscal disparities not only thanks Kathy and Sunny, but also thanks "participants in the State and Local Lunch Group at the MIT-Harvard Joint Center for Urban Studies." I guess SLLG was pretty formal by then!

Unlike the other core members of SLLG, I had the opportunity to work with many Ph.D. students after I left Cambridge. As a result, the reverberations of SLLG have appeared in another generation of scholars. Moreover, three of my students (Bob Bifulco, Steve Ross, and Bo Zhao) have worked with other core members of SLLG. Sunny has published three articles with Bob on charter schools (Bifulco and Ladd, 2006a, Bifulco and Ladd, 2006b, Bifulco and Ladd, 2007) and two articles with both Bob and Steve on school choice (Bifulco *et al.*, 2009a, Bifulco *et al.*, 2009b). Bo has published two articles with Kathy on local public finance (Bradbury and Zhao, 2009, Zhao and Bradbury, 2009). Finally, Bob has written a report, not yet published, with Howard (Bifulco *et al.*, 2014). The spirit of SLLG lives on.

Sunny was, of course, a central player in all the SLLG-inspired research. In fact, she was a little bit ahead of the rest of us, as her well-known paper, "Local Education Expenditures, Fiscal Capacity, and the Composition of the Property Tax Base" (Ladd, 1975), had already been published when she and Howard and I first got together. This paper, which has been widely cited (with 245 citations as counted by Google Scholar), had a large influence on the Massachusetts aid project and the associated *NTJ* publication.

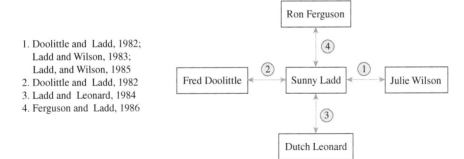

Figure 2 Sunny's other co-authors linked to the state and local lunch group.

Sunny's leadership and commitment to collaboration are also demonstrated by the large number of partnerships she formed with other young faculty members at KSG, several of whom participated in at least some of the SLLG meetings. Her junior co-authors on state and local public finance papers during the SLLG years include not only those mentioned above, but also Julie Wilson, Fred Doolittle, and Dutch Leonard. Julie and Sunny co-authored a series of insightful articles on support for Proposition 2 1/2 (Ladd and Wilson, 1982; 1983; 1985). Fred and Sunny published a 1982 paper in *NTJ* ("Which Level of Government Should Assist the Poor?"). Finally, Dutch and Sunny wrote a chapter on "Taxes and the Poor" in a 1984 book (see Figure 2).

As it turns out, I can document how I felt about Sunny's scholarship just before she and I left KSG, because she was competing for a chair at the Kennedy School and I wrote a letter of recommendation for her in November 1985, which I not only kept, but also managed to find after all these years. Here are a couple of quotes from that letter:

> Professor Ladd's research on state and local public finance is excellent and wide ranging. Her papers display theoretical insight, institutional knowledge, good judgement, clear writing, and careful empirical analysis. As a researcher in these fields myself, I have relied heavily on her work.

> Professor Ladd and I worked together on an analysis of state aid in Massachusetts. This project was unusual in that it combined original research on disparities across communities in the costs of providing local services with the actual policy-making process in Massachusetts. This combination would not have been possible without the special skills of Professor Ladd. ... The fact that Massachusetts now accounts for cost disparities in its aid program is testimony to Professor Ladd's skills.

My views obviously were not decisive, and in 1986 Sunny moved on, much to Harvard's loss and Duke's great gain.

Each of the core participants in SLLG has gone on to have a productive scholarly career. This presentation is meant to emphasize how fortunate we all were to have participated in SLLG as our careers began. The conversations and collaborations linked to SLLG gave us all a base of knowledge about theories, institutions, and methods that we could build on in our future work. It showed us the value of collaboration and of high standards. It was a great launching pad. I learned so much from Sunny and the other SLLG participants. I hope they learned something from me, too.

Before I move on, I have to mention that Sunny inspired me on a totally different topic, as well. In 1981 she co-authored an excellent book with Robert Schafer, a colleague of ours at CRP and KSG, called *Discrimination in Mortgage Lending*. A little over a decade later, the Urban Institute asked me to write a survey chapter on discrimination in mortgage lending, and I immediately turned to Bob and Sunny's book to get me started. Building on this strong foundation, my research on mortgage discrimination eventually led to several more book chapters, a 2002 book called *The Color of Credit*, and a 2006 article in the *American Law and Economics Review*. Steve Ross was my co-author for most of this work, including the last two entries. In my experience, it pays to build on Sunny's work.

The reader can see that I was very fortunate to start my career working with so many talented young scholars in the field of state and local public finance. Many of the chapters in this book (not just Chapter 13, which is co-authored with Sunny Ladd) build on lessons I learned through my connections with the State and Local Lunch Group.

References

Bifulco, Robert and Helen F. Ladd. 2006a. The impacts of charter schools on student achievement: evidence from North Carolina (with H. Ladd). *Education Finance and Policy* **1**(1) (Winter): 50–90.

Bifulco, Robert and Helen F. Ladd. 2006b. Institutional change and the coproduction of public services: the effect of charter schools on parental involvement. *Journal of Public Administration Research and Theory* (October): 553–572.

Bifulco, Robert and Helen F. Ladd. 2007. School choice, racial segregation and test-score gaps: evidence from North Carolina's charter school program. *Journal of Policy Analysis and Management* **26**(1) (Winter): 31–56.

Bifulco, Robert, Helen F. Ladd and Stephen Ross. 2009a. The effects of public school choice on those left behind. *Peabody Journal of Education* (Spring): 130–149.

Bifulco, Robert, Helen F. Ladd and Stephen Ross. 2009b. Public school choice and integration. *Social Science Research* (March): 71–85.

Bifulco, Robert, Rebecca Unterman and Howard S. Bloom. 2014. The relative costs of New York city's new small public high schools of choice. MDRC Working Paper, October.

Bloom, Howard S. and Helen F. Ladd. 1982. Property tax revaluation and tax levy growth. *Journal of Urban Economics* **11**(1) (January): 73–84.

Bradbury, Katharine L. 1982. Fiscal distress in large U.S. cities. *New England Economic Review* (November/December): 33–44.

Bradbury, Katharine L. 1983. Structural fiscal distress in cities: causes and consequences. *New England Economic Review* (January/February): 32–43.

Bradbury, Katharine L. 1984. Urban decline and distress: an update. *New England Economic Review* (July/August): 39–57.

Bradbury, Katharine L. and Bo Zhao. 2009. Measuring non-school fiscal disparities among municipalities. *National Tax Journal* **62**(1): 25–56.

Bradbury, Katharine L and Helen F. Ladd. 1982a. Proposition 2 1/2: initial impacts, Part II. *New England Economic Review* (March/April): 48–62.

Bradbury, Katharine L. and Helen F. Ladd. 1982b. Proposition 2 1/2: initial impacts, Part I. *New England Economic Review* (July/August): 13–24.

Bradbury, Katharine L. and Helen F. Ladd. 1985. Changes in the revenue-raising capacity of U.S. cities: 1970–1982. *New England Economic Review* (March/April): 20–37.

Bradbury, Katharine L. and Helen F. Ladd. 1987. City property taxes: the effects of economic change and competitive pressures. *New England Economic Review* (July/August): 22–36.

Bradbury, Katharine L. and Helen F. Ladd. 1988. City taxes and city property tax bases. *National Tax Journal* **41**(4) (December): 503–524.

Bradbury, Katharine L. and John Yinger. 1984. Making ends meet: Boston's fiscal situation in the 1980s. *New England Economic Review* (March/April): 18–28.

Bradbury, Katharine L., Helen F. Ladd, Mark Perrault, Andrew Reschovsky and John Yinger. 1984. State aid to offset fiscal disparities across communities. *National Tax Journal* **37**(2) (June): 151–170.

Doolittle, Fred C. and Helen F. Ladd. 1982. Which level of government should assist poor people? *National Tax Journal* **35**(3) (September): 323–336.

Ferguson, Ronald and Helen F. Ladd. 1986. Measuring the fiscal capacity of U.S. cities. In Clyde Reeves, (ed.), *Measuring Fiscal Capacity* Oelgeschlager, Gunn and Hain, 141–168.

Ladd, Helen F. 1975. Local education expenditures, fiscal Capacity and the composition of the property tax base. *National Tax Journal* **28**(2) (June): 145–158.

Ladd, Helen F. and Herman B. Leonard. 1984. Taxation and the poor. In Manuel Carballo and Mary Jo Bane (eds.), *The State and the Poor in the 1980's* (Auburn House), pp. 235–278.

Ladd, Helen F. and John Yinger. 1994. The case for equalizing aid. *National Tax Journal* **47**(1) (March): 211–224.

Ladd, Helen F. and John Yinger. 1989. *America's Ailing Cities: Fiscal Health and the Design of Urban Policy*, Johns Hopkins University Press. (Updated Edition in 1991.)

Ladd, Helen F. and Julie Boatright Wilson. 1982. Why voters support tax limitations: evidence from Massachusetts' Proposition 2 1/2. *National Tax Journal* **35**(2) (June): 121–148.

Ladd, Helen F. and Julie Boatright Wilson. 1983. Who supports tax limitations: evidence from Massachusetts' Proposition 2 1/2. *Journal of Policy Analysis and Management* **2**(2) (Winter): 256–279.

Ladd, Helen F. and Julie Boatright Wilson. 1985. Education and tax limitations: evidence from Massachusetts' Proposition 2 1/2. *Journal of Education Finance* **10**(3) (Winter): 281–296.

Ladd, Helen F., Andrew Reschovsky and John Yinger. 1992. City fiscal condition and state equalizing aid: the case of Minnesota. *Proceedings of the 84th Annual Conference of the National Tax Association and Tax Institute of America, 1991*: 42–49.

Ross, Stephen L. and John Yinger. 2002. *The Color of Credit: Mortgage Lending Discrimination, Research Methodology and Fair-Lending Enforcement*, MIT Press.

Ross, Stephen L. and John Yinger. 2006. Uncovering discrimination: a comparison of the methods used by scholars and civil rights enforcement officials. *American Law and Economics Review* 8(3) (Fall): 562–614.

Schafer, Robert and Helen F. Ladd. 1981. *Discrimination in Mortgage Lending*, MIT Press.

Yinger, John. 1982. Capitalization and the theory of local public finance. *Journal of Political Economy* 90(5) (September): 917–943.

Yinger, John. 1986. On fiscal disparities across cities. *Journal of Urban Economics* 19(3) (May): 316–337.

Yinger, John and Helen F. Ladd. 1989. The determinants of state assistance to central cities. *National Tax Journal* 42(4) (December): 413–428.

Yinger, John, Howard S. Bloom, Axel Boersch-Supan and Helen F. Ladd. 1988. *Property Taxes and House Values: The Theory and Estimation of Intrajurisdictional Property Tax Capitalization*, Academic Press.

Zhao, Bo and Katharine Bradbury. 2009. Designing state aid formulas. *Journal of Policy Analysis and Management* 28(2): 278–295.

Appendix C

In Memory of Wallace Oates[*]

John Yinger

*Departments of Public Administration and International Affairs and
of Economics, Syracuse University, Syracuse, NY, United States
jyinger@maxwell.syr.edu*

Professor Wallace Oates, a long-time faculty member at the University of Maryland and a star in the field of local public finance, passed away in October 2015. In the fall of 1971, Wally was my public finance professor at Princeton, where he taught before moving to Maryland. His class had a profound impact on my career.

Wally taught me about three local public finance topics out of his own research that I have continued to think and write about ever since I took his class: capitalization, the impact of poverty and other environmental factors on public service costs, and the equivalence between intergovernmental aid and resident income.[1] I have touched on each of these topics in many previous columns.

---

[*]This appendix originally appeared as the November 2015 "It's Elementary" column posted at http://cpr.maxwell.syr.edu/efap/about_efap/ie/Nov_2015.pdf.

[1]Wally did not introduce me to local public finance. That distinction goes to Dr. Joseph Pechman, who was my boss when I was a research assistant at the Brookings Institution for 2 years before I went to graduate school. Joe asked me to write a report comparing the finances of Washington, DC with the nation's city-counties, such as San Francisco. This episode provides more evidence that I like to stick to topics, as I went on to write a book with Helen Ladd on the finances of all the nation's large cities (Ladd and Yinger, 1991). But it also provides more evidence of Wally's impact on my career, because a central part of that book was the estimation of public service costs — topic two in this column.

To students of local public finance, "capitalization" is the impact of local public service quality and property tax rates on the price of housing. Wally taught me about his now-famous paper (Oates, 1969) in which he both estimated service and tax capitalization for a sample of cities in northern New Jersey and connected his analysis with the article by Tiebout (1956) that initiated the field of local public finance. Oates' article inspired dozens, if not hundreds, of imitators.[2] I wrote a paper on capitalization for his class and I have continued to write about the topic over the years. In fact, here it is, 44 years since I took Wally's class, and I just published an article that presents a new way to estimate public service capitalization (Yinger, 2015). Moreover, this topic continues to be vital to understanding the US system of local governments, and many scholars continue to investigate capitalization and related issues.[3]

Wally also taught me about his now-famous article on the costs of local public services (Bradford, Malt, and Oates, 1969). This article explains that the cost of public services depends on the environment in which they are provided. The same level of fire protection costs more, for example, in a community with old, wooden apartment buildings than in one with brick ranch houses on two-acre lots. Working mainly with William Duncombe, who was also fascinated by this topic, I have contributed many articles to the large literature that builds on this insight (e.g., Duncombe and Yinger, 2005). A review of this literature can be found in Duncombe, Nguyen-Hoang, and Yinger (2015).

Finally, Wally taught me that intergovernmental aid flowing into a community is in some sense equivalent to an increase in the income of the voters who live in that community (Bradford and Oates, 1971; Oates, 1972). This equivalence requires an adjustment for the fact that $1.00 of aid does not necessarily save a voter $1.00 in taxes. Suppose, for example, that half the property taxes in a community are paid by a large factory. If the community receives another dollar of aid and uses it to reduce property taxes, then the voters only save $0.50. In another community with no factory, they might save the full dollar. A more formal statement of this result is that state aid adjusted for voters' tax share is equivalent to voter income.

---

[2] Tax capitalization studies are reviewed in Yinger *et al.* (1988) and studies of school quality capitalization are reviewed in Nguyen-Hoang and Yinger (2011).

[3] The literature on local public finance related to capitalization is reviewed in Ross and Yinger (1999). This review cites eleven of Wally's articles. He did not stop being my teacher in 1971!

Although this equivalence makes sense in theory, it does not work out so well in practice; $1.00 of aid has a much larger impact on the demand for local public services than $1.00 of voter income. This is called the flypaper effect: the money sticks where it hits. There is also a large literature on the flypaper effect, to which Wally contributed (see Gamkar and Oates, 1996). For some reason, however, this literature largely skips the Bradford/Oates logic; that is, it estimates a flypaper effect without adjusting for tax share. As a result, most studies greatly underestimate this effect. My work on this topic is based on the Bradford/Oates logic and it finds much larger flypaper effects than most other studies (see Eom, Duncombe, Nguyen-Hoang, and Yinger, 2014). One of my current projects (with Phuong Nguyen-Hoang) investigates the extent to which a correctly specified flypaper effect can be explained by the notion from behavioral economics that people place resources received from different sources in different mental accounts. I'm still pursuing this topic, too.

Wally published articles on many topics in local public finance other than these three, of course, and he also made important contributions to environmental economics. He will be greatly missed. I will remember Wally as a stimulating and supportive teacher, a pioneering scholar, and the man who put three big ideas in my head that I cannot seem to stop thinking about.

References

Bradford, David F. and Wallace E. Oates. 1971. Towards a predictive theory of intergovernmental grants. *American Economic Review* **61**(2): 440–448.

Bradford, David F., R. A. Malt, and W. E. Oates. 1969. The rising cost of local public services: Some evidence and reflections. *The National Tax Journal* **22**(2): 185–202.

Duncombe, William D. and John Yinger. 2005. How much more does a disadvantaged student cost? *Economics of Education Review* **24**(5): 513–532.

Duncombe, William D., Phuong Nguyen-Hoang, and John Yinger. 2015. Measurement of cost differentials. In M.E. Goertz and H.F. Ladd (eds.), *Handbook of Research in Education Finance and Policy*, 2nd edition, pp. 260–278, New York: Routledge.

Eom, Tae Ho, William Duncombe, Phuong Nguyen-Hoang, and John Yinger. 2014. The unintended consequences of property tax relief: New York state's STAR program. *Education Finance and Policy* **9**(4): 446–480.

Gamkhar, Shama and Wallace E. Oates. 1996. Asymmetries in the response to increases and decreases in intergovernmental grants: some empirical findings. *National Tax Journal* **49**(4): 501–512.

Ladd, Helen F. and John Yinger. 1991. *America's Ailing Cities: Fiscal Health and the Design of Urban Policy*, Updated Edition. Johns Hopkins University Press.

Oates, Wallace E. 1969. The effects of property taxes and local public services on property values: An empirical study of tax capitalization and the tiebout hypothesis. *Journal of Political Economy* **77**(6): 957–971.

Oates, Wallace E. 1972. *Fiscal Federalism.* New York: Harcourt Brace Jovanovich.

Ross, Stephen and John Yinger. 1999. Sorting and voting: A review of the literature on urban public finance. In P. Cheshire and E.S. Mills (eds.), *Handbook of Urban and Regional Economics, Volume 3, Applied Urban Economics,* pp. 2001–2060, New York: North-Holland.

Tiebout, Charles M. 1956. A pure theory of local expenditures. *Journal of Political Economy* **64**: 416–424.

Yinger, John. 2015. Hedonic markets and sorting equilibria: Bid-function envelopes for public services and neighborhood amenities. *Journal of Urban Economics* **86**: 9–25.

A Tribute to William D. Duncombe*

John Yinger

*Departments of Public Administration and International Affairs and
of Economics, Syracuse University, Syracuse, NY, United States*

My dear friend and colleague, Bill Duncombe, passed away on May 11. He was 57 years old. The losses to his family, friends and colleagues, to the Maxwell School, and to scholarship on education finance are incalculable.

Bill was a Ph.D. student in public administration when I arrived at the Maxwell School in the fall of 1986. He and I hit it off right away and we started working together. Our first publication together grew out of his dissertation, and we went on to publish 23 more articles or book chapters together, along with many working papers, reports, op-eds, and policy briefs. We also served on many committees together, especially dissertation committees, and became fast friends.

Bill was an extraordinary scholar and person.

His data-gathering skills were legendary. One time he came into my office and told me that he had put together a detailed data set covering a couple of decades for all the rural school districts in New York State, including twelve pairs of districts that had consolidated. He asked me if I thought this data set would be useful for studying consolidation. He knew the answer, of course, and was just trying to rope me in — which he did. The eventual

---

*This appendix originally appeared as the May 2013 "It's Elementary" column posted at http://cpr.maxwell.syr.edu/efap/about_efap/ie/May_2013.pdf. The last paragraph has been updated.

result was an article in *Education Finance and Policy* in 2007 and dozens of phone calls from school officials interested in our finding that consolidation can save small school districts a great deal of money.

Bill also assembled complex data sets on education finance for California, Kansas, Maryland, Missouri, Nebraska, and New York. These data sets led to publications, court documents, or Bill's testimony, all of which had a significant impact on education finance reform in these states. Bill was also a master at devising and programming complex statistical procedures to apply to these data sets. Moreover, he was very well informed about the conceptual issues that arise in studying education finance, and our thousands of conversations on the topic invariably led to better formulations than either of us would have come up with on our own.

Actually, I think it is our conversations that I will remember the most. Not our individual conversations. In fact, I have trouble remembering conversations I had this morning! Instead, I remember how we pushed each other to come up with the best theory, data, and methods we possibly could; how amazed I often was at the amount Bill had accomplished since our last conversation; how committed Bill was to the fair treatment of our colleagues and students; how we made each other laugh; and how unfailingly kind Bill was in all his dealings with me and, for that matter, with everyone else.

Most of Bill's and my joint research addresses topics in education finance, particularly education cost functions and their implications for state aid to education. I have published a few articles on education finance without Bill as a formal co-author, but he has had an enormous influence on my thinking about this subject, and his fingerprints are all over everything I have written on education finance since I started working with him — and will be all over everything I write on this subject in the future.

The Public Administration Department in the Maxwell School is pretty amazing. Ever since I came to Maxwell, it has been a very collegial place with high, but fair standards for scholarship and teaching. This type of environment does not arise by accident, but is instead sustained by the commitment and character of the people involved. Since he joined the faculty in 1991, Bill set the standard for us all. He was the first person at work in the morning and the last person to leave at night — with the possible exception of a junior faculty member about to come up for tenure. He treated everyone with kindness and respect. He was remarkably generous with his time, scheduling extra sessions for his MPA students, writing detailed comments on draft after draft of his Ph.D. students' dissertations, providing extensive feedback to his colleagues on their research projects, and volunteering for time-consuming committee assignments. Bill's exceptional example will undoubtedly continue to contribute to the PA Department for many, many years to come.

Bill's publications on education finance are listed below in alphabetical order. The website of the Education Finance and Accountability Program, which is a program inside Syracuse University's Center for Policy Research, provides additional information on Bill and his scholarly legacy. See http://cpr.maxwell.syr.edu/efap/Duncombe/index.html.

William D. Duncombe's Publications on Education Finance

Ammar, Salwa, Robert Bifulco, William D. Duncombe, and Ronald Wright. 2000. Identifying low-performance public schools, *Studies in Educational Evaluation* **26**: 259–287

Ammar, Salwa, William D. Duncombe, Bernard Jump, and Ronald Wright. 2004. Constructing a fuzzy-knowledge-based system: an application for assessing the financial condition of public schools. *Expert Systems with Applications* **27**(3): 349–364.

Ammar, Salwa, William D. Duncombe, Bernard Jump, and Ronald Wright. 2005. A financial condition indicator system for school districts: a case study of New York. *Journal of Education Finance* **30**(3) (Winter): 231–258.

Ammar, Salwa, William D. Duncombe, Bernard Jump, and Ronald Wright. 2005. Avoiding fiscal stress: the use of expert systems to assess school district financial condition. *Developments in School Finance: 2004–05, Fiscal Proceedings from the Annual State Data Conferences of July 2004.* Washington, DC: National Center for Education Statistics.

Andrews, Matthew, William D. Duncombe, and John Yinger. 2002. Revisiting economies of size in education: are we any closer to a consensus? *Economics of Education Review* **21**: 245–262.

Baker, Bruce and William D. Duncombe. 2004. Balancing district needs and student needs: the role of economies of scale adjustments and pupil need weights in school finance formulas. *Journal of Education Finance* **29**(3) (Winter): 195–222.

Balter, Dana and William D. Duncombe. 2008. Recruiting highly qualified teachers: do district recruitment practices matter? *Public Finance Review* **36**(1) (January): 33–62.

Bifulco, Robert and William D. Duncombe. 2002. Evaluating school performance: are we ready for prime-time? In William J. Fowler (ed.), *Developments in School Finance, 1999–2000*, vol. 316, pp. 11–28. Washington, DC: National Center for Education Statistics.

Bifulco, Robert, William D. Duncombe, and John Yinger. 2005. Does whole-school reform boost student performance: the case of New York city. *Journal of Policy Analysis and Management* **24**(1) (Winter): 47–72.

Chung, Il Hwan, William D. Duncombe, and John Yinger. (2018). The impact of state aid reform on property values: a case study of Maryland's bridge to excellence in public schools act. *Education Finance and Policy* **13**(3) (Summer): 369–394. [Chapter 16]

Duncombe, William D. 2006. Responding to the charge of alchemy: strategies for evaluating the reliability and validity of costing-out research. *Journal of Education Finance* **21**(2) (Fall): 137–159.

Duncombe, William D. and Lloyd Blanchard. 1999. Tax policy and public school finance. In B. Hildreth and J. Richardson (eds.), *Handbook on Taxation*. vol. 7, pp. 345–400. New York: Marcel Dekker Inc.

Duncombe, William D. and Yilin Hou. 2014. The savings behavior of special purpose governments: a panel study of New York school districts. *Public Budgeting and Finance* **34**(3) (Fall): 1–23.

Duncombe, William D. and Jocelyn Johnston. 1998. Balancing conflicting policy objectives: the case of school finance reform, *Public Administration Review* **58**(2) (March/April): 145–166.

Duncombe, William D., Anna Lukemeyer, and John Yinger. 2003. Financing an adequate education: a case study of New York. *Developments in School Finance: 2001-02, Fiscal Proceedings from the Annual State Data Conferences of July 2001 and July 2002.* Washington, DC: National Center for Education Statistics, NCES 2003-403: 127–154. [Chapter 9]

Duncombe, William D., Anna Lukemeyer, and John Yinger. 2008. Dollars without sense: the mismatch between the No Child Left Behind Act accountability system and Title 1 funding. In R. Kahlenberg (ed.), *Improving On No Child Left Behind*, New York: The Twentieth Century Foundation.

Duncombe, William D., Anna Lukemeyer, and John Yinger. 2008. The No Child Left Behind Act: have federal funds been left behind? *Public Finance Review* **36**(4) (July): 381–407. [Chapter 6]

Duncombe, William D., Phuong Nguyen-Hoang, and John Yinger. 2015. Measurement of cost differentials. In M.E. Goertz and H.F. Ladd (eds.), *Handbook of Research in Education Finance and Policy*, 2nd edition, pp. 260–278. New York: Routledge.

Duncombe, William D., Mark Robbins, and Jeff Stonecash. 2003. Measuring citizen preferences for public services using surveys: does a "Gray Peril" threaten funding for public education? *Public Budgeting & Finance*, **23**(1) (Spring): 45–72.

Duncombe, William D. and Cynthia Searcy. 2007. Can the use of recommended procurement practices save money? *Public Budgeting & Finance* **27**(2) (Summer): 68–87.

Duncombe, William D. and Cynthia Searcy. 2007. Out with the old, in with the new? A case study of procurement practices in New York state school districts. *Journal of Public Budgeting, Accounting, and Financial Management* **19**(4) (Winter): 514–545.

Duncombe, William D. and Wen Wang. 2009. School facilities funding and capital outlay distribution in the states. *Journal of Education Finance* **34**(3) (Winter): 324–350.

Duncombe, William D. and John Yinger. 1998. An analysis of two educational policies in New York state: performance standards and property tax relief. In James H. Wyckoff (ed.), *Educational Finance to Support High Learning Standards*, New York State Board of Regents Final Report, pp. 97–136. Albany, New York: State Education Department, The University of the State of New York.

Duncombe, William D. and John Yinger. 1998. School finance reform: aid formulas and equity objectives. *National Tax Journal* **51**(2) (June): 239–262. [Chapter 12]

Duncombe, William D. and John Yinger. 1999. Performance standards and educational cost indexes: you can't have one without the other. In *Equity and Adequacy in Education Finance: Issues and Perspectives*, National Academy Press, Committee on Education Finance. Irvine, California: National Research Council, February 1999, 260–297.

Duncombe, William D. and John Yinger. 2000. Financing higher student performance standards: the case of New York State. *Economics of Education Review* **19**(October): 363–386.

Duncombe, William D. and John Yinger. 2001. Alternative paths to property tax relief. In Wallace Oates (ed.), *Property Taxation and Local Government Finance*. Cambridge, Massachusetts: Lincoln Institute of Land Policy.

Duncombe, William D. and Jocelyn Johnston. 2004. The impacts of school finance reform in Kansas: equity is in the eye of the beholder. In J. Yinger (ed.), *Helping Children Left Behind*, pp. 147–194. Cambridge, Massachusetts: The MIT Press.

Duncombe, William D. and John Yinger. 2005. How much more does a disadvantaged student cost? *Economics of Education Review* **24**(5) (October): 513–532. [Chapter 7]

Duncombe, William D. and John Yinger. 2007. Does school district consolidation cut costs? *Journal of Education Policy and Finance* **2**(4) (Fall): 341–376. [Chapter 22]

Duncombe, William D. and John Yinger. 2007. Measurement of cost differentials. In H. Ladd and T. Fiske (eds.), *Handbook of Research in Education Finance and Policy*, pp. 257–275. Mahwah, New Jersey: Lawrence Erlbaum Associates, Inc.

Duncombe, William D. and John Yinger. 2011. Are education cost functions ready for prime time? An examination of their validity and reliability. *Peabody Journal of Education* **86**(1): 28–57. [Chapter 5]

Duncombe, William D. and John Yinger. 2011. Making do: State constraints and local responses in California's education finance system. *International Tax and Public Finance* **18**: 337–368. [Chapter 10]

Duncombe, William D., John Yinger, and Pengju Zhang. 2016. How does school district consolidation affect property values: a case study of New York. *Public Finance Review* **44**(1): 52–79. [Chapter 19]

Eom, Tae Ho, William D. Duncombe, Phuong Nguyen-Hoang, and John Yinger. 2014. The unintended consequences of property tax relief: New York state's STAR program. *Education Finance and Policy* **9**(4) (Fall): 446–480. [Chapter 8]

Wang, Wen, William D. Duncombe, and John Yinger. 2011. School district responses to matching aid programs for capital facilities: a case study of New York's building aid program. *National Tax Journal* **64**(3) (September): 759–794. [Chapter 20]

Index

CPSIA information can be obtained
at www.ICGtesting.com
Printed in the USA
BVHW012105280220
573339BV00016B/18

9 789811 201608